March 1–2, 2014
Salt Lake City UT, USA

I0038036

**Association for
Computing Machinery**

Advancing Computing as a Science & Profession

VEE '14

Proceedings of the 10th ACM SIGPLAN/SIGOPS International Conference on

Virtual Execution Environments

Sponsored by:
ACM SIGOPS and ACM SIGPLAN

In-cooperation with:
USENIX

Supported by:
VMware, Facebook, IBM and Microsoft Research

Association for Computing Machinery

Advancing Computing as a Science & Profession

The Association for Computing Machinery
2 Penn Plaza, Suite 701
New York, New York 10121-0701

ISBN: 978-1-4503-2764-0 (Digital)

ISBN: 978-1-4503-3099-2 (Print)

Additional copies may be ordered prepaid from:

ACM Order Department
PO Box 30777
New York, NY 10087-0777, USA

Phone: 1-800-342-6626 (USA and Canada)
+1-212-626-0500 (Global)
Fax: +1-212-944-1318
E-mail: acmhelp@acm.org
Hours of Operation: 8:30 am – 4:30 pm ET

Printed in the USA

VEE 2014 Foreword

Welcome to the 10th ACM SIGPLAN/SIGOPS Conference on Virtual Execution Environments (VEE'14). We are happy to present the community with a strong program covering a wide range of virtualization topics.

This year, authors registered 56 papers, of which 49 were finalized as complete submissions. The program committee (PC) consisted of 2 chairs and 18 researchers active in virtualization-related aspects of programming languages and operating systems. Members were allowed to submit papers; the co-chairs chose not to submit anything. Reviewing was double-blind and was done almost entirely by the committee, with a little assistance from outsiders with special expertise. All submissions received 4–5 reviews, and authors were given the opportunity for rebuttal before the PC meeting.

The program committee meeting was held in January at the IBM T.J. Watson Research Center in New York. Most of the committee members were present in person. In an 8-hour session, we individually discussed all papers but those that were marked as early rejects due to receiving only negative reviews. We followed conventional rules for conflict of interest, with conflicted members (including co-chairs) leaving the room during discussion of the conflicted papers. In the end, we accepted 18 papers for presentation at the conference, of which about half were shepherded by PC members.

In addition to the 18 accepted papers, the VEE'14 program includes two keynote presentations by Galen Hunt and Jan Vitek. We hope that the resulting proceedings will serve as a valuable reference for researchers and practitioners in the area of virtualization.

Putting together VEE'14 was a team effort. Without the contributions of all the authors, the conference would not continue to be relevant and interesting. The program committee worked hard in reviewing papers and shepherding accepted submissions into their final forms. Our colleagues on the organizing committee of ASPLOS 2014 were helpful in coordinating the local arrangements, registration, and logistics for the conference itself. Lastly, we would like to thank our sponsors (ACM SIGPLAN and SIGOPS) and our corporate supporters (VMware, Facebook, IBM, and Microsoft Research) for their continued support.

We hope that you find the conference interesting and stimulating, and that it provides the opportunity to meet and engage with colleagues new and old from around the world.

Martin Hirzel
IBM Research, USA
VEE'14 General Chair

Erez Petrank
Technion, Israel
VEE'14 Program Chair

Dan Tsafrir
Technion, Israel
VEE'14 Program Chair

Table of Contents

Session 1: Keynote #1
Dan Tsafrir *(Technion - Israel Institute of Technology)*

Session 2: Bridging the Semantic Gap
Don Porter *(Stony Brook University)*

Session 3: Memory
Galen Hunt *(Microsoft Research)*

Session 4: Runtimes
Eric Eide *(University of Utah)*

VEE 2014 Organization

Sub-Reviewers	Orna Agmon Ben-Yehuda *(Technion)*
	Samer Al-kiswany *(UW Madison)*
	Vijay Chidambaran *(UW Madison)*
	Florian David *(INRIA)*
	Thanh Do *(UW Madison)*
	Peter Goodman *(University of Toronto)*
	Abel Gordon *(Stratoscale)*
	Jun He *(UW Madison)*
	Benoit Hudzia *(Stratoscale)*
	William Jannen *(Stony Brook University)*
	Rafal Kolanski *(Purdue University)*
	Julia Lawall *(INRIA)*
	Lanyue Lu *(UW Madison)*
	Thanu M. Pillai *(UW Madison)*
	Lior Segev *(Stratoscale)*
	Gaël Thomas *(INRIA)*
	Zev Weiss *(UW Madison)*
	Suli Yang *(UW Madison)*
	Yang Zhan *(Stony Brook University)*
	Tao Zhang *(Stony Brook University)*
	Yupu Zhang *(UW Madison)*

VEE 2014 Sponsors and Supporters

Sponsors

In-cooperation with

Supporters

Experiences in the Land of Virtual Abstractions

Galen C. Hunt

Microsoft Research
Redmond, WA USA
{galen.hunt}@microsoft.com

Abstract

The Microsoft Research Drawbridge Project began with a simple question: *Is it possible to achieve the benefits of hardware virtual machines without the overheads?* Following that question, we have built a line of exploratory prototypes. These prototypes range from an ARM-based phone that runs x86 Windows binaries to new forms of secure computation. In this talk, I'll briefly describe our various prototypes and the evidence we have accumulated that our first question can be answered in the affirmative.

Categories and Subject Descriptors D.4.7 **[Operating Systems]**: Organization and Design

Keywords virtualization; drawbridge

Biography

Galen Hunt is Principal Researcher of Operating Systems at Microsoft Research. He joined Microsoft Research in 1997, where he has stayed except for two sabbaticals in Microsoft engineering groups.

Galen's more successful past efforts include Drawbridge, Singularity, Experiment 19, Detours, and the first prototype of Windows Media Player. Singularity pioneered the concept of the modern sealed process, which can be found now in nearly every major commercial OS. Experiment 19 prototyped the OS architecture now found in Windows Phone 8. Detours is Microsoft's most widely licensed non-product intellectual property.

Galen's less successful efforts include the first prototype of Cloud Computing, work in Distributed Shared Memory, and a fully distributed version of the CLR. Galen shipped bugs in several Windows operating systems.

Galen holds a Ph.D. in Computer Science from the University of Rochester (where he contributed code to GCC 2.1), a B.S. in Physics from the University of Utah (where he contributed code to Linux 0.11), and over 70 patents. Before graduate school, Galen worked at a startup that reverse engineered the data structures of tax programs. Aside from systems research, Galen's biggest interests are his wife, daughter, son, and practicing to be a good a Mormon.

VEE '14, March 1–2, 2014, Salt Lake City, Utah, USA.
ACM 978-1-4503-2764-0/14/03.
http://dx.doi.org/10.1145/2576195.2576212

Real-Time Deep Virtual Machine Introspection
and Its Applications

Jennia Hizver

Department of Computer Science
Stony Brook University
Stony Brook, USA
jhizver@cs.stonybrook.edu

Tzi-cker Chiueh

Cloud Computing Center
Industrial Technology Research Institute
Taiwan
tcc@itri.org.tw

Abstract

Virtual Machine Introspection (VMI) provides the ability to monitor virtual machines (VM) in an agentless fashion by gathering VM execution states from the hypervisor and analyzing those states to extract information about a running operating system (OS) without installing an agent inside the VM. VMI's main challenge lies in the difficulty in converting low-level byte string values into high-level semantic states of the monitored VM's OS. In this work, we tackle this challenge by developing a real-time kernel data structure monitoring (RTKDSM) system that leverages the rich OS analysis capabilities of Volatility, an open source computer forensics framework, to significantly simplify and automate analysis of VM execution states. The RTKDSM system is designed as an extensible software framework that is meant to be extended to perform application-specific VM state analysis. In addition, the RTKDSM system is able to perform real-time monitoring of any changes made to the extracted OS states of guest VMs. This real-time monitoring capability is especially important for VMI-based security applications. To minimize the performance overhead associated with real-time kernel data structure monitoring, the RTKDSM system has incorporated several optimizations whose effectiveness is reported in this paper.

Categories and Subject Descriptors D.4.6 [**Operating Systems**]: Security and Protection; D.4.8 [**Operating Systems**]: Performance - Monitors.

Keywords Virtual machine introspection; Security monitoring; Forensics; Performance

1. Introduction

Virtualized data centers are witnessing increasing adoption of the virtual machine introspection (VMI) technology for building a wide range of agentless VM monitoring applications including intrusion detection systems, virtual firewalls, malware analysis, and live memory forensics [1-4]. Using VMI, a VM monitoring application reconstructs the internal state of a monitored VM from the byte values in the VM's memory pages. Access to a VM's memory pages is possible because the hypervisor on which the monitoring application runs has complete access to all memory pages of the VMs that run on it. Given a VM's entire physical memory, it is possible for a VM monitoring application to access the contents of the monitored VM's kernel and user-space memory and extract its critical OS data structures. From these data structures, a VM monitoring application can then infer exactly what the guest OS is doing. With agentless VM monitoring, users can focus on how to effectively utilize their VMs without worrying about any VM monitoring issues. Furthermore, this agentless approach makes it possible to build a VM monitoring system that is not tightly knitted with specific types or versions of a guest VM OS.

To support effective VM monitoring, VMI has to overcome the so-called semantic gap. Without access to the kernel's data structure layouts and semantics, the abstraction level at which the hypervisor captures a VM's memory pages is too primitive to extract high-level semantic views of the VM's OS state that are needed to make meaningful decisions. The first step in bridging this semantic gap is to gather information about a guest OS by locating and examining the OS's internal data structures used in system calls or internal kernel calls. This step generally requires labor-intensive, time-consuming, and error-prone efforts to accurately translate captured memory pages into kernel data structure views of monitored VMs. The lack of a general VMI framework that is able to apply kernel data structure knowledge of multiple OS types and versions to minimize the effort of closing semantic gaps presently poses a significant challenge for developers of VMI applications.

The RTKDSM system presented in this paper is designed to address this challenge by automating the process of kernel data structure extraction and enabling VMI applications to monitor any real-time changes to selective guest OS data structures. The RTKDSM system leverages the vast kernel data structure knowledge in an existing open source computer forensics framework called Volatility [9] to remove the burden of bridging semantic gaps from VMI application developers. Moreover, the RTKDSM system does not require users to specify anything about a monitored VM beforehand, since it is able to accurately fingerprint the OS used in the monitored VM on the fly; nor does it require access to the guest OS's source code, making it particularly compelling for use in real-world production IT environments. Because responding to changes in monitored kernel data structures in real time requires tracking of a large volume of kernel events and thus entails serious performance penalty, the RTKDSM system incorporates a tuneable performance optimization to mitigate this performance overhead problem for VMI applications that need to track rapid changes to a large number of kernel data structures.

To demonstrate the effectiveness and applicability of the RTKDSM system, we used it to develop three substantial VMI applications that applied VM monitoring in virtualized IT environments: a payment card data flow tracking tool, an application whitelisting system, and a security tool for detection of privilege escalation attacks.

2. Background

2.1 Semantic Awareness

VMI applications fall into either of the following two categories: semantically aware [1-4] and semantically unaware [5-8]. A VMI application is semantic aware if it seeks to extract information from the guest VM it monitors to carry out its monitoring operations. Semantically unaware VMI applications are largely unaware of the OS semantics associated with the VMs they monitor. The RTKDSM system is designed to significantly facilitate the development of semantically aware VMI applications.

2.2 Volatility Forensic Memory Analysis Framework

As computer forensic memory analysis tools aim to tackle many of the same issues that plague VMI application development, the computer forensics community has already done much work in addressing the semantic gap problem, including supporting multiple operating systems and a large number of kernel data structures in them. The RTKDSM system utilizes the open-source Python-based Volatility forensic memory analysis framework to extract OS data structures from the memory pages of monitored VMs [9].

Volatility supports several versions of Windows, Linux, and Mac OSes.

Volatility is a modular framework in which most of the functionality is implemented by *plugins,* each of which performs a certain function, such as identifying a list of running processes. One could further extend Volatility with new plugins without injecting them into the framework.

Volatility provides support for a variety of processor architectures through the use of *address spaces* (AS), which is intended to abstract the handling of different memory image formats and to facilitate random access to a memory image by a plugin. A valid AS for a given memory image is derived by Volatility automatically. The derived AS is used to satisfy memory read requests issued by a plugin. Exactly how a memory read request is satisfied is not important to the plugin code, so long as the read request is satisfied.

Once an AS is loaded, most plugins begin accessing data structures within the AS as objects, which are declared as Python classes by extending the base object class. Examples of objects include EPROCESS and ETHREAD objects, which correspond to the process and thread kernel data structures in Windows OS, respectively. Volatility's object manager parses objects using *profiles*, which are collections of data structure definitions (member fields and offsets) used in a certain OS.

3. Design

3.1 Assumptions and Requirements

The development of the RTKDSM system was driven by the following requirements and assumptions:

- No modifications to the OS and no additional software agents are needed in the monitored VM.
- Kernel data structures of the introspected guest OS must conform to known semantic and syntactic data structure layouts. This assumption is common to most existing VMI-based solutions. Although Bahram et al. [10] demonstrated the feasibility of semantic and syntactic data structure manipulation attacks to subvert introspection, this type of attacks could be defeated using data structure invariant inference and enforcement tools [11] and by generating robust signatures for kernel data structures [12].
- Kernel data structures of interest were assumed to be memory-resident at the time of scan and, once identified, were never moved (paged) between physical memory and the page file. While the kernel in general might keep some data in the paged memory whose contents might be swapped to a file, the most critical and frequently accessed kernel data structures, such as those used in this study, were known to be permanently kept in the non-paged memory. Therefore, we focused only on non-paged kernel data structures in this work.

3.2 Service Model

The RTKDSM system is designed to operate in two modes. In the *identification and analysis mode*, VMI applications use the RTKDSM system to discover locations of specific kernel data structures and values of specific fields within those data structures, and then deduce the semantic meanings of the returned values. In the *monitoring mode,* VMI applications rely on the RTKDSM system to monitor real-time changes to selected kernel data structures, and then respond to these changes appropriately.

VMI applications make VMI requests to the RTKDSM system. Each VMI request is of the following form: (*mode, data_structure_type, data_structure_offset, field_name1, field_name2, ..., field_nameN*). Examples of data structure types (*data_structure_type*) include: EPROCESS (process), TOKEN (token), and ETHREAD (thread) in Windows OS. Examples of field names (*field_name*) include: ImageFileName (process name) and CreateTime (thread creation time). The RTKDSM system is pre-configured with lists of supported data structure types and field names for each data structure type. These lists are derived from the Volatility supported types.

Examples of VMI requests in the identification mode include:

- *(identification, EPROCESS, 0x0, '')* - identifies all EPROCESS data structures and returns the memory locations of the identified data structures to the VMI monitor.

- *(identification, EPROCESS, 0x0, 'ImageFileName')* - identifies all EPROCESS data structures and returns the names of the corresponding processes.

- *(identification, EPROCESS, 0x000fabcd, 'ImageFileName')* - returns the name of the process whose EPROCESS data structure is located at the 0x000fabcd offset.

Examples of VMI requests in the monitoring mode include:

- *(monitoring, EPROCESS, 0x000fabcd, 'ImageFileName')* - calculates the offset of the ImageFileName field within the EPROCESS data structure located at the 0x000fabcd offset and monitors the ImageFileName field for changes in real-time. When a change in the field is detected, the new value is returned to the VMI monitor.

- *(monitoring, EPROCESS, 0x000fabcd, '')* - monitors the entire data structure for changes in real-time. When a change in the data structure is detected, the VMI monitor is notified of the change.

3.3 System Architecture

The RTKDSM system is composed of two agents: the *introspection* agent and the *monitoring* agent. As shown in Figure 1, the introspection agent gathers and analyzes kernel data structures in the monitored VM, while the monitoring agent detects write attempts to the monitored kernel data structures.

Upon receiving a request from a VMI application (Step 1 of Figure 1), the introspection agent searches the physical memory of the monitored VM (Step 2 of Figure 1) to locate data structures specified in the request. If this VMI request is an identification mode request, the introspection agent extracts the memory offsets of the identified data structures or values of the requested fields, and returns the results to the requesting VMI application (Step 8 of Figure 1). If the request is a monitoring mode request, the introspection agent extracts the physical page frame numbers (PFN) of those memory pages where the monitored data structures reside including their address ranges within the page (Step 3 of Figure 1).Then the introspection agent delivers the list of PFNs to the monitoring agent (Step 4 of Figure 1).

The monitoring agent continuously monitors data structures in real time by intercepting all memory writes to the pages in the monitored PFN list (Step 5 of Figure 1). On intercepting a write on a monitored page, the monitoring agent allows the write operation to proceed if the write is within one of the monitored address ranges and notifies the introspection agent of the corresponding PFN (Step 6 of Figure 1) for real-time analysis of the updated page (Step 7 of Figure 1). If the memory page hosts a data structure known to cross page boundaries and to reside on multiple pages, the analysis involves the entire set of page frames comprising the data structure. Subsequently, the VMI monitor is notified of the new state of the data structure (Step 8 of Figure 1). If the write is not within any of the known monitored memory ranges, the monitoring agent allows the write operation to proceed without notifying the introspection agent.

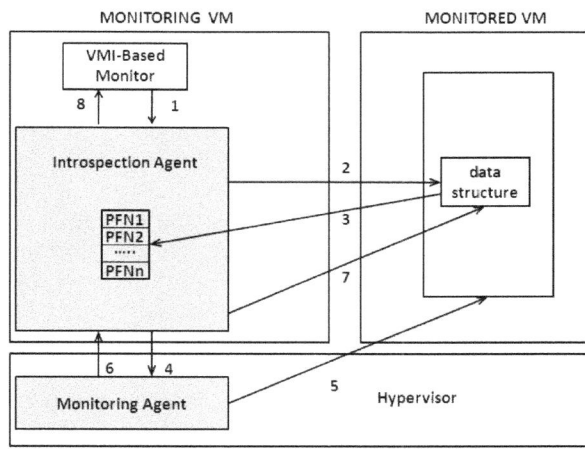

Figure 1. The RTKDSM system consists of an Introspection agent, residing in the same VM as the VMI application, and a Monitoring agent, which is inside the hypervisor.

4. Prototype Implementation

The current RTKDSM prototype is implemented on an x86 server that supports Intel VT technology, runs the Xen hypervisor and is designed to support guest VMs running both Windows and Linux. However, due to space constraints, in the following we focus only on guest VMs running Windows OS, because Windows VMS are more challenging than Linux VMs as far as VMI is concerned.

In our implementation, the introspection agent was deployed in the Dom0 domain. The monitoring agent was implemented inside the Xen hypervisor. The RTKDSM system receives VMI requests from a VMI monitor or application (Step 1 of Figure 2), which could be in the identification or monitor mode.

Memory Mapping: To analyze the memory of a running VM, the RTKDSM system first has to be able to access the memory of the monitored VM. The RTKDSM system uses the XenAccess API [13] to set up necessary memory mappings required to access the monitored VM's memory pages (Step 2 of Figure 2). Specifically, it leverages the PyXaFS file system in the XenAccess tool suite to make the physical memory pages of a monitored VM available to Dom0. PyXaFS exposes the memory of a VM as a regular file and allowes the introspection agent to read a live VM's memory as if it were a normal file.

Data Structure Search: To enable the RTKDSM system to effectively search a monitored VM's physical memory space for application-specified kernel data structures, we extended the Volatility framework with a new plugin called *rtkdsm* (real time kernel data structure monitoring). The *rtkdsm* plugin is written in Python and utilizes the existing Volatility scanning algorithms for extraction of kernel data structures from memory pages. The *rtkdsm* plugin functions as an on-line incremental analysis tool that is capable of directly accessing a memory page and identifying data structures of interest within that page by calling on Volatility with the corresponding data structure type and offset. The *rtkdsm* plugin calculates offsets and lengths of data fields that applications request monitoring, using Volatility's built-in profiles. For instance, a VMI monitor or application might issue a request to monitor the ImageFileName field, which stores a process's name. This field was defined by a Volatility profile as 16 bytes long and located at the 0x174 offset from the top of the EPROCESS data structure. Given a monitored VM's physical memory mapped as a PyXaFS file, the introspection agent searches the mapped pages for target data structures (Step 3a of Figure 2) or analyzes a particular data structure at a known offset (Step 3b of Figure 2). This *live* system analysis is unobtrusive to the execution of the monitored VM and does not change the VM's system state during the data acquisition process. In the monitoring mode, the data structure and fields offsets are converted to PFNs (Step 4a of Figure 2) and then delivered to the monitoring agent for real-time monitoring.

Run-Time Monitoring: The hypervisor maps the list of PFNs for monitored memory pages in such a way that it is shared between the introspection agent and the monitoring agent (Step 4b of Figure 2). We added a new hypercall to the hypervisor to set up this sharing. All writes to the memory pages corresponding to entries in the PFN list are intercepted by the monitoring agent. This is achieved by marking the pages as read-only (Step 5 of Figure 2) and configuring the hypervisor to recognize page faults caused by writes to these read-only pages (Step 6 of Figure 2). To reduce the amount of code modifications in the hypervisor required to implement this mechanism, we develop an extension to the Xen hypervisor's *log dirty* mode to support continuous tracking of modifications to memory pages. Specifically, we leverage the shadow paging infrastructure to configure the hypervisor to intercept writes to monitored memory pages. Unlike the log dirty mode where all shadow entries are destroyed on its activation, we destroy only those shadow page table entries that correspond to the PFNs of memory pages that contain kernel data structures being monitored. When the monitored VM attempts to access a page without an existing shadow page table entry, a shadow page fault occurs, and the corresponding shadow page table entry is constructed with its read-only bit turned on if the physical memory page referenced by the PTE contains a kernel data structure in the PFN list. The shadow PTE flags are otherwise identical to the original guest PTE flags. With this set-up, all the shadow page table entries corresponding to the monitored pages are effectively marked as read-only.

At run time, any write to these read-only pages causes the CPU to trap into the hypervisor, transferring control to the Xen's page fault handler. In the log dirty mode, such writes result in the page marked as dirty and read-write, so as to avoid traps on subsequent writes. For the RTKDSM system, if the write is within a monitored address range on the page, it processes the write using a three-step procedure as follows:

- Marks the page as writable and re-executes the faulting instruction as if no fault ever occurs,

- Sets the trap flag, commonly used by single-stepping debuggers for the guest OS, to trigger, after the write instruction is re-executed, a debug exception, which the hypervisor handles by re-setting the page to read-only again, and

- Notifies the introspection agent of the write (Step 7 of Figure 2) via an event channel established between the introspection and the monitoring agents at the beginning of the monitoring session, if the write is within a monitored range.

Continuous Monitoring and Analysis: Upon receiving a notification from the monitoring agent, the introspection agent only re-analyzes the page (or a set of pages if the data structure was known to span multiple pages) where the

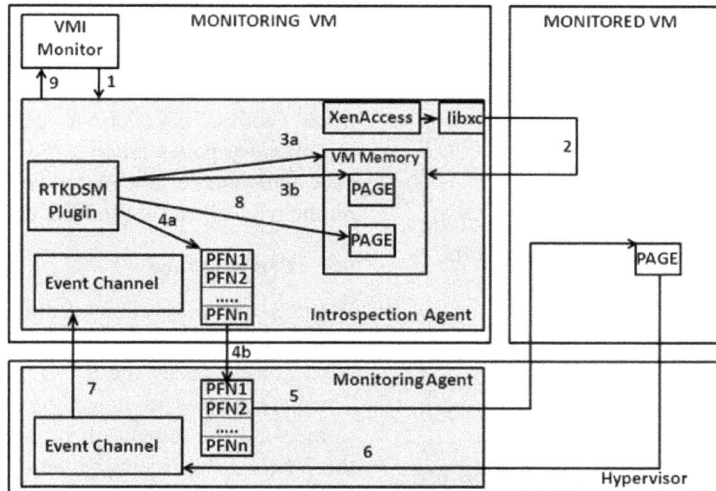

Figure 2. The control and data flow of how the RTKDSM system monitors application-specified kernel data structures and their real-time changes at run time.

modification occurs (Step 8 of Figure 2). The *rtkdsm* plugin extracts the new value of the data structure fields where the change takes place and returns it to the calling VMI monitor or application (Step 9 of Figure 2).

Run-time modifications to the monitored list: The PFN list is designed to be modified at run-time by adding new or deleting existing entries. Every time when an update is made to the monitored list, the RTKDSM system forces propagation of new PTE mappings into the shadow page table.

5. Performance Optimization

A major limitation of the RTKDSM system is its performance penalty in the monitoring mode. While the OS inside the monitored VM accesses and manipulates data at the granularity of machine words, the RTKDSM system intercepts writes only at the page level, because commodity x86 processors do not offer any mechanism to generate faults upon access to specific byte address ranges. Even though the RTKDSM system is able to distinguish between monitored and non-monitored addresses within a monitored page, writes to non-monitored addresses within a monitored page still cause page faults nonetheless and entail performance overheads.

Consequently, two types of page faults arise in the RTKDSM system. First, when the shadow page table entry for an accessed page does not exist, both read and write access to that page generate a shadow page fault. Second, when a write access to a page whose shadow page table exits but is marked as read-only, a shadow page fault occurs. The second type of page faults is the predominant source of performance overhead in the RTKDSM system, and is likely to exert a significant performance penalty on the monitored guest VM, especially if the VMI monitor requests monitoring of a large number of kernel data struc-

tures that are modified frequently. Therefore it is essential to bound the performance impacts on the monitored VM so as to make the RTKDSM system usable in real-world deployments.

We extend the RTKDSM system to operate in two modes: 1) the *always-on* mode: the application-specified kernel data structures are constantly and continuously monitored; 2) the *periodic polling* mode: the application-specified kernel data structures are checked and compared once in every fixed-sized time interval. In the periodic polling mode, the monitoring agent intercepts the first write to a monitored page and enables the write flag on the page for a fixed time period. Once the time period elapses, the introspection agent re-analyzes the page for any change, and the monitoring agent turns on its read-only flag to re-protect the page. As the next write is intercepted, another detection cycle comprising the above steps is repeated.

Although the periodic polling mode spares the hypervisor from unrelated and/or spurious modifications to monitored pages, reducing the frequency of checks introduces false negatives and the possibility of evasion when used in VMI-based security systems. A malicious data structure modification could go undetected if it occurs between two consecutive checks. This is especially possible when the polling interval is predictable. To prevent adversaries from exploiting the periodic nature of the polling mode, the RTKDSM randomizes the time interval size parameter T by selecting it from a uniform distribution in the (T-∂t, T+∂t) interval, with ∂t < T.

The choice of the *always-on* mode or the *periodic polling* mode represents a trade-off between performance penalty and false negative rate. Such trade-offs may not be possible for certain VMI applications. It is possible to choose a different T for each monitored page and even vary T dynamically over time by further analyzing the detailed profiles of modifications to monitored and non-monitored addresses within each monitored page. However, this analysis is outside the scope of this paper.

6. Evaluation

We evaluated the effectiveness and performance cost of the framework. This section presents the experimental results.

6.1 Experimental Setup

Our testbed consisted of a virtualized server that used Xen version 3.3 as the hypervisor and Ubuntu 9.04 (Linux kenel 2.6.26) as the kernel for Dom0. The host system had Duo CPU P8600 processor running two cores at 2.4GHz and 2GB of system memory. The RTKDSM system was installed in the Dom0 domain. In addition, the virtualized server hosted 2 VMs running a default installation of Windows XP OS with the IIS web server, MSSQL database server, Internet Explorer, and MS Office installed on each of the machines. These VMs were configured with 512Mb RAM.

6.2 Spurious Page Faults

We conducted experiments to estimate the probability of spurious updates, i.e. updates that might occur outside of monitored kernel data structures. The experiments included:

1. Monitoring of the 10 processes listed in Table 1 and their associated data structures listed in Table 2 over the period of one minute in an idle VM. For each listed process, we monitored one EPROCESS data structure (10 total for the 10 processes), one TOKEN (10 total for the 10 processes), one PEB (10 total for the 10 processes), one TEB (10 total for the 10 processes), two randomly selected ETHREADs (20 total for the 10 processes), two randomly selected FILE_OBJECTs (20 total for the 10 processes), two randomly selected KEVENTs (20 total for the 10 processes), two randomly selected KTIMERs (20 total for the 10 processes), and two randomly selected MMVADs (20 total for the 10 processes).

2. Monitoring of the PsActiveProcessHead structure over the period of one minute in an idle VM.

3. Monitoring of the TCBTable structure over the period of one minute in an idle VM.

The RTKDSM system located the PsActiveProcessHead structure, the TCBTable structure, and enumerated EPROCESS, TOKEN, PEB, TEB, ETHREADs, FILE_OBJECTs, KEVENTs, KTIMERs, and MMVADs data structures corresponding to the processes. The enumerated data structures were then monitored for updates in real-time. The results of these experiments are presented in Table 3 and Table 4. The memory pages containing EPROCESS, ETHREAD, and KTIMER data structures experienced

updates both inside and outside the monitored data structures. Although no updates were recorded inside the PsActiveProcessHead, TCBTable, TOKEN, FILE_OBJECT, KEVENT, and MMVAD data structures, the memory pages hosting these structures contained other data, which experienced updates. No updates were recorded on the pages hosting the PEB and TEB data structures.

6.3 Performance

We used a combination of micro/synthetic and application benchmarks to understand the direct computational overhead introduced by the RTKDSM system on the test VMs. The benchmarks included the PCMark05 benchmark [14] to measure the impact of the running RTKDSM system on the VM's CPU, memory, and hard drive and the Apache HTTP performance benchmark as an application benchmark [15] heavily relying on both threading and I/O operations. We assessed the performance of the RTKDSM system both in the "always-on" and the "periodic polling" monitoring modes.

The experiments included: (1) monitoring of the PsActiveProcessHead structure, (2) monitoring of the TCBTable structure, (3) monitoring of 2, 4, 6, 8, and 10 data structure sets corresponding to the first 2, 4, 6, 8, and 10 processes listed in Table 1. Each data structure set contained 14 data structures including 1 EPROCESS, 1 TOKEN, 1 PEB, 1 TEB, 2 randomly selected ETHREADs, 2 randomly selected KEVENTs, 2 randomly selected KTIMERs, 2 randomly selected FILE_OBJECTs, and 2 randomly selected MMVADs for each process.

6.3.1 "Always-On" Mode

#	Process Name	Description
1	System	First system process
2	smss	Handles sessions
3	csrss	Manages the graphical instruction sets
4	winlogon	Handles the login and logout procedures
5	services	Manages the operation of starting and stopping services
6	lsass	Enforces the security policy on the system
7	spoolsv	Communicates with the printing interfaces
8	inetinfo	A component of Microsoft Internet Information Services (IIS)
9	alg	Involved in client-server network communications
10	PCMark05	A computer benchmark tool

Table 1. Windows processes used in the experiments.

Data Structure	Describes
EPROCESS	A running process and all the information about the process
ETHREAD	A thread and contains all the information about the thread
TOKEN	The security context of a running process
PEB	Process Environment Block containing user-mode parameters
TEB	Thread Environment Block containing user-mode parameters
KEVENT	An event
KTIMER	A timer
FILE_OBJECT	An open instance of a device object
MMVAD	Virtually contiguous memory regions in a process's virtual address space
PsActiveProcessHead	Points to the first and the last EPROCESS data structure.
TCBTable	Transmission Control Block Table listing network connections

Table 2. Kernel data structures used in the experiments whose results are reported in this section.

The performance overhead was first measured with only 1 running VM and then with 2 VMs running concurrently. Each benchmark was run 3 times against the test VM. Figures 3 and Figure 4 show the average results of running the PCMark05 and Apache benchmarks. In the Apache bench-mark, the average process time per request was used for comparison. The results shown were calculated with respect to the speed of the Xen system with the RTKDSM system enabled with zero pages monitored.

The performance results demonstrated the performance overhead generally increased as the number of monitored structures increased. Additionally, the performance overhead also increased as the number of monitored VMs grew within the host. The performance was also affected by the type of a benchmark used in the experiments. Particularly, the Apache benchmark had a significant impact on the performance due to spurious page faults resulting from running this benchmark. In spite the significantly reduced performance, the outputs generated by the RTKDSM system would be sufficiently fast for use in systems that could tolerate reduced performance, for instance, in a VM replay for live forensic analysis of running VMs [16].

6.3.2 "Periodic Polling" Mode

The performance was assessed using the Apache HTTP benchmark only. Since this benchmark caused significant performance deteriorations in the "always-on" monitoring mode, switching to the "periodic polling" monitoring mode was expected to improve the performance.

In each experiment, the benchmark was run three times against one test VM. The average process time per request was used for comparison. Figure 5 shows the average results of running the Apache benchmarks with the timing parameter T set to 50 msec and 5 msec. The results shown were calculated with respect to the speed of the Xen system with the RTKDSM system enabled with zero pages monitored.

The performance results demonstrated the "periodic polling" approach significantly decreased the performance

Number of page faults inside the data structure	Data structure type and number of data structures with updates inside them										
	EPROCESS	TOKEN	PEB	TEB	ETHREAD	KTIMER	KEVENT	FILE_OBJECT	MMVAD	PsActiveProcessHead	TCBTable
0	4	10	10	10	18	8	20	20	20	1	1
1-100	5	0	0	0	1	11	0	0	0	0	0
101-500	0	0	0	0	1	0	0	0	0	0	0
501-1000	0	0	0	0	0	1	0	0	0	0	0
1001-5000	1	0	0	0	0	0	0	0	0	0	0

Table 3. Number of data structures with updates inside the data structure grouped by the data structure type and number of page faults. The page faults were recorded over the period of one minute in an idle VM.

Number of page faults outside the data structure on the monitored page	Data structure type and number of data structures with updates outside the data structure										
	EPROCESS	TOKEN	PEB	TEB	ETHREAD	KTIMER	KEVENT	FILE_OBJECT	MMVAD	PsActiveProcessHead	TCBTable
0	6	2	10	10	5	10	13	12	11	0	0
1-100	1	3	0	0	7	7	2	5	5	0	0
101-500	1	3	0	0	4	1	2	1	1	0	0
501-1000	0	1	0	0	1	0	0	1	2	0	0
1001-5000	2	1	0	0	2	2	2	1	1	0	1
5001-10000	0	0	0	0	1	0	1	0	0	0	0
10001-15000	0	0	0	0	0	0	0	0	0	1	0

Table 4. Number of data structures with updates outside the data structure grouped by the data structure type and number of page faults. The page faults were recorded over the period of one minute in an idle VM.

overhead observed in the "always-on" mode. The recorded write bursts involving spurious updates caused by the Apache benchmark to the monitored pages lasted in the 1 to 15 msec range. Hence, the improvement in the performance was due to a significantly reduced number of page fault interceptions that excluded page faults caused by such write bursts.

6.4 Effectiveness

In this section, we briefly describe three VMI-based applications that are built on top of the RTKDSM system to demonstrate the effectiveness of the RTKDSM system.

6.4.1 Payment Card Data Flow Tracking

All merchants that store, process, or transmit credit and debit card data are required to comply with the Payment Card Industry Data Security Standard (PCI-DSS) security requirements to ensure the card processing infrastructure is protected from unauthorized accesses from malicious attacks [17]. To help merchants to comply with the PCI-DSS, a VMI-based tool was implemented to automatically discover the card processing components and the payment card data flow in commercial distributed card data processing systems running on virtualized servers across multiple VMs [18].

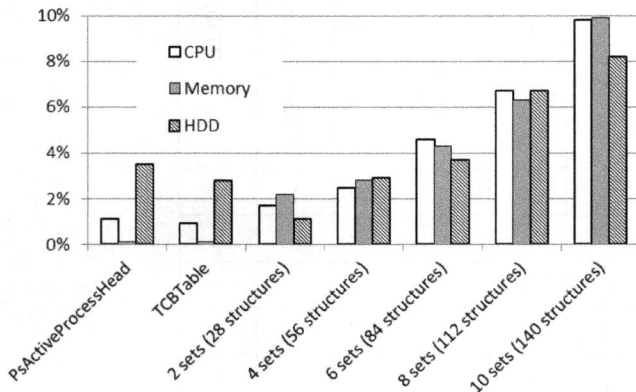

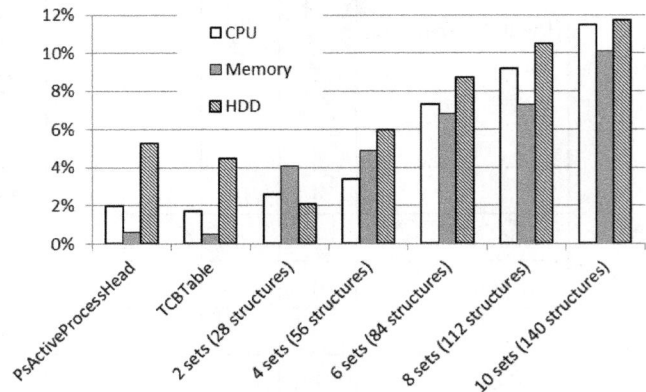

Figure 3. Performance overhead in the "always-on" mode using the PCMark05 benchmark with 1 test VM (left) and 2 test VMs (right).

To identify the trajectory of the card data flow, the tool leveraged the centralized monitoring capability of the RTKDSM framework to determine the set of VMs and the corresponding processes exchanging network packets as a result of card processing requests. On intercepting each inter-VM network connection, the tool initiated a VMI request to the RTKDSM introspection agent to identify the EPROCESS data structures bound to the network connections in the TCBTable data structure and inspected the memory spaces of the communicating processes for the card data. Even though card data might be encrypted during their transmissions, they would get decrypted and operated on during their processing, and therefore the clear text version of card data could be traced in the interacting processes' memory. Once the processes whose memory contained card data were found, the machines involved in the card data flow were readily identified.

Effectiveness of the tool was demonstrated through its successful discovery of the system components and the data flow of several commercial payment data processing systems. The availability of the tool could significantly decrease the efforts and costs in meeting the security regulations stipulated in the PCI-DSS standard.

6.4.2 Application Whitelisting

A cloud service that has proven commercially significant, especially in the private cloud space, is virtual desktop infrastructure (VDI), which gives each end user a dedicated VM as her desktop computer and manages these VMs in a centralized manner. To prevent unapproved software from running on a VDI, a VMI tool leveraging the centralized monitoring capability of the RTKDSM framework was designed and implemented to guarantee that only approved application were allowed to run on VMs under its management [19].

The tool checked an executable file or a library module against a whitelist of known good programs before it was loaded into the address space of a user process, and aborted the program load operation if the executable file or library module was not in the whitelist. By applying the RTKDSM system, the tool monitored the PsActiveProcessHead data structure for new process creation events so it could verify the new process's executable image through its EPROCESS data structure. The tool also monitored the PEB data structure of each process to detect new library modules loaded into the process.

The tool reliably identified whitelisted application codes and effectively blocking non-approved codes. The run-time overhead incurred by monitoring the PsActiveProcessHead and PEB data structures was 2.6% for the CPU suite, 1.3% for the memory suite, and 3.8% for the hard drive suite of the PCMark05 benchmark.

6.4.3 Privilege Escalation Attack Detection

With advances in protection measures against control flow hijacking attacks, attackers are devising a new group of attacks targeting at sensitive OS data structures. These attacks directly access and write to OS data structures stored in memory without using any APIs. The current range of defensive techniques against these types of non-control-related data attacks is limited.

We designed and implemented a tool to thwart malicious non-control data attacks specifically targeting at authorization and authentication data structures assigned to a

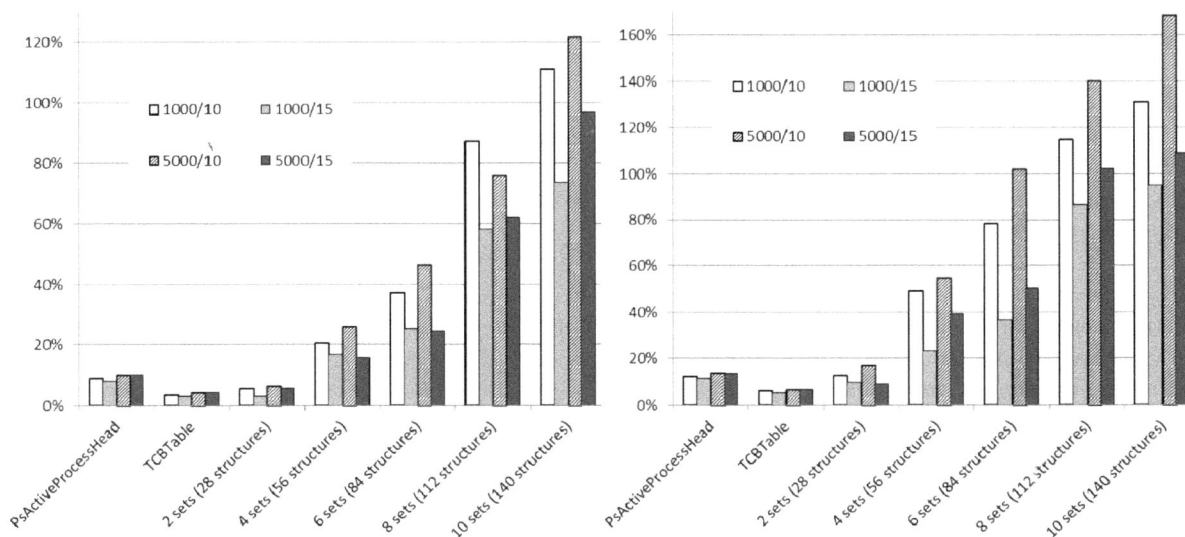

Figure 4. Performance overhead in the "always-on" mode using the Apache HTTP benchmark with 1 test VM (left) and 2 test VMs (right). We tested the benchmark using 4 different configurations for number of requests/concurrency: (1) 1000/10; (2) 1000/15; (3) 5000/10; and (4) 5000/15.

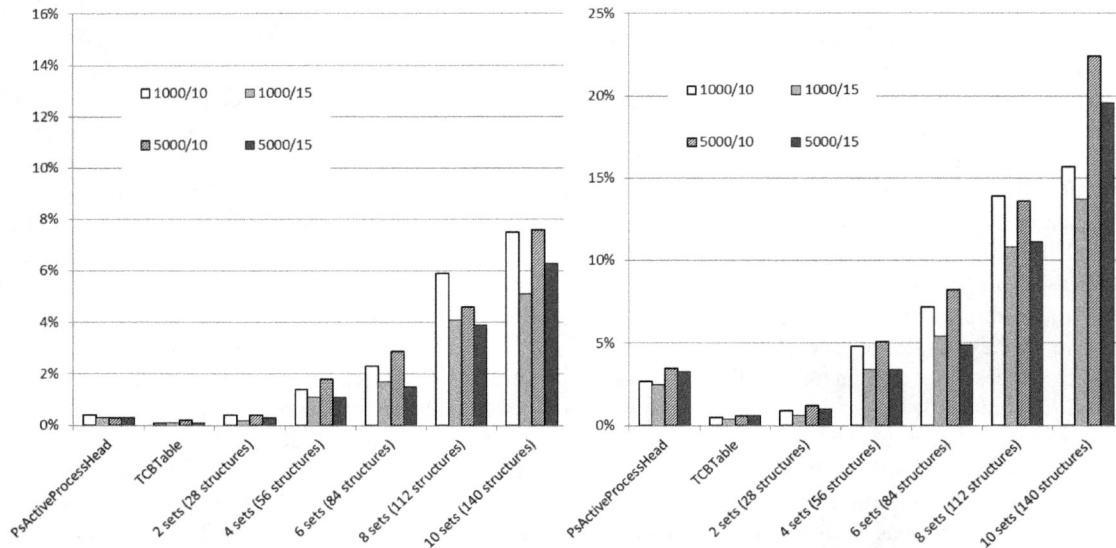

Figure 5. Performance overhead in the "periodic polling" mode using the Apache HTTP benchmark with the timing parameter T set to 50 msec (left) and 5 msec (right). We tested the benchmark using 4 different configurations for number of requests/concurrency: (1) 1000/10; (2) 1000/15; (3) 5000/10; and (4) 5000/15.

running process in the Windows OS. These attacks allow an attacker to raise privileges of a malicious process without making a single call to any related APIs by modifying data contained in the EPROCESS and TOKEN data structures directly in memory. By leveraging the real-time monitoring capability of the RTKDSM system, the tool monitors all write accesses to memory pages containing EPROCESS and TOKEN data structures of running processes and their real-time analysis when updates targeting these data were detected.

This tool indeed could successfully detect all privilege escalation attacks tested. Moreover, the run-time performance overhead was kept under 10%.

7. Related Work

7.1 Bridging the Semantic Gap

Several research studies have attempted to developed frameworks to make it easier for researchers to experiment with VMI without focusing on low-level details.

XenAccess framework was developed as a monitoring library for the Xen hypervisor. The purpose of this library was to provide memory and disk monitoring capabilities for both open source and closed source OSes. Hay and Nance created the VIX tools to perform forensic analysis of VMs running on Xen [20, 21]. The VIX tools were designed to allow a forensic investigator to perform live analysis of a VM system. Compared to the RTKDSM framework, XenAccess and VIX did not provide active monitoring, and their memory analysis capabilities were quite limited.

A whole-system binary code extractor, called Virtuoso, generated out-of-box code for use in VMI [22]. Using Virtuoso, developers could create VMI programs to monitor VMs running a variety of different OSes.

A novel technique, called process implanting, was proposed to narrow the semantic gap by implanting a process into the monitored VM and executing it under the cover of an existing running process [23]. The downside of this approach was that any reliance on functionality on the monitored VM ran the risk of deception by malware present in that VM, as if the implanted process were running as a process on the VM itself.

In another study, a lightweight introspection framework, called Pathogen, was proposed to streamline detection of the exact OS version and data structure definitions eliminating the use of hard-coded symbolic information relied upon by forensic analysis tools [24]. This framework is in an early stage of development supporting analysis of a limited number of data structures and lacking active data structure monitoring capabilities.

7.2 Real-Time Data Structure Monitoring Systems

A number of studies have developed out-of-VM real-time data structure monitors to detect integrity violations. Petroni et al. [25] proposed a framework for detection of attacks against dynamic kernel data structures using a coprocessor-based external monitor that periodically compared actual observed dynamic kernel data structures with specifications of correct kernel data structures and reported any semantic integrity violations. The data structure extractions were performed asynchronously with the monitored system's execution rendering this approach vulnerable to dynamic data attacks occurring between consecutive checks. On the contrary, the RTKDSM system developed was able to extract and analyze data structures synchronously, overcoming the limitation of the coprocessor-based approach.

In another related study, Srivastava et al. [26] developed Sentry, a VM-based system to prevent illegitimate changes to critical kernel data structures. Sentry's memory protection introduced modifications to the monitored OS to identify locations of dynamically-allocated kernel data objects and allowed only alterations invoked by legitimate kernel functionality. This kind of protection was difficult to design for a closed source operating system such as Windows. Compared to Sentry, the RTKDSM system offered an advantage of not requiring modifications to the monitored OS.

Rhee et al. [27] proposed a solution to prevent attacks on kernel data structures using QEMU emulator as an external monitor. At runtime, the system identified data structures in memory and intercepted all writes to their address ranges. Their approach was only portable to VM monitors that supported memory interposition to translate guest instructions into host instructions. Unlike in the RTKDSM system, such approach could not be extended to support commercial hypervisors that did not support memory interposition, such as Xen and VMWare ESX.

8. Future Work

An important problem that needs to be addressed by the future research is how to enable the RTKDSM system to automatically and dynamically choose between the "always-on" and the "periodic polling" mode without compromising monitored VMs' performance or the accuracy and effectiveness of change detection. Our research showed that some kernel data structures are likely to be allocated on memory pages that suffer from frequent spurious updates unrelated to the data structure itself, and the "periodic polling" mode is a better choice for monitoring such data structures. For this group of data structures, the next step is to quantify the number of changes that may be missed as a result of different polling frequencies in the "periodic polling" mode to help determine the optimal polling interval to achieve a certain level of accuracy of change detection.

Our research also indicated that some data structures are allocated on memory pages that are rarely updated; therefore monitoring of such data structures can be done in the "always on" mode without impacting the performance. In the next phase of this work, we will profile memory pages that hold common kernel data structures in multiple operating systems and add to the RTKDSM system a capability to dynamically choose the most appropriate monitoring mode according to the application-specified data structure types. Alternatively, we may apply machine learning techniques to efficiently train the RTKDSM system to choose between the "always-on" and "periodic polling" mode for various kernel data structure types.

9. Conclusion

VMI is a powerful technique that allows examination of a running VM's execution time in an agentless fashion. However, VMI applications are notoriously difficult to build because of the semantic gap between the byte value contents of memory pages and meaningful interpretations of the data structured contained within. This paper describes the design, implementation and evaluation of the RTKDSM system, whose goal is to facilitate the development of VMI applications by alleviating them of the task of closing the semantic gap. Specifically, a VMI application just needs to specify kernel data structures of interest, and the RTKDSM system is responsible for tracking down the memory locations of these data structures in the monitored guest OS, and notifying the application immediately when these data structures change at run time.

The RTKDSM achieves this feat by combining an offline computer forensic memory analysis tool called Volatility, with real-time dirty page tracking. By leveraging Volatility, the RTKDSM system is able to discover and analyze kernel data structures in multiple versions of the Windows and Linux OS without needing access to their source code. The result is a system that is able to receive high-level VMI requests, then *automatically* derive physical memory locations holding kernel data structures of interest and then *continuously* monitor the specified kernel data structures in real time to support active monitoring. The RTKDSM system is the first known VMI application development framework that is capable of this kind of real-time introspection.

The usefulness and effectiveness of the RTKDSM system has been demonstrated by successfully developing three applications: a data flow tracking tool for payment data that uses VMI to accurately track the trajectory of payment data through a distributed system, an application whitelisting tool to lock down a VDI by ensuring every piece of binary code used to start a thread, process or a DLL is in an approved list, and a privilege escalation monitoring tool to prevent direct un-authorized modifications to kernel data structures without using any API. Moreover, the fact that the performance penalty of monitored VMs in these VMI applications is relatively modest shows that the RTKDSM system is practical, usable, and ready for real-world VMI applications.

References

[1] A. Srivastava and J. Giffin. Tamper-resistant, application-aware blocking of malicious network connections. In *Proceedings of the 11th International Symposium on Recent Advances in Intrusion Detection (RAID 2008)*, pages 39-58, September 2008.

[2] B. D. Payne, M. Carbone, M. Sharif, and W. Lee. Lares: An architecture for secure active monitoring using virtualization.

In *Proceedings of the IEEE Symposium on Security and Privacy (IEEE SP 2008)*, pages 233-247, May 2008.

[3] X. Jiang, A. Wang, and D. Xu. Stealthy malware detection through VMM-based "out-of-the-box" semantic view reconstruction. In *Proceedings of the 14th ACM Conference on Computer and Communications Security (CCS 2007)*, pages 128-138, October 2007.

[4] T. Garfinkel and M. Rosenblum. A virtual machine introspection based architecture for intrusion detection. In *Proceedings of the Network and Distributed Systems Security Symposium (NDSS 2003)*, pages 191-206, February 2003.

[5] L. Litty and D. Lie. Manitou: A layer-below approach to fighting malware. In *Proceedings of the 1st Workshop on Architectural and System Support for Improving Software Dependability (ASID 2006)*, pages 6-11, October 2006.

[6] S. T. Jones, A. C. Arpaci-Dusseau, and R. H. Arpaci-Dusseau. VMM-based hidden process detection and identification using Lycosid. In *Proceedings of the 4th ACM SIGPLAN/SIGOPS International Conference on Virtual Execution Environments (VEE 2008)*, pages 91-100, March 2008.

[7] S. T. Jones, A. C. Arpaci-Dusseau, and R. H. Arpaci-Dusseau. Antfarm: Tracking processes in a virtual machine environment. In *Proceedings of the 2006 USENIX Annual Technical Conference (USENIX ATEC 2006)*, pages 1-14, June 2006.

[8] L. Litty, H.A. Lagar-Cavilla, and D. Lie. Hypervisor support for identifying covertly executing binaries. In *Proceedings of the 17th USENIX Security Symposium (USENIX SS 2008)*, pages 243-258, July 2008.

[9] https://www.volatilesystems.com/default/volatility.

[10] S. Bahram, X. Jiang, Z. Wang, M. Grace, J. Li, and D. Xu. DKSM: Subverting virtual machine introspection for fun and profit. In *Proceedings of the 29th IEEE Symposium on Reliable Distributed Systems (SRDS 2010)*, pages 82-91, November 2010.

[11] A. Baliga, V. Ganapathy, and L. Iftode. Automatic inference and enforcement of kernel data structure invariants. In *Proceedings of the 24th Annual Computer Security Applications Conference (ACSAC 2008)*, pages 77-86, December 2008.

[12] B. Dolan-Gavitt, A. Srivastava, P. Traynor, and J. Giffin. Robust signatures for kernel data structures. In *Proceedings of the 16th ACM Conference on Computer and Communications Security (CCS 2009)*, pages 566-577, November 2009.

[13] Z. Gu, Z. Deng, D. Xu, and X. Jiang. Process implanting: A new active introspection framework for virtualization. In *Proceedings of the 30th IEEE Symposium on Reliable Distributed Systems (SRDS 2011)*, pages 147-156, July 2011.

[14] http://www.futuremark.com/benchmarks/pcmark05/

[15] http://httpd.apache.org/docs/2.2/programs/ab.html.

[16] G. Dunlap, S. King, S. Cinar, M. Basrai, and P. Chen. Revirt: Enabling intrusion analysis through virtual-machine logging and replay. In *Proceedings of the 5th USENIX Symposium on Operating Systems Design and Implementation (OSDI 2002)*, pages 211-224, 2002.

[17] PCI Council. https://www.pcisecuritystandards.org/.

[18] J. Hizver and T. Chiueh. Tracking payment card data flow using virtual machine state introspection. In *Proceedings of the 27th Annual Computer Security Applications Conference (ACSAC 2011)*, pages 277-285, December 2011.

[19] J. Hizver and T. Chiueh. Cloud-based application whitelisting. In *Proceedings of the 6th IEEE International Conference on Cloud Computing (CLOUD 2013)*, pages 636-643, July 2013.

[20] B. Hay and K. Nance. Forensics examination of volatile system data using virtual introspection. *ACM SIGOPS Operating Systems Review*, vol. 42, issue 3, pages 75-83, April 2008.

[21] K. Nance, M. Bishop, and B. Hay. Investigating the implications of virtual machine introspection for digital forensics. In *Proceedings of the International Conference on Availability, Reliability and Security (ARES 2009)*, pages 1024-1029, March 2009.

[22] B. Dolan-Gavitt, T. Leek, M. Zhivich, J. Giffin, and W. Lee. Virtuoso: Narrowing the semantic gap in virtual machine introspection. In *Proceedings of the 32nd IEEE Symposium on Security and Privacy (IEEE SP 2011)*, pages 297-312, May 2011.

[23] Z. Gu, Z. Deng, D. Xu, and X. Jiang. Process implanting: A new active introspection framework for virtualization. In *Proceedings of the 30th IEEE Symposium on Reliable Distributed Systems (SRDS 2011)*, pages 147-156, July 2011.

[24] A. Roberts, R. McClatchey, S. Liaquat, N. Edwards, M. Wray. Introducing Pathogen: a real-time virtual machine introspection framework. In *Proceedings of the 20th ACM Conference on Computer and Communications Security (ACM CCS 2013)*, November 2013.

[25] N. Petroni, T. Fraser, J. Molina, and W. Arbaugh. Copilot—a coprocessor-based kernel runtime integrity monitor. In *Proceedings of the 13th USENIX Security Symposium (USENIX SS 2004)*, pages 179-194, August 2004.

[26] A. Srivastava, I. Erete, and J. Giffin. Kernel data integrity protection via memory access control. *Georgia Institute of Technology*, 2009. http://hdl.handle.net/1853/30785.

[27] J. Rhee, R. Riley, D. Xu, and X. Jiang. Defeating dynamic data kernel rootkit attacks via VMM-based guest-transparent monitoring. In *Proceedings of the International Conference on Availability, Reliability and Security (ARES 2009)*, pages 74-81, March 200

Tesseract: Reconciling Guest I/O and Hypervisor Swapping in a VM

Kapil Arya *

Northeastern University
kapil@ccs.neu.edu

Yury Baskakov

VMware, Inc.
ybaskako@vmware.com

Alex Garthwaite *

agarthwaite@acm.org

Abstract

Double-paging is an often-cited, if unsubstantiated, problem in multi-level scheduling of memory between virtual machines (VMs) and the hypervisor. This problem occurs when both a virtualized guest and the hypervisor overcommit their respective physical address-spaces. When the guest pages out memory previously swapped out by the hypervisor, it initiates an expensive sequence of steps causing the contents to be read in from the hypervisor swapfile only to be written out again, significantly lengthening the time to complete the guest I/O request. As a result, performance rapidly drops.

We present Tesseract, a system that directly and transparently addresses the double-paging problem. Tesseract tracks when guest and hypervisor I/O operations are redundant and modifies these I/Os to create indirections to existing disk blocks containing the page contents. Although our focus is on reconciling I/Os between the guest disks and hypervisor swap, our technique is general and can reconcile, or deduplicate, I/Os for guest pages read or written by the VM.

Deduplication of disk blocks for file contents accessed in a common manner is well-understood. One challenge that our approach faces is that the locality of guest I/Os (reflecting the guest's notion of disk layout) often differs from that of the blocks in the hypervisor swap. This loss of locality through indirection results in significant performance loss on subsequent guest reads. We propose two alternatives to recovering this lost locality, each based on the idea of asynchronously reorganizing the indirected blocks in persistent storage.

We evaluate our system and show that it can significantly reduce the costs of double-paging. We focus our experiments

on a synthetic benchmark designed to highlight its effects. In our experiments we observe Tesseract can improve our benchmark's throughput by as much as 200% when using traditional disks and by as much as 30% when using SSD. At the same time worst case application responsiveness can be improved by a factor of 5.

Categories and Subject Descriptors D.4.2 [*Storage Management*]: Virtual memory, Main memory, Allocation/deallocation strategies, Storage hierarchies

Keywords Virtualization; memory overcommitment; swapping; paging; virtual machines; hypervisor

1. Introduction

Guests running in virtual machines read and write state between their memory and virtualized disks. Hypervisors such as VMware ESXi [1] likewise may page guest memory to and from a hypervisor-level swap file to reclaim memory. To distinguish these two cases, we refer to the activity within the guest OS as *paging* and that within the hypervisor as *swapping*. In overcommitted situations, these two sets of operations can result in a two-level scheduling anomaly known as "double paging". Double-paging occurs when the guest attempts to page out memory that has previously been swapped out by the hypervisor and leads to long delays for the guest as the contents are read back into machine memory only to be written out again.

While the double-paging anomaly is well known [6–8, 13, 17], its impact on real workloads is not established. In addition, recent studies show that other factors significantly impact the performance of guests in the presence of uncooperative hypervisor swapping activity [5]. This paper also does not address the question of how often the double-paging anomaly occurs in real workloads. Nonetheless, we do show its effects can be mitigated in a virtual environment.

Our approach addresses the double-paging problem directly in a manner transparent to the guest. First, the virtual machine is extended to track associations between guest memory and either blocks in guest virtual disks or in the hypervisor swap file. Second, the virtual disks are extended to support a mechanism to redirect virtual block requests

---

* Work done while all authors were at VMware.

to blocks in other virtual disks or the hypervisor swap file. Third, the hypervisor swap file is extended to track references to its blocks. Using these components to restructure guest I/O requests, we eliminate the main effects of double-paging by replacing the original guest operations with indirections between the guest and swap stores. An important benefit of this approach is that where hypervisors typically attempt to avoid swapping pages likely to be paged out by the guest, the two levels may now cooperate in selecting pages since the work is complementary.

We have prototyped our approach on the VMware Workstation [3] platform enhanced to explicitly swap memory in and out. While the current implementation focuses on deduplicating guest I/Os for contents stored in the hypervisor swap file, it is general enough to also deduplicate redundant contents between guest I/Os themselves or between the hypervisor swap file and guest disks.

We present results using a synthetic benchmark that show, for the first time, the cost of the double-paging problem. We also show the impact of an unexpected side-effect of our solution: loss of locality caused by indirections to the hypervisor swap file which can substantially slow down subsequent guest I/Os. Finally, we describe techniques to detect this loss of locality and to recover it. These techniques isolate the expensive costs of the double-paging effect and making them asynchronous with respect to the guest.

We begin, in Section 2, with an exploration of the problems we are solving. In Section 3, we offer a high-level overview of our solution and the challenges it addresses. In Section 4, we describe the implementation of our basic prototype, in Section 5 we consider extensions to recover guest locality through defragmentation, and in Section 6, we offer some initial results. In Section 7, we turn to related work. Finally, in Sections 8 and 9, we outline possible future directions and conclude.

2. Motivation: The Doubly-Paging Anomaly

Tesseract has four objectives. First, to extend VMware's host platforms to explicitly manage how the hypervisor pages out memory so that its swap subsystem can employ many of the optimizations used by the ESX platform. Second, to prototype the mechanisms needed to identify redundant I/Os originating from the guest and virtual machine monitor (VMM) and eliminate these. Third, to use this prototype to justify restructuring the underlying virtual disks of VMs to support this optimization. Finally, to simplify the hypervisor's memory scheduler so that it need not avoid paging out memory that guest may decide to page. To address these, the project initially focused on the double-paging anomaly.

One of the tasks of the hypervisor is to allocate and map host (or machine) memory to the VMs it is managing. Likewise, one of the tasks of the guest operating system in a VM is to manage the guest physical address space, allocating and mapping it to the processes running in the guest. In both

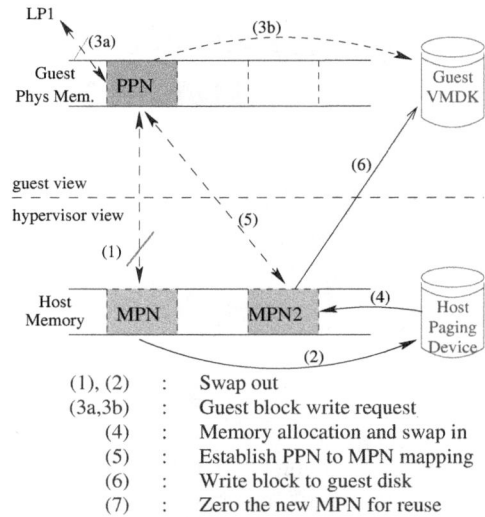

(1), (2)	:	Swap out
(3a,3b)	:	Guest block write request
(4)	:	Memory allocation and swap in
(5)	:	Establish PPN to MPN mapping
(6)	:	Write block to guest disk
(7)	:	Zero the new MPN for reuse

Figure 1: *An example of double-paging.*

cases, either the set of machine memory pages or the set of guest physical pages may be oversubscribed.

In overcommitted situations, the appropriate memory scheduler must repurpose some memory pages. For example, the hypervisor may reclaim memory from a VM by swapping out guest pages to the hypervisor-level swap file. Having preserved the contents of those pages, the underlying machine memory may be used for a new purpose. The guest OS may reclaim memory within a VM too to allow a guest physical page to be used by a new virtual mapping.

As hypervisor-level memory reclamation is transparent to the guest OS, the latter may choose to page out to a virtualized disk pages that were already swapped by the hypervisor. In such cases, hypervisor must synchronously allocate machine pages to hold the contents and read the already swapped contents back into that memory so they can be saved, in turn, to the guest OS's swap device. This multi-level scheduling conflict is called double-paging.

Figure 1 illustrates the double-paging problem. Suppose the hypervisor decides to reclaim a machine page (MPN) that is backing a guest physical page (PPN). In step 1, the mapping between the PPN and MPN is invalidated and, in step 2, the contents of MPN is saved to the hypervisor's swap file. Suppose the guest OS later decides to reallocate PPN for a new guest virtual mapping. It, in turn, in step 3a invalidates the guest-level mappings to that PPN and initiates an I/O to preserve its contents in a guest virtual disk (or guest VMDK). In handling the guest I/O request, the hypervisor must ensure that the contents to be written are available in memory. So, in step 4, the hypervisor faults the contents into a newly allocated page (MPN2) and, in step 5, establishes a mapping from PPN to MPN2. This sequence puts extra pressure on the hypervisor memory system and may further cause additional hypervisor-level swapping as a result of allocating MPN2. In step 6, the guest OS completes the I/O by writing the contents of MPN2 to the guest VMDK. Finally, the guest OS is able to zero the contents of the new MPN so that the PPN that now maps to it can be used for a new virtual mapping in step 7.

A hypervisor has no control over when a virtualized guest may page memory out to disk, and may even employ reclamation techniques like ballooning [17] in addition to hypervisor-level swapping. Ballooning is a technique that co-opts the guest into choosing pages to release back to the platform. It employs a guest driver or agent to allocate, and often pin, pages in the guest's physical address-space. Ballooning is not a reliable solution in overcommitted situations since it requires guest execution to choose pages and release memory and the guest is unaware of which pages are backed by MPNs. Hypervisors that do not also page risk running out of memory. While preferring ballooning, VMware uses hypervisor swapping to guarantee progress. Because levels of overcommitment vary over time, hypervisor swapping may interleave with the guest, under pressure from ballooning, also paging. This can lead to double paging.

The double-paging problem also impacts hypervisor design. Citing the potential effects of double-paging, some [13] have advocated avoiding the use of hypervisor-level swapping completely. Others have attempted to mitigate the likelihood through techniques such as employing random page selection for hypervisor-level swapping [17] or employing some form of paging-aware paravirtualized interface [7, 8]. For example, VMware's scheduler uses heuristics to find "warm" pages to avoid paging out what the guest may also choose to page out. These heuristics have extended effects, for example, on the ability to provide large (2MB) mappings to the guest. Our goals are to address the double-paging problem in a manner that is transparent to the guest running in the VM and identifies and elides the unnecessary intermediate steps such as steps 4, 5 and 6 in Figure 1 and to simplify hypervisor scheduling policies. Although we do not demonstrate that double-paging is a problem in real workloads, we do show how its effects can be mitigated.

3. Design

We now describe our prototype's design. First, we describe how we extended the hosted platform to behave more like VMware's server platform, ESX. Next, we outline how we identify and eliminate redundant I/Os. Finally, we describe the design of the hypervisor swap subsystem and the extensions to the virtual disks to support indirections.

3.1 Extending The Hosted Platform To Be Like ESX

VMware supports two kinds of hypervisors: the hosted platform in which the hypervisor cooperatively runs on top of an unmodified host operating system such as Windows or Linux, and ESX where the hypervisor runs as the platform kernel, the *vmkernel*. Two key differences between these two platforms are how memory is allocated and mapped to a VM, and where the network and storage stacks execute.

In the existing hosted platform, each VM's device support is managed in the *vmx*, a user-level process running on the host operating system. Privileged services are mediated by the *vmmon* device driver loaded into the host kernel, and control is passed between the vmx and the VMM and its guest via vmmon. An advantage of the hosted approach is that the virtualization of I/O devices is handled by libraries in the vmx and these benefit from the device support of the underlying host OS. Guest memory is mmapped into the address space of the vmx. Memory pages exposed to the VMM and guest by using the vmmon device driver to pin the pages in the host kernel and return the MPNs to the VMM. By backing the mmapped region for guest memory with a file, hypervisor swapping is a simple matter of invalidating all mappings for the pages to be released in the VMM, marking, if necessary, those pages as dirty in the vmx's address space, and unpinning the pages on the host.

In ESX, network and storage virtual devices are managed in the vmkernel. Likewise, the hypervisor manages per-VM pools of memory for backing guest memory. To page memory out to the VM's swap file, the VMM and vmkernel simply invalidate any guest mappings and schedule the pages' contents to be written out. Because ESX explicitly manages the swap state for a VM including its swap file, it is able to employ a number of optimizations unavailable on the current hosted platform. These optimizations include the capturing of writes to entire pages of memory [4], and the cancellation of swap-ins for swapped-out guest PPNs that are targets for disk read requests.

The first optimization is triggered when the guest accesses an unmapped or write-protected page and faults into the VMM. At this point, the guest's instruction stream is analyzed. If the page is shared [17] and the effect of the write does not change the content of the page, page-sharing is not broken. Instead, the guest's program counter is advanced past the write and it is allowed to continue execution. If the guest's write is overwriting an entire page, one or both of two actions are taken. If the written pattern is a known value, such as repeated 0x00, the guest may be mapped a shared page. This technique is used, for example, on Windows guests because Windows zeroes physical pages as they are placed on the freelist. Linux, which zeroes on allocation of a physical page, is simply mapped a writeable zeroed MPN. Separately, any pending swap-in for that PPN is cancelled. Since the most common case is the mapping of a shared zeroed-page to the guest, this optimization is referred to as the PShareZero optimization.

The second optimization is triggered by interposition on guest disk read requests. If a read request will overwrite whole PPNs, any pending swap-ins associated with those PPNs are deferred during write-preparation, the pages are pinned for the I/O, and the swap-ins are cancelled on successful I/O completion.

We have extended Tesseract so that its guest-memory and swap mechanisms behave more like those of ESX. Instead of mmapping a pagefile to provide memory for the guest, Tesseract's vmx process mmaps an anonymously-backed region of its address space, uses madvise to mark the range as NOTNEEDED, and explicitly pins pages as they are accessed by either the vmx or by the VMM. Paging by the hypervisor becomes an explicit operation, reading from or writing to an explicit swap file. In this way, we are able to also employ the above optimizations on the hosted platform. We consider these as part of our baseline implementation.

3.2 Reconciling Redundant I/Os

Tesseract addresses the double-paging problem *transparently* to the guest allowing our solution to be applied to unmodified guests. To achieve this goal, we employ two forms of interposition. The first tracks writes to PPNs by the guest and is extended to include a mechanism to track valid relationships between guest memory pages and disk blocks that contain the same state. The second exploits the fact that the hypervisor interposes on guest I/O requests in order to transform the requests' scatter-gather lists. In addition, we modify the structure of the guest VMDKs and the hypervisor swap file, extending the former to support indirections from the VMDKs into the hypervisor swap disk. Finally, when the guest reallocates the PPN and zeroes its contents, we apply the PShareZero optimization in step 7 in Figure 1.

In order to track which pages have writable mappings in the guest, MPNs are initially mapped into the guest read-only. When written by the guest, the resulting page-fault allows the hypervisor to track that the guest page has been modified. We extend this same tracking mechanism to also track when guest writes invalidate associations between guest pages in memory and blocks on disk. The task is simpler when the hypervisor, itself, modifies guest memory since it can remove any associations for the modified guest pages. Likewise, virtual device operations into guest pages can create associations between the source blocks and pages. In addition, the device operations may remove prior associations when the underlying disk blocks are written. This approach, employed for example to speed the live migration of VMs from one host to another [14], can efficiently track which guest pages in memory have corresponding valid copies of their contents on disks.

The second form of interposition occurs in the handling of virtualized guest I/O operations. The basic I/O path can be broken down into three stages. The basic data structure describing an I/O request is the scatter-gather list, a structure that maps one or more possibly discontiguous memory extents to a contiguous range of disk sectors. In the *preparation* stage, the guest's scatter-gather list is examined and a new request is constructed that will be sent to the underlying physical device. It is here that the unmodified hypervisor handles the faulting in of swapped out pages as shown in steps 4 and 5 of Figure 1. Once the new request has been constructed, it

is *issued asynchronously* and some time later there is an *I/O completion* event.

To support the elimination of I/Os to and from virtual disks and the hypervisor block-swap store (or BSST), each guest VMDK has been extended to maintain a mapping structure allowing its virtual block identifiers to refer to blocks in other VMDKs. Likewise, the hypervisor BSST has been extended with per-block reference counts to track whether blocks in the swap file are accessible from other VMDKs or from guest memory.

The tracking of associations and interposition on guest I/Os allows four kinds of I/O elisions:

swap - guest-I/O a guest I/O follows the hypervisor swapping out a page's contents

swap - swap a page is repeatedly swapped out to the BSST with no intervening modification

guest-I/O - swap the case in which the hypervisor can take advantage of prior guest reads or writes to avoid writing redundant contents to the BSST

guest-I/O - guest-I/O the case in which guest I/Os can avoid redundant operations based on prior guest operations where the results known reside in memory (for reads) or in a guest VMDK (for writes)

For simplicity, Tesseract focuses on the first two cases since these capture the case of double-paging. Because Tesseract does not introspect on the guest, it cannot distinguish guest I/Os related to memory paging from other kinds of guest I/O. But the technique is general enough to support a wider set of optimizations such as disk deduplication for content streamed through a guest. It also complements techniques that eliminate redundant read I/Os across VMs [13].

3.3 Tesseract's Virtual Disk and Swap Subsystems

Figure 2 shows our approach embodied in Tesseract. The hypervisor swaps guest memory to a block-swap store (BSST) VMDK, which manages a map from guest PPNs to blocks in the BSST, a per-block reference-counting mechanism to track indirections from guest virtual disks, and a pool of 4KB disk blocks. When the guest OS writes out a memory page that happens to be swapped out by the hypervisor, the disk subsystem detects this condition while preparing to issue the write request. Rather than bringing memory contents for the swapped out page back to memory, the hypervisor updates the appropriate reference counts in the BSST, issues the I/O, and updates metadata in guest VMDK and adds a reference to the corresponding disk block in BSST.

Figure 3 shows timelines for the scenario when guest OS is paging out an already swapped page with and without Tesseract. With Tesseract we are able to eliminate the overheads of a new page allocation and a disk read.

To achieve this, Tesseract modifies the I/O preparation and I/O completion steps. For write requests, the memory pages in the scatter-gather list are checked for valid associations to

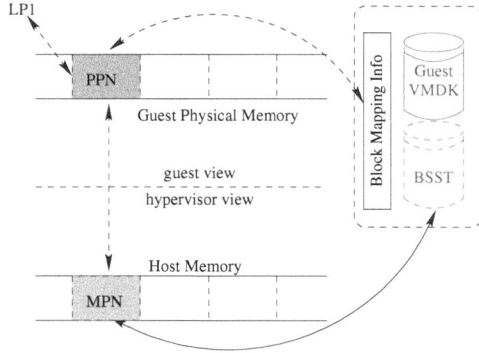

Figure 2: *Double-paging with Tesseract.*

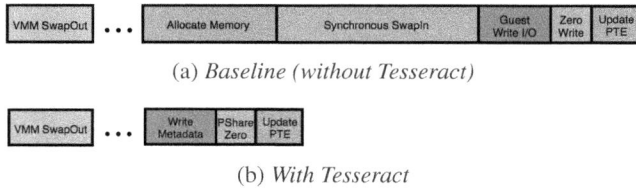

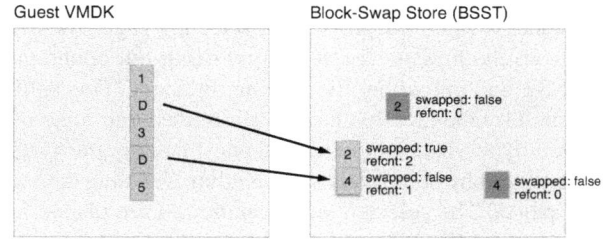

(a) *Baseline (without Tesseract)*

(b) *With Tesseract*

Figure 3: *Write I/O and hypervisor swapping.*

(a) *With Tesseract*

(b) *With Tesseract and BSST defragmentation*

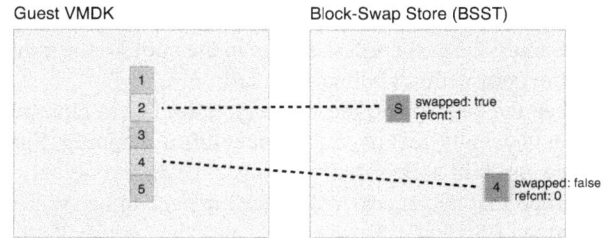

(c) *With Tesseract and guest VMDK defragmentation*

Figure 4: *Examples of Tesseract and of defragmentation.*

blocks in the BSST. If these are found, the target VMDK's mapping structure is updated for those pages' corresponding virtual disk blocks to reference the appropriate blocks in the BSST and the reference counts of these referenced blocks in the BSST are incremented. For read requests, the guest I/O request may be split into multiple I/O requests depending on where the source disk blocks reside.

Consider the state of a guest VMDK and the BSST as shown in Figure 4a. Here, a guest write operation wrote five disk blocks in which two were previously swapped to the BSST. In this example, block 2 still contains the swapped contents of some PPN and has a reference count reflecting this fact and the guest write. Hence, its state has "swapped" as true and a reference count of 2. Similarly, block 4 only has a nonzero reference count because the PPN whose swapped contents originally created the disk block has since been accessed and its contents paged back in. Hence, its state has "swapped" as false and a reference count of 1. To read these blocks from the guest VMDK now requires three read operations: one against the guest VMDK and two against the BSST. The results of these read operations must then be coalesced in the read completion path.

One can view the primary cost of double-paging in an unmodified hypervisor as impacting the write-preparation time for guest I/Os. Likewise, one can view the primary cost of these cases in Tesseract as impacting the read-completion time. To mitigate these effects, we consider two forms of defragmentation. Both strategies make two assumptions:

- the original guest write I/O request (represented in blue) captures the guest's notion of expected locality, and

- the guest is unlikely to immediately read the same disk blocks back into memory

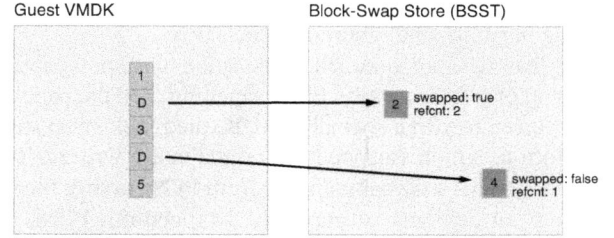

Based on these assumptions, we extended Tesseract to asynchronously reorganize the referenced state in the BSST. In Figure 4b, we copy the referenced blocks into a contiguous sequence in the BSST and update the guest VMDK indirections to refer to the new sequence. This approach reduces the number of split read operations. In Figure 4c, we copy the references blocks back to the locations in the original guest VMDK where the guest expects them. With this approach, the typical read operation need not be split. In effect, Tesseract asynchronously performs the expensive work that occurred in steps 4, 5, and 6 of Figure 1 eliminating its cost to the guest.

4. Implementation

Our prototype extends VMware Workstation as described in section 3.1. Here, we provide more detail.

4.1 Explicit Management of Hypervisor Swapping

VMware Workstation relies on the host OS to handle much of the work associated with swapping guest memory. A pagefile is mapped into the vmx's address space and calls to the vmmon driver are used to lock MPNs backing this memory as needed by the guest. When memory is released through hypervisor swapping, the pages are dirtied, if necessary, in the vmx's address space and unlocked by vmmon. Should the host OS need to reclaim the backing memory, it does so as if the vmx were any other process: it writes out the state to the backing pagefiles and repurposes the MPN.

For Tesseract, we modified Workstation to support explicit swapping of guest memory. First, we eliminated the pagefile and replaced it with a special VMDK, the block swap store (BSST) into which swapped-out contents are written. The BSST maintains a partial mapping from PPNs to disk blocks tracking the contents of currently swapped-out PPNs. In addition, BSST maintains a table of reference counts on the blocks in the BSST referenced by other guest VDMKs.

Second, we split the process for selecting pages for swapping from the process for actually writing out contents to the BSST and unlocking the backing memory. This split is motivated by the fact that having eliminated duplicate I/Os between hypervisor swapping and guest paging, the system should benefit by both levels of scheduling choosing the same set of pages. The selected swap candidates are placed in a victim cache to "cool down". Only the coldest pages are eventually written out to disk. This victim cache is maintained as a percentage of locked memory by the guest—for our study, 10%. Should the guest access a page in the pool, it is removed from the pool without being unlocked.

When the guest pages out memory, it does so to repurpose a given guest physical page for a new linear mapping. Since this new use will access that guest physical page, one may be concerned that this access will force the page to be swapped in from the BSST first. However, because the guest will either zero the contents of that page or read into it from disk and because the VMM can detect that the whole page will be overwritten before it is visible to the guest, the vmx is able to cancel the swap-in and complete the page locking operation.

4.2 Tracking Memory Pages and Disk Blocks

There are two steps to maintaining a mapping between disk blocks and pages in memory. The first is recognizing the pages read and written in guest and hypervisor I/O operations. By examining scatter-gather lists of each I/O, one can identify when the contents in memory and on disk match. While we plan to maintain this mapping for all associations between guest disks and guest memory, we currently only track the associations between blocks in the BSST and main memory.

The second step is to track when these associations are broken. For guest memory, this event happens when the guest modifies a page of memory. The VMM tracks when this happens by trapping the fact that a writable mapping is required and this information is communicated to the vmx. For device accesses, on the other hand, this event is tracked either through explicit checks in the module which provides devices the access to guest memory, or by examining pagelists for I/O operations that read contents into memory pages.

4.3 I/O Paths

When the guest OS is running inside a virtual machine, guest I/O requests are intercepted by the VMM, which is

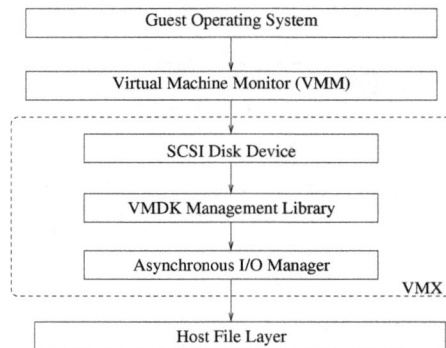

Figure 5: *VMware Workstation I/O Stack*

(a) *Scatter-gather prepared by the guest OS for disk write.*

(b) *Modified scatter-gather to avoid double-paging*

☐ pages in host memory   ■ pages swapped out to BSST   ▨ dummy page

Figure 6: *The pages swapped out to BSST are replaced with a dummy page to avoid double-paging. Indirections are created for the corresponding guest disk blocks.*

responsible for storage adaptor virtualization, and then passed to the hypervisor, where further I/O virtualization occurs.

Figure 5 identifies the primary modules in VMware Workstation's I/O stack. Tesseract inspects scatter-gather lists of incoming guest I/O requests in the SCSI Disk Device layer, where a request to the guest VMDK may be updated and extra I/O requests to the BSST may be issued as shown in Table 2. Waiting for the completion of all the I/O requests needed to service the original guest I/O request is isolated to the SCSI Disk Device layer as well. When running with defragmentation enabled (see Section 5), Tesseract allocates a pool of worker threads for handling defragmentation requests.

4.3.1 Guest Write I/Os

Guest I/O requests have PPNs in scatter-gather lists. The vmx rewrites the scatter-gather list, replacing guest PPNs with virtual pages from its address space before passing it further to the physical device. Normally, for write I/O requests, if a page was previously swapped, so that PPN does not have a backing MPN, the hypervisor allocates a new MPN and brings page's contents from disk.

With Tesseract, we check if the PPNs are already swapped out to BSST blocks by querying the PPN BSST-block mapping. We then use a virtual address of a special dummy page in the scatter-gather list for each page that resides in the BSST. On completion of the I/O, metadata associated with the guest VMDK is updated to reflect the fact that the contents of guest disk blocks for BSST-resident pages are in the BSST. This sequence allows the guest to page out memory without inducing double-paging.

Figure 6 illustrates how write I/O requests to the guest VMDK are handled by Tesseract. Tesseract recognizes that

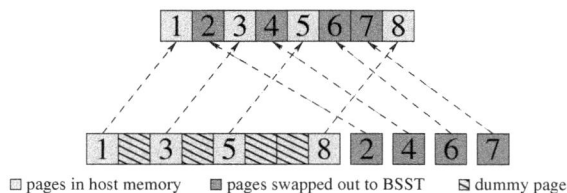

□ pages in host memory ■ pages swapped out to BSST ▨ dummy page

Figure 7: *Original guest read request split into multiple reads requests due to holes in the guest VMDK.*

contents for pages 2, 4, 6 and 7 in the scatter-gather list provided by the guest OS reside in the BSST (Figure 6a). When a new scatter-gather list to be passed to the physical device is formed, a dummy page is used for each BSST resident (Figure 6b).

4.3.2 Guest Reads I/Os and Guest Disk Fragmentation

Recognizing that data may reside in both the guest VMDK and the BSST is a double-edged sword. On the guest write path it allows us to dismiss pages that are already present in the BSST and thus avoid swapping them in just to be written out to the guest VMDK. However, when it comes to guest reads, the otherwise single I/O request might have to be split into multiple I/Os. This happens when some of the data needed by the I/O is located in the BSST.

Since data that has to be read from the BSST may not be contiguous on disk, the number of extra I/O requests to the BSST may be as high as the number of data pages in the original I/O request that reside in the BSST. We refer to a collection of pages in the original I/O request for which a separate I/O request to the BSST must be issued as a *hole*. Read I/O requests to the guest VMDK which have holes are called *fragmented*.

We modify a fragmented request so that all pages that should be filled in with the data from the BSST are replaced with a dummy page which will serve as a placeholder and will get random data read from the guest VMDK. So in the end for each fragmented read request we issue one modified I/O request to the guest VMDK and N requests to the BSST, where N is the number of holes. After all the issued I/Os are completed, we signal the completion of the originally issued guest read I/O request.

In Figure 7, the guest read I/O request finds disk blocks for pages 2, 4, 6 and 7 located on the BSST, where they are taking non-contiguous space. Tesseract issues one read request to the guest VMDK to get data for pages 1, 3, 5 and 8. In the scatter-gather list sent to the physical device, a dummy page is used as a read target for pages 2, 4, 6 and 7. Together with that one read I/O request to the guest VMDK, four read I/O requests are issued to the BSST. Each of those four requests reads data from one of the four disk blocks in the BSST.

4.3.3 Optimization of Repeated Swaps

In addition to addressing the double-paging anomaly by tracking guest I/Os whose contents exist in the BSST, we also implemented an optimization for back-to-back swap-out

requests for a memory page whose contents remain clean. If a page's contents are written out to the BSST, and later swapped back in, we continue to track the old block in the BSST as a form of victim cache. If the same page is chosen to be swapped out again and there has been no intervening write, we simply adjust the reference count for the block copy that is already in the BSST.

4.4 Managing Block Indirection Metadata

Tesseract keeps in-memory metadata for tracking PPN-to-BSST block mappings and for recording block indirections between guest and BSST VMDKs. The PPN-to-BSST block mapping is stored as key-value pair using a hash table. Indirection between guest and BSST VMDKs are tracked in a similar manner.

Tesseract also keeps reference counts for the BSST blocks. When a new PPN-to-BSST mapping is created, the reference count for the corresponding BSST block is set to 1. The reference count is incremented in the write prepare stage for PPNs found to have PPN-to-BSST block mappings. This ensures that such BSST blocks are not repurposed while the guest write is still in progress. Later, on the write completion path, the guest-VMDK-to-BSST indirection is created. The reference count of the BSST blocks is decremented during hypervisor swap in operation. It is also decremented when the guest VMDK block is overwritten by new contents and the previous guest block indirection is invalidated. Blocks with zero reference counts are considered free and reclaimable.

4.4.1 Metadata Consistency

While updating metadata in memory is faster than updating it on the disk, it poses consistency issues. What if the system crashes before the metadata is synced back to persistent storage? To reduce the likelihood of such problems, Tesseract periodically synchronizes the metadata to disk on the same schedule used by the VMDK management library for virtual disk state. However, because reference counts in the BSST and block-indirections in VMDKs are written at different stages in an I/O request, crashes must be detected and a `fsck`-like repair process run.

4.4.2 Entanglement of guest VMDKs and BSST

Once indirections are created between guest and BSST VMDK, it becomes impossible to move just the guest VMDK. To disentangle the guest VMDK, we must copy each block from the BSST to its guest VMDK for which there is an indirection. This can be done both online and offline. More details about the online process are in Section 5.2.

5. Guest Disk Fragmentation

As mentioned in Section 4.3.2, when running with Tesseract, guest read I/O requests might be fragmented in the sense that some of the data the guest is asking for in a single request may reside in both the BSST and the guest VMDK.

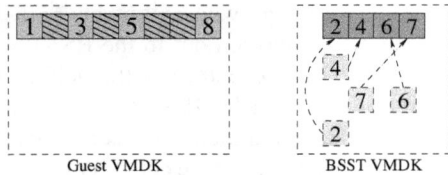

Figure 8: *Defragmenting the BSST.*

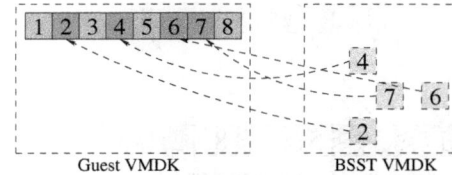

Figure 9: *Defragmenting the guest VMDK.*

The fragmentation level depends on the nature of the workload, the guest OS, and swap activity at the guest and the hypervisor level. Our experiments with SPECjbb2005 [16] showed that even for moderate level of memory pressure as much as 48% of all read I/O requests had at least one hole.

By solving double-paging problem Tesseract significantly reduced write-prepare time of the guest I/O requests since synchronous swap-in requests no longer cause delays. However, a non-trivial overhead was added to read-completion. Indeed, instead of waiting for a single read I/O request to the guest VMDK, the hypervisor may now have to wait for several extra read I/O requests to the BSST to complete before reporting the completion to the guest.

To address these overheads, Tesseract was extended with a *defragmentation* mechanism that improves read I/O access locality and thus reduces read-completion time. We investigated two approaches to implementing defragmentation - *BSST defragmentation* and *guest VMDK defragmentation*. While defragmentation is intended to help reduce read-completion time, it has its own cost. Defragmentation requests are asynchronous and reduce time to complete affected guest I/Os, but, at the same time, they contribute to a higher disk load and in the extreme cases may have an impact on read-prepare times. The defragmentation activity can be throttled on detecting performance bottlenecks due to higher disk load. ESX, for example, provides a mechanism, SIOC, that measures latencies to detect overload and enforce proportional-share fairness [9, 12]. The defragmentation mechanism could participate in this protocol.

5.1 BSST Defragmentation

BSST defragmentation uses guest write I/O requests as a hint of which BSST blocks might be accessed together in a single I/O read request in the future. Given that information we then group together the identified blocks in the BSST.

Figure 8 shows a scatter-gather list of the write I/O request that goes to the guest VMDK. In that request, the contents of pages 2, 4, 6 and 7 is already present in the BSST. As soon as these blocks are identified, a worker thread picks up a reallocation job that will allocate a new block in BSST and will copy the contents of BSST blocks for pages 2, 4, 6 and 7 into that new block.

BSST defragmentation is not perfect. If multiple guest VMDK writes create indirections to the same BSST blocks, multiple copies of those blocks may be made in the BSST. Further, since blocks are still present in both the guest VMDK and the BSST, extra I/O requests to the BSST cannot be entirely eliminated. In addition, BSST defragmentation tries to predict read access locality from write access locality and obviously the boundaries of read requests will not match with the boundaries of the write requests. So each read I/O request that without defragmentation would have required reads from both the guest VMDK and the BSST will still be split into the one which goes to the guest VMDK and one or more requests to the BSST. All this contributes to longer read completion times as shown in Table 4.

However, it is relatively easy to implement BSST defragmentation without worriying too much about data races with the I/O going to the guest VMDK. It can significantly reduce the number of extra I/Os that have to be issued to the BSST to service the guest I/O request as shown in Table 3.

If a guest read I/O request preserves the locality observed at the time of guest writes, we need more than one read I/O request from the BSST only when it hits more than one group of blocks created during BSST defragmentation. Although this is entirely dependent on a workload, one can expect read requests to typically be smaller than write requests, and, so, the number of extra I/O requests to BSST being reduced to one (fits into one defragmented area) or two (crosses the boundary of two defragmented areas) in many cases.

5.2 Guest VMDK Defragmentation

Like BSST defragmentation, guest VMDK defragmentation uses the scatter-gather lists of write I/O requests to identify BSST blocks that must be copied. But unlike BSST defragmentation, these blocks are copied to the guest VMDK. The goal is to restore the guest VMDK to the state it would have had without Tesseract. Tesseract with guest VMDK defragmentation replaces swap-in operations with asynchronous copying from the BSST to the guest VMDK. For example, in Figure 9, blocks 2, 4, 6 and 7 are copied to the relevant locations on the guest VMDK by a worker thread.

We enqueue a defragmentation request as soon as the scatter-gather list of the guest write I/O request is processed and blocks to be asynchronously fetched to the guest VMDK are identified. The defragmentation requests are organized as a priority queue. If a guest read I/O request needs to read data from the block that has not been copied from the BSST, the priority of the defragmentation request that refers to the block is raised to highest and the guest read I/O request is blocked until copying of all the missing blocks finishes.

While Tesseract with guest defragmentation can have an edge over Tesseract without defragmentation, it is not always a win. With guest defragmentation, before a guest I/O read

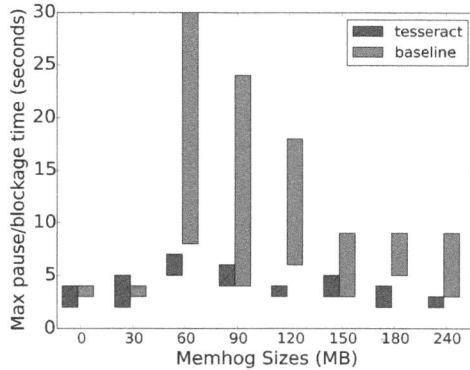

Figure 10: *Maximum single pauses observed in SPECjbb instantaneous scoring with various levels of guest memory pressure. Host memory overcommitment is 10%.*

request has a chance to be issued to the guest VMDK, it may become blocked waiting for a defragmentation request to complete. This may end up being slower than issuing requests to the BSST and the guest VMDK in parallel.

Disentanglement of Guest and BSST VMDKs. Guest defragmentation has an added benefit of removing the entanglement between guest and BSST VMDK. Once there are no block indirections between guest and BSST VMDK, the guest VMDK can be moved easily. This also allows us to disable Tesseract double-paging optimization on-the-fly.

6. Evaluation

We ran our experiments on an AMD Opteron 6168 (Magny-Cours) with 12 1.9 GHz cores, 1.5 GB of memory and a 1 TB 7200rpm Seagate SATA drive, a 1 TB 7200rpm Western Digital SATA drive, and a 128 GB Samsung SSD drive. We used OpenSUSE 11.4 as the host OS and a 6 VCPU 700 MB VM running Ubuntu 11.04. We used Jenkins [2] to monitor and manage execution of the test cases.

To ensure same test conditions for all test runs, we created a fresh copy of the guest virtual disk from backup before each run. For the evaluation we ran SPECjbb2005 [16] that was modified to emit instantaneous scores every second. It was run with 6 warehouses for 120 seconds. The heap size was set to 450 MB. The SPECjbb benchmark creates several warehouses and processes transactions for each of them.

We induced hypervisor-level swapping by setting a maximum limit on the pages the VM can lock. The BSST VMDK was preallocated. Swap-out victim cache size was chosen to be 10% of the VM's memory size.

Figure 11 and Figures 12–14, represent results from five trial runs. Figure 17 represents results from three trial runs.

6.1 Inducing Double-Paging Activity

To control hypervisor swapping, we set a hypervisor-imposed limit on the machine memory available for the VM. Guest paging was induced by running the SPECjbb benchmark with a working set larger than the available guest memory.

To induce double-paging, the guest must page out the pages that were already swapped by the hypervisor. Since, the hypervisor would choose only the cold pages from the guest memory, we employed a custom memhog that would lock some pages in the guest memory for a predetermined amount of time inside the guest. While the pages were locked by this memhog, a different memhog would repeatedly touch the rest of available guest pages making them "hot". At this point the pages locked by the first memhog are considered "cold" and swapped out by the hypervisor.

Next, memhog unlocks all its memory and the SPECjbb benchmark is started inside the guest. Once the warehouses have been created by SPECjbb, the memory pressure increases inside the guest. The guest is forced to find and page out "cold pages". The pages unlocked by memhog are good candidates as they have not been touched in the recent past.

We used memhog and memory locking in our setup to make the experiments more repeatable. In real world the conditions we were simulating could have been observed, for example, when execution phase shift of an application occurs, or when an application that caches a lot of data in memory and not actively uses is descheduled and another memory intensive application is woken up by the guest.

As a baseline we ran with Tesseract disabled. This effectively disabled analysis and rewriting of guest I/O commands so that all pages affected by an I/O command that happened to be swapped out by the hypervisor had to be swapped back in before the command could be issued to disk.

6.2 Application Performance

While it is hard to control and measure the direct impact of individual double-paging events, we use the pauses or gaps observed in the logged instantaneous scores of each SPECjbb run to characterize the application behavior. Depending upon the amount of double-paging activity, the pauses can be as big as 60 seconds in a 120 second run and negatively affect the final score. Often the pauses are associated with garbage collection activity.

6.2.1 Varying Levels of Guest Memory Pressure

Figure 11 shows scores and pause times for different sizes of memhog inside the guest with 10% host overcommitment. When the guest is trying to page out pages which are swapped by the hypervisor, the latter is swapping them back in and is forced to swap out some other pages. This cascade effect is responsible for increased pause period for the baseline. With Tesseract, however, the pause periods grow at a lower rate. This growth can be explained by longer wait times due to increased disk activity. Although the scores are about the same for higher guest memory pressure, the total pauses for Tesseract are less than that for the baseline.

Figure 10 shows the effect of increased memory pressure on the length of the biggest application pause. The bars represent the range of maximum pauses for individual sets of runs. There are five runs in each set. Notice that Tesseract clearly

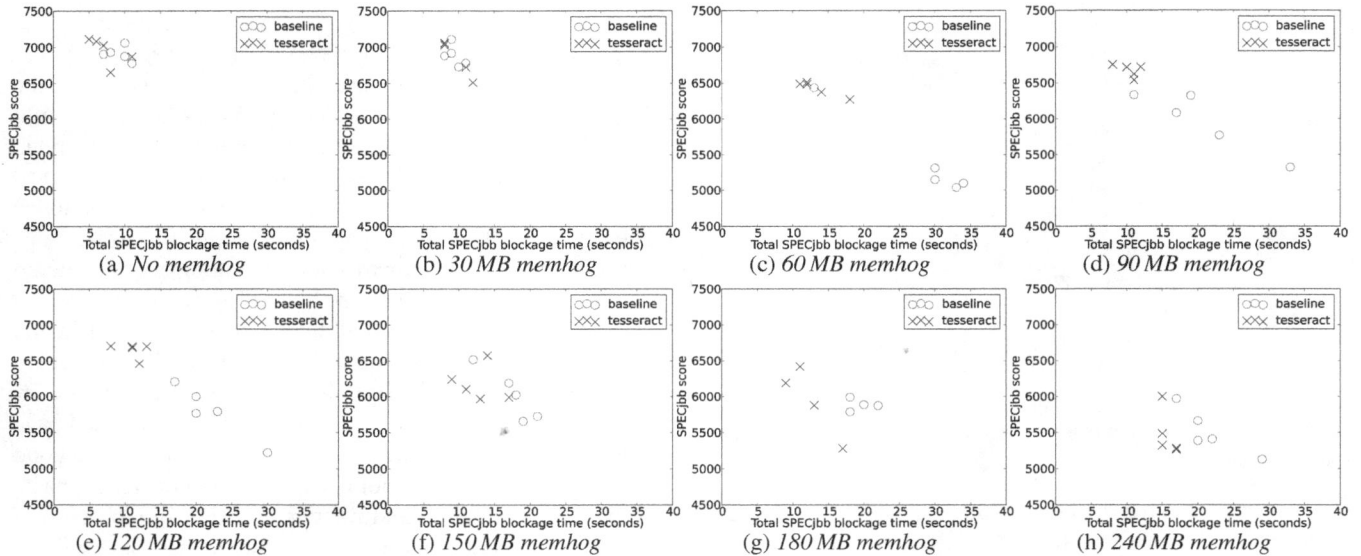

Figure 11: *Trends for the score and pauses in SPECjbb runs with various levels of guest memory pressure. Host overcommitment is 10%.*

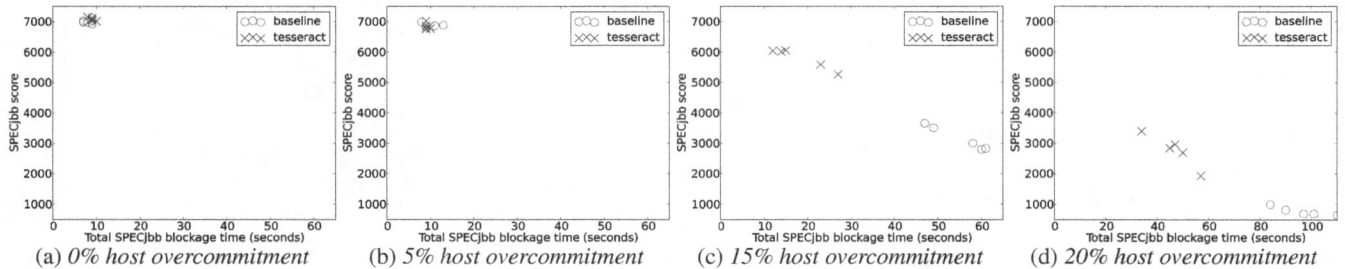

Figure 12: *Scores and total pause times obtained for SPECjbb runs with various levels of host overcommitment and 60 MB memhog.*

outperforms the baseline. The highest maximum pause time with Tesseract is 7 seconds, compared to 30 seconds for the baseline. This shows that the application is more responsive with Tesseract.

Host (%)	Guest I/Os Issued	I/Os with holes	I/Os 1 − 20 holes	I/Os 21 − 50 holes	I/Os > 50 holes	Double-paging cases
0	1,030	0	0	0	0	0
5	981	537	343	106	88	11,254
10	1,042	661	358	132	171	19,381
15	1,292	766	377	237	152	22,584
20	1,366	981	524	177	280	32,547

Table 1: *Holes in write I/O requests for various levels of host overcommitment. The memhog inside the guest is 60 MB.*

6.2.2 Varying Levels of Host Memory Pressure

To study the effect of increasing memory pressure by the hypervisor, we ran the application with various levels of host overcommitment with 60 MB memhog inside the guest.

Figure 12 shows the effect of increasing host memory pressure on the application scores and total pause times. For lower host pressure (0% and 5%), the score and pause times for the baseline and Tesseract are about the same. However, for higher memory pressure there is a significant difference in the performance. For example, in the 20% case, the

baseline observes total pauses in the range of 80–110 seconds. Tesseract, on the other hand, observes total pauses in a much lower range of 30–60 seconds.

Figure 16 focuses on the maximum pauses seen by the application as host memory pressure grows. While the maximum pauses are insignificant at lower memory pressure, with a higher pressure Tesseract clearly outperforms the baseline.

6.3 Double-Paging and Guest Write I/O Requests

Table 1 shows why double-paging is affecting guest write I/O performance. As expected, if the host is not experiencing memory pressure, none of the 1,030 guest write I/O requests refer to pages swapped by the hypervisor.

As memory pressure builds up, more and more guest write I/O requests require one or more pages to be swapped in before a write can be issued to the physical disk. All of this contributes to a longer write-prepare time for such a requests.

Consider a setup with 20% host memory is overcommitment. Of 1,366 guest write I/O requests 981 had at least one page that had to be swapped in. Then, 524 guest write I/O requests needed between 1 and 20 swap-in requests completed by the hypervisor in order to proceed, 177 needed between 21 and 50 swap-in requests completed, and, finally, 280 guest write I/O requests needed more than 50 swap-in requests.

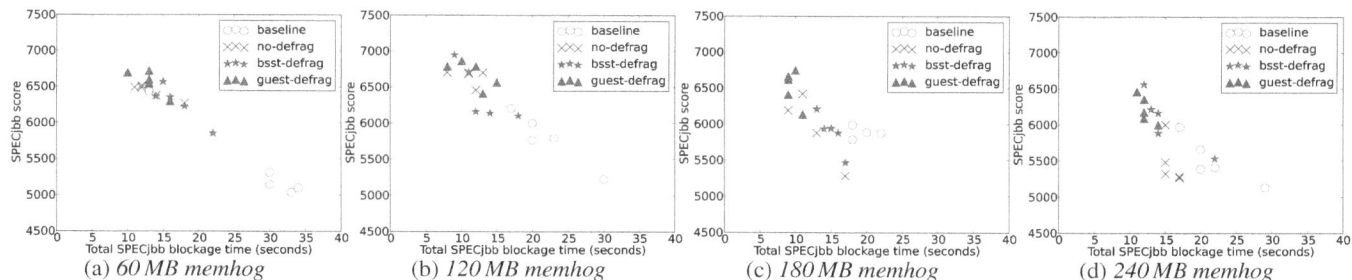

(a) *60 MB memhog*   (b) *120 MB memhog*   (c) *180 MB memhog*   (d) *240 MB memhog*

Figure 13: *Score and pauses in SPECjbb runs under various defragmentation schemes with 10% host overcommitment.*

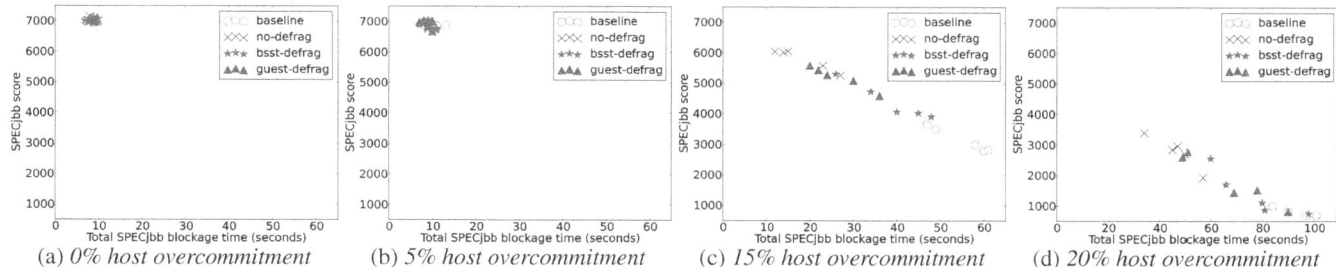

(a) *0% host overcommitment*   (b) *5% host overcommitment*   (c) *15% host overcommitment*   (d) *20% host overcommitment*

Figure 14: *Score and pauses in SPECjbb under various defragmentation schemes with varying host overcommitment and 60 MB memhog.*

Host (%)	Guest I/Os Issued	I/Os w/ Holes	Total Holes	Total I/Os Issued	Score
0	5,152	0	0	5,152	7,010
5	5,230	708	1,675	6,197	6,801
10	5,206	2,161	5,820	8,865	6,271
15	4,517	2,084	6,990	9,423	6,048
20	5,698	2,739	11,854	14,813	2,841

Table 2: *Holes in read I/O requests for Tesseract without defragmentation for various levels of host overcommitment. The memhog inside the guest is 60 MB.*

Defrag Strategy	Reads w/o Holes	Reads w/ Holes	Total Holes	BSST Reads Issued	Total Reads Issued	Defrag I/Os Reads Issued	Defrag I/Os Writes Issued
No-Defrag	3,025	1,203	2,456	2,456	6,684	0	0
BSST	2,946	1,235	2,889	1,235	5,416	12,674	616
Guest	3,909	0	0	0	3,909	11,538	11,538

Table 3: *Total I/Os with BSST and guest defragmentation.*

6.4 Fragmentation in Guest Read I/O Requests

Table 2 quantifies the number of extra read I/O requests that have to be issued to the BSST if defragmentation is not used.

If the host is not under memory pressure there is no hypervisor level swapping activity and all 5,152 guest read I/O requests can be satisfied without going to the BSST.

At higher levels of memory pressure, the hypervisor starts swapping pages to disk. Tesseract detects pages in guest write I/O requests that are already in the BSST to avoid swap-in requests for such pages. The amount of work saved by Tesseract on the write I/O path is quantified in the final column of Table 1.

When host memory is 20% overcommitted we can see that out of 5,698 guest read I/O requests 2,739 will require extra read I/Os to be issued to read data from the BSST. The total number of such an extra I/Os to the BSST was 11,854, which

made the total number of read I/O requests issued to both the guest VMDK and the BSST equal 14,813.

6.5 Evaluating Defragmentation Schemes

Figures 13 and 14 show the impact of using BSST and guest VMDK defragmentation on SPECjbb throughput, while Figures 15 and 16 give insight into SPECjbb responsiveness.

Guest defragmentation performs better than the baseline in all situations and is as good or better than BSST defragmentation. With low levels of host memory overcommitment Tesseract with guest VMDK defragmentation secures better SPECjbb scores than Tesseract without defragmentation and performs on par in responsiveness metrics.

With increasing host memory overcommitment, Tesseract without defragmentation starts outperforming Tesseract with either of the defragmentation schemes in both the application throughput and responsiveness as the total and maximum pause times grow slower for the no-defragmentation case. This is due to the fact that at higher levels of hypervisor level swapping, guest read I/O becomes more and more fragmented and pending defragmentation requests become a bottleneck leading to longer read completion times.

Table 3 shows the I/O overheads of the two defragmentation schemes compared to Tesseract without them. For this table, 3 runs with similar scores and similar number of guest read I/O requests were selected. With BSST VMDK defragmentation enabled, Tesseract was able to reduce the number of synchronous I/O requests to BSST VMDK from 2,889 (2.23 reads per I/O with holes on average) to 1,235 (1 read per I/O with holes). To do BSST VMDK defragmentation, 12,674 asynchronous reads from BSST VMDK and 616 asynchronous writes to BSST VMDK had to be issued. This number of writes equals the number of guest write I/O requests

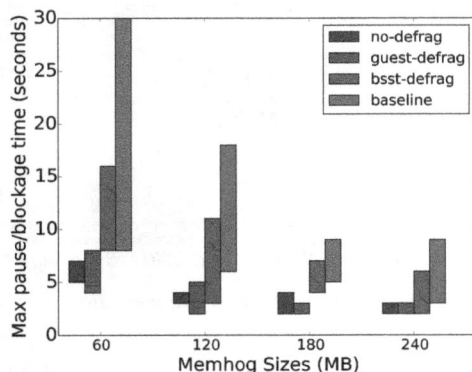

Figure 15: *Comparing maximum single pauses for SPECjbb under various defragmentation schemes with 10% host memory overcommitment.*

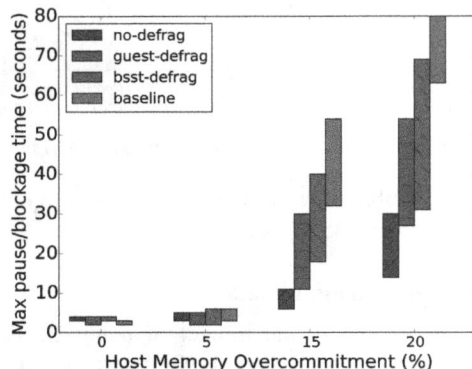

Figure 16: *Comparing maximum single pauses for SPECjbb under various defragmentation schemes with various levels of host memory overcommitment. Memhog was sized at 60 MB.*

with holes. Guest VMDK defragmentation eliminated holes in guest read I/O requests entirely, so there were no guest-related reads from BSST VMDK. To achieve this, 11,538 asynchronous reads from BSST VMDK and the same number of asynchronous writes to the guest VMDK were issued.

6.6 Using SSD For Storing BSST VMDK

SSDs have dramatically better performance over magnetic disk in terms of lower latencies for random reads. However, their relatively higher cost keeps them from getting into mainstream server market. They are used in smaller units for boosting performance. One potential application for SSDs in servers is as a hypervisor swap device allowing for higher memory overcommitment as the cost of swapping is reduced.

In our experiment, we placed the BSST VMDK on a SATA SSD. Figure 17 shows the performance of the baseline and Tesseract. At lower memory pressure, there is no difference in the performance, but as the memory pressure increases, at both guest and hypervisor level, Tesseract starts to show benefits over the baseline.

6.7 Overheads

I/O Path Overhead   Table 4 presents Tesseract overheads on I/O paths. The average overhead per I/O is on the order of

I/O Path	Baseline	No-defrag	BSST defrag	Guest defrag
Read prepare	0	37	30	109
Read completion	0	232	247	55
Write prepare	24,262	220	256	265
Write completion	0	49	91	101

Table 4: *Average read and write prepare/completion times in microseconds for baseline and Tesseract with and without defragmentation. Host overcommitment was 10%; memhog size was 60 MB.*

microseconds. Read prepare time for guest defragmentation is higher than the others due to the contention on guest VMDK during defragmentation. At the same time, the read completion time for guest defragmentation case is much lower than the other two cases as there are no extra reads going to the BSST. On the write I/O path, the defragmentation schemes have larger overhead. This is due to the background defragmentation of the disks which is kicked off as soon as the write I/O is scheduled.

Memory Overhead   Per Section 4.4, Tesseract maintains in-memory metadata for three purposes: tracking (a) associations between PPN and BSST blocks; (b) reference counts for BSST blocks; and (c) indirections between guest VMDK and BSST VMDK. We use 64 bits to store a (4 KB) block number. To track associations between PPN and BSST blocks we re-use MPN field in page frames maintained by the hypervisor so there is no extra memory overhead here. In general case where associations between PPN and blocks in guest VMDK have to be tracked we will need a separate memory structure with a maximum overhead of 0.2% of VM's memory size. Each BSST block's reference count requires 4 bytes per disk block. To optimize the lookup for free/available BSST blocks, a bitmap is also maintained with one bit for each block. The guest VMDK to BSST VMDK indirection metadata requires 24 bytes for each guest VMDK block for which there is a valid indirection to BSST. A bitmap similar to that for BSST is maintained for guest VMDK blocks to determine if an indirection to BSST exists for a given guest VMDK block.

7.   Related Work

Our project intersects three areas. The first is that of uncooperative hypervisor swapping and the double-paging problem. The second concerns the tracking of associations between guest memory and disk state. The third concerns memory and I/O deduplication.

7.1   Hypervisor Swapping and Double Paging

Recent, concurrent work by Amit, Tsafrir, and Schuster [5] systematically explores the behavior of uncooperative hypervisor swapping and implement an improved swap subsystem for KVM called VSwapper. The main components of their implementation are the Swap Mapper and the False Reader Preventer. The paper identifies five primary causes for performance degradation, studies each, and offers solutions to address them. The first, "silent swap writes", corresponds to our notion of guest-I/O–swap optimization which we do not

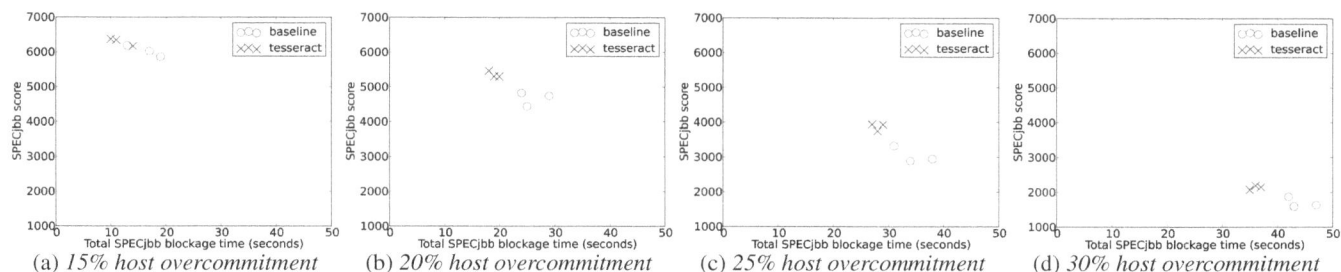

Figure 17: *Tesseract performances with BSST placed on an SSD disk. The memhog size was 60 MB.*

yet support because we do not support reference-counting on blocks in guest VMDKs. The second and third, "stale swap reads" and "false swap reads", and their solutions are similar to the existing ESX optimizations that cancel swap-ins for memory pages that are either overwritten by disk I/O or by the guest. For "silent swap writes" and "stale swap reads", the Swap Mapper uses the same techniques Tesseract does to track valid associations between pages in guest memory and blocks on disk. Their solution to "false swap reads", the False Reader Preventer, is more general, however, because it supports the accumulation of successive guest writes in a temporary buffer to identify if a page is entirely overwritten before next read. The last two, "decayed swap sequentiality" and "false page anonymity", are not issues we consider. In their investigation, they did not observe double-paging to have much impact on performance. This is likely due to the fact that they followed guidelines from VMware and provisioned guests with enough VRAM that guest paging was uncommon and most of the experiments were run with a persistent level of overcommitment. We view their effort as complementary to ours.

The double-paging problem was first identified in the context of virtual machines running on VM/370 [6, 15]. Goldberg and Hassinger [6] discuss the impact of increased paging when the virtual machine's address exceeds that with which it is backed. Seawright and MacKinnon [15] mention the use of *handshaking* between the VMM and operating system to address the issue but do not offer details.

The Cellular Disco project at Stanford describes the problem of paging in the guest and swapping in the hypervisor [7, 8]. They address this double-paging or redundant paging problem by introducing a virtual paging device in the guest. The paging device allows the hypervisor to track the paging activity of the guest and reconcile it with its own. Like our approach, the guest paging device identified already swapped-out blocks and creates indirections to these blocks that are already persistent on disk. There is no mention of the fact that these indirections destroy expected locality and may impact subsequent guest read I/Os.

Subsequent papers on scheduling memory for virtual machines also refer in passing to the general problem. Waldspurger [17], for example, mentions the impact of double-paging and advocates random selection of pages by the hypervisor as a simple way to minimize overlap with page-selection

by the guest. Others projects, such as the Satori project [13], use double-paging to advocate against any mechanism to swap guest pages from the hypervisor.

Our approach differs from these efforts in several ways. First, we have a system in which we can—for the first time—measure the extent to which double-paging occurs. Second, we have an approach that directly addresses the problem of double-paging in a manner *transparent* to the guest. Finally, our techniques change the relationship between the two levels of scheduling: by reconciling and eliding redundant I/Os, Tesseract encourages the two schedulers to choose the *same* pages to be paged out.

7.2 Associations Between Memory and Disk State

Tracking the associations between guest memory and guest disks has been used to improve memory management and working-set estimation for virtual machines. The Geiger project [10], for example, uses paravirtualization and intimate knowledge of the guest disks to implement a secondary cache for guest buffer-cache pages. Lu et al. [11] implement a similar form of victim cache for the Xen hypervisor.

Park et al. [14] describe a set of techniques to speed live-migration of VMs. One of these techniques is to track associations between pages in memory and blocks on disks whose contents are shared between the source and destination machines. In cases where the contents are known to be resident on disk, the block information is sent to the destination in place of the memory contents. In the paper, the authors describe techniques for maintaining this mapping both through paravirtualization and through the use of read-only mappings for fully virtualized guests.

7.3 I/O and Memory Deduplication

The Satori project [13] also tracks the association between disk blocks and pages in memory. It extends the Xen hypervisor to exploit these associations, allowing it to elide repeated I/Os that read the same blocks from disk across VMs immediately sharing these pages of memory across those guests.

Originally inspired by the Cellular Disco and Geiger projects, Tesseract shares much in common with these approaches. Like many of them, it tracks valid associations between memory pages and disk blocks that contain identical content. Like Park et al., it employs techniques that are fully transparent to the guest allowing it to be applied in a wider set of contexts. Unlike the Satori projects which focused on eliminating redundant read operations across VMs, Tesseract uses that mapping information to deduplicate I/Os *from* a specific guest *and* its hypervisor. As such, our approach complements and extends these others.

8. Future Work

We plan to extend our prototype to support reconciliation and elimination of all redundant I/Os whether from guest operations or the hypervisor. For this, we need to do a cleaner job of restructuring the VMDK structure to support indirections and reference-counting of blocks. Following this redesign to its logical conclusion, one would structure a set of guest VMDKs as (thinly-provisioned) maps from guest block identifiers to a general sea-of-blocks in some datastore.

Second, we plan to investigate the interaction of ballooning and hypervisor-level swapping. Ballooning is often used first and more frequently than swapping. Used in this order, one typically does not see much double paging because the balloon has already applied pressure within the guest before swapping commences. However, over a longer period of oscillation, one can imagine double paging occurring because of later inflations of ballooning in the guest.

Finally, our experience in this project has led us to question the existing interface for issuing I/O requests with scatter-gather lists. Given that the underlying physical organization of the disk blocks can differ significantly from the virtual disk structure, it makes little sense for a scatter-gather list to require that the target blocks on disk be contiguous. Having a more flexible structure may allow I/Os to be expressed more succinctly and to be more effective at communicating expected relationships or locality among those disk blocks.

9. Conclusion

We present Tesseract, a system that directly and transparently addresses the double-paging problem. We have described how this issue may arise in the context of guests and hypervisors as each attempts to overcommit its memory resources. We have outlined the design and implementation of Tesseract describing how it reconciles and eliminates redundant I/O activity between the guest's virtual disks and the hypervisor swap subsystem by tracking associations between the contents of pages in guest memory and those on disk. We have identified how, implemented naively, Tesseract interferes with the guest's notion of locality and we have offered two approaches to recover that locality through defragmentation. We have presented the first empirical data on the cost of the double-paging problem. Finally, we have outlined a number of directions we plan to investigate.

10. Acknowledgements

We thank Maxime Austruy for his help with the hosted I/O path and discussions about the BSST. We owe much to Joyce Spencer and Jerri-Ann Meyer for continued support of the project, and to Ron Mann who got telemetry on overcommitment from shipped hosted products. The paper has been improved much by thoughtful comments and feedback from Gene Cooperman, from anonymous reviewers, and especially from our shepherds, Dan Tsafrir and Nadav Amit.

References

[1] VMware vSphere hypervisor. http://www.vmware.com/go/ESXiInfoCenter.

[2] Jenkins. http://jenkins-ci.org.

[3] VMware Workstation. http://www.vmware.com/products/workstation.

[4] O. Agesen. US patent 8380939: System/method for maintaining memory page sharing in a virtual environment, 2011.

[5] N. Amit, D. Tsafrir, and A. Schuster. VSwapper: A memory swapper for virtualized environments. In *Proceedings of the 19th International Conference on Architectural Support for Programming Languages and Operating Systems*, ASPLOS-XIX, 2014.

[6] R. P. Goldberg and R. Hassinger. The double paging anomaly. In *Proceedings of the May 6-10, 1974, National Computer Conference and Exposition*, AFIPS '74, pages 195–199, 1974.

[7] K. Govil. *Virtual Clusters: Resource Management on Large Shared-Memory Multiprocessors*. PhD thesis, Stanford University, Palo Alto, CA, USA, 2001.

[8] K. Govil, D. Teodosiu, Y. Huang, and M. Rosenblum. Cellular Disco: Resource management using virtual clusters on shared-memory multiprocessors. *ACM Trans. Comput. Syst.*, 18:229–262, August 2000.

[9] A. Gulati, I. Ahmad, and C. A. Waldspurger. Parda: Proportional allocation of resources for distributed storage access. In *Proceedings of the 7th Conference on File and Storage Technologies*, FAST '09, pages 85–98, 2009.

[10] S. T. Jones, A. C. Arpaci-Dusseau, and R. H. Arpaci-Dusseau. Geiger: monitoring the buffer cache in a virtual machine environment. In *Proceedings of the 12th International Conference on Architectural Support for Programming Languages and Operating Systems*, ASPLOS-XII, pages 14–24, 2006.

[11] P. Lu and K. Shen. Virtual machine memory access tracing with hypervisor exclusive cache. In *Proceedings of the 2007 USENIX Annual Technical Conference*, USENIX'09, pages 3:1–3:15, 2007.

[12] P. Manning and J. Dieckhans. Storage I/O control technical overview and considerations for deployment. 2010. URL http://www.vmware.com/files/pdf/techpaper/VMW-vSphere41-SIOC.pdf.

[13] G. Miłós, D. G. Murray, S. Hand, and M. A. Fetterman. Satori: enlightened page sharing. In *Proceedings of the 2009 USENIX Annual Technical Conference*, USENIX'09, 2009.

[14] E. Park, B. Egger, and J. Lee. Fast and space-efficient virtual machine checkpointing. In *Proceedings of the 7th ACM SIGPLAN/SIGOPS International Conference on Virtual Execution Environments*, VEE '11, pages 75–86, 2011.

[15] L. Seawright and R. MacKinnon. VM/370 - a study of multiplicity and usefulness. *IBM Sys. Jrnl*, 18(1):4–17, 1979.

[16] Standard Performance Evaluation Corporation. SPECjbb2005. http://www.spec.org/jbb2005.

[17] C. A. Waldspurger. Memory resource management in VMware ESX server. *SIGOPS Oper. Syst. Rev.*, 36:181–194, Dec. 2002.

Virtual Asymmetric Multiprocessor for Interactive Performance of Consolidated Desktops

Hwanju Kim   Sangwook Kim   Jinkyu Jeong   Joonwon Lee

Sungkyunkwan University, Suwon, South Korea

hwandori@gmail.com, swkim@csl.skku.edu, jinkyu@skku.edu, joonwon@skku.edu

Abstract

This paper presents virtual asymmetric multiprocessor, a new scheme of virtual desktop scheduling on multi-core processors for user-interactive performance. The proposed scheme enables virtual CPUs to be dynamically performance-asymmetric based on their hosted workloads. To enhance user experience on consolidated desktops, our scheme provides interactive workloads with fast virtual CPUs, which have more computing power than those hosting background workloads in the same virtual machine. To this end, we devise a hypervisor extension that transparently classifies background tasks from potentially interactive workloads. In addition, we introduce a guest extension that manipulates the scheduling policy of an operating system in favor of our hypervisor-level scheme so that interactive performance can be further improved. Our evaluation shows that the proposed scheme significantly improves interactive performance of application launch, Web browsing, and video playback applications when CPU-intensive workloads highly disturb the interactive workloads.

1. Introduction

Virtual desktop infrastructure (VDI) [1, 2, 35] has drawn attention as a type of virtualized environments where individual desktops are consolidated in a server farm. The desktop consolidation is particularly appealing in organizations that manage personal desktops for a large number of their members or employees. By locating desktops as virtual machines (VMs) in a centralized data center, those organizations are capable of managing considerable desktop machines flexibly and securely. In addition, high density of desktop consolidation can lead to significant cost savings due to efficient resource utilization. Case studies about the real-world adoptions of VMware VDI show that virtual desktops are successfully deployed with the consolidation ratio of 15:1 or greater [35].

VDI hypervisors, however, provide limited support for consolidated desktops with respect to interactive performance, which is crucial for desktop user experience. For interactive performance, user-interactive workloads can be prioritized with larger CPU bandwidth and dispatch preference over background ones in a user's desktop VM. Most hypervisors shift the discretion of preferentially scheduling interactive workloads to guest operating systems (OSes) while themselves fulfilling workload-oblivious CPU provisioning. Hence, existing hypervisors provide a VM with virtual symmetric multiprocessor (vSMP) whose virtual CPUs (vCPUs) have identical computing bandwidth (i.e., CPU shares) as general workload containers. Since vSMP does not differentiate a VM's vCPUs regardless of their hosted workloads, an interactive workload running on a vCPU cannot benefit from any scheduling preference over background ones on the other vCPUs. In highly consolidated desktops, vSMP could restrict the performance of interactive workloads whose hosting vCPUs compete with those of other VMs for limited physical CPUs (pCPUs).

In this paper, we propose *virtual asymmetric multiprocessor* (vAMP), which is capable of dynamically adjusting the computing capacity of vCPUs in order to surmount the limitation of vSMP regarding interactive performance. The vAMP enables CPU shares allocated to a VM to be asymmetrically distributed to the vCPUs that belong to the VM. Since the asymmetric provisioning of CPU shares is allowed only within per-VM share budget, CPU fairness is preserved between independent VMs. By means of vAMP, we propose a VDI-friendly scheduling scheme that allows interactive workloads to run on faster vCPUs, which are given scheduling preference with larger CPU shares on contended pCPUs, than those hosting background workloads. To this end, we introduce a hypervisor extension that requests the hypervisor scheduler to allocate more CPU shares to vCPUs that host interactive workloads based on the estimation of workload characteristics.

VEE '14,   March 1–2, 2014, Salt Lake City, Utah, USA.
Copyright © 2014 ACM 978-1-4503-2764-0 /14/03. . . $15.00.
http://dx.doi.org/10.1145/2576195.2576199

The primary role of our hypervisor extension is to infer which vCPUs are involved in user-interactive workloads. Accurately identifying interactive workloads, however, is challenging in the hypervisor layer, which can access only a small set of hardware interactions (e.g., I/O operations and privileged instructions). Considering this challenge, we devise background workload identification on the basis of user I/O and per-task CPU loads rather than tracking interactive tasks. By using hypervisor-level task tracking [16], this scheme detects a set of tasks that have been generating nontrivial CPU loads before a user I/O event as background tasks. In this manner, non-background tasks are regarded as potentially interactive workloads. In addition, our hypervisor extension excludes CPU-intensive multimedia workloads such as video playback from background workloads by monitoring audio-generating tasks. To be more practical, multimedia tasks that indirectly generate audio output through server/client-based sound systems [27] can be also filtered by tracking remote wake-up recognized as an interprocessor interrupt (IPI).

Finally, we propose a guest OS extension for vAMP towards further improvement of interactive performance. Our hypervisor-level scheme has an intrinsic problem where it cannot manipulate OS scheduling policy in favor of vAMP. A vAMP-oblivious OS scheduler could multiplex interactive and background tasks on a single vCPU, which can thus be frequently changed between fast and slow modes. The frequent mode changes ineffectively increase the scheduling latency of interactive workloads. To avoid such multiplexing, our guest OS extension allows the OS scheduler to isolate interactive tasks from background ones on separate vCPUs. This extension is meant to be optionally installed in a guest OS to assist our hypervisor extension with vAMP-friendly isolation.

The proposed scheme was evaluated based on a KVM/SPICE VDI environment [1]. We chose application launch, Web browsing, and video playback as representative interactive workloads. For evaluation, we replayed a recorded interactive session to an 8-vCPU VM that ran a CPU-bound multithreaded workload (*freqmine* in the PARSEC suite) while another CPU-bound 8-vCPU VM was corunning. Our evaluation shows that the vAMP hypervisor extension alone improves application launch time by up to 41% and Web browsing time by up to 31% compared to vSMP, while achieving further improvement by up to 70% and 41% for launch and browsing time if assisted by our guest OS extension. In addition, the vAMP significantly improves video playback quality by reducing the frame drop rate from 28.1% to 1.5–2.2%.

The remainder of this paper is organized as follows: Section 2 describes background and related work on CPU scheduling schemes for interactive performance. Section 3 introduces the design and implementation of our vAMP extensions for hypervisor and guest OS. In Section 4, we present our measurement methodology and evaluation results. Finally, Section 5 concludes our work and presents future direction.

2. Background and Related Work

This section describes existing proportional share (PS) based scheduling mechanisms by which the hypervisor gives an illusion of an SMP to each VM. We then argue why the hypervisor scheduler should be enhanced for user-interactive performance in consolidated desktops.

2.1 PS-based Schedulers for SMP VMs

PS-based CPU scheduling [10, 14, 36, 37] is a simple and powerful scheme that provides performance isolation in CPU resources to each schedulable entity. PS-based schedulers guarantee available CPU bandwidth to be proportionally allocated to schedulable entities on the basis of their given shares. By doing so, fairness can be preserved between independent entities (e.g., processes or vCPUs), which time-share CPU resources. Since performance isolation is one of primary objectives in the hypervisor [15, 31], most commodity hypervisors have adopted PS-based CPU scheduling [9, 23, 34].

PS-based schedulers in hypervisors perform hierarchical share distribution in order to support SMP VMs. Firstly, each individual VM is given shares in proportion to its assigned weight. Inter-VM fairness is ensured in this level. Then, the VM's shares are redistributed to its own vCPUs. In order to provide a virtual SMP (vSMP), per-VM shares are equally distributed to each vCPU in the same VM. This simple scheme, however, could reduce effective shares given to active vCPUs in the case where per-VM shares are unnecessarily distributed to inactive (i.e., idle) vCPUs. To alleviate such wastage of shares, most schedulers keep track of idleness of vCPUs based on their recent CPU utilization. Once a vCPU is regarded as an idle vCPU, it is excluded from the target of share distribution, thereby increasing effective shares for active vCPUs.

2.2 Why Hypervisor Support for Interactive Performance?

In OS research communities, huge volume of work on CPU scheduling has focused on interactive performance enhancement. Most proposals improved user responsiveness by giving an interactive task higher priority or weight than throughput-oriented ones [11, 14, 24, 25, 40]. Such scheduling allows unfair CPU allotment between interactive and background tasks, for the first class support for user experience. In order to distinguish user-involved tasks from background ones, researchers have proposed various classification methods such as user-driven [24, 38], application-directed [25], middleware-assisted [11], and OS-level [40] schemes.

[1] http://www.spice-space.org

As a virtualization layer has been introduced and become prevalent as the most privileged layer in conventional software stack, we should rethink the support of CPU scheduling for interactive workloads hosted on consolidated systems. In a virtualized environment, a hypervisor scheduler sits on the bare-metal CPUs dictating how much and when to provide hosted VMs with shared CPU resources. Since OS schedulers work only on online vCPUs, which are scheduled by the hypervisor, OS scheduling policy for interactive performance could be invalidated if the hypervisor is oblivious to user-interactive workloads hosted on vCPUs. Making the hypervisor aware of user interaction is a challenging issue, because only a small set of hardware interactions are visible to the hypervisor.

3. Virtual Asymmetric Multiprocessor for Interactive Performance

This section presents vAMP, which dynamically adjusts the shares of vCPUs within a VM's share budget depending on workloads hosted on the vCPUs. As mentioned in the previous section, for high quality of user experience, vCPUs that are involved in user interaction need to be given more shares than others running background workloads. To differentiate vCPUs dynamically, the hypervisor should be able to determine whether a vCPU is currently hosting user-interactive workloads. In designing vAMP, we consider several challenges with regard to the different characteristics of the hypervisor from OSes.

Firstly, a vCPU, a minimum schedulable entity in the hypervisor, is a general container of various types of workloads. Since a thread can be migrated across vCPUs in a very fine-grained manner by an OS scheduler, the characteristic of a vCPU is dynamically changed at any given time. Secondly, available information for identifying workload characteristics is restrictive at the hypervisor. A small set of hardware accesses (e.g., I/O operations and privileged instructions [3]) can be unobtrusively monitored by the hypervisor, whereas upper layers in a VM can access abundant information to infer interactive workloads; this characteristic leads to semantic gap [8]. Thirdly, performance isolation between VMs limits the best-effort boosting of computing power required for interactive performance. Since VM-based consolidation environments typically have multi-tenant nature, favoring a certain VM is not allowed to compromise the computing power of other independent VMs [15, 31]. Finally, the hypervisor and guest OSes make their own scheduling decisions independently without considering the intent of each other, letting the decision of one layer less effective.

Based on the issues, we have the following design goals in mind:

1. **A simple hypervisor extension aiding the hypervisor scheduler**: Our hypervisor extension can identify user-involved vCPUs based on user I/O, per-task CPU loads,

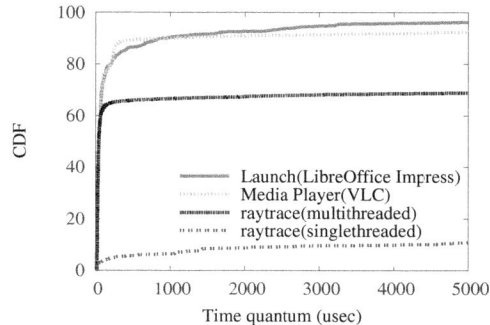

Figure 1. The cumulative distribution of time quanta observed by the hypervisor for interactive and throughput-oriented workloads.

and IPIs, all of which are unobtrusively monitored by the hypervisor.

2. **Asymmetric share distribution to sibling vCPUs within per-VM share budget**: No share exchange is allowed between independent VMs for performance isolation, but the shares of a VM are flexibly distributed to its sibling vCPUs. Nonetheless, idle CPU cycles of dormant VMs, which idle all vCPUs, can be used by other active VMs in a work-conserving manner.

3. **An optional guest OS extension for further enhancement of interactive performance**: A guest OS extension can further improve interactive performance by preventing an OS scheduler from making ineffective decisions against vAMP. Such an extension can optionally be installed in a guest OS if a user needs more enhanced interactive performance.

3.1 Which vCPUs Have More Computing Power?

The challenging part of vAMP is to identify user-interactive workloads at the hypervisor. To cope with the issue, we investigated some possible ways proposed in previous work.

3.1.1 Limitations on Alternatives

We first look into the I/O-bound task tracking, which is previously proposed in [18, 19]. In this scheme, a task with short time quanta in response to I/O events is regarded as an I/O-bound task on the basis of the traditional heuristic of distinguishing I/O-bound and CPU-bound tasks. Since task execution time can be measured on address space switches [16], which are visible to the hypervisor, this technique is a viable solution for the hypervisor to identify interactive tasks. However, modern interactive applications based on GUI and multimedia are not always I/O-bound tasks with short time quanta because of their nontrivial computation. Conversely, as many throughput-oriented workloads such as RMS (recognition, mining and synthesis) applications [6] have been multithreaded, frequent synchronizations between the threads in a throughput-oriented task can lead to short time quanta.

Figure 1 shows the cumulative distribution of per-task time quanta of various workloads: application launch and video playback as interactive workloads and *raytrace* as a throughput-oriented one. Per-task time quantum was measured at the hypervisor by monitoring address space switches as with the I/O-bound task tracking [18]. We ran an 8-vCPU VM on eight pCPUs. As shown in the figure, 10% time quanta of the interactive workloads are longer than 1ms, whereas the multithreaded raytrace has its 62% time quanta shorter than 100 microseconds. Note that the single-threaded raytrace is clearly distinguished from the interactive workloads by its sufficiently long time quanta (90% is longer than 5ms). In the case of the multithreaded version, however, inter-thread synchronization significantly shortens the time quantum by frequently blocking and waking up communicating threads. Based on the result, the I/O-bound task tracking based on time quanta may not identify non-I/O-bound interactive workloads.

The second alternative is user I/O-driven detection of interactive tasks by tracking user I/O and inter-process communications (IPCs) [40]. This work exploits the general knowledge in which user-interactive tasks are scheduled being derived from user I/O such as keyboard, mouse, and audio events. More importantly, multiple tasks are involved in a single user interaction in most cases. For example, a keyboard event is firstly delivered to an X server, which then forwards it to a specific task with which a user directly interacts. Although this technique is powerful in identifying a group of tasks involved in a user interaction, it heavily relies on OS-level structures and information for tracking various types of IPCs, which are solely carried out by an OS and inaccessible by the hypervisor.

3.1.2 Background Task Identification

Considering the strength and limitation of the previous work, we propose *background task identification* based on user I/O and per-task CPU loads. As opposed to existing ways of tracking interactive tasks, the proposed scheme identifies background tasks at the moment of a user I/O event and then regards the non-background ones as potentially interactive workloads. To this end, our scheme inspects recent CPU load imposed by each task when a user I/O event occurs. If a task has generated nontrivial CPU load within a certain period prior to the user I/O event, it is tagged as a background task that likely interferes with the following user interaction.

The rationales behind the proposed scheme are as follows: Firstly, a user I/O event typically initiates a user-interactive workload, so-called an *interactive episode*, for which corresponding tasks begin consuming CPU resources [12, 13]. Secondly, background workloads literally mean the CPU loads (or noises) being generated at the moment of user interaction, which typically triggers a foreground job. Finally, identifying background tasks enables a simple hypervisor extension to unobtrusively monitor user I/O and per-task CPU loads.

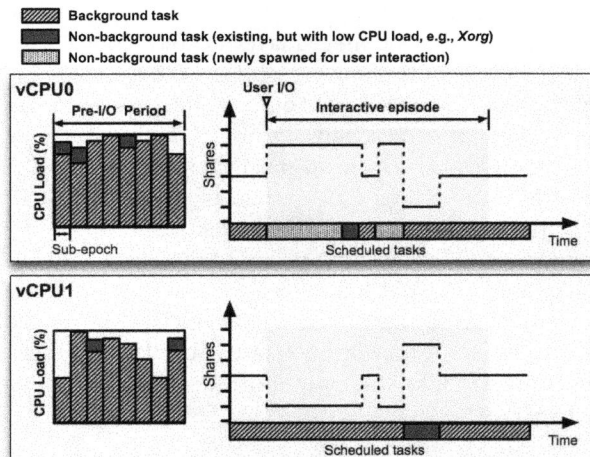

Figure 2. The background task identification based on user I/O and per-task CPU loads, and share adjustment during an interactive episode. In this example, the total amount of the VM's shares is six and the weight ratio of slow and fast vCPUs is 1:5.

In order to monitor per-task CPU loads, as with the I/O-bound task tracking [18], our hypervisor extension measures the time elapsed between two address space switches. In x86 architecture, a CR3 update with a different value represents an address space switch; an update with the same value is mainly used to invalidate translation lookaside buffer. While trapping a CR3 update by the hypervisor is essential for software-based memory virtualization, it is not mandatory and disabled by default in hardware-assisted one such as Intel EPT (Extended Page Tables) [32] and AMD RVI (Rapid Virtualization Indexing) [5]. Nonetheless, tracking address space switches is still feasible simply by enabling VMEXIT in the event of a CR3 update [19]. Although additional VMEXITs come at a cost of hypervisor intervention, improvement achieved by vAMP (hundreds of milliseconds to a few seconds shown in Section 4.3) outweighs VMEXIT overhead of hundreds of CPU cycles [4] by many orders of magnitude. Furthermore, CR3 trap can be selectively enabled when a VM is likely to take advantage of vAMP (e.g., while user interactions frequently take place with high background load). Such optimization can avoid the VMEXIT overhead while interactive workloads are solely running.

The algorithm of background task identification is illustrated in Figure 2 and performs as follows. Per-task CPU loads are maintained for each vCPU within a certain time window, named *pre-I/O period*; task execution time is accumulated by sub-epoch in a round-robin manner. Once a user I/O event occurs, per-task CPU loads are examined. If a task has generated higher CPU load than *background load threshold* (bgload_thresh), it is tagged as a background task. This threshold is used to consider only nontrivial loads that likely disturb a following interactive workload. More importantly, it helps filter daemon tasks (e.g., X server) that generate low CPU loads and possibly serve the invoked interactive tasks. After tagging tasks, the algorithm starts an interactive episode during which non-background tasks are assumed to be potentially interactive workloads. The episode is finished when another user input occurs or the episode lasts for *maximum interactive period* (max_int_period), which is long enough to generally cover a user-interactive period. After the episode ends, background tasks return to normal by removing their background tags.

When checking per-task loads, the algorithm also accounts *stolen time* as a potential load. Stolen time is the time taken to wait on a runqueue since a vCPU became runnable; the CPU time, which would otherwise be consumed without time-sharing, is stolen by another one during the wait-time. For example, a 100% CPU-bound task shows only 20% CPU load when running on a vCPU that contends with four CPU-bound vCPUs. Since stolen time is measured per vCPU, it should be accounted to existing tasks on a vCPU. In our algorithm, per-vCPU stolen time is accounted to a task in proportion to the amount of CPU time it has actually consumed while running on a vCPU.

For user-interactive I/O detection, the hypervisor extension monitors keyboard and mouse events as user input, and audio device accesses as user output by default. Most GUI-based applications in virtual desktops are interacted with a user via keyboard and mouse input devices. In addition, multimedia applications such as a media player typically involve audio output. Therefore, the default setting generally covers user interactions with virtual desktops. Other types of user I/O (e.g., user interaction via *ssh*) can also be monitored by simply interposing I/O virtualization layer; a packet with a well-known port number (e.g., 22 for ssh) can be inspected at network virtualization layer.

Inspecting per-task CPU loads on every user I/O may adversely affect the response time of a user event itself. For example, fast keyboard typing can degrade user-perceived responsiveness by repeatedly inspecting per-task loads on every keyboard input. To reduce the overheads, specific key codes are registered as a signal of when an interactive episode begins. In our current prototype, the Enter key is registered by default, since pressing it typically triggers interactive loads such as application launch and Web browsing. Regarding mouse inputs, the release event of a click is regarded as a start signal. Finally, since an audio device is intensively accessed for audio playback, it is heavyweight to start a new interactive episode by inspecting per-task loads on every audio output. To address this problem, once an audio device access initiates an interactive episode, subsequent accesses are ignored until the episode is finished.

3.1.3 Multimedia Task Identification

Although interactive CPU loads typically start to be generated in response to a user input, a user output may not be a start signal of CPU loads for output-based interactive workloads, which generate audio/video output to interact with a

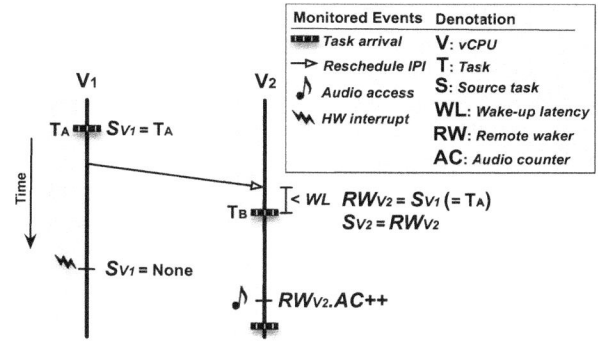

Figure 3. Remote wake-up tracking for identifying sound clients. In this example, T_A and T_B is a sound client and server, respectively.

user. For example, a media player continuously generates CPU load required for video decoding and rendering while accessing audio/video devices. Hence, the media player task could be misidentified as a background workload by our scheme if its CPU load is higher than bgload_thresh. In order to prevent this misidentification, output-based multimedia tasks should be excluded from background ones.

A simple solution is to exclude audio-generating tasks from background workloads, since multimedia applications generally accompany audio output [40]. To this end, the hypervisor can consider a task that is running when audio device is accessed as an audio-generating task. Since an audio device, however, can also be accessed in audio interrupt handler, which is asynchronously invoked, such an audio device access cannot be associated with a currently running task. As in [20], our scheme does not associate a currently running task with an audio device access in the interrupt handler within which an audio interrupt vector bit is set in the interrupt service register of a corresponding vCPU.

The simple method, however, cannot identify the multimedia tasks that indirectly generate audio output through server/client-based sound systems [27] where a user-level sound server is in charge of all audio accesses requested from other tasks. In most Linux OS distributions, *pulseaudio* [2] is a user-level sound server by default for the sake of compatible and flexible sound service [27]. In this case, the current solution can identify only the sound server as a multimedia task, while missing actual audio-requesting tasks (i.e., sound clients). It is challenging to exactly identify a sound client, since server-client communication is done by IPCs without hypervisor intervention.

Our scheme is enhanced to identify sound clients as well by introducing *remote wake-up tracking*, which is a statistical method based on IPIs between vCPUs. IPI is a signaling mechanism used to send a message to a remote CPU (vCPU in our case). In particular, *reschedule IPI* is used for a vCPU to wake up a task on a remote vCPU and notify it of

---

[2] www.pulseaudio.org

the newly runnable task [21]. If a client sends a request to a server via IPC, this communication could involve a reschedule IPI if the server is woken up on a remote vCPU. Since the hypervisor is in charge of delivering IPIs between vCPUs, it can infer server-client communication by tracking such IPI-driven remote wake-up. Although this scheme cannot track local communication on the same vCPU, remote wake-up more frequently happens than local wake-up in a multiprocessor VM so that the communication can be captured statistically.

Figure 3 illustrates how the remote wake-up tracking works in the case of a server/client-based sound system. Each vCPU (V_i) maintains a source task (S_{V_i}), which holds a currently running task (e.g., $S_{V_1} = T_A$) updated at each task arrival (i.e., scheduling). If V_1 sends V_2 a reschedule IPI, the hypervisor checks whether a task (T_B) is woken up on V_2 immediately within *wake-up latency* (*WL*) after the IPI being injected; we set *WL* to $20\mu s$ by profiling the time between reschedule IPI injection and its corresponding task wake-up using a micro-benchmark. If so, V_2 sets its remote waker (RW_{V_2}) to S_{V_1} ($= T_A$) based on the assumption that T_A and T_B are the source and destination of the communication, respectively. At this point, S_{V_2} is set to RW_{V_2} in order to maintain an initial source task of the communication in the case of consecutive remote wake-ups across more than two vCPUs. Such consecutive remote wake-ups can happen if a sound server or client is multithreaded; pulseaudio is multithreaded. Finally, if T_B accesses an audio device during this time slice on V_2, the remote waker's audio counter ($RW_{V_2}.AC = T_A.AC$) is incremented. In this manner, T_A and T_B are regarded as a sound client and server, respectively.

As illustrated in Figure 3, S_{V_i} is updated as None when an external interrupt is injected to V_i (V_1 in the figure). A sound server can be remotely woken up by an audio interrupt handler, which is invoked asynchronously regardless of any task context. In this case, a task currently running on a vCPU where the handler is invoked may not be a sound client. Without this update, we observed that the audio counter of a background task is often falsely incremented.

To consider recent audio activity, an audio counter is moving-averaged at every interactive episode. In the case where a multimedia application is generating audio output without any user input, it is averaged at every max_int_period. In addition, before calculating the average, the audio counter of a task is divided by how many times the task is tagged as background in order to curtail the false increment of background tasks. To this end, *background confidence* is incremented when it is tagged as a background task and is decremented otherwise; the maximum background confidence is 10 by default.

Using this tracking, the hypervisor can statistically filter sound clients out of background tasks on the basis of their audio counters. If a task is a sound client that continuously sends requests to a sound server, it could have relatively larger audio counter than others. This property enables a threshold-based classification. In our prototype, we use a simple policy that filters a dominant sound client with the highest audio counter. This simple policy is reasonable in practice, since it is uncommon to simultaneously run multiple sound clients.

3.2 Asymmetric Share Distribution

After identifying background tasks excluding multimedia ones, a VM's shares start to be asymmetrically distributed to active vCPUs during an interactive episode. Since a vCPU can host either a background or non-background task at any given time, per-vCPU shares are dynamically adjusted during the period. To this end, as shown in Figure 2, every time a background task arrives at a vCPU during an interactive episode, the vAMP hypervisor extension gives the scheduler a command to throttle the weight of the vCPU to which relatively smaller shares are distributed. Conversely, once a non-background task is switched back, the weight is restored. By doing so, the vCPUs that host potentially interactive tasks (i.e., non-background tasks) have more computing power as fast vCPUs to improve interactive performance.

Although the asymmetric share distribution is effective for improving interactive performance, there is an intrinsic limitation arising from manipulating only a single scheduling layer (i.e., the hypervisor scheduler). With the hypervisor extension alone, guest OS schedulers are agnostic about the presence of underlying vAMP. Commodity OSes typically assume their online CPUs to have identical computing power. As real AMP has drawn attention as an energy-efficient architecture, several efforts have been done to make OS schedulers aware of performance-asymmetric computing cores [29]. They have focused on, however, which workloads are beneficially scheduled on fast cores that are statically wired in architecture. Moreover, most proposals aimed at high throughput per watt for throughput-oriented workloads without considering interactive workloads.

An OS scheduler can make an ineffective decision without the knowledge of vAMP. A vAMP-oblivious OS scheduler may schedule an interactive task on a slow vCPU, which has smaller shares. In PS-based schedulers, a vCPU with smaller shares suffers higher scheduling latency while waiting its turn until those with larger shares exhaust their time slices. Therefore, the scheduling latency of the interactive task is increased when it is multiplexed with a background task on the same vCPU. Furthermore, an interactive task is frequently scheduled on a slow vCPU when a background workload tries to occupy all available vCPUs. Such workload mix is common in a multiprocessor VM, since many throughput-oriented applications are parallelized and commonly run with the configuration to use all available cores for high throughput.

In order to prevent the ineffective multiplexing from offsetting the benefit of vAMP, the weight ratio between slow and fast vCPUs should be carefully chosen. Since the hypervisor is unaware of where a guest OS will schedule its task, it is challenging to completely avoid the adverse effect of the multiplexing. Instead, a conservative setting for the ratio can reduce the extent of adverse effect while achieving high interactive performance. From the evaluations in Section 4, vAMP shows large and stable improvement with conservative weight ratio (e.g., 1:3).

3.3 Guest OS Extension for vAMP

To eliminate the intrinsic limitation of the hypervisor-only scheme, a guest OS can be enlightened about vAMP. We propose a lightweight OS extension by which vAMP becomes more effective. The design goals of the guest OS extension are as follows. Firstly, the OS extension is not mandatory for vAMP so that it can be optionally installed in an OS for further improvement of interactive performance. With this goal, main decisions for vAMP are still made by the hypervisor while the OS extension plays a role of reducing adverse effect of OS scheduling. Since the adverse effects stem from multiplexing interactive and background workloads on a vCPU, its primary role is to isolate interactive tasks from background ones on separate vCPUs during an interactive episode. Secondly, kernel changes are kept as small as possible for low maintenance cost. To this end, the primary functionalities of the extension are performed in user space, to which the kernel exports necessary information. Most OSes commonly provide user land with a knob to place a task on a specific set of CPUs (e.g., *cpuset* [23] and *sched_setaffinity* in Linux, and *SetThreadAffinityMask* in Windows).

Keeping the design goals in mind, we implemented a Linux extension for vAMP. To isolate non-background workloads from background ones, the kernel exposes the list of background tasks identified by the hypervisor extension to user space via *procfs*. The kernel obtains the information from the structure shared with the hypervisor. This small addition requires a few lines of source codes in the kernel. A user space extension, named *vamp-daemon*, refers to the exposed list of background tasks and carries out the isolation between background and non-background tasks. The vamp-daemon performs by responding to user I/O in an event-driven fashion. To this end, it listens the Linux input interface (i.e., /dev/input/eventN) for user inputs, while communicating with a sound server (pulseaudio in our case) via IPC for audio output; *pacmd*, which is a helper tool for pulseaudio, was used to inspect audio output generation. Finally, the vamp-daemon performs isolation by using cpuset [23], which provides a filesystem-based interface for user space to manipulate CPU affinity of a group of tasks.

In addition to the task placement, interrupts from I/O devices that can serve interactive workloads are isolated to fast vCPUs where non-background tasks are placed. Since interactive workloads can involve disk or network I/O operations during an interactive episode, delivering an interrupt from such an I/O device to a slow vCPU could increase the latency of interrupt delivery. To solve this problem, interrupts from

I/O devices that are involved in user interaction are isolated to fast vCPUs. In the Linux extension, it can be simply done by vamp-daemon via /proc/irq/number/smp_affinity.

The guest OS extension has an isolation policy of how vCPUs are partitioned (i.e., how many vCPUs are dedicated to interactive tasks). Interactive workloads typically require a small number of vCPUs, since they have low thread-level parallelism in general [7, 13]. Based on this characteristic, one or two vCPUs are enough to be initially dedicated to interactive tasks, while remaining vCPUs run background ones. In the case of audio output, the number of vCPUs for interactive tasks is set at least two in order for the hypervisor to track remote wake-up between a sound server and client. Interactive workloads may need more vCPUs as their given vCPUs become saturated involving in multiple tasks and threads. To address such demand, the vamp-daemon periodically monitors the CPU utilization of the vCPUs that host interactive workloads, so that it provisions an additional vCPU when they are fully utilized. This periodic monitoring also detects the end of an interactive episode at which all tasks become normal and therefore isolation is revoked. In our current vamp-daemon, an initial number of vCPUs for interactive tasks and a monitoring interval are given as configurable parameters.

One possible opportunity is that the guest OS extension performs workload identification and forwards the result of it to the hypervisor. Since a guest OS can access much more information about workloads than hypervisor, the guest-side workload identification could more precisely guide vAMP to boost interactive performance. In this case, only the substrate that adjusts vCPU shares is implemented in the hypervisor while any policy to use the substrate is implemented in guest OSes. As a simple method, task priority can be provided to hypervisor as a hint [17]. This type of separation could enhance accuracy and modularity while eliminating the overheads for hypervisor-level task tracking, but requires the guest OS extension to be mandatory, not optional. In this work, we aim to have vAMP not rely on guest OS extension, but benefit from it if any. We will explore guest-side workload identification for vAMP in the future work.

4. Evaluation

The vAMP hypervisor extension was implemented based on the KVM, a Linux module for virtualization, in Linux kernel 3.0.0. In the KVM-based virtualization, I/O requests from guest OSes are handled by a QEMU (version 1.0) running in the host Linux. Once QEMU handles a predefined user I/O event, it notifies the vAMP hypervisor extension, which then initiates an interactive episode. The extension adjusts vCPU weight interacting with Completely Fair Scheduler (CFS), which is the default PS-based scheduler in Linux. KVM uses CFS group scheduling [23], which allows multiple threads to share per-group (per-VM) shares; all threads of vCPUs and QEMU in the same VM are grouped in the VM's share budget. We set per-VM shares to the default shares (1024) multiplied by the number of pCPUs.

The prototype was installed on Dell PowerEdge R410, equipped with a quad-core Intel Xeon X5550 2.67GHz processor and 8GB RAM. In this setting, eight pCPUs are available with hyperthreading enabled. We used Ubuntu 11.04 with Linux kernel 3.0.0 as a guest OS and gave each VM eight vCPUs and 3.5GB memory. A remote desktop client ran on a separate machine (identical hardware with the server) connected through a 1Gbps Ethernet switch.

4.1 Measurement Methodology

A KVM-based desktop environment is effectively built by means of SPICE, a remote desktop solution optimized to access virtualized hardware. A SPICE server handles user I/O requests from remote SPICE clients by interacting with QEMU. Since consolidated virtual desktops are remotely accessed by end-users in general, we evaluated interactive performance at a client side.

To measure interactive performance, user-perceived response time should be properly quantified. Previous work used snapshot-based record/replay for robust replay of user-recorded interactive sessions [28, 39]. In the case where system loads (or computing power) may be different between the times of record and replay, snapshot can be used as a user-perceived (or synchronization) point to avoid unsynchronized replay. We implemented such measurement functionality in a SPICE client. As with *DeskBench* [28], at every interaction to be evaluated, a user can explicitly mark the completion of perception (by inserting a special key), at which a snapshot is recorded. During an evaluation, recorded user inputs are replayed by synchronizing the their corresponding snapshots; similar to fuzzy matching [28], small snapshot differences are allowed to continue a replay for reducing replay failure due to unexpected screen update.

We evaluated a multimedia workload using the VLC open-source media player. In a video playback workload, the performance metric is displayed frames per second (FPS). Since a media player drops frames when it cannot meet the defined rate of a video, FPS is used to evaluate how well a CPU scheduler satisfies the computing demand for video playback. We measured FPS at the server side in order to evaluate the CPU scheduling impact, because client-side performance of video playback highly depends on remote desktop protocols. Protocol supports of graphical operation offloading affects the performance of client-side video quality.

The evaluation of interactive performance was done in a consolidated environment where VMs are competing for available pCPUs. Since evaluated workloads have different completion times from each other, we fully overlapped each workload by repeated executions and considered only the overlapped runs for averaged results. Each throughput-oriented workload was repeatedly run at least five times (ten

Parameter	Role	Default
Pre-I/O period	Background task identification	1024msec
bgload_thresh	Background task identification	50%
max_int_period	Duration of an interactive episode	5sec

Table 1. The vAMP parameters, their roles, and default values used in the evaluations.

times in the case of the Web browsing evaluation), while an interactive session made progress.

4.2 Parameters

Table 1 summarizes the parameters, their roles, and default values for the vAMP hypervisor extension. The pre-I/O period and bgload_thresh are used to identify background tasks. The main role of bgload_thresh is to prevent a daemon task that is supposed to service interactive workloads from being misidentified as a background task. Since such daemons typically have low CPU utilization in the common case while handling requests in an event-driven manner, the threshold can be empirically set to a value higher than the maximum achievable CPU utilization of well-known daemon tasks. One thing to consider is a display service daemon such as an X server, since display can service both background and non-background ones [11, 40]. We determined the default value of bgload_thresh considering the highest CPU utilization of the display daemon; in our case, an X server showed less than 50% CPU utilization during the high rate of display service from video playback.

Our asymmetric share distribution is not sensitive to max_int_period as long as it sufficiently covers a general interactive episode. If an interactive workload is prematurely finished and thus background tasks solely run until the end of an interactive episode, all vCPUs have eventually the equal shares. Although previous research suggested that two seconds are reasonable as an interactive period [26, 30, 40], we used five seconds by default considering that modern interactive applications show relatively longer response time such as application launch.

As mentioned in Section 3.2, the weight ratio of slow and fast vCPUs can affect the interactive performance. A higher ratio can improve interactive performance if interactive tasks are scheduled on fast vCPUs, whereas it may degrade the performance otherwise. The Linux CFS scheduler associates pre-set shares with each *nice* value [22], with which vAMP adjusts weight. We used three configurations for the weight ratio: low (L), medium (M), and high (H) ratios, which approximately match 1:3, 1:9, and 1:18, respectively. With these configurations, we show the performance impact by different weight ratios.

4.3 Application Launch

Application launch is a representative interactive workload where desktop users desire low response time. Many GUI-based applications require considerable CPU bandwidth for initialization during launch period. We used *LibreOffice Im-*

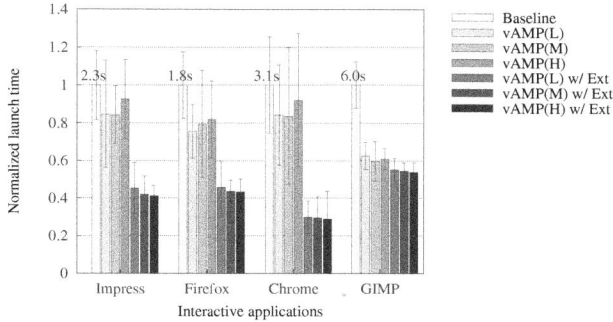

(a) The Normalized average launch time of interactive tasks

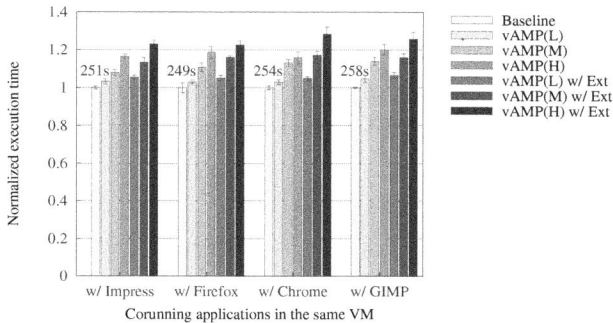

(b) The normalized average execution time of background tasks (freqmine)

Figure 4. Application launch time and the execution time of background workloads mixed with launched applications (error bars represent standard deviations and the value over a box is the elapsed time in each baseline case).

press, *Mozilla Firefox*, *Google Chrome*, and *GNU Image Manipulation Program (GIMP)* for the evaluation. Each application was repeatedly launched and closed at a user-perceived point. We inserted one-second interval between close and relaunch during replay. We used freqmine, a multi-threaded data mining application in the PARSEC benchmark suite [6], as a background workload; this type of application (e.g., data mining, data analysis, simulation, encoding) represents the workloads of knowledge workers [33]. Among PARSEC applications, freqmine is one of CPU-bound applications with a little communication while fully utilizing all vCPUs. We ran freqmine with eight threads each in two 8-vCPU VMs while repeated application launch was performed in one of the VMs. For comparison, we used the default CFS scheduler (vSMP) as the baseline.

Figure 4(a) shows the average launch time of each interactive application. Ext stands for our guest OS extension, in which one vCPU is initially assigned for interactive tasks and, if fully utilized, is increased at every one second. As shown in the figure, the vAMP hypervisor extension alone improves the average launch time by up to 41%, while achieving further improvement by up to 70% if assisted by the guest OS extension. One important thing to note is that higher weight ratio shows less improvement without the guest OS extension. In addition, the applications

that show such adverse effect by higher weight ratio (Impress, Firefox, and Chrome) show significant performance improvement in the case where the guest OS extension assists vAMP. On the other hand, GIMP shows larger improvement by about 40% even without the guest OS extension, which has a little impact in this case.

As mentioned in Section 3.2, the vAMP hypervisor extension alone may have negative effect when an OS scheduler multiplexes interactive and background tasks on a single vCPU. Since higher weight ratio leads to larger scheduling delay of a slow vCPU, the negative effect could offset the benefit of vAMP if such multiplexing frequently happens. In order to show the multiplexing behavior of a vAMP-oblivious OS scheduler, we obtained the scheduling traces of Chrome and GIMP launches. Figure 5 shows the scheduling traces where gray and black colors represent background and non-background tasks, respectively. In the figure, Chrome shows frequent multiplexing of background and non-background tasks, whereas GIMP shows that different types of tasks are mostly isolated on separate vCPUs for its launch time.

These behaviors come from the different characteristics of the applications. Chrome involves many threads in a fine-grained manner during launch so that the threads spread over multiple vCPUs with communicating with each other. By this characteristic, ineffective multiplexing with background tasks frequently happens. In GIMP, on the other side, one thread is dominantly compute-intensive conducting most of the jobs for launch, while the others perform small computation. Hence, the compute-intensive thread occupies one vCPU for most of its launch time, thereby leading to spontaneous isolation from background tasks (except for the last 500ms). Such isolation results in large performance improvement even without the guest OS extension.

We also measured how much the performance of a background workload is degraded by throttling the shares of its hosting vCPU (i.e., slow vCPU). Figure 4(b) shows the average execution time of freqmine mixed with each launched application. Note that the performance degradation of background workloads depends on how intensively an interactive application requires computation. As mentioned earlier, we used a 1-second interval between close and relaunch to simulate highly interactive workloads. As shown in the figure, the performance of freqmine is degraded by 3–20%. The higher weight ratio is used, the more degradation is observed due to the smaller shares of slow vCPUs. With the same weight ratio, the guest OS extension more degrades the performance of freqmine by preventing it from using the vCPU that is dedicated to interactive tasks during an interactive episode. The degradation of background workloads is reasonable considering the highly interactive workloads and their significant improvement by up to 70%.

Finally, we evaluated the impact of I/O interrupt isolation, which forwards an I/O interrupt to a fast vCPU during

(a) Chrome

(b) GIMP

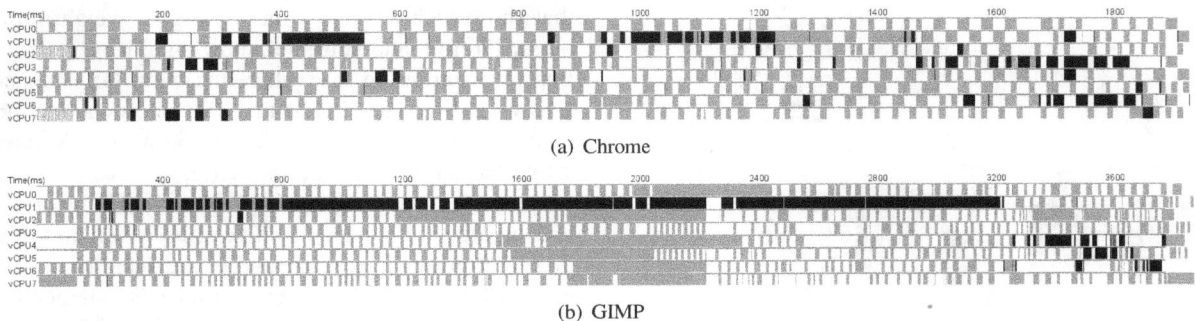

Figure 5. Scheduling traces during launch for Chrome and GIMP; gray and black colors represent the execution of a background task (freqmine) and a non-background task, respectively. No color means that a vCPU is not scheduled on a pCPU due to the time-sharing with another VM, which runs freqmine.

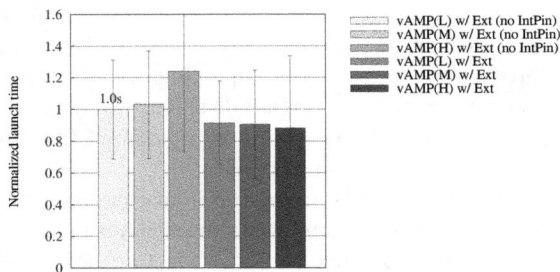

Figure 6. The normalized launch time of Chrome for vAMP with the guest OS extension. `IntPin` represents the interrupt isolation scheme in the guest OS extension.

an interactive episode. We chose Chrome for this evaluation, since it involves synchronous file writes during launch. The synchronous file write requires disk I/O even for warm launch, in which file reads are served from disk cache without I/O. Figure 6 shows the normalized launch time of Chrome for vAMP with our guest OS extension; `IntPin` means the I/O interrupt isolation (pinning). As shown in the figure, without the interrupt isolation, higher weight ratio worsens the launch performance, since the interrupt delivery of synchronous file writes can be delayed if a disk interrupt is pending to a slow vCPU. The isolation of disk interrupts resolves this problem by ensuring that the interrupts are delivered to fast vCPUs, which are scheduled with shorter latency.

4.4 Web Browsing

Web browsing has been a prevalent interactive workload as desktop users usually have their jobs done by using Web and cloud services. Web browsing is computationally intensive during an interactive period especially for rendering a Web page with complex structures and images. For evaluation, we used the contents of Web sites in *bbench* and placed them in a VM local disk in order to preclude the effects of network I/O. An interactive session of Web browsing consecutively visits ten Web sites: Amazon, BBC, CNN, Craigslist, eBay,

ESPN, Google, MSN, Slashdot, and Twitter. [3] We used Firefox as a web browser and inserted three-second interval between visits.

Figure 7 shows the normalized response time of browsing each Web site in the same consolidation scenario as the evaluation of application launch. For the average, the vAMP hypervisor extension improves the browsing time by up to 31% while achieving the further improvement by up to 41% if assisted by the guest OS extension. As with the result of application launch, higher weight ratio without the guest OS extension shows less performance. In the case of Amazon and Google pages, the baseline outperforms vAMP(H) that is not assisted by the guest OS extension. This result implies that negative effect of multiplexing outweighs the benefit of vAMP. Considering the results of application launch and Web browsing, vAMP with conservative weight ratio, vAMP(L), achieves stable and noticeable performance improvement both for the hypervisor and guest OS extensions.

4.5 Media Player

As an output-based interactive workload, we evaluated a video playback application by using the VLC media player. For a video playback workload, the requirement of CPU bandwidth relies on video contents. For highly compute-intensive video playback, we chose a high definition video clip with 1920x800 resolution, *The Simpsons Movie Official Trailer HD*; its running time and FPS are 137 seconds and 23.976 FPS. Since it shows higher CPU utilization than bgload_thresh (50%), it can be misidentified as background workloads without the multimedia workload identification. Regarding audio playback, the VLC media player requests pulseaudio to generate the audio output of the video clip.

Figure 8 shows the video playback quality (FPS) in the same consolidation scenario as the evaluation of application launch. `Mult` means our multimedia identification scheme, and percentage over each bar represents a drop rate (= dropped frames × 100 / total frames). In the baseline case,

---

[3] YouTube was excluded for robust replaying, since it automatically plays a video when visited.

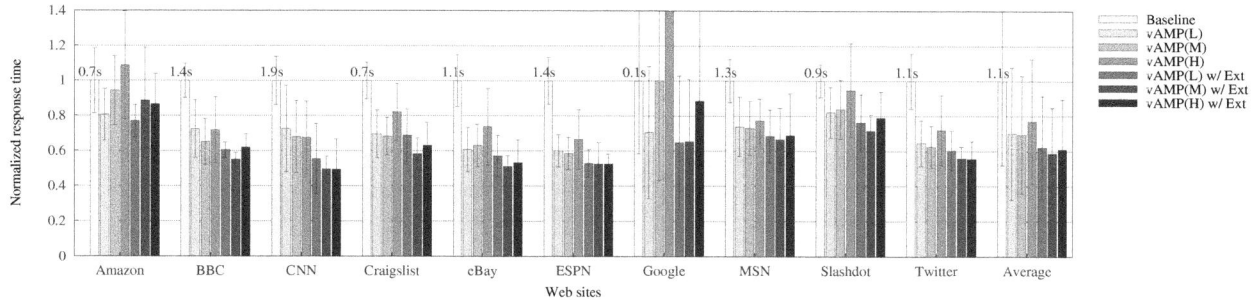

Figure 7. Normalized browsing time for each Web site in bbench. The error bars represent standard deviations and the value over a box is the elapsed time in each baseline case.

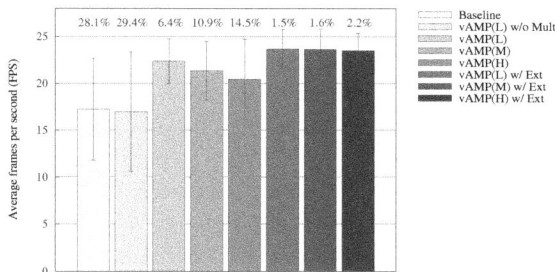

Figure 8. The displayed FPS of a 1920x800 video with 23.976 FPS. `Mult` means the multimedia identification support, and percentage over each bar is a drop rate.

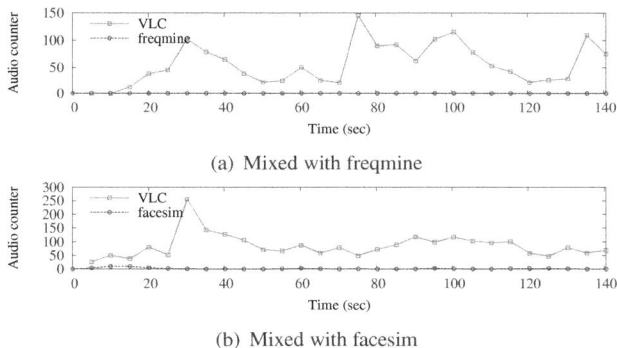

(a) Mixed with freqmine

(b) Mixed with facesim

Figure 9. Audio counters during video playback

vSMP significantly degrades video quality with 28.1% drop rate. Without the multimedia identification scheme, vAMP also shows similar degradation by classifying the CPU-intensive VLC as a background task. Once the multimedia identification filters VLC out of background workloads, the video playback quality is improved. Without the guest OS extension, as with the other evaluations, higher weight ratio shows less improvement due to the negative effect of multiplexing of video playback and background tasks on a single vCPU. The guest OS extension remedies the problem by achieving much better quality with only 1.5–2.2% drop rate.

To figure out how well VLC is filtered out of background workloads, Figure 9(a) shows the moving-averaged audio counter as time progresses. In the figure, VLC has always much higher audio counter than freqmine so that it can be

identified as a dominant sound client. We also ran VLC with *facesim*, which intensively generates reschedule IPIs for the repeated wake-up of worker threads, to disturb our remote wake-up tracking. In Figure 9(b), VLC also shows higher audio counter than facesim, which increases its audio counter only up to ten. As a result, our remote wake-up tracking effectively filters the multimedia workloads that indirectly generate audio output through server/client sound systems.

5. Concluding Remarks

In this paper, we present the design and implementation of vAMP for improving user-interactive performance of consolidated desktops. For differentiating the computing power of vCPUs, we devised a simple and effective scheme for identifying background workloads at the hypervisor layer. One important finding is that manipulating only the hypervisor scheduler for interactive performance limits the improvement due to the negative effect of multiplexing of interactive and background tasks on a single vCPU. To address this limitation, the lightweight guest OS extension prevents such ineffective multiplexing, thereby achieving significant improvement of interactive performance. With the hypervisor and guest OS extensions for vAMP, the consolidated desktops enable high quality of user experience while compute-intensive jobs are concurrently running with interactive workloads. We plan to investigate collaborative scheduling between the hypervisor and guest OSes for vAMP. In addition, we are exploring the applicability of vAMP for various workloads other than interactive applications.

Acknowledgments

This work was partly supported by the National Research Foundation of Korea (NRF) grant funded by the Korea government (MEST) (No. 2013-003871), and by the IT R&D program of MKE/KEIT [10041244, Smart TV 2.0 Software Platform].

References

[1] Sun virtual desktop infrastructure software. `http://www.sun.com/software/vdi/`.

[2] Virtual desktop infrastructure (VDI). White paper of VMware.

[3] K. Adams and O. Agesen. A comparison of software and hardware techniques for x86 virtualization. In *Proc. of ASPLOS*, 2006.

[4] O. Agesen, J. Mattson, R. Rugina, and J. Sheldon. Software techniques for avoiding hardware virtualization exits. In *Proc. of USENIX Annual Technical Conference*, 2012.

[5] AMD. AMD64 virtualization codenamed "pacifica" technology: Secure virtual machine architecture reference manual, May 2005.

[6] C. Bienia, S. Kumar, J. P. Singh, and K. Li. The PARSEC benchmark suite: characterization and architectural implications. In *Proc. of PACT*, 2008.

[7] G. Blake, R. G. Dreslinski, T. Mudge, and K. Flautner. Evolution of thread-level parallelism in desktop applications. In *Proc. of ISCA*, 2010.

[8] P. M. Chen and B. D. Noble. When virtual is better than real. In *Proc. of HotOS*, 2001.

[9] L. Cherkasova, D. Gupta, and A. Vahdat. Comparison of the three CPU schedulers in Xen. *SIGMETRICS Perform. Eval. Rev.*, 35(2):42–51, 2007. ISSN 0163-5999.

[10] K. J. Duda and D. R. Cheriton. Borrowed-virtual-time (BVT) scheduling: Supporting latency-sensitive threads in a general-purpose scheduler. In *Proc. of SOSP*, 1999.

[11] Y. Etsion, D. Tsafrir, and D. G. Feitelson. Process prioritization using output production: Scheduling for multimedia. *ACM TOMCCAP*, 2(4):318–342, 2006. ISSN 1551-6857.

[12] K. Flautner and T. Mudge. Vertigo: Automatic performance-setting for linux. In *Proc. of OSDI*, 2002.

[13] K. Flautner, R. Uhlig, S. Reinhardt, and T. Mudge. Thread-level parallelism and interactive performance of desktop applications. In *Proc. of ASPLOS*, 2000.

[14] P. Goyal, X. Guo, and H. M. Vin. A hierarchical cpu scheduler for multimedia operating systems. In *Proc. of OSDI*, 1996.

[15] D. Gupta, L. Cherkasova, R. Gardner, and A. Vahdat. Enforcing performance isolation across virtual machines in Xen. In *Proc. of Middleware*, 2006.

[16] S. T. Jones, A. C. Arpaci-Dusseau, and R. H. Arpaci-Dusseau. Antfarm: Tracking processes in a virtual machine environment. In *Proc. of USENIX Annual Technical Conference*, 2006.

[17] D. Kim, H. Kim, M. Jeon, E. Seo, and J. Lee. Guest-aware priority-based virtual machine scheduling for highly consolidated server. In *Proc. of Euro-Par*, 2008.

[18] H. Kim, H. Lim, J. Jeong, H. Jo, and J. Lee. Task-aware virtual machine scheduling for I/O performance. In *Proc. of VEE*, 2009.

[19] H. Kim, H. Lim, J. Jeong, H. Jo, J. Lee, and S. Maeng. Transparently bridging semantic gap in cpu management for virtualized environments. *JPDC*, 71(6):758 – 773, 2011. ISSN 0743-7315.

[20] H. Kim, J. Jeong, J. Hwang, J. Lee, and S. Maeng. Scheduler support for video-oriented multimedia on client-side virtualization. In *Proc. of MMSys*, 2012.

[21] H. Kim, S. Kim, J. Jeong, J. Lee, and S. Maeng. Demand-based coordinated scheduling for SMP VMs. In *Proc. of ASPLOS*, 2013.

[22] R. Love. *Linux Kernel Development*. Addison-Wesley Professional, 3rd edition, 2010. ISBN 0672329468, 9780672329463.

[23] P. B. Menage. Adding generic process containers to the linux kernel. In *Proc. of OLS*, 2007.

[24] C. Mercer, S. Savage, and H. Tokuda. Processor capacity reserves: operating system support for multimedia applications. In *Proc. of ICMCS*, 1994.

[25] J. Nieh and M. S. Lam. A SMART scheduler for multimedia applications. *ACM TOCS*, 21(2):117–163, 2003. ISSN 0734-2071.

[26] J. Nielsen. *Designing Web Usability: The Practice of Simplicity*. New Riders Publishing, Thousand Oaks, CA, USA, 1999. ISBN 156205810X.

[27] L. Poettering. Cleaning up the linux desktop audio mess. In *Proc. of OLS*, 2007.

[28] J. Rhee, A. Kochut, and K. Beaty. Deskbench: Flexible virtual desktop benchmarking toolkit. In *Proc. of IM*, 2009.

[29] J. C. Saez, M. Prieto, A. Fedorova, and S. Blagodurov. A comprehensive scheduler for asymmetric multicore systems. In *Proc. of EuroSys*, 2010.

[30] B. Shneiderman. Response time and display rate in human performance with computers. *ACM Comput. Surv.*, 16(3): 265–285, Sept. 1984. ISSN 0360-0300.

[31] G. Somani and S. Chaudhary. Application performance isolation in virtualization. In *Proc. of CLOUD*, 2009.

[32] R. Uhlig, G. Neiger, D. Rodgers, A. L. Santoni, F. C. M. Martins, A. V. Anderson, S. M. Bennett, A. Kagi, F. H. Leung, and L. Smith. Intel virtualization technology. *Computer*, 38 (5):48–56, 2005. ISSN 0018-9162.

[33] VMware. VMware Infrastructure 3: VDI server sizing and scaling, May 2006.

[34] VMWare. VMware, Inc. VMware vSphere 4: The CPU scheduler in VMware ESX 4.1. Technical report, 2010.

[35] VMware Inc. Enabling your end-to-end virtualization solution. http://www.vmware.com/solutions/partners/alliances/hp-vmware-customers.html.

[36] C. A. Waldspurger and W. E. Weihl. Lottery scheduling: Flexible proportional-share resource management. In *Proc. of OSDI*, 1994.

[37] C. A. Waldspurger and E. Weihl. W. Stride scheduling: Deterministic proportional- share resource management. Technical report, Cambridge, MA, USA, 1995.

[38] T. Yang, T. Liu, E. D. Berger, S. F. Kaplan, and J. E. B. Moss. Redline: first class support for interactivity in commodity operating systems. In *Proc. of OSDI*, 2008.

[39] N. Zeldovich and R. Chandra. Interactive performance measurement with vncplay. In *Proc. of USENIX Annual Technical Conference*, 2005.

[40] H. Zheng and J. Nieh. RSIO: Automatic user interaction detection and scheduling. In *Proc. of SIGMETRICS*, 2010.

Ginseng: Market-Driven Memory Allocation

Orna Agmon Ben-Yehuda[1] Eyal Posener [1] Muli Ben-Yehuda[1,2] Assaf Schuster[1] Ahuva Mu'alem[1,3]

[1]Technion – Israel Institute of Technology   [2]Stratoscale   [3]Ort Braude

{ladypine, posener, muli, assaf, ahumu}@cs.technion.ac.il

Abstract

Physical memory is the scarcest resource in today's cloud computing platforms. Cloud providers would like to maximize their clients' satisfaction by renting precious physical memory to those clients who value it the most. But real-world cloud clients are *selfish*: they will only tell their providers the truth about how much they value memory when it is in their own best interest to do so. How can real-world cloud providers allocate memory efficiently to those (selfish) clients who value it the most?

We present *Ginseng*, the first market-driven cloud system that allocates memory efficiently to selfish cloud clients. Ginseng incentivizes selfish clients to bid their true value for the memory they need when they need it. Ginseng continuously collects client bids, finds an efficient memory allocation, and re-allocates physical memory to the clients that value it the most. Ginseng achieves a $6.2\times - 15.8\times$ improvement (83%–100% of the optimum) in aggregate client satisfaction when compared with state-of-the-art approaches for cloud memory allocation.

Categories and Subject Descriptors   D.4.2 Operating Systems [*Storage Management*]: Main memory

Keywords   KVM; Memory Overcommitment

1. Introduction

Infrastructure-as-a-Service (IaaS) cloud computing providers rent computing resources to their clients. As competition between providers gets tougher and prices decrease, providers will need to continuously and ruthlessly reduce expenses, primarily by improving their hardware utilization. Physical memory is the most constrained and thus precious resource in cloud computing platforms today [12, 15, 17, 25, 27, 37]. Google, for example, had to begin charging for memory usage in addition to CPU usage: not charging for memory made the scaling of applications that use a lot of memory and little CPU time "cost-prohibitive to Google." [8]. Other platforms (such as Amazon EC2) offered virtual machines with varying amounts of memory to begin with, thereby charging clients for memory usage in addition to CPU and I/O usage. In general, today's cloud computing clients buy a supposedly-fixed amount of physical memory for the lifetime of their guests.

Providers can greatly reduce their expenses by using less memory to run more client guest virtual machines on the same physical hosts. This can be done transparently by means of memory overcommitment [23, 37]. When memory is overcommited, the clients have no way to discern how much physical memory they are actually getting. Due to the lack of transparency and difficulties with providing a given level of quality of service when overcommitting memory, some providers refrain from memory overcommitment and let their hardware go underutilized. Others simply reduce their clients' quality of service.

Clients would much prefer to have full visibility and control over the resources they receive [2, 28]. They would like to pay only for the physical memory they need, when they need it [3, 11]. By granting clients this flexibility, providers can increase client satisfaction: clients interested in high quality of service (QoS) will be able to choose a non-overcommited machine, while budget-conscious clients will be able to enjoy the cloud at low prices when demand is low. Finding an efficient allocation of physical memory on each cloud host—an allocation that gives each guest virtual machine precisely the amount of memory it needs, when it needs it, at the price it is willing to pay—yields benefits for clients, whose satisfaction is improved, and providers, whose hardware utilization is improved.

Previous physical memory allocation schemes assumed that guest virtual machines are *white boxes*: that they are run by fully cooperative clients, who let the host know precisely what each guest is doing, how well it performs, how much benefit additional memory would bring to it, and the importance of the workload to the client [12, 15, 17, 27]. These systems allocated memory efficiently and improved the overall system's performance, but were unsuitable for real-world commercial clouds, because the assumption that the host has full, accurate information on all aspects of guest performance is unrealistic.

As recent commercial cloud trends of price dynamicity and fine-grained resource granularity [2] indicate, real-world cloud clients act *rationally* and *selfishly*. They are *black boxes* with private information such as their performance statistics, how much memory they need at the moment, and what it is worth to them. Rational, selfish black-boxes will not share this information with their provider unless it is in their own best interest to do so.

When the host allocates memory solely according to guest-provided input, rational and selfish guests have an incentive to manipulate the host into granting them more memory than their fair share. For example, if the host gives memory to those guests that will benefit more from it, each guest will say it benefits from memory more than any other guest. If the host gives memory to those guests that perform poorly with their current allocation, each guest will say it performs poorly.

Alternatively, the host can allocate memory according to passive *black-box* measurements taken outside of the guests [18, 25, 37, 39, 40]: for example, by monitoring I/O and inferring major page faults [18], or by monitoring use of physical pages to balance the guests' need for physical memory [39]. However, in such cases the guests have an incentive to bias the measurement results, e.g., by inducing unnecessary page faults or accessing unnecessary memory. Furthermore, such passive measurements can only compare the guests by externally visible metrics such as throughput and latency, which are valued differently by different guests under different circumstances.

We address the cloud provider's fundamental memory allocation problem: How should it divide the physical memory on each cloud host among selfish black-box guests? A reasonable meta-approach would be to give more memory to guests who would benefit more from it. But how can the host compare the benefits of additional memory for each guest?

Our first contribution towards solving this problem is the **Memory Progressive Second Price (MPSP) auction**, a game-theoretic market-driven mechanism which induces auction participants to bid (and thus express their willingness to pay) for memory according to their true economic *valuations* (how they perceive the benefit they get from the memory, stated in monetary terms).

Our second contribution is **Ginseng** itself, a market-driven cloud system for allocating memory efficiently to selfish black-box virtual machines. It is the first full implementation of a single-resource Resource-as-a-Service (RaaS) cloud [2]. Ginseng is the first cloud platform to optimize overall client satisfaction for black box guests. In Ginseng, the host periodically auctions memory using the MPSP auction. Guests bid for the memory they need as they need it; the host then uses these bids to compare the benefit that different guests obtain from physical memory, and to allocate it to those guests which benefit from it the most. The host is not manipulated by guests and does not require unreliable black-box measurements. We also build a strategic agent for the MPSP auction.

Ginseng supports static-memory applications—legacy applications that require some fixed quantity of memory and do not perform better with more memory, but is tailored for *elastic-memory applications*—applications that can improve

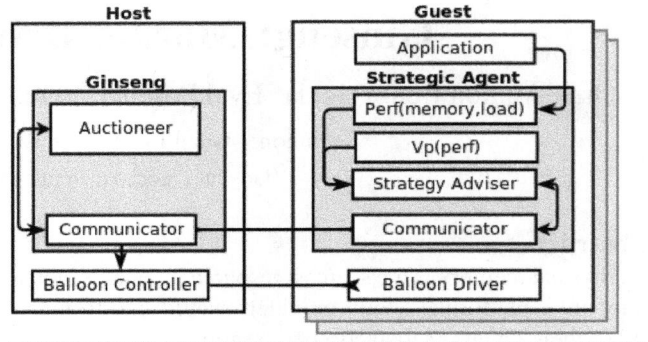

Figure 1. Ginseng system architecture

their performance when given more memory on-the-fly over a large range of memory quantities and can return memory to the system when needed. Elastic-memory applications are becoming more common thanks to platforms that facilitate their development, such as Salomie et al.'s database [29], Java runtime with balloons [12, 17, 29], CRAMM [38], or dynamic heap adjustment for garbage-collected environments [14, 16]. In addition, applications designed for the Linux mempressure control group are elastic by design. **Our third contribution** is two elastic-memory benchmark applications: an **elastic-memory version of Memcached**, a widely-used key-value cloud application, and **MemoryConsumer**, an elastic memory benchmark we developed.

Ginseng achieves a $6.2\times$ improvement in aggregate client satisfaction for MemoryConsumer and $15.8\times$ improvement for Memcached, when compared with state-of-the-art approaches for cloud memory allocation. Overall, it achieves 83%–100% of the optimal aggregate client satisfaction.

2. System Architecture

Ginseng is a market-driven cloud system that allocates memory to guests using guest bids for memory. It is implemented for cloud hosts running the KVM hypervisor [20] with Litke's memory overcommit manager MOM [23]. It controls the exact amount of physical memory allocated to each guest via libvirt using *balloon drivers* [37]. The *balloon driver* is installed in the guest operating system. The host's *balloon controller* controls the balloon driver, inflating or deflating it. When inflating, the balloon driver allocates memory from the guest OS and pins it, so that the guest OS won't attempt to swap it out; the balloon driver then transfers this memory to the host. When deflating, the balloon driver frees memory back to its OS, in effect giving the OS more memory from the host. Libvirt supplies an API to balloon drivers in different hypervisors, improving portability.

Ginseng has a host component and a guest component, as depicted in Figure 1. The host component includes the *Auctioneer*, which runs the MPSP auction. The auctioneer's *communicators* communicates asynchronously with the guests' *communicators* according to the auction's protocol specified in **Section 4**. The host's communicator also instructs the balloon controller how to allocate memory between guests. The balloon controller inflates and deflates the balloon drivers inside the guests. The guest's economic learning agent acts on behalf of the client. The *strategy adviser* is the agent's brains. Our implementation of an adviser is described in **Section 6**, but the client is free to choose a different logic.

3. Memory Auctions

Ginseng allocates memory efficiently because its guests bid for the memory they want in a specially-designed auction that the host conducts in quick rounds. We begin by supplying the background to the auction, whose protocol is defined in Section 4.

In Ginseng, each guest has a different, changing, private (secret) *valuation* for memory. This valuation reflects how much additional memory is worth to each guest. We define the aggregate benefit of a memory allocation to all guests—their satisfaction from auction results—using the game-theoretic measure of *social welfare*. The social welfare of an allocation is defined as the sum of all the guests' valuations of the memory they receive in this allocation. An efficient memory auction allocates the memory to the guests such that social welfare—guest satisfaction—is maximized.

VCG [7, 13, 34] auctions optimize social welfare by incentivizing even selfish participants with conflicting economic interests to inform the auctioneer of their true valuation of the auctioned items. VCG auctions do so by charging each participant for the damage it inflicts on other participants' social welfare, rather than directly for the items it wins. VCG auctions are used in various settings, including Facebook's repeated auctions [24].

Various auction mechanisms, some of which resemble the VCG family, have been proposed for *divisible* resources, in particular for *bandwidth sharing* [19, 21, 26]. For practical reasons, bidders in these auctions do not communicate their valuation for the full range of auctioned goods. One of these VCG-like auctions is Lazar and Semret's Progressive Second Price (PSP) auction [21]. None of the auctions proposed so far for divisible goods are suitable for auctioning memory, because memory has two characteristics that set it apart from other divisible resources. First, transferring memory too quickly between two participants leads to waste; Second, the participants' valuation functions might not be concave; that is, the law of diminishing marginal utility might not always apply to memory, e.g., as in Figure 2b. However, the PSP auction optimally allocates a divisible resource if and only if all the valuation functions are monotonically rising and concave. Other bandwidth auctions also rely on the monotonically rising concave property of the valuation functions.

The *memory valuation function*, which describes how much the guest is willing to pay for different memory quantities, depends on the load the guest is under, the performance gain or loss it expects from more memory given that load, and the value of performance to the guest. Formally, it is $V(mem, load) = V_{perf}(perf(mem, load))$, where $V_{perf}(perf)$ refers to the valuation of performance as described below, and $perf(mem, load)$ describes the performance the guest can achieve given a certain load and a certain memory quantity.

Performance might be measured in page hits per second for a webserver, "get" hits per second for a caching service, transactions per second for a database, trades per second for a high-frequency trading system, or any other guest-specific metric. For our experiments, an offline mapping of performance as a function of memory and load (as done by Hines et al. [17] and Gordon et al. [12]) was accurate enough, as we demonstrate in Section 8.2. However, real-world performance may depend on many variable conditions. To this end, performance can be measured online as several works demonstrate [39–41]. An important feature of the MPSP auction is that it does not require the guest to have its performance defined for any memory value. Hence, the guest can keep a moving window of its latest performance measurements, which reflect best the current conditions under which it operates.

The guest's owner's (i.e., the client's) valuation of performance function, $V_{perf}(perf)$, describes the value the client derives from a given level of performance from a given guest. This client-specific function is private information of each client. It is based on economic considerations and business logic.

For example, an e-commerce website that typically makes $100 sales and needs to display $10,000$ web pages on average to generate a single sale might measure its performance in displayed pages per second, and value each displayed page at $0.01. For this client, $V_{perf}(perf) = \frac{\$0.01}{page} \cdot perf$. Another client might require the same average number of displayed pages to make a sale, but its typical sale would be $10 only. For this client, $V_{perf}(perf) = \frac{\$0.001}{page} \cdot perf$. Both clients will need to know $perf(mem, load)$: how many pages they can display per second when given various amounts of memory and under the current conditions (e.g., load).

If either of these functions is non-concave or not monotonically rising, the composed function may be non-concave or not monotonically rising as well. Indeed, guest performance $perf(mem, load)$ is not necessarily a concave, monotonically rising function of physical memory. For example, the performance graph of off-the-shelf memcached in our experimental environment is monotonically rising, but not concave (Figure 2b). This non-concave function resembles a step function, and is typical of the operating system's efforts to handle memory pressure through swapping. Nonconcavity may also result from differences in the size and frequency of use of various working sets, swapping policies, or garbage collection operations [31]. Our *elastic memcached*, in contrast, has a concave, monotonically rising performance graph in the same experimental environment

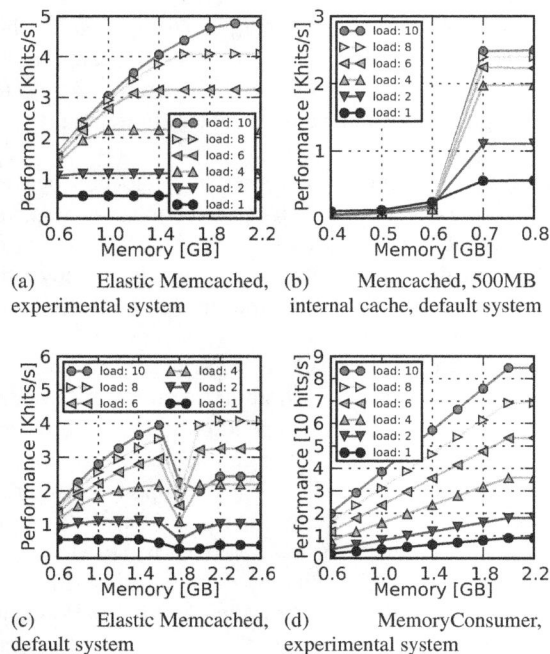

Figure 2. Application performance ("get" hits per second for Memcached, hits per second for MemoryConsumer) as a function of guest physical memory, for different load values. The load is defined as the number of concurrent requests made to the application.

(Figure 2a). However, in a default system configuration, its performance graph is neither concave nor monotonically rising (Figure 2c), due to a network bottleneck that was prevented in the experimental environment. This bottleneck is an example of a problem that a real production system might encounter. It cannot fine-tune its setup parameters and re-design its software on-the-fly; it has to make do with what it measures. Ginseng is designed to support such ad hoc, real-life valuation-of-memory graphs that are neither concave nor monotonically rising.

Auction protocols that assume monotonically rising concave valuation functions either interpret a bid of unit **p**rice and **q**uantity (p, q) as willingness to buy exactly q units for unit price p or as willingness to buy up to q units at price p. In the first case, the bidding language is limited to exact quantities. In the second case, if the valuation function is non-concave, the guest may get a quantity that is smaller than the one it bid for, and pay for it a unit price it is not willing to pay. If the function is not, at the very least, monotonically rising, it may even get a quantity it would be better off without.

MPSP supports monotonically rising concave memory valuation functions in the same way that the PSP auction supports them. In addition, it supports non-concave and non-monotonic valuation functions by specifying *forbidden*

ranges. These are forbidden memory-quantity ranges for a single price bid. The guest can use forbidden ranges to cover domains in which its average valuation per memory unit is lower than its bid price. By definition, MPSP will not allocate the guest a memory quantity within its forbidden ranges. Rather, it will optimize the allocation given the constraints. The guest can thus avoid getting certain memory quantities in advance while still expressing a variety of desired quantities. The forbidden ranges are designed to efficiently convey information about functions which are concave, monotonically rising in separate ranges. However, the terminology does not restrict the guest valuation functions in any way. In particular, the guest can bid for a specific desired point (p, q) by setting the open range $(0, q)$ as a forbidden range.

4. MPSP: Repeated Auction Protocol

In Ginseng, each guest has some permanent *base memory*. Guests pay a constant hourly fee for their base memory, and it is theirs to keep as long as they run. In each auction round, each guest can bid for extra memory. Ginseng calculates a new memory allocation after every auction round and guests rent the extra memory they won. In the next auction round the same memory will be put up for auction again.

The constant fees for base memory are designed to provide the lion's share of the host's revenue from memory, such that the host can afford to rent the extra memory for the sole purpose of optimizing social welfare, thereby attracting more guests. The price of base memory is not affected by the prices paid for extra memory.

Ultra high-end clients with hard QoS requirements are expected to pre-pay for all the memory they need in advance, to ensure that they always get the resources they need. Ultra low-end clients are expected to pre-pay only for as much memory as they need to operate the guest OS and limit their bids, so that they can temporarily rent additional resources later while staying within their budget. The clients spanning the range between those extremities are expected to choose a flexible deal according to their needs.

Here we describe one MPSP auction round, accompanied by a numeric example.

Initialization. Each guest i is set up with its *base memory* as it enters the system. For example, guest 1 runs memcached and pre-pays for 1.4GB, while guest 2 runs MemoryConsumer and pre-pays for 0.6GB.

Auction Announcement. The host computes the *free memory*—the maximal amount of memory each guest can bid for—as the *excess* physical memory beyond the amount of memory in use by the host and the sum of base memories. It then informs each guest of the free memory and the auction's closing time, after which bids are ignored. In the example, the machine has 4GB. The host uses 1.6GB, and the guests pre-paid for 2GB, so the host announces an auction for 0.4MB.

Bidding. Interested guests bid for memory. Agent i's *bid* is composed of a *unit price* p_i—memory price per GB per hour (billing is still done per second according to exact rental duration) and a list of *desired ranges*: mutually exclusive, closed ranges of desired memory quantities, sorted in ascending order. We denote the desired ranges by $[r_j, q_j]$ for $j = 1 \ldots m_i$, where r and q stand for restriction and quantity. The bid means that the guest is willing to rent any memory quantity within the desired range list for a unit price p_i.

In the example, both guests experience a load of 10 concurrent requests. Guest 1 values its performance at \$1 per Khit/second, and bids \$1 per GB of memory per second ($p = 1\frac{\$}{GBs}$) for any amount of memory between 0 and 0.4GB ($r_1 = 0, q_1 = 0.4GB$), on the basis of the performance data in Figure 2a. Guest 2 values its performance at \$0.1 per hit/second, and bids \$5 per GB of memory per second for the same amount of memory ($p = 5\frac{\$}{GBs}, r_1 = 0, q_1 = 0.4GB$), on the basis of the performance data in Figure 2d.

Bid Collection. The host asynchronously collects guest bids. It considers the most recent bid from each guest, dismissing bids received before the auction round was announced. Guests that did not bid lose the auction automatically, and are left with their base memory.

Allocation and Payments. The host computes the allocation and payments according to the MPSP auction protocol described in Section 5. For each guest i, it computes how much memory it won (denoted by q'_i) and at what unit price (denoted by p'_i). The payment rule guarantees that the price the guest will pay is less than or equal to the unit price it bid. The guest's account is charged accordingly. In the example, guest 1 loses ($p'_1 = 0, q'_1 = 0$), and guest 2 wins all of the free memory ($p'_2 = 1\frac{\$}{GBs}, q'_2 = 0.4GB$).

Informing Guests. The host informs each guest i of its personal results p'_i, q'_i. The host also announces *borderline bids*: the lowest accepted bid's unit-price and the highest rejected bid's unit-price ($5\frac{\$}{GBs}$ and $1\frac{\$}{GBs}$ in the example, respectively). This is information that guests can work out on their own; having the host supply it makes for a more efficient system. The guests use this information in on-line algorithms that decide how much to bid in future rounds, as described in Section 6.

Adjusting and Moving Memory. After an *adjustment period* following the announcement, the host actually takes memory from those who lost it and gives it to those who won, by inflating and deflating their balloons as necessary. The purpose of the adjustment period is to allow each guest's agent to notify its applications of the upcoming memory changes, and then allow the applications time to gracefully reduce their memory consumption, if necessary. The applications are free to choose when to start reducing their memory consumption, according to their memory-release agility. This early notification approach makes it possible for the guest operating systems to gracefully tolerate sudden large memory changes and spares applications the need to monitor second-hand information on memory pressure. Which applications to notify and when to notify them is left to the guest's agent. In the absence of elastic applications, it is left to the guest kernel to deal with memory pressure, e.g., by shrinking internal caches.

5. MPSP: Auction Rules

Every auction has an allocation rule—who gets the goods?—and a payment rule—how much do they pay? To decide who gets the goods, the MPSP auction determines the optimal allocation of memory. This is the allocation that maximizes social welfare—client satisfaction—as described in Section 3. To determine the optimal allocation, the MPSP auction solves a constrained divisible good allocation problem, as detailed in Section 5.1. To determine how much they pay, the MPSP auction takes into account the damage they inflict on other guests, as detailed in Section 5.2. After explaining the rules we discuss their run-time complexity and provide an example for executing them. A correctness proof is also available but has been omitted for brevity.

5.1 Allocation Rule

Ginseng finds the optimal allocation using a constrained divisible-good allocation algorithm, which works in stages as described below. In each stage, Ginseng attempts a divisible good allocation by sorting the guests lexically, first by their bid unit-price, second (to break ties) by their current holdings, and last by a random shuffle. Preferring the current holder when breaking ties reduces memory waste due to back-and-forth transfers of memory between guests [39]. It also reduces the waste in comparison to a single PSP auction, in which tied guests are excluded from the allocation. Ginseng then allocates each guest its maximal desired quantities according to this order.

If there are a guest g and a forbidden range R such that g ends up with a memory quantity inside R, then the allocation is *invalid*. This can happen if g is the last guest allocated some memory and there is not enough memory left to fulfill g's entire request. Ginseng examines the social welfare of such invalid allocations. If such an invalid allocation gives a higher social welfare than the highest social welfare seen to date in a valid allocation, then Ginseng considers two constrained allocations instead of the invalid one. In the first, guest g gets a memory quantity large enough to cover all of R. In the second, g gets a memory quantity small enough such that none of it is in R. The social welfare of the *valid* allocations is compared to find the optimal allocation.

5.2 Payment Rule

The payments follow the *exclusion compensation* principle, as formulated by Lazar and Semret [21]. Let q''_k denote the memory that would have been allocated to guest k in an auction in which guest i does not participate and the rest of the guests bid as they bid in the current auction. Then guest i is charged a unit price p'_i, which is computed as follows:

$$p'_i = \frac{1}{q'_i} \sum_{k \neq i} p_k \left(q''_k - q'_k \right). \tag{1}$$

According to this payment rule, when guest i is charged $p'_i q'_i$, it actually pays for the damage its bid inflicted on the other guests. We note that to compute the payment for a guest that gets allocated some memory, the constrained divisible good allocation algorithm needs to be computed again without this guest. In total, the allocation procedure needs to be called one time more than the number of winning guests.

5.3 Complexity

The problem that the MPSP algorithm solves—finding the memory allocation that maximizes the social welfare function—is defined over the domain of memory quantities that guests agree to rent. This domain is not convex because the forbidden ranges create "holes" in it. Maximizing a function over a non-convex domain is at least as hard as the knapsack problem, and therefore NP-hard. In the worst case the algorithm needs to compute the social welfare which results from each forbidden range being completely allocated or completely denied: 2^M different divisible allocations, where M is the number of all the forbidden ranges in all the bids. Each such allocation takes $O(N)$ to compute, where N is the number of bids, and each payment rule requires $O(N)$ allocations to be computed. Hence, the time complexity of MPSP is $O(N^2 \cdot 2^M)$.

Nevertheless, for real life performance functions, a few forbidden ranges should be enough to cover the non-concave regions. We observed one forbidden range for off-the-shelf memcached and zero forbidden ranges for elastic-memory applications. Given the relatively small number of guests on a physical machine, the algorithm's run-time is reasonable: we observed less than one second using a single hardware thread, even in experiments with 23 guests.

6. Guest Strategy

So far, we discussed the Ginseng system's architecture, and the MPSP memory auction from the auctioneer's point of view. But what should guests who participate in MPSP auctions do? How much memory should they bid for and how much should they offer to pay? In an exact VCG auction, the guests can inform the host about their valuation for different memory quantities. However, the reduced MPSP bidding language lightens the computational burden on the host and leaves the choice of memory quantity with the guest. An intermediate approach—the multi-bid auctions—is discussed in Section 10.

In this section we present the bidding strategy we developed. It is used by the guests in the performance evaluation in Section 8. Our guest wishes to maximize the utility it estimates it will derive from the next auction. This is a natural class of bidding strategies in ad auctions [5].

Our guest needs to decide how much memory to bid for, and at what price. We show in Section 6.1 that for any memory quantity, the best strategy for the guest would be to bid its true valuation for that quantity. To choose the maximal quantity it wants to bid for, the guest compares its estimated utility from bidding for the different quantities, as described in Section 6.2.

6.1 Choosing a Bid Price

In this subsection we assume the guest has decided how much memory (q_m, or q for short) it wants to bid for and show how much it should bid for it. For the simple case of an exact desired memory quantity ($m = 1$, $r_m = q_m = q$), for any value q, bidding the mean unit valuation of the desired quantity (the slope $s(q) = \frac{V(base+q)-V(base)}{q}$) is the best strategy, no matter what the other guests do. By bidding lower than $p = s(q)$, the guest risks losing the auction; by bidding higher it risks operating at a loss (paying more than what it thinks the memory is worth).

For less simple cases when the guest bids for a range of memory quantities up to q, if the valuation function is (at least locally, in the range up to q) concave monotonically rising, bidding $p = s(q)$ is still the best strategy for q regardless of other guests' bids: $s(q)$ is the guest's minimal valuation for the range because the unit valuation drops with the quantity. See, for example, Figure 3a, where the valuation function is above the line connecting the valuation of 1200 MB with the base (400 MB) valuation. Since the connecting line's slope is the mean unit valuation of 1200MB, any point above the line is a point whose mean unit valuation is higher than the mean unit valuation of 1200MB.

In the remaining cases, the valuation function is non-concave or not even monotonically rising. In such functions, the mean unit-valuation $s(q)$ may rise locally with quantity: in Figure 3b, for example, $s(2200MB) > s(1800MB)$. This means that simply bidding for 2200MB with a unit-price of $s(2200MB)$ may result in getting a memory quantity for which the guest is not willing to pay that much. The guest can avoid getting quantities for which the mean unit valuation is lower than its bid price by excluding those quantities from its bid using the forbidden ranges mechanism. In this example, the guest uses a forbidden range to exclude the quantities $[1700, 2000]$ MBs of memory from its range, since it is not economical to bid for them with a unit price of $s(2200MB)$.

The forbidden ranges mechanism allows the guest to bid $s(q)$ without the risk of operating at a loss. However, the guest may have something to gain by bidding with a unit-price that is less than $s(q)$. If the guest does not get the maximal memory quantity it bid for, it can try exploring its strategy space. It can retain q, lower the bid price, and decrease the forbidden ranges. Thus the guest allows the host to give it a partial allocation in more cases, when the alternative might be not getting any memory at all. In Figure 3b, the lowest bid-price worth exploring is labeled the *low slope*: it eliminates the need for forbidden ranges.

When the auction has reached a *steady state*—when a guest's won goods and payment turn out the same in subsequent auctions in response to the same strategy—the guest already knows how much memory it can get for any bid. The

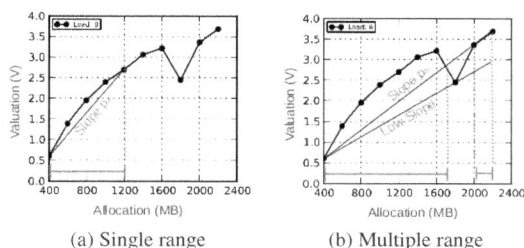

(a) Single range (b) Multiple range

Figure 3. Strategies for choice of unit price for two maximal quantities, using the same valuation function. Figure 3a demonstrates a single desired range strategy for a concave monotonically rising part of the valuation function. Figure 3b demonstrates a multiple desired range strategy for a non-concave, not even monotonically rising part of the valuation function.

guest is incentivized to raise its bid price to a maximum, thus increasing the exclusion compensation that other guests pay and making them more considerate. Hence, our guests always bid $s(q_m)$.

6.2 Choosing a Maximal Memory Quantity q_m

To maximize the guest's estimated utility from the next auction, the guest chooses q_m. Our guest assumes it is in a steady state, and estimates its utility using past auction results. The guest assumes, for simplicity, that it will get a memory quantity of q_m if $p > p_{min}$, and 0 otherwise. p_{min} is the lowest price the guest can offer and still have a chance of getting any memory at all. It is evaluated on the basis of ten recent borderline bids that are announced by the host.

The utility estimation also requires an estimation of the unit price to be paid for the allotted memory amount. The guest estimates its utility from bidding (p, q_m) by dividing it to two components: (1) a valuation improvement from winning the memory it expects to win and (2) a charge. For concave valuation functions $V(\cdot)$, the estimated utility is maximized when $s(q_m) = p_{min}$. In such cases, the guest need only estimate and predict p_{min} to bid optimally. For other (non-concave) functions, the guest must evaluate the estimated charge to find the memory quantity that maximizes the estimated utility To this end it assesses the unit price it will pay on the basis of a historical table of (p', q') pairs, and further bounds it from above by the highest losing bid price in the last auction round. If several values of q_m maximize the estimated utility, the guest prefers to bid with higher p values, to improve its chances of winning the auction.

7. Experimental Setup

In this section we describe the experimental setup in which we evaluate Ginseng.

Alternative Memory Allocation Methods. We compared Ginseng with memory overcommitment and allocation methods available to commercial IaaS providers: *static*, *host-swapping* and *MOM*. In the *static* method, each guest is allocated a fixed amount of memory without any overcommitment. This is a common method in public clouds. When relying on *host-swapping*, each guest gets a fixed memory quantity regardless of the number of guests, and the host is allowed to swap guest memory to balance memory between guests as it sees fit. This method is the fallback of many overcommitment methods. The *Memory Overcommitment Manager (MOM)* [23] collects data from its guests to learn about their memory pressure and continuously adjusts their balloon sizes to make the guests feel the same memory pressure as the host. This is a state-of-the-art overcommitment method that is freely available, but it is not a black-box method: it relies on probes inside the guests and can be easily circumvented by a malicious one.

Workloads. To experiment with overcommitment trade-offs, we used benchmarks of *elastic memory applications*: applications that can improve their performance when given more memory on-the-fly over a large range of memory quantities, and can return memory to the system when needed. We experimented with a modified *elastic memcached* and with *MemoryConsumer*, a dedicated dynamic memory benchmark. Both applications interacted with the Ginseng guest agent to dynamically adjust their heap sizes when they won or lost memory: the Ginseng agent informed the application of the upcoming change and the application reacted by reducing its working-set size accordingly, so that the system would not run out of memory when the balloon is inflated.

Elastic memcached is a version of memcached that changes its heap size on-the-fly to respond to guest memory changes. It can free the less-needed internal-cache slabs or alternatively increase its internal cache size. Memcached was driven by a *memslap* client, a standard memcached benchmarking utility. To test a large number of guests quickly, we configured memslap such that memcached's performance graphs saturated at 2GB. To this end we ran memslap with a key size of 249 bytes, a value size of 1024 bytes, a window size of 100K, and a get/set ratio of 30:70, for 200 seconds each time. The application's performance is defined as the "get" hits per second. [1]

MemoryConsumer is an elastic memory benchmark. It tries to write to a random 1MB-sized cell from a predefined range. If the address is within the range of memory currently available to the program, then 1MB of data is actually written to the memory address and it is considered a hit. After each attempt, whether a hit or a miss, it sleeps for 0.1 seconds, so that misses cost time. The application's performance is defined as the hits per second. This application is tailored as a pure memory overcommitment benchmark, in order to create clean tests, unhindered by resource bottlenecks other than memory. As with memcached, we chose a range of 1950 cells, so that performance graphs would saturate at 2GB.

---

[1] Elastic-memcached is available from `https://github.com/ladypine/memcached`.

We profiled the performance of each workload with varying amounts of memory to create its *perf(mem, load)* function. We measured performance under different loads for four concurrent guests without memory overcommitment, as also done by Hines et al. [17]. We gradually increased and decreased the physical memory in small steps, waiting in each step for the performance to stabilize. For memcached we measured the performance over 200 seconds, and for MemoryConsumer over 60 seconds. The *perf(mem, load)* graphs can be seen in Figure 2a for the elastic Memcached and Figure 2d for MemoryConsumer.

Load. We defined "load" for memcached and MemoryConsumer as the number of concurrent requests. Loads are in the range $[2, 10]$. The total load is always the number of guests $\times 6$, so that the aggregate hits per second of different experiments will be comparable. Each pair of guests exchanged their loads every T_{load}. The load values and their exchange timing were chosen to increase the diversity among the guests, as expected in a real system. Guests were further diversified by assigning them with different memory valuation functions.

Machine Setup. We used a cloud host with 12GB of RAM and two Intel(R) Xeon(R) E5620 CPUs @ 2.40GHz with 12MB LLC. Each CPU had 4 cores with hyper-threading enabled, for a total of 16 hardware threads. The host ran Linux with kernel 2.6.35-31-server-#62-Ubuntu, and the guests ran 3.2.0-29-generic-#46-Ubuntu. To reduce measurement noise, we disabled EIST, NUMA, and C-STATE in the BIOS and KSM in the host kernel. To prevent networking bottlenecks, we increased the network buffers. We dedicated hardware thread 0 to the host and pinned the guests to hardware threads $1 \ldots N$.

Memory Division. 0.75GB were dedicated to the host. To allow guests to both grow and shrink their memory allocations, we configured all guests with a high *maximal memory* of 10GB, most of which was occupied by balloons, leaving each guest with a smaller *initial memory*. However, when using *host-swapping* and *MOM*, extensive host-swapping caused the host to freeze when the maximal guest memory was set to 10GB. Hence we also created a hinted (*white-box*) version of each of these methods to compare against: we informed the host that the applications actually cannot benefit from the full 10GB, and that a rational guest would only need 2GB. As a result, the provider in the *hinted-MOM* and *hinted-host-swapping* methods configured the guests with at most 2GB. This white-box configuration, which is based on our knowledge of the experiment design, is intended to get the best performance out of the alternative memory allocation methods. The initial and maximal memory values are summarized in Table 1.

Reducing Guest Swapping. Bare metal operating systems shield applications from memory pressure by paging memory out and by clearing buffers and caches, but elastic-memory applications should be exposed to memory-pressure

Method/Memory (GB)	Initial	Maximal
Ginseng	0.6	10
Static	11.25/N	11.25/N
Host-swapping	10	10
MOM	0.6	10
Hinted host-swapping	2	2
Hinted MOM	0.6	2

Table 1. Guest configuration: initial and maximal memory values for each overcommitment method. N denotes the number of guests.

in order to enable them to respond. To this end we minimized guest swapping by setting vm.min_free_kbytes to 0. Note that this did not hinder performance of host-swapping.

Reducing Indirect Overcommitment. Bare metal operating systems keep some memory free, in case of sudden memory pressure. The host can indirectly overcommit such memory by giving it to other guests while it is unused; the host relies on its ability to page out guests if and when sudden memory pressure occurs. Since we focus on direct overcommitment (e.g., using balloons), we made the accounting more accurate by setting vm.overcommit_memory to 1 in our guests, thus making the guest physical memory the exact limitation for guest memory allocations. These settings make more sense for a production VM than the default bare-metal OS settings (vm.overcommit_memory=0). A VM with default settings would have required and not used 300MB more on our system. These 300MB would only be available for use by other VMs.

Time Scales. Three time scales define the usability of memory borrowing and therefore the limits to the experiments we conducted: the typical time that passes before the change in physical memory begins to affect performance (e.g., *cache-warming* time—time for the cache to be filled with relevant data), T_{memory}; the time between auction rounds, $T_{auction}$; a typical time scale in which conditions (e.g., load) change, T_{load}. Useful memory borrowing requires $T_{load} >> T_{memory}$. This condition is also necessary for on-line learning of performance with different memory quantities. To evaluate T_{memory}, we performed large step tests, making abrupt, sizable changes in the physical memory and measuring the time it took the performance to stabilize. We empirically determined good values for T_{load} on the basis of step tests results: 1000 seconds for memcached experiments, whereas for MemoryConsumer 200 seconds are enough. We also used those step tests to verify that major page faults in the guest were insignificant (indicating hardly any guest thrashing), and to verify that there was enough time for the performance measurement method to evaluate the performance. For example, memslap required 200 seconds to start experiencing cache misses.

In realistic setups, providers should set $T_{auction} << T_{load}$, to get a responsive system. Therefore, we set $T_{auction}$

to 12 seconds. In each 12-second auction round the host waited 3 seconds for guest bids and then spent 1 second computing the auction's result and notifying the guests. The guests were then allowed 8 seconds to prepare in case they lost memory. We note that due to the long T_{load}, most of the auctions in the experiments did not result in memory changes, and the cache warmth was not affected.

8. Performance Evaluation

This section answers the following questions: (1) Which memory allocation method provides the most satisfied guests (i.e., the highest social welfare)? (2) How accurate is off-line profiling of guest performance?

8.1 Comparing Social Welfare

We evaluate the social welfare achieved by Ginseng vs. each of the five other methods listed in Table 1 for a varying number of guests on the same physical host. We evaluate memcached guests and MemoryConsumer guests in separate sets of experiments. Each Memcached experiment lasted 60 minutes, with $T_{load} = 1000$ seconds. Each MemoryConsumer experiment lasted 30 minutes with $T_{load} = 200$ seconds. For each set we present average results of 5 experiments. Ginseng guests use the strategy described in Section 6.

In both benchmarks, *perf(mem)* is a concave function. To evaluate Ginseng's abilities over non-concave functions, we used performance valuation functions $V_{perf}(perf)$ that make the resulting composed valuation function $V(mem)$ non-concave.

In the first experiment set (MemoryConsumer), each guest i's valuation function is defined as $V_i(mem) = f_i \cdot (perf(mem))^2$, where the f_i values were drawn from the *Pareto distribution*, a widely used model for income and asset distributions [22, 32]. We bounded the distribution because on-line trading does not span the whole range of human transactions: some are too cheap or too expensive to be made on-line. We used a reasonable Pareto index for income distributions (1.1) [32], and a lower bound of $10^{-4}\frac{\$}{Khit}$. The "square of performance" valuation function is characteristic of on-line games and social networks, where the memory requirements are proportional to the number of users, and the income is proportional to user interactions, which are proportional to the square of the number of users. The composed valuation function is illustrated in Figure 4a.

In the second experiment set (elastic memcached), each guest i's valuation function is defined as $V(mem) = f_i \cdot perf(mem)$, where the f_i values were Pareto-distributed with a Pareto index of 1.36 (an empirical wealth distribution [22]), and bounded in the range $[10^{-4}, 100]\frac{\$}{Khit}$. The highest coefficient was set as:

$$f_1 = \begin{cases} 0.1\frac{\$}{Khit} & perf(mem) < 3.4\frac{Khit}{s} \\ 1.8\frac{\$}{Khit} & otherwise. \end{cases} \quad (2)$$

The piecewise-linear valuation function characterizes service level agreements that distinguish usage levels by unit

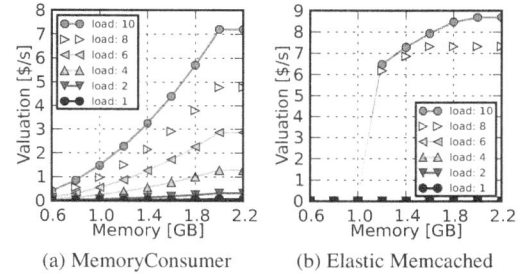

(a) MemoryConsumer   (b) Elastic Memcached

Figure 4. Valuation functions for different loads

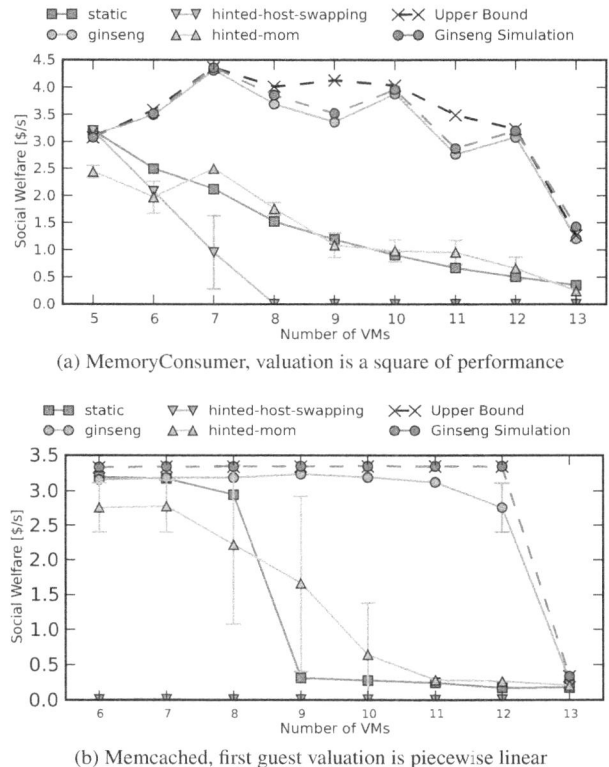

(a) MemoryConsumer, valuation is a square of performance

(b) Memcached, first guest valuation is piecewise linear

Figure 5. Social welfare (mean and standard deviation) under different allocation schemes as a function of the number of guests. The dashed lines indicate simulation-based upper bounds on Ginseng's social welfare.

price. The valuation function for the first guest is shown in Figure 4b.

We calculated the social welfare for each experiment using each VM's measured performance and that VM's valuation function. The social welfare of the different experiments is compared in Figure 5. The figures contain two upper bounds for the social welfare, achieved by simulating Ginseng's auction and assuming the guests perform exactly according to their predicted performance (e.g., ignoring cache warmup). The tighter bound results from a simulation of Ginseng itself. The looser bound results from a white-

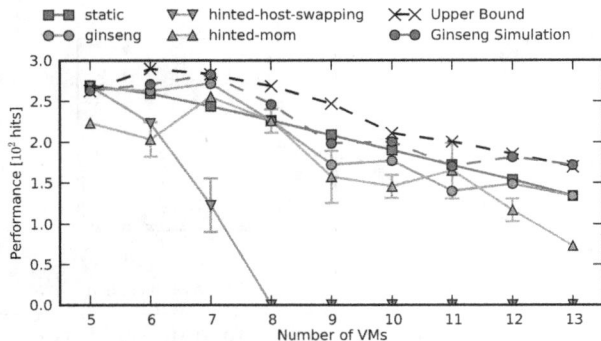

(a) MemoryConsumer, valuation is a square of performance. Performance is in terms of hits per second.

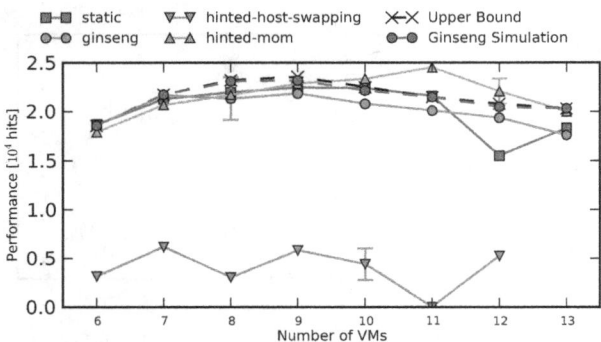

(b) Memcached, first guest valuation is piecewise linear. Performance is in terms of "get" hits per second.

Figure 6. Performance (mean and standard deviation) under different allocation schemes as a function of the number of guests. The dashed lines indicate the performance according to the simulation from which the upper bounds on Ginseng's social welfare were derived. They are not the upper bound on aggregate performance: memory allocation schemes with lower social welfare may have higher aggregate performance.

box on-line simulation, which results in the theoretically optimal allocations given full offline information. The MOM and host-swapping methods yield negligible social welfare values for these experiments, and are not shown.

As can be seen in Figure 5, Ginseng achieves much better social welfare than any other allocation method for both workloads. It improves social welfare by up to $15.8\times$ for memcached and up to $6.2\times$ for MemoryConsumer, compared both with black-box (static) and white-box approaches (hinted-mom). As the number of guests increases, so does the potential for increased social welfare, because more individual utilities are aggregated to compose the social welfare. However, each guest is allocated a fixed amount of memory (*base*) on startup, reducing our host's free memory, which is available for auction; hence the relative peak in social welfare for 7 guests (MemoryConsumer). In the Memcached experiment the relative peak is flat because the first guest's valuation is much higher than the valuations of the rest of

the guests. In both experiment sets, Ginseng achieves 83%–100% of the optimal social welfare. The sharp decline in Ginseng's social welfare for 13 guests comes when Ginseng no longer has enough free memory to answer even the needs of the most valuable guest. This improved social welfare does not come at the cost of overall aggregate performance: it is roughly equivalent to the performance of the better performing competitors, as can be seen in Figure 6.

8.2 Influence of Off-Line Profiling

In our experiments we used performance graphs that were measured in advance in a controlled environment. In real life, such data should be collected on-line, considering both data accumulation and data freshness in view of changing environment conditions. Since the accuracy of the best on-line methods is bounded by the accuracy of hindsight, we can bound the influence of refraining from on-line evaluation on the performance graphs. In Figure 7 we compare our benchmarks' predicted performance (deduced from measured load and memory quantities using the functions in Figure 2, which were measured without memory overcommitment) with performance values measured during Ginseng experiments for the same loads and memory quantities. The experimental values were collected after the memory usage stabilized. The comparison shows that the profiled data is accurate enough, as can be seen when comparing Ginseng's results in the full experiments to its results with simulated guests in Figure 5.

9. Discussion: Host Revenue and Collusion

Ginseng does not maximize host revenue directly. Instead, it assumes that the host charges an admittance fee for the seed virtual machine and maximizes the aggregate client satisfaction (the social welfare). Maximizing social welfare improves host revenues indirectly because better-satisfied guests are willing to pay higher admittance fees. Likewise, improving each cloud host's hardware (memory) utilization should allow the provider to run more guests on each host. To ensure that guests cover power-related operational costs, the host can introduce a dummy bidder that bids with a unit price that equals these costs.

Our guests reach a steady state using indirect interactions that result from their on-line strategy. More sophisticated guests may collude and negotiate to ease their way into a steady state of their choice. While collusion can hasten reaching a steady-state, it may also result in a non-optimal resource allocation. However, collusion which involves bidding with non-truthful unit prices is risky if bidders can join or leave and bids can change. The risk can be increased by randomly limiting the auctionable memory [1].

10. Related Work

Grey-Box and Black-Box Techniques. Magenheimer [25] used the guests' own performance statistics to guide overcommitment. Zhao et al. [40] balanced memory between VMS on the basis of on-the-fly intermittently-built miss-rate curves. Waldspurger [37] randomly sampled pages to esti-

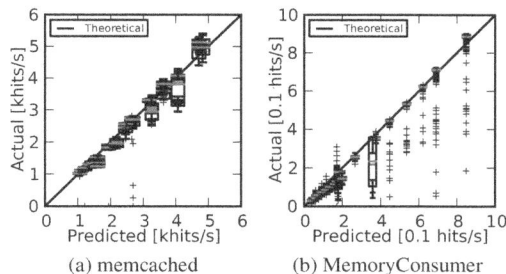

Figure 7. Comparison of predicted performance values (according to the profile graphs, given load and memory allocation) with measured performance.

mate the quantity of unused guest memory, to guide page reclaim. These methods can be circumvented by a selfish guest, and like white-box methods, ignore the client's valuation of performance. Gong, Gu and Wilkes [11] and Shen et al. [30] used learning algorithms to predict guest resource requirements.

Market Driven Resource Allocation Drexler and Miller suggested auctioning memory chunks to reach a market clearing price [10]. Waldspurger et al. used multiple concurrent sealed-bid, second price auctions to auction processor time slices [35]. Waldspurger [36] allocated resources in proportion to tickets that had to be allocated by a centralized know-all control. In a cloud, no know-all control can allocate tickets to separate economic entities. However, real clouds do not need to allocate tickets—the real money that they use has intrinsic value.

Resource Allocation For Monotonically Rising, Concave Valuations. Maillé and Tuffin [26] extended the PSP [21] to multi-bids, increasing the auction's complexity to instantly reach equilibrium. Though a multi-bid auction is more efficient for static problems, it loses its appeal in dynamic problems which require repeated auction rounds anyhow. Other drawbacks of the multi-bid auction are that the guest needs to know the memory valuation function for the full range; that frequent guest updates pose a burden to the host; and that the guest cannot directly explore working points which currently seem less than optimal. (It can do so indirectly by faking its valuation function.) In contrast, the MPSP auction leaves the control over the currently desired resource allocation to the guest, who best knows its own current and future needs.

Chase et al. [6] allocated CPU time assuming client valuations of the resource are fully known, concave, and monotonically increasing. Urgaonkar, Shenoy, and Roscoe [33] overbooked bandwidth and CPU given full profiling data.

Auctions With Non-concave Valuations. Bae et al. [4] supported a single bidder with a non-concave valuation function. Dobzinski and Nisan [9] presented truthful polynomial time approximation algorithms for multi-unit auctions with not-necessarily-concave k-minded valuations. They only as-

sumed that the valuations are non-decreasing (because they allow shedding of unneeded goods). Our bidding language of forbidden ranges creates more efficient allocations, because it allows undesired memory to be auctioned to guests who value it more, instead of disposing of it. Ginseng is based on a divisible good auction, and not on *bundles* in a *multi-unit* auction. Hence, its fine-grained allocation accuracy does not increase its algorithmic complexity.

11. Conclusion

Ginseng is the first cloud platform that allocates physical memory to selfish black-box guests while maximizing their aggregate benefit. It does so using the MPSP auction, in which even guests with non-concave valuation of memory are incentivized to bid their true valuations for the memory they request. Ginseng achieves an order of magnitude of improvement in the social welfare function when compared with alternative cloud memory allocation methods.

Although Ginseng focuses on selfish guests, it can also benefit altruistic guests (e.g., when all guests are owned by the same economic entity). In this case, guests that perform the same function for different purposes, such as a test server vs. a production server, can be distinguished by their economic valuation functions.

The MPSP auction is suitable for memory auctioning, but is not limited to this purpose. When used for the allocation of another divisible resource, e.g., bandwidth, whose valuation functions are concave and monotonically rising, it is as efficient as the PSP auction. Hence, Ginseng is not just a memory auctioning platform, but rather the first concrete step towards the Resource-as-a-Service (RaaS) cloud [2]. In the RaaS cloud, all resources, not just memory, will be bought and sold on-the-fly. Extending Ginseng to resources other than physical memory remains as future work.

12. Acknowledgments

We thank Sharon Kessler, Abel Gordon, Michael Hines, Nadav Amit, Gala Yadgar, Yaron Singer, Hadas Shachnai and Erez Petrank for fruitful discussions. This research was partially supported by THE ISRAEL SCIENCE FOUNDATION (grant No. 605/12) and by the Prof. A. Pazi IAEC-UPBC joint research foundation.

References

[1] O. Agmon Ben-Yehuda, M. Ben-Yehuda, A. Schuster, and D. Tsafrir. Deconstructing Amazon EC2 spot instance pricing. In *IEEE Conf. on Cloud Computing Technology and Science (CloudCom)*, 2011.

[2] O. Agmon Ben-Yehuda, M. Ben-Yehuda, A. Schuster, and D. Tsafrir. The resource-as-a-service (raas) cloud. In *USENIX Conf. on Hot Topics in Cloud Computing (HotCloud)*, 2012.

[3] M. Armbrust, A. Fox, R. Griffith, A. D. Joseph, R. Katz, A. Konwinski, G. Lee, D. Patterson, A. Rabkin, I. Stoica, and M. Zaharia. A view of cloud computing. *Communications of the ACM*, 53(4):50–58, 2010.

[4] J. Bae, E. Beigman, R. Berry, M. L. Honig, and R. Vohra. An efficient auction for non concave valuations. In *Int'l Meeting of the Society for Social Choice and Welfare*, 2008.

[5] M. Cary, A. Das, B. Edelman, I. Giotis, K. Heimerl, A. R. Karlin, C. Mathieu, and M. Schwarz. Greedy bidding strategies for keyword auctions. In *ACM Conf. on Electronic Commerce (EC)*, pages 262–271, 2007.

[6] J. S. Chase, D. C. Anderson, P. N. Thakar, A. M. Vahdat, and R. P. Doyle. Managing energy and server resources in hosting centers. In *ACM Symposium on Operating Systems Principles (SOSP)*, 2001.

[7] E. H. Clarke. Multipart pricing of public goods. *Public Choice*, 11(1):17–33, Sep 1971.

[8] G. D'Alesandre. Updated app engine pricing faq! Web site, June 2011. http://tinyurl.com/D-Alesandre.

[9] S. Dobzinski and N. Nisan. Mechanisms for multi-unit auctions. *J. of Artificial Intelligence Research*, 37:85–98, 2010.

[10] K. E. Drexler and M. S. Miller. Incentive engineering for computational resource management. In *The Ecology of Computation*, pages 231–266. Elsevier Science Publishers, 1988.

[11] Z. Gong, X. Gu, and J. Wilkes. Press: Predictive elastic resource scaling for cloud systems. In *Int'l Conf. on Network and Service Management (CNSM)*, pages 9–16, 2010.

[12] A. Gordon, M. Hines, D. Da Silva, M. Ben-Yehuda, M. Silva, and G. Lizarraga. Ginkgo: Automated, application-driven memory overcommitment for cloud computing. In *Runtime Environments/Systems, Layering, & Virtualized Environments Workshop (ASPLOS RESOLVE)*, 2011.

[13] T. Groves. Incentives in teams. *Econometrica*, 41(4):617–631, Jul 1973.

[14] C. Grzegorczyk, S. Soman, C. Krintz, and R. Wolski. Isla vista heap sizing: Using feedback to avoid paging. In *Int'l Symposium on Code Generation and Optimization (CGO)*, pages 325–340, 2007.

[15] J. Heo, X. Zhu, P. Padala, and Z. Wang. Memory overbooking and dynamic control of xen virtual machines in consolidated environments. In *IFIP/IEEE Symposium on Integrated Management (IM)*, 2009.

[16] M. Hertz, S. Kane, E. Keudel, T. Bai, C. Ding, X. Gu, and J. E. Bard. Waste not, want not: resource-based garbage collection in a shared environment. In *Int'l Symposium on Memory Management (ISMM)*, 2011.

[17] M. Hines, A. Gordon, M. Silva, D. D. Silva, K. D. Ryu, and M. Ben-Yehuda. Applications know best: Performance-driven memory overcommit with ginkgo. In *IEEE Conf. on Cloud Computing Technology and Science (CloudCom)*, 2011.

[18] S. T. Jones, A. C. Arpaci-Dusseau, and R. H. Arpaci-Dusseau. Geiger: monitoring the buffer cache in a virtual machine environment. In *ACM Architectural Support for Programming Languages & Operating Systems (ASPLOS)*, 2006.

[19] F. Kelly. Charging and rate control for elastic traffic. *European Trans. on Telecommunications*, 8:33–37, 1997.

[20] A. Kivity, Y. Kamay, D. Laor, U. Lublin, and A. Liguori. KVM: the Linux virtual machine monitor. In *Ottawa Linux Symposium (OLS)*, pages 225–230, 2007.

[21] A. Lazar and N. Semret. Design and analysis of the progressive second price auction for network bandwidth sharing. *Telecommunication Systems—Special issue on Network Economics*, 20:255–263, 1999.

[22] M. Levy and S. Solomon. New evidence for the power-law distribution of wealth. *Physica A*, 242:90–94, 1997.

[23] A. G. Litke. Memory overcommitment manager. website, 2011. https://github.com/aglitke/mom.

[24] B. Lucier, R. Paes Leme, and E. Tardos. On revenue in the generalized second price auction. In *Int'l World Wide Web Conf. (WWW)*, 2012.

[25] D. Magenheimer. Memory overcommit... without the commitment. In *Xen Summit*. USENIX association, June 2008.

[26] P. Maillé and B. Tuffin. Multi-bid auctions for bandwidth allocation in communication networks. In *IEEE INFOCOM*, 2004.

[27] R. Nathuji, A. Kansal, and A. Ghaffarkhah. Q-clouds: Managing performance interference effects for qos-aware clouds. In *ACM SIGOPS European Conf. on Computer Systems (EuroSys)*, 2010.

[28] Z. Ou, H. Zhuang, J. K. Nurminen, A. Ylä-Jääski, and P. Hui. Exploiting hardware heterogeneity within the same instance type of amazon EC2. In *USENIX Conf. on Hot Topics in Cloud Computing (HotCloud)*, 2012.

[29] T.-I. Salomie, G. Alonso, T. Roscoe, and K. Elphinstone. Application level ballooning for efficient server consolidation. In *ACM SIGOPS European Conf. on Computer Systems (EuroSys)*, pages 337–350, 2013.

[30] Z. Shen, S. Subbiah, X. Gu, and J. Wilkes. Cloudscale: elastic resource scaling for multi-tenant cloud systems. In *ACM Symposium on Cloud Computing (SOCC)*, 2011.

[31] S. Soman, C. Krintz, and D. F. Bacon. Dynamic selection of application-specific garbage collectors. In *Int'l Symposium on Memory Management (ISMM)*, 2004.

[32] W. Souma. Universal structure of the personal income distribution. *Fractals*, 9(04):463–470, 2001.

[33] B. Urgaonkar, P. Shenoy, and T. Roscoe. Resource overbooking and application profiling in a shared internet hosting platform. *ACM Trans. Internet Technol.*, 9(1), 2009.

[34] W. Vickrey. Counterspeculation, auctions, and competitive sealed tenders. *J. of Finance*, 16(1), 1961.

[35] C. Waldspurger, T. Hogg, B. A. Huberman, J. O. Kephart, and W. S. Stornetta. Spawn: a distributed computational economy. *IEEE Trans. on Software Engineering*, 18(2):103–117, 1992.

[36] C. A. Waldspurger. *Lottery and Stride Scheduling: Flexible Proportional-Share Resource Management*. PhD thesis, Massachusetts Institute of Technology, 1995.

[37] C. A. Waldspurger. Memory resource management in Vmware ESX server. In *USENIX Symposium on Operating Systems Design & Implementation (OSDI)*, 2002.

[38] T. Yang, E. D. Berger, S. F. Kaplan, and J. E. B. Moss. CRAMM: virtual memory support for garbage-collected applications. In *USENIX Symposium on Operating Systems Design & Implementation (OSDI)*, pages 103–116, 2006.

[39] W. Zhao and Z. Wang. Dynamic memory balancing for virtual machines. In *ACM/USENIX Int'l Conf. on Virtual Execution Environments (VEE)*, pages 21–30, 2009.

[40] W. Zhao, X. Jin, Z. Wang, X. Wang, Y. Luo, and X. Li. Low cost working set size tracking. In *USENIX Annual Technical Conf. (ATC)*, 2011.

[41] P. Zhou, V. Pandey, J. Sundaresan, A. Raghuraman, Y. Zhou, and S. Kumar. Dynamic tracking of page miss ratio curve for memory management. In *ACM Architectural Support for Programming Languages & Operating Systems (ASPLOS)*, 2004.

Mortar: Filling the Gaps in Data Center Memory

Jinho Hwang[†]   Ahsen Uppal   Timothy Wood   H. Howie Huang

[†]IBM T.J. Watson Research Center   The George Washington University

jinho@us.ibm.com   {auppal, timwood, howie}@gwu.edu

Abstract

Data center servers are typically overprovisioned, leaving spare memory and CPU capacity idle to handle unpredictable workload bursts by the virtual machines running on them. While this allows for fast hotspot mitigation, it is also wasteful. Unfortunately, making use of spare capacity without impacting active applications is particularly difficult for memory since it typically must be allocated in coarse chunks over long timescales. In this work we propose repurposing the poorly utilized memory in a data center to store a volatile data store that is managed by the hypervisor. We present two uses for our Mortar framework: as a cache for prefetching disk blocks, and as an application-level distributed cache that follows the memcached protocol. Both prototypes use the framework to ask the hypervisor to store useful, but recoverable data within its free memory pool. This allows the hypervisor to control eviction policies and prioritize access to the cache. We demonstrate the benefits of our prototypes using realistic web applications and disk benchmarks, as well as memory traces gathered from live servers in our university's IT department. By expanding and contracting the data store size based on the free memory available, Mortar improves average response time of a web application by up to 35% compared to a fixed size memcached deployment, and improves overall video streaming performance by 45% through prefetching.

Categories and Subject Descriptors   D.4.2 [*Operating Systems*]: Storage Management

General Terms   Design; Experimentation; Performance

Keywords   Memory Management; Virtualization; Memcached; Disk Prefetching

VEE '14,   March 1–2, 2014, Salt Lake City, Utah, USA.
Copyright © 2014 ACM 978-1-4503-2764-0/14/03...$15.00.
http://dx.doi.org/10.1145/2576195.2576203

1. Introduction

Cloud data centers can comprise thousands of servers, each of which may host multiple virtual machines (VMs). Making efficient use of all those server resources is a major challenge, but a cloud platform that can obtain better utilization can offer lower prices for a competitive advantage. A resource such as the CPU is relatively simple to manage because it can be allocated on a very fine time scale, greatly simplifying how it can be shared among multiple VMs. Memory, however, typically must be allocated to VMs in large chunks at coarse time scales, making it far less flexible. Since memory demands can change quickly and new VMs may frequently be created or migrated, it is common to leave a buffer of unused memory for the hypervisor to manage. Even worse, operating systems have been designed to greedily consume as much memory as they can—the OS will happily release the CPU when it has no tasks to run, but it will consume every memory page it can for its file cache. The result is that many servers have memory allocated to VMs that is inefficiently utilized, *and* have regions of memory left idle so that the machine can be ready to instantiate new VMs or receive a migration.

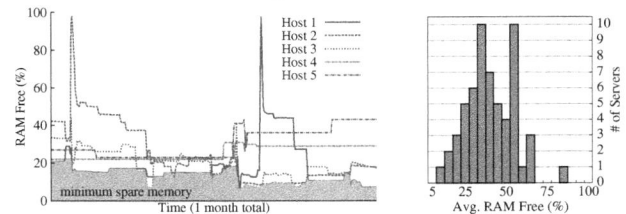

Figure 1: The amount of free memory on a set of five hosts varying over time (left), and the histogram on 58 servers from our university's data center (right).

To illustrate this inefficiency, we have gathered four months of memory traces from over fifty servers within our university's IT department. Each server is used to host an average of 15 VMs running a mix of web services, domain controllers, business process management, and data warehouse applications. The servers are managed with VMware's Distributed Resource Management software [24], which dynamically reallocates memory and migrates virtual machines based on their workload needs. Figure 1 shows the amount of memory left idle on a set of five representative machines

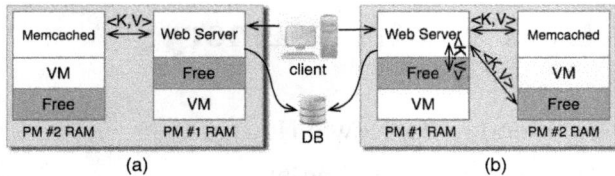

Figure 2: Physical RAM map shows how a physical machine (PM) composes its memory. (a) Traditional Memcached uses only dedicated memcached space for cache; (b) Mortar uses all the spare memory in the whole system.

over the course of a month, and the histogram of the amount of free memory on the full set of 58 servers, ignoring maintenance periods where VMs have not yet been started and nearly all memory is free. We find that at least half of the machines have 30% or more of their memory free. This level of overprovisioning was also shown in the resource observations from [4]. Clearly it would be beneficial to make use of this spare memory, but simply assigning it back to the VMs does not guarantee it will be used in a productive way. Further, reallocating memory from one VM to another can be a slow process that may require swapping to disk.

To improve this situation, we present the design of Mortar, a system that enhances the Xen hypervisor to pool together spare memory on each machine and expose it as a volatile data cache. When a server has spare memory capacity, VMs are free to add data to the hypervisor managed cache, but if memory becomes a constrained resource, the hypervisor can immediately evict objects from the cache to reclaim space needed for other VMs. This grants the hypervisor far greater control over how memory is used within the data center, and improves performance by making opportunistic use of any spare memory available.

We present two example usages for the Mortar framework. Our first prototype aggregates free memory throughout the data center for use as a distributed cache following the standard memcached protocol. This allows unmodified web applications to achieve performance gains by opportunistically using spare data center memory. Next, we demonstrate how Mortar can be used at the OS-level to transparently cache and prefetch disk blocks for applications. Prefetching is an ideal candidate for Mortar's volatile data store because the aggressiveness of the algorithm can be tuned based on the amount of free memory available.

The contributions of this paper are as follows:

- A framework for repurposing spare system memory that otherwise would be idle or poorly utilized.
- A prototype disk prefetching system that aggressively reads disk blocks into spare hypervisor memory to reduce the latency of future disk reads.
- An enhanced memcached server that can utilize this hypervisor controlled memory to build a distributed application-level cache accessible by web applications.
- Cache allocation and replacement algorithms for prioritizing access to spare memory and balancing the need to

retain hot data in the cache against the goal of being able to immediately reclaim memory for other uses.

We have thoroughly evaluated Mortar using microbenchmarks, realistic web applications, and disk access traces. Our results demonstrate that Mortar incurs an overhead under 0.03ms on individual read accesses, and illustrates the benefit of making use of all free memory in a data cecnter. Our fast cache release algorithm can reclaim gigabytes of memory within 0.1ms. In experiments driven by real server memory traces, Mortar improves web performance by over 35% by using a spare memory based cache. When using only 500MB of idle server memory for a prefetch cache, Mortar makes disk reads in an OLTP benchmark three times faster.

2. Background and Motivation

In this work we assume Mortar is run in a public or private cloud environment that makes use of a virtualized infrastructure to adapt quickly to different user demands. As is now common, we assume that dynamic resource provisioning techniques [3, 11, 19, 23–25] are frequently readjusting resource shares for virtual machines based on their workloads. Even in these automated systems, overprovisioning is still common since some spare capacity is left on each machine to handle rising workloads locally without resorting to more expensive VM migrations.

Ideally, this spare capacity would be opportunistically used, but then freed when it is needed for a more important purpose. For resources such as CPU time, this can be easily accomplished using existing CPU schedulers that can assign weights for different VMs and can adjust scheduling decisions on the order of milliseconds. Unfortunately, memory cannot be reassigned as efficiently or as effectively as CPU shares.

There are two challenges that prevent memory from being used as a flexible resource like CPU time. First, memory is generally only helpful if it is allocated in large chunks over coarse time scales (i.e., minutes or hours). If a VM has processing to do, it can immediately make use of more CPU time, but an increased memory allocation can take time to fill up with useful data. Further, rapidly increasing and decreasing a VM's memory share can lead to disastrous swapping. The second challenge is that adjusting a VM's memory share generally has an unpredictable impact on performance. This is partly because operating systems have been designed to greedily hoard whatever memory they can make use of. Over time, a VM will consume any additional memory pages it is given for its disk cache, but this will not necessarily have a significant impact on application-level performance.

One approach that has gained popularity for directly translating more memory into better performance is the use of in-memory application-level caches such as memcached. Many web applications, such as Wikipedia, Flickr, and Twitter, use memcached to store volatile data such as the results

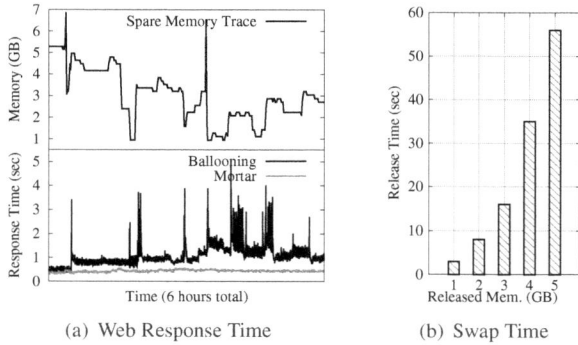

(a) Web Response Time   (b) Swap Time

Figure 3: Ballooning vs. Mortar

of database queries, allowing for much faster client response times as depicted in Figure 2(a). Each memcached node holds a simple key-value based data store, and these nodes are then grouped together to create a distributed in-memory cache. However, memcached works by allocating fixed size caches on each server. Thus by itself, memcached is not effective for making use of varying amounts of spare memory.

Our goal in Mortar is to expose unallocated system memory so that applications such as memcached can make better use of it. By having the hypervisor control access to this volatile storage area, Mortar can prioritize how different guests access the memory and allows it to be reclaimed much more quickly than if it must be ballooned out of the guest. Mortar uses a modified Xen hypervisor that exposes a new hypercall interface for putting and retrieving data in the free memory pool. We believe that this interface will be useful for a wide range of scenarios at both the system and application level. In this paper we present two examples: a modified version of memcached that taps into spare hypervisor memory and an OS-level disk block prefetching system.

3. Hypervisor-Managed Resources

Traditionally, the guest OS and applications controlled resources that were statically assigned to the VM, and the hypervisor primarily provided isolation. While this offered the strictest performance guarantees, the overall resource utilization of the physical machine could be low because the hypervisor did not take different workload demands and spare resources into consideration.

To overcome this limitation, dynamic resource management [25] emerged to control the usage of memory according to priority and necessity. For instance, the balloon drivers in the hypervisor can monitor memory access patterns of each VM and grant more memory to more aggressive ones. This has many benefits by allowing VMs to grow and shrink based on their demand, but it can still cause some serious problems since the hypervisor does not know what memory is being used for and the VM does not know when it will get more or less RAM.

To show this, we run a memcached VM in an environment with automated memory ballooning. In the experiment, a memcached VM is first assigned all spare memory, but then

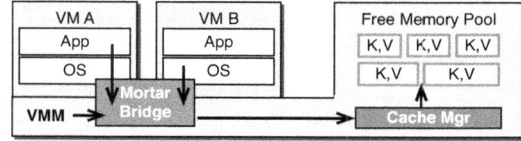

Figure 4: Mortar allows an application or OS to store Key-Value data in the hypervisor's free memory pool.

the allocation changes based on the memory trace shown in the upper part of Figure 3(a) (see Section 6.5 for the full experimental setup). As the memory allocated to the VM varies over time, pages from memcached must be swapped to disk, causing the response time to rise to several seconds, worse than not using the cache at all.

Not only is performance terrible due to swapping, the fact that data needs to be written to disk for each memory reconfiguration can dramatically increase the amount of time required for resource management operations. Figure 3(b) shows the time needed to reduce the memory allocation when using ballooning on a VM with resident data in memory. This can easily take tens of seconds if multiple gigabytes must be written to disk.

Both of these problems occur because of the *semantic gap* between the hypervisor and VM: the operating system and applications within the VM cannot distinguish between memory dedicated to the VM and memory which may soon be reclaimed by the hypervisor. In Mortar, we bridge this gap by not only allowing the hypervisor to dynamically allocate memory at fine granularity, but to understand how that memory is being used—it separates a VM's memory into that used for crucial application data and that used for volatile pages which can be recovered elsewhere if needed. While we focus on using this for disk (Guest OS level) and application level caches, our approach of granting the hypervisor greater knowledge and control of memory holds promise for a wide variety of general purposes.

4. Mortar Framework

The Mortar framework is divided into two main components as shown in Figure 4. The Mortar Bridge is composed of a pair of interfaces at the hypervisor and kernel levels that allow user applications to transfer data to and from the hypervisor's free memory pool. This interface can be accessed via system calls within user-space, or with direct hypercalls in kernel-space. The request to put or retrieve data from the hypervisor is passed to the Mortar Cache Manager, which is responsible for managing the hypervisor's free memory pool. This section describes the interface of the Mortar Bridge and how it is used by our two prototype applications. We then describe the eviction and management policies supported by Mortar in Section 5.

4.1 Repurposing Unallocated Memory

A hypervisor maintains a list of spare memory that can be allocated to VMs on demand. In order to use this spare mem-

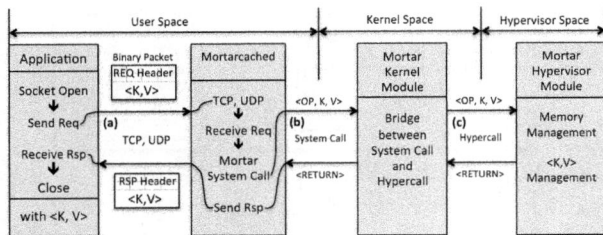

Figure 5: Mortar Protocol Processing Flow: (a) Equivalent protocol with memcached supports the same access method to Mortar so that we do not need to change applications; (b) System call moves data from user to kernel; (c) Hypercall bridges between kernel and hypervisor.

ory as a cache, we need a way to easily and quickly transfer data between a guest VM and the hypervisor controlled free memory pool. Mortar does this by defining a new Linux system call and a Xen hypercall which together provide the interface to a key-value store. Both of these calls take a key, a value, an operation (put, get, or invalidate), and an optional field that can set an expiration time for a new object. Communication between a VM and the hypervisor in Xen can be done through hypercalls, event channels plus shared memory, or the xenstore. Event channels plus shared memory and xenstore have limitations when transferring large amounts of data, whereas a hypercall delivers a physical address to the hypervisor, which can translate the physical address into the machine address and copy the data, so we use this approach. Depending on how Mortar is being used, these calls can originate in a user-space application or inside the guest VM's kernel; for this explanation we assume requests originate in user-space since this subsumes all the steps needed for the kernel case.

On a *put* operation, the calling application provides a key and value to the Mortar kernel module, which copies the data from user space to kernel space and invokes a hypercall. Moving objects from user space to hypervisor space via kernel space is necessary because no direct connection is possible from the user perspective. While the memory copies from user space to kernel space and then hypervisor space has a processing overhead, directly copying non-contiguous memory from user space is a non-trivial problem since the hypervisor does not know how the virtual address space is organized. If the hypervisor has enough unallocated pages to store the object, it is copied into the host's free memory. The pages used for the object are then moved from the hypervisor's free page list to a new "volatile page list", indicating that the page is being used to store cache data, but that it can be immediately reclaimed if necessary. A *get* operation reverses this procedure: the key is used as an index to a chained hash table which verifies the object is still in memory and copies it back to the kernel and then the user space application. Since the hypervisor is invoked on each operation it can verify the VM should have access rights to the data and can enforce prioritization across VMs.

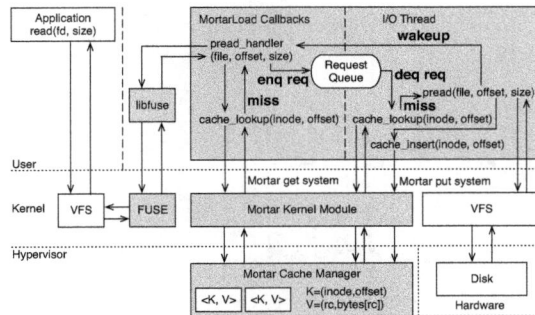

Figure 6: MortarLoad disk caching and prefetching.

4.2 Mortar-based Memcached

While Mortar's data store could be used for many purposes, our first prototype uses it to store data following the memcached architecture. We have modified the memcached application so that instead of using a fixed memory region to store all cached data, it invokes the Mortar system call to ask the hypervisor to hold the data. This modified memcached process can then be run in Dom-0 or a guest VM, and can be seamlessly merged with an existing memcached server pool. This lets Mortar instantly be used by many existing applications to access a distributed memory pool available throughout the data center.

Mortar modifies the backend memory management routines in memcached to change the course of the put and get functions so they route data to the hypervisor rather than user memory. Since the hypervisor may revoke memory storing an object without notifying memcached, a get request may return an error code for a missing object. Note that this is no different from what would happen in a regular memcached server if the object has been evicted, so we require no changes to existing applications.

Figure 5 shows the protocols of applications, Mortarcached (our modified memcached), kernel, and hypervisor. First, a web application issues a request to Mortarcached using the standard memcached protocol. Mortarcached receives the binary packet and checks the operation code. A get or put system call is then issued to the Mortar kernel module, then the kernel module simply delivers the request to hypervisor space by calling a new hypercall. Later in Section 6.2, we will show how much overhead occurs due to this additional processing. Modifying an application such as memcached to work with Mortar is a straightforward process (e.g., adding about 500 lines of code).

4.3 Mortar-based Prefetching

This section describes the design and implementation of our prefetching and caching system, MortarLoad. This system leverages the easy access to the free memory pool that is provided by Mortar to automatically prefetch data from storage systems (local or network disks) based on access predictions, and store the data in Mortar memory to expedite future accesses. MortarLoad is completely transparent to user applications. At the highest level, an application requests I/O operations through standard read() and write() system calls, which will be forwarded to MortarLoad. Depending on where the data is, MortarLoad will fetch it from Mortar, or pass the request to underlying storage systems.

MortarLoad can be implemented in both kernel and user spaces. In this work for easy implementation, we implement a prototype of MortarLoad in Linux as a FUSE filesystem with backend calls through the Mortar hypervisor API. We leave a kernel implementation as future work and expect to achieve higher efficiency and performance. Figure 6 presents the overall architecture of MortarLoad.

MortarLoad adds an additional cache layer beyond the operating system's standard disk cache. This second-level cache uses spare memory provided by the Mortar framework. The cache management and replacement algorithms are managed by Mortar in the same way as memcached. In fact, requests from memcached and the disk can be stored simultaneously.

MortarLoad translates every I/O request into a tuple of <key, value>, where the key into the cache represents the inode of the requested file, file offset, and size of the operation, i.e., a function f(inode, size, offset). Requests are automatically aligned to 128KB-sized blocks by the FUSE layer.

For a read request, the Mortar cache is checked for the presence of this key. This call crosses the system call boundary into the kernel and then as a hypervisor call across the VM boundary. If the request can be satisfied from cache, a copy of the data is copied back from the hypervisor by Mortar. If the request is not in cache, it is enqueued for a separate I/O thread to handle. Serializing disk I/Os through a separate thread is to improve the performance when there are many simultaneous readers, especially when there are prefetch requests. This thread has an input request queue and an associated condition variable that it waits on.

Each request enqueued to the I/O thread also has a destination buffer and a blocking semaphore. When the I/O thread wakes up, it dequeues the latest request, performs an additional cache lookup (in case different threads requested the same block), and if not found, reads the data from the disk with a call to pread(). The resulting data and return code are copied to the location pointed to by the request and the associated semaphore increased. Another call is also made to place the key inode, size, offset and data result code, data bytes into the cache. When the calling context is woken up after waiting on the semaphore, it copies the data back into FUSE which then copies it to the application.

Prefetching is handled by having the calling thread place additional requests on the I/O queue that read several blocks ahead of the current request. The amount of prefetching is an adjustable start-up parameter. These requests have no waiting semaphore, but are still placed into the cache after being read from disk. Our experiments have shown that the prefetching accuracy is very high ($> 99\%$) for many workloads that perform sequential reads. As an enhancement, we plan to investigate the use of feedback-directed prefetching to vary the aggressiveness based on recent performance and the size of memory available to Mortar.

For a write request, MortarLoad currently puts the request straight into the I/O thread's input queue without any cache lookup. In other words, writes are handled with a simple write-through policy. If the I/O request is a write and is writing to an already-cached block, that block is first removed from the cache, and then written to disk normally. As a possible enhancement, we plan to investigate optimizations including a write-back cache.

There are other filesystem operations which as currently implemented do not make use of the cache at all, to name a few, getattr, access, readdir, chmod, chown, and fsyn. Instead, these operations write directly to the disk, bypassing the I/O thread, and invalidate the corresponding cache entries as needed.

5. Cache Management Mechanisms

Mortar's cache management has two important roles: (1) handling data replacement/eviction; (2) enforcing VM priorities based on weights.

5.1 Cache Replacement Algorithms

Mortar uses inactive memory to store application data, but it is possible that this memory will suddenly be needed for either a new, migrated, or overloaded VM. Fortunately, since the data store is considered volatile, Mortar can invalidate cache entries without needing to worry about consistency. Ideally, cache eviction should follow an intelligent policy such as removing the least recently used (LRU) entries first, however, this can be too slow if gigabytes must be freed and each cache entry is on the order of kilobytes.

The Xen hypervisor uses Two-Level Segregate Fit (TLSF) [17], which is a general purpose dynamic memory allocator specifically designed to meet real-time bounded response times. The worst-case execution time of TLSF memory allocation and deallocation has to be known in advance and be independent of application data. With this, Mortar must support two different memory release schemes: a slower, but more intelligent scheme used to replace objects when the cache is full or when only a relatively small amount of memory needs to be freed, and a fast release approach that can quickly purge a large portion of memory. This allows efficient cache management in the normal case, but still allows memory to be rapidly reclaimed when needed for other purposes.

Slow Cache Replacement Algorithm (SCRA): We use a hybrid cache replacement algorithm, which prefers to evict expired objects, but falls back to a combination of LRU and least frequently used (LFU), called LRFU, to improve the combined results [12]. LRU requires keeping age records for caches, and LFU needs to keep reference counts; Mortar tracks this information on a per-object basis, and also indexes objects by VM in order to support the cache prioritization scheme described in the next section. The algorithm works by alternating between removing the least recently used item or the least frequently used one. The combination of LRU and LFU tries to balance the drawbacks of each: unpopular objects that happen to have been accessed recently may still be evicted, and content that was briefly popular some time in the past may be removed if it has not been touched recently. Mortar uses SCRA when replacing objects in the cache, or when a relatively small amount of memory (e.g., up to 1GB) must be freed for other uses.

Fast Cache Replacement Algorithm (FCRA): Since Mortar tries to fill all the spare memory in the system, it must be prepared for the situation when the system needs to free a large amount of memory instantly. Dynamic resource management techniques may require additional RAM to be allocated to an important VM, and since the cloud service model is pay-as-you-go, users may turn off and turn on their VMs frequently, causing sudden demands for large amounts of memory. In these scenarios, Mortar must guarantee fast cache eviction to prevent delays in resource management operations.

Mortar's fast cache eviction algorithm works by simply stepping through the hash-chain used to store all of the object keys, removing them in order. Since the hash function essentially randomizes the object keys, this results in a random eviction policy. Since no cache frequency or recency information needs to be used or updated, this can be performed very quickly. While FCRA allows large numbers of objects to be removed from the cache in a short period of time, it may harm the performance of applications since hot data may be inadvertently evicted from the cache.

5.2 Weight-based Fair Share Algorithm

Mortar uses a weight-based prioritization system to determine how cache space is divided when multiple VMs compete for cache memory. If one VM is assigned twice the weight of another, then the higher weight VM will be allocated twice as much cache space. However, if a high weight VM does not use its entire allocation, a lower weight VM will be able to fill the spare capacity with its own data. If the high weight VM later needs more storage space, the lower priority VM's data will be evicted.

Mortar's weight-based proportional fair partitioning scheme works as follows. Let $W = \{w_1, w_2, ..., w_N\}$ be a set of weights and $C = \{c_1, c_2, ..., c_N\}$ be a set of current cache utilizations, where w_i and c_i are the weight and current cache use of VM i, and N is the number of VMs. We denote P as the total cache capacity. The weight ratio of VM i is $r_i = \frac{w_i}{\sum_{j=1}^{N} w_j}$, and the fairness parameter is $f_i = \frac{c_i/P}{r_i}$. If a virtual machine has $f_i > 1$, this indicates that it is using more than its weighted fair share of the cache.

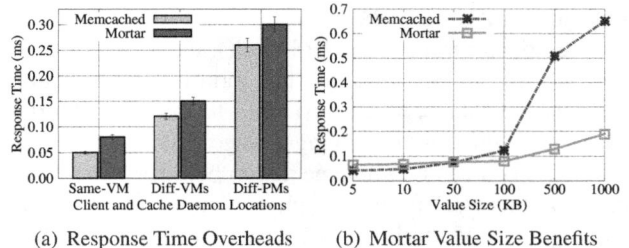

(a) Response Time Overheads   (b) Mortar Value Size Benefits

Figure 7: (a) The overhead of Mortar is on the order of 0.03ms compared to memcached; (b) Mortar has better performance over memcached when the value size becomes larger than 50KB.

When the cache is fully utilized, the objective is to ensure:

$$f_1 = f_2 = ... = f_N. \tag{1}$$

Equation (1) divides the cache size proportionally based on the N virtual machines' weights. This is achieved by Mortar's Cache Manager with consideration of the fairness metrics when handling a put request. If there is spare capacity in the cache, then Mortar will always allow a VM to add the object, regardless of its current fairness value. However, when there is no cache space left, Mortar finds the VM with the largest fairness metric f and evicts data stored by that VM in order to fit the new object. This ensures that VMs unfairly utilizing excess capacity must release their data when another VM wishes to use its weight-based allocation.

6. Experimental Evaluation

Our goals for the evaluation is to see the overheads of Mortar through micro-benchmarks, and to check the performance for both Mortar-based memcached and prefetching through real workload-based benchmarks.

6.1 Environmental Setup

System Setup: Six experimental servers, each of which has quad-core Intel Xeon X3450 2.67GHz processor, 16GB memory, and a 500GB 7200RPM hard drive. Dom-0 is deployed with Xen 4.1.2 and Linux kernel 3.5.0-17-generic, and the VMs use Linux kernel 3.3.1.

Memslap[1] **(micro-benchmark):** For our micro-benchmark experiments, memslap from a memcached client library is used. It generates a load against a cluster of memcached servers with configuration options including number of concurrent users, operation type, and number of calls.

CloudStone Benchmark [21]: CloudStone is a multi-platform benchmark for Web 2.0 and Cloud Computing. It is composed of a load injection framework called Faban (client), and a social online calendar Web application called Olio (server). CloudStone provides a framework to generate

---

[1] http://www.libmemcached.org

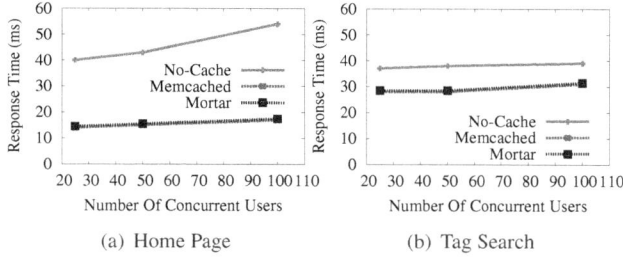

(a) Home Page   (b) Tag Search

Figure 8: When combined with a realistic web application, Mortar's overheads are insignificant.

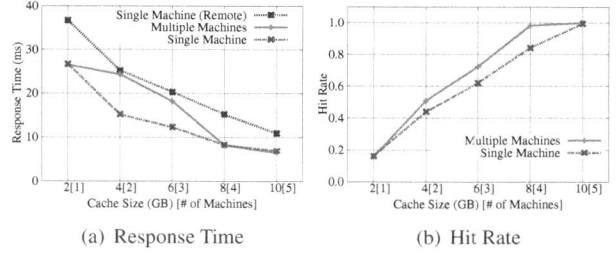

(a) Response Time   (b) Hit Rate

Figure 9: Increasing the total cache size (either on a single machine, or divided across multiple), increases hit rate and reduces respones time when Mortar is accessed with a Zipf ($\alpha = 0.8$) request distribution.

workloads of varying strengths and measure application performance. The PHP-based Olio web application queries a memcached node before issuing read requests to its MySQL database.

6.2 Mortar Overheads

Mortar keeps data in hypervisor space, but allows it to be accessed from both kernel modules and user space applications. To evaluate the overhead of Mortar's operations, Figure 7(a) shows the time to perform a *get* request using both standard memcached and our Mortar-based version. Kernel-based applications that make use of Mortar's data store should see a lower level of overhead since data will not need to be moved to user space. Since Mortar requires two data copies for each request, it incurs a higher overhead than a traditional memcached server, which uses only preallocated user space memory.

We test each system using the memslap benchmark, and report the average response time and standard deviation for 100 requests, each of which has a 100B key and 5KB value. We test three scenarios: 1) when the memslap client is in the same VM as the cache daemon, 2) when in a different VM but the same host, and 3) when the client is on an entirely different physical machine (the most common case in practice). In each case, we find that the overhead of Mortar is quite small, on the order of 0.03ms, less than 15% overhead if the cache must be accessed over the network. We believe this overhead is a small price to pay in exchange for opening up a larger amount of memory for the cache. Of course, our approach can be used in conjunction with regular memcached servers, allowing for fast, guaranteed access for priority applications and slower, best-effort service to applications using the Mortar memory pool.

We next consider how the data value size affects Mortar's overhead. Figure 7(b) shows that data size does not have a significant impact on Mortar's response time. Memcached is designed primarily for web applications that must store relatively small objects (maximum size $\leq$ 1MB), but Mortar is a general data storage framework, so we specifically use a memory allocator, TLSF, that supports a more consistent memory (de)allocation speed regardless of size.

6.3 Web App. Performance Overheads

The previous experiments show the low-level overheads of Mortar, but it is also important to see how it performs with a more realistic web application. We use the CloudStone benchmark [21] to measure how Mortar's overheads affect the performance of a real application. We dedicate an identical amount of memory to both Mortar and regular memcached and measure the client performance under a range of workloads.

Figure 8 shows the performance of CloudStone when 25 to 100 concurrent users connect to Olio. We consider the four most common operation types since together they make up over 95% of all requests; the other request types perform similarly. The results show that the Home Page (Figure 8(a)) operation has the biggest difference between no-cache and cache because they involve many database accesses to a small set of hot content. We find that Mortar and memcached have essentially no difference in application-level response time, despite the minor overheads shown by Mortar when handling small requests in the previous section.

The Tag Search operation shown in Figures 8(b) has similar performance. Since these operations access a much wider range of database records, it is less likely that requests will be found in cache, reducing the overall performance benefit compared to the no-cache case. Once again, we find that Mortar incurs no overhead compared to a standard memcached deployment.

In all of the tests, we find that the performance for Mortar and standard memcached scales identically as the number of clients rises. This suggests that our Mortar-enhanced version of memcached has both minimal additional latency and can support a similar level of concurrency as traditional memcached.

6.4 Impact of Cache Size

The goal of Mortar is to opportunistically make use of all free memory, so we next consider how application performance varies with the size of cache available. We use a simple web application that maintains a database filled with 10GB worth of entries, each sized at 50KB. We vary the size of the cache and measure Mortar's response time and hit rate.

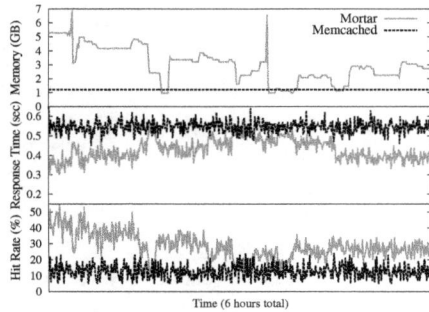

Figure 10: Mortar makes use of all spare memory, leading to lower response times and a higher hit rate than memcached.

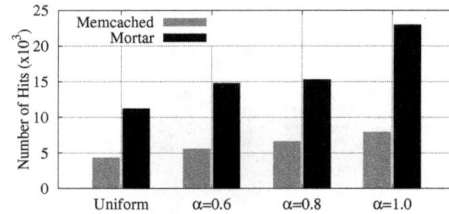

Figure 11: Varying the request distribution affects the likelihood of data being within the cache. In all cases, Mortar has substantially more cache hits since it has more memory available to it.

We allow the cache to warm up to a consistent hit rate after each size changes.

To demonstrate the benefits of more cache space, Figure 9 shows how cache performance changes while varying the available memory both in a single machine (accessed either locally or by a remote client) and for multiple machines (one local and up to four remotes, each adding 2GB of cache space). As expected, performance improves as the size rises.

6.5 Dynamic Cache Sizing

To truly see the benefits of using Mortar, we need to consider a scenario where the amount of memory available for the cache varies over time—a scenario which memcached is unable to take advantage of since the cache is statically sized. To demonstrate this, we take one of the memory traces from our IT department shown in Figure 1 and condense it down to a six hour period. We compare two cases: 1) a traditional memcached server with a fixed cache size of 1.2 GB (the largest a fixed sized cache can be over the entire trace) and 2) our Mortar implementation that can scale the cache size up and down based on the server's free memory. We use the cache as a frontend to a MySQL database that is filled with 16GB of data, with an average record size of 50KB. When memory needs to be reclaimed from the cache, we use Mortar's slower, but more accurate, eviction policy; as will be shown in Section 6.8, this still allows memory to be freed in under one second.

Figure 10 illustrates the memory available to each cache, the response time, and the hit rate as web requests are processed over the course of the experiment. The clients make requests at a constant rate, but queries follow a Zipf distribution with $\alpha = 0.8$, resulting in the type of skewed distribution commonly seen by web applications that have a relatively small portion of more popular content [29]. Since memcached has a fixed size cache throughout the trace, its performance is relatively steady with an average response time of 0.57 seconds and a hit rate consistently below 20%. In contrast, Mortar's performance varies based on the amount of available cache space, with a response time ranging from 0.3 to 0.52 seconds. Overall, Mortar has an average response time of 0.38 seconds, a 35% improvement over memcached.

We next study the impact of the request distribution on cache performance. Figure 11 shows the total number of cache hits when changing the request distribution for the experiment described above. With a uniform distribution or a Zipf distribution with a low α value, it is less likely that requested content will have been seen recently enough to still be in the cache. In all cases, Mortar provides a substantial benefit over memcached since it is able to make use of about 2.6 times as much cache memory over the course of the experiment.

6.6 Multi-Server Caching

The previous experiment illustrates the benefits of Mortar, but also shows how the variability in free memory on the caching server can result in less predictable performance. To mitigate this drawback, we next experiment with Mortar in a larger scale setting where multiple hosts each run both applications and a Mortar cache. We use a set of five memory traces from our university's data center, which have been scaled down to prevent the free memory on each host from becoming over half of the total memory size, as shown in Figure 12(a). The total spare memory is initially close to 25GB, but goes through several changes before ending around 13GB. No host has memory size below 1.2GB (min memory).

Our goal is to understand how having a larger number of servers available for caching data can reduce the performance variability of the applications using the cache. Towards this end, we compare two setups: the *single-server* case where a single server acts as a cache, and the *multi-server* case where five servers use their combined spare memory for the cache. In each case we vary the number of applications active *on each physical host* from one to five. For the single-server case we select the trace that on average has the most free memory available, and this is used to cache data by up to five applications. In the multi-server case, up to twenty-five applications distribute their data across all five hosts. If the data cannot be stored in the cache it must be retrieved from a MySQL database.

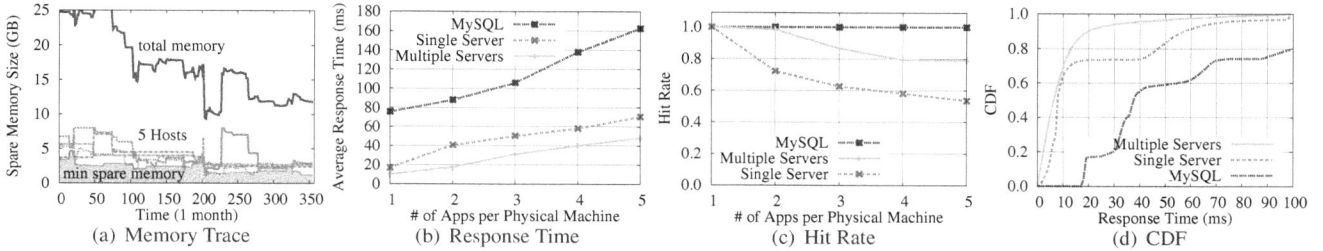

Figure 12: Running Mortar on more servers reduces performance variability; (a) depicts the system memory traces over time; (b) shows the average response times; (c) illustrates the hit rates; (d) cumulative density functions (CDFs) for response time.

Figures 12(b) and 12(c) illustrate the average response time and the hit rate over the entire memory trace. Even though the multiple server scenario has a larger number of total applications running, it has both a 20ms better response time and 20% better hit rate than the single server setting. This happens because the variations in free memory on each of the five hosts do not generally occur at the same time, increasing the chance that at least some application data will be found in the cache compared to the single server case where periods of memory scarcity significantly impact all applications. Figure 12(d) depicts the distribution on response times, and further reaffirms the result that spreading Mortar's data across multiple servers leads to not only improved response times, but a lower standard deviation.

6.7 Disk Prefetching with Mortar

We next evaluate the overheads and benefits of MortarLoad using the following I/O benchmarks: **Slowcat** is a synthetic benchmark written by us to compute typical I/O times in a carefully controlled manner. This program will read in a file in increments of a configurable block size and sleep for a configurable amount of time per read. It reports several usage statistics, including the total time spent waiting for read operations to complete. **Videoserver** is part of the Filebench suite of I/O benchmarks [8]. It is intended to mimic the behavior of a streaming video server that reads and writes to several video files at a time. In our configuration, we set it up for reading three videos and writing one. The overall I/O amount is approximately 8GB read and 1.5GB written. **OLTP** is the database application benchmark in Filebench, which has a significant percentage of non-sequential reads.

MortarLoad Overheads: We first study the overheads of our FUSE based MortarLoad when prefetching is turned off. Figure 13(a) shows the average read time in milliseconds measured with slowcat for a 1GB input file read with 1 MB block sizes under different conditions. We first measure the uncached base Linux time by forcibly dropping caches, and executing the program. Once this completes, we re-run it to measure the time taken when the entire file fits in the Linux page cache. To measure the impact of MortarLoad, we mount the MortarLoad file system to act like a caching loop back file system with a Mortar cache size greater than the input file size. We perform a similar measurement, this time flushing the Mortar cache (and Linux cache) before the first pass and re-running for a second pass (with just Linux caches dropped) over the Mortar cached data. The final bar measures the cache miss cost on vanilla FUSE, which is known to actually improve performance for certain cases, which turns out to be the case for this particular workload.

Our results show that MortarLoad has similar performance to Linux when they experience a cache miss and must read from disk. A MortarLoad cache hit is slower than a standard Linux cache hit but in normal operation, the Linux page cache acts as a first-level cache, only reading from Mortar when it fails to hit in the page cache. This means there is not a performance reduction to regular cache hits from using MortarLoad, but that a second-level cache hit to the prefetched data is somewhat slower than the base cache. We expect that the MortarLoad cache hit latency can be reduced by further optimizing our implementation and moving it into the kernel.

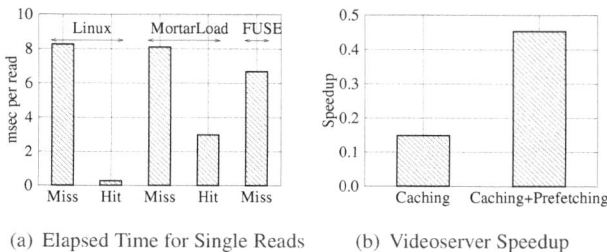

(a) Elapsed Time for Single Reads   (b) Videoserver Speedup

Figure 13: Caching + Prefetching Experiments

	Cache Size (MB)		
	100	500	1000
Avg. Read Latency Speedup	2.84	3.14	3.79
Avg. Hit Percentage	4.51	22.06	59.72

Table 1: Data prefetching with different memory sizes running the OLTP benchmark.

Cache and Prefetching Benefits: We next study how MortarLoad can improve the performance of the Videoserver benchmark by providing both a larger cache and prefetching. Figure 13(b) shows the overall speedup with and without prefetching compared to a baseline without FUSE. These

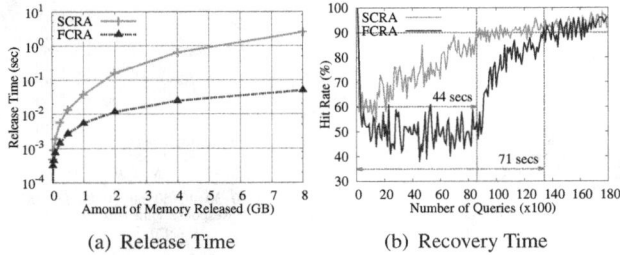

(a) Release Time   (b) Recovery Time

Figure 14: (a) FCRA releases memory an order of magnitude faster than SCRA. (b) However, the speed of FCRA has the cost of reducing cache performance for a longer period.

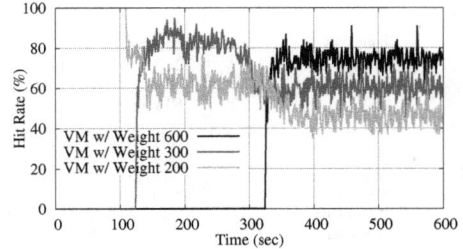

Figure 15: Three VMs with weights 200, 300, and 600 run web applications starting at times 0, 100, and 300, respectively.

results are measured using an initially empty 1GB cache. The benefits of using prefetching are substantial over using a plain LRU disk cache (speedup of 45% compared to 15%).

We next evaluate the performance of the OLTP server while we vary the size of Mortar cache. As shown in Table 1, with a 100MB cache, the server sees 2.8× speedup on average read latency when compared to the case of native read. When the cache size is set to 1GB, the hit rate is further increased to 60% and as the result the read improvement reaches 3.8×.

Our results illustrate how re-purposing spare memory for an extended disk cache with prefetching provides substantial performance improvements. Further, Mortar transitions the management of memory from inside each VM's OS to the hypervisor, which allows for higher-level decision making as shown in the following sections.

6.8 Responding to Memory Pressure

Mortar's goal is to opportunistically use all free memory, but it must be ready to release memory for various situations: when a new VM enters the system, when a VM in another physical machine live migrates to this host, or when a VM's memory allocation needs to be adjusted.

In this experiment, we measure how much time it takes to release the demanded amount of memory when the cache is filled with 50KB objects. We compare the two cache replacement algorithms, SCRA (slow but accurate) and FCRA (fast but random), discussed in Section 5.1. Figure 14(a) shows the release time as the amount of memory requested increases. As expected, both approaches take more time for larger requests, but the FCRA approach can keep the release time under 0.1 seconds even when releasing the full 8GB cache (approximately 168 thousand objects), while SCRA takes more than ten times as long.

Depending on the speed with which memory requests must be handled, Mortar can be tuned to select which replacement algorithm is used for different size requests. In many systems, a two second latency for memory requests is acceptable, meaning that SCRA can be used exclusively, increasing the likelihood that hot data will remain in cache. Other systems may not be able to tolerate this latency, so, for example, a 1GB threshold might be used to switch between

SCRA and FCRA. This would allow all memory reallocation requests to be handled within only 0.1 seconds.

While FCRA is clearly faster at relinquishing memory, this comes at a cost since it removes objects without considering cache locality. To study how the eviction algorithm affects cache performance, we next test a scenario where the cache is rapidly resized, and then the time it takes to rewarm the cache is measured. We start the experiment with a hot cache filled with 15GB of data. We then cut the cache size by 8GB, causing more than half of the data to be evicted by one of our two replacement algorithms. We then immediately increase the Mortar memory pool back to 15GB and observe the time required to recover the previous hit rate.

Figure 14(b) shows how the hit rate of the FCRA and SCRA managed caches recover over time. During the mass eviction, SCRA is able to preserve a larger amount of hot data by using frequency and recency data, so its initial hit rate is higher than FCRA which randomly removes data from the cache. This gives SCRA a significant edge on rebuilding its cache, allowing it to reach a 90% hit rate 39 percent faster than FCRA.

6.9 Weight-based Memory Fairness

Mortar supports weight-based proportional fair partitioning to divide the cache between competing VMs. VM's receive cache space proportional to their weight, but if there is spare capacity, even a lower weight VM can make use of it. Figure 15 shows hit rates of three VMs when they are assigned different weights. Each VM uses web server-type applications with request arrival rates following Zipf distribution ($\alpha = 0.8$). Each VM starts at a different time, causing the relative weights to adjust over the course of the experiment. A VM with weight 200 (VM_200) starts at time 0, and uses the whole cache because no other VMs are active. At time 100, a VM with weight 300 (VM_300) starts pushing data into the cache, so VM_200 surrenders cache space to VM_300 according to Equation (1). At time 300, a VM with weight 600 (VM_600) starts causing the cache to be rebalanced again.

While Mortar is able to correctly reallocate cache space to each of the VMs based on their weights (e.g., VM_600 receives $\frac{6}{11}$ of the cache), the same proportion does not necessarily hold for the hit-rate or response time achieved by each VM. This is because in a skewed distribution like Zipf a smaller cache may still fit the most important hot data. This illustrates one of the challenges in partitioning a shared cache such as Mortar: weights can be used to control resource shares, but they may not be directly proportional to performance.

7. Related Work

Our system draws inspiration from the Transcendent Memory (tmem) system [16]. Tmem is made up of a set of pools in the hypervisor that can be used to store the disk cache pages of each VM. Tmem provides an efficient way to manage the cache by providing functions such as compression and remote cache access. Mortar provides a general purpose data store, while tmem focuses on swapping the ownership of full memory pages between the guest and hypervisor to facilitate disk cache management.

Dynamic memory management systems automatically control memory allocations for multiple VMs, typically by using a "ballooning" mechanism to add and subtract pages from the guest [25, 28]. Waldspurger [25] tracks individual VM memory usage by monitoring page access rates. This allows it to grow and shrink VM allocations as needed. Zhao et al. [28] look at multiple VMs at once and decide how to divide up memory. Perfectly allocating memory is impossible since workloads may change over time, so even when using these systems system admins often leave spare memory to handle new or rising workloads. The Overdriver system proposes using network based RAM in times of high load [27]. In contrast, Mortar focuses on opportunistically using memory during periods of light load.

Page sharing schemes such as transparent page sharing (TPS) [10, 25] have been proposed to maximize memory efficiency. TPS provides a level of abstraction over physical memory and is able to share pages by identifying identical content. TPS is another way of freeing up a moderate amount of memory, but this memory often does not last for long periods of time, as shown by the Satori [18] system. We believe that Mortar can be used very effectively in conjunction with TPS systems by allowing even small numbers of briefly shared pages to be put to an effective purpose.

Data prefetching has been extensively studied on CPU cache [22], hard drives [7, 9], and most recently, solid-state drives [14]. Another very related topic, disk caching, also draws a great amount of interests for improved performance, as well as energy efficiency, and here we cannot possibly present a complete list. To name a few, [2, 5] propose a gray-box approach to infer and utilize OS and file caches, and [6] present work combining the study of both.

Smart caching mechanisms in the hypervisor have also been proposed, for example, [26] combines all persistent storage in a virtualized cluster and uses local persistent storage as cache to VMs, [13] infers disk block liveness to manage VMM memory cache, and [15] describes a caching policy split between the hypervisor and guest VMs. While [1] argues lack of disk locality for certain workloads, it suggests to use memory as a cache in data centers based on the observation of memory locality. MortarLoad focuses on data prefetching for file-level accesses within each guest VM, and is able to leverage the free memory pool managed by Mortar, which is otherwise unavailable to the guest VMs.

8. Discussion

Performance Unpredictability: To be effective, Mortar needs to have some amount of spare memory available throughout the data center. While the traces from our IT department and anecdotal discussions with system administrators indicate that this is commonly the case, a valid concern is that Mortar will lead to deceptively high performance when workloads are light, and poor performance when workloads rise and there is less spare capacity. Of course one solution is to use Mortar as a supplemental cache in addition to a set of regular memached nodes. In practice however, if Mortar is deployed in a cloud-scale data center we do not expect this to be a major concern since different applications will see workload spikes at different times.

Security: Memory and cache-induced side channel attacks are a concern in shared environments [20]. To increase security guarantees, Mortar allows to choose whether to put objects in shared memory (potentially reducing redundancy among trusting VMs) or private memory. This separation does not affect how memory is managed, but allows Mortar to control permission for each data access. While this prevents data leakage, Mortar does potentially expose information about the amount of spare capacity on the host, and in turn the memory utilization level of co-located VMs. Still, the random behavior of VMs and unknown memory partitions make hard to infer the real metrics.

Private Clouds: Within a private data center, system administrators can use Mortar both for exploiting spare capacity and as a way to gain finer control over memory allocations. Mortar moves memory management from within each VM's operating system down into the hypervisor, which may have more information about the relative priority of different virtual machines. If an important application is known to require a memcached size ranging from 100MB to 1GB depending on its workload, then the administrator can assign 1GB of memory to Mortar, and mark the application with a high priority so that it will be able to get the cache space it needs when its workload is high, but allow another VM to use the spare memory (perhaps for disk prefetching), when the workload is low. This kind of flexible, fine grained memory management is impractical with existing memory ballooning techniques.

Public Clouds: We envision that a public cloud may use Mortar to pool together its spare memory resources and sell them at a discounted price. For example, Amazon's spot-instance market auctions off spare resource capacity in the form of VMs which may be instantly shutdown if the provider needs those resources for a higher paying customer. Mortar allows a similar approach to be used for memory at a very fine grain. The popularity of the spot market illustrates that developers will eagerly make use of even highly transient resource capacity if the price is right.

9. Conclusion

Mortar represents the start of our vision for new techniques that opportunistically consume idle resources in a data center without imposing overheads on other active applications. It does this by taking the unallocated memory on each server and exposing it as a volatile data store that can be rapidly reclaimed by the hypervisor if needed. Our prototype modifies the Xen hypervisor to expose this interface to a memcached server and a disk prefetcher. This allows existing web applications and the OS to immediately make use of memory that currently is left idle as a buffer for rising workloads. Mortar moves the control of memory from within each VM's operating system to the hypervisor level, and allows it to be managed at finer granularity than existing approaches that rely on resizing VM memory allocations. In our future work we will investigate further uses of the Mortar framework, as well as how shifting the control of resources from inside a VM's operating system to the hypervisor can allow cloud platforms to make smarter management decisions.

Acknowledgments

We thank the reviewers for their help improving this paper. This work was supported in part by NSF grants CNS-1253575, CNS-1350766, and OCI-0937875.

References

[1] G. Ananthanarayanan, A. Ghodsi, S. Shenker, and I. Stoica. Disk-locality in datacenter computing considered irrelevant. In *Proceedings of the 13th USENIX conference on Hot topics in operating systems*, HotOS'13, pages 12–12, Berkeley, CA, USA, 2011. USENIX Association.

[2] A. C. Arpaci-Dusseau and R. H. Arpaci-Dusseau. Information and control in gray-box systems. In *Proceedings of the eighteenth ACM symposium on Operating systems principles*, pages 43–56, Banff, Alberta, Canada, 2001. ACM.

[3] P. Barham, B. Dragovic, K. Fraser, S. Hand, T. Harris, A. Ho, R. Neugebauer, I. Pratt, and A. Warfield. Xen and the art of virtualization. *In Proceedings of the ACM Symposium on Operating Systems Principles*, 2003.

[4] L. A. Barroso and U. Holzle. *The Datacenter as a Computer: An Introduction to the Design of Warehouse-Scale Machines.* 2009.

[5] N. C. Burnett, J. Bent, A. C. Arpaci-Dusseau, and R. H. Arpaci-Dusseau. Exploiting Gray-Box knowledge of Buffer-Cache management. In *Proceedings of the annual conference on USENIX Annual Technical Conference*, pages 29–44, 2002.

[6] A. R. Butt, C. Gniady, and Y. C. Hu. The performance impact of kernel prefetching on buffer cache replacement algorithms. In *Proceedings of the 2005 ACM SIGMETRICS international conference on Measurement and modeling of computer systems*, SIGMETRICS '05, pages 157–168, New York, NY, USA, 2005.

[7] X. Ding, S. Jiang, F. Chen, K. Davis, and X. Zhang. Diskseen: exploiting disk layout and access history to enhance i/o prefetch. In *USENIX Annual Technical Conference*, pages 20:1–20:14, 2007.

[8] FileBench. http://sourceforge.net/projects/filebench/.

[9] B. S. Gill and D. S. Modha. SARC: sequential prefetching in adaptive replacement cache. In *Proceedings of the USENIX Annual Technical Conference*. Berkeley, CA, USA, 2005.

[10] D. Gupta, S. Lee, M. Vrable, S. Savage, A. C. Snoeren, G. Varghese, G. M. Voelker, and A. Vahdat. Difference engine: Harnessing memory redundancy in virtual machines. *USENIX*, 2008.

[11] J. Hwang and T. Wood. Adaptive performance-aware distributed memory caching. *USENIX Internation Conference on Autonomic Computing*, 2013.

[12] P. R. Jelenkovic and A. Radovanovic. Optimizing lru caching for variable document sizes. *Combinatorics, Probability & Computing*, 13(4-5):627–643, 2004.

[13] S. T. Jones, A. C. Arpaci-Dusseau, and R. H. Arpaci-Dusseau. Geiger: monitoring the buffer cache in a virtual machine environment. In *Proceedings of the 12th international conference on architectural support for programming languages and operating systems*, pages 14–24, 2006.

[14] Y. Joo, J. Ryu, S. Park, and K. Shin. FAST: quick application launch on solid-state drives. In *Proceedings of the 9th USENIX conference on File and stroage technologies*, pages 19–19. USENIX Association, 2011.

[15] P. Lu and K. Shen. Virtual machine memory access tracing with hypervisor exclusive cache. In *Proceedings of the USENIX Annual Technical Conference*, ATC'07, pages 3:1–3:15, Berkeley, CA, USA, 2007.

[16] D. Magenheimer, C. Mason, D. McCracken, and K. Hackel. Transcendent memory and linux. *Oracle Corp.*, 2009.

[17] M. Masmano, I. Ripoll, A. Crespo, and J. Real. Tlsf: A new dynamic memory allocator for real-time systems. *ECRTS*, 2004.

[18] G. Milos, D. G. Murray, S. Hand, and M. A. Fetterman. Satori: Enlightened page sharing. *USENIX*, 2009.

[19] R. Nishtala, H. Fugal, S. Grimm, M. Kwiatkowski, H. Lee, H. C. Li, R. McElroy, M. Paleczny, D. Peek, P. Saab, D. Stafford, T. Tung, and V. Venkataramani. Scaling memcache at facebook. *USENIX Symposium on Networked Systems Design and Implementation*, 2013.

[20] R. Owens and W. Wang. Non-interactive os fingerprinting through memory de-duplication technique in virtual machines. In *Proceedings of the 30th IEEE International Performance Computing and Communications Conference*, PCCC '11, pages 1–8. IEEE Computer Society, 2011.

[21] W. Sobel, S. Subramanyam, A. Sucharitakul, J. Nguyen, H. Wong, A. Klepchukov, S. Patil, O. Fox, and D. Patterson. Cloudstone: Multi-platform, multi-language benchmark and measurement tools for web 2.0, 2008.

[22] S. Srinath, O. Mutlu, H. Kim, and Y. N. Patt. Feedback directed prefetching: Improving the performance and bandwidth-efficiency of hardware prefetchers. In *Proceedings of the 2007 IEEE 13th International Symposium on High Performance Computer Architecture*, pages 63–74, 2007.

[23] C. Stewart, A. Chakrabarti, and R. Griffith. Zoolander: Efficiently meeting very strict, low-latency slos. *USENIX ICAC*, 2013.

[24] VMware. Resource management with vmware drs. *Technical Resource Center*, 2006.

[25] C. A. Waldspurger. Memory resource management in vmware esx server. *OSDI*, 2002.

[26] A. Warfield, R. Ross, K. Fraser, C. Limpach, and S. Hand. Parallax: managing storage for a million machines. In *Proceedings of the 10th conference on Hot Topics in Operating Systems - Volume 10*, HOTOS'05, pages 4–4, Berkeley, CA, USA, 2005.

[27] D. Williams, H. Jamjoom, Y.-H. Liu, and H. Weatherspoon. Overdriver: handling memory overload in an oversubscribed cloud. In *7th International Conference on Virtual Execution Environments*, pages 205–216. ACM, 2011.

[28] W. Zhao and Z. Wang. Dynamic memory balancing for virtual machines. *VEE*, 2009.

[29] T. Zhu, A. Gandhi, M. Harchol-Balter, and M. A. Kozuch. Saving cache by using less cache. *HotCloud*, 2012.

CMD: Classification-based Memory Deduplication through Page Access Characteristics

Licheng Chen[†§], Zhipeng Wei[†§], Zehan Cui[†§], Mingyu Chen[†], Haiyang Pan[†§], Yungang Bao[†]

[†]State Key Laboratory of Computer Architecture, Institute of Computing Technology, Chinese Academy of Sciences
[§]University of Chinese Academy of Sciences
{chenlicheng, weizhipeng, cuizehan, cmy, panhaiyang, baoyg}@ict.ac.cn

Abstract

Limited main memory size is considered as one of the major bottlenecks in virtualization environments. Content-Based Page Sharing (CBPS) is an efficient memory deduplication technique to reduce server memory requirements, in which pages with same content are detected and shared into a single copy. As the widely used implementation of CBPS, Kernel Samepage Merging (KSM) maintains the whole memory pages into two global comparison trees (a stable tree and an unstable tree). To detect page sharing opportunities, each candidate page needs to be compared with pages already in these two large global trees. However since the vast majority of pages have different content with it, it will result in massive futile page comparisons and thus heavy overhead.

In this paper, we propose a lightweight page Classification-based Memory Deduplication approach named **CMD** to reduce futile page comparison overhead meanwhile to detect page sharing opportunities efficiently. The main innovation of CMD is that pages are grouped into different classifications based on page access characteristics. Pages with similar access characteristics are suggested to have higher possibility with same content, thus they are grouped into the same classification. In CMD, the large global comparison trees are divided into multiple small trees with dedicated local ones in each page classification. Page comparisons are performed just in the same classification, and pages from different classifications are never compared (since they probably result in futile comparisons). The experimental results show that CMD can efficiently reduce page comparisons (by about 68.5%) meanwhile detect nearly the same (by more than 98%) or even more page sharing opportunities.

VEE '14, March 1–2, 2014, Salt Lake City, Utah, USA.
Copyright © 2014 ACM 978-1-4503-2764-0 /14/03. . . $15.00.
http://dx.doi.org/10.1145/2576195.2576204

Categories and Subject Descriptors D.4.2 [*Storage Management*]: Main Memory; D.4.8 [*Performance*]: Measurements

Keywords Memory Deduplication; Page Classification; Page Access Characteristics

1. Introduction

Cloud computing becomes increasingly popular and competitive both in industry and academia. In cloud computing, multiple virtual machines (VMs) can be collocated on a single physical server, and they can operate independently with virtualization technology [16, 25], which is promising to provide flexible allocation, migration of services, and better security isolation. In the virtualization environment, physical resources (such as processor, main memory) are managed by a software layer called hypervisor (or Virtual Machine Monitor, VMM), and the primary goal of a hypervisor is to provide efficient resource sharing among multiple co-running virtual machines.

However, as the number of VMs collocated on a physical server keeps increasing (e.g. it can collocate up to 8 virtual machines on a physical core in desktop cloud environment), meanwhile with the increasing size of working set of applications running in a virtual machine, virtualization has placed heavy pressure on memory system for larger capacity. However, since the increasing speed of main memory capacity falls behind with the demand, the limited main memory size has been considered as one of the major bottlenecks to consolidate more number of guest VMs on a hosting server [17, 22]. Memory deduplication is an efficient technique to alleviate the memory capacity bottleneck, which detects and reduces page duplication to save memory. A large volume of prior work has shown that there are great opportunities in memory deduplicaion, e.g. Difference Engine [17] reported absolute memory savings of 50% across VMs, and VMware [29] reported about 40% memory savings.

Content Based Page Sharing (CBPS) is one of the most widely used memory deduplication techniques to improve memory efficiency, since CBPS can be performed transparently in the hypervisor layer and it doesn't require any modification to guest operating systems (OS). In CBPS, a memory scanner is adopted to scan memory pages of guest VMs periodically and to detect all identical pages that have same content, these identical pages can then be shared into a single physical page[1], and the redundant memory pages can be reclaimed and free back to the hypervisor. Thus CBPS can efficiently reduce the memory footprint of guest VMs and provide good opportunity to increase the number of VMs collocated on a host server.

In this paper, we mainly focus on Kernel Samepage Merging (KSM) [6], which is a widely-used implementation of CBPS, and it has been integrated into the Linux kernel archive [3]. In KSM, there are two global red-black comparison trees for the whole memory pages of a hosting server, named **stable tree** and **unstable tree** respectively. The stable tree contains already shared pages with write-protected, and the unstable tree contains only pages that are not shared yet (without write-protected). In each scan round, each candidate page needs to be compared with pages already in these two large global trees to detect page sharing opportunities. We define the term **futile comparison** as the page content comparison of a candidate page with other pages (both in the stable tree and unstable tree), which fails to find any page with the same content. Since KSM only maintains two global comparison trees for the whole memory pages, each global tree will contain a large number of nodes (or pages), e.g. 1M nodes (4KB page) for 4GB memory. For each candidate page, it needs to be compared with a large number of uncorrelated pages in the global trees, thus it will result in massive futile page comparisons and heavy overhead. And as the page scan performs repeatedly, the number of futile page comparisons will increase proportionally.

In this paper, we propose a lightweight page Classification-based Memory Deduplication approach named **CMD** to reduce futile comparison overhead meanwhile to detect page sharing opportunities efficiently. In CMD, pages are grouped into different classifications based on page access characteristics. Pages with similar access characteristics are suggested to have higher possibility with same content, thus they are grouped into the same classification. And the large global comparison trees are divided into multiple small trees that there are dedicated local comparison trees in each page classification. For each candidate page, its classification is firstly determined based on its access characteristics (e.g. write access count, write access distribution of sub-pages), and then it is searched and compared with pages only in the local comparison trees of its classification. Thus page comparisons are performed just in the same classification, and pages from different classifications are never compared, since they probably result in futile comparisons. In this paper, we mainly focus on page write access, which will modify page content and thus affect page sharing opportunities.

We monitor write access of pages with a hardware-snooping based memory trace monitoring system, which is able to capture all memory write references with fine cache-block granularity, thus we can use not only the count of write accesses for each page (coarse granularity), but also write access distribution of sub-pages (fine granularity), which will be a better hint for page classification. Additionally, hardware-assisted page access monitor introduces negligible overhead, thus our implementation of CMD is lightweight and efficient.

Overall, we have made the following contributions:

- We perform a detailed profiling of KSM, we find that page content comparisons contribute a certain portion of the whole KSM run-time (about 44%). And futile comparisons contribute most of the page comparison overhead (about 83%).

- To reduce futile comparison overhead meanwhile to detect page sharing opportunities efficiently, we propose a lightweight page Classification-based Memory Deduplication approach named **CMD**. In CMD, pages are grouped into different classifications based on page access characteristics, the large global comparison trees are divided into multiple trees with dedicated local ones in each classification. Page comparisons are performed just in the same classification, and pages from different classifications are never compared (since they probably result in futile comparisons).

- We implement the CMD in our real experimental system. The experimental results show that, compared with the baseline KSM, the CMD can efficiently detect page sharing opportunities (by more than 98%) meanwhile reduce the number of page comparisons (by about 68.5%), and the futile comparison rate is also reduced by about 12.15% on average.

The rest of the paper is organized as follows: Section 2 introduces the background and motivation. Section 3 describes the design and implementation of page classification based memory deduplication. We describe the experimental methodology in Section 4 and demonstrate experimental results and discussion in Section 5. Related work and conclusion are in Section 6 and Section 7 respectively.

2. Background and Motivation

2.1 Kernel Samepage Merging

KSM (Kernel Samepage Merging) [6] is a scanning based implementation of CBPS, which detects and shares pages with same content into a single copy. Nowadays KSM is implemented as a kernel thread, which periodically scans memory pages of guest virtual machines co-running on a hosting server. Each candidate page is compared content with pages already in the comparison trees, and then it is inserted into the global trees based on comparison result.

---

[1] With all identical guest physical pages pointing back to the same machine physical page in the hypervisor's page table.

If multiple pages with same content are detected during a scan round, one of the pages is selected as the KSM page (or identical page), then other duplicate pages are merged and shared with the single KSM page, which is implemented by replacing the page table entries of duplicate pages to map to the KSM page, and the original space of duplicate pages are reclaimed and saved. Duplicated Pages are shared with Copy-On-Write (COW) mechanism, which means that all page table entries of duplicate pages are mapped with read-only permission. If a VM attempts to write a shared page, a page fault named COW fault will be triggered. The hypervisor handles the fault by allocating a new page frame and making a private copy of the page for the requesting VM, then the VM writes data in this new private page.

Nowadays, KSM maintains only two global red-black comparison trees for the whole memory pages of a hosting server, as shown in Figure 1: the stable tree and the unstable tree. Nodes of these two global trees are indexed directly with the content of pages (as key of red-black nodes). The stable tree maintains search structure for shared pages, while the unstable tree maintains only pages that are not yet shared. In each scan round, a candidate page is firstly compared with pages in the stable tree. If there is a match with an existed KSM page, the candidate page will be merged and shared with this matched KSM page. Otherwise, it needs to be further searched in the unstable tree: If there is a match in the unstable tree, the matched page will be removed from the unstable tree, then it will be merged with the candidate page and migrated into the stable tree with write-protected; if no match is found, the candidate page is inserted into the unstable tree (as a leaf node). In each full scan round, the unstable tree needs to be reconstructed, which means that pages in the unstable tree need to be re-inserted into the unstable tree to get the correct node position. This is because that pages in the unstable tree are not write-protected, and content of these pages might be modified during the scan round. As the increasing capacity of main memory, the size of these two global trees expands proportionally. Since KSM does not take any page access characteristics into account, for a candidate page, it needs to be compared content with a large number of uncorrelated pages which will induce massive futile comparisons.

There is a tradeoff of controlling the page scan speed of KSM. Fast scan can detect more page sharing opportunities, especially for short-lived page-sharing, however it will induce heavy CPU overhead due to frequent page content comparisons. Slow scan, on the other side, might lose some short-lived page sharing opportunities, but the CPU overhead is relatively lightweight. In KSM, the kernel thread scans pages of VMs in a batch-by-batch manner: all candidate pages are firstly separated into batches with each batch having the same number of pages; after scanning all pages in a batch, the KSM thread goes to sleep for a specified time; then it continues to scan pages in the next batch. The scan

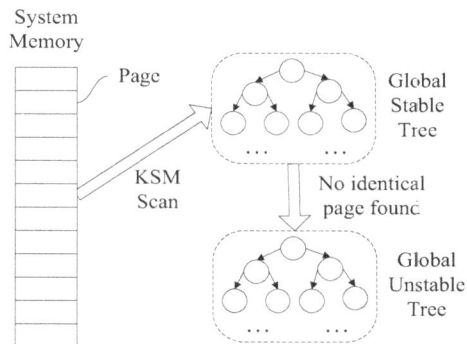

Figure 1. The global stable tree and global unstable tree in KSM. A candidate page is firstly searched and compared with pages in the stable tree. If no match is found, it needs to be further searched and compared with pages in the unstable tree.

speed can be controlled by configuring the number of pages in a batch (it is 100 by default) and the sleep time between batches (20ms by default). Before a page is searched in the unstable tree, the checksum of it is re-calculated and then compared with its last checksum. The checksum serves as a filter of page comparisons in the unstable tree: if the checksum remains the same, it is a candidate page, and the page can be searched and compared with pages in the unstable tree; otherwise, it is considered as a volatile page and it will not be searched in the unstable tree. The computation of page checksum also induces some CPU overhead to the system (as shown in Figure 2).

2.2 Profiling of KSM

Table 1. KSM characteristics with different Configurations

Configuration	C0	C1	C2	C3	C4	C5
Pages to scan in each batch	100	200	400	800	1600	3200
Full scan time (seconds)	400	200	100	50	25	12.5

Table 1 shows the KSM characteristics with different configurations in our experimental system with 8GB memory (please refer to Section 4 for detailed system configuration). In KSM, there are two parameters that control scan-speed which can affect KSM sharing efficiency and run-time overhead: *pages_to_scan* and *sleep_millisecs*, which represents the number of pages to be scanned in a batch before the KSM thread goes to sleep, and how many milliseconds of time the KSM thread will sleep before turning to scan pages of the next batch of respectively. We adopt the default value of *sleep_millisecs* as 20ms and vary *pages_to_scan* from 100 (default, as C0) to 3200 (as C5). For our experimental system with 8GB physical memory, the corresponding of a full

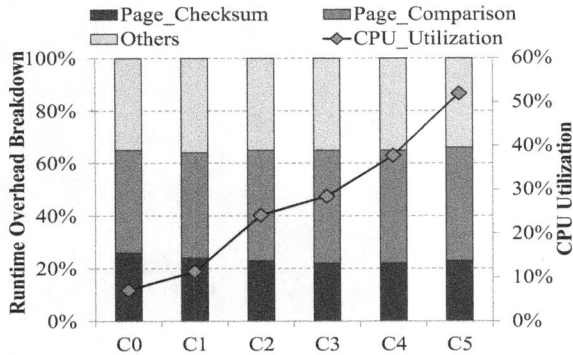

Figure 2. KSM run-time overhead breakdown and the CPU Utilization of the KSM thread as the number of pages to be scanned in a batch varied from 100 to 3200 with four guest VMs collocated on the host server.

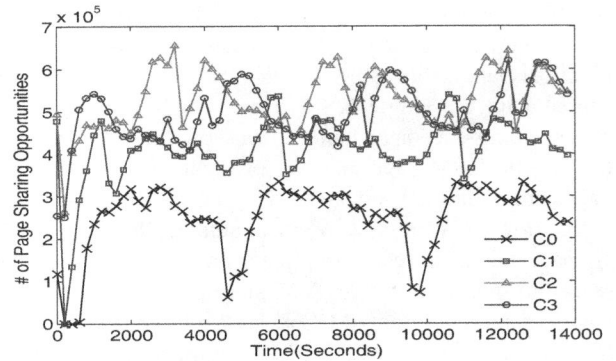

Figure 3. The number of page sharing opportunities with 4 VMs as the number of pages to scan in a batch varied from 100 (C0) to 800 (C3).

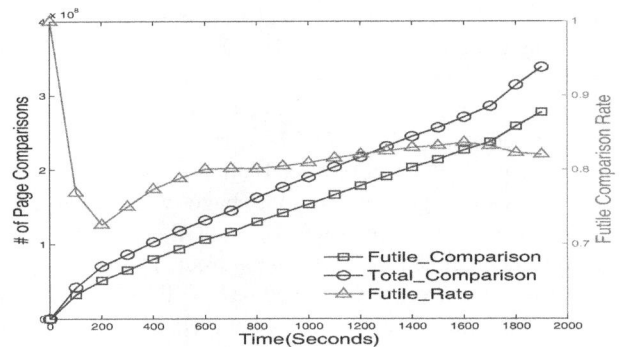

Figure 4. The number of total page comparisons and futile comparisons as the KSM thread running with 4 VMs, where KSM is configured to scan 400 pages and then sleep 20 milliseconds (default) in each batch.

scan time is varied from 400 seconds to 12.5 seconds respectively.

Figure 2 shows the KSM run-time overhead breakdown and the CPU Utilization of the KSM thread as the number of pages to be scanned in a batch varied from 100 (C0) to 3200 (C5) with four guest VMs collocated on the host server. We can see that as the number of pages scanned in a batch increasing, the CPU utilization increase correspondingly, it is about 8.52% for C1, it increase up to 24.13% for C3 and 53.09% for C5. The induced CPU overhead will degrade the performance of VMs, although it can find more page sharing opportunities (as shown in Figure 3). The KSM run-time overhead can be divided into 3 parts: *page checksum*, *page comparison*, and *others*. *Page checksum overhead* represents the time spending on calculating checksum of candidate pages to check whether it is volatile; *page comparison overhead* represents the time spending on page content comparison in both the global stable tree and unstable tree, and *others* represent the other KSM run-time overhead, such as inserting nodes in trees or removing nodes from trees, merging pages to be shared with COW, breaking COW when a shared page is modified. We can see that the overhead of *page checksum* and *page comparison* portions remain nearly the same (they don't not change with the scan speed). The *page comparison* contributes about 44% and the *page checksum* contributes about 22% of the total KSM run-time, while *others* contributes about 34%.

Figure 3 shows the number of page sharing opportunities with 4 VMs as the number of pages to be scanned in a batch varied from 100 (C0) to 800 (C3). The page sharing opportunities are varied with time as the phases of VMs changing. We can see that, the KSM can detect more page sharing opportunities as scan-speed increasing, since it can detect more short-lived page sharing in time. Normalized to C0, it can detect about 1.63x of page sharing opportunities for C1, about 2.08x for C2, and about 2.088x for C3 respectively. We can also see that, with 4 VMs running on our experimental sys-

tem, C2 with 400 pages scanned in a batch is fast enough to detect almost all potential page sharing opportunities. Thus in the latter of this paper, without particularly pointed out, we will adopt C2 as our default KSM configuration.

Figure 4 shows the number of total page comparisons and futile page comparisons as the KSM thread running with 4 VMs. We can see that, as the KSM thread scans and compares pages periodically, the total number of page comparisons increases linearly. We can also see that although periodically repeated page comparisons can detect some additional page sharing opportunities, most of them are futile comparisons, which also increase almost linearly along with page scans periodically. We define the term **Futile_Rate** as follows:

$$Futile\_Rate = Futile\_PC\_Num/Total\_PC\_Num \quad (1)$$

Where *Futile_PC_Num* represents the number of futile page comparisons (failed to find sharing page), and *Total_PC_Num* represents the total number of page comparisons as periodically scans.

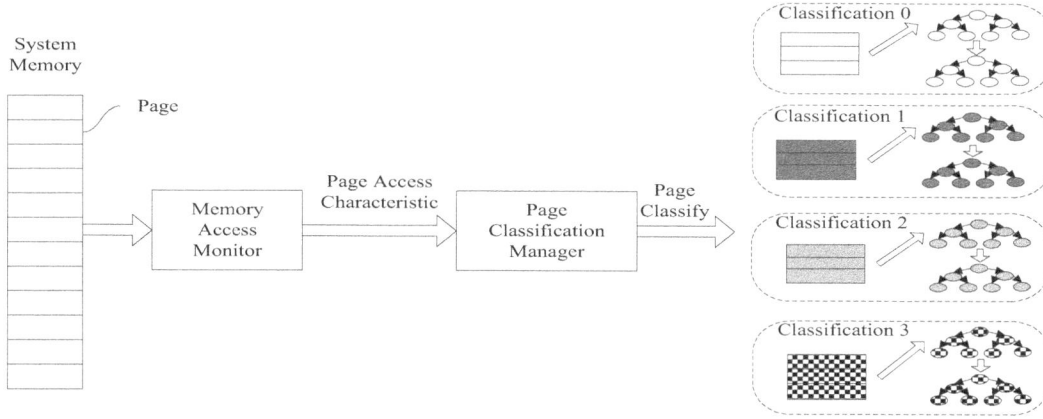

Figure 5. The page classification based memory deduplication implemented with KSM.

We can see that the **Futile_Rate** is finally become steady at about 83.64%. Thus we can conclude that: since nowadays the KSM compares pages with two large global trees and it does not take page access characteristics into account, most of the page comparisons are futile and do nothing help to find page sharing opportunities, thus it will induce heavy CPU overhead (about 44% as shown in Figure 2). And our goal of this paper is to reduce futile page comparisons overhead meanwhile detect page sharing opportunities efficiently in KSM page scans.

3. Classification-Based Memory Deduplication

In this section, we firstly introduce the overview of page Classification-based Memory Deduplication in subsection 3.1. Then we introduce a lightweight hardware-assisted approach to monitor page access characteristics in subsection 3.2. Finally, we introduce three different page classification approaches and analyze their Pros and Cons in subsection 3.3.

3.1 Overview

Since the KSM simply maintains two global comparison trees for all memory pages of a hosting server. To detect page sharing opportunities, each candidate page needs to be compared with a large number of uncorrelated pages in the global trees repeatedly, which will induce massive futile comparisons. The key innovation to reduce futile comparison is to break the global comparison trees into multiple small trees (with less page nodes in each one). Pages are grouped into multiple classifications, with dedicated local comparison tree in each page classification. A candidate page needs only to be compared with pages in its local comparison tree of its classification, which contains less page nodes. But the pages in its local tree are having much higher probability to have same content with the candidate page,

thus it can reduce futile comparisons meanwhile detect page sharing opportunities efficiently.

There are two requirements for page classification approaches: (1) pages with high probability to have same content should be grouped into the same classification, thus the scan thread can detect page sharing opportunities in its local classification tree, as efficient as scanning pages in the global trees. And pages with low probability to have same content should be separated into different classifications, thus they will never be compared with each other. This can reduce futile page comparisons. (2) The page classification approach needs to be balanced, which means that the number of page nodes in each page classification should be nearly the same. Unbalanced page classification will result in a few of page classifications having large number of page nodes, and page comparisons in them will still induce massive futile comparisons as in the global comparison trees.

Figure 5 shows the page classification based memory deduplication named CMD. In CMD, there is a memory access monitor to capture all memory accesses to pages, especially write memory accesses, since write accesses modify pages content and thus affect page sharing opportunities. The memory access monitor maintains page access characteristics for each page: once a write access to a page is captured, it updates the page access characteristics of the corresponding page (e.g. write count). The page classification manager is responsible to group pages into different classifications based on page access characteristics: pages with similar access characteristics are grouped into the same classification. The page classification are performed in each scan round, which means that the access characteristics of pages captured during the last scan round are used to guide page classification in this scan round. And the memory access monitor continues to capture access characteristics of pages during this scan round, which will be used in the next scan round.

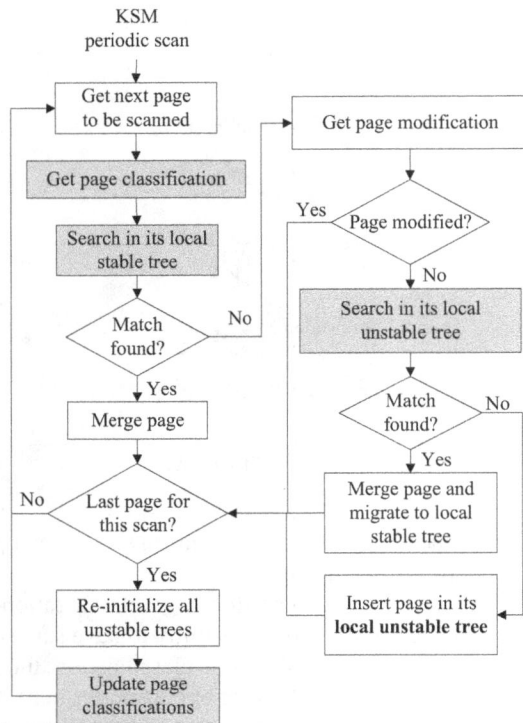

Figure 6. The Classification based KSM Tree algorithm flowchart.

After pages are grouped into classifications, there is a dedicated stable tree and a dedicated unstable tree in each page classification. In each scan, pages searching and comparison are performed in a classification-by-classification manner. In each page classification, a candidate page is firstly compared with pages in the local stable tree of its classification, if no match is found, the candidate page needs to be further compared with pages in the local unstable tree. When searching and comparison of all candidate pages in a classification finished, it starts to scan pages in the next classification. After finishing all pages scanning in all classifications, the the KSM thread will start the next scan round.

Figure 6 shows the classification based KSM tree algorithm flowchart. In each KSM periodic scan, the KSM kernel thread gets next page to be scanned, it firstly gets page classification from page classification manager and then searches in its local stable tree. If a match is found, the candidate page is merged with its identical page into its local stable tree. Otherwise, it gets page modification information (by comparing new calculated checksum with last checksum of the page), if the page is modified during last scan, it is considered to be volatile, and it will not be searched in the local unstable tree; if it is not modified, it is searched and compared with pages in its local unstable tree. If a match is found, they are merged into a shared page and migrated to its local stable tree; if no match is found, the candidate page is inserted into its local unstable tree. After finishing all pages searching

Figure 7. The HMTT board.

in each scan round, all unstable trees in all page classifications need to be destroyed and re-constructed in the next scan round. Pages classifications also need to be updated based on page access characteristics which is monitored in this scan round.

3.2 Page Access Monitor

In this paper, we adopt a hybrid hardware/software memory trace monitoring system named HMTT [7], which is based on hardware snooping technology. HMTT is DDR3 SDRAM compatible[2], and it is able to monitor full-system memory reference traces, including OS, VMMs, libraries, applications, and it has also been enhanced to support fine-grained objects [13], locks [18]. Figure 7 shows the HMTT board. It acts as a DIMM adaptor between the motherboard DIMM and the DRAM DIMM[3], thus it can monitor all memory transaction signals (issued to DRAM devices plugged on the HMTT board) on the DDR3 command bus. Then the corresponding memory read/write access references can be reconstructed based on interpreting DDR3 protocol with the FPGA on the HMTT board, thus HMTT can capture all memory traces at cache block granularity (since processors access DRAM memory when last level cache miss) on a real system. We have also implemented a PCIe interface on the HMTT to send memory traces to another machine with high bandwidth, thus the HMTT can support monitoring workloads with long-time running (e.g. hours). For more implementation detail, please visit the HMTT home page at http://asg.ict.ac.cn/hmtt/.

In this work, we don't need to get detailed memory access traces, instead, we just need write access characteristics of pages, such as write access count, write distribution of sub-pages. Thus we can directly maintain the access information of pages with a SDRAM buffer on the HMTT board. When a write access is monitored, it gets the physical page

---

[2] In this version, it can work with DDR3-800MHz.

[3] The HMTT is plugged directly on the motherboard DIMM, and the DRAM DIMM is plugged on the HMTT board.

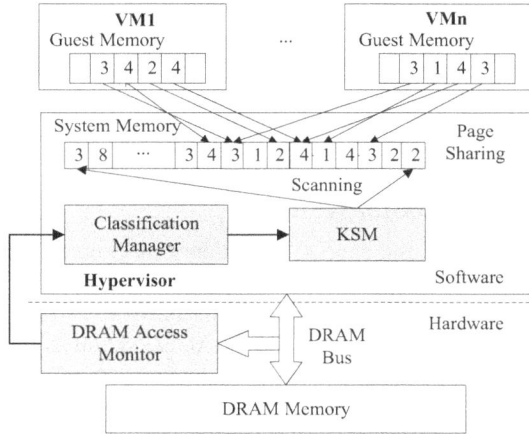

Figure 8. The overview of partitioned based KSM.

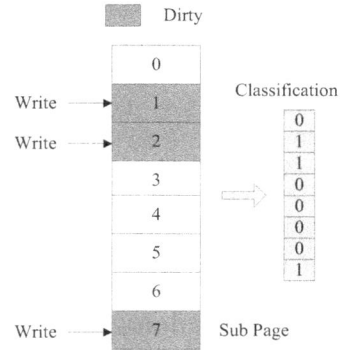

Figure 9. An example of CMD_Subpage_Distribution page classification.

frame number (pfn) from request address, then it updates the access characteristics of the page. Furthermore, we have also implemented a Gigabit Ethernet interface on the HMTT as shown in Figure 7, and the page access information is sent periodically back to the experimental server with this Ethernet interface (the time interval is smaller than the KSM scan period). In software, we have implemented a shared memory buffer between the receiving process and the kernel (as a kernel module), thus the KSM thread can get the feedback page access characteristics periodically, and this feedback information is used to guide page classification. Since the HMTT adopts hardware snooping technology, monitoring page access characteristics introduces negligible overhead to the hosting server. And furthermore, HMTT can capture memory accesses at fine granularity (e.g. cache block), thus we can get more detailed and fine-grained page access characteristics, such as write access distribution among sub-pages. In contemporary processors, there is only an access bit and a dirty bit for each page can be used to indicate whether it is accessed or written recently. Although HMTT is an assistant device that can not be deployed in every server node, the main logic for memory access monitoring and counting can be easily integrated into on-chip memory controller. Here we only evaluate the benefit of such a mechanism while leaving the architecture issue for future research.

3.3 Page Classification

Page classification algorithm is critical to reduce futile page comparisons meanwhile to detect page sharing opportunities efficiently. In this paper, we consider the following three simple page classification algorithms:

- **CMD_Address**: pages are statically classified by their physical addresses (or page frame number). For example, in our experimental system with 8GB physical memory, pages are grouped into 8 classifications like that: pages with address from 0B to 1GB are classified into classification 0, pages with address from 1GB to 2GB are

classified into classification 1, and so on. CMD_Address approach is probably to group pages into different partitions in balance, thus it can reduce page comparisons within each classification. However, it might lose some page sharing opportunities since it does not take page access characteristics into account, pages with the same content might be placed into different classifications, and they have no chance to be compared and shared with each other.

- **CMD_PageCount**: the memory access monitor captures count of write accesses for each page during each scan round, and pages are simply partitioned by their write access count. For example, when we set the write access threshold as 8, then pages with the count of write accesses from 0 to 8 are placed into classification 0, and pages with the count from 8 to 16 are placed into classification 1, and so on. CMD_PageCount considers access characteristics as a whole page, thus it can improve classification accuracy rate and detect more page sharing opportunities.

- **CMD_Subpage_Distribution**: each page is divided into multiple sub-pages (e.g. 4 1KB sub-pages), and the memory access monitor maintains write access characteristics for all sub-pages. Pages with the same sub-page access distribution are grouped into the same classification. Figure 9 shows an example of page classification based on sub-page distribution. A page is divided into 8 sub-pages, each sub-page is with a dirty bit to indicate whether it is written (or modified) during a scan round. In this example, the page has only three sub-pages of 1,2,7 being written, thus the classification of this page is (0,1,1,0,0,0,0,1). With fine grained sub-page access characteristics, CMD_Subpage_Distribution has more opportunity to group pages with the same content into the same classification, thus it can detect page sharing opportunities more efficient.

In addition to the above page classification approach, we can make some optimizations to further reduce page comparison overhead. Pages that have not been modified during last scan round can be treated as a special classification. And they don't need to be searched and compared with each other, because the content of these pages have been compared and failed to find any sharing opportunities before. If the content of them are not modified, page comparisons in this classification will definitely result in futile page comparisons. Thus for this page classification, we can just put pages in a set without maintaining any comparison trees.

4. Experimental Methodology

We carried out our experiments with two 2.00GHz Intel Xeon E5504 processors with EPT enabled. Each E5504 processor has 4 physical cores and we have disabled the Hyper-Thread. There are 3-level caches in each processor, the L1 instruction and data caches are 32KB each and the L2 cache is 256KB, both the L1 and L2 are private in each core. The L3 cache is 16-way 4MB and shared by all four cores in each processor. The cache block size is 64-Byte for all caches in the hierarchy. The total capacity of physical memory is 8GB with one dual-ranked of DDR3-800MHz. The host server runs CentOS-6.2 with Linux kernel 3.6.0. We implement CMD based on KSM of Linux 3.6.10. We use libpcap [5] to get ethernet packets with feedback page access characteristics from Ethernet interface of the HMTT board. We use QEMU [9] with KVM [2] (qemu-kvm-1.2.0) to support guest VMs. Each guest VM is configured with 1 virtual CPU and 2GB main memory, we boot 4 VMs in parallel as our default configuration. The guest VMs are running 64-bit CentOS-6.3 with Linux kernel 2.6.32-279. We choose to run the following workloads inside guest VMs:

- **Kernel Build**: we compile the Linux kernel 3.6.10 in guest VMs. We begin this benchmark after the VMs are fully booted and static sharing opportunities are detected.

- **Apache Server**: we run the ab [1] benchmark on Apache httpd server. We test a local web site in guest VMs with 24 of concurrency requests.

- **MySQL Database**: we run the SysBench [4] with MySQL database in guest VMs. We test database with 1-thread and the oltp-table-size is configured as 1500000.

The CMD configuration parameters are set as follows[4]. For CMD_Address, we separate the 8GB machine physical memory into 8 page classifications with 1GB memory in each page classification. For CMD_PageCount, we adopt the write access count threshold for each page of 64, and since we adopt 16 page classifications, all pages that with write accesses exceeding 1024 are placed into the last page classification. And for CMD_Subpage_Distribution, we adopt 4 sub-pages access distribution (with 1KB in each sub-page) to guide 16 page classifications. And to get the page classifi-

cation as sub-page dirty map, we adopt a threshold of 16 for the number of write access to each sub-page, which means that when the number of write access for a sub-page exceeds 16, the dirty bit of this sub-page is set to 1; otherwise it is set to 0.

5. Experimental Results

Figure 10 shows the page sharing opportunities of different workloads with 4VMs. For *Kernel Build* workload in Figure 10(a), we can see that the KSM can detect the most page sharing opportunities (it is about 1.02E6 sharable pages). But since it maintains pages into large global comparison trees, candidate pages needs to be compared with a large number of uncorrelated page nodes, thus it takes a little longer time to reach its maximum page-sharing state. On the other hand, The CMD_Addr detects the least page sharing opportunities, it is only about 71% of the KSM (about 7.25E5). That is because the CMD_Addr groups pages into different classifications simply based on physical page frame number, but without taking any page access characteristics (which affect page content) into account. Pages with same content but with long-distance page frame number will be separated into different page classifications. And since this classification approach is static, these pages have no chance to be detected and shared with each other. The CMD_PageCount can detect about 87.1% (about 8.89E5) page sharing opportunities as the KSM, this is because it adopts coarse granularity page access characteristics (the count of write accesses in each scan round) to guide page classification. It can achieve higher accuracy, however there is still some room for improvement. Finally the CMD_Subpage is able to detect nearly the same page sharing opportunities (about 1.00E6), which is about 98% of the KSM. This result proves that fine-granularity sub-page write access distribution is a better guide for page classification. We can also see that the CMD_Subpage can detect page sharing opportunities more quickly than the KSM, since each candidate page costs less time overhead to be scanned and compared in its local comparison trees.

For *Apache* workload as shown in Figure 10(b), we can see that the KSM can detect almost the same page sharing opportunities (about 7.45E5) with the CMD_PageCount and the CMD_Subpage approach. However the CMD_Addr performs quite poor, it can detects about only 38.9% page sharing opportunities of the KSM (about 2.9E5). This further indicates that static page classification has poor adaptivity, and it needs to adopt dynamic page classification approach. In this paper we prove that fine granularity dynamic page access characteristics is a good hint for page classification, since it has a close relationship with page content and thus page sharing opportunities.

For *MySQL* workload as shown in Figure 10(c), we can see that the CMD_Addr and the CMD_PageCount detects almost the same page sharing opportunities (about 3.54E5),

[4] However they are not the best configurations, since we just choose them based on some coarse parameters searching.

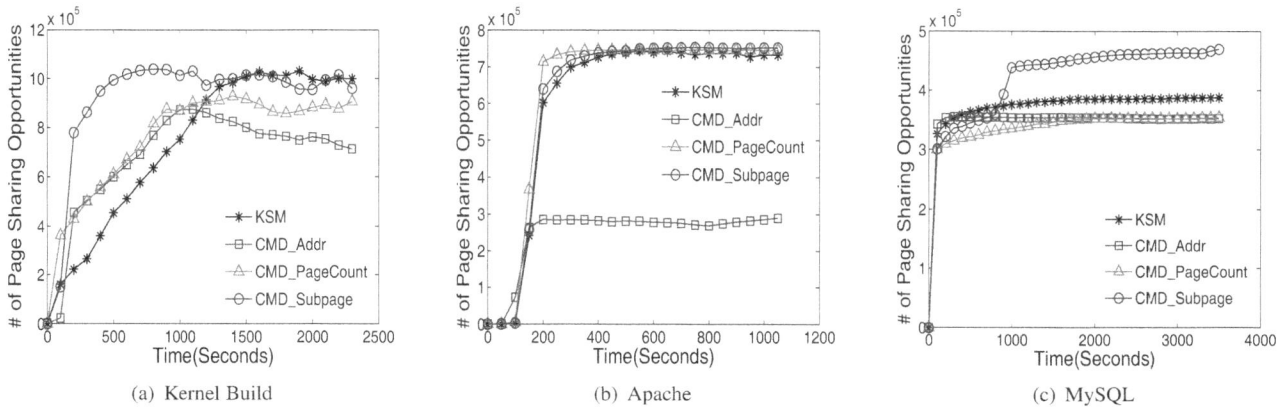

Figure 10. The page sharing opportunities with 4 VMs.

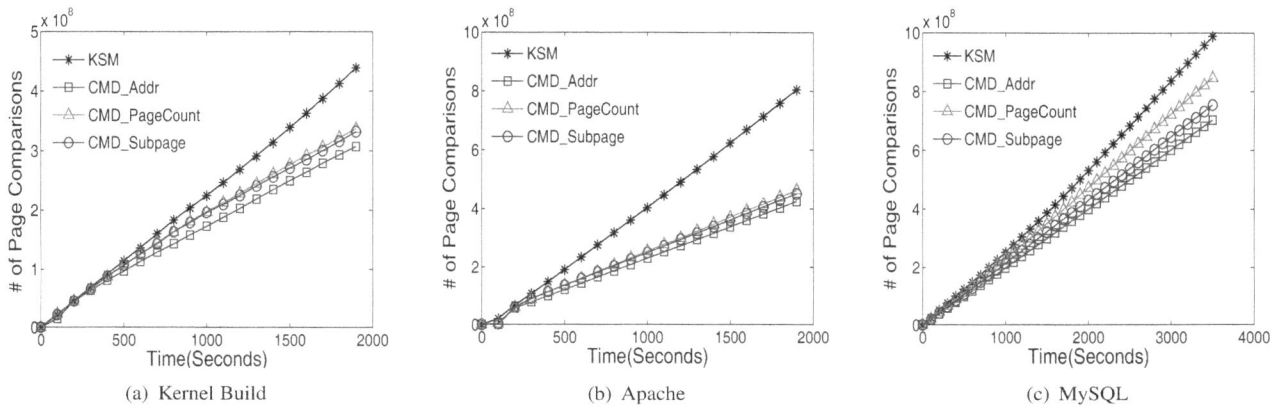

Figure 11. The number of page comparisons of different workloads with 4VMs.

which is about 91.5% of the KSM (about 3.87E5). It is worth noting that the CMD_Subpage can detect even more page sharing opportunities (about 4.69E5), which is about 1.21x of the KSM. The probable reason for it is that, in MySQL workload, there exists abundant short-lived page sharing opportunities. However the KSM is failed to detect them since it costs longer comparison time for each candidate page which inducing massive futile comparisons. They can be detected by the CMD_Subpage approach, because for each candidate page, it can be scanned more quickly just in its local comparison tree, which makes it detect short-lived page sharing opportunity more efficient.

Figure 11 shows the number of pages comparisons of different workloads with 4 VMs. For *Kernel Build* workload as shown in Figure 11(a), we can see that the KSM with large global comparison trees induces the most number of page comparisons. While the CMD_Addr has the least number of page comparisons, it is about 56.8% of the KSM, since CMD_addr has the best balanced page classifications (with address). The CMD_PageCount and the CMD_Subpage have nearly the same number of page comparisons, it is about

73.3% of the KSM. Although the CMD_Subpage induces about 1.08x of page comparisons than the CMD_Addr, it can detect page sharing opportunities more efficient (as shown in Figure 10). For *Apache* workload as shown in Figure 11(b), the KSM also has the most number of page comparisons, and the CMD_Addr has the least number of page comparisons which is about 55.5% of the KSM. The CMD_PageCount and the CMD_Subpage have almost the same page comparisons, which is about 55.7% of the KSM. For *MySQL* workload as shown in Figure 11(c), The CMD_Addr also has the least number page comparisons, which is about 71.2% of the KSM. While the CMD_Subpage is about 76.6% of the KSM, this is less than the CMD_PageCount, which is about 86% of the KSM. Thus we can conclude that the CMD_Subpage is the best tradeoff between detecting page sharing opportunities and reducing page comparisons (especially futile comparisons).

Figure 12 shows the percentage of futile rate reduction with 4 VMs, where the baseline is with the KSM approach. We can see that all these three approaches can reduce futile rate. On average it can reduce at about 4.77%,

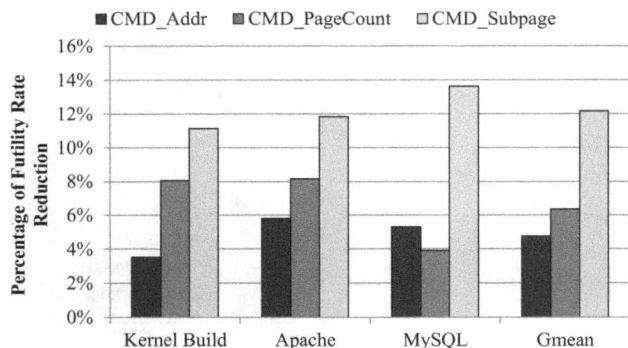

Figure 12. The percentage of futile rate reduction with 4 VMs, where the baseline is with the KSM approach.

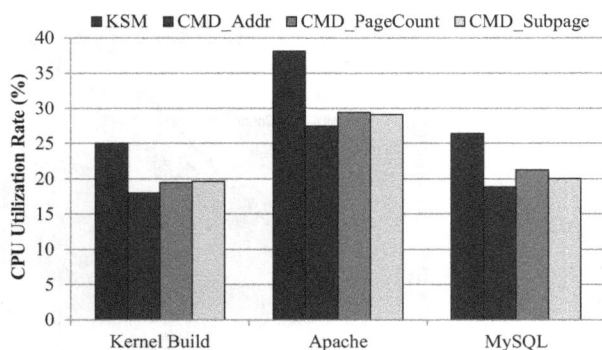

Figure 13. The average CPU Utilization Rate of the KSM kernel thread for different approaches. The CPU Utilization is got from top measurements taken every second.

6.35% and 12.15% for the CMD_addr, CMD_PageCount and CMD_Subpage respectively. The maximum reduction of the CMD_Subpage approach is about 13.62% for *MySQL* workload. This result prove the accuracy of the CMD_Subpage approach for page classification, which is based on fine granularity sub-page access distribution characteristics.

Figure 13 shows the average CPU Utilization Rate of the KSM kernel thread for different approaches. We get the CPU Utilization from top measurements taken every second. We can see that all the other three CMD approaches (dividing the global comparison tree into multiple comparison trees) can reduce the CPU overhead compared with the KSM. For *Kernel Build* workload, the CPU Utilization Rate is about 24.98% for the KSM, which is reduce to 18.00%, 19.45% and 19.65% for the CMD_Addr, CMD_PageCount and CMD_Subpage respectively. This is main because that the CMD approaches can reduce the number of futile page comparisons and reduce the CPU run-time overhead. For the *Apache* workload, the CPU Utilization Rate is about 38.12% for the KSM, and it reduces to 27.48%, 29.44% and 29.12% for the CMD_Addr, CMD_PageCount and CMD_Subpage respectively. For the *MySQL* workload, the CPU Utilization Rate is about 26.40% for the KSM, and it reduces to 18.86%, 21.28% and 20.05% for the CMD_Addr, CMD_PageCount and CMD_Subpage respectively.

6. Related Work

Limited main memory size has become one of the major bottlenecks in virtualization environment, and as an efficient approach to reduce server memory requirement, memory deduplication thus has attracted a large body of work on it. Disco virtual machine monitor (VMM) [10] was one of the first systems that implemented page sharing technique, however it needed to modify the guest OS to explicitly track page changes to build knowledge of identical pages. The content-based page sharing (CBPS) technique was firstly exemplified by VMWare's ESX server [29], in which CBPS required no assistance from the guest OS and it was performed transparently in the hypervisor layer. Thus CBPS had become the most widely used page sharing technique both in industry and academia. Kloster et al. [20] designed and implemented content based page sharing in the Xen hypervisor. They found that the unified disk caches were often the most significant cause of redundancy in virtualized systems.

KSM (Kernel Samepage Merging) [6] is a scanning based mechanism to detect page sharing opportunities. KSM is implemented as a kernel thread, which periodically scans pages of guest VMs to detect identical pages (based on page content comparison). Chang et al. [12] conducted empirical study on the effectiveness of KSM for various kind of workloads. They found KSM achieved effective memory sharing which could reduce memory usage by around 50% for I/O-bound applications. And they also found KSM would cause higher run-time overhead for CPU-bound applications caused by futile page comparisons. Rachamalla et al. [24] studied the trade-off between KSM performance and CPU overhead with different KSM configurations, then they developed an adaptive scheme to maximize sharing opportunities at minimal overhead. Barker et al. [8] proposed an empirical study of memory sharing in virtual machines through an exploration and analysis of memory traces captured from real user machines and controlled virtual machines, they found that sharing tended to be significantly more modest, and the self-sharing contributed a significant majority of the total sharing potential. Yang et al. [32] evaluated memory overcommit features of memory sharing and swapping in Xen, they also proposed an adaptive memory overcommit policy to reach higher VM density without sacrificing performance.

Gupta et al. proposed Difference Engine [17] to firstly support sub-page sharing, in which full memory pages were broken down into multiple sub-pages and memory sharing was performed at the fine sub-page granularity. They further proposed patching technique which would store similar pages by constructing patches, and worked together with compression of non-shared pages to reduce the memory footprint. With these optimizations, it could save memory up to 90% between VMs running similar applications and operating systems and up to 65% even across VMs running disparate workloads. Wood et al. [30] proposed Memory Buddies which adopted intelligent VM collocation within a data center to aggressively exploit page sharing benefits. KSM++ [21] adopted I/O-based hints in the host to make the memory scanning process more efficient and to exploit short-lived sharing opportunities. Miller et al. [22] proposed a more effective memory deduplication scanner XLH, which could exploit sharing opportunities earlier. XLH generated page hints in the host's virtual file system layer, then moved them earlier into the merging stage. Thus XLH could find short-lived sharing opportunities. However, the XLH could only worked for virtual machines with intensive file, and it still adopted the KSM with global trees for the whole system memory. Chiang et al. [14] proposed a Generalized Memory de-duplication engine that leveraged the free memory pool information in guest VMs and treated the free memory pages as duplicates of an all-zero page to improve the efficiency of memory de-duplication.

Satori system [23] implemented sharing by watching for identical regions of memory when read from disk, it could find short-lived sharing opportunities effectively, however it required modifications to the guest operating systems. Sharma et al. [27] extended the page deduplication of KSM for page caches, they proposed Singleton to address the double-caching problem, which implemented an exclusive cache for the host and guest page cache hierarchy. Kim et al. [19] proposed a group-based memory deduplication scheme that allowed the hypervisor to run with multiple deduplication threads, each of which was in charge of its dedicated group. However their sharing group was aimed to provide performance isolation and secure protection among different groups. Deng et al. [15] also proposed a similar memory sharing mechanism based on user groups to support isolation and trustworthiness mechanism between different users on the same host. Both of the above work did not take futile page comparison overhead into account, while our goal of page classification in this paper is to reduce futile page comparison overhead based on page access characteristics. Sha et al. proposed SmartKSM [26] to divide memory footprints into several sets in KSM based on page types and process aspect. Sindelar et al. [28] proposed the design of graph models to capture page sharing across VMs. They also developed sharing-aware algorithms that could collocate VMs with similar page content on the same physical server. Xia and Dinda [31] argued that in virtualized large scale parallel systems, both intra- and inter- node memory content sharing was common, they then proposed an effective sharing memory detection system by using a distributed hash table. In IBM Active Memory Deduplication [11], the hypervisor created signatures for physical pages (in a deduplication table) to reduce full page content comparison overhead.

7. Conclusion

In this paper, we firstly perform a detailed profiling of the KSM run-time, and we find that there exists massive futile page comparisons, because the KSM thread scans on two large global comparison trees. We then propose a lightweight page Classification-based Memory Deduplication approach named CMD. In CMD, pages are divided into different classifications based on page access characteristics, and the large global comparison trees are divided into multiple trees with dedicated ones in each page classification. Page comparisons are performed just in the same classification, and pages from different classifications are never searched and compared with each other, since they are probably futile comparisons. We adopt a lightweight hardware assisted memory trace monitoring system to capture fine granularity page access characteristics. We implement CMD based on KSM in our real experimental system, and the experimental results show that the CMD can detect page sharing opportunities efficiently (more than 98% of the KSM), meanwhile reduce page comparisons and reduce the futile rate by about 12.15% on average with fine granularity sub-page access distribution characteristics.

Acknowledgements

The authors thank the anonymous reviewers for their constructive suggestions. This work is partially supported by the National Natural Science Foundation of China (NSFC) under Grant Nos. 60925009, 61221062, 61331008, the National Basic Research Program of China (973 Program) under Grant No. 2011CB302502, the Strategic Priority Research Program of the Chinese Academy of Sciences under Grant No. XDA06010401, and the Huawei Research Program under Grant No. YBCB2011030. Yungang Bao is partially supported by the CCF-Intel Young Faculty Research Program (YFRP) Grant.

References

[1] ab - apache http server benchmarking tool. http://httpd.apache.org/docs/2.2/programs/ab.html.

[2] Kvm-kernel based virtual machine. http://www.linux-kvm.org/page/Main_Page.

[3] Linux 2 6 32 - linux kernel newbies. http://kernelnewbies.org/Linux_2_6_32.

[4] Sysbench: a system performance benchmark. http://sysbench.sourceforge.net/.

[5] Tcpdump and libpcap. http://www.tcpdump.org/.

[6] A. Arcangeli, I. Eidus, and C. Wright. Increasing memory density by using ksm. In *Proceedings of the Linux Symposium (OLS'09)*, pages 19–28, 2009.

[7] Y. Bao, M. Chen, Y. Ruan, L. Liu, J. Fan, Q. Yuan, B. Song, and J. Xu. Hmtt: a platform independent full-system memory trace monitoring system. In *Proceedings of the 2008 ACM SIGMETRICS international conference on Measure-*

ment and modeling of computer systems, SIGMETRICS '08, pages 229–240, 2008.

[8] S. Barker, T. Wood, P. Shenoy, and R. Sitaraman. An empirical study of memory sharing in virtual machines. In *Proceedings of the 2012 USENIX conference on Annual Technical Conference*, USENIX ATC'12, pages 273–284, 2012.

[9] F. Bellard. Qemu, a fast and portable dynamic translator. In *Proceedings of the annual conference on USENIX Annual Technical Conference*, ATEC '05, pages 41–46, 2005.

[10] E. Bugnion, S. Devine, K. Govil, and M. Rosenblum. Disco: running commodity operating systems on scalable multiprocessors. *ACM Trans. Comput. Syst.*, 15(4):412–447, Nov. 1997.

[11] R. Ceron, R. Folco, B. Leitao, and H. Tsubamoto. Power systems memory deduplication. In *IBM Redbooks*, 2012. http://www.redbooks.ibm.com/abstracts/redp4827.html.

[12] C.-R. Chang, J.-J. Wu, and P. Liu. An empirical study on memory sharing of virtual machines for server consolidation. In *Parallel and Distributed Processing with Applications (ISPA), 2011 IEEE 9th International Symposium on*, pages 244–249, 2011.

[13] L. Chen, Z. Cui, Y. Bao, M. Chen, Y. Huang, and G. Tan. A lightweight hybrid hardware/software approach for object-relative memory profiling. In *Performance Analysis of Systems and Software (ISPASS), 2012 IEEE International Symposium on*, pages 46–57, 2012.

[14] J.-H. Chiang, H.-L. Li, and T.-c. Chiueh. Introspection-based memory de-duplication and migration. In *Proceedings of the 9th ACM SIGPLAN/SIGOPS international conference on Virtual execution environments*, VEE '13, pages 51–62, 2013.

[15] Y. Deng, C. Hu, T. Wo, B. Li, and L. Cui. A memory deduplication approach based on group in virtualized environments. In *Proceedings of the 2013 IEEE Seventh International Symposium on Service-Oriented System Engineering*, SOSE '13, pages 367–372, 2013.

[16] R. P. Goldberg. Survey of virtual machine research. *Computer*, 7(9):34–45, Sept. 1974.

[17] D. Gupta, S. Lee, M. Vrable, S. Savage, A. C. Snoeren, G. Varghese, G. M. Voelker, and A. Vahdat. Difference engine: harnessing memory redundancy in virtual machines. In *8th USENIX Symposium on Operating Systems Design and Implementation*, OSDI'08, pages 309–322, 2008.

[18] Y. Huang, Z. Cui, L. Chen, W. Zhang, Y. Bao, and M. Chen. Halock: hardware-assisted lock contention detection in multithreaded applications. In *Proceedings of the 21st international conference on Parallel architectures and compilation techniques*, PACT '12, pages 253–262, 2012.

[19] S. Kim, H. Kim, and J. Lee. Group-based memory deduplication for virtualized clouds. In *6th Workshop on Virtualization in High-Performance Cloud Computing*, VHPC 2011, pages 387–397, 2011.

[20] J. F. Kloster, J. Kristensen, and A. Mejlholm. Determining the use of interdomain shareable pages using kernel introspection. In *Tech. rep., Aalborg University, 2007.* http://mejlholm.org/uni/pdfs/dat7_introspection.pdf.

[21] K. Miller, F. Franz, T. Groeninger, M. Rittinghaus, M. Hillenbrand, and F. Bellosa. Ksm++: Using i/o-based hints to make memory-deduplication scanners more efficient. In *Proceedings of the ASPLOS Workshop on Runtime Environments, Systems, Layering and Virtualized Environments (RESoLVE'12)*, 2012. http://www.dcs.gla.ac.uk/conferences/resolve12/papers/session3_paper2.pdf.

[22] K. Miller, F. Franz, M. Rittinghaus, M. Hillenbrand, and F. Bellosa. Xlh: More effective memory deduplication scanners through cross-layer hints. In *Proceedings of the 2013 USENIX conference on Annual Technical Conference*, USENIX ATC'13, pages 279–290, 2013.

[23] G. Miłós, D. G. Murray, S. Hand, and M. A. Fetterman. Satori: enlightened page sharing. In *Proceedings of the 2009 conference on USENIX Annual technical conference*, USENIX'09, pages 1–14, 2009.

[24] S. Rachamalla, D. Mishra, and P. Kulkarni. All page sharing is equal, but some sharing is more equal than others. 2013. http://www.cse.iitb.ac.in/internal/techreports/reports/TR-CSE-2013-49.pdf.

[25] M. Rosenblum and T. Garfinkel. Virtual machine monitors: current technology and future trends. *Computer*, 38(5):39–47, 2005.

[26] S. Sha, J. Li, N. Li, W. Ju, L. Cui, and B. Li. Smartksm: A vmm-based memory deduplication scanner for virtual machines. http://act.buaa.edu.cn/lijx/pubs/sosp2013.smartksm.pdf.

[27] P. Sharma and P. Kulkarni. Singleton: system-wide page deduplication in virtual environments. In *Proceedings of the 21st international symposium on High-Performance Parallel and Distributed Computing*, HPDC '12, pages 15–26, 2012.

[28] M. Sindelar, R. K. Sitaraman, and P. Shenoy. Sharing-aware algorithms for virtual machine colocation. In *Proceedings of the 23rd ACM symposium on Parallelism in algorithms and architectures*, SPAA '11, pages 367–378, 2011.

[29] C. A. Waldspurger. Memory resource management in vmware esx server. *SIGOPS Oper. Syst. Rev.*, 36(SI):181–194, Dec. 2002.

[30] T. Wood, G. Tarasuk-Levin, P. Shenoy, P. Desnoyers, E. Cecchet, and M. D. Corner. Memory buddies: exploiting page sharing for smart colocation in virtualized data centers. In *Proceedings of the 2009 ACM SIGPLAN/SIGOPS international conference on Virtual execution environments*, VEE '09, pages 31–40, 2009.

[31] L. Xia and P. A. Dinda. A case for tracking and exploiting inter-node and intra-node memory content sharing in virtualized large-scale parallel systems. In *Proceedings of the 6th international workshop on Virtualization Technologies in Distributed Computing Date*, VTDC '12, pages 11–18, 2012.

[32] X. Yang, C. Ye, and Q. Lin. Evaluation and enhancement to memory sharing and swapping in xen 4.1. In *XenSubmitt 2011*. http://www-archive.xenproject.org/files/xensummit_santaclara11/aug3/3_XiaoweiY_Evaluation_and_Enhancement_to_Memory_Sharing_and_Swapping_in_Xen%204.1.pdf.

MuscalietJS: Rethinking Layered Dynamic Web Runtimes

Behnam Robatmili[†]   Călin Caşcaval[†]   Mehrdad Reshadi[‡1]   Madhukar N. Kedlaya[‖]

Seth Fowler[§1]   Vrajesh Bhavsar[†]   Michael Weber[†]   Ben Hardekopf[‖]

[†]Qualcomm Research Silicon Valley   [‖]University of California, Santa Barbara   [‡]InstartLogic   [§]Mozilla

mcjs.devel@qti.qualcomm.com

Abstract

Layered JavaScript engines, in which the JavaScript runtime is built on top another managed runtime, provide better extensibility and portability compared to traditional monolithic engines. In this paper, we revisit the design of layered JavaScript engines and propose a layered architecture, called MuscalietJS[2], that splits the responsibilities of a JavaScript engine between a high-level, JavaScript-specific component and a low-level, language-agnostic .NET VM. To make up for the performance loss due to layering, we propose a two pronged approach: high-level JavaScript optimizations and exploitation of low-level VM features that produce very efficient code for hot functions. We demonstrate the validity of the MuscalietJS design through a comprehensive evaluation using both the Sunspider benchmarks and a set of web workloads. We demonstrate that our approach outperforms other layered engines such as IronJS and Rhino engines while providing extensibility, adaptability and portability.

Categories and Subject Descriptors   D.3.4 [*Programming Languages*]: Processors–Run-time environments

Keywords   JavaScript; layered virtual machine; dynamic languages

1. Introduction

JavaScript is a language in which almost everything is dynamically modifiable: it is dynamically typed, object properties (the JavaScript name for object members) can be dynamically inserted and deleted, inheritance hierarchy (via prototype chains) can be changed dynamically, new code

---

[1] Work performed while at Qualcomm Research Silicon Valley.

[2] MuscalietJS can be found at http://www.github.com/mcjs/mcjs.git

VEE '14,   March 1–2, 2014, Salt Lake City, Utah, USA.
Copyright © 2014 ACM 978-1-4503-2764-0 /14/03. . . $15.00.
http://dx.doi.org/10.1145/2576195.2576211

can be injected dynamically, and so on. These properties make JavaScript application development flexible. However, they also make compiling JavaScript a significant challenge. In addition, JavaScript is still a relatively new and evolving language, requiring an extensible compilation engine to enable easy exploration of new language features. Adding language-level compiler optimizations should be easy, especially in an engine architecture that supports different compilers and optimization levels. JavaScript engines are used in a variety of environments, from web page loading to web applications and server processing [14]. As such, an engine needs to adapt the quality of generated code and the time spent compiling to the particular workload. Finally, portability is critical, especially in the browser case, as JavaScript engines run on a wide variety of platforms.

Given the significant advancements in virtual machines such as .NET and JVM, both in terms of improved efficiency and large number of available features, a fundamental question is whether we can exploit these VMs to efficiently build and run a dynamic language like JavaScript in an adaptable manner. Such an approach can potentially ease new language feature extensions and improve portability. Concentrating almost exclusively on performance, traditional engines [9, 18] implement the entire dynamic managed runtime using an unmanaged language such as C or C++. In these engines, the basic constructs of the dynamic runtime such as object layout, heap, garbage collector, compilers, profilers and call frames, have been designed and implemented from scratch in the low-level language. This approach achieves high performance and requires significant effort. Since everything is designed together, the monolithic architecture ends up less extensible, making it more challenging to implement an evolving dynamic language.

Recently, there have been several efforts [1, 2, 10, 16] for building a high-level dynamic VM runtime (such as JavaScript) on top of another low-level VM (such as JVM or .NET). We call such a runtime a *layered* runtime. Although a layered runtime can experience a performance hit due to the presence of the low-level VM, it can significantly ease development and improve extensibility. In this paper, we reexamine and reenvision the architecture of layered JavaScript engines with the goal of providing a flexible and performant framework for optimization. The specific contributions of this paper are:

- A new, layered JavaScript engine, MuscalietJS (or MCJS), for decent performance, rapid prototyping and exploration of research ideas implemented on top of the .NET common language runtime (CLR). This architecture is different than any previously proposed layered engines such as SPUR [1], IronJS [10] or Rhino [16] in how it divides responsibilities between high-level and low-level engines and achieves better performance (Section 3). JavaScript-specific optimizations, such as property lookup and type inference, are performed in the high-level engine (Section 4). Code generation and hardware-specific optimizations are performed at the low-level VM. MuscalietJS exploits features provided by the low-level VM runtime, such as *Reflection* and *Runtime Method Attributes*, to emit efficient code for hot functions (Section 5).

- Insights into the low-level VM features that will maximize the performance benefits of the JavaScript runtime without losing generality. Examples include eliminating array bounds checks on data structures that are either used by the JavaScript JIT or generated by it, and which are guaranteed not to overflow, explicit object initialization, and avoiding JITed code validation checks (Section 5.3).

- We demonstrate the validity of our approach by comparing the performance of MuscalietJS to previously proposed layered engines implemented in managed languages, including Rhino [16] and IronJS [10] and also monolithic engines such as V8 [9] (Section 6). We find that on both traditional JavaScript benchmarks and several record-and-replay benchmarks based on real websites, MuscalietJS significantly outperforms other layered engines such as Rhino and IronJS (by a factor of 2 to 3), while still supporting extensibility and portability.

2. Design Space of JavaScript Engines

Given the pace of change experienced in web development and the growing ubiquity of JavaScript, we identify the following criteria for evaluating JavaScript engines:

- **Performance.** Performance is the key criterion by which production JavaScript engines are evaluated. Given the increase in dynamic execution of web pages [15] and the trend toward web apps, better JavaScript performance in browsers is increasingly important.

- **Adaptability.** A JavaScript engine must be adaptable enough to recognize different workloads, ranging from server-side [14] to latency-sensitive page-load and iterative hot-spot workloads, and react accordingly to provide the best possible quality of service.

- **Extensibility.** The JavaScript language is constantly evolving both formally, (e.g., the new ECMAScript standard [7]), and informally [19–21]. This means that JavaScript engines must evolve constantly and must be designed such

that extensions can be added and integrated easily, while taking advantage of the full feature set of optimizations. Changes must be localized and modular, and avoid re-engineering the engine flow.

- **Portability.** Browsers, and hence JavaScript, are widely used on many platforms, from desktops to mobile devices; thus an engine should be easily portable to different hardware architectures. This implies that engines should be decoupled from the underlying hardware, treating the hardware interface as a separate concern. However, it is still critical for performance that an engine take advantage of any available hardware-specific features.

2.1 Traditional Monolithic Architectures

The traditional engines are designed to achieve the best performance and adapt to different Web workloads. For example, the Google V8 JavaScript engine [9] is a native C++ application that has two just-in-time (JIT) compilers and no interpreter. One is a quick, simple compiler that generates very fast generic code using inline caches, and the second is a profile-based optimizing JIT compiler called Crankshaft. The optimizing compiler applies a wide range of low-level optimizations such as SSA (Static Single Assignment) redundancy elimination, register allocation, and static type inference when generating native code. It also uses type feedback from the inline caches from the simple compiler. V8 does not use a bytecode-based IR (intermediate representation); instead, it uses both high-level and low-level graph-based IRs for different levels of optimization. SpiderMonkey [18], Firefox's JavaScript engine, is another monolithic engine written in C/C++ and comprised of a bytecode-based interpreter, a baseline JIT compiler, and an optimizing JIT compiler (IonMonkey). The baseline compiler is similar to the V8 engine's simple compiler and uses inline caches to generate fast code.

While these runtimes are usually implemented and compiled in a low-level unmanaged language such as C++, they need to provide complete JIT compilers with several IRs and optimizations at different levels, and assembly code generators for all target machines. The compiler stack and the code generators must be updated frequently to support newly added language features. Significant development effort is required to extend and maintain such engines and port them to new platforms. Researchers have been experimenting with various JIT compilers in the Mozilla framework, such as the tracing JIT in Gal et al. [8], and highlight the complexity of implementing such components in monolithic engines. Additionally, in these architectures, there is an impedance mismatch between the runtime call stack (generally C++) and the call stack of the executing generated code in the target language (JavaScript). Consequently, communication between the executing JITed code and the runtime is complex and has high overhead.

Table 1. Traditional vs. Layered JavaScript Engines.

Architecture	Name	Host Language	Compilation methodology	LOC
Monolithic	V8	C++	Adaptive: Inline-cache based fast compiler wit no IR for cold code; an JavaScript optimizing compiler (HIR and LIR) for hot code	1M
Monolithic	SpiderMonkey	C++	Adaptive: A byte-code based interpreter for cold code; a trace JIT and method JIT for hot JavaScript code	300K
Layered	MuscalietJS	CLR (C#)	Adaptive: an IR-based interpreter implemented in CIL for cold code; an JavaScript optimizing compiler (implemented in CIL) and a CIL code generator for hot code	95K
Layered	SPUR	CLR (C#)	Translate JavaScript to CIL; leaves dynamic optimizations to tracing CIL JIT	N/A
Layered	IronJS	DLR (F#)	Translate JavaScript to DLR; leaves dynamic optimizations to DLR	23K
Layered	Rhino	JVM (Java)	Non-adaptive but can be reconfigured ahead of time (AOT); supports various degrees of optimizations (interpreter to optimized code)	115K

2.2 Layered Architectures

In layered JavaScript (also called Repurposed JIT) architectures, the target dynamic runtime is built on top of another runtime engine, rather than building an entire compiler from scratch. These designs are typically more portable than monolithic ones, as hardware-specific optimizations and functionality are provided by the low-level VM. Additionally, the target runtime may take advantage of features and resources provided by the host runtime including object layout, garbage collection and code generators. Therefore, these designs can better fit the quick development cycles needed for evolving dynamic languages. For example, as shown in Table 1, the code size for these architecture is significantly smaller (up to 10x) than the code size of traditional engines. Adding new features to the layered engines is usually easier. For example, adding support for parallel execution or parallel compilation to monolithic engines is a significant task as it requires major changes to the memory system, garbage collector and runtime. Whereas, basic parallelism support in a layered engine that runs on top of .NET for example, such as MuscalietJS, can be provided using Task-Parallel Library (TPL) already available in the .NET runtime.

Table 1 compares MuscalietJS against three common layered JavaScript engines and two traditional engines. MuscalietJS is a layered JavaScript engine architecture built on top of the .NET Common Language Runtime (CLR). Most other layered engine provide a thin layer on the top and rely on the low-level engine to provide the optimizations. MuscalietJS, however, implements many language-level optimizations at the high-level, where the semantics of the language allows for better decisions. And it delegates the traditional compiler optimizations to the low-level engine (e.g. register allocation). MuscalietJS performs adaptive JavaScript-specific optimizations and uses CIL code generation to JIT optimized versions of hot function after applying high-level JavaScript optimizations. These high-level optimizations include hidden classes, property lookup, type analysis, and restricted dataflow analysis. MuscalietJS also exploits special features in CLR runtimes to generate high-performance optimized code. For example, MuscalietJS uses reflection and inlining hints to generate optimized code for dynamic JavaScript operations. MuscalietJS communicates special hints to the CLR engine to avoid array-bounds checks and object initialization for JavaScript property access and JavaScript object creation.

SPUR [1] is a tracing JIT compiler for Common Intermediate Language (CIL) in which JavaScript is directly compiled to CIL and CIL is trace-compiled by SPUR for better optimization. The authors show that tracing CIL generated by compiling JavaScript programs gives similar performance gains to a JavaScript tracing compiler. Due to the modular nature of our engine, we believe that it is possible for MuscalietJS to run on top of any CIL compiler including SPUR. Given the effectiveness of SPUR over Microsoft's .NET runtime, MuscalietJS might benefit from it; unfortunately, SPUR is not available for general use and thus we could not test this setup. IronJS [10] translates JavaScript to Dynamic Language Runtime (DLR) expression trees [5] and leaves dynamic optimizations to the DLR. DLR uses the concept of *dynamic callsites* to generate type specialized versions of each operation. This is similar to polymorphic inline caches. Rhino [16] is a JavaScript engine on top of the JVM which offers various levels of optimization. The default configuration of the runtime invokes a naïve bytecode-based interpreter written in Java. Other optimization levels invoke a code generator that generates Java class files. When set to the highest optimization level, Rhino performs optimizations such as detection of numerical operations, common sub-expression elimination, and function call target caching. Though the current implementation lacks adaptive compilation, optimizations can be enabled or disabled ahead of time. Nashorn [13] is a more recent implementation of a JavaScript runtime on the JVM. Nashorn uses the *invoke-dynamic* bytecode instruction, which was added to recent versions of the JVM to enable efficient implementation of dynamic language runtimes. We were not able to find a performant version of Nashorn to compare against.

Some prior studies [2] have stressed the importance of having matching semantics of the two layers. We believe semantics of the low-level VM might be of some importance but the overall architecture and work breakdown between high-level and low-level VMs are more important. For example, by moving JavaScript optimizations (similar to the one explained in Section 4) to the high-level engine, it is possible to achieve significant speedups regardless of the semantics of the lower-level language. As our results show while semantics of DLR used by IronJS are relatively close to dynamic languages such as JavaScript, with better engineering MuscalietJS outperforms IronJS.

3. MuscalietJS Architectural Overview

MuscalietJS's architecture is shown in Figure 1. It splits responsibilities across two levels: a JavaScript-specific engine and a language-agnostic low-level VM. In principle, any managed language VM can serve as the low-level engine. Our current implementation uses the Common Language Runtime (CLR), as implemented by Mono [12]. The low-level VM provides traditional compiler optimizations: instruction scheduling, register allocation, constant propagation, common subexpression elimination, etc., as well as code generation and machine specific optimizations. In addition it provides managed language services such as garbage collection, allowing us to focus on the JavaScript-specific aspects of the engine.

The JavaScript specific layer is further decomposed into several components:

- **JavaScript runtime.** The high-level runtime consists of a parser, an interpreter, a parallel JIT compiler, and a profiler. The parser takes in JavaScript code and produces a custom IR (see Sec. 4.1). The interpreter executes the IR directly, while the JIT compiler applies JavaScript-specific transformations and optimizations, and generates CIL bytecodes for hot functions. Some examples of performed optimizations are: type analysis and type inference, array analysis, and signature-based specialization; these are further discussed in Section 4.

  The combination of interpreter, JIT, and profiler provides adaptability in our design by deciding which compilation path is more appropriate given the workload. For latency-sensitive scenarios, like browser page load, we provide an interpreter which can directly execute the output of the parser without any intermediate bytecode generation. As functions are invoked multiple times and become hot, the JIT compiler will optimize them since the compilation time can be amortized. For the hottest, most performance-sensitive code, we apply more expensive optimizations at both the high-level JavaScript engine layer and the low-level VM layer.

- **Dynamic runtime.** The dynamic runtime provides the necessary support to enable compilation for dynamic, prototype-based languages. This includes dynamic values, objects, types, and hidden classes.

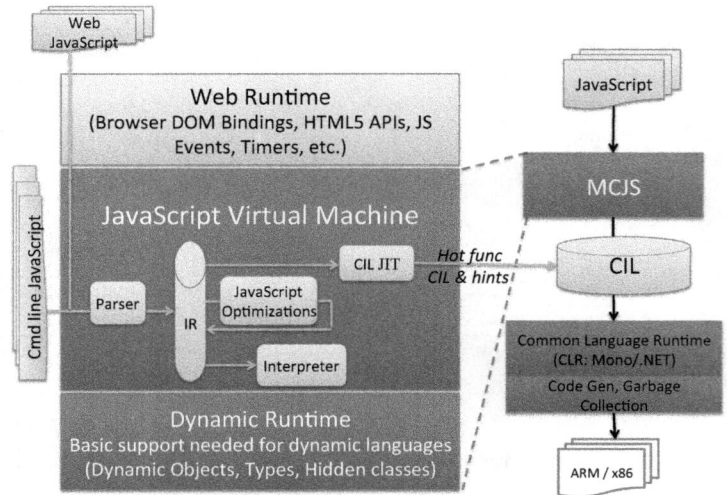

Figure 1. MuscalietJS Architecture.

- **Web runtime.** The web runtime handles the integration with the browser. MuscalietJS was designed in concert with a browser architecture [?] to optimize the bindings between the browser and the engine. The web runtime understands the semantics of the DOM and implements DOM bindings as well as other browser-related services like events and timers.

Running the JavaScript engine inside another VM has performance implications. Our split design relies on JavaScript specific optimizations at the high-level to help mitigate the overhead of running on the CLR. The JavaScript engine code generator exploits advanced high-level techniques combined with type analysis and special hints to lead the low-level VM to generate high-quality optimized code. There are performance advantages to running on top of the CLR.

4. JavaScript Specific Optimizations

This section discusses JavaScript-specific optimizations applied to the input JavaScript code in the JavaScript runtime (JSR) and dynamic runtime (DR) components.

4.1 Parsing and IR Generation

The MuscalietJS engine uses a graph-based intermediate representation (IR) that describes JavaScript code using simple operations that are easy to analyze. The IR describes the flow of data through operations by placing edges in the graph between expressions that generate values (*Writers*) and expressions that use those values (*Users*). It also represents implicit operations like type conversions explicitly so that they can be taken into account during later phases. This simplifies the implementation of analyses like type inference. The interpreter, optimization passes, and code generator all operate using this IR.

We depart from common practice when constructing the IR. Rather than building a temporary abstract syntax tree (AST) which is then used to build the IR in a separate pass, the parser directly generates the IR. The structure of the IR is designed such that constructing it also performs some of analyses. For example, dataflow analysis is performed completely at parse time by connecting Writers and Users as they are constructed. We build a symbol table for each function and determine useful metadata like whether the function uses *eval* or closes over its environment. This has significant advantages in the context of a latency-sensitive system like a web browser: it reduces the number of passes, improves locality (since multiple passes are fused), and eliminates the overhead of constructing temporary AST nodes that will later be discarded. The disadvantage is the complexity involved in implementing the semantic actions of the parser. To address it, we separate the parser's view of the IR from that of the *IR factory* which constructs the IR nodes. From the parser's perspective, we maintain the illusion that we are building an AST that follows the structure of the EC-MAScript 5 [7] grammar very closely, by tagging the real IR node classes with empty interfaces corresponding to non-terminals in the grammar. These interfaces have no effect at runtime, but they provide static type-level constraints that make it easier to ensure the parser behaves correctly when constructing the IR graph. They also hide the complexity of the underlying graph nodes by presenting the parser with a simple, uniform interface. The IR factory, meanwhile, works with the concrete IR node types, and does not concern itself with the structure of the grammar at all.

Since there is such an impedance mismatch between the grammar and the IR, we cannot always hide the truth from the parser perfectly. However, by obeying two requirements when designing the IR and the factory code that constructs it, we were able to isolate these issues to a few small parts in the parser. One requirement was that the IR could be constructed in a recursive fashion, matching the parser's algorithmic structure. This was fundamentally needed to allow the construction of the IR without using a separate pass. We also needed to allow the parser to backtrack in certain circumstances. To support this, we required that the IR factory act only on local state stored within the IR nodes themselves, so that IR subgraphs could be thrown away without corrupting global data structures. The combination of these constraints also has another advantage: the designs of the parser and the IR factory lend themselves nicely to parallelism. We leave further exploration of that approach for future work. Once the IR for a parsed function is created, it can be used by the interpreter to run the function or by the CIL JIT engine to apply type optimizations and eventually generate optimized code.

4.2 Adaptive Function-level Execution

To achieve adaptability and performance, traditional JavaScript engines support different modes of execution (interpretation,

basic JIT and advanced JIT with specialization) at function granularity. For example, V8 first quickly generates an unoptimized version of the code for each function. After a certain number of executions a trampoline code section replaces the code pointer with a runtime function that generates a heavily optimized version of the code. The code pointer is then changed to point to the optimized code. It remains in this state unless the assumptions made during optimization prove false, in which case a *deoptimization* happens which restores the unoptimized code.

Providing this type of dynamic code adjustment (especially across the runtime function and JITed code) requires access to stack frames, control over stack semantics, and sometimes support for self-modifying code. This is hard to achieve in a layered design given the restrictions imposed by host VMs like the CLR. We therefore take a different approach to achieve the same degree of adaptability. Each JavaScript function object in MuscalietJS has a *codePtr*: a function pointer (C# delegate) that takes as its only argument a *CallFrame* object. The CallFrame includes a reference to the function object for that function as well as the actual input arguments and their types. A codePtr can point to different runtime functions that manage the execution and optimization of the function, or to different JITed specializations of the function. Each JavaScript function object also stores *function metadata*, which includes the current compilation state of the function (parse, analyze, JIT, specialized JIT), the IR graph of the function, and a code cache to store the function's JITed CIL code. The *codePtr* of a JavaScript function can point to one of the following functions:

- **FirstExecute (runtime function):** When the JavaScript function is called by the JavaScript code for the first time, this function performs pre-JIT analysis and the initialization of the JIT code cache for that function. At the end, the codePtr is changed to point to another runtime function responsible for normal execution.

- **NormalExecute (runtime):** Depending on the status of the JavaScript function, the normal execution function either calls the interpreter (for "cold" functions) or JITs the function at one of several optimization settings.

- **Interpret:** The interpreter executes the function by traversing its IR graph and calling runtime functions that implement operations, property lookup, and other JavaScript semantics.

- **CIL JITed code:** For hot functions, normal execution starts the JIT to generate a specialized version of the function for the current arguments' types. The generated code will be added to the code cache and *codePtr* will be updated to point to it.

Tight coupling between the target and host runtime allows low overhead switching between interpreter and JIT code similar to traditional monolithic runtimes.

4.3 Type Analysis

Advanced monolithic engines employ type analysis to JIT efficient code for hot functions. MuscalietJS also implements an advanced type analysis by combining type feedback and type inference before JITing optimized code for hot functions. An initial type inference pass is first applied to reduce type feedback overhead by enabling more intelligent placement of profiling hooks. After profiling, when a hot function is detected in the next invocation of that function, a second type inference pass uses the profiling type information to infer the types of most variables or expressions in the function.

MuscalietJS supports type signature-based method dispatch for JavaScript. The basic concept is to dynamically generate different JITed implementations of the same function, each specialized for one observed signature [4], i.e. the types of the function's arguments for a particular invocation. At each invocation of the method the current signature is used to dispatch to an appropriate implementation. The type analysis and signature-based method dispatch algorithm used by MuscalietJS is similar to the type inference and analysis explained in [11].

4.4 Property Lookup

As in any dynamic runtime, the way objects and their fields are stored in memory affects the performance and efficiency of the memory allocation and object and field accesses [3]. In monolithic engines such as V8 [9], object layouts are complex and tightly coupled to the garbage collector, imposing a huge burden on extending the engine with new object types and features. For JavaScript, engines also have an internal data structure representing the implicit class of each object at a given point during execution, known as a *hidden class* or *map*. The hidden class of an object can change at any point given the dynamic nature of the language. This affects the way optimizing compilers generate efficient JITed code, and the JIT must take this layout into account in order to provide efficient property lookups using low-level optimizations such as inline caches. In MuscalietJS, both JavaScript objects and their hidden classes are normal CIL objects. Adding new features is easy, since it requires no translation between layers. This extensibility does not come at the cost of speed; the MuscalietJS representation is capable of fast property lookups using techniques like multi-level caching and property propagation. The same lookup mechanism is used directly by the interpreter and the JIT engine in the JSR.

MuscalietJS employs a data structure for representing hidden classes that is customized for prototype-based languages. In such languages, objects act as multi-level dictionary, where each level adds or replaces properties and inherits the rest from another object, its *prototype*. Since an object may both be a prototype and have a prototype of its own, a *prototype chain* is formed. The prototype chain is highly dynamic in nature because any of the objects forming

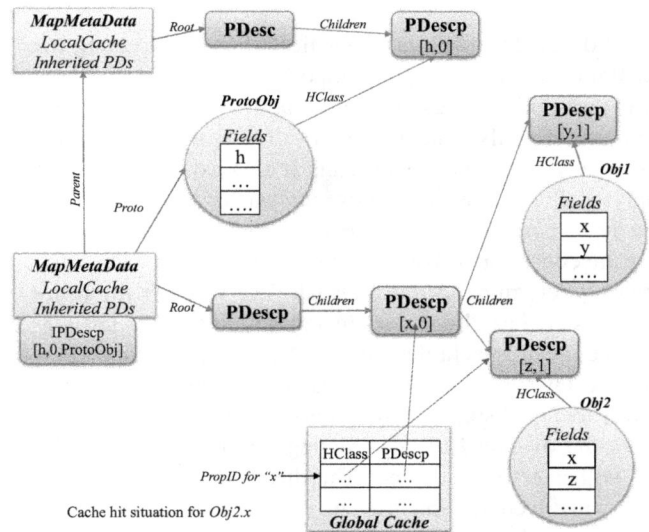

Figure 2. Property description data structure for representing hidden classes (maps) in MuscalietJS DR.

the chain may be changed at any time. To address the challenge of inferring hidden classes from these chains of objects at runtime, we use a data structure with a tree of *property descriptors* at each level of inheritance or *prototype depth*. Each node in the tree represents an *owned* property – that is, a property which is set directly on the object rather than being inherited. Each property descriptor includes the property name and the offset at which the corresponding field is stored in the objects that share this prototype. Every path from a node to the root of the tree represents the fields of an object in the order they were added. Each node thus corresponds to a particular hidden class, shared by all objects whose fields were constructed in the same manner. This data structure makes it easy to keep the inferred hidden class of an object up to date as properties are added at runtime. The root of the tree has no property info. Therefore, the root node alone represents any object with no properties of its own. Note that such an object may still inherit properties from its prototype chain.

All of the property descriptors in a tree share a *map metadata* structure that includes a reference to the prototype object, a list of properties inherited through the prototype, and a cache for recently accessed property descriptors. Figure 2 shows an example of the two-level map data structure used by MuscalietJS for managing dynamic objects and properties. In this particular example, the prototype has one field called *"h"*. Objects *Obj1* and *Obj2* inherit *"h"* from that prototype and add { *"x"*, *"y"* } and {*"x"*, *"z"*}, respectively as sets of owned fields stored directly on each object.

Slow Path Lookup: The default process for looking up a property name in an object (e.g. *obj1.x* in Figure 2) includes walking the tree of property descriptors, starting at the node corresponding to the hidden class (map) of the object and continuing towards the root of the tree. If a property descriptor with the desired property name is found, the value is retrieved from the field at the corresponding offset in the object. Otherwise, the search is continued on the next object in the prototype chain. For instance, looking up *obj1.h* in Figure 2 will cause the property descriptors to be walked starting from *Obj1* until the root property descriptor is reached. Since the property won't be found, this will be followed recursively by a walk of *ProtoObj*'s property descriptors (since *ProtoObj* is the prototype of *Obj1*), eventually reaching the property descriptor for *"h"*. To reduce the cost of future lookups, when a lookup on an object results in an inherited property being found, an *inherited property descriptor* is added to the map metadata structure at the object's prototype depth. The inherited property descriptor indicates the prototype object that owns the property and the offset of the corresponding field in the prototype object.

Fast Path Lookup: MuscalietJS employs two levels of caching to speed up the property lookup process: a global cache shared between all hidden classes and objects and a cache at the map metadata level. For faster lookups in these caches, the MuscalietJS runtime globally assigns an integer ID (called a *propID*) to each statically known string property name and manages the propIDs during code generation and use these IDs to access these caches for known property names. The global cache is a small array, indexed by the low-order bits of the propID, that contains tuples composed of a hidden class (identified by a node in the tree of property descriptors) and the last property descriptor retrieved for that propID. If the looked up hidden class matches the hidden class of the object on which we are performing the lookup, then the property descriptor is still correct and can be used to access the corresponding value. A global cache hit for *Obj2.x* (or any other object with the same hidden class accessing property *"x"*) is shown in Figure 2. If there is no hit in the global cache, we check a second-level cache associated with the map metadata of that object (for example the cache in *Obj1.HClass.MapMetadata* for Obj1 in the example). This map metadata local cache similarly maps a property name to the last property descriptor matched for that name and the hidden class the match was for. While slower, this cache achieves better locality than the global cache given that it is limited to the hidden classes associated with a particular map metadata.

If the propID cannot be obtained for a property statically, the generated code bypasses the cache and uses the runtime property name as a string through the slow lookup path. Using these compile time assigned propIDs, the caching overhead is significantly reduced. Some engines, such as V8 [9], use transient maps for representing hidden classes and use inline caches for fast property lookup and requires deoptimization in case of inline cache miss. MuscalietJS's hidden class model requires a tree walk for cache misses and is amenable to property caching at the runtime level.

Also it uses two levels of caching and the results in Section 6 report good hit rates for different types of workloads using this mechanism.

5. CIL Code Generation for Hot Functions

In JavaScript, most operations are dynamically defined depending on the types of their operands. For example, a property load operation such as *object.a* can turn into a direct field access in *object*, a field access in *object*'s prototype chain, a call to a getter function call, or a call back to a browser function. A binary addition can translate to integer or double addition, a string concatenation or a complicated user-defined conversion on operands followed by a numerical addition or a concatenation, depending on the value types of the operands.

Given the heavy use of the dynamic operations in JavaScript (and most other dynamic languages), generating efficient code based on the inferred or profiled types is very important when JITing code for hot functions. With the large number of variants for each of these operations, producing low-level code for all of the variants, as is done in traditional engines, is challenging and hard to debug. MuscalietJS exploits the rich features of the host engine such as reflection and special code-generation hints to JIT efficient code while maintaining scalability and debuggability. This section discusses how MuscalietJS performs code generation for operations in hot functions.

5.1 Operation Implementation

Initially, we generated the CIL bytecode implementing each operation manually; there were many variations depending on the operand type information extracted during type inference. However, this approach is very tedious and hard to maintain because the relationships between the input and output types of the operations and their corresponding implementations were separated and implicitly captured in multiple places, including the type inference and JIT algorithms. Debugging was also very difficult.

To address these problems, we created an operation database. This is essentially a series of overloaded functions, each implementing one particular instance of an operation's behavior. During type inference, we use reflection to map operand types (function argument types) to operation result types (function return value types). During JIT we again use reflection to look up the appropriate operation implementation function based on the types of the operand and simply generate a call to that function. Figure 3 (B) shows a simplified code for binary addition operator for three of the possible many cases including *(Int, Int)*, *(Undefined, Bool)* and *(Bool, Float)* in the MuscalietJS operation code database.

This approach produces very robust, maintainable, and easy to debug code. Since we use reflection to take advantage of the overloading functionality of the host language, we do not even need to generate lookup code. By assigning proper CIL method attributes to these operator implementa-

```
/**** (A) CodeGen for binary operations ***********/
Visit(BinaryExp node, OpCache operation)
{
    var ltype = Visit(node.Left);
    var rypet = Visit(node.Right);
    /* Using reflection to extract the expected type and call*/
    var methodInfo = operation.Get(ltype, rtype);
    var resultType = operation.ReturnType(ltype, rtype);
    GenerateCall(methodInfo, resultType);
}

/**** (B) Addition operation ***********/
public static class Add
{
    ...
    [MethodImplAttribute(MethodImplOptions.AggressiveInlining)]
    public static float Run(bool i0, float i1)
    { return Run((float)Convert.ToNumber.Run(i0), i1); }
    ...
    [MethodImplAttribute(MethodImplOptions.AggressiveInlining)]
    public static double Run(mdr.DUndefined i0, bool i1)
    { return double.NaN; }
    ...
    [MethodImplAttribute(MethodImplOptions.AggressiveInlining)]
    public static int Run(int i0, int i1) { return i0 + i1); }
    ...
}
```

Figure 3. CodeGeneration (JIT) code for binary operation IR nodes (A) and *Addition* operation implementation (B).

tion functions, the runtime is forced to inline them, and the compiled code achieves the same performance as the previous manually-generated CIL bytecode implementation. We developed a template-based code generator to generate most of the C# code for the various possible implementations of each operation, and used the "partial classes" feature of the C# language to manually implement the corner cases and integrate them with the rest of the auto-generated code.

5.2 CIL Code Generation

The MuscalietJS code generator (JIT engine) traverses the IR of the function being JITed and uses information added to the IR during type inference or other pre-JIT phases to generate efficient CIL code. This section discusses some of the techniques used by the engine and how it interacts with the low-level VM to achieve high performance.

The engine generates CIL for JavaScript code using the CLR's reflection API. The various JavaScript-level expressions are implemented by generating calls to appropriate operation functions specialized for the inferred types of their operands as shown in Figure 3. To show how our code generator uses operand types and hints to the low-level VM to help the underlying platform generate efficient code, Figure 4 illustrates: (A) a sample JavaScript function, (B) its corresponding CIL code generated by MuscalietJS and, (C) the x86 code generated by the low-level engine. The call to the `doublePlusOne` function shown in the figure passes an *Int* value (a) as argument, and the literals in the function are all integer constants. Therefore, the type inference pass infers the type of the operands to both the multipli-

```
/********* (A) JavaScript Source ***********/
function doublePlusOne(a)
{
    return 2 * a + 1;
}
doublePlusOne(20)
...........
/*** (B) Generated CIL code for doublePlusOne ***/
...........
0.0 ldarg.0 ;loading call frame
1.1 ldflda ;loading arg0 in callframe (a)
2.1 call Int32 DValue:AsInt32 () ;unboxing arg0
2.2 stloc.1
3.0 ldarg.0
4.0 ldflda
5.1 ldc.i4 2
5.2 ldloc.1
5.3 call Int32 Binary.Mul:Run (Int32, Int32)
6.1 ldc.i4 1
6.2 call Int32 Binary.Add:Run (Int32, Int32)
7.0 call Void DValue:Set (Int32) ;boxing for return
...........
/*** (C) x86 assembly code generated by mono ***/
...........
0 addl $0x10,%esp
1 leal 0x34(%edi),%eax ;load arg0 (a)
2 movl 0x04(%eax),%ecx
3 movl %ecx,0xf4(%ebp)
4 leal 0x0c(%edi),%eax
5 shll %ecx ;inlined/optimized integer multiply
6 incl %ecx ;inlined/optimized integer addition
7 movl %ecx,0x04(%eax) ; boxing for return
8 movl $0x00000009,(%eax)
9 leal 0xfc(%ebp),%esp
```

Figure 4. JITed CIL and assembly for a sample code.

cation and addition operations to be *Int*. During JIT compilation, as shown in Figure 3, the JIT engine uses reflection to look up the multiplication and addition functions for *(Int, Int)* operands. The resulting functions, which are called in the JITed code (CIL lines 5.3 and 6.2), are the basic integer addition and multiply functions `Binary.Mul:Run` and `Binary.Add:Run`, which are implemented in terms of CIL-level primitive operations. Since these functions return *Int* as well, the intermediate value passing the multiplication result to the addition operation is inferred to be an *Int* as well, and so it does not generate any boxing or unboxing operations. All the operations in the function are pure integer operations except the unboxing of the function argument read from the call frame (CIL line 2.1) and the boxing for the return (CIL line 7.0).

When the low-level VM sees this specialized version of `doublePlusOne`, it is guaranteed to inline the calls to `Binary.Mul:Run`, `Binary.Add:Run`, and the runtime functions that handle boxing, because we annotate them with CIL attributes that require this behavior (*AggressiveInlining*). After inlining, the calls are replaced with simple integer + and * operations. The low-level VM then applies other optimizations such as dead code elimination, register allocation, and constant folding on the resulting code. Finally, optimized code is generated for the target hardware architecture. For example, as shown in Figure 4, the x86 generated code implements the multiplication and addition operations in the original JavaScript function with a `shift left` instruction and an `increment` instruction.

We implement property access expressions (the . operator) at the JavaScript level with calls to the property lookup runtime operation discussed in Subsection 4.4. These calls are also inlined by the low-level VM. For indexing operations (the `[]` operator), MuscalietJS performs special optimizations: if the inferred type of the expression that is being indexed is *Array*, and the indexing expression's inferred type is *Int*, then we can skip the property lookup code and cache accesses. Instead, the engine generates a simple array access, using the integer to directly index the internal CIL-level array used to implement the array object.

In traditional JavaScript engines, calls to runtime functions from the JITed code is usually very costly, given that the runtime is unmanaged while the JITed code exists in a managed environment. The primary source of overhead is the difference in stack frame models between the two environments. In the MuscalietJS runtime, however, JavaScript objects, the runtime, calls to operations, boxing and unboxing, and JITed code all exist in the same managed world and so communication between them has essentially no overhead. As shown, MuscalietJS effectively exploits this low-overhead during CIL code generation for hot functions.

5.3 Special Hints

Through significant profiling and evaluation of the Mono and .NET VMs, we designed a set of hints that can be passed to the low-level VM to significantly improve the generated code in a layered architecture like MuscalietJS. Most of these hints can be provided as per-value or function attributes passed to the runtime once. We were able to implement some of these features in the Mono runtime:

- **Avoiding array bound check for property access operations:** MuscalietJS can guarantee the validity of the length of the property array in the objects through hidden classes, so the low-level code that would be generated by the low-level .NET VM for those checks is redundant.

- **Avoiding object zero initialization for JavaScript objects created by MuscalietJS:** MuscalietJS explicitly sets the fields of JavaScript objects after creating them in JITed CIL codes.

- **Avoiding IL validation security checks for CIL code emitted by MuscalietJS:** We found that the Microsoft .NET runtime [6] spends a huge amount of time on security validation of our JITed CIL code. Our profiling shows that with .NET, Sunspider benchmarks are slowed on average by $2\times$ (and sometimes as much as $5\times$) because of the JIT method access check done on every invocation of MuscalietJS generated code for hot methods. This is observed in the .NET runtime, but we did not observe this issue with the Mono runtime [12]. This security check is redundant because MuscalietJS performs code validation for type safety during code generation. We were not able to fix

this issue and so could not fully evaluate MuscalietJS on .NET. Having a selective IL validation check can improve the code quality of layered designs such as MuscalietJS.

- **Allowing on-stack replacement (OSR) between two CIL emitted methods:** As MuscalietJS employs type profiles as well as type inference, it sometimes generates speculative code protected by guards. As a result, it needs support for deoptimization and jumps back to the interpreter if the guard condition is violated. Switching contexts between the optimized method and the interpreter and continuing execution is a challenging task given the current limitations of the CIL stack machine. Since both Mono and .NET internally support OSR, having high-level access to that feature would have simplified the implementation of such a deoptimizer.

6. Evaluation

We evaluated MuscalietJS against three existing JavaScript engines: Rhino [16] and IronJS [10], which both have layered architectures (one running on top of JVM and the other one on top of .NET DLR) similar in some respects to MuscalietJS (MuscalietJS performs many more high-level JavaScript-specific type analysis and optimizations), and V8 [9], which is a state-of-the-art native engine. We were not able to evaluate against SPUR [1] as SPUR is not publicly available. We used the latest release of each engine as of this writing: Rhino v1.7, and IronJS v0.2.0.1. Our engine, MuscalietJS v0.9, and IronJS run on top of Mono 2.10. All experiments were carried out on a 2.80GHz Intel Core i7 machine with 8 GB of RAM, running Ubuntu 11.04.

Table 2. JavaScript Engines Configurations.

Name	Description
MCJS_I	MuscalietJS interpreter only
MCJS_J	MuscalietJS JIT
MCJS_J+	MuscalietJS JIT + type inference/specialization and array optimization
MCJS_IJ	MuscalietJS interpreter/JIT for cold/hot functions
Rhino_I	Rhino interpreter only
Rhino_C	Rhino basic compiler (-O 0)
Rhino_C+	Rhino compiler with maximum optimizations (-O 9)
IronJS	IronJS translates to DLR expression trees, DLR performs dynamic optimizations

Our test configurations are described in Table 2. Note that Rhino does not JIT code on a per-function basis as MuscalietJS does; instead, depending on its configuration, it is either a pure interpreter or a pure AOT compiler. To reduce variation, we run each benchmark four times on each engine and average the execution times. For the results, we measured confidence intervals of 1%, 2%, 5%, and 2% for V8, Rhino, IronJS, and MuscalietJS, respectively.

Benchmark Selection: Selecting the right set of benchmarks across all platforms and configuration was challenging. Rhino and IronJS fail to execute JSBench [17] benchmarks and several Octane benchmarks require typed arrays

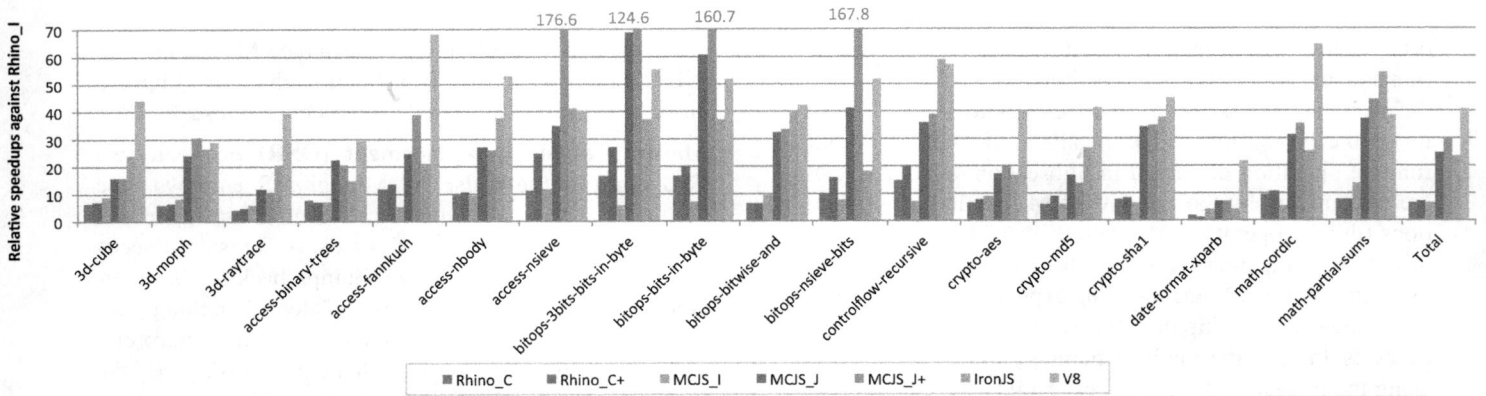

Figure 5. Relative speedups against Rhino_I for Sunspider benchmarks.

not yet supported by MCJS. We present results for the Sunspider and V8 benchmark suites. We run each test in loop 4 times to increase the running time and improve the confidence of our results.

In addition we want to capture workloads that are characteristic of web page loading, in which large amounts of JavaScript code are downloaded, but only small portions are executed most of the time, and these portions are usually only executed once [15]. To evaluate these types of workloads, we generate a set of benchmarks using a record-and-replay mechanism. For a given web page, we record the process of loading the web page in the browser. Then, our benchmark generation tool reconstructs all the JavaScript code locally, modeling the DOM-based interaction between the browser and the JavaScript engine as follows: prefix each script with additional code that initializes a simulated DOM tree represented by a tree of JavaScript objects, each of which has the same properties that were read from their real counterparts during execution. The performance overhead introduced by the simulated DOM tree is similar to the browser-integration, as the JavaScript side of the DOM bindings also wraps native objects and accesses them in the managed JavaScript heap.

6.1 Traditional Benchmarks

Figure 5 presents average execution time for the Sunspider benchmark suite on the configurations of MuscalietJS, Rhino, and IronJS listed in Table 2. The last column (*total*) shows the total Sunspider score speedup, also relative to the Rhino interpreter. A few benchmarks crash on IronJS running with Mono; therefore we present 18 benchmarks running correctly on all platforms. The IJ and IJ+ results for MuscalietJS are very close to I and J+ so the table does not include them. On Sunspider, the MuscalietJS interpreter (I) performs close to the Rhino AOT compiler (C). The MuscalietJS JIT (J) improves performance over the MuscalietJS interpreter by a factor of 2 to 3, and delivers almost 3× the performance of the Rhino AOT compiler at its maximum optimization level (C+), despite the overhead of JIT-ing code at runtime. This is slightly higher than the speedups

achieved by IronJS using .NET DLR. This is not surprising, since we implemented hidden classes and property lookup directly in the managed runtime using its internal data structures. In addition, when we enable JavaScript-specific type optimizations, such as array optimization and type analysis (J+), MuscalietJS outperforms IronJS (1.3× on average up to 4× on some benchmarks such as access-nsieve). The speed ups over Rhino_C+ is about 4×. These significant speedups emphasize the effectiveness of our JavaScript-specific optimizations such as property lookup, array optimizations and type analysis. On average MCJS_J+ achieves about 75% of the speed of the V8 engine on Sunspider benchmarks, which is by far the highest reported performance for a layered engine.

Table 3. Speedups vs. Rhino_I for V8 benchmarks.

Benchmark	Rhino		MCJS			IronJS
	C	C+	I	J	J+	
deltablue	3.05	2.69	1.37	2.50	3.78	1.53
navier-stokes	5.43	7.93	1.42	5.84	10.62	4.20
regex	1.22	1.19	0.56	0.59	0.58	0.58
richards	2.17	2.20	1.55	3.05	3.09	1.90
splay	2.50	2.40	1.25	1.49	1.48	2.10
Average	2.88	3.28	1.23	2.69	3.91	2.06

Table 3 presents average execution time for a subset of the V8 benchmark suite that runs on all of MuscalietJS, Rhino, and IronJS configurations. Rhino AOT compiler performs very well, achieving an average speed up of 3.8 compared to Rhino interpreter, since for these long-running benchmarks, the compilation time is negligible and several static optimizations pay off. On the other hand, the MuscalietJS optimizing CIL compiler, relies on JavaScript-specific optimizations and outperform both IronJS and Rhino best configurations. On average, the best MuscalietJS configuration (MCJS_J+) outperforms the IronJS and Rhino best configurations by about 2× and 1.2×, respectively. The two slow benchmarks for MuscalietJS are *Splay* and *Regex*. *Splay* stresses garbage collector and the slowdown can be related

```
function nsieve(m, isPrime) {
  var i, k, count;
  for (i=2; i<=m; i++) { isPrime[i] = true; }
  count = 0;
  for (i=2; i<=m; i++){
    if (isPrime[i]) {
      for (k=i+i; k<=m; k+=i) isPrime[k] = false;
      count++;
    }
  }
  return count;
}
function sieve() {
  for (var i = 1; i <= 3; i++ ) {
    var m = (1<<i)*10000;
    var flags = Array(m+1);
    nsieve(m, flags);
  }
}
sieve();
```

Figure 6. *access-nsieve* sunspider benchmark.

to the Mono garbage collection mechanism and changing the garbage collection mechanism can potentially improve the results. *Regex* on the other hand, runs in .NET regex operations most of the time, and these have not been optimized for performance.

Speedup contributions breakdown: There are two factors contributing to speedups: JavaScript optimizations and hints to low-level VM. Figure 5 shows MCJS_J+ speeding up Sunspider benchmarks about 4.7× compared to the interpreted execution (29.71/6.37). 75% of this speedup is due to MuscalietJS CIL code generation boosted by array optimization, type analysis and function specialization combined with our operation implementation and property lookup. The additional 25% of the speedup is due to our special hints passed to the Mono runtime (Section 5.3).

Individual Benchmark Analysis: Figure 5 also provides details on the execution time of each benchmark in the Sunspider suite, normalized against the execution time of the same benchmarks on the Rhino interpreter. The benefit for type inference and array optimization (J+) for benchmarks like *access-nsieve*, *bitops-bit-in-bytes*, and *bitops-nsieve-bits* is very significant – 3 to 4× compared to the standard MuscalietJS JIT, which is already optimized. These benchmarks make heavy use of arrays, and the combination of type analysis and signature-based specialization makes very effective array optimizations possible.

Figure 6 shows part of the *access-nsieve* benchmark source code. In function *nsieve*, the argument *isPrime* is indexed several times in multiple loops. The standard MuscalietJS JIT converts *isPrime* accesses such as *isPrime[k]* into direct calls to property lookup functions; these require accesses to the global property cache and indirection through property descriptors (explained in Section 4.4) before finally loading the value in the internal array of the *isPrime Array* object. Applying static type analysis on this function in isolation is not enough to infer the type of *isPrime*, *k*, and *i* correctly because *isPrime* is an argument, and the values

of *k* and *i* depend on another argument *m*. Instead, with signature-based function dispatch enabled, the first hot execution of the function *nsieve* triggers type inference based on the runtime types of the actual arguments, *m* and *flags*, which are passed in from the *sieve* function. The algorithm determines that *m* and *isPrime* are of type *Int* and *Array*, respectively. As a result, the type of *i* and *k* are inferred to be *Int*. This allows all accesses to *isPrime* to be converted to direct array accesses, which speeds up the algorithm significantly. For this simple example, inlining the internal function and then applying a range-based flow-sensitive type analysis may achieve similar results. However, such an analysis cannot always infer the types given the dynamism in the language, and even when it can it may need to generate extra guards in the JITed code. This type of analysis can also be expensive for long scripts. MuscalietJS is able to exploit dynamic types of arguments to provide effective optimizations using a simple, fast type inference algorithm.

For a few of the benchmarks, such as *date-format-xparb*, the speedups are not significant. Our investigation shows that these benchmarks spend a high portion of their time in JavaScript builtin functions, some of which are not implemented very efficiently in MuscalietJS. We are redesigning those builtins to improve performance and to allow them to be optimized along with the rest of the JITed code.

6.2 Web Replay Benchmarks

Table 4. Speedup vs. Rhino_I for WebReplay benchmarks.

Benchmark	Rhino		MCJS			
	C	C+	I	IJ	J	J+
BBC	0.79	0.74	1.62	0.60	0.60	0.60
Yahoo	0.99	0.99	3.36	1.67	1.29	1.24
Google	0.98	0.95	3.98	2.18	0.62	0.60
Wikipedia	0.70	0.70	2.03	1.81	0.69	0.67
Mozilla	1.01	0.95	2.08	1.61	0.64	0.62
Amazon	0.99	0.96	2.12	1.83	0.60	0.60

This section presents the results for 6 web replay benchmarks, which are based on the page load behavior of six popular websites: *BBC*, *Yahoo*, *Google*, *Wikipedia*, *Mozilla*, and *Amazon*. IronJS does not support this benchmark as it only supports ECMA3, but the other evaluated engines support ECMA5 [7]. These page load benchmarks involve large JavaScript codes, but most of the code is not executed, and most code that is executed is only run once [15]. This means that JITing can account for a significant portion of overall execution time and result in major slowdown, and our results bear this out. Table 4 presents the speedups we measured for each configuration, normalized against the performance of the Rhino interpreter. For these benchmarks, Rhino performs better with just the interpreter than when using the AOT compiler at any optimization level. Similarly, MuscalietJS's interpreter (I) outperforms its JIT compiler (J and

J+). The MuscalietJS interpreter also outperforms the Rhino interpreter by a factor of up to 3.98 (2.53× on average).

6.3 Effectiveness of Property Lookup Operations

To study the difference between these workloads and measure the effectiveness of the property lookup algorithm used by MuscalietJS, Table 5 reports the hit rate of our global property lookup cache (Section 4.4) and also percentage of inherited properties. For the traditional benchmarks, nearly 90% of property lookups hit in the global cache. Although not shown here, the hit rate for the second-level local property lookup caches is also very high for these benchmarks. However, for the web replay benchmarks less than half of the lookups could be found in the global cache. This reflects the fact that during page load, not only is execution time distributed across many more functions than in the data processing benchmarks, but data access patterns are also distributed across a much larger set of properties. Another interesting point here is that even for web non-repetitive Web replay benchmarks, the property cache hit rate is more than 40% which mean for over 40% of property accesses in the MuscalietJS interpreter the slow path lookup is avoided; speeding up execution as shown in Table 4.

Table 5. MuscalietJS benchmark optimization statistics.

Benchmark	Global property cache hit	Percent of Inherited properties
Traditional	88.0%	33.6%
Web Replay	41.2%	33.4%

7. Conclusions

In this paper, we argue that JavaScript engines can be architected for performance without sacrificing other desirable properties. We presented a layered JavaScript engine, with a high-level runtime handling language-specific optimizations, relying on a low-level host virtual machine to provide runtime services and machine-specific optimizations. This layered architecture combined with general-purpose code-generation hints passed from the top-level VM to the .NET VM achieves significantly performance when compared to prior layered architectures. The layered approach lets us focus on language-level optimizations, while relying on the low-level VM for efficient code generation, and using host VM features like reflection to improve performance. We see significant value in this approach, and we believe this trend will continue for other languages. As existing low-level managed VMs like CLR continue to mature, there will be an incentive to expose APIs to some of their low-level features to ease the development of layered engines.

References

[1] M. Bebenita, F. Brandner, M. Fahndrich, F. Logozzo, W. Schulte, N. Tillmann, and H. Venter. SPUR: a trace-based JIT compiler for CIL. In *Proceedings of the ACM international conference on Object oriented programming systems languages and applications*, pages 708–725, Reno/Tahoe, Nevada, USA, 2010.

[2] J. Castanos, D. Edelsohn, K. Ishizaki, P. Nagpurkar, T. Nakatani, T. Ogasawara, and P. Wu. On the benefits and pitfalls of extending a statically typed language jit compiler for dynamic scripting languages. In *International Conference on Object Oriented Programming Systems Languages and Applications*, pages 195–212, Tucson, 2012.

[3] C. Chambers, J. Hennessy, and M. Linton. The design and implementation of the self compiler, an optimizing compiler for object-oriented programming languages. Technical report, Stanford University, Department of Computer Science, 1992.

[4] J. Dean, C. Chambers, and D. Grove. Selective specialization for object-oriented languages. In *ACM Conference on Programming Language Design and Implementation*, pages 93–102, La Jolla, 1995.

[5] Dynamic Language Runtime. http://msdn.microsoft.com/en-us/library/dd233052.aspx.

[6] .NET Framework. http://msdn.microsoft.com/en-us/vstudio/aa496123.aspx.

[7] ECMAScript. http://www.ecmascript.org/.

[8] A. Gal, B. Eich, M. Shaver, D. Anderson, D. Mandelin, M. R. Haghighat, B. Kaplan, G. Hoare, B. Zbarsky, J. Orendorff, J. Ruderman, E. W. Smith, R. Reitmaier, M. Bebenita, M. Chang, and M. Franz. Trace-based just-in-time type specialization for dynamic languages. In *ACM conference on Programming language design and implementation*, pages 465–478, Dublin, Ireland, 2009.

[9] Google Inc. V8 JavaScript virtual machine. http://code.google.com/p/v8/.

[10] IronJS. https://github.com/fholm/IronJS.

[11] M. N. Kedlaya, J. Roesch, B. Robatmili, M. Reshadi, and B. Hardekopf. Improved type specialization for dynamic scripting languages. In *Dynamic Languages Symposium*, pages 37–48, October 2013.

[12] Mono Project. http://www.mono-project.com.

[13] Nashorn JavaScript engine. http://openjdk.java.net/projects/nashorn.

[14] Node.js. http://nodejs.org.

[15] P. Ratanaworabhan, B. Livshits, and B. G. Zorn. Jsmeter: comparing the behavior of javascript benchmarks with real web applications. In *USENIX Conference on Web Application Development*, WebApps'10, pages 3–3, 2010.

[16] Rhino JavaScript engine. https://developer.mozilla.org/en-US/docs/Rhino.

[17] G. Richards, A. Gal, B. Eich, and J. Vitek. Automated construction of javascript benchmarks. In *ACM International Conference on Object Oriented Programming Systems Languages and Applications*, OOPSLA '11, pages 677–694, Portland, Oregon, USA, 2011.

[18] SpiderMonkey: Mozilla's JavaScript engine. https://developer.mozilla.org/en-US/docs/Mozilla/Projects/SpiderMonkey.

[19] ECMAScript typed arrays. http://www.khronos.org/registry/typedarray/specs/latest/.

[20] Typescript. http://www.typescriptlang.org/.

[21] ECMAScript web workers. http://www.whatwg.org/specs/web-apps/current-work/multipage/workers.html#workers.

A Fast Abstract Syntax Tree Interpreter for R

Tomas Kalibera   †Petr Maj   ‡Floreal Morandat   Jan Vitek

Purdue University   †ReactorLabs   ‡University of Bordeaux

Abstract

Dynamic languages have been gaining popularity to the point that their performance is starting to matter. The effort required to develop a production-quality, high-performance runtime is, however, staggering and the expertise required to do so is often out of reach of the community maintaining a particular language. Many domain specific languages remain stuck with naive implementations, as they are easy to write and simple to maintain for domain scientists. In this paper, we try to see how far one can push a naive implementation while remaining portable and not requiring expertise in compilers and runtime systems. We choose the R language, a dynamic language used in statistics, as the target of our experiment and adopt the simplest possible implementation strategy, one based on evaluation of abstract syntax trees. We build our interpreter on top of a Java virtual machine and use only facilities available to all Java programmers. We compare our results to other implementations of R.

Categories and Subject Descriptors   D.3.4 [*Programming Languages*]: Processors—interpreters, optimization; G.3 [*Probability and Statistics*]: statistical computing

Keywords   R language; specialization; lazy evaluation

1.   Introduction

Dynamic languages are gaining in popularity in many areas of science. Octave and R are perfect examples of widely adopted domain specific languages that were developed by scientists, chemical engineers and statisticians respectively. They are appealing because of their extensive libraries and support for exploratory programming. Yet, both are painfully slow and memory hungry; R programs can run hundreds of times slower than equivalent C code [10]. Inefficiencies sometime force end-users to rewrite their applications in more performant languages. This is clearly undesirable and could be mitigated by better language implementations. Unfortunately, as is often the case for community-supported languages, domain scientists lack the manpower to build a high-performance runtime and often also the skills to do so. Their expertise lies elsewhere, chemistry or statistics, they are language implementers by necessity, not by choice. Also, even if a high-performance runtime were to be handed to them, maintenance would likely prove to be a stumbling block.

We explore how far one can push simple implementation techniques – techniques that are portable and leverage widely deployed technologies – to obtain a performing language implementation. We aim to show that a relatively performant interpreter and runtime system can be obtained without requiring deep knowledge of compiler techniques. For concreteness, we have chosen to implement a subset of the R language and to restrict ourselves to an abstract syntax tree (AST) interpreter built on top of an off-the-shelf Java virtual machine (JVM). Choosing Java as an implementation language simplifies maintenance as it is type safe and provides a high-quality runtime that includes a garbage collector and a threading system. Relying on the JVM gives us portability across all supported architectures and operating systems, as well as some basic security guarantees. Of course this comes at a cost, writing an interpreter in a managed language is likely to be less efficient than in C as we only have limited access to memory and pay for Java's runtime safety checks. Furthermore, implementing R data types on top of Java objects can lead to less than optimal memory usage. These costs and benefits have to be balanced when evaluating the viability of the approach.

R was designed by Ihaka and Gentleman [8] based on the S language [2]. GNU-R is maintained by a core group of statisticians and is available under the GPL license [12]. R is extensible and widely extended, currently there are nearly 6,000 packages available from the CRAN[1] and Bioconductor[2] repositories. R is heavily used for data analysis, visualization, data mining, or machine learning in fields including biology, environmental research, economics and marketing. R has an estimated 2 million installed base [13].

VEE '14,   March 1–2, 2014, Salt Lake City, Utah, USA.
Copyright © 2014 ACM 978-1-4503-2764-0/14/03... $15.00.
http://dx.doi.org/10.1145/2576195.2576205

---

[1] http://cran.r-project.org   [2] http://www.bioconductor.org

For its first fifteen years or so, R was implemented as an AST interpreter. This was likely due to the fact that an AST interpreter is simple to write, portable, easy to maintain. In 2011, Luke Tierney added a bytecode interpreter to improve performance. For compatibility reasons, the AST interpreter was retained and users can switch between the two engines freely. Both interpreters (we will refer to them as GNUR-AST and GNUR-BC) are written in C. We will use the AST as our baseline for performance comparisons. With R programs that spend mostly time out of numerical libraries, bytecode is about 2x faster than the AST. For context, we also consider Renjin, a rewrite of the GNUR-AST in Java. Renjin is roughly 2x slower than the GNUR-AST. So, if speedups compose, one could expect that a Java AST interpreter should be roughly 4x slower than a hand-tuned C bytecode interpreter.

This paper introduces FastR v0.168, an AST interpreter for the R language written in Java and capable of running on any off-the-shelf JVM. FastR leverages the ANTLR parser generator and the Java runtime for garbage collection and runtime code generation; native code is invoked via the Java Native Interface. What makes the implementation stand out is the extensive use of runtime feedback to perform AST-specialization [17], data specialization, as well as data and code co-specialization. These techniques enable the program to optimize itself by in-place rewriting of AST-nodes. To this we added a number of interpreter optimization tricks. The result is an interpreter that runs roughly **5x** faster than GNUR-BC and about **8x** faster than GNUR-AST. The remainder of the paper will describe our implementation techniques and argue that they remain simple enough to be maintained and extended by domain experts.

2. The R language and its implementation

R is a dynamically-typed, lazy functional language with limited side-effects and support for computational reflection. The authoritative description of R is its source code [12].

Data types. R has few primitive data types, namely, `raw` (unsigned byte), `logical` (three-valued booleans), `integer` (signed 32-bit), `double`, `complex`, and `string`. Missing observations are denoted by `NA`. For integers, `NA` is the smallest integer representable, for doubles, one of the IEEE NaNs is used, and for logicals, `NA` is a special value. Integer overflow results in an `NA`. All values are vectors of zero or more data points of a base type. Values can have *attributes*, which are lists of name-value pairs that can be manipulated programmatically. Built-in attributes define dimensions, names, classes, etc. Operations are vectorized; they perform type conversions when values are not of the same type, and for vectors of different lengths, re-use elements of shorter vectors. R has several other data types including lists – polymorphic vectors capable of holding values of different types – closures, built-ins, language objects, and environments.

Functions. Functions are first class. They nest and have read/write access to their lexical environment. R also supports dynamic scoping with a global environment and package environments. Copy semantics provides the illusion of referential transparency; each assignment semantically creates a deep copy of the original value. An exception is environments, which are passed by reference. Functions may have formal arguments with default expressions. Arguments are matched by name, by unique prefix match on name, and as a last resort, by position. Arguments are evaluated lazily, using *promises*. Default expressions are packed in promises that evaluate in the called function while accessing data from the caller scope. Promises cache their results to avoid wasting computational resources and performing any included side-effects multiple times.

Meta-programming. Environments can be created synthetically and attached to the current variable search path or to closures. Reflection allows to change variable values, add new variables, or even remove variables from any environment unless the variables are locked. Code can be stored as a "language object", passed around and evaluated using `eval` in any environment. Language objects can also be created dynamically, e.g. by parsing a string.

Environment. R runs in a read-eval-print loop. R has about 700 built-in functions. R supports calling into native code, particularly with focus on C and Fortran. It interfaces with the BLAS and LAPACK numerical libraries and includes a modified version of LINPACK.

Interpreter. GNU-R is implemented in C and Fortran. GNU-R parses source code and generates an AST represented by lists of language objects. Evaluation follows the AST structure. Most nodes translate to function calls. Special functions, such as assignment, loops, or even braces, are dispatched to native C code that also evaluates argument expressions. Calls to closures are dispatched to evaluation of their bodies, with argument expressions packed into promises. The interpreter keeps a stack of execution contexts for stack traces in case of errors and for control flow operations such as loop break, continue, function return, or exception. Each execution context includes a target for C level non-local jump. Function environments are linked lists, where each element has a value slot and a symbol. Function environments are searched linearly whenever looking up a variable. Arguments are passed in heap-allocated lists of name/value pairs. Argument matching is done by reordering argument lists in three passes: for exact name matching, unique name prefix matching, and positional matching. Excessive copying is avoided through dynamic alias analysis (or bounded reference counting) — each value has a reference count 0 (temporary), 1 (bound to at most one variable), 2 (possibly bound to more than one variable). Vector update operations avoid copying when the reference count is at most 1. The reference count is never decremented and is not relevant for memory reclamation. GNU-R implements a non-moving generational mark-sweep collector with free-list based allocation.

3. Architecting a new R engine

FastR is a Java-based interpreter for a subset of the R language including most of the features of the language such as data types, functions, global environment, lazy evaluation, language objects, and eval. FastR is currently lacking support for packages and the different object systems implemented on top of R.

FastR is implemented in Java 7 and runs on any JVM. It relies on the ANTLR 3.4 to generate a Java parser. Mathematical operations are implemented by a mixture of Java and native code linked from GNU-R's library (mostly NMath and modified LINPACK), BLAS, LAPACK, and the system Math library. We use Javassist 3.18 to generate Java source code on the fly for operator fusion.

The current code base consists of 1358 classes, and 66KLoc (including comments and empty lines). The package structure is given in Figure 1; the majority of programming effort is split between data types (13KLoc), built-in functions (18KLoc) and basic operations (26KLoc in package r.nodes.exec). The ANTLR generated parser and lexer account for additional 10KLoc. In comparison, the core of GNU-R is 141KLoc of C code and the whole GNU-R code base goes up to 1.3MLoc.

R code can be entered at the console or input from a file. The parser creates a *parse tree* from source code. For execution, a more suitable kind of ASTs, called *executable trees*, is used. The conversion from parse trees to executable trees happens on demand, nodes lazily convert themselves whenever they are encountered during evaluation. Executable nodes retain a reference to their parse tree so as to produce user-friendly error messages. During execution, the interpreter continuously rewrites executable trees, selecting optimal implementations of operations based on runtime information available at each node. This form of *code specialization* is one of our key optimizations. FastR supports *data specialization* with multiple implementations of common data types optimized to take advantage of character-

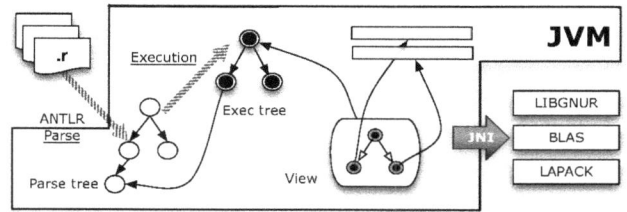

Figure 2. FastR Architecture. R code is turned into parse trees. As execution proceeds, parse trees are transformed into executable trees. Data is allocated in the Java heap and views are created to delay and bunch the execution of vector operations. Native code is accessed through JNI.

istics of the actual data. The other important optimization is the delayed evaluation of vector operations. FastR introduces *views* which perform *data and code co-specialization*. A view represents a vector operation that can be performed element-wise or in bulk and that can depend on other views, forming a *view tree*. Individual views in a view tree can also be fused together. Figure 2 summarizes the high-level architecture of the interpreter.

3.1 A traditional AST interpreter

FastR, at its core, has a naive abstract syntax tree interpreter that uses the native Java stack to store the execution state (a pointer to an executable node) and `Frame` objects to hold name-value bindings for arguments and local variables. Execution of a node boils down to calling that node's `execute()` method. Figure 3 shows an `If` node with children representing the condition and the true and false branches. The call to `executeScalarLogical` speculates that the condition evaluates to a scalar logical, as opposed to a vector or any other type, otherwise an exception is thrown and conversion or subseting is performed.

```
class If extends BaseR {
  RNode cond, tBr, fBr;
  Object execute(Frame frame) {
    int c;
    try {
      c = cond.executeScalarLogical(frame);
    } catch (SpecException e) { ... } //Recovery
    return (c==TRUE ? tBr:fBr).execute(frame);
} }
```

Figure 3. Sample executable node (simplified).

3.2 Data layout

Basic R data types are represented by Java objects in the most straightforward fashion. Classes `ComplexImpl`, `DoubleImpl`, `IntImpl`, `ListImpl`, `LogicalImpl`, `RawImpl`, `StringImpl` denote vectors of the corresponding base types. Each holds a Java array for the payload, an array of dimensions in case the vector is used as a matrix or n-dimensional matrix, a list of names, a set of attributes and an integer reference count. FastR has two other data types, `Closure` which

Package	# of files	# lines of code
r	8	1625
r.builtins	179	18715
r.data	20	4659
r.data.internal	28	8252
r.errors	2	1789
r.ext	3	110
r.ifc	1	172
r.nodes.ast	56	1794
r.nodes.exec	32	26113
r.nodes.tools	5	1880
r.runtime	7	1436

Figure 1. FastR package structure.

bundles a `Frame` with the attached code as executable node and `Language` which represents source code using AST tree and can be passed to eval.

4. FastR optimizations

We detail the optimizations applied to our base interpreter.

4.1 Pre-processing

The pre-processing step that translates parse trees into executable trees is an opportunity to perform optimizations. After profiling of our workloads, we identified three transformations as being profitable: *return elision*, *loop unrolling* and *variable numbering*.

Return elision. In R, `return` is a one-argument call which terminates execution of the current function and returns the argument to the function's caller. FastR implements it using a Java exception — `return` throws a pre-allocated singleton and the return value is stored in the `Frame`. The semantics of R specifies that, absent an explicit `return`, a function yields the value of the last expression evaluated. Thus, semantically, any function that has, as its last statement, a `return`, is equivalent to the same function without it.

Trailing `return`s are elided by a simple control-flow analysis and rewriting to deal with control flow patterns such as:

```
function(...) {                 function(...) {
  if (condition) {                if (condition) {
    ...                   ⟹         ...
    return(value)                   value
  }                               } else {
  rest                            rest
}                               } }
```

As `return` can be redefined by the user, FastR monitors redefinitions and rewrites the executable tree to implement the semantics of the non-optimized form.

Loop unrolling. The code specialization optimization that we will describe next requires a certain amount of stability in the code executed. We have observed that many loops must be evaluated once before they stabilize, i.e. the type information required for specialization be apparent to the interpreter. Consider a loop that performs double arithmetic on an integer vector. The first iteration of the loop will cause coercion of the vector and the change of type from integer to double will confuse the specialization optimization. To avoid this, all loops are unrolled once by rewriting loop nodes to special nodes that have two bodies. The first loop body runs for the first loop iteration, while the second runs for the following iterations. We have observed significant performance improvements after adding this optimization to `for` loops.

Variable numbering. R has baroque variable declaration and lookup rules which allow new variables to be injected into an existing environment. Thus, a naive implementation would implement an environment as a hash map of symbols to values (or a list of pairs), and the lookup would have to check all lexically enclosing environments up to the global scope, making variable access expensive. FastR attempts to speed up the common case when local variables are looked up and reflection is not employed.

Environments use different `Frame` classes: `GenericFrame` has an `Object[]` to hold values and 5 specialized `Frame` classes for environments of 0 to 4 variables hold their values in fields, avoiding the need for indirection through the array. A `FrameDescriptor` holds the names of frame's variables. Descriptors are shared across multiple invocations of a function, while each invocation has its own frame. Additional variables can be kept with their names in a `FrameExtension`, which can be either linear (values searched sequentially by name), or hashed. A frame extension is private to an invocation of a function.

To avoid hashing on local variable lookup, a simple static analysis runs at parse tree translation time. We collect a *write set* W of variables written to in each function. Each variable in W is assigned a unique number. This number is the index of the variable's value in the frame. Accessing a variable by index side steps hashing. A reflective operation may introduce a new variable to a frame: if a variable does not occur in W, it will be installed in the frame extension. The new variable may also shadow a variable defined in an enclosing environment. If this happens, the corresponding frame is marked dirty.

Reads are slightly tricky. For a non-reflective read of a variable in W, the variable's index in the frame can be used. If the variable is not in W of the current function, but is in W of some lexically enclosing function, its index and the number of hops required to get from the current frame to the target are recorded during the static analysis and are used to speed up the lookup. When performing a non-local read, the dirty bit of the frame that has the variable in W must be checked. If a dirty frame is encountered, then the interpreter reverts to the slower hashed lookup. A read must also check that the variable has indeed been defined, because entries in W include all possible variable declarations, some of which may be in branches not taken or not-yet-taken.

4.2 Code specialization

Specialization is used pervasively. As a program executes, its executable tree is continuously updated to leverage runtime information. Execution of a program represented by an executable tree P (or AST in systems that execute it directly) and a program state S proceeds stepwise. Evaluation of a node updates both program and state:

$$P, S \hookrightarrow P', S'$$

In practice, we restrict ourselves to local modifications of executable trees. Assume a tree with nodes $n_0, n_1, n_2 \ldots$ such that $n_0 \to n_1 \to \{n_2 \ldots\}$ ($\to$ denote the parent relationship). If the current node is n_1, we allow:

1. Replace node: $n_0 \to \mathbf{n} \to \{n_2 \ldots\}$.

2. Replace child: $n_0 \rightarrow n_1 \rightarrow \{\mathbf{n} \dots\}$.

3. Insert above: $n_0 \rightarrow \mathbf{n} \rightarrow n_1 \rightarrow \{n_2 \dots\}$.

Specializations are driven by runtime information with no inherent guarantee of soundness. Any rewriting may alter the meaning of the program to yield incorrect results when the node is encountered again. To prevent this, we perform *guarded* specialization. There are two kinds of guards: inline guards and watchpoints. Inline guards simply check that the predicate that was used to specialize a node holds when the node is evaluated again. Watchpoints can register node rewritings to be performed if a particular event occurs, such as redefinition of a symbol in the global scope. Inline guards can sometimes be replaced with watchpoints or elided. For instance, an `If` node is specialized on the assumption that the condition yields a scalar, non-`NA`, value; if the condition happens to be a call to, say, `is.na`, FastR infers that unless the built-in is redefined it will return either `TRUE` or `FALSE`. Thus, no guard is required, instead a watchpoint is registered for changes to `is.na`. If we further assume that changes to built-ins are disallowed, the check disappears entirely.

When a guard fails, a Java exception is thrown and the programmer must provide recovery code to rewrite the tree to a semantically meaningful version. Our implementation does not mandate convergence of rewritings. This can be the right behavior for code that processes different types at different stages in the program, but pathological cases are possible where a node keeps getting optimized only to be de-optimized right after. If this is a risk, programmers can choose to maintain a bound on rewriting any given node, which we do in FastR.

Dealing with recursion is tricky as a node may appear multiple times on the call stack. This can lead to an inconsistent tree rewrite. Consider the evaluation of $n \rightarrow \{\dots n_i \dots\}$ in function `f`. Rewriting n to n' can occur at any time, say after child n_i has been evaluated. If another instance of `f` is also in evaluating n, it may not realize that the node has been removed from the tree and it may try to perform a replacement itself. To prevent this, developers must check that a node is in the tree to execute it. When a node is kicked out of a tree, it retains a reference to its replacement node. Consider the `execute()` method of the `If` node. It checks if the current node has been replaced during evaluation of the condition node, and if so, proceeds with the replacement (Figure 4).

We have described the mechanics of specialization. But *what* and *when* should one specialize? The key for performance is choosing specializations with inexpensive guards and reducing the risk that hot code gets stuck in generic nodes. Careful profiling of workloads is necessary along with a deep understanding of the semantics of the language and its libraries. As to when to specialize, we sometimes create uninitialized nodes which have no other behavior than wait to see the shape of their arguments and immediately rewrite themselves. In other cases, we have generic nodes that im-

```
Object execute(Frame f) {
  int c;
  try {
    c = cond.executeScalarLogical(f);
  } catch (SpecializationException e) {
    return (replaced() ? replacement : this).
        executeWithFailedCond(f, e.getResult());
  }
  return (replaced() ?
    replacement : this).executeWithCond(f, c);
}
```

Figure 4. The `If` node's execute method.

plement the full, but slow, semantics of the operation, and rewrite themselves, after execution, to a more specific version. Lastly, some specializations are eager, speculating on likely values and properties of arguments.

Arithmetic. The `Arithmetic` class is one of the largest with close to 8KLoc; it contains nested classes that implement the `Add`, `Sub`, `Div`, `Mod`, `Mult`, and `Pow` operations for numeric data types. Figure 5 shows an extract of this class. This executable node has two fields for children and fields that describe the specific operation to be performed by the node. The `execute` method first evaluates both children, checking, each time, that the current node was not replaced. Equipped with values of subexpressions, a specialized version of the node is constructed. The `SpecializedConst` class is used if one of the arguments was a constant expression. This class specializes the evaluation by hard-wiring a constant. The node is then replaced and the `execute` method of the specialized node is invoked to perform the actual computation. From that point on, the specialized node will be called directly.

```
class Arithmetic extends BaseR {
  RNode l, r; ValArit arit;

  Object execute(Frame f, ASTNode src) {
    Object lx = l.execute(f);
    if (replaced())
      return replacement.execute(f, lx, src);
    Object rx = r.execute(f);
    if (replaced())
      return replacement.execute(lx, rx, src);
    Arithmetic s = (l instanceof Constant
    || r instanceof Constant) ?
      SpecializedConst.mk(lx, rx, src, l, r, arit) :
      Specialized.mk(lx, rx, src, l, r, arit);
    return replace(s).execute(lx, rx, src);
} }
```

Figure 5. The `Arithmetic` node is the entry point for arithmetics.

Arithmetics specializes on scalar arguments with inline guards for particular combination of argument types such as: both are integers, left is double and right is integer, etc. Specialized nodes include necessary casts and `NA` checks. FastR has nodes for operations where argument types alternate between integer and double as this shows up in our workloads.

For vector arithmetics, specializations exist for common shapes, i.e. combinations of types and dimensions, e.g. when vectors are of the same length. Vector operations check the reference count of the arguments; if the reference count is zero then that vector is a temporary and can be reused for the result. Some arithmetic operations like `mod` and `pow` can be off-loaded to native code, as their Java implementation is notoriously slow. Data is passed as primitive array without copying.

Variable access. Variable access is a frequent operation with a number of specialized nodes. Pseudo-code for the uninitialized read node is in Figure 6. If the node executes in the global environment (the frame is null), it will always execute that way, and hence goes directly to the symbol table without checking dirty bits (`readOnlyTopLevel`). Otherwise, if the variable has a local slot (is in W), it will always be at the same index, the read unconditionally accesses the slot in the frame (`readLocalSmallFrame`) or in an array referenced from the frame (`readSimpleLocal`). Otherwise, the value has to be searched in the global environment, but checking the dirty bit to ensure it had not been inserted reflectively (`readTopLevel`).

We observe that variables in the global environment rarely get changed after initialized. Hence, if the uninitialized read node is able to find a value for the variable in the global environment and the symbol is clean, it creates a specialized node to always return this value (`readStableTopLevel`). If the value changes or is shadowed by a reflective write, a watchpoint will undo the rewrite.

Last, in the uninitialized read node, if there is no local slot for the variable, but there is one in a lexically enclosing function, that enclosing slot will always be there when this read node executes and it will be the closest one — `EnclosingIdx` contains the number of hops to a lexically enclosing frame and the index of the slot in that frame. The read node hence specializes to one that always checks that enclosing slot (`readEnclosing`) for the value and also the dirty bit of that enclosing frame. When a dirty frame or symbol is found, the read operation has to check extensions of all frames on the lexical stack, up to the one that has a fixed slot for the variable.

```
class UninitializedRead extends ReadVariable {
  Object execute(Frame f) {
    ReadVariable node;
    int idx; EnclosingIdx eidx;
    if (f == null)
      node = readOnlyTopLevel(ast, symbol);
    else if ((idx = f.findVariable(symbol)) != -1)
      node = f instanceof SmallFrame ?
        readLocalSmallFrame(ast, symbol, idx, f):
        readSimpleLocal(ast, symbol, idx);
    else if ((eidx = f.readSetEntry(symbol))==null) {
      node = readStableTopLevel(ast, symbol);
      if (node == null)
        node = readTopLevel(ast, symbol);
    } else
      node = readEnclosing(ast, symbol, eidx);
    return replace(node).execute(f);
} }
```

Figure 6. This class is the entry point for all variable reads.

`ReadSimpleLocal` (Figure 7) reads a variable from a known index of a frame. If the read value is a promise, it is forced. The node speculates that the variable has been initialized. If this assumption fails, the node rewrites to `readLocal`, which can handle the general case (looking up through enclosing slots, their dirty bits, possibly frame extensions and global environment). Generally, we observed that keeping performance critical nodes small helps the JIT compiler of the JVM generate faster code.

```
class ReadSimpleLocal extends ReadVariable {
  final int idx;
  Object execute(Frame f) {
    Object value = f.getForcing(idx);
    return value != null ? value :
      replace(readLocal(ast,symbol,idx)).execute(f);
} }
```

Figure 7. This class implements read of local variables by index.

Functions. Function calls are costly as function arguments can be passed in any order and, thus, they must be matched. However, we observe that programs almost always call the same function at a particular call-site. We therefore compute the matching once and re-use it over subsequent calls. The closures expect their arguments to be provided in declaration order. Each call must create a frame for the closure and populate it with arguments in the expected order. Figure 8 shows the generic call node; `argsPos` holds the mapping of argument positions.

We have observed that it is common for functions to be defined in the global environment and not re-defined. Moreover, functions quite often take only a few arguments passed by position. Thus, specialized nodes exist for a positional closure call through a global environment for 0, 1, 2 and 3 arguments. Except a watchpoint for re-definition, this specialization requires no guards.

Built-ins are slightly different. A *builtin* is a function that, unlike a closure, does not have its own environment. A custom instance of an executable node is created for each builtin call, specializing for a particular set of arguments. The specialization covers values of literals, e.g. `log(base=10, x)` will use a node specialized for log10. Builtin call sites directly refer to the body of the built-in and they are protected by a watchpoint which will rewrite them if needed.

4.3 Data specialization

Data types are represented using Java interfaces, such as `RInt`, as to allow data specialization. There is a most general implementation, e.g. `IntImpl`, which holds multiple values, names, dimensions, attributes and a reference count. For numeric types values are held in primitive arrays so that they can be passed to native code without conversions or copying. Figure 9 shows an interface to a double vector. Mutating operations, such as `set` and `setAttributes`, may return a new value of the whole data type (i.e. possibly copying a vector). We support immutable values, which always return a copy

```
class GenericCall extends FunctionCall {
  RClosure lastClosure;
  int[] argsPos; RFunction fun;
  RBuiltin lastBuiltin; RNode bnode;

  Object execute(Frame f) {
    Object callable = callableExpr.execute(f);
    if (callable == lastClosure) {
      Frame nf = fun.newFrame(lastClosure.frame());
      placeArgs(callerFrame, fun, argsPos);
      return fun.call(nf);
    } else if (callable == lastBuiltin) {
      return bnode.execute(f);
    } else {
      //if closure, set lastClosure, argsPos, fun,
      //if builtin, set lastBuiltin, bnode; and call
} } }
```

Figure 8. This class implements generic function/builtin call.

of themselves on an update. The `materialize` method performs the conversion to the general representation. Method `getContent` returns a primitive array in the standard format, which, may require materialization. Method `ref` increments the internal reference count, `isTemporary` means `ref` has not been called, `isShared` means `ref` was called more than once. For an immutable representation, there is no reference count and the value is always shared.

Simple scalars. Scalars with no names, dimensions, or attributes have an immutable representation with a single field to hold the payload, e.g. a double for `ScalarDoubleImpl`. Literals are represented as simple scalars, and results of computations that can be represented by simple scalars are automatically converted to those. This speeds up code by removing the indirection required by the primitive array. Also, checking that a value is a simple scalar is just a simple type check, making guards in specialized code cheaper.

Simple range. A sequence of integers, written in R as `1:n`, is immutable and has no attributes. The upper bound is remembered instead of creating a primitive array (`RIntSimpleRange`). Simple ranges often appear in `for` loops and vector indexing. The data specialization allows code specialization of such loops and vector indexing through a type check for `RIntSimpleRange`.

```
interface RDouble extends RAny {
  int size();
  Attributes attributes();
  double getDouble(int i);
  double[] getContent();
  double sum(boolean narm);
  RDouble materialize();
  RDouble set(int i, double val);
  RDouble setAttributes(Attributes attributes);
  void ref();
  boolean isShared();
  boolean isTemporary();
}
```

Figure 9. This interface represents a double vector (simplified).

Integer sequence. An integer sequence has an arbitrary starting point, arbitrary (possibly negative) step, and a size (`RIntSequence`). Integer sequences result from R expressions like `m:n` and from calls to `seq`. FastR has immutable specialization for these sequences, saving memory and allowing code specialization of loops and vector indexing.

4.4 Code and data co-specialization

Our last optimization intertwines code and data specialization by turning code into data. More precisely, rather than performing operations on vectors, FastR can defer them constructing expression trees (or *views*). Views are first class values, transparent to the users, which can provide both speed and memory improvements by defining a different evaluation order for the vector operations.

Views should not be mistaken with the lazy semantics introduced with promises. First, promises are rather eager [10], any assignment or sequencing operation will cause them to get evaluated. Second, promises are exposed to the programmer as they are used for meta-programming.

A view is an implementation of one of the R data types that contains a mixture of data objects and unevaluated operations. It supports materialization to compute the entire result, individual reads to obtain subsets of the result, and selected aggregate operations such as `sum` to perform computation on the result without materializing it. Views are stateless trees of arbitrary size. Views can cache their results and still appear stateless to the rest of the interpreter.

Views are built incrementally as the program performs vector operations. The actual computation is deferred. The operations allowed in a view include arithmetic and logical operations (`+`, `/`, `%/%`, `%%`, `*`, `-`, `!`, `&`, `&&`, ...), casts (int to double,...), builtin functions (`ceiling`, `floor`, `ln`, `log10`, `log2`, `sqrt`, `abs`, `round`, `exp`, `Im`, `log`, `Re`, `rev`, `is.na`, `tolower`, `toupper`), vector index (`x[1:10]`, `x[[1]]`, `x["str"]`, `x[-1]`, ...). The key criterion for inclusion is operations whose behavior is solely defined by the value of their inputs, where computation of individual vector elements is independent, and that do not have observable side-effects.[2] Views form trees that have values at their leaves. R semantics (and FastR's dynamic alias analysis) ensure that these values will not be modified after the view is created.

In R expressions, operations on vectors can include vectors of different lengths (shorter vectors are reused) and types (conversions are applied). The size and type of a view thus depends on its leaves and on the operations applied to them. FastR uses a view only when determining the result type and size is cheap. This is true for arithmetics, but not for many vector indexing modes, such as indexing with a logical index. Consider the following R program, on the left, and the view it creates, on the right:

---

[2] Warning messages are one exception, views report warnings retrospectively and in a different order from the original computation.

```
add1 <- function(a) a+1

x <- 1:1000
y <- add1( x )
z <- y + x
```

```
"+"(
  "+"(
    "cast"(Seq(1000)),
    1
  ),
  "cast"(Seq(1000))
)
```

```
boolean shouldBeLazy() {
  if (isRecursive || size == 0) return false;
  if (noAccesses) return true;
  if (size < 20) return false;
  if (externalMaterializeCount > 0 || externalGetCount
     > size || internalGetCount > size) return false;
  return true;
}
```

Figure 10. Heuristic choice of lazy/eager arithmetic.

Executing the above code will leave z pointing to the view on the right, with no actual computation performed. The benefits of views come into play when we try to access the result, for instance print(z). In this example, we can avoid allocating temporary vectors for x and y. No temporary is needed and, if print accesses z element-by-element, there will even be no allocation for the result vector: if the user requested only one value, e.g. print(z[[1]]), then no allocation would be needed and the value would be computed directly for the first element only.

Deferred element-wise computation is not always going to help. For very small vectors avoiding temporaries will not make a big impact and the overhead of interpreting the tree will not be amortized. Moreover, views can lead to redundant computation due to element vector re-use (repeatedly computing data points of a shorter vector) or simply by reusing the view in the R program for multiple computations. An extreme example of a redundant computation would be a recursive view, e.g. a computation such as x = x * x + c performed in a loop.

Specialization is used to heuristically find when it pays off to compute using a view. Every executable node that performs an operation supported by views will return a profiling view (*PView*) when first executed. PViews record the number of calls to methods of the view that access individual elements (get), access all values (materialize) and call to aggregators (e.g. sum), as well as other statistics about the views such as size and type. A PView also installs a listener on assignment of a view to detect recursion. The profile filled in by a PView is attached to the executable node which created it. When this node executes next, it will rewrite itself based on the profile, either to a node that always creates a view, or to a node that always materializes its inputs and performs the computation on them eagerly. The heuristic of Figure 10 decides when to be eager. There could be adversary programs which will not work well with it, such as when multiple views are created by a node before the first one is used, but the view is not recursive. Or, when the size of a vector created by a particular node will significantly increase during execution. Or, when a PView is passed to a very expensive computation.

Even eager computation can be optimized, for instance when an operation has a temporary input (ref count 0) of the same type as the result, it can be re-used. Performing operations one vector at a time can be easily off-loaded: we have obtained big speed-ups for pow and FP mod by evaluating them in native code as these functions are notoriously slow in Java. Some operations can be off-loaded even if they are in a view

that is being materialized. When materializing, one needs first to obtain a vector for the result; this is done by allocating a fresh vector. This vector can be used to store temporary results and allow some views of a view tree to be materialized eagerly, possibly off-loading the operations. FastR implements a heuristic when it performs materialization of a view using eager computation, whenever possible without allocating an extra buffer.

In addition to avoiding temporaries, view trees encode a simple program with semantics far simpler than Java or R. This program is easier to optimize. E.g., a view tree that is externally only used from its root can be automatically *fused* into a single view, which implements all operations of the view tree. FastR implements fusion using Java bytecode generation and dynamic loading. As we have observed with our benchmarks, even without explicit fusion, the JIT of the underlying JVM can often devirtualize the get call from a parent view to its child and inline it, essentially doing the fusion. This is, however, unlikely to work well in complicated programs.

4.5 Implementation complexity

The optimizations we describe have a cost in code complexity and code bloat. This cost is hard to measure, as the optimizations are not encapsulated like e.g. phases in a compiler. Instead, they are mostly rules and tricks for how to write the interpreter code, and they make the code harder to understand and bigger compared to a hypothetical naive AST interpreter. Our design choice was to isolate complex code and reduce code bloat with standard Java features (polymorphism, etc) rather than using additional tools e.g. for code generation or meta-programming.

The *code complexity* is increased by self-optimization. The AST tree has to be copied into the executable tree. Each executable node has to be written so that it can be safely removed from the tree, and even so while an instance of it is executing. After executing each child, a node has to check if it has been replaced, possibly continuing execution in the replacement node. This replacement logic has to be implemented specifically for each node and each of its children. The replacement code (catch blocks of SpecializationException) is about 3% Loc of the code base excluding the generated parser. There is an additional overhead in execute methods related to checking if a node has been replaced and some overhead with maintaining replacement nodes. While the replacement logic is complex, it does not add many lines of code, because it is shared by executable nodes of a similar kind (e.g. arithmetics, logical operations, comparison, unary Math function, etc). Also, the replacement code is expected to run rarely, so it does not have to be fast.

Code specialization by definition increases the code size. For example, the `ReadVector` class implements nodes for indexing a vector (2KLoc), but 70% of this code is for specialized cases, such as that the index is a scalar integer within bounds or the index is a logical vector of the same length as the base vector. Implementing these cases is no harder than implementing the general case any AST interpreter will need to have. Still, they pose substantial code bloat: over two thirds of the specialized cases in `ReadVector` require thought and in their present form could not be generated. This increases the amount of maintenance work needed, but not the set of skills to do the maintenance.

Less than a third of specialized cases in `ReadVector` are copy-pasted with mundane edits, e.g. the implementation of a subset of a double vector using an integer sequence is essentially the same as of an integer vector, but has to be implemented as a distinct class. Similar types of mundane bloat appear in the whole code base. Such bloat is due to the choice of Java, not because of our optimizations. In C/C++, one could avoid it using templates, macros, multiple inheritance, and unsafe casts.

5. Related Work

Our work was inspired by Truffle [17], a framework for writing AST interpreters under development at Oracle Labs. It encourages programming in a self-optimizing style. Future version of FastR will use it and the companion optimizing JIT compiler called Graal. Our approach to code specialization is related to techniques developed for Self [3] and trace-based compilation [7]. Earlier work on program specialization, e.g. [4], used the term *data specialization* to mean memoization of expensive computations, where we actually specialize the data types themselves. In the terminology of [9], we perform code specialization that is both dynamic and optimistic. The idea of data specialization can be traced back all the way to the notion of *drag-along* in APL implementations [1].

The GNU R bytecode interpreter [15] translates AST to bytecode on-the-fly at the granularity of a generalized call (e.g. a function or a loop). The only optimizations performed by the compiler are constant folding, inlining, and tail call optimizations. Many non-local jumps can be replaced by local transfers of control. No specialization is performed. The bytecode compiler optimizes local variable look-up by caching them into a constant-indexed array, but unlike FastR, variables in enclosing environments are not optimized. GNU-R can be extended with RcppArmadillo which is a lazy vector Math library [5]. But unlike FastR,

lazy vector operations have to be extracted manually by programmers from their R code.

Renjin[3], like FastR, is an AST interpreter for a subset of R running on a JVM. Unlike FastR, it mirrors the implementation of GNUR-AST, including internal data structures. Renjin implements lazy computation similar to views. Certain views can be cached, parallelized and sometime fused, but arithmetic vector operations are not parallelized and are prone to repeated computation. Work on compiling simple basic blocks into Java bytecode is ongoing.

Riposte [14] implements a subset of R. It defers vector operations, producing a trace with operations on typed vector futures analog to our views. Traces are limited to operate on vectors of the same length, but the operations may originate from different expressions in the R source code. Traces are compiled to 64-bit Intel machine code with optimizations that include vector instructions, algebraic simplification, constant folding, and common subexpression elimination. Traces can be fused and parallelized. To avoid redundant computation, Riposte computes and caches all futures reachable from R variables at the time the trace is compiled and executed. This may lead to unnecessary computation of futures. Scalar code is not optimized.

pqR[4] is a modified version of GNU-R 2.15.0. It adds some data specialization, e.g. for integer sequences. It replaces the bounded reference counts by full reference counting with decrements to reduce the need of copying on vector update. It offloads some numerical computations to helper threads, running them asynchronously.

6. Performance

We compare performance of FastR against the GNUR-AST to evaluate the impact of all optimizations implemented to date. We also compare against GNUR-BC with its highest optimization level, as it is the best performing official implementation of R. We are targeting longer-running programs (benchmarks are dimensioned to run 1-2 minutes with GNUR-BC). There are fixed costs of starting up a JVM, JIT compilation, and FastR self-optimization. We include the whole execution into the measurement, including these start-up costs.

6.1 Benchmarks

We run all benchmarks from the Benchmark 2.5 suite [16] (b25) and the Language Shootout benchmarks [6] (shootout).

Benchmark 2.5. The *b25 benchmarks*[5] comprise of three groups, each with five micro-benchmarks: matrix calculation (`mc`), matrix functions (`mf`) and programming (`pr`). The workloads are summarized in Figure 11. Most but not all of the workloads include a trivial amount of R code and R interpretation only takes a small fraction of their execution

---

[3] http://www.renjin.org

[4] http://radfordneal.github.io/pqR

[5] Sometimes referred to as AT&T R Benchmarks.

mc1	Double square matrix transposition
mc2	Power function, double vector over scalar
mc3	Quicksort on a double vector
mc4	Cross-product of a double square matrix ($A^T \times A$)
mc5	QR decomposition of a double square matrix
mf1	Fast Fourier transformation of a double matrix
mf2	Eigenvalues of a double matrix
mf3	Determinant of a double matrix
mf4	Cholesky decomposition, cross-product of a double matrix
mf5	Solve equations via QR decomposition
pr1	Power function scalar over double vector, arithmetics
pr2	Square integer matrix transpose, arithmetics
pr3	Grand common divisors, vectorized
pr4	Toeplitz matrix (nested loops with scalars)
pr5	Escoufier's method (vectors, loops, function calls)

Figure 11. Benchmark 2.5.

time. Much time is spent in numerical algorithms in native code. The benchmarks use BLAS and LAPACK numerical libraries. Most of the benchmarks use random number generators implemented in native code (NMath part of GNU-R). One of the benchmarks uses the native `fft`. FastR uses the same code through JNI. Some numerical algorithms are harder to re-use and were re-implemented in Java following the original C implementation, an example is the estimation of correlation coefficients. Two of the benchmarks use matrix transposition. We implemented a blocked version of a square matrix transposition in Java that is faster than the simple implementation in GNU-R. We also specialized the random number generators for batch generation from one distribution with identical parameters because calling through JNI for every single number was too slow. The most R intensive workloads are `pr5` and `pr3`; `pr4` also spends all time in R, but is quite simple. Workloads `mc2`, `pr1` and `pr2` are based on arithmetics on long vectors, so they are still somewhat affected by the R interpreter design. None of the original benchmarks outputs any results, which makes validation of the computation hard. Worse yet, FastR with lazy computation can run some of them without actually doing most of the computation. We modified the benchmarks so that they aggregate their result and print it. This forces computation and provides a value to check.

Shootouts. The shootouts are R implementations of problems from the Computer Language Benchmarks Game [6]. The R implementation was written by a computer science student and optimized for speed on GNUR-BC. The programs are small applications, they produce an output to check, and stress different parts of an R implementation. Unlike b25, most of the shootouts are dominated by execution in the interpreter. The exceptions are sn6 (spends a lot of time in BLAS) and `rd` (dominated by regular expressions matching library). For each problem, the R version of the shootout suite [11] includes a "main" implementation and several alternative implementations. We run all variants unmodified, except for a performance irrelevant fix needed to run kn3 in R. We also replace the use of internal calls to the GNU-R interpreter by more standard equivalents (kn1-4).

binarytrees	Allocates and traverses binary trees
bt	*GC benchmark, recursive calls, recursive lists*
pfannkuchred	Solves a combinatorial problem
pr	*Loops, indexing short vectors*
fasta	Generates DNA sequence by copying, rand. selection
fa	*String operations, scalar arithmetic*
fastaredux	Solves same problem as fasta
fr	*Adds more loops, vector indexing and arithmetic*
knucleotide	Finding patterns in gene sequences
kn	*Uses environment as a hashmap, string operations*
mandelbrot	Calculates a Mandelbrot set (fractal image)
ma	*Vector arithmetic on complex numbers*
nbody	Solves the N-body problem (simulation)
nb	*Arithmetic, Math with short vectors*
pidigits	Calculate digits of pi using spigot algorithm
pd	*Arbitrary precision arithmetic in R (diverse code)*
regexdna	Matching, replacing regex-specified gene sequences
rd	*Regular expressions (falls back to regex library)*
reversecompl	Computing reverse-complements for gene sequence
rc	*String vector indexing using string names*
spectralnorm	Computing eigenvalue using power method
sn	*Loops, function calls, scalar arithmetic*

Figure 12. Shootout.

The shootout problems are listed in Figure 12, including which aspect of an R interpreter does the main implementation stress. The alternative implementations always solve the same problem as the main one, but may stress different parts of an R interpreter from the main version. In particular, some of the alternative versions of sn and fa use more vector arithmetic than the main version. The biggest and most complicated program is pd (400 lines of code).

6.2 Measurement Methodology

We dimensioned benchmarks to run approximately 60 seconds with GNUR-BC on a development laptop and fit to 7G heap (sn3 needed a shorter run to fit in memory). On the measurement platform, the benchmarks run mostly over a minute, some about 2 minutes. We dimensioned the shootouts via their size parameter (those that accept output from the fa benchmark via sizing fa). We dimensioned b25s by finding the best iteration count for the outer loop, hence the same computation is repeated, but on different data (these benchmarks generate random inputs and set the random seed prior to entering the outer iteration loop). For Renjin and the b25 experiments, however, we measure b25 with a smaller number of iterations (so that Renjin runs about a minute), and then scale the result to the iteration count of the other VMs. This was needed at least for pr4 which has a two orders of magnitude slow-down, and we did it for all b25 benchmarks with Renjin.

We run each benchmark from either suite 10 times, for each VM, and then report a ratio of mean execution times of FastR, GNUR-BC, and Renjin each against GNUR-AST. We calculate a 95% confidence interval for the ratio of means using the percentile bootstrap method. For a quick summary, we also calculate the geometric mean of the ratios (that is the ratios of means) over each benchmark suite. The geometric mean has to be taken with a grain of salt, though, as performance changes tend to be dominated by several benchmarks from each suite (pr4 from b25 and kn from shootout). The overall speedup is thus a measure of how many of outlying benchmarks are in the suite. If the author chose to add say one more variant of kn to the shootouts, FastR speedups will likely be also great for it, and the geometric mean would increase a lot, as opposed to adding another variant of say rd. Similarly, if the author of b25 chose to add yet another benchmark that spends all time in LAPACK, the overall FastR speedup will drop. If that was another benchmark like pr4, it would increase. Still, the choice of geometric mean is more robust against the outlying benchmarks than would e.g. an arithmetic mean be. We intentionally do not calculate an error bar for the overall mean, as it would be giving a false level of confidence given the described issues.

6.3 Platform

We run our benchmarks on Dell PowerEdge R420 (2x Intel Xeon CPU 2.10GHz, 48G RAM) with 64-bit Ubuntu 12.04. We use GNU-R 3.0.2 compiled with default options by GCC. For GNUR-BC, we use the highest optimization level available (3). We run FastR on 64-bit Oracle JDK 1.8 (early access release), linking against system libraries including the R library. We run Renjin on the same JDK8, but compile it with JDK7 due to build problems with JDK8. We use the Oct-15-2013, github version of Renjin. We run all VMs with the Ubuntu version of openBLAS.

6.4 Results

The relative execution time of FastR and GNUR-BC normalized to GNUR-AST is shown in Figure 14 (b25) and 13 (shootout). The plots include error bars (95% confidence intervals), but the variation with most benchmarks is small.

Shootout benchmarks. On geometric average, FastR is 8.5x faster than GNUR-AST (while GNUR-BC is 1.8x faster than GNUR-AST). The biggest speed-ups are on the kn benchmarks. The benchmark uses a hash-map to look up gene sequences, and individual versions of kn differ in how they represent the hash-map (kn1 uses an environment, kn2 and kn3 use an attribute list, kn4 uses a named vector). FastR speed-ups come from optimization of these structures, e.g. a named vector in FastR remembers a hash-map of its names; this hash-map and the names are immutable, and hence can be propagated through operations with no cost. Attributes in FastR have a trie structure for fast matching of attributes based on their prefix. This trie is mutable, but can still be propagated through operations (the originating owner looses the trie and will have to re-build it in case matching becomes needed again). Most benchmarks then benefit from code and data specialization, and few from lazy vector computation. bt particularly benefits from function call optimizations and data/code specializations for scalars. pr particularly benefits from data specialization for integer sequences and from loop and vector indexing specializations. nb particularly benefits from optimized vector computation (not computing small

vectors lazily). rc particularly benefits from vector indexing optimizations. sn benefits from vector and matrix indexing optimizations, loop optimizations, and lazy vector arithmetics. fa and particularly pd are relatively diverse and benefit from various optimizations.

Benchmark 2.5. On geometric average, FastR is 1.7x faster than GNUR-AST (and GNUR-BC is 1.1x faster than GNUR-AST). The relatively small speedup is explained by the preponderance of native calls. FastR offers biggest speed-up with the pr4 benchmark. This is due data/code specialization for scalars, including loops, matrix indexing, arithmetic and Math operations. pr3 speedups are thanks to specialization of vector operations (arithmetics, comparison, vector indexing using the result of a comparison). pr2 and mc1 benefit from optimized matrix transposition, pr2 also from lazy vector arithmetic. pr5 benefits from specialization for integer sequences and from code/data specializations of vector operations. Also, pr5 takes advantage of function call optimizations. The remaining speed-ups are mostly from specialization of the random number generator wrappers.

Renjin. Renjin performance results are shown in Figures 16 (b25) and 15 (shootout). We only show benchmarks that run; the other did not due to missing features. On geometric average over supported benchmarks, Renjin is 2.2x slower than GNUR-AST on b25 and 1.8x on the shootouts. The pr4 benchmark from b25 fills in a matrix of 500x500 elements in a loop. Semantically in R, any element update of a matrix creates a new matrix. Renjin copies the matrix in each iteration of the loop. GNUR-AST (and FastR) know through dynamic alias analysis that the matrix is private and avoid the copy, hence the 107x overhead of Renjin.

The 15x slowdown of Renjin on sn2 is because of redundant computation of a view. sn2 pre-computes two matrices (one using an outer product, another as the transpose of the first) and uses them read-only in a loop for computation. In Renjin, due to lazy computation, the matrices are not in fact pre-computed. Instead, each element is repeatedly recomputed on-the-fly. Renjin supports views that can cache the computed result, but they are not used for these operations. We do not have a definitive advice for Renjin on this. FastR implements profiling views to fight redundant computation, but they are based on a heuristic that does not work in the sn2 benchmark — redundant computation is avoided by coincidence (the particular computation of the initial matrices in sn2 happens to be always eager in FastR). GNUR does not run into these problems, because it always computes eagerly.

The nearly 5x slowdowns of Renjin on bt benchmarks (shootout) is due to the return statement (the benchmark is dominated by calls to a cheap recursive function which uses a return statement). In Renjin, every single call to return allocates a new Java exception and throws it. GNUR-AST, instead, uses a C non-local jump, which is much cheaper. In

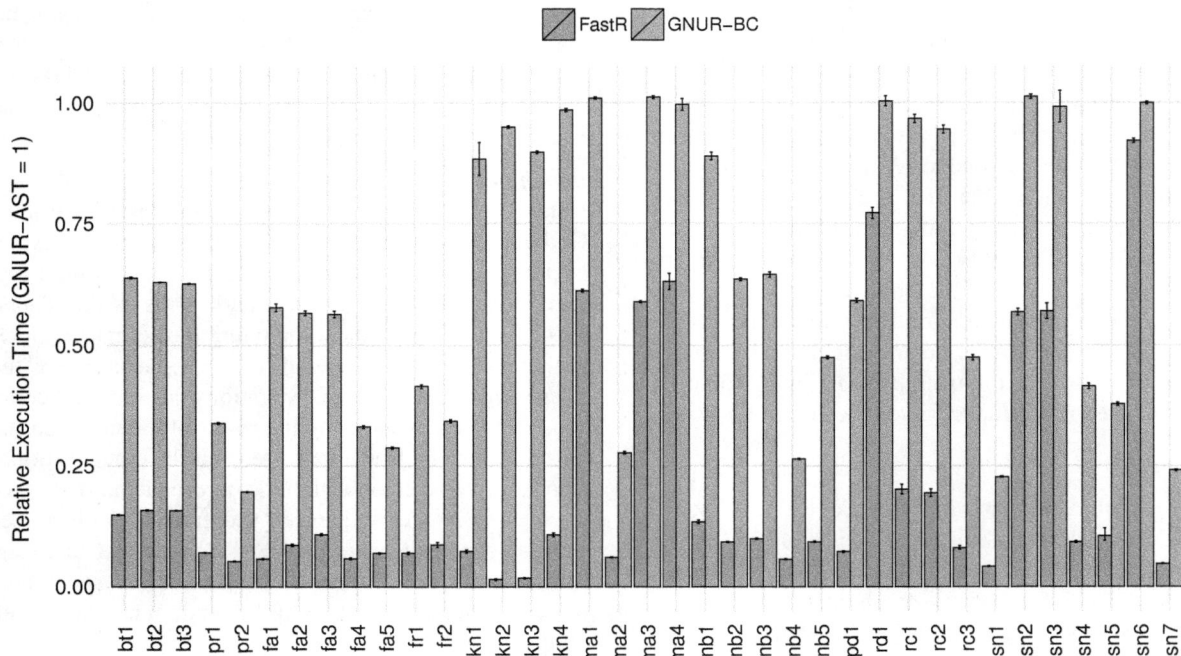

Figure 13. **Shootout Relative Execution Times** (lower is better). Geo. mean speedup for FastR is 8.5x and 1.8x for GNUR-BC.

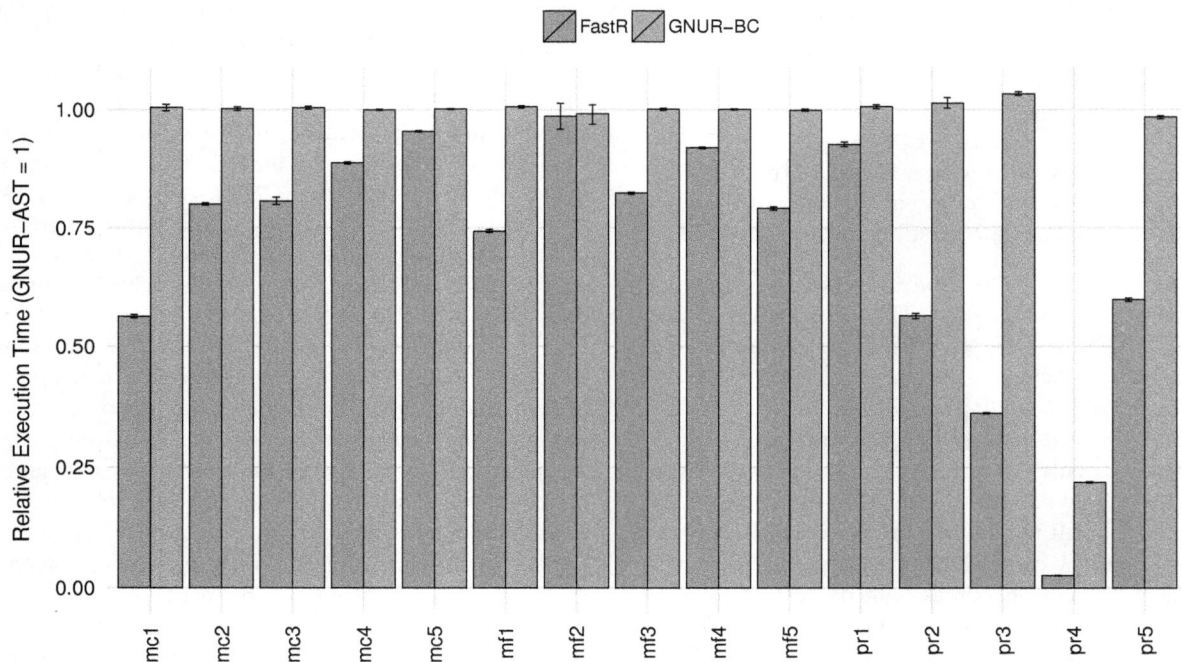

Figure 14. **Benchmark 2.5 Relative Execution Times** (lower is better). Geo. mean speedup FastR is 1.7x and 1.1x for GNUR-BC.

FastR, we use a pre-allocated exception (the return value is stored in the R Frame). Moreover, FastR's return elision optimization avoids executing the return statement completely in the bt benchmarks.

Fusion. Our implementation of fusion of view trees into Java byte-code, on average, provides no performance change on the b25 and the shootout benchmarks (numbers shown in graphs are without fusion). Lacking a realistic application that would stress vector computation, we use a trivial micro-benchmark to validate the potential speed-up of fusion. We

100

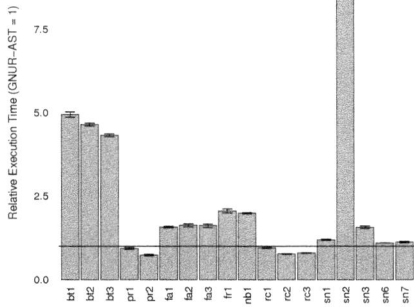

Figure 15. Shootout Relative Execution Times: Renjin (lower is better). Y-axis cut off at 10x slowdown (sn2 slowdown is 15x). Geo mean slowdown is 1.8x.

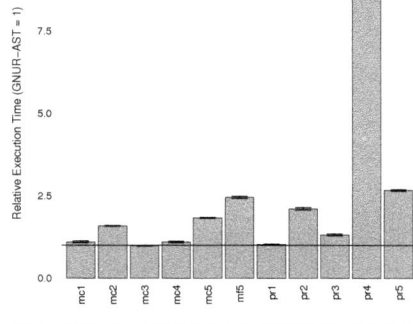

Figure 16. Benchmark 2.5 Relative Execution Time: Renjin (lower is better). Y-axis cut off at 10x slowdown (pr4 slowdown is 107x). Geo. mean slowdown is 2.2x.

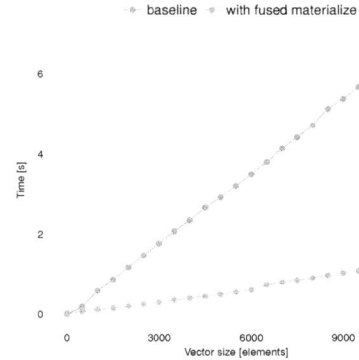

Figure 17. FastR Fusion. (smaller is better). Fusion speeds up materialization on a micro-benchmark as vector size increases. Approx. 7x speedup.

measure the time to compute a sequence of commands $x = y + z * y + z - 2 * (8 + z)$; $x[[1]] = 3$ for primitive vectors y and z of increasing size. Note the vector update of x which triggers materialization of the full vector x. With fusion enabled, the materialization will be performed using automatically fused and dynamically loaded byte-code for the particular computation. We report average time to calculate 10,000 repetitions of the code sequence (Figure 17) for increasing vector size. We exclude initial 30,000 iterations, focusing on peak performance of repeated computation rather than fixed cost of fusing a view tree.

7. Conclusions

Many languages start with a straightforward AST interpreter. As their popularity grows, the initial implementation usually starts to feel slow. This paper shows that the battle is not necessarily over. We have implemented a Java-based AST interpreter for a subset of the R language which, on some benchmarks, is 8.5x faster than a C AST interpreter and 4.9x faster than a byte-code interpreter. The techniques we used are all, individually, simple and require understanding of the application domain rather than heroic compiler skills. These techniques can be ported to a C interpreter and the ideas to other languages.

Our implementation leveraged the Java runtime system in a number of ways. We benefited from Java's garbage collector, from its ability to generate and load code dynamically, and from the productivity that comes with a type safe object-oriented language. But, there is a price too. Integration with the myriad of native functions used by GNU R is painful as JNI is cumbersome and slow. The lack of complex numbers and accompanying complex number arithmetics complicates the implementation. Math functions implemented in Java are often slow compared to their native equivalent.

Specialization worked well on our workloads, but one should be careful about generalizing. On one hand, the problems we looked at are kernels that are simpler than real code. On the other hand, they manipulate relatively small amounts of data. Some of our speedups will be more pronounced with large vectors. But this remains to be shown in practice. As we increase coverage of the language we will be in a position to better evaluate the true benefits of our optimizations.

Drawbacks of specialization are that it greatly increases code size of the interpreter and result in a non-linear body of code. We found we were writing boiler plate code for multiple variants of a node, yet it was not sufficiently repetitive, so there was not a clear way to generate it automatically. Understanding control flow in the interpreter is made difficult by the fact that classes are related by rewriting relationship.

Working at the AST level was convenient because tree rewriting is easy to implement, but it is a less efficient representation than bytecode and each node is optimized in isolation, with no information from its context. An extension to our work would be to look at how to perform similar changes directly on the bytecode and combine them with some program analysis. It is not clear if going to bytecode rewriting would raise the complexity bar too high for non-experts, though. We plan to add parallelism to our implementation, hence we will be forced to deal with concurrency.

Availability

FastR v0.168 is released under a GPL license and can be downloaded from:

```
http://github.com/allr/fastr
```

Acknowledgments

The authors thank Leo Osvald, Brandon Hill and Gaël Thomas for their help early in the project. Michael Haupt, Helena Kotthaus, Luke Tierney and Duncan Temple Lang provided us with feedback. We thank Tomas Würthinger, Mario Wolczko and the Truffle team for the idea of using code specialization. This work was supported in part by grants from the NSF and the ONR, and by gifts from the Oracle Corporation.

References

[1] P. S. Abrams. *An APL machine*. Ph.D. thesis, Stanford University, 1970.

[2] R. A. Becker, J. M. Chambers, and A. R. Wilks. *The new S language: a programming environment for data analysis and graphics*. Wadsworth and Brooks/Cole Advanced Books & Software, 1988.

[3] C. Chambers and D. Ungar. Making pure object oriented languages practical. In *Proceedings of Object-Oriented Programming Systems, Languages and Applications (OOPSLA)*, 1991.

[4] S. Chirokoff, C. Consel, and R. Marlet. Combining program and data specialization. *Higher-Order and Symbolic Computation*, 12(4), 1999.

[5] D. Eddelbuettel and C. Sanderson. RcppArmadillo: accelerating R with high-performance C++ linear algebra. *Computational Statistics & Data Analysis*, 71, 2014.

[6] B. Fulgham and D. Bagley. The computer language benchmarks game. `http://benchmarksgame.alioth.debian.org`, 2013.

[7] A. Gal, B. Eich, M. Shaver, D. Anderson, D. Mandelin, M. R. Haghighat, B. Kaplan, G. Hoare, B. Zbarsky, J. Orendorff, J. Ruderman, E. W. Smith, R. Reitmaier, M. Bebenita, M. Chang, and M. Franz. Trace-based just-in-time type specialization for dynamic languages. In *Proceedings of Programming Language Design and Implementation (PLDI)*, 2009. .

[8] R. Ihaka and R. Gentleman. R: A language for data analysis and graphics. *Journal of Computational and Graphical Statistics*, 5(3), 1996.

[9] D. McNamee, J. Walpole, C. Pu, C. Cowan, C. Krasic, A. Goel, P. Wagle, C. Consel, G. Muller, and R. Marlet. Specialization tools and techniques for systematic optimization of system software. *ACM Transactions on Computer Systems*, 19(2), 2001.

[10] F. Morandat, B. Hill, L. Osvald, and J. Vitek. Evaluating the design of the R language. In *Proceedings of European Conference on Object-Oriented Programming (ECOOP)*, 2012.

[11] L. Osvald. R shootout. `http://r.cs.purdue.edu/hg/r-shootout`, 2012.

[12] R Development Core Team. *R: A Language and Environment for Statistical Computing*. R Foundation for Statistical Computing, 2008. `http://www.r-project.org`.

[13] D. Smith. The R ecosystem. In *R User Conference (UseR)*, 2011.

[14] J. Talbot, Z. DeVito, and P. Hanrahan. Riposte: a trace-driven compiler and parallel VM for vector code in R. In *Proceedings of Parallel Architectures and Compilation Techniques (PACT)*, 2012.

[15] L. Tierney. *A Byte Code Compiler for R*. University of Iowa, 2012. `http://homepage.stat.uiowa.edu/~luke/R/compiler/compiler.pdf`.

[16] S. Urbanek. R benchmark 2.5. `http://r.research.att.com/benchmarks`, 2008.

[17] T. Würthinger, C. Wimmer, A. Wöß, L. Stadler, G. Duboscq, C. Humer, G. Richards, D. Simon, and M. Wolczko. One VM to rule them all. In *Proceedings of Onward!, the ACM Symposium on New Ideas in Programming and Reflections on Software*, 2013.

Deoptimization for Dynamic Language JITs on Typed, Stack-based Virtual Machines

Madhukar N Kedlaya[†]   Behnam Robatmili[*]   Călin Caşcaval[*]   Ben Hardekopf[†]

[†]University of California, Santa Barbara   [*]Qualcomm Research Silicon Valley
{mkedlaya,benh}@cs.ucsb.edu   mcjs@qti.qualcomm.com

Abstract

We are interested in implementing dynamic language runtimes on top of language-level virtual machines. Type specialization is a critical optimization for dynamic language runtimes: generic code that handles any type of data is replaced with specialized code for particular types observed during execution. However, types can change, and the runtime must recover whenever unexpected types are encountered. The state-of-the-art recovery mechanism is called *deoptimization*. Deoptimization is a well-known technique for dynamic language runtimes implemented in low-level languages like C. However, no dynamic language runtime implemented on top of a virtual machine such as the Common Language Runtime (CLR) or the Java Virtual Machine (JVM) uses deoptimization, because the implementation thereof used in low-level languages is not possible.

In this paper we propose a novel technique that enables deoptimization for dynamic language runtimes implemented on top of typed, stack-based virtual machines. Our technique does not require any changes to the underlying virtual machine. We implement our proposed technique in a JavaScript language implementation, MCJS, running on top of the Mono runtime (CLR). We evaluate our implementation against the current state-of-the-art recovery mechanism for virtual machine-based runtimes, as implemented both in MCJS and in IronJS. We show that deoptimization provides significant performance benefits, even for runtimes running on top of a virtual machine.

Categories and Subject Descriptors D.3.4 [*Programming Languages*]: Processors–Run-time environments, Optimization

VEE '14,   March 1–2, 2014, Salt Lake City, Utah, USA.
Copyright © 2014 ACM 978-1-4503-2764-0 /14/03... $15.00.
http://dx.doi.org/10.1145/2576195.2576209

Keywords deoptimization; JavaScript; type specialization; virtual machine; language implementation

1. Introduction

Language-level virtual machines (VMs) provide a number of advantages for application development. These advantages extend to implementing language runtimes on top of existing VMs, which we call *layered architectures*—for example, dynamic language runtimes like Rhino, IronJS, IronRuby, JRuby, IronPython, and Jython, which implement JavaScript, Ruby, and Python runtimes respectively, either on top of the Java Virtual Machine (JVM) or the Common Language Runtime (CLR).

However, VMs can also impose performance penalties that make language implementation unattractive. These penalties include not only VM overheads, but also *opportunity costs* arising from optimizations common to native runtime implementations[1] but difficult or impossible within a VM. Our goal in this work is to alleviate an important opportunity cost for implementing dynamic language runtimes on top of VMs. Specifically, we introduce a novel technique for *deoptimization* on typed, stack-based VMs that enables efficient type specialization, a critical optimization for dynamic language runtimes (explained further in Section 2).

Why Implement Languages on a VM?   There are many advantages to using a layered architecture. Layered architectures provide nice program abstractions, free optimizations, and highly-tuned garbage collection, which are all required for a performant engine. Leveraging an existing VM allows the language developers to focus on language-specific optimizations without bothering with machine-specific optimizations that are handled by the existing VM. Layered architectures also offer a good platform for experimenting with new language features and different optimization techniques for language runtimes. Finally, using a layered architecture enables interoperability between different languages implemented on the same runtime.

---

[1] By which we mean runtimes implemented in a low-level language such as C and compiled to native binaries.

Opportunity Costs. The existing VM often imposes restrictions on the language developer that can prevent important optimizations. For example, a key optimization for dynamic languages is *type specialization*, which uses dynamic profiling to specialize code based on observed type information. Type specialization is unsound and thus requires a recovery mechanism to deal with unexpected types by transferring execution from the type-specialized code to the original unspecialized code. However, the very nature of typed, stack-based VMs such as the JVM or CLR means that the most effective known recovery mechanism, deoptimization, cannot be implemented using any known techniques that are used in native runtimes [12, 15, 20, 22].

Key Insights. We have developed a novel technique for effective deoptimization on typed, stack-based VMs. Our key insight is that we can leverage the VM's existing exception mechanism to perform the deoptimization. Doing so is non-trivial, because exceptions throw away the current runtime stack whereas deoptimization should preserve the stack information from the specialized code in order to re-start execution at the equivalent program point in the unspecialized code. Our technique leverages the code generator's bytecode verifier to track and transfer appropriate values on the runtime stack between the specialized code and the unspecialized code when a deoptimization exception is thrown.

Contributions. Our specific contributions are:

- We describe a novel deoptimization technique to enable type specialization for dynamic language runtimes running on top of a typed, stack-based virtual machine. (Section 3)
- We describe a specific instantiation of this technique for MCJS[2] [21], a JavaScript engine implemented on top of the CLR. (Section 4)
- We evaluate our MCJS implementation and compare against (1) a non-type specializing version of MCJS, (2) a type specializing version of MCJS using an alternate fast-path + slow-path recovery technique, and (3) IronJS[3], a JavaScript engine implemented using the DLR (which performs type specialization using the fast path + slow path technique). We use both standard benchmarks (i.e., Sunspider and V8) and long-running web JavaScript applications, and show that our deoptimization technique significantly outperforms existing type specialization techniques for layered architectures. On an average (geomean) our deoptimization technique is $1.16\times$ and $1.88\times$ faster than MCJS with fast-path + slow-path recovery technique and IronJS respectively. (Section 5)

Before describing our technique, we provide background on type specialization, the two dominant recovery mecha-

---

[2] http://www.github.com/mcjs/mcjs.git

nisms used by type specialization, and the challenges they face when implemented on top of a VM (Section 2).

2. Type Specialization

In this section we give background on type specialization, the two dominant recovery mechanisms (*fast path + slow path* and *deoptimization*) used to implement type specialization, and the challenges faced by these techniques when implemented on top of VMs.

2.1 Type Specialization

Dynamic languages are dynamically typed, i.e., a variable can refer to values of different types at different points during a program's execution. However, dynamic language runtimes implemented in a typed language must declare a single type for each variable in the underlying implementation. Therefore, runtimes must wrap base values (e.g., integers, booleans, strings, etc) inside a wrapper type called a *DValue*, which stands for "dynamic value". Wrapping a base value inside a DValue is called *boxing*, and extracting a base value from a DValue is called *unboxing*.

The semantics of dynamic language operations depend heavily on the types involved. For example, the simple expression a + b can mean many different things depending on the types of a and b at the time the expression is evaluated. The runtime must unbox a and b to determine the types of the wrapped base values, perform the appropriate operation, and then box the result back into a DValue. Thus every expression encountered during execution requires unboxing values, performing a series of branch conditions based on type, performing the desired operation, and finally boxing a value. These operations tend to dominate the execution time of any dynamic language program.

In response, dynamic language implementors have developed an optimization called *type specialization*. During execution the observed types of each variable's values are monitored. The runtime then dynamically generates code that is specialized for the observed types. In the previous example, if a and b are always observed to hold integer values, then the runtime can generate specialized code that declares them to be int types instead of DValues and thus avoid all of the unboxing, branching, and boxing. However, this optimization is unsound—for example, while a and b have been integers so far, they may hold strings at some point later in the execution. Runtimes that use type specialization must have some sort of *recovery mechanism* that detects unexpected types and falls back to the standard, generic evaluation algorithm. There are two dominant approaches for this recovery mechanism; we describe each below along with their challenges with respect to being implemented on VMs.

2.2 Recovery Option 1: Fast Path + Slow Path

For the *fast path + slow path* recovery mechanism, type-specialized code is guarded by a conditional that tests the current types of the specialized variables. If the current types

```
if (GetType(a) == Int && GetType(b) == Int) {
  c = ToDValue(IntAdd(a.ToInt(), b.ToInt()));
}
else { // Slow path
  c = GenericAdd(a, b);
}
// c is of the type DValue here.
```

```
if (GetType(a) == Int && GetType(b) == Int) {
  c = IntAdd(a.ToInt(), b.ToInt());
}
else {
  // Jump to deoptimization routine.
}
// c is of the type int here.
```

(a) C-like pseudocode representing the fast path + slow path approach for the statement c = a + b

(b) C-like pseudocode representing the deoptimization approach for the statement c = a + b

Figure 1: Two approaches for generating type specialized code for the statement c = a + b where a and b are observed to be integers.

match the expected types then the true branch containing the type-specialized code is taken, otherwise the false branch containing the generic, unspecialized code is taken. In pseudocode, where variable is a DValue:

```
if (unbox(variable).type == type T) {
  T variable' = unbox(variable)
  // fast path: specialized code for type T
  // computes the result using variable'
  box(result)
}
else {
  // slow path: unspecialized code computes
  // the result using variable
}
// use result
```

Notice that variables are still unboxed and boxed for the fast path; this is because the type of result must be the same regardless of whether the fast path or slow path is taken. However, there may be multiple operations contained in the fast path and so the cost of boxing and unboxing is amortized; in addition, there is no branching on types in the fast path.

Figure 1a gives C-like pseudocode showing how the runtime implements the fast path + slow path operation for a simple binary add operation. Based on the previously observed types of a and b, say int and int, the runtime generates code to perform integer addition in the fast path and a generic add operation in the slow path.

Challenges. This technique is the one used in current layered architectures for dynamic languages that perform type specialization, such as IronJS and MCJS. There is no technical difficulty in implementing it, however the constant boxing and unboxing severely limits the benefits of type specialization. Deoptimization is known to out-perform fast path + slow path in native code implementation of dynamic language runtimes; however as we describe below deoptimization is difficult for VMs.

2.3 Recovery Option 2: Deoptimization

For the *deoptimization* recovery mechanism, type-specialized code is again guarded by a conditional that tests the current types of the specialized variables. The key difference is that the fast path and slow path are not contained inside the branches of the condition; instead, the slow path is placed in an entirely separate routine. If the condition fails then control leaves the current, type-specialized routine and jumps to the generic, unspecialized routine, where it resumes execution at the unspecialized program point that is equivalent to the specialized program point where the type mismatch was detected. In pseudocode, where variable is a DValue:

```
if (unbox(variable).type == expected type T) {
  T variable' = unbox(variable)
  // fast path: specialized code for type T
  // computes the result using variable'
}
else {
  // jump to equivalent program point in
  // unspecialized code
}
// use result
```

The benefit of this approach is that the remaining code in the routine can assume that the fast path succeeds, and hence we do not need to box the result—we can leave it as whatever type it was specialized to, because if it wasn't supposed to be that type then the code would have jumped completely out of the specialized routine and into the unspecialized routine.

Figure 1b gives C-like pseudocode describing the deoptimization approach for the statement c = a + b. Similar to the fast path + slow path approach, the guard condition checks whether the observed types of a and b are integers. If so, the runtime unboxes the integer values of a and b and performs the integer addition operation. This constitutes the fast path. A difference here with respect to the fast path + slow path approach is that resultant value is not boxed back into a DValue before assigning it to c. Instead, the type of c is initialized to be an integer. This prevents further unboxing of c when it is used later in the function. The deoptimization code captures the current state of execution of the code

105

and transfers it to either an interpreter or to non-optimized compiled code.

Challenges. Deoptimization has been used in native code implementations of dynamic language runtimes. However, the techniques used there do not translate to typed, stack-based VMs such as the CLR or JVM. Native code uses either *code patching/on-stack replacement* or *long jumps*. In the former strategy, deoptimization is implemented by dynamically replacing the specialized code in the runtime stack with the generic unspecialized code. However, in managed VMs runtime modification of generated functions is not allowed. In the latter strategy, deoptimization is implemented as a long jump to the unspecialized code. However, in managed VMs long jumps are not allowed, for two reasons: first, it disables all optimizations that can be performed within a basic block, and second, these jumps can violate the *Gosling principle* which dictates that stack-based VMs should guarantee the *typestate* at any given program point. Typestate refers to the types of a function's local variables and the types of the values in the operand stack; stack-based VMs enforce the Gosling principle to help ensure correctness and performance. Thus, implementing the deoptimization strategy for type specialization using known techniques is not possible without modifying the underlying VM.

3. Deoptimization on Layered Architectures

In this section we give a high-level overview of our approach to solving the deoptimization problem on layered architectures. We discuss two aspects: (1) how to jump from the specialized code to the correct place in the unspecialized code; and (2) how to transfer the current state from the specialized code to the unspecialized code.

Jump to Unspecialized Code. When specialized code detects a type mismatch, it must jump from the current program point in the specialized code to the equivalent program point in the unspecialized code. As explained in Section 2, we cannot use the standard techniques of code patching or long jump to implement this behavior. Instead, we leverage the underlying VM's exception-handling mechanism. The jump from specialized code is done by throwing a `GuardFailure` exception. The body of every optimized method is wrapped in a try block, and deoptimization for every expression in that body is handled in a common catch block. Figure 3b illustrates the structure of the specialized code that is generated for a specific example.

The catch block must then transfer control to the unspecialized code, specifically the point equivalent to where the exception was thrown in the specialized version. To achieve this, we assume that the dynamic language runtime implements something like a subroutine-threaded interpreter [5]. A subroutine-threaded interpreter implements each operation of the program (e.g., reading a value of a variable, or performing binary addition) as a separate, unspecialized subroutine implemented in the underlying VM bytecode;

each subroutine returns a pointer to the next subroutine that should be executed, and so interpretation consists of a series of subroutine calls with each call returning the address of the next subroutine to call.

Assuming the interpreter is subroutine-threaded, each language expression has an unspecialized implementation in the form of a subroutine with a known address. At each deoptimization guard, a pointer to the appropriate expression's subroutine is hardcoded into the thrown exception's value. The catch block then calls the appropriate subroutine to transfer control to the unspecialized code. We illustrate this process with an example in Section 4.

State Transfer. It is not sufficient to simply transfer control from the specialized code to the unspecialized code; we must also transfer the current state of the program, i.e., the values of the local variables on the runtime stack *and* the values on the operand stack used to store intermediate values during expression evaluation. Transferring the local variables is straightforward: we insert code immediately before the `GuardFailure` exception to read the values of each local variable and store them in a separate data structure shared by both specialized and unspecialized code. We describe such a data structure in Section 4.

The tricky part of state transfer is the operand stack. This stack is cleared whenever an exception is thrown, and its values are not stored in local or temporary variables. For example, suppose while evaluating the expression a + b + c that there is a deoptimization guard around c that throws an exception. The value of a + b resides (only) in the operand stack, and must be transferred to the unspecialized code that will evaluate c before the operand stack is cleared by the thrown exception. What makes this process tricky is that the number and types of values on the operand stack vary across deoptimization points; therefore we must have access to the stack size and type information at each deoptimization point in order to correctly transfer state. Unfortunately, managed VMs do not provide the ability to reflect on the operand stack during runtime.

We solve this problem by using compile-time[3] validation of the generated intermediate representation. To achieve this, the code generator is combined with a bytecode verifier which verifies the generated code line-by-line during code generation (as opposed to the normal order, which completely generates the code and then validates it). The benefit of this approach is that, in order to verify type safety, the code verifier maintains a shadow stack of value types present in the operand stack at any program point. The code generator can take advantage of this information during code generation, whereas it could not do this if the validator waited until after generation is complete.

---

[3] Throughout this paper, "compile" refers to generation of the typed bytecode of the underlying VM from the dynamic language being implemented on that VM. This should not be confused with the native code generation that happens at the VM level.

```
function foo(a)
{
  var b = 10;
  return a + b + global;
}
```

Figure 2: Running example in JavaScript.

Index	Subroutine Name	Expression	Operand Stack
0	WriteIndentifier	b = 10	[]
1	ReadIdentifier	a	[a]
2	ReadIdentifier	b	[a, b]
3	AddExpression	a+b	[a+b]
4	ReadIdentifier	global	[a+b, global]
5	AddExpression	a+b+global	[a+b+global]
6	Return	return	[]

Table 1: Subroutines generated for a subroutine-threaded interpreter corresponding to the example in Figure 2. Subroutine 5 is the unspecialized code where control is transferred by the deoptimizer if `global` contains an unexpected type during the specialized code evaluation.

This approach has two benefits beyond enabling correct state transfer. First, it enables runtime validation of the VM intermediate bytecode generated by the dynamic language runtime, which aids the language implementor in detecting compiler errors early rather than waiting until the code is actually run and the underlying VM gives an "Invalid IR" message. Secondly, there are certain unusual circumstances where the values on the operand stack cannot be transferred correctly to the unspecialized code, and hence deoptimization is not feasible (this is discussed further in Section 4.3). The code verifier will detect such circumstances and mark the code as un-optimizable.

4. Deoptimization for MCJS

This section concretely explains the algorithm for deoptimization that we have implemented in MCJS, a JavaScript engine implemented on top of the Common Language Runtime (CLR). MCJS performs type feedback based type inference to generate type specialized code. The type inference algorithm implemented in MCJS is described in the paper by Kedlaya et al [18]. The explanation in this section uses a running example given in Figure 2: a JavaScript function foo that takes an argument a which the example assumes is always an integer value.

The function foo is initially interpreted by the MCJS runtime. When foo becomes warm, it is compiled by the fast compiler into CIL[4] bytecode. This fast compilation also: (1) uses the code verifier to detect the types of values present on the operand stack for each potential deoptimization point, and determines for each point if deoptimization is feasible;[5] and (2) instruments the code to collect type profiling information. Finally, if foo becomes hot then it is re-compiled by the optimizing compiler into (1) a type-specialized CIL bytecode version based on the collected profile information; and (2) an unspecialized subroutine-threaded version used by the deoptimizer to recover from unexpected types.

The remaining subsections expand on the optimizing compiler pass: we explain first the subroutine-threaded code generator and then the specialized code generator that handles deoptimization.

4.1 Subroutine-Threaded Interpreter

When a hot function is compiled, the optimizing compiler first generates subroutine-threaded code for that function be-

fore generating type-specialized code. The order is important, because the specialized code needs to have pointers to the appropriate subroutines for each potential deoptimization point. Table 1 shows the subroutines that are generated for the example function in Figure 2. The only possible place for deoptimization (assuming a is always an integer) is if the type of global changes during some subsequent execution of foo. Thus, subroutine 5 is the subroutine that the runtime will jump to if deoptimization occurs. Since the subroutine-threaded interpreter executes a sequence of subroutines for each operation in the function, it is important to maintain an explicit stack that mimics the operand stack across the subroutines. MCJS implements this operand stack in the callFrame data structure described in Figure 4. The operand stack generated by subroutine 4 needs to be reconstructed by the deoptimizer before jumping into subroutine 5. The method to do so is explained below.

4.2 Specialized Code Generator

The generated type-specialized code contains deoptimization hooks at each potential deoptimization point. These hooks are filled in with the addresses of the appropriate subroutines generated as per the above description. In the example, the deoptimization code in the guard around global is compiled with a pointer to subroutine 5. Figure 3a shows the CIL code that is generated for the expression a+b+global.

It remains to explain how a deoptimization point transfers control to the unspecialized code subroutine while maintaining the current program state. We first explain how control is transferred from the specialized code into the unspecialized code, and then we explain how program state is transferred along with the control.

Control Transfer. The jump to the deoptimization code is implemented using the exception handling feature of the CLR. Each specialized method is wrapped in a try-catch block. Before a GuardFailure exception is thrown at a deoptimization point, the runtime updates the profiler with the new type that was observed, in order to improve the profiler's type information. The operand stack is then captured

---

[4] Common Intermediate Language, a typed bytecode IR used by the CLR.
[5] This is discussed further in Section 4.3.

```
...
0055    ldloc a
0056    ldloc b
0057    call Int32 Binary.Add:Run (Int32, Int32)

...  ;   TYPE CHECK
...  ;   Load the global variable
0071    dup
0072    call int DValue:get_ValueType()
007b    ldc.i4 9 ; 9 = observed type = Int32
0080    beq fast ; jump to fast path

...  ;   DEOPTIMIZATION CODE
...  ;   Update the profiler with observed type.
...  ;   Transfer the operand stack to the
...  ;   callFrame->stack data-structure.
...  ;   Explained in Table 2.
00d4    ldc.i4 5 ; 5 is the index of the
                 ; subroutine to jump into.
00db    throw GuardFailedException(Int32)

...  ;   FAST PATH
fast    call Int32 DValue:AsInt32() ; Unboxing
00e5    call Int32 Binary.Add:Run(Int32, Int32)
...  ;   Set the return value in the callFrame
00f4    ret

...  ;   CATCH BLOCK
...  ;   Store the current values of the local
...  ;   variables into the callFrame->symbols array.
...  ;   BlackList this function.
...  ;   Load the callFrame object that contains
...  ;   the updated stack and symbols.
...  ;   Load the subroutine index obtained from
...  ;   the exception value.
0147    ldc.i4 subroutineIndex
014c    call Void STInterp(Int32, CallFrame)
```

(a) CIL code generated by the type-specializing code generator for the expression a + b + global.

```
void __foo(CallFrame *callFrame)
{
  int a, b;

  try {
    b = 10;
    a = callFrame->argument[0].ToInt();

    int _temp0 = a + b;
    DValue _temp1 = callFrame->getGlobal("global");

    /* TYPE CHECK */
    if (_temp1.type != Int) { // Int is the profiled type
      /* DEOPTIMIZATION CODE */
      /* Update the profiler with newly observed type */
      UpdateProfiler(global, Int);
      /* Capture the current values of _temp* */
      callFrame->stack.Enqueue(_temp1); // Enqueue(DValue);
      callFrame->stack.Enqueue(_temp0); // Enqueue(int);
      /* 5 is the pointer to the subroutine */
      throw new GuardFailureException(5);
    }
    else { // FAST PATH
      callFrame->retVal = DValue(_temp0 + _temp1.AsInt32());
      return;
    }
  }
  catch (GuardFailureException e) {
    /* Update the callFrame->symbols array with the
       current values of local variables */
    callFrame->symbols[symbolsIndex++] = DValue(a);
    callFrame->symbols[symbolsIndex]   = DValue(b);
    BlackList(this); // BlackList this function code.
    STInterp(e.subRoutineIndex, callFrame);
  }
}
```

(b) C-like psuedocode that describes the generated CIL for the JavaScript code in Figure 2. The values pushed onto the stack are made explicit using _temp variables.

Figure 3: The code generated for the JavaScript example in Figure 2.

at the point the exception is thrown. The function locals, in contrast, are captured inside the catch block; this is because the operand stack is specific to a particular deoptimization point while the locals are common across all deoptimization points in the function. Capturing the values of the local variables in a single place avoids code duplication and reduces code bloat.

Once inside the catch block and with all local variables captured, the runtime must clean up and then transfer control to the appropriate subroutine. First, the runtime calls the Blacklist function which deletes the specialized code that had to be deoptimized and updates the function metadata with this information; this prevents the function from entering a cycle of specialization followed by deopti-

mization over and over again. Secondly, the runtime calls the appropriate subroutine whose pointer was passed inside the GuardFailure exception, passing it the updated callFrame data structure as explained below.

State Transfer. In MCJS, the callFrame data structure tracks the state of execution for the current function. It also holds a link to the scoping structure used to resolve the scope of the variables used in the function. Figure 4 shows the definition of callFrame. MCJS uses the callFrame object to transfer program state from the specialized code to the unspecialized subroutine-threaded code. The two relevant fields are symbols, which holds the values of the function's local variables at the deoptimization point, and stack, which holds the operand stack at the deoptimization point.

```
struct CallFrame {
    // Arguments passed to the function
    DValueArray arguments;
    // Return value of the function
    DValue retVal;

    // Fields and functions to track the scope
    // and other bookkeeping.
    Scope currentScope;
    Scope parentScope;

    // Fields below are only used by the
    // subroutine-threaded interpreter.
    // symbols array is used to store the values of
    // local variables at the deoptimization point.
    DValueArray symbols;

    // stack array is used to capture the state of
    // operand stack at the deoptimization point.
    DValueArray stack;
}
```

Figure 4: The callFrame data structure which tracks the state of execution for the current function.

Instruction	Operand Stack	TypeStack
;before state transfer	global a + b	DValue Int32
LdLoc callFrame	callFrame global a + b	DValue Int32
LdFld stack	stack global a + b	DValue Int32
Call stack.Enqueue(DValue)	a + b	Int32
LdLoc callFrame	callFrame a + b	Int32
LdFld stack	stack a + b	Int32
Call stack.Enqueue(Int32)		

Table 2: The different steps taken when popping values from the operand stack.

The symbols field is computed inside the specialized function's catch block, as explained above. This is straightforward for the MCJS implementation because the runtime maintains a list of local symbols; the catch block merely iterates over this list and copies the values into the callFrame.symbols field.

The stack field must be computed separately for each deoptimization point. For each point, the type and number of values that need to be pushed onto the stack are different. The code generator used to generate the specialized CIL code uses the bytecode verifier to track this information. The verifier is reponsible for inferring and checking type information, which means that it already needs to know the required information. We simply piggyback on the verifier to determine what code to emit for enqueueing the operand stack values at each deoptimization point. The verifier maintains a data structure called the TypeStack which holds the types of values inside the operand stack at each program point. At each deoptimization point, we record the current TypeStack and emit code to enqueue the operand stack values onto callFrame.stack. Each value is wrapped inside a DValue before being enqueued. Because in CIL value types are not subtypes of the Object type, the runtime cannot use a generic Enqueue(Object) method to enqueue the values which is why we need the verifier's TypeStack information.

Table 2 shows how the state transfer code is generated for the example in Figure 2. Maintaining a TypeStack during code generation helps to determine which variation of Enqueue has to be called to enqueue the value in the top of the operand stack to callFrame.stack. In the example, while enqueuing global from the operand stack, the top of the TypeStack is referred for the appropriate type. Since the type of global is DValue, the CIL code to call Enqueue(DValue) is emitted by the code generator. Similarly, a call to Enqueue(Int32) is emitted to capture the value of a + b from the operand stack.

4.3 Limitations

Our deoptimization technique assumes that all values present on the operand stack at a deoptimization point are subtypes of DValue. If so, then all of the values are easily convertable to value types used in the JavaScript runtime. However, there are rare cases where this assumption is not true. Some optimizations, such as polymorphic inline caches, store the map or class of an object in the operand stack of the CLR. If a deoptimization is triggered at this point, state transfer is not possible because map cannot be converted to a DValue and stored in callFrame.stack.

Fortunately, it is easy to detect this ahead of time during code generation. During the fast compilation phase which translates warm functions to CIL bytecode and instruments the code with type profiling hooks, the types of the values in the operand stack are tracked by the code verifier as previously described. For every deoptimization point, the type stack is checked to see whether it contains values that cannot be converted to DValue. If so, then the function is

Benchmark	Type
breakout.js	Game
chopper.js	Game, Animation
colorfulPointer.js	Utility, Animation
conways.js	Animation, Algorithm
flyingWindows.js	Animation, Utility
loadingSpinner.js	Utility
sierpinskiGasket.js	Algorithm
analogClock.js	Utility
halloweenAnim.js	Animation
growingGrass.js	Animation
kaboom.js	Game
mandelbrot.js	Animation, Algorithm
plasma.js	Animation
primesAnim.js	Algorithm
springPond.js	Algorithm, Animation
tetris.js	Game
waveGraph.js	Algorithm, Utility

Table 3: Table describing JS1k web applications used as benchmarks.

marked as non-optimizable. The profile hooks are removed and the function is compiled directly to CIL without any type feedback-based type specialization. Our evaluation shows that this circumstance rarely happens.

5. Evaluation

We evaluate our deoptimization technique on MCJS using the standard JavaScript benchmark suites Sunspider [1] and V8 [2] [6]. Because the Sunspider benchmarks run for a short duration of time (average of 180ms), each benchmark was wrapped in a $20\times$ loop. We also evaluate our technique on real-world long-running web applications from the JS1k [4] website. Due to the unstable nature of IronJS, we selected only the benchmarks that IronJS was able to execute without any problem. The JS1k benchmarks are described in the Table 3.

Experimental Setup. We perform our experiments on a machine with two 6-core 1.9 GHz Intel Xeon processors with 32GB of RAM, running the Ubuntu 12.04.3 Linux OS and Mono v3.2.3. We used the latest version of IronJS, v0.2.1.0 from its Github repository [3].

Calculating Speedups. To calculate execution times, each of the benchmarks is run eleven times and the average execution time of the last ten executions is recorded.

Configurations. Speedup numbers were collected for the following five configurations.

- MCJS without type feedback-based type specialization (the base configuration against which results for other configurations are normalized).

---

[6]MCJS and IronJS do not implement typed arrays. Therefore, we not evaluate our implementation on Octane benchmarks.

- MCJS with type specialization using the standard fast path + slow path recovery mechanism (MCJS_FS).
- MCJS with type specialization using the deoptimization recovery mechanism, i.e., our technique (MCJS_D).
- MCJS with optimal type specialization (MCJS_OPT) as described below.
- IronJS in its default configuration.

The optimal type specialization configuration means that code is type-specialized but there is no deoptimization or any other recovery mechanism; this is unsound, but provides a maximal speedup due to type specialization against which we can compare our technique and the cost of deoptimization. IronJS is implemented on top of DLR [10] which mimics the fast path + slow path approach to optimizing type specializable code, hence we use it to show that MCJS is not a strawman JavaScript implementation.

5.1 Speedups

Figure 5 shows the speedups achieved by the type specializing configurations with respect to the MCJS base configuration for the Sunspider benchmark suite. The approaches without a local slow path (i.e., MCJS_D and MCJS_OPT) perform significantly better than the fast path + slow path approaches implemented in MCJS and IronJS. The MCJS_OPT configuration does not emit any deoptimization code and the runtime exits when any deoptimization should occur, which is why the 3d-cube.js benchmark sees a speedup of $0\times$ for the MCJS_OPT configuration.

On an average (geomean) MCJS_D, MCJS_FS, and IronJS are $1.5\times$, $1.31\times$, and $0.77\times$ faster than the base configuration, respectively. On comparing the execution times of MCJS_D against MCJS_FS and IronJS, we see an average speedup (geomean) of $1.14\times$ and $1.97\times$ respectively. An important observation is that for a few of the benchmarks like access-fannkuch.js, access-nbody.js, access-nsieve.js, bitops-bitwise-and.js, etc, the runtime does not benefit from type feedback-based type specialization. This is because these benchmarks are relatively small and execute for a very short period of time (average of 237.2ms). For these benchmarks profiling overhead is not amortized over time.

Figure 6 shows the speedups achieved by the type specializing configurations with respect to the MCJS base configuration for the V8 benchmark suite. We selected the benchmarks for which IronJS executed without crashing. Following a similar trend as the Sunspider benchmarks, MCJS_D, MCJS_FS, and IronJS are $2.13\times$, $1.74\times$, and $1.21\times$ faster than the MCJS base configuration. On comparing the execution times of MCJS_D against MCJS_FS and IronJS, we see an average (geomean) speedup of $1.22\times$ and $1.75\times$ respectively. Excluding regexp.js (for which MCJS spends most of the time executing the inefficient regexp library code) and splay.js (which is a benchmark designed for stressing the garbage collection of the engine rather than the runtime

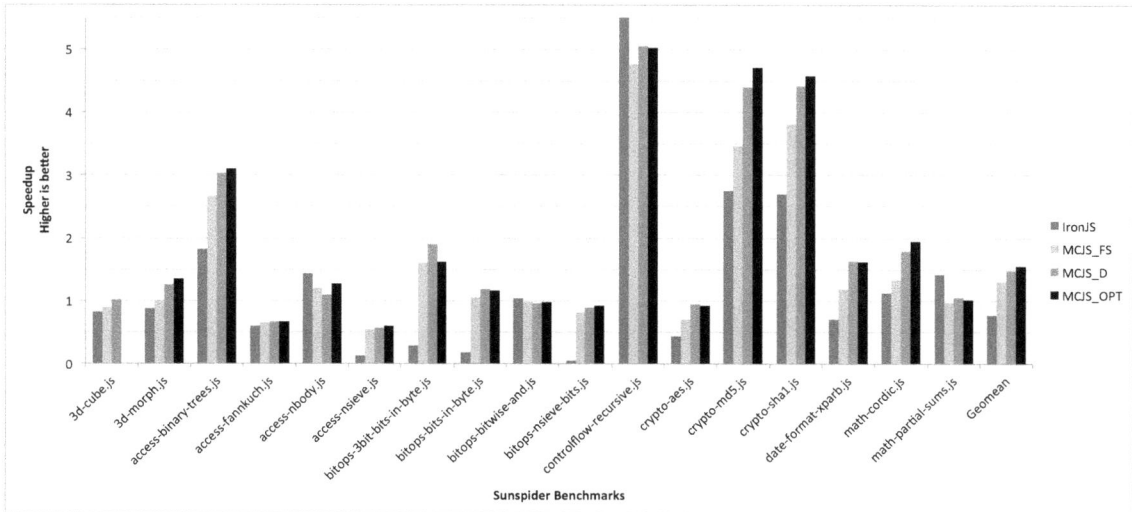

Figure 5: This figure shows the speedup numbers for various configurations of MCJS and IronJS for the Sunspider benchmark suite. FS = fast path + slow path, D = deoptimization, OPT = optimal.

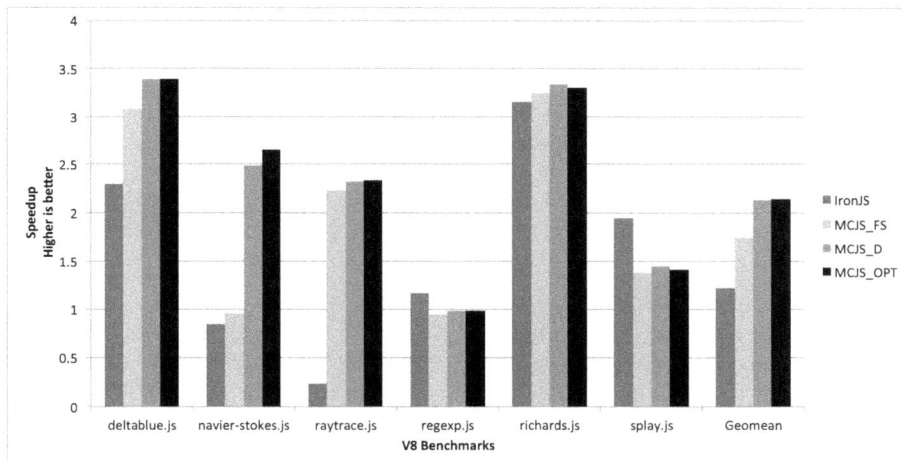

Figure 6: This figure shows the speedup numbers for various configurations of MCJS and IronJS for the V8 benchmark suite. FS = fast path + slow path, D = deoptimization, OPT = optimal.

performance), MCJS_D consistently performs better than all other configurations.

The JS1k benchmarks represent a diverse set of applications including games, utilities, algorithms, and animations. We manually modified the JavaScript code to eliminate or substitute code that interacted with the browser DOM. We substituted setTimeOut and setInterval functions with JavaScript functions that execute the passed-in function in a loop for a considerable number of times. For the benchmarks that require user interactions like mouse clicks, the user events were simulated using a fixed set of event objects embedded in the code. These applications run for a relatively long duration with the average execution time for the base configuration being 10.66 seconds.

Figure 7 shows the speedups achieved by the type specializing configurations with respect to the MCJS base configuration for the JS1k web application benchmark suite. As expected, MCJS_D, MCJS_FS and IronJS are 1.76×, 1.5×, and 0.94× times faster than the MCJS base configuration. Similar to the other benchmark suites, on comparing the execution times of MCJS_D with MCJS_FS and IronJS, we see an average speedup of 1.18× and 1.87× respectively.

Speedup vs. V8: MCJS achieves on an average about 75% of the V8 engine performance on the Sunspider benchmarks. The speedup is significantly lower for few of the

111

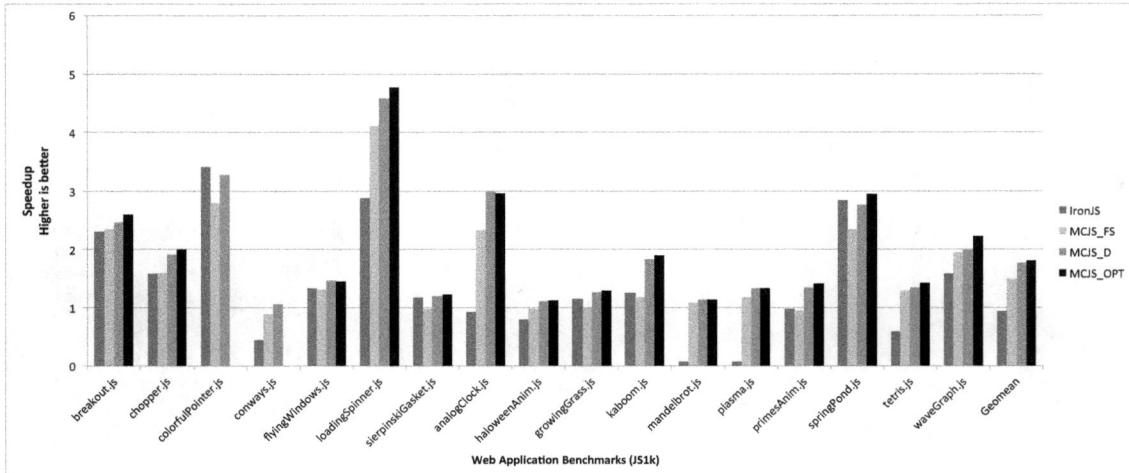

Figure 7: This figure shows the speedup numbers for various configurations of MCJS and IronJS for the web application benchmark suite. FS = fast path + slow path, D = deoptimization, OPT = optimal.

benchmarks in V8 benchmark suite. This is mainly because the regexp and string library implementations of MCJS (which are based on CLR's implementations) are very slow. Those affects dominate performance for those benchmarks, rather than anything due to recovery. However, this is not a fair comparison because V8 implements both the recovery mechanisms as part of its compilers along with many other optimizations, making it very difficult to tease out and isolate the effect of each of the recovery mechanisms.

5.2 Effect of Deoptimization

Deoptimization is a rare occurrence and it is observed only during the execution of the 3d-cube.js, colorfulPointer.js, and conways.js benchmarks. The speedup numbers for these benchmarks indicate that the overhead of the actual deoptimization process is negligible.

There are two ways of measuring the effect of the deoptimization code. First, we compare the speedup achieved by the MCJS_D and MCJS_OPT configurations. Figures 5, 6, and 7 indicate that the runtime overhead of the deoptimization code is negligible.

Secondly, we compare the size of the extra code that is generated to achieve deoptimization for each of the benchmarks. Figure 8 shows the comparison on code size of MCJS_D and MCJS_FS with respect to MCJS_OPT. Though the amount of code that is generated in MCJS_D is approx. 30% higher compared to the MCJS_OPT configuration, the impact on performance is negligible. This is because most of the extra code that is generated is to enable deoptimization. This deoptimization code is rarely ever executed for most of the benchmarks.

Another important metric used while comparing two implementations is the memory consumption. The amount of data captured in the stackFrame data-structure is very mini-

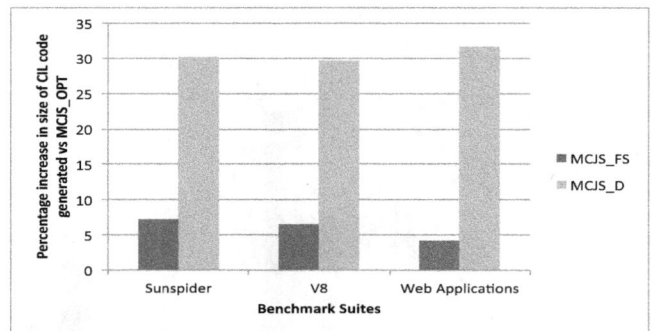

Figure 8: This figure shows the percentage increase in CIL code generated for MCJS_FS and MCJS_D in comparison to MCJS_OPT. FS = Fast + Slow Path, D = Fast Path with Deoptimization, and OPT = Fast Path with No Deoptimization.

mal; the operand stack and values associated with local variables are usually a few bytes in size. Therefore, the stack-Frame data-structure has little to no impact on memory when we consider a managed runtime system.

5.3 Boxing/Unboxing

The amount of boxing and unboxing of DValues performed during the execution of the benchmarks is a major cause of overhead for the MCJS_FS configuration. Figure 9 shows the percentage increase in boxing and unboxing performed in MCJS_FS configuration when compared to the MCJS_D configuration for each of the benchmark suites. As expected, MCJS_FS performs more boxing and unboxing of values when compared to MCJS_D across all benchmark suites.

An important observation is that the percentage of boxing for web applications is significantly higher compared to other benchmarks. This is because the number of variables

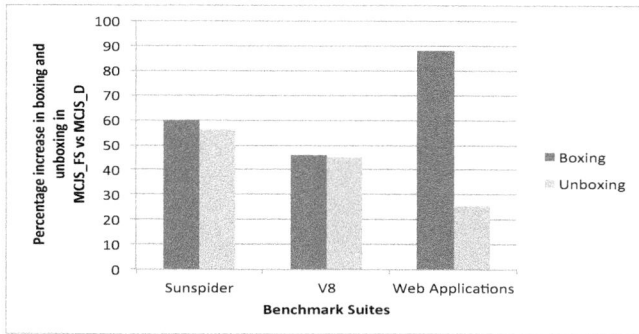

Figure 9: This figure shows the percentage increase in boxing and unboxing in MCJS_FS in comparison to MCJS_D. FS = fast path + slow path and D = deoptimization.

that are typed in the MCJS_D configuration is significantly higher compared to the number of local variables which are typed in the MCJS_FS configuration. This means that for the MCJS_FS configuration almost all the values need to be boxed before assigning them to the variable.

5.4 Non-optimizable Code

In some benchmarks, the deoptimization approach is not possible because some values present in the operand stack cannot be converted to DValues, as explained in Section 4.3. Among all benchmarks from the various benchmark suites that were executed, the runtime was not able to generate deoptimization code for only 35 out of 448 functions that were classified as hot. This shows that the deoptimization approach is viable for type specialization on top of VMs.

6. Related Work

Both the fast path + slow path and the deoptimization approaches for type specialization have been used in various dynamic language runtimes implemented natively (rather than on top of a VM). The baseline compilers of popular JavaScript engines V8 [9, 24] and SpiderMonkey [23] use the fast path + slow path approach for initial compilation of JavaScript functions to native code. Once a function becomes hot, the optimizing compilers for both of these engines generate type-specialized code with deoptimization hooks. If the types used for specialization change during execution, the runtime performs deoptimization by initiating long jumps to deoptimization routines in the compiled machine code. Language runtimes written on top of typed, stack-based runtimes cannot implement such a deoptimization technique because of the typed nature of the IR and the runtime type safety guarantees enforced by the VM.

TraceMonkey [13], PyPy [6], and LuaJIT [19] are popular tracing JIT compilers. Deoptimization is a common approach to use in runtimes with trace-based compilers. These traces span across function boundaries and are compiled to native code with deoptimization hooks. Implementing such

a trace-based compiler on top of a VM is very complicated, especially from the perspective of deoptimization.

Brunthaler et al [7, 8] describe a purely interpretative optimization technique called *Quickening* implemented in CPython runtime. Quickening involves rewriting generic instructions to optimized alternatives based on the runtime information. This is analogous to the fast-path + slow-path approach of optimization. Quickening with deoptimization can be an alternative to the existing approach of optimization.

Hackett et al [14] describe an approach of combining type inference with type feedback to generate type specialized code. This approach uses recompilation approach instead of classic deoptimization technique to bail out whenever the type related assumptions do not hold anymore in the compiled code. Their approach tracks the type of values held by a variable or object field, and recompile all the type specialized code to generic version when the new types are observed.

Dynamic Language Runtime (DLR) [10] based language implementations like IronJS [3], IronRuby, and IronPython compile the program written in the dynamic language into DLR's *ExpressionTrees*. DLR performs the optimizations and native code generation required for the runtime. DLR employs polymorphic inline caches to specialize any operation observed during execution, which is analogous to the fast path + slow path approach of type specialization. As observed in Section 5, such an optimization does not always result in good performance when compared to the deoptimization approach.

Ishizaki et al [17] implement a dynamically-typed language runtime by modifying a statically-typed language compiler. Their approach to type specialization modifies the compiler to generate fast path + slow path code for arithmetic, logical, and comparison operators. Similarly to the MCJS original fast path + slow path approach, their approach also has to deal with incessant boxing and unboxing of values.

Duboscq et al [11] describe a way of inserting and coalescing deoptimization points in the IR of the Graal VM. This technique is orthogonal to and complementary to our own. In our approach, the deoptimization points are determined while generating the subroutine threaded code for the interpreter. Our implementation can benefit from the techniques like coalescing and movement of deoptimziation points described in their paper.

On-stack replacement (OSR) is a deoptimization / reoptimization strategy that has been explored and implemented in language runtimes to enable speculative optimizations [12, 15, 20, 22] and to enable debugging of optimized code [16]. Hölzle et al [16] implement deoptimization for the SELF programing language for debugging optimized code. The main focus of this work is to maintain the mapping from optimized compiled code to source code. As the authors have complete control over the underlying VM, such deoptimization is relatively easy to implement when compared to our implementation which does not modify the underlying VM. Fink et al [12] describe an on-stack replacement strategy for deoptimization implemented in JikesRVM. As described in the paper, capturing the state of the execution is straightforward given the access to the JVM scope descriptor object of the executing code. Our implementation is not straightforward due to the fact that part of the state that needs to be transferred resides in the underlying operand stack which is not easily accessible by any code currently executing in the VM. Soman et al [22] present a new general-purpose OSR technique on JikesRVM which is decoupled from the optimization performed by the runtime. Similar to this approach our deoptimization technique is also general-purpose. Applying the current deoptimization technique to other optimizations would involve minor modifications to the subroutine threaded interpreter to indicate the expected points of deoptimization specific to that optimization.

7. Conclusion

Deoptimization is a recovery mechanism which allows the runtime to bail out of type specialized code when type assumptions are violated, capture the state of current execution and continue execution form an equivalent point in a unspecialized code. This paper proposes a novel deoptimization based type-specialized code generation for a dynamic language runtime implemented on top of a typed, stack-based virtual machine. Our approach does not require any modification to the underlying virtual machine. Our implementation uses the exception handling feature offered by the underlying VM to perform deoptimization. Just using exception handling feature to jump into unspecialized code is not enough because throwing an exception clears the operand stack of the VM. The operand stack is an important part of state that needs to be transferred during deoptimization. We leverage the shadow type stack maintained by the bytecode verifier, which verifies the validity of the code generated during its generation, to safely transfer the values in the operand stack to the unspecialized code.

We implement our proposed technique in MCJS, a research JavaScript engine running on top of the Mono runtime. We evaluate our implementation against the fast path + slow path approach implemented in MCJS and IronJS. Our results show that deoptimization approach is on an average (geomean) $1.16\times$ and $1.88\times$ faster than fast path + slow path approach implemented in MCJS and IronJS respectively on Sunspider, V8 and web application benchmark suites.

Our implementation is generic and can be extended to enable other optimizations like function inlining. A few minor modifications to the existing approach are required to implement it in a sound manner. Currently, the location of deoptimization is determined by the placement of type checking guards. This needs to be extended to incorporate possible places where function inlining is possible in the code.

Acknowledgments

We would like to thank the the anonymous reviewers for their valuable input. The work described in this paper was significantly supported by Qualcomm Research.

References

[1] Sunspider benchmark suite. http://www.webkit.org/perf/sunspider/sunspider.html.

[2] V8 benchmark suite. http://v8.googlecode.com/svn/data/benchmarks/v7/README.txt.

[3] Ironjs javascript engine. https://github.com/fholm/IronJS, 2013.

[4] Js1k. http://js1k.com, 2013.

[5] M. Berndl, B. Vitale, M. Zaleski, and A. D. Brown. Context threading: A flexible and efficient dispatch technique for virtual machine interpreters. In *Proceedings of the international symposium on Code generation and optimization*, 2005.

[6] C. F. Bolz, A. Cuni, M. Fijalkowski, and A. Rigo. Tracing the meta-level: Pypy's tracing jit compiler. In *Proceedings of the 4th workshop on the Implementation, Compilation, Optimization of Object-Oriented Languages and Programming Systems*, 2009.

[7] S. Brunthaler. Efficient interpretation using quickening. In *Proceedings of the 6th Symposium on Dynamic Languages*, 2010.

[8] S. Brunthaler. Inline caching meets quickening. In *Proceedings of the 24th European Conference on Object-oriented Programming*, 2010.

[9] Crankshaft compiler. V8 engine. http://www.jayconrod.com/posts/54/a-tour-of-v8-crankshaft-the-optimizing-compiler, 2013.

[10] DLR. Microsoft Dynamic Language Runtime. http://dlr.codeplex.com/, 2013.

[11] G. Duboscq, T. Würthinger, L. Stadler, C. Wimmer, D. Simon, and H. Mössenböck. An intermediate representation for speculative optimizations in a dynamic compiler. In *Proceedings of the sixth ACM workshop on Virtual machines and intermediate languages*, 2013.

[12] S. J. Fink and F. Qian. Design, implementation and evaluation of adaptive recompilation with on-stack replacement. In *Proceedings of the international symposium on Code generation and optimization: feedback-directed and runtime optimization*, 2003.

[13] A. Gal, B. Eich, M. Shaver, D. Anderson, D. Mandelin, M. R. Haghighat, B. Kaplan, G. Hoare, B. Zbarsky, J. Orendorff, J. Ruderman, E. W. Smith, R. Reitmaier, M. Bebenita, M. Chang, and M. Franz. Trace-based just-in-time type specialization for dynamic languages. In *Proceedings of the 2009 ACM SIGPLAN conference on Programming language design and implementation*, 2009.

[14] B. Hackett and S.-y. Guo. Fast and precise hybrid type inference for javascript. In *Proceedings of the 33rd ACM SIGPLAN conference on Programming Language Design and Implementation*, 2012.

[15] U. Hölzle and D. Ungar. A third-generation self implementation: reconciling responsiveness with performance. In *Proceedings of the ninth annual conference on Object-oriented programming systems, language, and applications*, 1994.

[16] U. Hölzle, C. Chambers, and D. Ungar. Debugging optimized code with dynamic deoptimization. In *Proceedings of the ACM SIGPLAN 1992 conference on Programming language design and implementation*, 1992.

[17] K. Ishizaki, T. Ogasawara, J. Castanos, P. Nagpurkar, D. Edelsohn, and T. Nakatani. Adding dynamically-typed language support to a statically-typed language compiler: performance evaluation, analysis, and tradeoffs. In *Proceedings of the 8th ACM SIGPLAN/SIGOPS conference on Virtual Execution Environments*, 2012.

[18] M. N. Kedlaya, J. Roesch, B. Robatmili, M. Reshadi, and B. Hardekopf. Improved type specialization for dynamic scripting languages. In *Proceedings of the 9th Symposium on Dynamic Languages*, 2013.

[19] LuaJIT. Lua Just-In-Time compiler. http://luajit.org/, 2013.

[20] M. Paleczny, C. Vick, and C. Click. The java hotspot server compiler. In *Proceedings of the 2001 Symposium on JavaTM Virtual Machine Research and Technology Symposium - Volume 1*, 2001.

[21] B. Robatmili, C. Cascaval, M. Reshadi, M. N. Kedlaya, S. Fowler, M. Weber, and B. Hardekopf. Muscalietjs: Rethinking layered dynamic web runtimes. In *Proceedings of the 10th ACM SIGPLAN/SIGOPS conference on Virtual Execution Environments*, 2014.

[22] S. Soman and C. Krintz. Efficient and general on-stack replacement for aggressive program specialization. In *Proceedings of the 2006 International Conference on Programming Languages and Compilers*, 2006.

[23] SpiderMonkey. SpiderMonkey JavaScript Engine. http://www.mozilla.org/js/spidermonkey/, 2013.

[24] V8. Google Inc. V8 JavaScript virtual machine. https://code.google.com/p/v8, 2013.

The Case for the Three R's of Systems Research: Repeatability, Reproducibility and Rigor

Jan Vitek

Purdue University

Abstract

Computer systems research spans sub-disciplines that include embedded systems, programming languages, networking, and operating systems. In this talk my contention is that a number of structural factors inhibit quality systems research. Symptoms of the problem include unrepeatable and unreproduced results as well as results that are either devoid of meaning or that measure the wrong thing. I will illustrate the impact of these issues on our research output with examples from the development and empirical evaluation of the Schism real-time garbage collection algorithm that is shipped with the FijiVM – a Java virtual machine for embedded and mobile devices. I will argue that our field should foster: repetition of results, independent reproduction, as well as rigorous evaluation. I will outline some baby steps taken by several computer conferences. In particular I will focus on the introduction of Artifact Evaluation Committees or AECs to ECOOP, OOPLSA, PLDI and soon POPL. The goal of the AECs is to encourage author to package the software artifacts that they used to support the claims made in their paper and to submit these artifacts for evaluation. AECs were carefully designed to provide positive feedback to the authors that take the time to create repeatable research.

Joint work with Kalibera, Pizlo, Hosking, Blanton and Ziarek [1–3].

Biography

Jan Vitek is a Professor of Computer Science at Purdue University since 1999 and University Faculty Scholar. He holds a PhD from the University of Geneva and a Masters from the University of Victoria.

Over the years, Jan worked on a number of topics related to programming languages, their design, use and implementation. With Noble and Potter, he proposed the notion of flexible alias control, which became know as Ownership Types. Jan led the Ovm project which produced the first real-time Java virtual machine to be flight tested on a ScanEagle drone (he is sure no one was harmed as a side effect). Two outcomes of this project were the Schism real-time garbage collection algorithm and the FijiVM – a production VM for embedded systems. More recently, Jan worked on dynamic languages, trying to make sense of JavaScript and to design a new language called, Thorn. Nowadays, he spends his time with statisticians and data scientists.

Jan Vitek believes that he was elected Chair of SIGPLAN be accident in 2012, and since has been busy trying to rock the boat to make sure this does not happen again.

In his spare time, Jan enjoys starting workshops series, sitting on conference program committees and organizing conferences. He founded the MOS (mobile objects), IWACO (alias control), STOP (gradual typing), and TRANSACT (transactional memory) workshop series. Was the first program chair of VEE and chairs ESOP, ECOOP, Coordination and TOOLS. Was the general chair of PLDI (in Beijing!), ISMM and LCTES. He may still be sitting on the steering committee of some of these conferences: ECOOP, JTRES, ICFP, OOPLSA, POPL, PLDI, LCTES, ESOP.

References

[1] J. Vitek, T. Kalibera. *Repeatability, Reproducibility and Rigor in Systems Research.* In EMSOFT, 2011.

[2] T. Kalibera, F. Pizlo, A. Hosking, J. Vitek. *Scheduling real-time garbage collection on uniprocessors.* ACM Trans. Comput. Syst. 29 (3), 2001.

[3] F. Pizlo, E. Blanton, A. Hosking, P. Maj, J. Vitek, L. Ziarek. *Schis: Fragmentation-tolerant real-time garbage collection.* In PLDI 2010.

VEE '14, March 1–2, 2014, Salt Lake City, Utah, USA.
Copyright is held by the owner/author(s).
ACM 978-1-4503-2764-0 /14/03.
http://dx.doi.org/10.1145/2576195.2576216

Efficient Memory Virtualization for Cross-ISA System Mode Emulation

Chao-Jui Chang, Jan-Jan Wu

Institute of Information Science,
Academia Sinica, Taiwan
{crchang,wuj}@iis.sinica.edu.tw

Wei-Chung Hsu, Pangfeng Liu

Dept. Computer Science &
Information Engineering
National Taiwan University
{hsuwc, pangfeng}@csie.ntu.edu.tw

Pen-Chung Yew

Dept. Computer Science
& Engineering
University of Minnesota at Twin
Cities, Minneapolis, USA
yew@cs.umn.edu

Abstract

Cross-ISA system-mode emulation has many important applications. For example, Cross-ISA system-mode emulation helps computer architects and OS developers trace and debug kernel execution-flow efficiently by emulating a slower platform (such as ARM) on a more powerful platform (such as an x86 machine). Cross-ISA system-mode emulation also enables workload consolidation in data centers with platforms of different instruction-set architectures (ISAs). However, system-mode emulation is much slower. One major overhead in system-mode emulation is the multi-level memory address translation that maps guest virtual address to host physical address. Shadow page tables (SPT) have been used to reduce such overheads, but primarily for same-ISA virtualization. In this paper we propose a novel approach called embedded shadow page tables (ESPT). EPST embeds a shadow page table into the address space of a cross-ISA dynamic binary translation (DBT) and uses hardware memory management unit in the CPU to translate memory addresses, instead of software translation in a current DBT emulator like QEMU. We also use the larger address space on modern 64-bit CPUs to accommodate our DBT emulator so that it will not interfere with the guest operating system. We incorporate our new scheme into QEMU, a popular, retargetable cross-ISA system emulator. SPEC CINT2006 benchmark results indicate that our technique achieves an average speedup of 1.51 times in system mode when emulating ARM on x86, and a 1.59 times speedup for emulating IA32 on x86_64.

Categories and Subject Descriptors   D.0 [*Computer Systems Organization*]: System Architectures;

General Terms   Design, Experimentation, Performance

Keywords   memory virtualization; cross-ISA dynamic binary translation; hardware MMU; embedded shadow page table

1. Introduction

Whole system emulation is very important for multi-cores and cloud computing. It allows applications running on such systems to be agnostic about the underlying operating systems and hardware platforms. For example, applications compiled for a particular instruction-set architecture (ISA) and operating system, such as an Intel x86 platform running Windows, can run on an ARM platform running Linux. With system mode emulation we can run legacy applications developed for older OSes and ISAs on newer ones. System mode emulation also enables the implementation of secure environments in which operating systems are isolated from one another. Finally system emulation speeds up CPU execution flow tracing and OS kernel debugging by emulating a slower platform (e.g., ARM) on a faster one (e.g., x86-64).

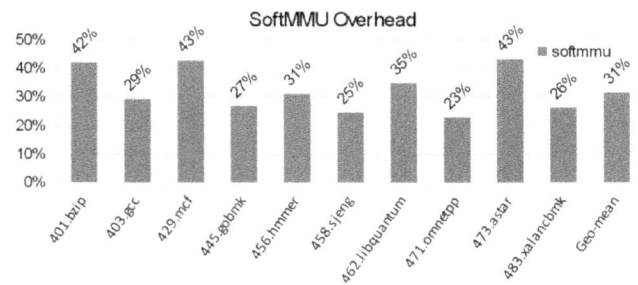

Figure 1-0. Percentage of the total execution time spent in address translation in QEMU system-mode emulation (ARM to x86_64)

For same ISA system emulation, efficiency is improved by recent hardware support, including Intel VT-x, AMD-V, and ARM-VE. This paper focuses on cross-ISA system-level emulation, i.e., the guest and the host are of different instruction set architectures, using dynamic binary translation (DBT) techniques.

QEMU is a popular retargetable cross-ISA, system-level emulator. It runs as a process and virtualizes memory through multi-level address translation by the software-based virtual memory management unit (vMMU). The address translation incurs significant overheads and is the main reason for slow emulation. For example, Figure 1-0 shows that in average QEMU spends 23%~43% of the total execution time in memory translation for SPEC CINT2006 benchmarks when running in system mode emulation.

In this paper, we propose an efficient memory virtualization scheme for cross-ISA system-level DBT. This scheme effectively incorporates shadow page tables (SPTs) [20] in DBT and uses the hardware MMU on the host machine to translate memory addresses without slow software MMU translation.

Using Shadow Page Tables (SPTs) or hardware assisted Second Level Address Translation (SLAT) [24,26] to support memory virtualization is a well-known technique for same-ISA virtualization [17]. However, adopting a shadow page table in a cross-ISA DBT is much more challenging for the three reasons. First, the host shadow page table must be carefully placed to avoid interfering with the virtual memory space of the guest OS, because we are collapsing the two address space. Second, the overheads in creating and maintaining a shadow page table must be minimized, because guest page tables modification is just a normal memory operation and tracing all guest memory update incurs extra overhead. Third, multi-process emulation with one address space, because multiple processes are executed at the same time in a guest OS.

We propose the notion of "*embedded shadow page table*" (ESPTs) to address these challenges. ESPT utilizes the larger address space of modern 64-bit CPUs to provide more space for mapping tables and to achieve address isolation. The rationale behind the embedded shadow page table is that by embedding the shadow page entries into the host page table of the DBT, the translated host binary code will be executed in the address space of the host machine, and thus avoiding switching between shadow and page tables while translating a guest virtual address.

The main contributions of this paper are as follows.

- We propose an efficient memory virtualization for cross-ISA system-level DBT by incorporating hardware MMU into the DBT. To the best of our knowledge, our work is the first effort to exploit hardware MMU support for cross-ISA, system-level memory virtualization.

- We propose the notion of embedded shadow page tables to avoid frequent switching between host page table and shadow page table during address translation.

- We adopt an interception-based methodology for tracing guest page modification, reducing the overhead of synchronizing guest page tables and embedded shadow page tables.

- Our implementation on QEMU demonstrates an average speedup of 1.51 times and 1.59 times on SPEC CINT2006 benchmarks for ARM-to-x86 and IA32-to-x86_64 system-mode emulation, respectively, when compared with the standard soft-MMU approach in QEMU. The results also show an average speedup of 1.15 times and 1.28 times on NBench benchmarks for ARM-to-x86 and IA32-to-x86_64 system-mode emulation, respectively.

The rest of the paper is organized as follows. Section 2 gives an overview on the various memory virtualization techniques and the motivation of our proposed ESPT-based approach for cross-ISA memory address translation. We also elaborate on the challenges in the design and implementation of such an approach. Section 3 presents our design and implementation details of the proposed ESPT-based approach. Section 4 reports our experiment results on ARM-to-x86 emulation and x86_32 to x86_64 emulation with SPEC CINT2006 and the NBench benchmarks. Section 5 describes some related work, and Section 6 gives our concluding remarks.

2. Memory Virtualization

In this section, we first briefly describe memory address translation and DBT emulation. Next, we introduce software-based same-ISA and cross-ISA emulation, and point out the source of inefficiency in such software-based implementation. We then introduce recent hardware approaches for same-ISA memory address translation, e.g., Intel's Extended Page Table (EPT) and AMD's Nested Paging, and explain why they cannot provide efficient support for cross-ISA emulation. Finally we describe the motivation behind our hardware-assisted approach for cross-ISA memory virtualization, and discuss the challenges in designing and implementing the proposed approach.

Virtual address technology provides a separate address space for each process to achieve process isolation in a multitasking operating system with the help of a memory management unit (MMU). MMU is a computer hardware component that provides memory access for CPU by translating virtual addresses from processes to physical addresses. A physical address is the memory address on a physical machine.

Figure 2-0 illustrates the components in a DBT emulation system and the execution flow. Virtualization technology allows multiple operating systems to run on a single physical machine. The operating system runs directly on the physical machine is the host operating system, and the operating systems running on the host operating system are guest operating systems. A DBT emulator is a process that runs on the host operating system and provides emulated hardware components, like a virtual MMU, CPU, and memory, to the guest operating systems.

The execution flow of a DBT is: 1) a user launches a DBT emulator to run a guest OS on host operating system; 2) an application in the guest OS issues a memory access instruction; 3-4) the software MMU refers to the guest's page table and performs the translation of virtual address (GVA) to physical address (GPA); 5-6) the DBT emulator has another layer of mapping guest physical address to host virtual address (HVA) to avoid occupying the whole host memory at beginning; 7-8) the host memory management unit refers to host's page table and performs host virtual address to host physical address (HPA) translation. Note that in a cross-ISA DBT, the guest physical address is not the same as the host virtual address, whereas in a same-ISA VM they are basically equivalent.

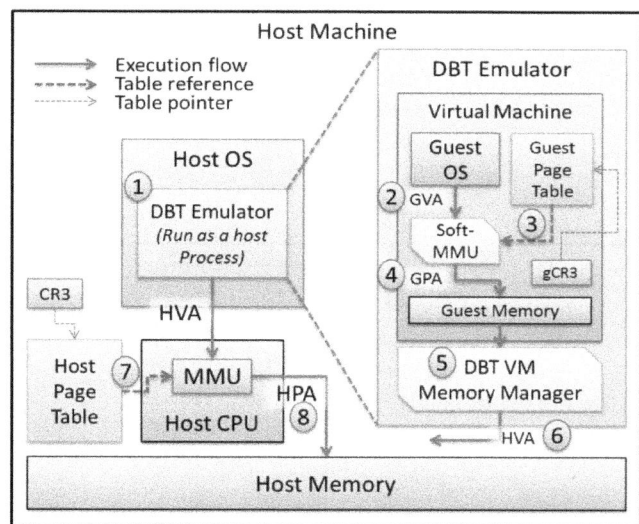

Figure 2-0. The components and the execution flow of a DBT emulator

For same-ISA virtualization, modern CPU provides hardware support to execute the guest OS seamlessly while use guest page table directly. When address translation is needed, the host CPU will first look up the guest page table and then host page table to get host physical address.

For cross-ISA emulation, the host cannot run a guest OS directly because the binary of the guest OS is not compatible with the host CPU. To execute the guest OS, we need a dynamic binary translator (DBT) to translate the guest binary into a host binary, then we run the host binary on host CPU. If the DBT needs to translate a memory address,

it needs to go through step 3 to 6 in Figure 2-0 to find the corresponding host virtual address (HVA). Then, the DBT emulator accesses the translated address just like a normal host user process accesses a memory address, and return the result to the guest OS. The DBT emulator must complete this multi-step translation for every memory access.

2.1 Design Goal for Memory Address Translation in Cross-ISA Emulation

A cross-ISA system-mode DBT needs to go through three levels of address translation for each guest memory access, while emulating a guest VM, as shown Figure 2-1-1(a). Only the last level of address translation is performed by hardware MMU on the host machine, and the first two levels of address translation between guest OS and host are implemented purely in software. This software-implemented address translation subsystem is referred to as soft-MMU, as shown within the circle of Figure 2-1-1(a). The soft-MMU approach is one of the biggest performance bottlenecks in cross-ISA system-mode DBT, such as QEMU.

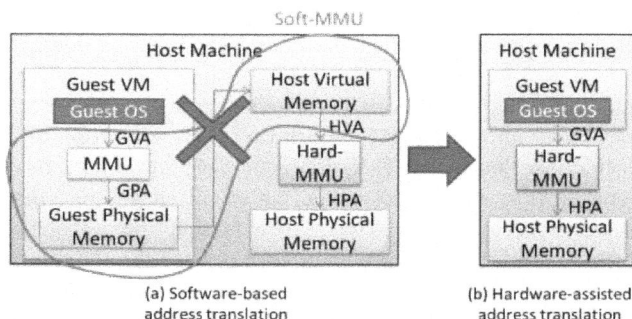

(a) Software-based address translation

(b) Hardware-assisted address translation

Figure 2-1-1. Address translation for cross-ISA emulation

We improve address translation performance by using hardware MMU to translate virtual address on virtual machine directly to physical address on physical machine without soft-MMU, as shown in Figure 2-1-1(b). We also take advantage of a larger address space available on modern 64-bit CPUs to isolate the DBT emulator from the guest operating system, as shown in Figure 2-1-2.

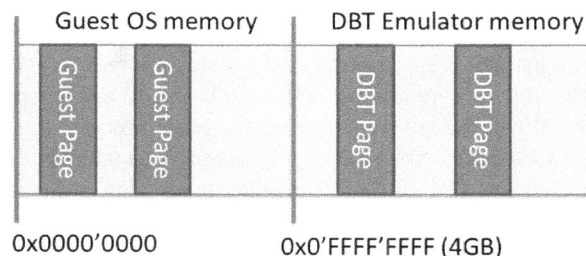

0x0000'0000   0x0'FFFF'FFFF (4GB)

Figure 2-1-2. Memory layout with wider memory space on 64-bit CPUS

In Section 2.2 and 2.3, we introduce two memory address translation techniques currently used for same-ISA memory virtualization: (1) software based shadow page table and (2) hardware assisted second level address translation. We then point out the reasons why these same-ISA techniques are not sufficient for cross-ISA memory address translation.

2.2 Same-ISA Address Translation

Shadow Page Table

For security reasons, guest processes are not allowed to access page tables on hardware without page table virtualization. Consequently, in a pure software implementation, the host Virtual Machine Monitor (VMM) creates a shadow page table (SPT) that maps guest address to host address for each guest page table and changes the page table base pointer (CR3) to the shadow page table. Then the guest process can use the shadow page table as if it were using its own guest page table for address translation.

Shadow page table is an effective technique in same-ISA address translation, but not in cross-ISA translation. In same-ISA virtualization, host CPU can execute guest OS binary directly, thus VMM only needs to switch between shadow page tables when the guest OS switches context. However, in cross-ISA, the guest OS has been translated into host binary and each guest memory access also been translated into Soft-MMU operations. If we adopt SPT technology into cross-ISA, frequent page table switching between host and shadow page table will cause huge performance degradation. The reason is that the translated guest binary and the DBT emulator now use the same host address space, so the DBT emulator must switch to shadow page table when it needs to translate addresses for the guest OS, and then switch back to the host page table of the DBT emulator to run the translated guest binary. The DBT engine needs to protect from being modified by guest OS. In same-ISA, Bugnion et al. propose a segmentation-based solution[19], however it only works on x86 machine. To achieve better portability, we check the translated host virtual address and make sure it doesn't touch the DBT engine before embedding into the host page table.

Second Level Address Translation

Intel Extended Page Tables (EPT) [24,25] and AMD Nested Paging [26] are x86 virtualization technologies to avoid overheads in maintaining software-based shadow page tables. When the host machine runs a guest process, it will first load the guest page table to translate guest address, and then load the EPT table to translate guest address to host address. In contrast with aforementioned software-based shadow page table approach, the EPT technology uses the guest page table directly and thus does not require the host virtual machine monitor to maintain a separate shadow page table.

EPT technology incurs extra overheads in cross-ISA DBT. Same-ISA virtualization can switch on EPT during the execution of a guest VM, and switched off EPT when the guest VM invokes a hypercall, thus CPU mode only switches on and off EPT when entering and exiting the VMM. A cross-ISA DBT, however, needs to switch CPU mode each time the guest accesses a virtual address. The reason is that the guest is not in the same address space with the DBT while EPT can only be activated in VM mode, and therefore, the emulator needs to switch to VM mode to perform the address translation with EPT and then exit the VM mode. Such frequent CPU mode switching incurs very high overhead in cross-ISA DBT. Another issue of EPT is that currently it is only available on x86 platform, thus making EPT not a general solution for address translation in cross-ISA DBT.

3. Design of Hardware-Assisted Memory Address Translation for Cross-ISA System Emulation

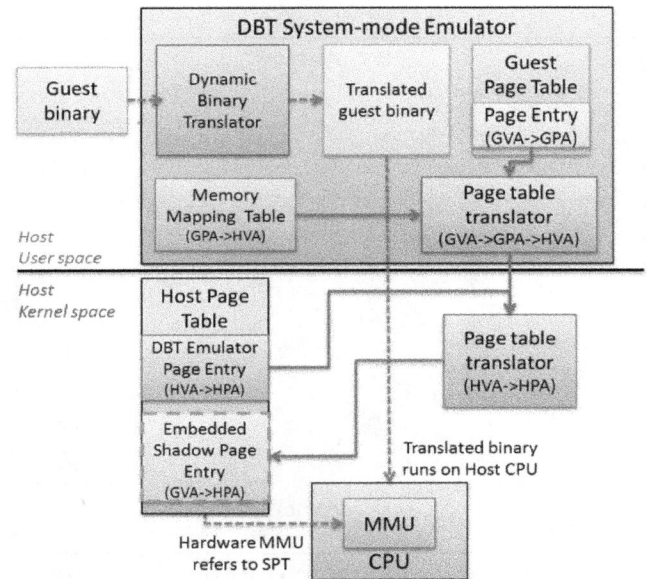

Figure 3-0. System architecture of hardware assisted memory address translation for cross-ISA system emulation

To eliminate the aforementioned bottlenecks, we propose an *"embedded shadow page table"* (ESPT). When a DBT emulates a guest memory access instruction, it creates an entry in shadow page table for mapping guest address to host address. To avoid frequent table pointer switching as described in section 2.2, we embed the shadow page table entries in the host page table of the cross-ISA DBT. As a result, the host page table now has two kinds of entries: (1) the original address mapping entries of the host DBT emulator, and (2) the embedded guest to host address mapping entries. Since we embed the shadow page entries into the host page table, the hardware MMU can use these "*embedded*" shadow page entries in the host page table to translate memory address transparently. Therefore, our ESPT approach does not need to switch between host page table and shadow page table, and can achieve the same efficiency as in a native environment.

Figure 3-0 illustrates the system architecture of the proposed hardware assisted memory address translation. The page table translator merges the multiple-level address translation into one level of guest-to-host address translation. After the merging, if the guest binary issues a memory operation the MMU of the host CPU looks up the embedded shadow page table to translate the guest address to a host address directly and transparently. To achieve this one level translation, the page table translator first walks the guest page table to find the corresponding guest physical address, then it searches the memory mapping table in the DBT emulator to find the corresponding host virtual address for the guest physical address. Finally, the page table translator walks the host page table to find the corresponding host physical address for the host virtual address.

There are two major challenges in designing such a framework. The first challenge is to find a memory region in the DBT address space that does not conflict with the DBT emulator itself. In system-mode DBT emulation, all guest instructions are translated and executed on a host CPU within the same address space as the DBT emulator. We need to find an efficient way that can adapt DBT to use hardware MMU to speed up cross-ISA emulation.

The second challenge is to reduce the overhead of creating and maintaining the embedded shadow page table. Recall that in our approach, the hardware MMU uses embedded shadow page entries to translate guest virtual address to host physical address directly. We can create the embedded shadow page table entries for the entire guest page table at the beginning of emulation, however, such an approach will incur a lot of inefficiency. The reasons are: (1) When an entry in the shadow page table is created for a guest page table entry, synchronization between guest and shadow page tables is required to ensure the correctness of the mapping, (2) Not all the entries of the guest page table will be accessed during the emulation. If we create shadow page entries for the entire guest page table at the beginning of emulation, it will incur excessive synchronization overhead. How to dynamically create embedded shadow page table entries to avoid unnecessary synchronization overhead is a challenging issue. In the following subsections we present our design approaches to tackle these issues.

3.1 Memory Allocation and Design of Shadow Page Table

A cross-ISA DBT runs as a process in the user space of the host virtual memory. As described in Figure 2-1, the host OS creates a page table for the DBT emulator process. We call the page table "host page table" (part (A) in Figure 3-1). The guest VM (including guest OS and the applications running on it), emulated by the DBT, has its own "guest page table" (part (B) in Figure 3-1). The DBT maintains an internal table (part (C) in Figure 3-1) to manage the memory allocation for the guest VM.

Before creating an embedded shadow page table, we must determine its location so that it will not interfere with the virtual memory space of the guest virtual machine. A guest operating system running on a 32-bit architecture, such as x86_32 and ARM_32, will only use the address space below 4GB, so the address above 4GB is free and can be used for other system components. To free the address space below 4GB, we can modify the linker script of the DBT so that it will place itself and its components above 4GB in the host virtual memory during runtime. We then use the free space of host page table entries below 4GB to store the embedded shadow page table. When our system emulates a 32-bit guest memory operation, the page table translator will find an unused page table entry below 4GB in the host page table to create a guest virtual address to host physical address mapping. We call such page table entry an embedded shadow page entry. Because the address space below 4GB is free, it is safe to map any 32-bit virtual address here.

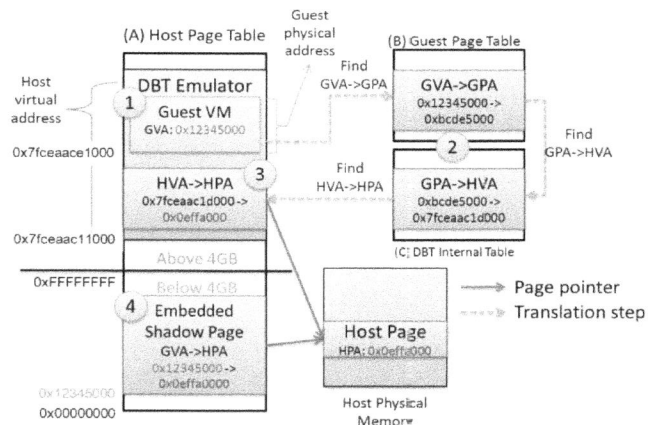

Figure 3-1. Memory allocation and design strategy for embedded shadow page table

In this paper, we focus on 32-bit guest and 64-bit host. Memory allocation for 64 bit guest to 64 bit host translation is more complicated but still possible. The main issue for 64-bit on 64-bit is how to find free space on host address space. We think this is still possible because 64-bit is a very large space and most OSes and applications do not use all the space. For example, Linux only uses virtual address from 0x7f00'0000'0000 and above. Thus, it is still possible to find a free space to place the ESPT. We leave it to our future work. We do not consider 64 bit guest to 32 bit host translation because such kind of translation is rarely needed.

Figure 3-1 illustrates our shadow page table design. We assume that we load the DBT at host virtual address 0x7ceaac11000, and the DBT uses virtual address 0xfceaace1000 as the starting point of the guest physical address space. When a guest operating system accesses a virtual address 0x12345000 (indicated in (1)), if the address does not exist in shadow page table, the host page fault exception triggers our page table translation mechanism. Next, our framework traverses the guest page table to find the corresponding guest physical address, and then looks up the internal table of the DBT to find the corresponding host virtual address (indicated in (2)). Next it searches the host page table to find the corresponding host physical address (indicated in (3)). Then it creates a shadow page table entry for that guest virtual address and embeds the entry into the host page table of the DBT (indicated in (4)). This entry has the guest virtual address 0x12345000 and points to the same corresponding host physical address.

3.2 Incorporating with DBT emulator

In this section, we discuss how to make this scheme work with a DBT system mode emulator. Here we use QEMU as an example. We need to modify the QEMU tiny code generator (TCG) to use the hardware to translate the guest address. QEMU uses a 'qemu_ld_helper' helper function to translate memory address in software. Figure 3-2 shows an example of translated host code from a guest memory operation 'mov 0x4(%ebp),%eax'. This guest memory instruction loads the memory address pointed by %ebp plus an offset 0x4 into %eax. QEMU maps the guest register %ebp as 0x20(%r14) in host memory. QEMU generates the following codes to emulate this instruction. (1) load guest register %ebp (0x20(%r14) in host binary) to host register %eax, (2) add the offset 0x4 to %eax. Now the guest virtual address is in host %eax, (3) use SoftMMU to find the host virtual address, and (4) load the data in the host virtual address.

In Figure 3-2, the left hand side is the original QEMU soft-MMU approach that employs two alternatives---soft-TLB (fast_path) and soft-MMU (slow_path). The fast_path is a series of instructions to search the table by a hash function, and the slow_path is a guest page table walking procedure. On the right hand side is our approach that generates only one 'mov' instruction to access the guest memory. Our approach uses 10 to 20 less instructions than the soft-TLB and soft-MMU approach in QEMU. In our approach QEMU is a process on the host so it can use the host page table, which already contains the shadow page table. As a

result we can run guest instruction and access the intended guest memory address without switching among multiple page tables.

Guest instruction: mov 0x4 (%ebp), %eax
→ Load %eax from the address in %ebp + offset 0x4
→ Guest %ebp is mapped in host 0x20(%r14)

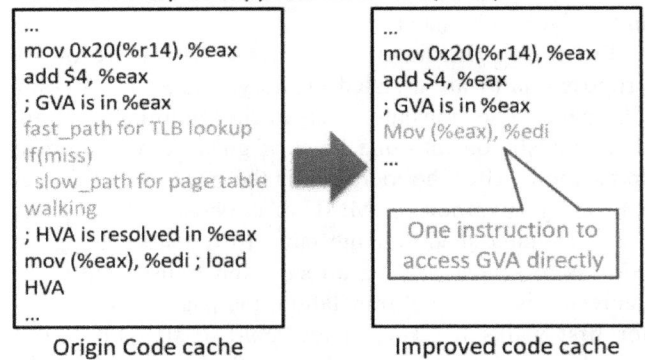

Figure 3-2. Improved QEMU code cache with hardware-assisted address translation

There are two types of branch instructions in DBT -- direct and indirect branch. Direct branch can be handled by ESPT efficiently. For indirect branch, we use Indirect Branch Translation Cache (IBTC) [14] to cache the lookup result so that we do not need to look up the entire table every time we need to determine a destination address.

3.3 Reducing Overhead of Creating Shadow Page Table

The shadow page table needs to be created before guest OS can access it. Usually a guest page table contains many page entries, therefore it is inefficient to translate all entries at once at the beginning because not all entries will be used. Moreover, synchronization between shadow and guest page tables also incurs heavy overhead because the guest OS modifies its page table very frequently, e.g., from lazy page allocation. Lazy allocation will not allocate the free memory page immediately when a guest application calls 'malloc' of glibc library to allocate memory space; instead it only allocates space when the application accesses the allocated address for the first time. As a result the lazy allocation will update the page table numerous times, and causes significant overheads.

Interception based methodology for reducing synchronization overhead. Our approach only creates pages that are needed or accessed by the guest operating system in order to reduce the overhead in creating the shadow page table. To synchronize entries in shadow page table, our framework intercepts the 'invalid TLB' instruction issued by the guest operating system when a guest application maps, unmaps or changes an existing mapping. By intercepting invalid TLB instructions, our framework only needs to update the modified page table without constant monitoring modifications made to the guest page table. This design significantly reduces overheads in tracing guest memory operations.

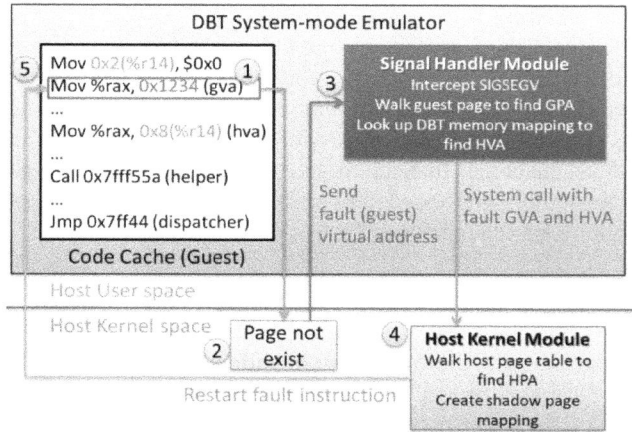

Figure 3-3. Signal notification approach for creating embedded shadow page table on demand

Signal notification mechanism for dynamic recreation of ESPT. We propose a signal notification mechanism that reduces the size and overheads in creating embedded shadow page table by only creating the shadow page table entries on demand. The flow of signal notification is illustrated in Figure 3-3. We add a host kernel module to help manipulate the host page table without modifying the host kernel. The host kernel provides the function to create memory alias and security checking on the memory address to make sure it will not touch the DBT emulator or other system components. When a guest virtual address is accessed for the first time (labelled as step 1), the host kernel raises a SIGSEGV signal (step 2) because right now this guest virtual address does not yet have a corresponding entry in the host page table. The signal event contains the faulty memory address that causes the signal. We also add a signal handler into the DBT to intercepts this SIGSEGV signal (step 3) and perform a series of address translation: a) walk the guest page table to retrieve corresponding guest physical address, b) look up the internal memory mapping table of DBT to get the corresponding host virtual address, c) pass the guest virtual address and the host virtual address to our kernel module by a system call, d) the kernel module walks the host page table to finds the corresponding host physical address of the host virtual address, and adds an entry from the guest virtual address to the host physical address in the embedded shadow page table (step 4). After adding the embedded shadow page table entry, the host kernel restarts the instruction (step 5). Now the 'mov' instruction will correctly read or write the requested guest virtual address.

3.4 Page fault handling

Page fault is an important system design issue in page table manipulation. There are two types of page faults in our approach -- shadow page fault and guest page fault. A shadow page fault occurs when the requested guest virtual address is not in the shadow page table. A guest page fault occurs when the address does not exist in the guest page table. Figure 3-4 illustrates our approach of two-level page fault handling and the Left hand side is a translation block in the DBT code cache. Our approach adds a 'mov' and a 'jmp' instruction before executing DBT SoftMMU. Our approach tries the shadow page first while trying to access a guest virtual address. If the entry for the guest virtual address does exist in the shadow page table, we translated it into host physical address by hardware MMU directly. If the entry for the guest virtual address does not exist in the shadow page table nor the guest page table, we will disable hardware MMU instruction by replacing the 'jmp' with a 'nop' so the DBT emulator will use soft-MMU to fill the guest page table.

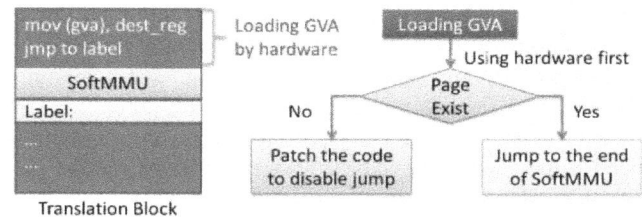

Figure 3-4. Page fault handling

3.5 ESPTs for Multi-Process Emulation

In this subsection, we describe how we handle multiple guest processes by using one host page table. In system mode emulation, there are usually more than one processes running in guest VM. The guest OS needs to do context-switching between each process periodically to enable multiple processes to share a single CPU. This is also an essential feature of a modern multitasking operating system.

We create one shadow page table per guest process to eliminate unnecessary re-creation of shadow page table. The x86_64 platform has a four-level page table, and in each level a page table maintains 512 tables of the next level. The top level page table is called page global description table (PGD). The tables in the next three levels are page upper description table (PUD), page middle description (PMD) table, and page table (PT) respectively. Each table in the first three levels has 512 entries and each entry points to a table in the next level. Each entry of a page description table in the last level points to a 4096-bytes physical memory page. As a result four entries in the second level table can address 4G memory ($4096*512*512*4$), which is sufficient to support a 32-bit guest operating system, as shown in Figure 3-5.

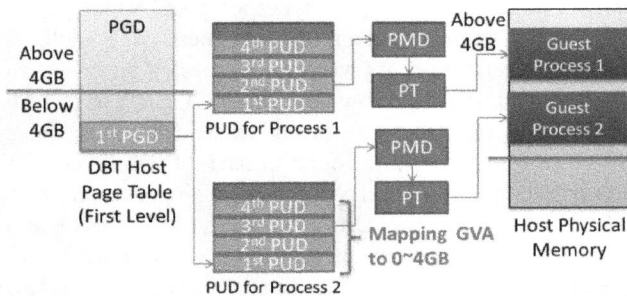

Figure 3-5. Multi-process emulation uses the first entry in the top level page table as the shadow page table pointer

Figure 3-5 illustrates the design of our embedded shadow page tables for multi-process support using only one host page table. We create four second level page table entries for each guest process and use the first entry in the top level table as the shadow page table pointer. When the guest OS switches context between two processes, our framework changes the first entry in the top level table from pointing to the four second level entries of the leaving process to the four second level entries of the incoming process. Our framework also set the write-protection on these switched-out shadow page table to keep it synchronized with guest page table. This design can reduce the time needed for recreating the shadow page table.

Our framework needs to identify the current running process in the guest operating system in order to achieve multi-process emulation. It is more precise to use the guest process id to identify the running process than to use the guest page table pointer, because guest operating system may reuse the same page table pointer for new processes without issuing page table modification instruction. The process id is an architecture information located in control registers on an ARM platform, but is not available on x86 platform. Thus we slightly modify the guest operating system kernel to retrieve the current running process id on an x86 platform.

4. Experimental Results

We implement our hardware-assisted ESPT based memory virtualization framework on QEMU, a popular retargetable cross-ISA dynamic binary translator. We evaluate the effectiveness of our framework on Intel x5550 machine with 2.67GHz CPU, 12G RAM, and an x86_64 Gentoo Linux operating system as QEMU host. We use Gentoo Linux 201308 as our guest OS and runs benchmarks in the guest VM. All the benchmarks we use can run correctly in such multi-tasking environment. Two benchmark suites are used as the guest applications in our experiments: SPEC CINT2006 and NBench. SPEC CINT2006 is an industry-standardized, CPU-intensive benchmark suite, stressing system's processor and memory subsystem. The reason we chose the SPEC integer benchmark suite is that QEMU v0.15 and up uses integer instructions to simulation floating point instructions for portability. Such software simulation approach causes significant slowdown on the SPEC floating point benchmarks.

NBench is a synthetic computing benchmark program and is intended for measuring a computer's CPU, FPU, and memory system speed. In our experiments, we emulate ARM and x86_32 platforms with Gentoo Linux OS on an x86_64 machine. In Section 4.1, we first describe the implementation work needed to make the ARM MMU system work on an x86 machine.

4.1 MMU on ARM Platform

ARM processor provides a set of CP15 registers to control the behavior of the processor, including cache and MMU. CP15:C1 register decides whether MMU is enabled or not. CP15:C2 register points to the translation table base which contains the mappings of guest virtual address to guest physical address. CP15:C8 register provides the TLB-related operations, such as 'TLBIMVAA', which invalidates a TLB entry of the virtual address, and 'TLBIALL', which invalidates all TLB entries. To do cross-ISA address translation, we first need to check if the MMU is enabled (C1). If it is enabled, we can walk the ARM page table starting from the translation table base (C2).

4.2 ARM 32bit to x86 64bit DBT

In this experiment, we emulate an ARM platform with Linux OS on an x86 machine. Figure 4-2(a) shows the performance of the CINT2006 benchmarks with train input size in ARM-to-x86 emulation. The reason that we use train instead of reference input size is the memory limitation. The ARM platform emulated by QEMU can only provide maximum 1GB memory for guest OS while some benchmarks require more than 1GB memory during execution. The performance will be affected by memory swapping, thus we use train input size for ARM-to-X86 emulation. The x-axis is the benchmarks and the y-axis is the execution time in seconds. The 'soft' legend is the execution time with QEMU Soft-MMU, and the 'hard' legend is the execution time with our hardware-assisted MMU. Figure 4-2(b) shows the speedup. On average, our approach achieves 1.51X speedup. We can also see that among the twelve benchmarks, 429.mcf has the largest speedup (2.95X), while 445.gobmk has the smallest (1.20X). We will explain the reasons in Section 4.4.

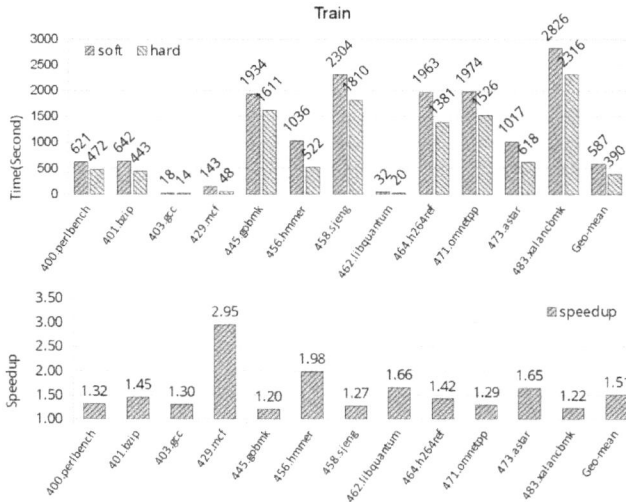

Figure 4-2. (a) Execution time and (b) Speedup by hardware MMU against software MMU for the SPEC CINT2006 benchmarks in ARM-to-x86 emulation (with train input).

We also compare the effectiveness of our hardware assisted memory virtualization on short running tasks versus long running tasks. We use SPEC CINT2006 with test input (short running) and reference input (long running) as the basis for comparison. The difference between short and long tasks is that longer running code will have more opportunities to exploit the ESPT entries once they are created. Comparing Figure 4-2(b) and Figure 4-2-2, we can see that the reference input (long running) results in larger speedup factors (1.51X on average) than the test input (short running), 1.37X on average. The reason is that, with the increase in execution time, the reuse ratio of the ESPT also increases, hence resulting in better performance.

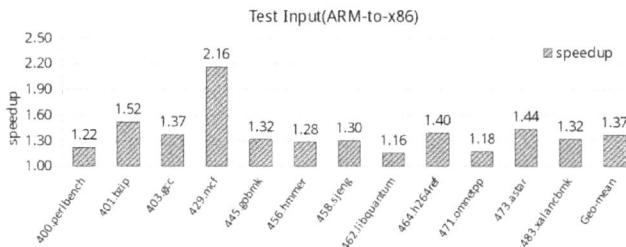

Figure 4-2-2. Speedup by hardware MMU against software MMU for the SPEC CINT2006 benchmarks in ARM-to-x86 emulation (with test input)

Figure 4-2-3 shows the experiment result on NBench. On average, our approach achieves 1.22X speedup against the original QEMU. Among the 7 benchmarks, String Sort achieves the most significant speedup (1.64x) because it is a memory-intensive program which performs a large number of memory read and compare. BitField has the lowest speedup (1.06x) because it has few memory operations. Its

computation mainly involves bit manipulation functions, such as: AND, OR, and XOR.

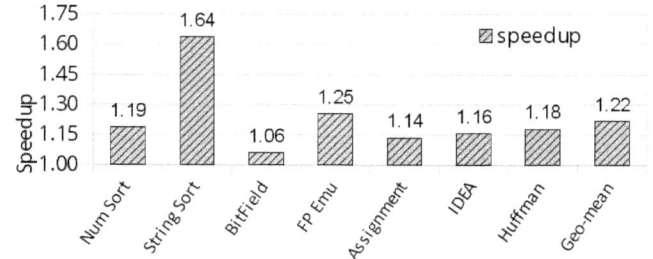

Figure 4-2-3. Speedup by hardware MMU against software MMU for the NBench benchmarks in ARM-to-x86 emulation.

The performance improvement for NBench is not as good as that of SPEC CINT2006. The main reason is that most of the NBench benchmarks do not have many memory operations as most of the SPEC CINT2006 benchmarks do.

4.3 x86 32bit to x86 64bit DBT

x86 32bit is one of the most popular computing platforms. Many applications (and operating systems) were developed on x86 32bit machines. With the increasing popularity of x86 64bit machines in recent years, there will be increasing need for emulating legacy operating systems and applications developed for x86 32bit on the newer x86 64bit platforms. Hence, we also conduct experiments on x86_32 to x86_64 DBT.

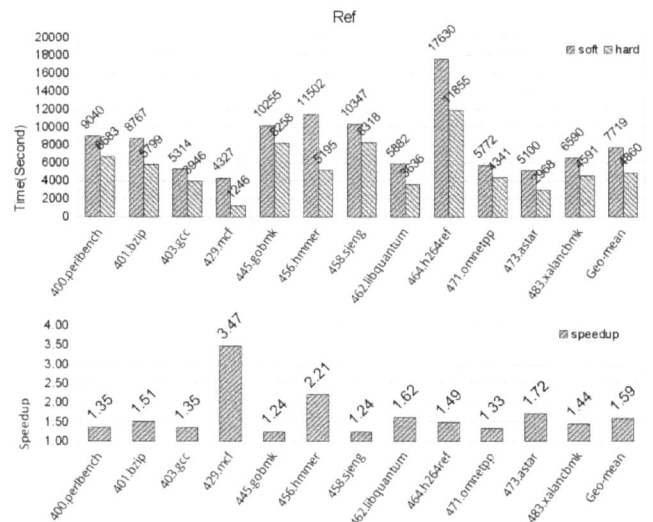

Figure 4-3. Speedup by hardware MMU against soft MMU on SPEC CINT2006 benchmarks for x86_32 to x86_64 DBT (with reference input)

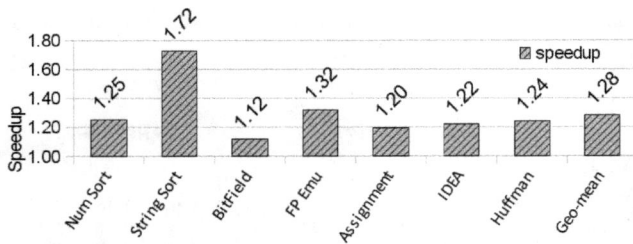

Figure 4-3-2. Speedup by hardware MMU against soft MMU on NBench benchmarks for x86_32 to x86_64 DBT

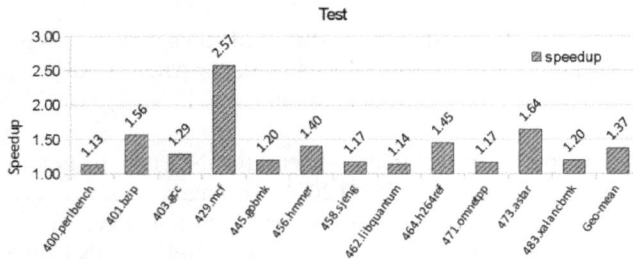

Figure 4-3-3. Speedup by hardware MMU against soft MMU on SPEC CINT2006 benchmarks for x86_32 to x86_64 DBT (with test input)

Figure 4-3 and 4-3-2 show the execution time and speedup factors of the SPEC CINT2006 and the NBench benchmarks respectively. The speedup factors on SPEC CINT2006 are quite consistent with those for ARM-to-x86_64 emulation, with an average speedup of 1.59x compared to SoftMMU. For NBench, the average speedup is 1.28x. String Sort achieves the most significant speedup (1.72x) while BitField has the lowest speedup (1.12x).

By comparing Figure 4-3 and Figure 4-3-3, we can see that short running tasks versus long running tasks have similar effect on the speedup factors of CINT2006. That is, long running tasks (with reference input) result in higher ESPT reuse ratios and hence larger performance improvement.

In the next subsections, we examine the effect of hardware assisted address translation on reduction of memory instructions and TLB miss rate.

4.4 Effect on Memory instructions Reduced

From processor microarchitecture point of view, memory operation is one of the slowest instructions, thus processor manufacturers add many mechanisms to reduce the frequency of memory accessing, such as multiple level memory caching and translation lookaside buffer. As mentioned in previous section, our framework can reduce the level of memory translation from 3 steps to just 1 step. Even in the case of QEMU Soft-TLB hit, our framework can also reduce the number of memory instructions from 3 to 1, because Soft-TLB needs (1) calculate guest virtual address (2) read host virtual address from hash table (3)

read the data in the host virtual address (and then the hardware MMU will translate the virtual address to the host physical address transparently). Figure 4-4 shows the percentage of memory instructions eliminated by our framework. In most benchmarks, the speedup is proportional to the reduction percentage of memory instructions.

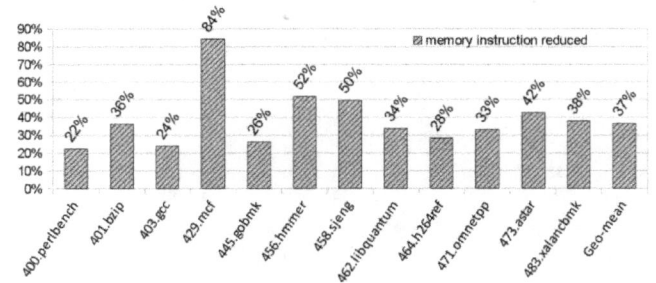

Figure 4-4. Reduction percentage of memory instructions by hardware-assisted address translation

4.5 Effect on TLB miss rate

429.mcf is the one that achieves the highest performance improvement. The reason is described as follows. Recall that in Figure 1-1, 429.mcf takes about 40% time in soft-MMU, and other benchmarks, such as 401.bzip and 473.astar, also take about 40% time in soft-MMU. Why is 429.mcf the only one that achieves 3.47X speedup while 401.bzip and 473.astar only has 1.51X ad 1.72X speedup respectively? Hardware MMU can reduce memory operation instructions, however, in Figure 4-5, all benchmarks contain about 26% memory accessing instructions, 429.mcf is not the one that has the highest number of memory access instructions. Therefore, reduction in the number of memory operations is not the main reason that makes 429.mcf achieve such high performance improvement.

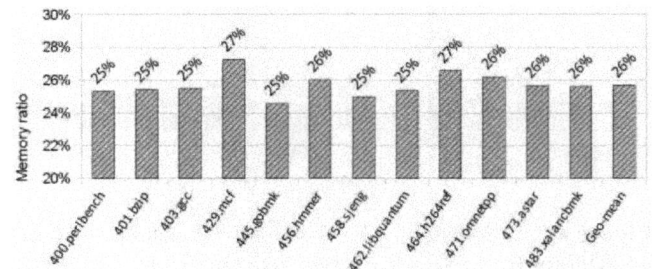

Figure 4-5. Percentage of memory access instructions in SoftMMU mode

Another possible reason would be SoftTLB in QEMU. A TLB is a cache that memory management hardware uses to improve virtual address translation speed. In order to speed up SoftMMU, QEMU also implements a TLB-like caching mechanism that records the guest virtual address to host virtual address mapping. Figure 4-5-2 shows TLB miss rate of SoftTLB(left bar) compared with our framework(right bar). 429.mcf causes 10%TLB miss in SoftTLB while others only 0.1% ~ 3%. The reason is that QEMU's SoftTLB is implemented using hash table that uses the last 8 bits of guest virtual address as the index, and therefore can hold up to 256 entries. The hash design has the best performance when finding an entry. However, this simple design will suffer from hash conflicts. For example, these two virtual addresses, 0x1234aa12 and 0x1234bb12, will compete for the same hash entry and causes SoftTLB invalidation and SoftTLB miss. For HardTLB, current processor provides larger and multiple level TLB. For instances, Intel's Nehalem microarchitecture has a L1 DTLB with 64 entries and a L2 TLB with 512 entries, both four-way associative. With the hardware support, our framework can decrease TLB miss rate of 429.mcf from 10% to 1%, and thus obtain 3.47 times speedup.

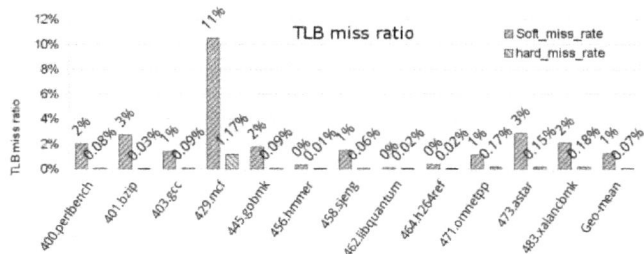

Figure 4-5-2. TLB miss rate of QEMU SoftTLB compared with Hardware-supported TLB

We also enlarged QEMU SoftTLB. We found that QEMU reaches its peak performance when the SoftTLB is increased to 2^{12}. However, even with peak performance of QEMU's SoftTLB hit, our approach still achieves 1.5X speedup against QEMU.

From the results presented in Section 4.4 and Section 4.5, we can see that hardware supported memory virtualization can not only reduce the memory address translation overhead but also reduce the TLB miss rate, because hardware provides more effective cache replacement mechanism.

5. Related work

There are generally two types of binary translators: (1) process-level binary translators and (2) system-level binary translators. Process-level binary translation emulates the functionality of the application binary interface (ABI) of the guest application. On the other hand, the system-level binary translators emulate the functionality of the entire guest ISA interface, including privileged instructions. We could further classify binary translators into four categories according to the relationship between the platform ISA and the operating system. Table 5-1 categorizes the binary translators into four possible scenarios.

Table 5-1. The classification of binary translators.

ISA / OS	Same ISA	Cross ISA
Same OS	DynamoRIO[4,15], Strata[5], Embra[2], Pin[3]	FX!32[6], memTrace[12], StarDBT[10], Valgrind[18]
Cross OS	VMware [7], Xen [8], KVM[9], VirtualBox [11].	QEMU[13], Quick-Transit [16]

Binary translators in the same-ISA-same-OS category are usually for improving performance, security, and binary instrumentation. Same-ISA-cross-OS virtualization works are usually for server virtualization, which is extremely important for cloud computing. Related works in the cross-ISA-same-OS are most for application migration, optimization and instrumentation. They are all bound for a specific guest-ISA/host-ISA combination. MemTrace [12] is a memory tracing framework for 32-bit applications. It uses the wider address space available on 64-bit machine to isolate the tracer from 32-bit guest program. StarDBT [10] is an optimizer which uses the new registers and instructions provided on 64-bit machine to optimize the legacy 32-bit code. Valgrind [18] is a framework for dynamic binary instrumentation. Users can use it to build dynamic analysis tools. In the Cross-ISA-cross-OS category, QuickTransit [16] supports multiple source and target ISAs, but also allows different source and target OS's. QEMU [13] is a retargetable binary translator. It currently supports six guest-ISAs (ARM, CRIS, m68k, MIPS, SPARC, IA32) and 3 host-ISAs (IA32, x86_64, PowerPC) with several operating systems.

Since memory virtualization usually relies on the underlying host architecture, we will focus on same-ISA and cross-ISA memory virtualization.

In same-ISA, memory virtualization can be achieved by software-based shadow page table [20,22] and hardware-supported Extended Page Table(EPT) technology [9]. The implementation of shadow page table used by VMware optimizes caching of guest virtual address translations so that expensive hardware faults resulting from memory access are minimized. Dynamic binary translation is also used to keep the cost of MMU-related operations low. With shadow page tables, the virtual machine's linear addresses can be mapped directly to the physical machine addresses, and therefore, accesses to memory can be performed at native hardware speed.

In cross-ISA system mode emulation, the guest page table structure is different from host, thus hardware cannot be used to translate guest address directly. Some cross-ISA emulators provide a software-based MMU[13] to translate guest address. QEMU is one of the cross-ISA system-mode emulators that use Soft-MMU for memory virtualization. However, as evidenced in this paper, Soft-MMU incurs high overhead and could become the performance bottleneck of cross-ISA emulators.

6. Conclusion

We have proposed an efficient memory virtualization scheme, *"embedded shadow page table"* (ESPTs), for cross-ISA system-level DBT that uses shadow page tables and host hardware MMU to reduce address translation overheads. By embedding the shadow page entries into the host page table of the DBT, we can avoid frequent switching between host and shadow page table during address translation. We have also proposed two optimizations for reducing ESPT overhead and hence increasing performance gain. We adopt an interception-based methodology to reduce the overhead of synchronizing guest page table and embedded shadow page table. We have also devised a signal notification mechanism which creates the shadow page table entries on demand. These optimizations have successfully reduced the overhead of creating embedded shadow page table. We also take the advantage of wider address space available on 64-bit CPUs embed our shadow page table and isolate the guest OS from DBT emulator.

Our experiment results demonstrate an average speedup of 1.51 times and 1.59 times on SPEC CINT2006 benchmarks for ARM-to-x86 and IA32-to-x86_64 system-mode emulation respectively, and an average speedup of 1.22 times and 1.28 times on NBench benchmarks for ARM-to-x86 and IA32-to-x86_64 system-mode emulation respectively, when compared with the standard softMMU approach in QEMU. We also show that our approach reduces the number of memory instructions by 37% on average and reduces TLB miss rate by more than 10 times compared with the original QEMU.

Acknowledgments

We would like to express our gratitude to Dr. Donald Porter for his very helpful comments and suggestions to improve this paper. This work is supported in part by National Science Council of Taiwan under grant number NSC102-2221-E-001-034-MY3.

References

[1] James Smith and Ravi Nair, "Virtual Machines: Versatile Platforms for Systems and Processes", Elsevier, 2005, ISBN: 1-55860-910-5

[2] E. Witchel and M. Rosenblum, "Embra: Fast and Flexible Machine Simulation", Proceedings of the ACM SIGMETRICS international conference on Measurement and modeling of computer systems, 1996

[3] Luk, C.-K., Cohn, R., Muth, R., Patil, H., Klauser, A., Lowney, G., and Wallace, S., Reddi, V. J., Hazelwood, K., "Pin: Building Customized Program Analysis Tools with Dynamic Instrumentation", Programming languages design and implementation, June 2005.

[4] N. Nethercote. Dynamic Binary Analysis and Instrumentation. A dissertation submitted for the degree of doctor of philosophy, University of Cambridge, November 2004.

[5] K. Scott and J. Davidson. Strata: A Software Dynamic Translation Infrastructure. In IEEE Workshop on Binary Translation (2001).

[6] A. Chernoff and Ray Hookway, "DIGITAL FX!32: Running 32-Bit x86 Applications on Alpha NT", the Proc. of the USENIX Windows NT Workshop, August 1997

[7] Vmware. http://www.vmware.com.

[8] Xen. http://www.xen.org.

[9] Sheng Yang, "Extending KVM with new Intel ® Virtualization technology", Intel Open Source Technology Center, KVM Forum 2008.

[10] WANG, C., HU, S., KIM, H.-S., NAIR, S., BRETERNITZ, M., YING, Z., and WU, Y. "'Stardbt: An efficient multiplatform dynamic binary translation system", In Advances in Computer Systems Architecture, vol. 4697. 2007

[11] Virtualbox. http://www.virtualbox.org/.

[12] Payer, M., Kravina, E., and Gross T. R., "Lightweight Memory Tracing". In USENIX ATC, 2013

[13] Bellard, F.; "QEMU, a Fast and Portable Dynamic Translator," in USENIX ATC 2005

[14] K. Scott, N. Kumar, B. R. Childers, J.W. Davidson, and M. L. Soffa, "Overhead reduction techniques for software dynamic translation," in Proc. IPDPS, 2004, pp. 200–207.

[15] D. Bruening, T. Garnett, S. Amarasinghe, "DynamoRIO: An Infrastructure for Adaptive Dynamic Optimization", Proceedings of the international symposium on code generation and optimization, 2003.

[16] Transitive corporation. quicktransit software. http://www.transitive.com/.

[17] Xiao Guangrong, "KVM MMU Virtualization", Linux Foundation Events, 2011.

[18] N. Nethercote and J. Seward, "Valgrind: A Framework for Heavyweight dynamic Binary Instrumentation", ACM SIGPLAN Conference on Programming Language Design and Implementation (PLDI 2007), June 2007

[19] E. Bugnion, S. Devine, M. Rosenblum, J. Sugerman and E. Y. Wang, "Bringing Virtualization to the x86 Architecture with the Original VMware Workstation", TOCS , volume 30 issue 4, Nov 2012

[20] K. Adams and O. Agesen, "A Comparison of Software and Hardware Techniques for x86 Virtualization", ASPLOS'06, San Jose, California, USA, October 21–25, 2006.

A Platform for Secure Static Binary Instrumentation *

Mingwei Zhang   Rui Qiao   Niranjan Hasabnis   R. Sekar

Stony Brook University

Abstract

Program instrumentation techniques form the basis of many recent software security defenses, including defenses against common exploits and security policy enforcement. As compared to source-code instrumentation, binary instrumentation is easier to use and more broadly applicable due to the ready availability of binary code. Two key features needed for security instrumentations are (a) it should be applied to all application code, including code contained in various system and application libraries, and (b) it should be non-bypassable. So far, dynamic binary instrumentation (DBI) techniques have provided these features, whereas static binary instrumentation (SBI) techniques have lacked them. These features, combined with ease of use, have made DBI the de facto choice for security instrumentations. However, DBI techniques can incur high overheads in several common usage scenarios, such as application startups, system-calls, and many real-world applications. We therefore develop a new *platform for secure static binary instrumentation* (PSI) that overcomes these drawbacks of DBI techniques, while retaining the security, robustness and ease-of-use features. We illustrate the versatility of PSI by developing several instrumentation applications: basic block counting, shadow stack defense against control-flow hijack and return-oriented programming attacks, and system call and library policy enforcement. While being competitive with the best DBI tools on CPU-intensive SPEC 2006 benchmark, PSI provides an order of magnitude reduction in overheads on a collection of real-world applications.

1. Introduction

Program instrumentation has played a central role in exploit detection/prevention, security policy enforcement, application monitoring and debugging. Such instrumentation may be performed either on source or binary code. Source code

instrumentations can be more easily and extensively optimized by exploiting higher level information such as types. However, binary instrumentations are more widely applicable since users have ready access to binaries. Moreover, security instrumentations should be applied to all code, including all libraries, inline assembly code, and any code inserted by the compiler/linker. Here again, binary based techniques are advantageous.

Binary instrumentation can either be static or dynamic. Static binary instrumentation (SBI) is performed offline on binary files, whereas *dynamic* binary instrumentation (DBI) operates on code already loaded into main memory. DBI techniques disassemble and instrument each basic block just before its first execution. DBI has been the technique of choice for security instrumentation of COTS binaries. Previous works have used DBI for sandboxing [15, 17], taint-tracking [23, 28], defense from return-oriented programming (ROP) attacks [11, 12], and other techniques for hardening benign code [16, 26]. This is because DBI platforms provide several features that simplify instrumentation development, while ensuring their security:

* *Non-bypassable instrumentation.* DBI tools check every control-transfer to ensure that the target is instrumented, and hence can block attempts to escape security checks enforced by the instrumentation, e.g., by returning/jumping to (i) data (code injection attacks), (ii) middle of an instruction (typical ROP attacks), or (iii) into the middle of added instrumentation or past its end.

* *Completeness.* DBI techniques instrument all executed code, regardless of whether they reside in executables or libraries. The alternative of omitting library instrumentation is unsatisfactory because the vast majority of code executed by today's applications resides in libraries, and all of this code will remain unprotected.

* *Ease of use.* Instrumenting an application is as simple as prefixing its invocation with the name of a wrapper program. There is no need to explicitly instrument the application prior to its run, nor is there a need to know (and instrument) the libraries used by it. Moreover, DBI platforms such as Pin [19], DynamoRIO [8] and Valgrind [22] provide a convenient API that greatly simplifies the development of new instrumentations (also called *tools*).

Previous SBI techniques have lacked these features, and moreover, were targeted at specific problems such as control-flow integrity (CFI) [2] or software fault isolation (SFI) [32]. Consequently, they don't address the issues in developing a general-purpose platform for binary instrumentation.

* This work was supported in part by AFOSR grant FA9550-09-1-0539, NSF grant CNS-0831298, and ONR grant N000140710928.

Main Results and Contributions

We present a general-purpose binary instrumentation platform PSI that addresses the shortcomings of previous SBI techniques. It combines the benefits of DBI with the advantages that are unique to SBI, including:

- the ability to trade off increased (offline) analysis/instrumentation time for faster runtime performance, and
- avoiding reliance on a potentially large and complex virtual environment at runtime

Moreover, PSI provides low overheads across a wide range of benchmarks, while avoiding some pitfalls of DBI platforms such as high application startup times and high overheads for systems applications. Our key contributions are summarized below.

Secure static instrumentation. Two key features needed for security instrumentations are completeness (instrumentation should be applied to all code that can get executed) and non-bypassability (instrumented code should not be able to bypass or subvert the added instrumentation). Many previous SBI techniques, including Native Client [35], PittSFIeld [20], PEBIL [18] and many others [2, 6, 14, 24, 36, 37], are not complete for COTS binaries since they require additional information (such as symbol or relocation information) for correctly instrumenting binaries.

Among techniques applicable to stripped binaries, Reins [33] and SecondWrite [4, 13] don't instrument all libraries. Moreover, several of these techniques, including Dyninst [10], SecondWrite and Binary stirring [34], do not prevent execution from escaping instrumentation since they do not check the validity of targets such as return addresses. Although our BinCFI [38] system performs such checks, it implements a single hard-coded instrumentation, and hence there is no general discussion or treatment of instrumentation non-bypassability.

A versatile, easy-to-use static instrumentation platform. Our platform provides an easy-to-use API with convenient abstractions for low-level instrumentation, including data structures to capture instructions, basic blocks, and control-flow graphs. We illustrate the API and demonstrate its versatility by developing several instrumentation tools:

- *Counting basic blocks:* This conceptually simple example has been used frequently to illustrate DBI platforms.
- *System call policy enforcement:* These policies are commonly used in security hardening and related applications.
- *Shadow stack:* This technique has been used by several previous works to defend against stack-smashing [27] and ROP [12]. While our instrumentation is similar to that of ROPdefender [12], it provides much better performance.

On-demand instrumentation of libraries. SBI techniques require all library dependences to be identified statically, and these libraries need to be instrumented ahead of time; otherwise, an instrumented application can fail at runtime. Tools for determining library dependencies (e.g., ldd on Linux) cannot identify libraries that are loaded after an application begins execution. For a collection of popular real-world applications, more that 40% of library loads occurred after the commencement of application execution. To support seamless instrumentation of such libraries, we have developed an on-demand static instrumentation technique.

Good performance across a wide range of applications We present a comparative performance evaluation of PSI against the two leading DBI tools, namely DynamoRIO and Pin. We summarize our results below:

- *BB counting on SPEC 2006.* PSI incurs an average overhead of 69% on SPEC 2006 for basic-block counting, compared with 53% for DynamoRIO and 97% for Pin.
- *Shadow stack.* PSI's overhead is less than a quarter of that reported by ROPdefender (18% vs 74%).
- lmbench *Microbenchmark.* The average overhead of PSI is about 10 times smaller than DynamoRIO, and 200 times smaller than Pin.
- *A collection of real-world applications.* PSI's overheads are about 7 to 13 times lower than DynamoRIO, and 60 times lower than Pin on several real-world applications, including compilation, software updates, etc.

Our PSI platform will be available for download from http://seclab.cs.stonybrook.edu/download.

Scope and Limitations. PSI is a general platform for the instrumentation of COTS applications. It is targeted at benign COTS binaries that do not employ obfuscation. If a binary employs obfuscation (as is common with malware), our disassembly technique can fail to detect all of its code, or perform incorrect disassembly. However, since control flows are checked at runtime, PSI will block all attempts to execute code that wasn't disassembled and instrumented. Thus, binaries employing obfuscation may fail at runtime due to control-flow transfers being blocked, but they won't be able to bypass PSI.

Similar to most SBI techniques, PSI does not support self-modifying code. In particular, any attempt to modify existing code (or to transfer control to runtime-generated code) will be denied, causing such applications to fail.

Our implementation targets x86/Linux, but our techniques are generally applicable to other architectures as well.

2. Background

Disassembly. Two of the basic algorithms used for disassembly are linear sweep and recursive disassembly. Linear sweep begins at the binary entry point, and sequentially disassembles instructions until the end. Data or padding embedded within code will also get disassembled. With variable-length instruction sets, this error can cascade past the data region. Recursive disassembly avoids this problem by following the control-flow, and limiting disassembly to those code fragments that are known to be reachable. However, it often fails to discover all code, since some code is reachable only via code pointers whose values aren't known statically. As a result, accurate disassembly of stripped binaries has been a challenging problem for variable-length instruction sets such as x86. Indeed, this is another reason for the popularity of DBI platforms, since they can side-step these difficulties by limiting disassembly to one basic block at a time, just before the block is executed for the first time.

Our BinCFI [38] work and binary stirring [34] have shown that robust instrumentation can be achieved despite the above challenges. Like many previous efforts in static disassembly, these works combine elements of linear sweep and recursive disassembly. Specific advances made in these works were: (a) expanding the coverage of recursive disassembly using static analysis techniques for code pointer discovery, and (b) the development of instrumentation techniques that tolerate disassembly of data. Our efforts were also helped by the fact that compilers have become more strict in avoiding data within code segments. As a result, we have achieved 100% disassembly accuracy on many complex binaries [38]. In PSI, we reused this disassembler.

Resolving Indirect Control Transfers. Insertion of instrumentation will cause the locations of subsequent code to change. This means that statically computed function pointers will have incorrect values in an instrumented program, pointing to code locations in the original rather than the instrumented code. DBI techniques solve this problem by performing *address translation* of indirect control flow targets at runtime. Our BinCFI work [38] uses the same approach, and we reused it in PSI. When an address is not found in the translation table, that indicates an attempt to transfer control to an invalid destination, which will be blocked by PSI.

We point out BinCFI's address translation approach is modular, and is performed in two steps. In the first step, a global translation table (GTT), maintained by our modified loader, is used to translate the upper 20-bits of an address to the entry point of a module-specific translation table (MTT) routine. This MTT, which is generated at the time the module is transformed by PSI, uses the remaining bits to look up the corresponding address in the transformed module.

3. System Overview

PSI instruments executables as well as all of the shared libraries used by them. On each invocation, PSI takes a binary file (executable or library) as input, and outputs an instrumented version of this binary. This invocation may occur before execution, or on-the-fly during program execution.

Figure 1 shows the architecture of PSI. It consists of three main components: a binary analyzer, an instrumentor and a binary generator. The binary analyzer takes a binary as input, disassembles it, and then constructs a control-flow graph. This control-flow graph becomes the input for static analysis and instrumentation components.

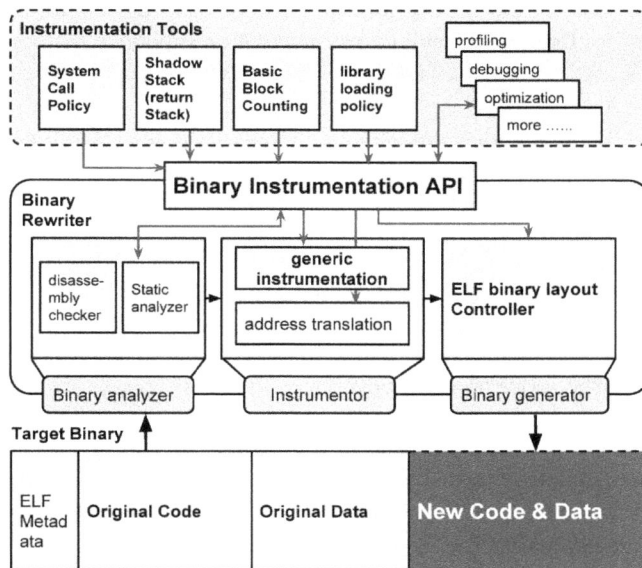

Figure 1. Architecture Overview of PSI

The heart of PSI is the instrumentor, which provides an expressive API for static binary instrumentation. Two levels of API are supported. The low-level API operates at the instruction level, and supports operations for inserting assembly language snippets at desired points. The high-level API allows insertion of calls to instrumentation functions that may be written in a language such as C. This code is compiled into a shared library, and our platform ensures that these functions can be called in a secure manner from (and only from) the calls inserted using the high-level instrumentation API. This API is further described in Section 3.2.

PSI uses the address translator from BinCFI [38], but its behavior can be modified using the instrumentation API.

The actual task of instrumentation is performed by *instrumentation tools*, which are programs that use the API provided by the platform to instrument applications and the libraries used by them.

Our API not only allows tools to control the instrumentation phase, but also other phases such as static analysis, address translation, etc. This allows instrumentation tools to enhance these phases.

3.1 Non-bypassable Instrumentation

PSI ensures that the added instrumentation is non-bypassable by enforcing the following properties.

- All direct and indirect control-flow transfers made from the original code must target instructions in the original code that were validly disassembled by the disassembler.

- If a snippet was specified for insertion before an instruction I, then all (direct or indirect) control-flow transfers targeting I will instead be made to target the first instruction of the added snippet.

- Only the added instrumentation code can transfer control to libraries containing instrumentation support functions. (Recall that the high-level instrumentation API relies on inserting calls to this library.)

All indirect branches, including jumps, calls and returns, are checked at runtime to ensure the above properties. Direct branches are checked at the time of generating the instrumented binary.

In addition to the above, our loader denies requests for loading uninstrumented libraries. If on-demand instrumentation option is turned on, the request isn't denied; instead, an instrumented version of the library is generated and loaded.

The above properties overlap with coarse-granularity CFI that limits control transfers to instruction boundaries. Specifically, we have enhanced such a CFI property with additional restrictions intended to protect the integrity of added instrumentation, as well as to deal with problems such as runtime loading of libraries, disassembly problems, etc.

Our platform is geared for instrumenting benign applications — applications that may contain vulnerabilities, but are not malicious themselves. For such applications, these checks ensure that control-flow cannot "escape" instrumentation. A non-exhaustive list of attacks prevented by PSI is as follows.

- *Branching to data segments.* As described above, the list of valid targets can only include addresses within validly instrumented code. Thus, data segments cannot appear in this table of valid targets.

- *Branching to code sections that were not recognized and instrumented.* If the disassembler fails to recognize some code fragments, they won't be instrumented. However, since branch targets are restricted to be valid instruction boundaries in disassembled code, any attempt to execute undiscovered code will be blocked.

- *Branching to middle of instructions.* ROP attacks are a prime example here. Since the targets are checked to be valid instruction boundaries, these attacks are stopped.

- *Bypassing the instrumentation code.* As noted above, if an instrumentation snippet was specified for insertion before an instruction, that instruction is no longer permitted to be a branch target.

- *Corrupting the integrity of instrumentation logic by jumping into its middle, or by accessing functions intended to be used exclusively by instrumentation.* As noted above, branches will be checked to preclude these targets.

Threats posed by untrusted code. Instrumentation of untrusted (and potentially malicious) applications can be supported, but it requires more extensive (and expensive) checks on instrumented code. Specifically, untrusted code can attempt to subvert PSI using one of the following means:

- *corrupting PSI data.* Untrusted code could intentionally corrupt data used by PSI instrumentations.

- *using race conditions.* Untrusted code may use data races to carry out time-of-check-to-time-of-use attacks on policies enforced by PSI, such as system call policies.

- *subverting the loader.* By subverting the loader, untrusted code may be able to load and execute uninstrumented libraries.

All of these threats can be addressed by isolating the memory used by the instrumented applications, using a technique such as software fault isolation (SFI) [32]. However, memory isolation incurs significant additional costs, and hence is typically not enabled on most instrumentation platforms, including most DBI platforms.

3.2 Instrumentation API

Our platform provides a simple API for custom instrumentation of binaries. This API is designed to operate at roughly the same level of abstraction as Pin and DynamoRIO. However, being a static rewriting tool, all instrumentation operations occur in one shot on our platform: the entire CFG for a binary is presented to the code instrumentor, which traverses the CFG and adds all the desired instrumentation. This contrasts with DBI tools where instructions and basic blocks are discovered one by one, just before their first execution, and the code instrumentor invoked separately on the newly discovered basic block.

After disassembly, PSI constructs a control-flow graph (CFG) of the program. The nodes in the CFG are basic blocks, each of which consists of a sequence of instructions. All incoming control transfers into a basic block go to its first instruction, while all control transfers out of the block occur on its last statement. Note that every indirect control flow target computed by our static analysis is considered in defining these basic blocks. Since this analysis estimates a superset of possible indirect targets, the basic blocks computed by our technique can be smaller than those computed by a compiler.

The entire CFG can be accessed using the API function `getCFG`, while the list of all basic blocks and instructions can be obtained using the functions `getBBs` and `getInsns`. The API also provides operations to iterate through instructions and basic blocks in a CFG, and instructions in a basic block. Also supported are operations to examine instructions. These operations are based on the Intel's xed2 instruction encoder/decoder library. Some of the most commonly used operations are `isCall`, `isRet`, `isTest`, `isSysCall`, `isMemRead`, `isMemWrite`, `getTarget`, and `getSrc`.

Insertion of Assembly Code Snippets. Instrumentation can be performed at a low or high level. At the low level, an instrumentation snippet is inserted as follows:

$$\texttt{ins\_snippet}(target, location, snippet)$$

Here, $target$ is a reference to an instruction or a basic block, and is specified using a reference to the corresponding object, or by using a label. The parameter $location$ is one of BEFORE or AFTER, and snippet is a string consisting of assembly code that is to be inserted. For call instructions, one extra location AFTER_CALL is defined. To ensure transparency of return addresses on the stack, a call is translated into a push instruction that pushes the original return address, followed by a jump that transfers control to the target function. AFTER_CALL corresponds to the point between push and jump.

Instead of inserting additional instrumentation, some applications may require replacement of existing instructions. This is done using the following API function:

$$replace\_ins(target, new\_snippet)$$

Instruction emulation is a purpose for which this API function comes handy: we replace the original instruction with a snippet that emulates it.

PSI provides a private thread local storage (TLS) area that can be used by assembly snippets to store their data. This private TLS, which is independent of the one used by glibc, is organized into two arrays TS and GS that are both initialized with all zeros. The size of these arrays is configurable, but they default to one memory page. Snippet code can use the identifiers TS_n and GS_n to access the nth word of the arrays TS and GS respectively. Example uses of these arrays can be found in Figures 2 and 3.

Insertion of Calls to Instrumentation Functions. The benefit of the snippet API is that it can be more efficient since the instrumentation writer can minimize the number of instructions executed. Its downside is that instrumentation has to be performed in assembly, and that it is more complex. In contrast, the higher level API simplifies instrumentation but is generally less efficient. It enables the insertion of calls to handler functions in a shared library defined by the instrumentor. Several low level details are handled automatically by the high-level API. These include saving/restoring of registers and flags, switching to a different stack, resolving the symbolic name of the user-defined handler function, making the program state available through a high-level data structure called Context, and so on. These factors simplify the instrumentation task, and allows the handler code to be written in higher level languages (currently, C/C++). This API is accessed using the following function:

$$ins\_call(target, location, name, args)$$

Here, *target* and *location* have the same meaning as the snippet API. The name of the function to be invoked is specified using the string parameter *name*. This function should have the following prototype:

$$void\ handler(struct\ Context\ *c, \ldots)$$

It takes a first parameter that represents the runtime context of the instrumented program, including all of the CPU registers, stack, etc. The subsequent parameters are exactly those that were included in the *args* parameter to ins_call.

Controlling Address Translation. As described earlier, address translation instrumentation, which regulates ICF transfers, is automatically added by our platform. We provide some API functions so that an instrumentation developer can exercise finer control over ICF transfers. These functions can be used by an instrumentation tool that implements a more sophisticated ICF target analysis to further restrict indirect branches. Even without performing more static analysis, an instrumentation tool may enforce a more restrictive policy, e.g.,

- all returns should go to instructions following calls
- (some or all) indirect jumps should not target addresses outside the current module

These restrictions can be specified using the API function:

$$rm\_indirect\_target(src\_addrs, target\_addrs)$$

The argument *src_addrs* is a list of the labels of the ICF transfer instructions whose targets should be restricted. If it is empty, then the operation is applied to all ICF transfer instructions in the module. The second argument is also a list of labels, but may include a special label $NONLOCAL$ that causes non-local addresses to be deleted from the list of valid targets.

Custom address translation instrumentation can also be used to relax a previously specified policy. This is done using the following API function:

$$add\_indirect\_target(src\_addrs, target\_addrs)$$

Any number of rm_indirect_target and add_indirect_target calls may be made. The platform will keep track of possible targets for each source address, and will generate a unique address translation trampoline for each set of source addresses that share the same set of possible targets.

Runtime event handling. Finally, the API supports registration of instrumentation functions that will be called when certain events occur at runtime, such as program/thread startup or exit, loading of libraries, and system calls:

- register_pre_syscall_handler()
- register_post_syscall_handler()
- register_library_load_handler()
- register_thread_start_handler()
- register_thread_terminate_handler()
- register_program_start_handler()
- register_program_terminate_handler()

These API calls take a function name as their argument.

Development of Instrumentation tools. To develop an instrumentation tool, user provides the tool code, and optionally, a *client library*. The tool code uses the API provided by our platform to realize an instrumentation tool. Tools that use the high-level API need a mechanism to provide the definitions of function calls inserted using that API. This is the role of the client library. Note that the tool code is used at the time of instrumenting a binary, whereas the client library functions are used during the execution of the instrumented applications. This is why tool code is separated from the client library.

The instrumentation tool code should be stored in a source file, say, bbcount.c. To instrument a binary file xyz, the tool developer will first compile this into a shared library, and then apply it to the binary. Specifically, the following sequence of commands is used for developing a instrumentation tool using the low-level API:

```
psic —o bbcount.so bbcount.c
psi_loader -t bbcount.so -- xyz
```

If a high-level API is used, the client library needs to be compiled first. At runtime, calls made by instrumentation to client library functions need to be resolved. In principle, resolving a client function name is straight-forward: use the standard C-compiler to produce a shared library from the client library source, and include this library in the dependency list for the instrumented binary. However, such an approach will violate our security requirement because client library functions would be callable by original code. Instead, we want these functions to be callable only from the added instrumentation. To satisfy this requirement, we have developed a dedicated symbol resolution technique for resolving function names in the client library.

To resolve client functions, the basic idea is to create a global address table (GAT) that contains the memory locations where the client functions have been loaded. To simplify the look-up process, we translate function names in the client library to integer indices. This enables GAT to be a simple array indexed by these integer indices. A mapping file specifying a name-to-index mapping is generated during the compilation of the client library:

```
psic —m bbclient.map —o bbclient.so bbclient.c
```

Now, this mapping file will be used by the instrumentor to translate calls to client library functions made in the instrumentation code. The mapping file is also used by our modified loader, which uses this mapping to populate the GAT. Specifically, for each function f defined in the client library, the loader finds its index i_f from the mapping file, and stores the location where f is loaded in $GAT[i_f]$. After populating GAT, it is made read-only. In addition, none of the locations in the client library are ever added to the translation tables. These two steps ensure that code in the client libraries can never be invoked by the original code.

Resolution of the variable names could be accomplished in a similar way with the help of another GAT and a corresponding name-to-index mapping.

3.3 On-demand Instrumentation

One of the drawbacks of a purely static instrumentation approach is that the user has to compute the list of all shared libraries that may be used when an instrumented program is run, and create instrumented version of these libraries. This is a difficult task, since many libraries are loaded long after program execution begins. Some of these libraries may reside at user-specified locations known only at runtime. In order to support seamless instrumentation of such libraries, our platform provides an option to generate instrumented libraries on-the-fly. In particular, we modified the loader to support an option to specify a configuration file that is consulted when an instrumented application requests to load an uninstrumented library. (If this option is not specified, then any request to load an uninstrumented library will be denied.) This configuration file must specify the name of the libraries containing the tool code, client library code, and the mapping file. The loader will then invoke PSI to create an instrumented version of the uninstrumented library, and then load this version.

Instrumented libraries are stored in a disk cache for subsequent uses. This cache can store multiple versions of the same library, each corresponding to a different tool.

In principle, PSI could be deployed on a system-wide basis, and use a shared cache across all users. However, currently we rely on a simpler scheme that uses a per-user cache. The cache is simply a directory owned by the user, say, /var/psi/bob/.

When the loader is asked to load a library, say, /usr/lib/abc.so by a process instrumented with a tool bbcount and owned by bob, the loader concatenates the library name to the cache location, i.e., looks for the file

/var/psi/bob/bbcount/usr/lib/abc.so.

If found, this file is loaded. If not, the loader invokes psi to instrument /usr/lib/abc.so with the tool bbcount and stores this result in the cache, and loads the instrumented version from the cache.

Note that libraries with the same instrumentation but with different compilation options or client libraries may cause compatibility problems. To avoid these, the loader checks the library version, compilation options, as well as the client library version. It also checks the timestamps on the tool code and client library code, and if they are newer than the cached version, then a new, instrumented version is generated and the copy in the cache is updated.

On-demand instrumentation can be applied to executables as well, and serve to support seamless instrumentation of applications that involve running multiple executables.

4. Instrumentation Applications

We illustrate the API described in the preceding section using several examples. These examples illustrate the flexibility, versatility and the ease-of-use benefits of PSI.

4.1 Basic Block Counting

Basic block counting has been used to illustrate previous DBI tools such as Pin and DynamoRIO. Moreover, an op-

```
unopt = "mov%eax, TS_0;
         lahf;
         incl TS_1;
         sahf;
         mov TS_0, %eax"
opt = "incl TS_1"
foreach bb in getBBs() {
  found = false
  foreach insn in bb {
    if isTest(insn) or isCmp(insn) {
      found = true
      ins_snippet(insn, BEFORE, opt)
      break
    }
  }
  if !found
    ins_snippet(bb, BEGIN, unopt)
}
```

Figure 2. An instrumentation tool for Basic Block Counting

timized version of this tool is available for these platforms, thus providing a good basis for performance comparison. For this reason, we illustrate our platform and API using this example. (See Figure 2.) The core of the instrumentation is to increment a memory location. However, since this operation affects CPU flags, it is necessary to save and restore them. This is performed in the snippet *unopt*.

It would be safe to avoid flag save/restore, and use the optimized snippet *opt*, if the flags aren't live at the snippet insertion point. To simplify the example, we avoid a general liveness analysis. Instead, we find two common instances of instructions that set the flags, namely, test and cmp, and insert the increment instruction just before them.

For brevity, we have omitted the code for printing results. This can be done by registering a thread termination handler that will accumulate the count from thread-local TS_1 into a global location, say, GS_1. Finally, a program termination handler needs to be registered that prints the value of GS_1.

4.2 System Call Policy Enforcement

System call policy enforcement is a well-known protection technique for sandboxing. Our platform provides a simple API to enforce system call policies. Performance overheads are minimal, comparable to library interposition. At the same time, it provides security comparable to ptrace, a much heavier-weight mechanism used in tools such as strace.

System call policy enforcement is implemented by registering system call event handlers register_pre_syscall_ handler() and register_post_syscall_handler(). Our platform is able to identify system calls that use int 0x80 mechanism as well as the faster method that uses the sysenter instruction. The handler function can use its Context argument to determine system call arguments, which are stored in registers. The handler can examine and/or modify these arguments.

4.3 Library Load Policy Enforcement

Unsafe library loading is a well known strategy employed by security exploits to circumvent injected code defenses such as those that prevent execution of data.

A library loading policy is implemented using a tool that registers a handler for the event register_library_load_ handler(). The handler can then examine the name of the library being loaded, and disallow it if need be. In our tool, rather than enforcing a policy, we simply logged a message that can be processed subsequently to identify how many libraries are loaded by an application, and what fraction of them are loaded after the application begins execution. We used this tool to on a collection of commonly used command-line and GUI applications and found that a significant fraction of libraries (specifically, over 40% in this experiment) were loaded after the commencement of application execution.

4.4 Shadow stack

Shadow stack [27] is a well-known technique for defending against return address corruption. The idea is to maintain a second copy of return addresses on a "shadow" stack, and check the two copies for consistency before each return. Successful exploits now require both copies of the return address to be compromised, which is harder than circumventing protection mechanisms such as stack canaries.

Binary based return address defender [27] was the first to use binary instrumentation to implement shadow stacks. It inserts additional code at function prologue and epilogue to respectively push and check return addresses on shadow stack. While their approach is useful against buffer overflow attacks on return addresses, they are not effective against ROP attacks that mainly use unintended return instructions, as there will be no shadow stack checks preceding such "instructions." Note that the initial exploit can be triggered without compromising a return address, e.g., by corrupting a function pointer.

ROPdefender [12] addresses this weakness using DBI. As DBI techniques ensure instrumentation of all code before execution, their approach will instrument unintended returns as well, and hence prevent ROP attacks. We compare the performance of their implementation, which is based on Pin, with our platform. For this purpose, we developed the shadow stack instrumentation tool shown in Figure 3. Our implementation emphasizes ease of development and compatibility with legacy software, and we did not make any significant effort at optimizing it. Thus, our performance results reflect the performance strengths of our platform, rather than the efficiency of our instrumentation tool.

Note that being a static instrumentation technique, our technique will not instrument unintended return instructions. However, our runtime checks on indirect targets will stop any attempts to jump to such instructions. Moreover, attacks aimed at evading shadow stack checks, such as those based

```
/* shadow stack pointer is stored in TS_2 */
chk_init_shadowstk= "
         cmp   $0x0, TS_2;
         jnz   L001;
         call  $alloc_stack;
      L001: ";

push_shadowstk = "
         mov   %eax, TS_0; mov %ebx, TS_1;
         subl  $4, TS_2;
         mov   TS_2, %eax;
         mov   (%esp), %ebx; mov %ebx, (%eax)
         mov   TS_0, %eax; mov TS_1, %ebx;"

check_return(Context*ctxt) {
   shadow_sp = ctxt->TS[2]
   ret = getmem(ctxt->ESP)
   while !empty(shadow_sp)
     if (pop(shadow_sp) == ret) {
        ctxt->TS[2] = shadow_sp
        return
     }
     abort()
}

foreach insn in getInsns()
   if isCall(insn) {
      ins_snippet(insn, BEFORE, chk_init_shadowstk)
      ins_snippet(insn, BEFORE, push_shadowstk)
   }
   else if isRet(insn)
      ins_call(insn, AFTER_CALL, check_return)
```

Figure 3. Shadow Stack Defense

on jumping into the middle of (or past the end of) checking code will be defeated as well.

In Figure 3, the shadow stack could be initialized at the time a new thread is spawned. However, we opted for a simpler (but less efficient) approach where the validity of shadow stack is checked on each call instruction, using chk_init_shadowstk. This snippet uses another support function to allocate a shadow stack if it is not already set up. Once the shadow stack is in place, push_shadowstk is used to push a copy of the return address to the shadow stack.

Checking the integrity of returns is more complex, so we use a high-level function to perform this action. Note that uses of longjmp can cause a mismatch between shadow and main stack. This occurs because stack frames have been popped off the main stack. The solution to this problem, used in previous works [12, 27], is to successively pop off entries from the shadow stack until the two match. However, if the bottom of shadow stack is reached, that implies an attack, and the program is aborted.

As noted by the authors of ROPdefender, real-world programs introduce a few benign violations of shadow stack checks, and these need to be handled. We already described how violations due to longjmp are handled. Other violations occur due to lazy binding used by the dynamic loader, the occurrence of C++ exceptions, UNIX signals, and System V thread context switches due to functions such as setcontext and getcontext. The core idea used in

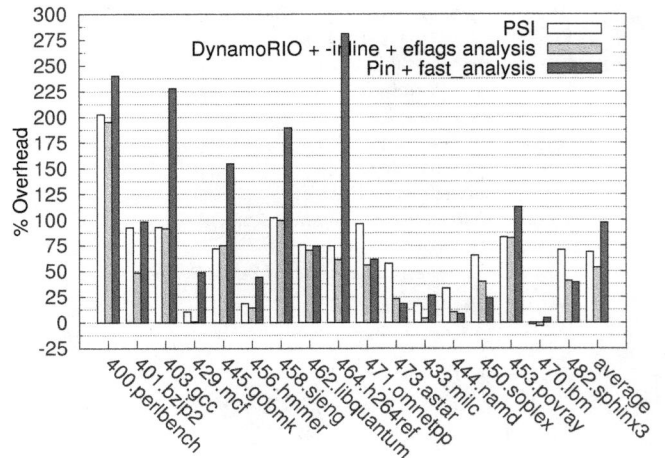

Figure 4. Overhead of basic block counting application of PSI, DynamoRIO, and Pin on SPEC 2006.

ROPdefender is that of recognizing which return instructions in the binary cause these exceptions (each of them occur within a specific routine in the loader or libc), and modifying the instrumentation of those instructions. We used the same idea in our implementation, but have omitted the details to conserve space.

5. Experimental Evaluation

5.1 Basic block counting on SPEC2006

Our instrumentation tool incorporates a simple optimization to skip flag saving in some common cases, but lacks a systematic liveness analysis. In spite of lacking this optimization, performance of PSI (average overhead of 69%) is only a slightly worse than DynamoRIO (53%), and better than Pin (97%). The result is shown in Figure 4. For this experiment, we used the most optimized version of basic-block counting applications distributed with Pin and DynamoRIO platforms.

Although PSI is designed for offline instrumentation, we turned on the on-demand instrumentation feature, emptied the library cache and reran the benchmark. In addition, we added back the time for instrumenting the executables to the totals. In this way, we can measure the total runtime that includes instrumentation time. This change causes the overhead to increase by another 3%.

5.2 Performance of shadow stack application

Figure 5 depicts the overhead of the shadow stack implementation using our platform in comparison to that of ROPdefender, which is based on Pin. While ROPdefender reports an overhead of 74%, PSI incurs just one-fourth of this overhead (18%).

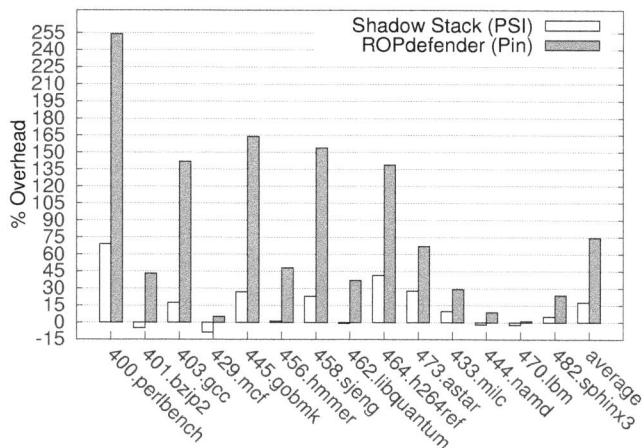

Figure 5. Overhead of shadow stack implementation using PSI and that of ROPdefender on SPEC 2006

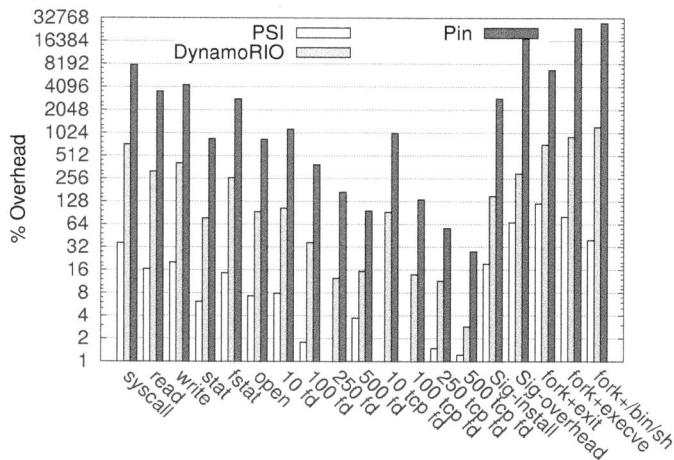

Figure 6. lmbench microbenchmark result

Prasad et al [27] report lower overheads, as low as a few percent. But as mentioned earlier, their technique does not defend against ROP attacks.

5.3 Evaluation of system call policy

On SPEC 2006 benchmark, our baseline system call policy enforcement introduced an average of 1.6% overhead. This is with a policy function registered for each system call, but the function body being empty.

5.4 Microbenchmark Evaluation

Although DynamoRIO performs well on CPU-intensive SPEC2006, real world programs can often exhibit different characteristics. To compare PSI with DynamoRIO and Pin for workloads that are system-call intensive, we used the lmbench [1] benchmark. Since lmbench (as well as the real-world evaluation in the next section) cause some DBI platforms to slow to the point where experiments take far too long to complete, we used the null instrumentation in these experiments to minimize their runtime.

Figure 6 shows the lmbench performance numbers. Note that the histogram is drawn to logarithmic scale on Y axis. The average system call overhead for PSI is 16.9%, whereas for DynamoRIO it is 312%, and for Pin it is 3300%. On system calls related to communication, PSI achieves almost native performance, whereas DynamoRIO has 36.1% overhead, and Pin has 378%. System calls related to signal handling and process spawning slow down PSI by 43.3% and 79.7% respectively, which increase to 222% and 948% for DynamoRIO, and 104x and 198x for Pin.

To summarize, the average overhead across the tests shown in Figure 6, while counting only one of the `select` operations (for 10 fds), is 33% for PSI (geometric mean:

30%), while for DynamoRIO it is 413% (geometric mean: 309%) and for Pin it is 7873% (geometric mean: 4083%).

DBI platforms are complex, and hence the reasons for their high overheads on lmbench (and the real-world applications discussed in the next section) aren't all obvious. But we can identify several factors that contribute to the high overhead. First, and most obvious, is that runtime disassembly and instrumentation incurs nontrivial overheads, unless this cost is amortized across many executions of instrumented code. Such amortization occurs on CPU-intensive benchmarks, but the real-world applications discussed in the next section tend to load much more code, and execute it far fewer times, thus causing the overheads of runtime instrumentation to rise significantly. This is one of the main reasons for the high overhead of applications that make frequent calls to `execve`.

A second factor that contributes to the overhead is the increased memory footprint of dynamically instrumented programs. We have observed that DynamoRIO can frequently use a code cache that is over a 100MB in size. We have also observed that such increased use of data memory can significantly slow down `fork` due to factors such as the increased time for copying page tables.

A third factor relates to threads and locking that is needed to ensure that accesses to data used by the DBI platform (including the code cache) are free of concurrency errors.

5.5 Performance on Real-world Applications

In this section, we compare the performance of PSI with that of Pin and DynamoRIO on a collection of commonly used applications. Once again we used the null instrumentation to minimize the runtime for the experiments.

We first measured the performance for two tasks that are commonly undertaken by typical Unix users: compilation of software, and running scripts that invoke other programs.

Program	PSI (%)	Dynamo-RIO (%)	Pin (%)	Description
coreutils	97%	1922%	3509%	Coreutils testsuite
gcc	63%	1376%	10250%	Compile openssh.
apt − get update	2%	326%	411%	Run command 5 times.
enscript	211%	5292%	15153%	Convert text and source code files to ps and pdf. [a]
postmark	2%	22%	64%	Run benchmark.
gpg	24%	382%	5994%	Operate on pdfs with an avg size of 500KB.
tar	19%	79%	1107%	Tar /usr/include.
find	21%	34%	38%	Find a file in /.
scp	-1%	18%	31%	Copy 10 mp3s, with an avg size of 5MB.
mplayer	32%	67%	211%	Play 10 mp3s.
vim	56%	92%	615%	Search and replace strings in 18MB text file.
latex	51%	185%	1806%	Compile tex files with an avg size of 17KB to dvi.
readelf	62%	71%	197%	Parse the DWARF sections of glibc.
python	33%	85%	96%	Run pystone 1.1 benchmark.
Average	**53%**	**887%**	**3421%**	

[a] We used a bunch of text files such that the their file sizes average to 8K. We used 2 types of source files for our purpose: C programs and Python programs. We averaged C file sizes from Openssl source package and used the same average of 18K for our test purpose. For Python, we averaged sizes of Python scripts found on a typical Ubuntu machine and used the same average of 8K for our test purpose.

Figure 7. Real World Program Performance

Specifically, we compiled OpenSSH with GNU make and gcc tool chain, and used the built-in testsuite of coreutils.

When testing gcc compilation with PSI, we instrumented all the executables in the gcc toolchain, including gcc, g++, cc1, cc1plus, f951, lto, ar, ranlib, as, ld.bfd, and collect2. We also instrumented make and all external tools used in makefile such as echo, sed, cat, perl, and gawk. Note that all libraries used by these programs were transformed too. The overhead incurred by PSI was 63%, while DynamoRIO and Pin incurred overheads of 1376% and 10250% respectively.

In the case of coreutils, for PSI, we transformed all coreutils binaries as well as other programs used in the coreutils test suite. But due to difficulties in invoking DynamoRIO on each coreutils program inside the test script, we used DynamoRIO to run make so that it will subsequently instrument all programs invoked from there. DynamoRIO incurred a 19.2x slowdown, as compared to 97% for PSI.

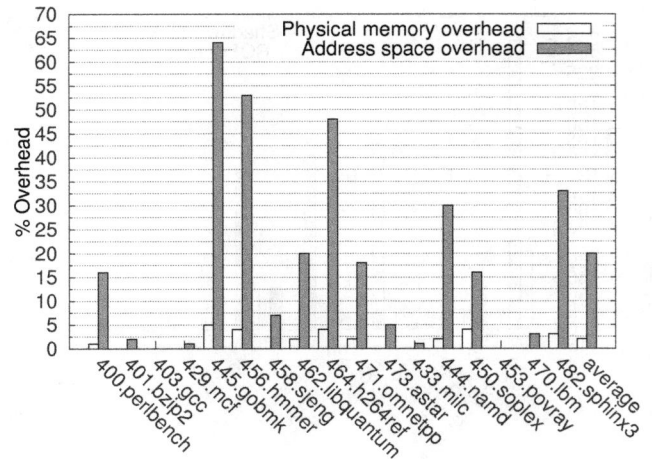

Figure 8. Space overhead of PSI on SPEC 2006

When we tested Pin, unfortunately, the testsuite did not stop after running for over an hour. We stopped the experiment at this point, and used that figure as the runtime of Pin, which worked out to be 3509%.

In addition to the above tests, we measured the overhead for several commonly used programs. The results are shown in Figure 7. It is worth mentioning that apt-get update invoked several executables including http, gpgv, dpkg and touch. All of the executables as well as libraries used were transformed in the tests.

Note that for about half the applications, there is more than 10x difference between PSI and DynamoRIO. The difference drops down to 3x to 5x for about a quarter of the applications, and for the remaining, the overhead difference is within a factor of two. When averaged across all of the applications, PSI's overhead was 53% (45% geometric mean), DynamoRIO's overhead was 887% (322% geometric mean), and Pin's overhead was 3421% (924% geometric mean).

5.6 Space Overhead

In addition to the runtime overhead on SPEC 2006 benchmark, we also measured the space overhead of our platform. Figure 8 describes the space overhead of our platform for SPEC 2006 benchmark. From the figure, the virtual memory overhead of our platform is 19.79%, while the physical memory overhead is merely 1.68%. In addition to the space overhead for physical and virtual memory, we also measured that our platform increased the on-disk size of the executables and shared libraries by around 139%. This is because PSI instruments a copy of original code, leaving the original code in place. However, this original copy is seldom accessed, which explains why the resident memory overhead is very small, at around 2%.

In comparison, we also measured the space overhead of DynamoRIO and PIN. We discover that their address space overhead is 272% and 72%. This is mainly because the DBI tools need to reserve address space for code cache allocation. The physical memory overhead is 7.5% and 34%, higher than our platform.

6. Related Work

This section is aimed at discussing related works that have not already been adequately described earlier in this paper.

Static Binary Rewriting A number of efforts in exploit protection and hardening of binaries have been based on static binary rewriting. However, supporting large and complex COTS binaries has proved elusive due to the twin challenges of accurate disassembly, and safe rewriting in the presence of embedded code pointers within binaries. To overcome the disassembly problem, most previous works have relied on a cooperative compiler [35], or worked on assembly code [6, 20, 24], or binary code containing symbol [18, 29], debugging [2, 14], or relocation information [36, 37].

SecondWrite [3] uses static binary rewriting to harden binaries, but applicability to large and complex binaries was not established. Recently, they showed that their platform can handle real world applications [4]. They develop powerful analysis and optimization techniques that provide excellent performance. However, this improved platform does not target security instrumentations that need to worry about low-level attacks such as return address corruption, or other attacks that may invalidate static analysis results.

Several earlier works such as BIRD [21] and Dyninst [10] used a combination of analysis, compiler idioms and heuristics to disassemble binaries. BIRD further improves results by incorporating a runtime disassembly component. However, use of heuristics means that there could be disassembly errors, and these can lead to instrumentation subversion, e.g., by jumping to the middle of an instruction. In-place randomization [25] also has this same drawback, but mitigates it through randomization of the binary, which significantly reduces the likelihood of finding exploit code within the binary. However, in-place transformations are insufficient for instrumentation.

Reins [33] targets sandboxing of untrusted COTS executables on Windows. Like us, they can also ensure that sandboxed code can never escape instrumentation (except to invoke certain trusted functions), but unlike our technique, their approach does not target instrumentation of all libraries used by the application. Moreover, their evaluation does not consider as many or as large applications as ours.

PSI builds on our earlier BinCFI work [38]. In particular, we reused the disassembler and ELF-related tools developed in that work. The main focus of this paper is the development of a general-purpose platform for static binary instrumentation. We demonstrated the power and flexibility of this platform by developing a variety of security instrumentations. In contrast, BinCFI targets just a single instrumen-

tation, namely, control-flow integrity. This instrumentation is hardcoded into the BinCFI platform, whereas this paper decouples the instrumentation platform for instrumentation tools. Another important contribution of this paper is a detailed performance comparison with DBI platforms.

Binary Analysis Binary Analysis Platform [9] is a platform that targets COTS binaries, but its main focus is sophisticated analysis rather than efficient instrumentation. For example, they have developed interesting applications such as automatic exploit generation [5]. BitBlaze [31] is also targeting powerful static and dynamic analysis of binary code, including malware. These and other binary analysis works are complementary to ours: whereas their focus is on accurate and powerful analysis techniques, ours is on robust and efficient instrumentation.

Dynamic Binary Instrumentation As mentioned earlier, several DBI platforms [7, 8, 19, 22, 30] are currently available. Many of these, including DynamoRIO [8], Pin [19], Strata [30] and StarDBT [7] are geared for efficient support of light-weight instrumentation, while Valgrind [22] targets heavy-weight instrumentations, e.g., memory debugging.

DBI techniques have formed the basis of many research proposals for hardening and securing COTS binaries. Program shepherding [17] enforces several low-level policies using DynamoRIO. Libdetox [26] improves on this work by supporting a more refined control-flow policy, including a shadow stack. They also provide an API for specifying customized system call policies. We also provide an easy-to-use API for specifying system call policies, but in addition, provide a low-level instrumentation API as well, so as to ease the development of customized inline security checks. Whereas Libdetox targets vulnerable but benign code, Vx32 [15] uses DBI techniques to sandbox untrusted code.

While PSI seeks to achieve many of the same goals of DBI platforms, in terms of the underlying techniques, PSI is mostly complementary to those of DBI: we emphasize static disassembly, static analysis and static transformation, whereas DBI tools excel in runtime disassembly, dynamic analyses and optimizations.

7. Summary and Conclusions

DBI platforms have been popular for instrumentation of COTS binaries because of their ability to handle large and complex binaries, instrument all code, ensure that applications cannot escape instrumentation, and easy-to-use APIs. SBI techniques have complementary strengths, such as the ability to perform offline instrumentation and the ability to support more powerful static analysis techniques. Unfortunately, previous SBI platforms have lacked some of main features needed to support robust security-related instrumentations on large and complex binaries.

The work presented in this paper demonstrates that indeed it is possible to realize the best of both worlds: PSI retains most of the advantages of DBI platforms, while also providing the central benefits of static instrumentation. The resulting platform can thus retain most of the strengths of DBI and SBI, while mitigating their drawbacks.

We illustrated the power of our platform and the simplicity of its programming model by developing several instrumentation tools. Among these is an implementation of efficient shadow stack defense that is resistant to ROP attacks. For many real-world usage scenarios, our platform achieves about an order of magnitude performance improvement over DBI platforms. Based on these results, we conclude that static binary rewriting can provide a powerful alternative to the popular dynamic rewriting platforms.

References

[1] Lmbench tool for performance analysis. http://lmbench.sourceforge.net/.

[2] M. Abadi, M. Budiu, U. Erlingsson, and J. Ligatti. Control-flow integrity principles, implementations, and applications. *ACM TISSEC*, 2009.

[3] K. Anand, M. Smithson, A. Kotha, K. Elwazeer, and R. Barua. Decompilation to compiler high IR in a binary rewriter. Technical report, University of Maryland, 2010.

[4] K. Anand, M. Smithson, K. Elwazeer, A. Kotha, and J. Gruen et al. A compiler-level intermediate representation based binary analysis and rewriting system. In *EuroSys*, 2013.

[5] T. Avgerinos, S. K. Cha, A. Rebert, E. J. Schwartz, and M. Woo et al. AEG: automatic exploit generation. In *NDSS*, 2011.

[6] T. Bletsch, X. Jiang, and V. Freeh. Mitigating code-reuse attacks with control-flow locking. In *ACSAC*, 2011.

[7] E. Borin, C. Wang, Y. Wu, and G. Araujo. Software-based transparent and comprehensive control-flow error detection. In *CGO*, 2006.

[8] D. Bruening. *Efficient, transparent, and comprehensive runtime code manipulation*. PhD thesis, 2004.

[9] D. Brumley, I. Jager, T. Avgerinos, and E. Schwartz. BAP: a binary analysis platform. In *CAV*, 2011.

[10] B. Buck and J. Hollingsworth. An API for runtime code patching. *Int. J. High Perform. Comput. Appl.*, 2000.

[11] P. Chen, H. Xiao, X. Shen, X. Yin, and B. Mao et al. DROP: detecting return-oriented programming malicious code. In *ICISS*, 2009.

[12] L. Davi, A.-R. Sadeghi, and M. Winandy. ROPdefender: a detection tool to defend against return-oriented programming attacks. In *ASIACCS*, 2011.

[13] K. ElWazeer, K. Anand, A. Kotha, M. Smithson, and R. Barua. Scalable variable and data type detection in a binary rewriter. In *PLDI*, 2013.

[14] U. Erlingsson, M. Abadi, M. Vrable, M. Budiu, and G. Necula. XFI: software guards for system address spaces. In *OSDI*, 2006.

[15] B. Ford and R. Cox. Vx32: lightweight user-level sandboxing on the x86. In *USENIX ATC*, 2008.

[16] J. Hiser, A. Nguyen-Tuong, M. Co, M. Hall, and J. Davidson. ILR: where'd my gadgets go? In *S&P*, 2012.

[17] V. Kiriansky, D. Bruening, and S. Amarasinghe. Secure execution via program shepherding. In *USENIX Security*, 2002.

[18] M. Laurenzano, M. Tikir, L. Carrington, and A. Snavely. PEBIL: efficient static binary instrumentation for Linux. In *IEEE International Symposium on Performance Analysis of Systems Software (ISPASS)*, 2010.

[19] C.-K. Luk, R. Cohn, R. Muth, H. Patil, and A. Klauser et al. Pin: building customized program analysis tools with dynamic instrumentation. In *PLDI*, 2005.

[20] S. McCamant and G. Morrisett. Evaluating SFI for a CISC architecture. USENIX Security, 2006.

[21] S. Nanda, W. Li, L.-C. Lam, and T.-c. Chiueh. BIRD: binary interpretation using runtime disassembly. In *CGO*, 2006.

[22] N. Nethercote and J. Seward. Valgrind: a framework for heavyweight dynamic binary instrumentation. In *PLDI*, 2007.

[23] J. Newsome. Dynamic taint analysis for automatic detection, analysis, and signature generation of exploits on commodity software. In *NDSS*, 2005.

[24] K. Onarlioglu, L. Bilge, A. Lanzi, D. Balzarotti, and E. Kirda. G-Free: defeating return-oriented programming through gadget-less binaries. In *ACSAC*, 2010.

[25] V. Pappas, M. Polychronakis, and A. Keromytis. Smashing the gadgets: Hindering return-oriented programming using in-place code randomization. In *S&P*, 2012.

[26] M. Payer and T. Gross. Fine-grained user-space security through virtualization. In *VEE*, 2011.

[27] M. Prasad and T.-c. Chiueh. A binary rewriting defense against stack based overflow attacks. In *USENIX ATC*, 2003.

[28] F. Qin, C. Wang, Z. Li, H.-s. Kim, and Y. Zhou et al. LIFT: a low-overhead practical information flow tracking system for detecting security attacks. In *MICRO*, 2006.

[29] P. Saxena, R. Sekar, and V. Puranik. Efficient fine-grained binary instrumentation with applications to taint-tracking. In *CGO*, 2008.

[30] K. Scott, N. Kumar, S. Velusamy, B. Childers, and J. Davidson et al. Retargetable and reconfigurable software dynamic translation. In *CGO*, 2003.

[31] D. Song, D. Brumley, H. Yin, J. Caballero, and I. Jager et al. BitBlaze: a new approach to computer security via binary analysis. In *ICISS*, 2008.

[32] R. Wahbe, S. Lucco, T. Anderson, and S. Graham. Efficient software-based fault isolation. In *SOSP*, 1993.

[33] R. Wartell, V. Mohan, K. Hamlen, and Z. Lin. Securing untrusted code via compiler-agnostic binary rewriting. In *ACSAC*, 2012.

[34] R. Wartell, V. Mohan, K. Hamlen, and Z. Lin. Binary stirring: self-randomizing instruction addresses of legacy x86 binary code. In *CCS*, 2012.

[35] B. Yee, D. Sehr, G. Dardyk, J. B. Chen, and R. Muth et al. Native Client: a sandbox for portable, untrusted x86 native code. In *S&P*, 2009.

[36] C. Zhang, T. Wei, Z. Chen, L. Duan, and S. McCamant et al. Protecting function pointers in binary. In *ASIACCS*, 2013.

[37] C. Zhang, T. Wei, Z. Chen, L. Duan, and L. Szekeres et al. Practical control flow integrity & randomization for binary executables. In *S&P*, 2013.

[38] M. Zhang and R. Sekar. Control flow integrity for COTS binaries. In *USENIX Security*, 2013.

DBILL: An Efficient and Retargetable Dynamic Binary Instrumentation Framework using LLVM Backend

Yi-Hong Lyu
Ding-Yong Hong
Tai-Yi Wu
Jan-Jan Wu

Institute of Information Science,
Academia Sinica, Taiwan
{mitnick, dyhong, rogerwu,
wuj}@iis.sinica.edu.tw

Wei-Chung Hsu
Pangfeng Liu

Dept. Computer Science &
Information Engineering
National Taiwan University, Taiwan
{hsuwc, pangfeng}@csie.ntu.edu.tw

Pen-Chung Yew

Dept. Computer Science &
Engineering,
University of Minnesota at Twin
Cities
Minneapolis, USA
yew@cs.umn.edu

Abstract

Dynamic Binary Instrumentation (DBI) is a core technology for building debugging and profiling tools for application executables. Most state-of-the-art DBI systems have focused on the same instruction set architecture (ISA) where the guest binary and the host binary have the same ISA. It is uncommon to have a cross-ISA DBI system, such as a system that instruments ARM executables to run on x86 machines. We believe cross-ISA DBI systems are increasingly more important, since ARM executables could be more productively analyzed on x86 based machines such as commonly available PCs and servers.

In this paper, we present DBILL, a cross-ISA and retargetable dynamic binary instrumentation framework that builds on both QEMU and LLVM. The DBILL framework enables LLVM-based static instrumentation tools to become DBI ready, and deployable to different target architectures. Using address sanitizer and memory sanitizer as implementation examples, we show DBILL is an efficient, versatile and easy to use cross-ISA retargetable DBI framework.

Categories and Subject Descriptors D.2.5 [*Software Engineering*]: Testing and Debugging; D.3.4 [*Processors*]: Runtime environments

General Terms Design, Performance

VEE '14, March 1–2, 2014, Salt Lake City, Utah, USA.
Copyright © 2014 ACM 978-1-4503-2764-0 /14/03... $15.00.
http://dx.doi.org/10.1145/2576195.2576213

Keywords dynamic binary instrumentation framework, LLVM-based instrumentation, LLVM enhanced dynamic binary translation and instrumentation, memory bugs

1. Introduction

Dynamic Binary Instrumentation (DBI) is a core technique used for building debugging and profiling tools for application executables. DBI frameworks such as PIN [13], DynamoRIO [8] and Valgrind [14] have been widely used to build program analysis tools. Such tools include memory checkers, security violation detectors, profilers for code optimizations, and race detectors for assisting parallel programming.

Most state-of-the-art DBI systems target the same instruction set architecture (ISA) where the guest binary and the host binary are based on the same ISA. For example, an x86 executable is instrumented to run on x86 machines. It is uncommon to have a cross-ISA DBI system, where the guest and the host are based on different ISAs. For example, a system that instruments ARM executables to run on x86 machines is a cross-ISA instrumentation system.

We believe cross-ISA DBI systems will be increasingly more important because of the success of the Android platform for mobile devices, which uses ARM based executables. On the surface, Android applications are supposed to run under the Dalvik VM, and thus should be in the form of Dalvik code rather than ARM binaries. In reality, many popular applications include ARM native binaries in the package to maintain good runtime performance. Many popular applications on both Google Play and the Apple Store either contain ARM native code or are entirely ARM based. Although ARM based application executables are everywhere, program analysis tools for them are not easy to deploy since the majority of ARM based systems are embedded devices, which are difficult to develop on. On the other hand, x86 based PCs and servers are productive development machines and are commonly available. They also have much higher performance than ARM based systems. Therefore, it is very attractive to build cross-ISA program analysis tools to debug, profile, and analyze ARM executables on x86 based systems.

Building a cross-ISA DBI system which runs ARM executables on an x86 machine has multiple advantages: (1) the host system (i.e., x86 PC/desktop/server) has much more resources in terms of memory and storage for collecting traces, (2) the host machine often has greater computing power so analysis tools run faster, and (3) the host machines ISA has a larger address space (i.e., 64bit vs. 32bit) and thus memory mapping of the virtual machine is easier. Although the latest ARMv8 architecture supports 64bit virtual address space, its ISA is not compatible with earlier ARM architectures. So, exploiting the 64bit address space of ARMv8 for running dynamically instrumented ARMv7 or earlier executables is still considered as a cross-ISA instrumentation system.

To build a cross-ISA DBI framework, we could leverage a retargetable Dynamic Binary Translators (DBT) such as QEMU [6]. QEMU is a widely used system emulator for running ARM executables on x86 machines. The main contributor of QEMU's high performance emulation is its DBT techniques. One drawback of QEMU is that its Tiny Code Generator (TCG) performs little code optimization. Recent research efforts [10, 11] have successfully combined LLVM [12] with QEMU, and with parallel code optimization and runtime optimization techniques [10], QEMU is not just a retargetable DBT framework, but a high performance, retargetable DBT framework. We intend to take advantage of such framework to build a cross-ISA DBI system.

Furthermore, because of the popularity of LLVM, there have been abundant static, compile-time instrumentation tools built upon LLVM, such as Address Sanitizer (detecting out-of-bound memory access) [18], Memory Sanitizer (detecting uninitialized read) [3], data flow sanitizer (for dynamic data flow analysis) [2], Thread Sanitizer (detecting race condition) [5], and profiling tools. This set of LLVM-based instrumentation tools are based on LLVM IR. A LLVM based DBI system can quickly leverage cross-ISA program analysis tools.

In this paper, using QEMU and LLVM as our building blocks, we propose a cross-ISA and retargetable dynamic binary instrumentation framework called DBILL (Dynamic Binary Instrumentation with LLVM). DBILL leverages both QEMU and the LLVM toolkit to enable LLVM-based instrumentations on binary code. DBILL leverages QEMU to translate guest binary code into TCG IR. It then translates TCG IR into LLVM IR to enable code optimizations and conduct instrumentation at the IR level. DBILL allows any instrumentation at the LLVM IR level and benefits from many existing static instrumentation tools based on LLVM IR.

The main contributions of this work are as follows.

1. Leveraging HQEMU [10], we have developed an efficient and retargetable dynamic binary instrumentation framework, DBILL, which supports cross-ISA, dynamic binary instrumentation.

2. We demonstrate that DBILL can easily transform LLVM IR based static instrumentation tools into DBI based tools. To the best of our knowledge, this is the first effort to successfully integrate LLVM-based instrumentation with a DBT system.

3. We demonstrate the effectiveness of DBILL in terms of performance and memory access counts using Address Sanitizer and Memory Sanitizer as implementation examples. DBILL achieves an average speed-up of 1.74X for x86-based instrumentation on SPEC CPU2006 INT benchmarks, and an average speed-up of 8.66X for ARM-based instrumentation, compared with Valgrind [14].

2. Background

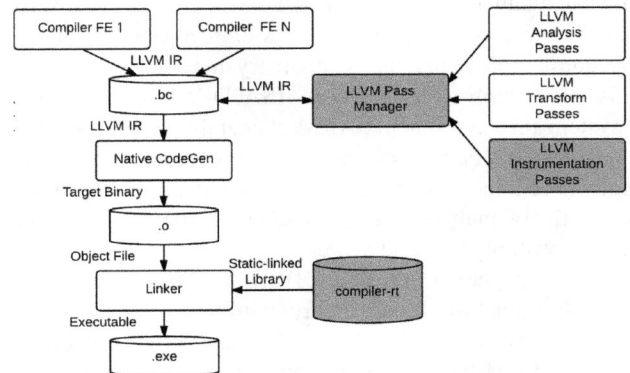

Figure 1. Compile-time instrumentation flow in LLVM

Figure 1 depicts the compile-time instrumentation process in LLVM. First, the user program (written with a programming language) is translated to the LLVM intermediate representation (IR). Then, the LLVM IR is compiled to the target binary by the code generator. LLVM IR serves as a good medium for program analysis, transformation, and instrumentation. All these functions are governed by the LLVM Pass Manager. Finally, the linker links the generated object code with necessary libraries (e.g., compiler-rt) and produces the instrumented executables.

We use Address Sanitizer, an out-of-bound memory access checker developed by Google, as an example to illustrate two important steps in developing a compile-time instrumentation tool in LLVM. Address Sanitizer (ASan) is a red-zone-based memory checker [18] designed to detect addressable bugs. ASan inserts *red-zones*, which are unaccessible areas of a program, at the boundary of variables, and uses *shadow memory* to store the state of each address. Implementing ASan in LLVM requires the following two steps: (1) intercept memory allocation/deallocation library calls, and replace them with a routine for inserting red-zone and updating shadow memory, and (2) insert analysis code before each memory access to check if it will be out-of-bound. Step (1) is implemented in compiler-rt as a modified standard library, and step (2) is implemented as an LLVM instrumentation pass, which instruments analysis code in the LLVM IR.

Existing LLVM-based instrumentation tools are mostly applied to LLVM IR derived from source programs. In the real world, many application programs and libraries are only available in binary form. By translating binary code to LLVM IR and incorporating LLVM-based instrumentation on the IR, a DBT system can leverage these LLVM-based instrumentation tools on binary code. Another benefit of such approach is that the shadow memory of the DBI system can be completely separated from the guest address space. We cannot achieve the same goal if we instrument program with LLVM static instrumentation tool first then run it on a DBT system.

3. System Architecture of DBILL

Incorporating an LLVM-based instrumentation tool in a DBT system would require the aforementioned two steps, but it raises two challenging issues. First, in a compile-time environment, function interception can be achieved simply by recompiling and relinking with the modified library in compiler-rt. In a DBT environment, however, recompiling and relinking is impossible, which makes function interception a challenging issue. Second, in a compile-time environment, the LLVM IR is all generated from the source code. Whereas, in a DBT environment, the LLVM IR includes those translated from the guest binary and others generated from the DBT itself for emulation purpose. An LLVM pass for instrumentation should only process those guest binary IR to ensure the correctness of the execution. A systematic annotation scheme to help an LLVM pass distinguish between guest binary IR and emulation IR is called for.

In this section, we present the system architecture of DBILL and the interaction between the system components. We also propose our solution to the two technical issues mentioned above. Finally, we present some optimizations to improve the performance of DBILL.

3.1 System Architecture of DBILL

Figure 2 shows the high-level architecture of DBILL. The input to DBILL is a guest program binary (e.g., executable, shared library or dynamic linker/loader). For a guest program binary, as indicated by the left path in Figure 2, the target front-end (FE) of QEMU emits code in the Tiny Code Generator (TCG) representation, which is translated by the TCG frond-end. The TCG front-end performs a TCG to

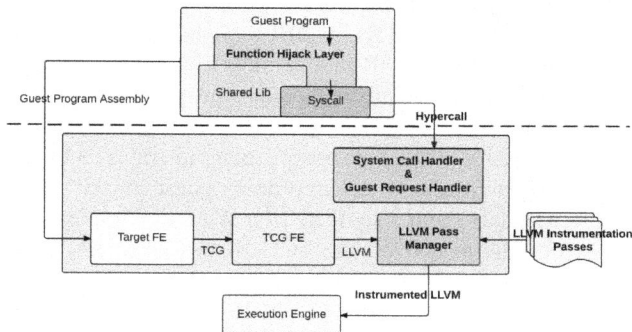

Figure 2. System architecture of DBILL

LLVM translation to emit code in LLVM IR representation. The LLVM Pass Manager inserts analysis code in the LLVM IR, and then a just-in-time (JIT) translator generates object code for the instrumented LLVM IR at runtime.

Some events, such as system calls and library function calls (e.g., memory allocation/deallocation routine calls), are pivotal in DBI. A DBI system needs to provide a mechanism to execute the corresponding callback functions when such events are triggered. Different DBI systems may use different mechanisms to handle system calls and library function calls. Our approach is adding two system components: the Function Hijack Layer and the Hypercall Handler (which is derived from the QEMU system call handler).

As indicated in the right path in Figure 2, the Function Hijack Layer intercepts the function calls to the shared library (e.g., memory allocation (malloc)/deallocation (free)), and then issues a hypercall, whose mission is to notify the DBI system when the event being monitored is triggered. When the DBI system receives a hypercall, it executes the corresponding hypercall Handler, which in turn executes the callback function registered for that particular event. For system calls, we adopt the approach of QEMU. When the guest program invokes a system call, QEMU executes the corresponding system call handler. If the system call is under the monitor of a DBI system/tool, then the system call handler will execute the callback function registered for that system call.

3.2 Interaction of System Components

In this subsection, we describe the interaction between the system components.

3.2.1 Disassemble Time - Target Front End and TCG Front End

The QEMU target front-end translates guest-binary executables into the TCG instruction set, called TCG IR. Then, the intermediate code is translated into target binary for execution. TCG IR is RISC-like, guest and host independent IR, and has only 142 opcodes in total. TCG IR can be classified into two categories: one that maps to guest executable instructions (e.g., ADD, SUB), and the other dedicated to DBT emulation (e.g., EXIT_TB). A DBI tool should only instrument codes in the TCG IR that belongs to the first category in order to accurately analyze the guest program itself.

We found that the TCG IR in the first category bears similarity to LLVM IR. This observation motivates us to use QEMU target front-ends to preprocess guest binary codes (i.e., to translate them into TCG IR). We then implement a TCG front end to convert the TCG IR to LLVM IR. Such a two-phase conversion significantly simplifies the effort of translating guest binary into LLVM IR. Furthermore, since DBILL uses QEMU as its building block, it inherits all guest ISAs of QEMU, such as i386 (32-bit), x86-64 (64-bit), ARM (32-bit), PowerPC (32-bit), MicroBlaze (32-bit) and MIPS (32-bit).

3.2.2 LLVM IR annotation in DBILL

The TCG front end converts TCG IR to LLVM IR. Since an LLVM pass for instrumentation should only process those guest binary IR to ensure the correctness of the execution result, a systematic annotation scheme to help the LLVM pass distinguish between guest binary IR and emulation IR is called for. Our solution is as follows. In the TCG front end, we adopt the metadata scheme in LLVM to add annotation to the LLVM IR generated from guest binary. For example, we annotate a guest binary LLVM IR "%22 = add i32 %19, 4" with metadata "!guest". The annotated IR will be "%22 = add i32 %19, 4, !guest !0". In this way, an LLVM pass will be able to distinguish between guest binary IR and emulation IR with a simple check on the annotation. For example, the Address Sanitizer LLVM pass

```
if (LoadInst *LI = dyn_cast<LoadInst>(I))
{
    //instrument analysis code
}
```

will perform instrumentation on the IR if the IR represents a load instruction (memory instruction). With a simple check, the modified Address Sanitizer LLVM pass as shown below will perform instrumentation on the load instruction only if the IR is annotated with "guest", meaning that it is generated from the guest binary.

```
if (LoadInst *LI = dyn_cast<LoadInst>(I))
{
    if (LI->getMetadata("guest") &&
        LI->isVolatile())
    {
        //instrument analysis code
    }
}
```

3.2.3 Instrumentation Time - Instrumentation Engine and LLVM Instrumentation Passes

The LLVM code block (LLVM IR) translated by the Target Front End and the TCG Front End is passed to the LLVM pass manager, which manages and processes all LLVM instrumentation passes. An LLVM instrumentation pass is a special kind of LLVM pass designed specifically for instrumentation purpose. The LLVM IR at this stage has been annotated as either guest binary IR or emulation IR. An LLVM instrumentation pass only analyzes and instruments codes to guest binary IR. Since the annotations are specific to DBILL, they have no effect on other LLVM passes.

3.2.4 Execution Time - Execution Engine

During execution, LLVM JIT (the Execution Engine) is used to invoke the appropriate code generator at runtime. LLVM JIT leverages the code generation ability of LLVM static compiler to generate high quality code, translating one basic block at a time. Since we use LLVM JIT in DBILL, the host ISA of DBILL is limited to the ISAs supported by LLVM JIT, including i386 (32-bit), x86-64 (64-bit), ARM (32-bit) and PowerPC (64-bit).

3.3 Optimizations for High-Performance Instrumentation

3.3.1 Helper Function Inlining

Most guest instructions are translated to TCG IR and then LLVM IR, and then the JIT compiler generates binary code from the LLVM IR. Some complicated instructions that are not supported by the TCG frontend can be implemented as helper functions. A helper function is implemented as a C function, and is compiled into a binary when compiling the QEMU source code. During emulation, a helper function is translated into a function call instruction. Such a function call incurs extra overhead, including arguments passing, adapting the arguments (the prolog), and retrieving the result (the epilog). The prolog/epilog increases memory accesses. Our approach to reduce memory accesses consists of the following three steps: (1) translate the helper function to LLVM IR using LLVM-GCC/Dragonegg, (2) inline the translated helper function IR in the LLVM IR translated from TCG FE, and (3) pass the LLVM IR translated from TCG FE to the LLVM JIT compiler.

3.3.2 Register Promotion for State Mapping

QEMU emulates the guest register file using host memory. Therefore, if a register is accessed twice in a basic block, host memory will also be accessed twice. We promote frequently accessed guest registers to host registers. At the beginning of the translated code, the guest register is loaded to a host register. Read/write operations to the guest register are all performed on the host register. At the end of the translated code, the value of the host register is stored to the host memory dedicated for emulating the guest register set. Such optimization can reduce memory accesses significantly.

3.3.3 Cross-ISA DBT

Like Valgrind, DBILL is a heavyweight DBI system. Current heavy weight DBI systems may suffer high overhead due to runtime recompilation of instrumentation code. We mitigate the performance problem by emulating the instrumented code on a faster machine through cross-ISA dynamic binary translation. As shown in Section 7, instrumentation on a machine with weak computing power (e.g., ARM) can cause substantial slowdown. By instrumenting an ARM executable on a machine with strong computing power (e.g., x86-64) through cross-ISA DBT, we could achieve better performance.

4. Implementation Details

In this section, we elaborate on general implementation details of DBILL, including the start up stage of DBILL, shadow registers and shadow memory management for metadata storage, and the function hijack layer. These principles are applicable to other dynamic instrumentation tools.

4.1 Start Up

The start-up stage is the period between invoking DBILL from command line and the first guest program binary fetch for instrumentation. The goal of this stage is to load DBILL, reserve address space for the guest program and shadow memory (to be introduced in Section 4.2), and load the guest program into the same process (see Table 1).

DBILL itself is loaded by dynamic linker/loader (ld-linux.so under Linux) in host environment. When DBILL is loaded, it first initializes some sub-systems, such as Target FE, TCG FE, LLVM JIT and stored code cache. Second, DBILL reserves address space for the guest program and shadow memory. Third, DBILL begins to load a guest program. DBILL uses the loader code ported from the Linux kernel. The ported version has replaced the host address space allocation routine with *target_mmap*, which is used to allocate address space within a guest program's address space.

Some earlier same-ISA DBI frameworks use the same dynamic linker/loader to load themselves and the guest program. This may harm robustness. Besides, many same-ISA DBI frameworks and their guest programs use the same shared library simultaneously. This may cause some potential complications and conflicts, such as reentrancy, side effect, idempotence and thread safety. However, the problems mentioned above do not occur in DBILL because of the following two reasons: (1) In a cross-ISA environment, the guest program binaries and the DBILL executable are incompatible and thus cannot be loaded with the same dynamic linker/loader, (2) In a cross-ISA environment, the guest program has been translated before execution, and thus DBILL and the guest program do not use the same shared library.

4.2 Shadow Registers and Shadow Memory

A DBI system usually provides a shadow mechanism for the DBI tools to store the metadata. The metadata related to guest registers are referred to as shadow registers, and those related to guest memory are referred to as shadow memory. QEMU uses separate parts of the host memory address space to simulate guest register and guest memory. Therefore, each guest register and guest memory location has a distinct address. This allows us to use the host virtual address of a guest state (register or memory) as the key to define the shadow address of the guest state. The case study presented in Section 5 describes the memory mapping for shadow registers and shadow memory in more details using Address Sanitizer as an example.

4.3 Function Hijack Layer

Function Hijack Layer is implemented as a shared library, which consists of the functions to be intercepted by the DBI system. We use the following example to explain the interception of the malloc function call:

```
void *malloc(size_t size)
{
    int ret = syscall(TARGET_NR_malloc, size);
    return (void *)ret;
}
```

First, the malloc function is compiled as a shared library. Then, the function hijack layer (shared library) is preloaded during guest binary loading time by the guest dynamic linker. After that, all malloc function calls from the guest program would be intercepted and replaced by our own version of malloc. Our malloc implementation uses the hyper call mechanism (syscall(TARGET_NR_malloc, size)) to notify DBILL that the guest program calls malloc. DBILL then accepts the notification and executes the corresponding handler.

5. Case Study: Incorporating Address Sanitizer

In this section, we describe the process of incorporating existing LLVM-based instrumentation tools in DBILL, using Address Sanitizer [18] as an example. Address Sanitizer (ASan) is a compile-time address sanity checker. ASan inserts red-zone at the boundary of variables. ASan then uses shadow memory to store the state of each address. To detect illegal memory access, it inserts a piece of code to check the shadow before any memory read/write.

As a compile-time tool, ASan can detect heap/stack/global variables out-of-bound access and heap use-after-free. Out-of-bound access checking relies on inserting red-zone at the boundary of variables. Since inserting red-zones will change the memory layout and will require recompilation of the instrumented code, it cannot be applied to global variables and stack variables at runtime. Hence, a DBI, such as Valgrind/Memcheck and Dr. Memory [7], can only detect heap out-of-bound access and heap use-after-free. DBILL is a runtime framework, and therefore, is subject to the same constraint as Valgrind/Memcheck and Dr. Memory. Other tools that do not change memory layout of the guest binary and thus do not require recompilation, such as data flow sanitizer, memory sanitizer, and thread sanitizer, can be fully incorporated in DBILL.

In the following subsections, we describe the process of porting Address Sanitizers heap out-of-bound access and heap use-after-free detection tools. Note that the guest we consider in this paper is 32-bit and the host is 64-bit.

5.1 Address Sanitizer

The state of a memory byte is either addressable or unaddressable. When a memory allocation routine (e.g., malloc, new) allocates memory, the memory state is changed from unaddressable to addressable. Calling a memory deallocation routine (e.g., free, delete) causes the deallocated memory to enter the unaddressable state. An access to memory that contains bytes that are currently in an unaddressable state causes memory violation.

To catch memory violations, Address Sanitizer [18] allocates a red-zone at the beginning and the end of each block returned by a memory allocation routine. The bytes in the red-zone are recorded as unaddressable. If a program accesses these bytes, Address Sanitizer signals a memory violation error. Address Sanitizer uses shadow memory to store the state of memory bytes. It also inserts a piece of code before any memory access instruction of an application to check the state of the memory bytes to be accessed by the application.

The implementation of Address Sanitizer consists of two parts: an LLVM pass named *AddressSanitizer* and library functions in the compiler-rt library. The former is a FunctionPass, which instruments the piece of code before memory access instructions at LLVM function level. The latter is a set of modified memory allocation/deallocation routines, which insert red-zones between the allocated memory and update the shadow memory during execution. AddressSanitizer redirects memory allocation/deallocation call of an executable to the corresponding function of compiler-rt during link-time.

5.2 Basic Structure

GNU libc uses mmap to allocate a block of memory and manages it by itself to implement memory allocation/deallocation routine. Dynamic memory management routine is almost an user level routine, which does not always trap into DBILL. However, this would be a problem for us because we need to update shadow memory. We use function hijack layer to replace the original dynamic memory management routine with our own, which would send a hypercall to DBILL when called. Then the hypercall handler uses the function in compiler-rt to update the shadow memory. Finally, the LLVM pass *AddressSanitizer* is added into the LLVM pass manager.

5.3 Memory Layout

Module	Host Virtual Address
DBILL	0x000060000000 - 0x000060ddd000
[heap]	0x0000680ce000 - 0x000068ce4000
Sadow	0x1ff1c0000000 - 0x1ff1dfffffff
Shared Lib	0x7f1e7ef34000 - 0x7f1e80867000
Guest Program	0x7f8e00000000 - 0x7f8ef7000000
[stack]	0x7fffb64e5000 - 0x7fffb6507000

Table 1. Memory layout when a guest program runs on DBILL

Table 1 shows the memory layout when a guest program runs on DBILL. An entry in the right column represents the location of the memory segment in the host virtual address space. Note that, from host OS point of view, DBILL and the guest program are user level processes. The Guest Program segment is used to store the loaded guest program and data, and the Sadow segment is used to store the metadata on memory use by the guest program.

All same-ISA shadow-based instrumentation tools, either compile-time or runtime, suffer the potential threats that address space may be exhausted. This issue arises because existing shadow-based tools put the guest program and its shadow memory into the same address space. Despite the advance of shadow memory encoding algorithms, such problem would not be perfectly solved in the same-ISA systems. In contrast, DBILL separates address space for shadow memory from that for a guest program when the word size of guest ISA is shorter than that of host ISA. Under such scenario, the guest program could use address space as much as the guest ISA granted, which preserves address space transparency. As shown in Table 1, all these memory segments do not overlap. The isolation between each of them provides protection.

Note that providing address space transparency requires that the host has sufficient memory space to store shadow memory separately from that for the guest program. 32-bit on 32-bit does not provide such transparency because the host machine does not have sufficient space to store shadow memory separately. In this paper, we demonstrate that address space transparency can be achieved for DBI on 32-bit guest and 64-bit host. We believe that address space transparency is also possible for 64-bit guest and 64-bit host because most operating systems and application programs do not use the complete address. We will study the address space transparency issue for 64-bit on 64-bit in the future.

5.4 Translating a Memory Access Instruction

In this subsection, we will describe the process of instrumenting a memory access instruction. We first use pseudo code to explain the process. We then show the code segment translated by DBILL.

A Memory access translated by a compiler looks like the following:

```
*address = ...;  // or: ... = *address;
```

After instrumentation, a memory access would be the following[1]:

```
byte *shadow_address = (address >> 3) | kOffset;  // (1)
byte shadow_value = *shadow_address;              // (2)
if (shadow_value)                                 // (3)
{
    last_accessed_byte = (address & 7) +
                    kAccessSize - 1;              // (4)
    if (last_accessed_byte >= shadow_value)       // (5)
    {
        ReportError(address, kAccessSize,
                kIsWrite);                        // (6)
    }
}
*address = ...;  // or: ... = *address;
```

We take one i386 memory access instruction to demonstrate how DBILL works. In the guest instruction, the eax register holds the address of one variable. The purpose of this guest instruction is to reset the variable, referenced by the address, as 0. Such assembly code is very common in variable initialization.

The guest instruction is translated into TCG IR by QEMU Target FE; meanwhile, the TCG FE of DBILL will know that the guest instruction is a guest memory store operation via qemu_st, a TCG OP, given by QEMU Target FE. Consequently, DBILL translates the TCG IR into LLVM store instruction (with attribute volatile and with metadata !guest !0).

With the !guest !0 metadata and volatile attributes of load/store LLVM instructions, the Address Sanitizer Pass will confirm the LLVM instructions as a memory access of the guest program and then insert check code in the LLVM IR. The %4 LLVM virtual register contains the guest virtual address (GVA). DBILL uses %5 and %6 LLVM instructions to calculate the host virtual address (HVA) via %4. Among the instrumented LLVM IRs, the number 0x7f8e00000000 represents the starting address position of GVA (e.g., the guest_base). HVA is computed as GVA + guest_base. HVA of (%eax) is used as a key for shadow memory as mentioned in Section 4.2.

Guest Instruction:

```
movl $0x0, (%eax)
```

TCG IR:

```
mov_i32 tmp2, eax
movi_i32 tmp0, $0x0
qemu_st32 tmp0, tmp2, $0xffffffffffffffff
```

LLVM IR:

```
%3 = load i32* %eax,!guest !0
```

```
%4 = inttoptr i32 %3 to i32 addrspace(256)*,!guest !0
store volatile i32 0,i32 addrspace(256)* %4,!guest !0
```

Instrumented LLVM IR:

```
%3 = load i32* %eax,!guest !0
%4 = inttoptr i32 %3 to i32 addrspace(256)*,!guest !0

# GVA -> HVA translation
%5 = ptrtoint i32 addrspace(256)* %4 to i64
%6 = add i64 %5,0x7f8e00000000

# (1)
%7 = lshr i64 %6,3
%8 = or i64 %7,0x100000000000
%9 = inttoptr i64 %8 to i8*

# (2)
%10 = load i8* %9

# (3)
%11 = icmp ne i8 %10,0
br i1 %11,label %12,label %18

# (4)
; <label>:12        ; preds = %entry
%13 = and i64 %6,7
%14 = add i64 %13,3
%15 = trunc i64 %14 to i8

# (5)
%16 = icmp sge i8 %15,%10
br i1 %16, label %17,label %18

# (6)
; <label>:17        ; preds = %12
call void @__asan_report_store4(i64 %6)
call void asm sideeffect "",""()
br label %18

; <label>:18        ; preds = %12, %17, %entry
store volatile i32 0,i32 addrspace(256)* %4,!guest !0
```

5.5 Memory (De-)Allocation Routine Called by Guest Program

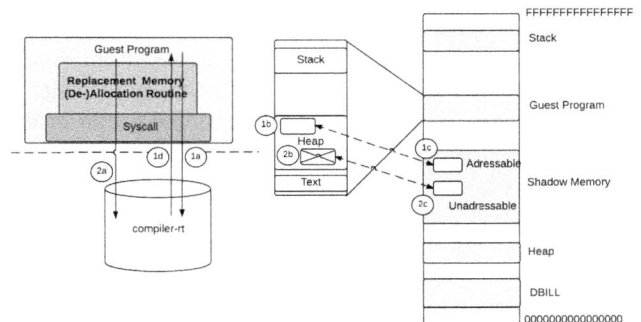

Figure 3. Control flow of memory allocation and deallocation

Steps (1a) to (1d) in Figure 3 show the interaction between DBILL components when the guest program calls memory allocation routine (e.g., malloc). (1a) The replacement memory allocation routine is invoked. We use syscall with a particular system call number SYS_MALLOC in the replacement to trap into DBILL, and invoke the compiler-rt routine incorporated from LLVM. The compiler-rt routine will perform the following: (1b) Allocate a block of memory for the guest program and its red-zone, (1c) mark the shadow of the memory region for the guest program as addressable, and on the contrary, mark the shadow of its red-zone as unaddressable, and (1d) return the address to the guest program.

Since a guest program can only access within its address space, we use target_mmap instead of host mmap to reserve a block of memory within guest address space and manipulate it. When we want to return the address back to the guest program, we need to subtract the address by guest_base because of the address translation from host to guest.

Steps (2a) to (2d) in Figure 3 show the interaction between DBILL components when the guest program calls memory deallocation routine (e.g., free). The replacement process is similar. DBILL would perform the following three steps: (2a) Retrieve the address (argument) from the guest program, (2b) deallocate the block of memory and its red-zone, and (2c) mark the shadow of the memory region for guest program as unaddressable. When we want to get the address passed from the guest program, we must add the address by guest_base because of the address translation from guest to host.

6. Limitation of DBILL

6.1 Limitation of Binary Instrumentation

In general, binary instructions can be categorized into three categories: arithmetic, logic, control flow and loads/stores. Both TCG IR and LLVM IR follow this categorization, and instructions of an ISA/IR in one category are always translated into the same category of instructions of another ISA/IR. Therefore, DBILL loses no binary-level semantics in the process of translation and instrumentation.

However, the LLVM IR translated from guest binary usually contains less information than that derived from source programs. Since high-level type information is unavailable in many binary codes, the loss of type information in the LLVM IR translated from guest binary makes any DBI framework, e.g. DBILL, Valgrind, or DynamoRIO, unable to leverage type-based optimizations. Despite this limitation, there are still many optimizations applicable with only binary information, such as register promotion, inlining of helper functions (corresponding to some guest instructions), etc.

Another limitation is caused by the fact that binary information is insufficient to insert red-zone for global and stack variables. Since one cannot tell merely from a binary to which variable a location refers, it is also difficult to change the memory layout of a guest binary.

6.2 Function Hijack of Static-linked Binary

The current implementation of function hijack layer depends on the preload mechanism provided by the guest dynamic loader. The preload mechanism can work on any instruction set architecture without writing additional codes. Though the preload mechanism applies to only dynamic-linked libraries, this fact does not limit the practicality of DBILL, since dynamic libraries are widely used to save memory and storage space.

Indeed, function hijack layer can also be implemented for functions in a static-linked library, which keeps a symbol table. With the symbol table, DBILL can learn when a function in a static-linked library is called and hijack the function call in advance. DBILL works for (1) dynamical-link libraries and (2) static binaries which are not stripped.

6.3 Floating Point Instruction

Currently DBILL only supports integer instructions because TCG IR in QEMU lacks representation for floating point instructions. The TCG translator of QEMU v 0.15.0 and up does not emit floating point instructions of the host machine. Instead, all floating point instructions are simulated by integer instructions. Such simulation causes significant slowdown of the guest application. One possible solution is to emulate all floating point instructions via helper functions provided by QEMU. By using the LLVM compiler infrastructure, such helper functions can be inline and get floating point host instructions generated directly. Another alternative is to extend TCG IR to support floating point operations.

DBILL can be applied to floating point instructions once either one of the solutions is implemented.

7. Evaluation

In this section, we present the experimental results to evaluate the effectiveness of DBILL. Since DBILL is a heavyweight DBI framework based on LLVM and LLVM IR, we compare with the widely used, state-of-the-art heavyweight DBI system, Valgrind. Comparison of performance and memory access counts of these two systems are reported.

7.1 Experiment Setting

All the x86-based experiments were conducted on a x86-64 machine with a 3.3 GHz quad-core Intel Core i7 processor and 12 GB main memory. The operating system is 64-bit Gentoo Linux with kernel version 3.5.0. The ARM-based experiments were conducted on pandaboard with dual-core ARM cortex-A9 MPcore processors at 1.2GHz each and 1 GB main memory. The operating system on pandaboard is 32-bit Gentoo Linux with kernel version 3.4.48.

SPEC CPU2006 integer benchmark suite (CINT) is tested with reference inputs in the x86-based experiment. All benchmarks are compiled by GCC 4.7.3 and with -O3 optimization level. QEMU version 1.3.0, LLVM version 3.2 and Dragonegg version 3.2 were used as the building blocks of our DBILL framework. We chose Valgrind version 3.9.0 as our comparison counterpart. The latest officially released Valgrind version 3.8.1 fails to run some SPEC benchmarks on pandaboard, such as 445.gobmk, since it does not support some ARM instructions. Therefore, we use the newest subversion 3.9.0 (retrieved from Valgrind repository) in our ARM-based and x86-based experiments.

As mentioned in Section 6, QEMU v 0.15.0 and up does not emit floating point instructions of the host machine, and thus causes significant slowdown of floating-point based guest application. For this reason, we only use SPEC CINT benchmarks in our experiments,

For ARM-based experiments, the benchmarks are cross-compiled by GCC 4.7.3 and with -O3 optimization level and full hardware floating point convention. In the ARM-based experiment, the large memory consumption of CINT reference inputs will make some benchmarks either swap or corrupt at run time. Therefore, for ARM, we test CINT with train inputs.

Although both Valgrind and DBILL are IR based (retargetable) heavy-weight DBI frameworks, Valgrind is designed for same-ISA environment. For i386 guest program, Valgrind translates i386 to i386. DBILL is a cross-ISA DBI framework. It translates i386 to x86-64. For fair comparison, we measured the SPEC CINT performance on i386 and x86-64bit with reference input. The geometric mean of the run time ratios (x86-64 over i386) is 0.97, with only 3% difference between the two architectures. Based on this observation, in the rest of our experiments, we will not take the individual discrepancy into consideration in x86 based performance comparison between Valgrind and DBILL.

7.2 Performance Comparison of Valgrind Memcheck and DBILL ASan

Valgrinds Memcheck supports both memory addressable bug detection and uninitialized read detection. On the other hand, DBILL Address Sanitizer (ASan) only supports memory addressable bug detection (uninitialized read detection is supported by the Memory Sanitizer tool). For fair comparison, we turn off the following Valgrind Memcheck options, –leak-check=no –show-possibly-lost=no – leak-resolution=low –undef-errors=no, to disable uninitialized read detection. Therefore, in this setting, both Valgrind Memcheck and DBILL Address Sanitizer can detect heap out-of-bound access and use-after-free bugs.

Figure 4 compares the performance of Valgrind Memcheck and DBILL Address Sanitizer on x86, with SPEC CINT2006 (reference input) as the guest binary. The y-axis is the normalized execution time against the native run of the SPEC CINT2006 benchmarks compiled with gcc -O3 -m32. On average, DBILL ASan achieves speedup of 1.74X against Valgrind Memcheck. Furthermore, DBILL has larger speedup factors on perlbench, sjeng, libquantum and astar. The reason is that DBILL incurs much lower memory ac-

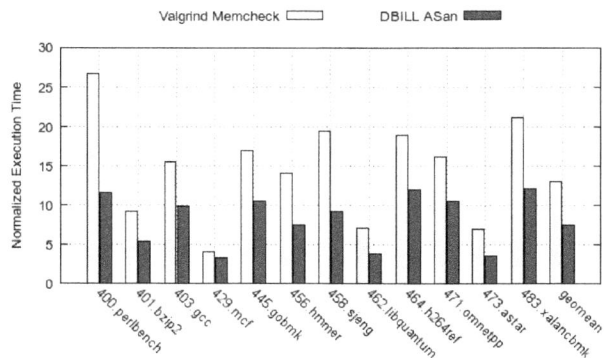

Figure 4. Performance of Valgrind Memcheck and DBILL Address Sanitizer on SPEC CINT2006 (reference inputs) on x86. The y-axis is the normalized execution time against the native run.

cess counts than Valgrind on these four benchmarks. More details are presented in Section 7.3.

7.3 Comparison of Memory Access Counts of Valgrind Memcheck and DBILL ASan

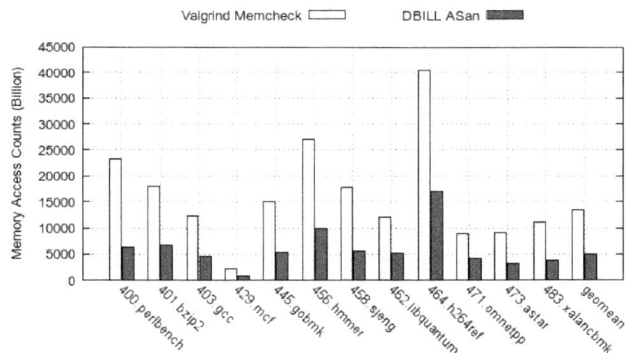

Figure 5. Comparison of memory access counts of Valgrind Memcheck and DBILL Address Sanitizer in SPEC CINT2006

We use the *perf* tool to monitor the memory access counts of Valgrind Memcheck and DBILL ASan in SPEC CINT. As Figure 5 shows, Valgrind Memcheck has more memory access counts than DBILL ASan. The geomean of the ratios (Valgrind Memcheck / DBILL ASan) of memory access counts is 2.71. The reasons are (1) Valgrind Memcheck uses page table-like approach to look up a shadow. It requires two memory accesses to look up one shadow. On the other hand, DBILL Address Sanitizer uses a linear mapping approach, which requires only one memory access for each shadow look-up. (2) DBILL implements special instructions via helper functions provided by QEMU. The LLVM infrastructure used by DBILL will inline all these helper functions. The result is that the number of prolog/epilog in basic blocks is reduced, which in turn also reduces the memory access counts. (3) DBILL also implements register promotion of architecture state mapping, which also helps reduce memory access counts.

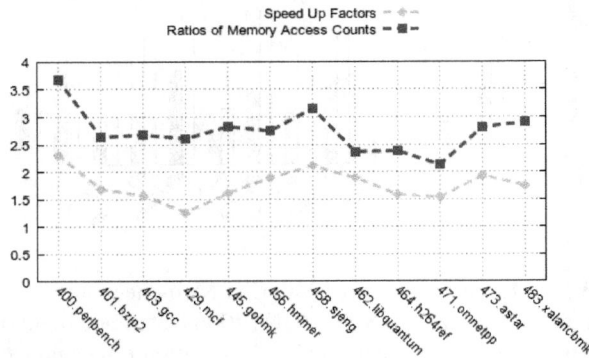

Figure 6. Relation between speed up factors (Valgrind time / DBILL time) and ratios of memory access counts (Valgrind memory access counts / DBILL memory access counts)

Figure 6 shows the relation between the ratios of memory access counts (Valgrind counts devided by DBILL counts) and the speedup factors (Valgrind time devided by DBILL time). The lower line represents the speedup factors, and the upper line represents the ratios of memory access counts. As can be seen in Figure 6, the curves of the two lines are quite similar. Higher ratio of memory access counts results in larger speed-up, while lower ratio results in smaller speed-up.

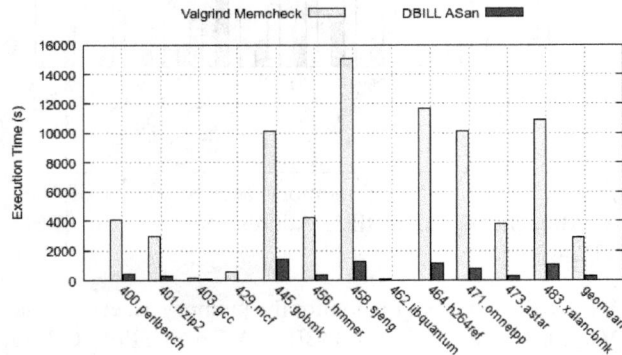

Figure 7. Performance Comparison of Valgrind Memcheck and DBILL Address Sanitizer on SPEC CINT2006 (with train inputs) on ARM

Figure 7 compares the performance of Valgrind Memcheck and DBILL Address Sanitizer on ARM. The ARM binary of the SPEC CINT benchmarks are given as the guest binary. Valgrind translates the ARM guest binary to ARM host binary of the same ISA. DBILL translates ARM guest binary to x86-64 host. In Figure 7, the left bars represent the execution time of Valgrind/Memcheck on ARM, and the right bars represent the execution time of DBILL ASan on

x86-64. Figure 7 demonstrates the benefit of instrumenting ARM codes on a faster machine such as x86-64 by cross-ISA DBT. The speed-up factors (Valgrind time on ARM / DBILL time on x86-64) are significantly higher than on x86 machine (Figure 4, geometric mean of 1.74X) with geometric mean of 8.66X

7.4 Time Breakdown

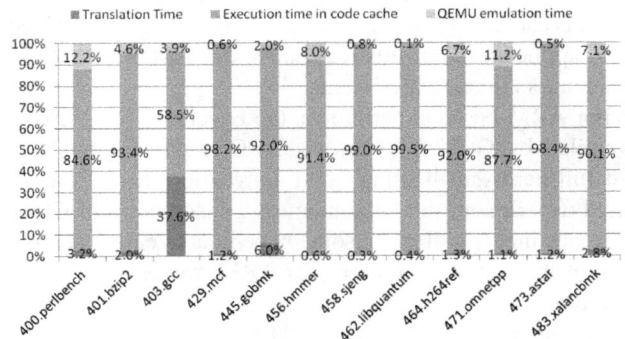

Figure 8. Time breakdown of DBILL

Figure 8 shows the time breakdown of DBILL ASan. The total execution time is divided into three parts: the translation time, the execution time in code cache, and QEMU emulation time. The translation time consists of the time from changing guest instructions into TCG and then being translated into LLVM IR and finally become instrumented LLVM IR. The Execution time in code cache is the time of running guest program. The QEMU emulation time is the time that the host system emulates the guest events, such as handling system call, finding the tranlated code, etc. Furthermore, 403.gcc has the highest proportion of translation time among these benchmarks. The reason is that QEMU generates large number of code blocks for 403.gcc; however, these code blocks are executed very few times.

7.5 Performance of DBILL Memory Sanitizer

Figure 9 illustrates the performance of DBILL Memory Sanitizer (DBILL MSan). The left bars represent DBILL MSan time, and the right bars represents the native run of the SPEC CINT2006 benchmarks on x86. The average slowdown of DBILL MSan is 5.7X.

7.6 Source Code Changes in Tools

Our implementation effort to incorporate Address Sanitizer and Memory Sanitizer is reported in Table 2. All sanitizer tools consist of two parts: the LLVM pass part and the compiler-rt part. Note that compiler-rt consists of a set of tool dedicated parts (e.g., only for Address Sanitizer or only for Mmeory Sanitizer) and a common part (i.e., shared by all sanitizer tools).

Since currently LLVM does not provide standard interface support for developing LLVM based DBI tools, to in-

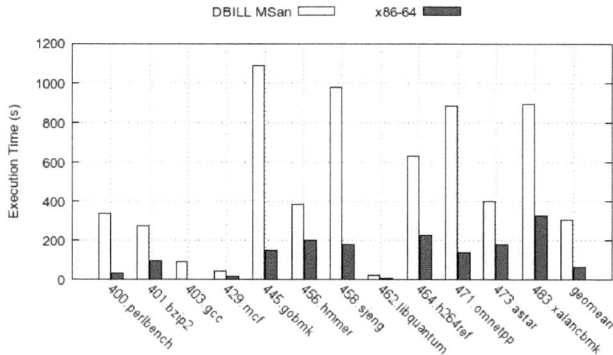

Figure 9. Execution time (in seconds) of DBILL MSan with train inputs

	LLVM Pass	Tool Dedicated	Common
ASan	26/1120	40/4392	98/4858
MSan	80/2055	28/2269	

Table 2. Source code changes in tools. The number on the left in each column indicates the lines of source code changed, and the number on the right indicates the total lines of source code in each part of the LLVM instrumentation tool.

corporate an LLVM instrumentation tool in DBILL, minor changes to the LLVM pass and the compiler-rt are required.

For Address Sanitizer, 26 lines of code are modified in the LLVM pass, 40 lines in the compiler-rt tool dedicated part, and 98 lines in the compiler-rt common part. For Memory Sanitizer, 80 lines of code are modified in the LLVM pass and 28 lines in the compiler-rt tool dedicated part. Note that the compiler-rt common part is shared by all sanitizer tools, and hence, the modification only needs be performed once.

7.7 Summary of Results

We compare the performance of dynamic binary translation (i.e., without any instrumentation code) of Valgrind and DBILL on x86, and found that Valgrind has 3.9X slowdown on SPEC INT compared with the native run, and DBILL has 3.4X slowdown. DBILL achieves speedup of 1.15X against Valgrind. The performance gains of DBILL DBT are mainly contributed by helper function inlining (about 5.5%), register promotion (default on), and other LLVM optimizations. With instrumentation codes (DBILL ASan and Valgrind MemCheck), on average, DBILL ASan achieves speedup of 1.74X against Valgrind Memcheck (Figure 4). The main reason is that DBILL ASan incurs lower memory access counts than Valgrind Memcheck (Figure 5). As explained in Section 7.3, the lower memory access counts is a result of more efficient shadow memory management in Address Sanitizer.

In the case of instrumenting ARM code on x86-64 machine, the speed-up factors (Valgrind Memcheck time on ARM vs. DBILL ASan time on x86-64) are significantly higher than on x86 machine, with geometric mean of 8.66X (Figure 7). Most of the performance gain is from cross-ISA DBI because x86-64 PC runs much faster than the ARM (Pandaboard) platform we used in the experiment.

8. Related Work

There are several fundamental ways for a DBI framework to represent code and allow instrumentation; probe-, copy-and-annotate- (C&A) and disassemble-and-resynthesise- (D&R) based. The probe-based way works by replacing instructions in the original program with trampolines that branch to the instrumentation code at runtime. On the contrary, C&A and D&R are JIT-based, which uses a code cache to store the compiled result. The difference between C&A and D&R is whether there exists an abstract form (intermediate representation) of the instruction during instrumentation.

The advantage of Probe-based instrumentation is the speed. In contrast, it cannot provide fine granularity because some instruction is hard to replace and maintain the semantic simultaneously, especially for variable instruction length ISA (e.g., x86).

To support the fine granularity, we usually introduce JIT-based binary instrumentation. The compiling overhead of C&A is less than D&R. In the meantime C&A cannot introduce more compiler optimization technology. The most drawbacks of C&A compared to D&R is the ability to implement cross-ISA instrumentation.

Pin [13] and DynamoRIO [8] are the most famous DBI frameworks on windows. Pin has two approaches to dynamic instrumentations: probe-based and C&A-based (JIT-based). The probe-based approach is a method to insert probe, which is a jump instruction that redirects the flow of control to the replacement function. Probes can only be placed on function boundaries. Pin and DynamoRIO also support C&A-based dynamic instrumentations. They copy the instruction from the guest program, manipulating it and store into code cache. The added analysis code is usually interleaved with the original code without perturbing its effects. Neither probe- nor C&A-based dynamic instrumentation are easy to support cross-ISA DBI.

Valgrind [14] is the most popular DBI frameworks on Linux. The binary translators in Valgrind and DBILL use the D&R-based dynamic instrumentation. That is, both of them translate the guest program into an architecture-independent IR, and the instrumentation and compilation are performed on the IR. Although the binary translation technology of Valgrind bears similarity to DBILL, it does not support cross-ISA instrumentation.

MemTrace [16] is a framework for memory tracing for 32-bit guest programs. Memory tracing means that execution of additional code (aka. memlet) for every memory access of a program. Tool writer uses the API provided by MemTrace to set and check shadows values for every byte used in the guest program. MemTrace use libdetox [15], a C&A-based binary translator during execution. Because libdetox relies on translation table, the translation overhead would be low but the retarget effort would be more. Unlike traditional DBI framework, MemTrace does not provide shadow registers mechanism.

LIFT [17] is an information flow tracking (also referred to as taint analysis) system for IA-32 guest programs. Information flow tracking is the technique that label the input data from unsafe source as taint data, propagates the labels of data through computation (any data derived from taint data is also taint data), and detects inappropriate use of taint data. LIFT is built on top of StarDBT [19], which is a C&A-based dynamic binary translator targets translation from IA-32 into x86-64 at user level.

PIRATE [20] and DBILL use D&R-based binary translator. Both of them rely on QEMU to translate guest program into TCG first, then translate TCG into LLVM to further generate host code. Although our implementation paradigm is relevant, the problem we aim to solve are different. PIRATE is dedicated to providing an architecture-independent dynamic information flow tracking system. In contrast, DBILL provides a general architecture-independent DBI framework.

RevGen [9] and x86-to-LLVM DBT [4] use dyngen, a translation engine of QEMU used before version 0.10, to translates x86 binary to micro operation first, then inline LLVM IR precompiled from micro operation implemented as C function. In QEMU 0.10 and newer versions, dyngen has been replaced by TCG.

9. Conclusion

In this paper, we have proposed an efficient and retargetable dynamic binary instrumentation framework called DBILL, which can incorporate LLVM-based instrumentation tools. We demonstrate that LLVM IR, which has only been used for compile-time instrumentation previously, is also an effective choice for implementing dynamic runtime instrumentation. We have successfully incorporated a number of existing LLVM-based instrumentation tools in DBILL. In this paper, we have presented the process of incorporating Address Sanitizer in DBILL. We have also conducted extensive experiments with two tools, an address sanitizer and a memory sanitizer, to evaluate the effectiveness of DBILL. The experiment results show that DBILL ASan has better performance and less memory access overhead than Valgrind Memcheck.

Acknowledgments

We would like to express our gratitude to Todd Mytkowicz and Mathias Payer for their very helpful comments and suggestions to improve this paper. We also thank Chun-Chen Hsu and Yi-Shan Lu for helpful discussions. This work is supported in part by National Science Council of Taiwan under grant number NSC102-2221-E-001-034-MY3.

References

[1] Address sanitizer algorithm. https://code.google.com/p/address-sanitizer/wiki/AddressSanitizerAlgorithm.

[2] Dataflow sanitizer. http://clang.llvm.org/docs/DataFlowSanitizer.html.

[3] Memory sanitizer. https://code.google.com/p/memory-sanitizer/.

[4] Dynamically translating x86 to llvm using qemu. http://infoscience.epfl.ch/record/149975/files/x86-llvm-translator-chipounov_2.pdf.

[5] Thread sanitizer. https://code.google.com/p/thread-sanitizer/.

[6] F. Bellard. QEMU, a fast and portable dynamic translator. USENIX ATC'05.

[7] D. Bruening and Q. Zhao. Practical memory checking with dr. memory. CGO '11.

[8] D. Bruening, T. Garnett, and S. Amarasinghe. An infrastructure for adaptive dynamic optimization. CGO '03.

[9] V. Chipounov and G. Candea. Enabling sophisticated analyses of x86 binaries with revgen. DSNW '11.

[10] D.-Y. Hong, C.-C. Hsu, P.-C. Yew, J.-J. Wu, W.-C. Hsu, P. Liu, C.-M. Wang, and Y.-C. Chung. HQEMU: A multi-threaded and retargetable dynamic binary translator on multi-cores. CGO '12.

[11] C.-C. Hsu, P. Liu, C.-M. Wang, J.-J. Wu, D.-Y. Hong, P.-C. Yew, and W.-C. Hsu. LnQ: Building high performance dynamic binary translators with existing compiler backends. ICPP '11.

[12] C. Lattner and V. Adve. LLVM: A compilation framework for lifelong program analysis & transformation. CGO '04.

[13] C.-K. Luk, R. Cohn, R. Muth, H. Patil, A. Klauser, G. Lowney, S. Wallace, V. J. Reddi, and K. Hazelwood. Pin: Building customized program analysis tools with dynamic instrumentation. PLDI '05.

[14] N. Nethercote and J. Seward. Valgrind: A framework for heavyweight dynamic binary instrumentation. PLDI '07.

[15] M. Payer and T. R. Gross. Fine-grained user-space security through virtualization. VEE '11.

[16] M. Payer, E. Kravina, and T. R. Gross. Lightweight memory tracing. USENIX ATC'13.

[17] F. Qin, C. Wang, Z. Li, H.-s. Kim, Y. Zhou, and Y. Wu. LIFT: A low-overhead practical information flow tracking system for detecting security attacks. MICRO '06.

[18] K. Serebryany, D. Bruening, A. Potapenko, and D. Vyukov. AddressSanitizer: A fast address sanity checker. USENIX ATC'12.

[19] C. Wang, S. Hu, H.-s. Kim, S. R. Nair, M. Breternitz, Z. Ying, and Y. Wu. StarDBT: An efficient multi-platform dynamic binary translation system. ACSAC '07.

[20] R. Whelan, T. Leek, and D. Kaeli. Architecture-independent dynamic information flow tracking. CC '13.

COMMA: Coordinating the Migration of Multi-tier Applications

Jie Zheng   T. S. Eugene Ng

Rice University

Kunwadee Sripanidkulchai

NECTEC, Thailand

Zhaolei Liu

Rice University

Abstract

Multi-tier applications are widely deployed in today's virtualized cloud computing environments. At the same time, management operations in these virtualized environments, such as load balancing, hardware maintenance, workload consolidation, etc., often make use of live virtual machine (VM) migration to control the placement of VMs. Although existing solutions are able to migrate a single VM efficiently, little attention has been devoted to migrating related VMs in multi-tier applications. Ignoring the relatedness of VMs during migration can lead to serious application performance degradation.

This paper formulates the multi-tier application migration problem, and presents a new communication-impact-driven coordinated approach, as well as a system called COMMA that realizes this approach. Through extensive testbed experiments, numerical analyses, and a demonstration of COMMA on Amazon EC2, we show that this approach is highly effective in minimizing migration's impact on multi-tier applications' performance.

Categories and Subject Descriptors   D.4.0 [*Operating Systems*]: General

Keywords   Virtual Machine; Live Migration; Coordination; Multi-tier Applications;

1. Introduction

Server virtualization is a key technology that enables infrastructure-as-a-service cloud computing, which is the fastest growing segment of the cloud computing market and is estimated to reach $9 billion worldwide in 2013 [11]. Optimally managing pools of virtualized resources requires the ability to flexibly map and move running virtual machines (VM) and their data across and within pools [23]. Live mi-

VEE '14,   March 1–2, 2014, Salt Lake City, Utah, USA.
Copyright © 2014 ACM 978-1-4503-2764-0 /14/03... $15.00.
http://dx.doi.org/10.1145/2576195.2576200

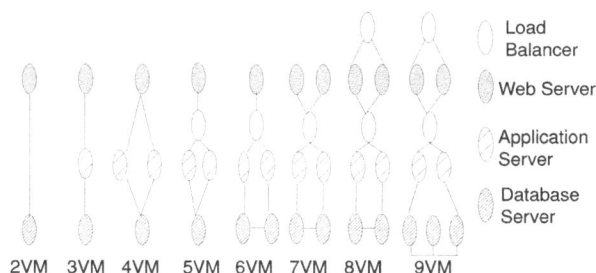

Figure 1. Examples of multi-tier web application architectures. Components that interact are connected by links.

gration of VM's disk, memory, and CPU states enables such management capabilities. This paper is a novel study on how to effectively perform live VM migration on multi-tier applications.

Applications that handle the core business and operational data of enterprises are typically multi-tiered. Figure 1 shows Amazon Web Services' [7] referential multi-tier architectures for highly-scalable and reliable web applications. A multi-tier application deployed in the cloud typically includes many interacting VMs, such as web server VMs, application server VMs, and database VMs. Such VMs are subjected to migration within a data center or across data centers. For instance, due to hardware maintenance, VMs running on physical machines sometimes need to be evacuated. For large corporations, multi-tier applications could be deployed in multiple data centers in different regions. Among the top 1 million domains that use EC2 or Azure to host their services, 44.5% are hosted in two geographical zones, and 22.3% are hosted in three or more geographical zones [14]. Live migration could potentially be used in cases where the enterprise needs to re-allocate computing resources over distant data centers or dynamically bring their services' presence into different regions.

1.1   The split components problem

Because the VMs in a multi-tier application are highly interactive, during migration the application's performance can severely degrade if the dependent components become split across a high latency and/or congested network path. Such a slow network path may be encountered within a data

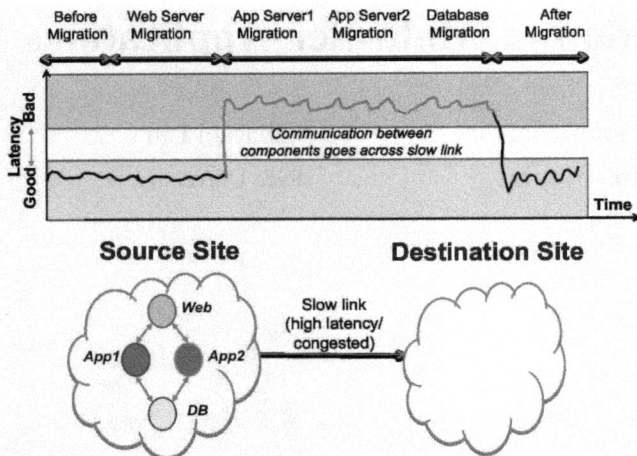

Figure 2. The split components problem in multi-tier application migration.

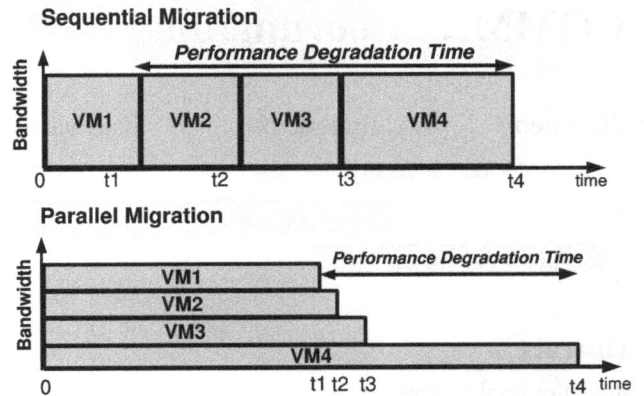

Figure 3. Sequential and parallel migration of a multi-tier application.

center network's aggregation layers, and in networks interconnecting data centers.

Figure 2 shows an example of migrating a 3-tier e-commerce application across a slow network path. The application has 4 VMs (shown as ovals) implementing a web server, two application servers, and a database server. An edge between two components in the figure indicates that those two components communicate with each other. Let us assume that the four VMs are migrated one by one in the sequence of web server, application server 1, application server 2, and database server. When the web server finishes migration and starts running at the destination site, the communication between the web server and application servers goes across the slow path, resulting in degraded end-to-end request handling latency. When the application servers finish migration, the communications between the web server and the application servers no longer need to traverse the slow path. However, it becomes necessary for the application servers to communicate with the database server over the slow path. Only when the database server finally finishes migration will the entire set of VMs be run in the destination site, and the request latency returns to the normal level.

Although existing solutions for migrating an *individual* VM are highly developed [10, 16, 18], when it comes to organizing the migration of a group of related VMs, existing solutions lack sophistication. They either employ *sequential migration*, where VMs are migrated one after another, or *parallel migration*, where VMs are migrated simultaneously. Figure 3 shows that these two migration strategies may result in poor performance when applied to multi-tier applications. Sequential migration results in a long period of performance degradation from when the first VM finishes migration until the last VM finishes migration. Parallel migration is not able to avoid such potential degradation either because the amount of data to migrate for each VM is different and therefore the VMs in general will not finish migration si-

multaneously. The application will experience performance degradation as long as components are split across a slow path.

1.2 Contributions

This paper makes the following contributions.

1. **Problem formulation (Section 2):** We formulate the multi-tier application migration problem as a performance impact minimization problem, where impact is defined as the volume of communications impacted by split components. An alternative definition of impact might be based on the amount of time during which application components are split. However, this alternative is not as suitable because it ignores the communication frequency between components of the application. A very different problem formulation would be aiming to finish migrating all VMs simultaneously. However, this formulation is inappropriate because it is impossible to achieve if the sum of the disk dirty rates of the VMs exceeds the available migration bandwidth.

2. **Communication-impact-driven coordinated system (Section 3):** We propose a centralized architecture to coordinate the migration of multiple VMs in order to minimize the impact on application communications. We have fully implemented our approach in a system called COMMA[1]. COMMA is general for all multi-tier applications, because it does not assume any application-specific information, and all measurements needed by COMMA are performed at the hypervisor level. The architecture consists of a centralized controller and a local process running inside each VM's hypervisor. COMMA is able to adapt to run-time variations in network bandwidth, I/O bandwidth, and application workload.

---

[1] COMMA stands for COordinating the Migration of Multi-tier Applications

3. **Algorithm for computing VM migration settings (Section 3):** We propose a novel algorithm that works in two stages. In the first stage, it periodically computes and coordinates the speed settings for migrating the static data of VMs. In the second stage, it coordinates the migration of dynamically generated data. VMs are grouped according to their migration resource requirements to ensure the feasibility of migration. The algorithm then performs *inter-group scheduling* to minimize the impact on application communications, and performs *intra-group scheduling* to efficiently use network bandwidth for migration.

4. **Extensive evaluation (Sections 4 & 5):** COMMA is evaluated through extensive testbed experiments on realistic applications and workloads: RUBiS (a realistic auction application modeled after eBay.com) and SpecWeb (an industry standard e-commerce website benchmark). We also perform numerical analyses and demonstrate COMMA on Amazon EC2. The experiments show that our approach is highly effective in minimizing migration's impact on multi-tier applications' performance.

2. Problem formulation and challenges

2.1 Background of live migration

Live migration refers to the process of migrating a running VM (**the entire disk, memory, CPU states**) between different physical machines without incurring significant application downtime. Live migration is widely used for planned maintenance, failure avoidance, server consolidation, and load balancing purposes. Live migration also enables a range of new cloud management operations across the wide area such as follow-the-sun provisioning [23]. Thus, live migration happens over a wide range of physical distances, from within a machine rack to across data centers located in different continents.

Full migration of a VM includes migrating (1) the running state of the VM (i.e., CPU state, memory state), (2) the storage or virtual disks used by the VM, and (3) the client-server connections.

Live migration is controlled by the source and destination hypervisors. Live migration has four phases: storage precopy, dirty iteration, memory migration and a barely noticeable downtime. During the pre-copy phase, the virtual disk is copied once and all new disk write operations are logged as dirty blocks. During the dirty iteration, the dirty blocks are retransmitted, and new dirty blocks generated during this time are again logged and retransmitted. This dirty block retransmission process repeats until the number of dirty blocks falls below a threshold, and then memory migration begins. The behavior of memory migration is similar to that of storage migration, but the size is much smaller. At the end of memory migration, the VM is suspended. The remaining dirty blocks and pages are copied, and then the VM resumes at the destination.

2.2 Problem formulation

Let n be the number of VMs in a multi-tier application and the set of VMs be $\{vm_1, vm_2, ..., vm_n\}$. The goal is to minimize the performance degradation caused by splitting the communicating components between source and destination sites during the migration. Specifically, we propose a communication-impact-driven approach. To quantify the performance degradation, we define the unit of impact as the volume of traffic between VMs that need to crisscross between the source and destination sites during migration. More concretely, by using the traffic volume to measure the impact, components that communicate more heavily are treated as more important. While many other metrics could be selected to evaluate the impact, e.g. the end-to-end latency of requests, the number of affected requests, performance degradation time, we do not adopt them for the following reasons. We do not adopt the end-to-end latency of requests and the number of affected requests because it is application dependent and requires extra application-specific support for measurement at the application level. We do not adopt performance degradation time because it ignores the communication rate between components. We define the communication impact as the volume of traffic which does not require any extra support from the application and is therefore *application-independent*.

Let traffic matrix TM represent the communication traffic rates between VMs prior to the start of migration. Our impact model is based on the traffic prior to migration rather than the traffic during migration. During migration, the traffic rate of the application may be distorted by a variety of factors such as network congestion between the source and destination sites and I/O congestion caused by the data copying activities. Therefore, we cannot optimize against the traffic rate during migration because the actual importance of the interaction between components could be lost through such distortions. Let the migration finish time for vm_i be t_i. Our goal is to minimize the total communication impact of migration, where:

$$impact = \sum_{i=1}^{n} \sum_{j>i}^{n} |t_i - t_j| * TM[i,j] \qquad (1)$$

2.3 Challenges

To tackle the above problem, we first introduce the challenges for managing the migration progress of a single VM addressed in our previous work Pacer [28]. In this paper, we address the new and unique challenges for managing the migration progress of multi-tier applications.

2.3.1 Managing the migration progress of a single VM

Managing the migration progress for a single VM comprises of the functions to monitor, predict and control VM migration time. The migration time of a VM is difficult to predict and control for the following two reasons:

- **Dynamicity and interference:** VM migration time depends on many static and dynamic factors. For example, the VM image size and memory size are static factors, but the actual workload and available resources (e.g. disk I/O bandwidth and network bandwidth) are dynamic. During migration, the network traffic and disk I/O from migration can interfere with the network traffic and disk I/O from the application, resulting in migration speed and disk dirty rate changes.

- **Convergence:** We define the term "*available migration bandwidth*" as the maximal migration speed that migration could achieve considering all bottlenecks such as network and disk I/O bottlenecks. If the available bandwidth is not allocated properly, the migration could fail because the application may generate new data that needs to be migrated at a faster pace exceeding the available migration bandwidth. For example, if the available migration bandwidth is 10MBps while the VM generates new data at the speed of 30MBps, migration will not converge in the dirty iteration phase and migration will fail. For a single VM migration, the mechanism to handle nonconvergence is either to set a timeout to stop migration and report a failure, or to throttle write operations to reduce the new data generation rate. The latter mechanism will degrade application performance.

For the above challenges of single VM migration, our previous work Pacer [28] is able to achieve accurate prediction and control of migration progress. Pacer provides algorithms for predicting dirty set and dirty rate in the pre-copy phase and the dirty iteration phase. These algorithms are leveraged by COMMA to gather information needed for coordination (details in Section 3).

2.3.2 Managing the migration of a multi-tier application

The management of the migration of a multi-tier application is more complicated because of the dependencies between VMs.

1. **Multiple VM migration coordination:** At the level of a single VM, the migration process can be predicted and controlled using Pacer [28]. However, if we rely on an architecture where all VM migration processes act independently, it would be difficult to achieve the joint migration goal for all VMs of the application. It is necessary to design a new architecture where a higher level control mechanism governs and coordinates all VM migration activities for the application.

2. **Convergence in multi-tier application migration:** For multiple VM migrations, the convergence issue mentioned above becomes more complicated. If the network bandwidth is smaller than any single VM's new data generation rate, the only reasonable option is sequential migration. If the network bandwidth is large enough to mi-

Challenge	Solution
Multiple VM migration coordination	Centralized architecture
Convergence in multi-tier application migration	Valid group and inter-group scheduling
Dynamicity in multi-tier application migration	Periodic measurement and adaptation
System efficiency	Inter-group scheduling heuristic and intra-group scheduling

Table 1. Challenges and solutions in COMMA.

grate all VMs together, the problem is easily handled by parallel migration. When the network bandwidth is in between the previous two cases, we need a mechanism to check whether it is possible to migrate multiple VMs at the same time, decide how to combine multiple VMs into groups that can be migrated together, and decide how to schedule the start and finish time of each group to achieve the goal of minimizing the communication impact.

3. **Dynamicity in multi-tier application migration:** For single VM migration, Pacer [28] can predict the migration time and control the migration progress. For multitier application migration, it is more complicated because the VMs are highly interactive and the dynamicity is more unpredictable; the traffic from multiple VM migrations and the application traffic from all VMs can interfere with each other. In this case, we need a measurement and adaptation mechanism that handles the dynamicity across all VMs.

4. **System efficiency:** The computation complexity for obtaining an optimal solution to coordinate the migration of a multi-tier application could be very high. It is important that the coordination system is efficient and has low overhead. Furthermore, the system should ensure that the available migration bandwidth is utilized efficiently.

3. System design

3.1 Overview

COMMA is the first migration coordination system for multiple VMs. It relies on a centralized architecture and a two-stage scheduling routine to conduct the coordination. The challenges mentioned in Section 2.3.2 and the corresponding key features that tackle those challenges are summarized in Table 1.

The centralized architecture of COMMA is the key to orchestrating the migration of multiple VMs. The architecture consists of two parts: 1) a centralized controller program, and 2) a local process running inside each VM's hypervisor. The local process provides three functions: 1) monitor the migration status (such as actual migration speed, migration progress, current dirty blocks and dirty rate) and periodically report to the controller; 2) predict the future dirty set and dirty rate to help estimate the remaining migration time. The dirty set and dirty rate prediction algorithms come from Pacer [28]; 3) a control interface that receives messages from the controller to start, stop or pace the migration speed. Based on the reported migration status from all VMs, the controller executes a scheduling algorithm to compute the proper settings, and sends control messages to each local process to achieve the performance objective. This periodic control and adaptation mechanism with controller coordination overcomes the migration dynamicity and interference problems, and helps to achieve the overall objective of finishing the migration with the minimal impact.

More specifically, COMMA works in two stages. In the first stage, it coordinates the migration speed of the static data of different VMs such that all VMs complete the static data migration at nearly the same time. Before migration, the user provides the list of VMs to be migrated as well as their source hypervisors and destination hypervisors to the controller, and then the controller queries the source hypervisors for each VM's image size and memory size. At the same time, COMMA uses `iperf` [1] to measure the available network bandwidth between the source and destination, and uses `iptraf` [4] to measure the communication traffic matrix of VMs. At the beginning, the measured network bandwidth is considered as the available migration bandwidth. Periodically (every 5 seconds in our implementation), the controller gathers the actual available bandwidth and the migration progress of each VM, and then it paces the migration speed of each VM so that their precopy phases complete at nearly the same time. Subsequently COMMA enters the second stage. COMMA provides mechanisms to check whether it is possible to migrate multiple VMs at the same time, to decide how to combine multiple VM migrations into a group to achieve convergence for all VMs in the group called *valid group*, and to decide how to schedule the starting and finishing time of each group to minimize the communication impact called *inter-group scheduling*. Furthermore, COMMA performs *intra-group scheduling* to schedule each VM inside the same group in order to best maximize the bandwidth utilization.

3.2 Scheduling algorithm

The algorithm works in two stages. In the first stage, it coordinates the migration speed of the static data of VMs (phase 1) so that all VMs complete the precopy phase at nearly the same time. In the second stage, it coordinates the migration of dynamically generated data (phase 2, 3, 4) by inter-group and intra-group scheduling. The definitions of the four phases of migration are in Section 2.1.

Phase 1 migrates static content, and there is no inherent minimum speed requirement. Phase 2 and 3 migrate dynamically generated content. The content generation rate implies a minimum migration speed that must be achieved or otherwise throttling might become necessary (which causes application performance degradation). Therefore, we should dedicate as much of the available bandwidth to phase 2 and 3 in order to prevent application performance degradation. This

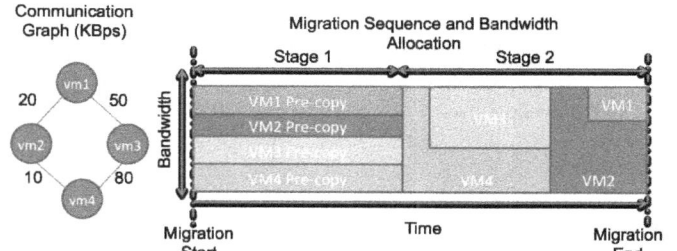

Figure 4. An example of coordinating a multi-tier application migration with COMMA.

clearly implies that the phase 1 migration activities should not overlap with phase 2 and 3.

3.2.1 First stage

The goal of the first stage is to migrate VMs in parallel and finish all VMs' phase 1 at the same time. Assuming the data copying for each VM is performed over a TCP connection, it is desirable to migrate VMs in parallel because the aggregate transmission throughput achieved by the parallel TCP connections tend to be higher than a single TCP connection.

In this stage, the amount of migrated data is fixed. The controller adjusts each VM's migration speed according to its virtual disk size (see Equation 2).

$$speed_{vm_i} = \frac{\text{DISK\_SIZE}_i * \text{BANDWIDTH}}{\text{TOTAL\_DISK\_SIZE}} \quad (2)$$

During migration, the controller periodically gathers and analyzes the actual available network bandwidth, migration speeds and the progress of VMs. Then it adjusts the migration speed settings of VMs to drive phase 1 migrations to finish at the same time.

Figure 4 shows an example of migrating 4 VMs with COMMA. In the first stage, the controller coordinates the migration of 4 VMs such that their precopy phases complete at the same time. At the end of the first stage, each VM has recorded a set of dirty blocks which require retransmission in the next stage.

3.2.2 Second stage

In the second stage, we introduce the concept of "valid group" to overcome the second challenge mentioned in Section 2.3.2. COMMA performs inter-group scheduling to minimize the communication impact and intra-group scheduling to efficiently use network bandwidth.

To satisfy the convergence constraint, the VMs in the multi-tier application are divided into valid groups according to the following rule: the sum of the VMs' maximal dirty rates in a group is no larger than the available network bandwidth (See Equation 3). The maximal dirty rate is usually achieved at the end of dirty iteration, since at this time most blocks are clean and they have a high probability of getting dirty again. The maximal dirty rate is needed before the second stage but it is unknown until the migration finishes, and thus we leverage the dirty rate estimation algorithm in Pacer [28] to estimate the maximal dirty rate before the second stage starts. In the second stage, we migrate the VMs in groups based on the inter-group scheduling algorithm. Once a group's migration starts in the second stage, we wait for this group to finish. At the same time, we continue to monitor the actual bandwidth, dirty rate and dirty set for other not-yet-migrated groups. We update the schedule for not-yet-migrated groups by adapting to the actual observed metrics.

$$\sum_{vm_i \in group} \{Max\_dirty\_rate_i\} \leq \text{BANDWIDTH} \quad (3)$$

3.3 Inter-group scheduling

In order to minimize the communication impact, COMMA needs to compute the optimal group combination and migration sequence, which is a hard problem. We propose two algorithms: a brute-force algorithm and a heuristic algorithm. The brute-force algorithm can find the optimal solution but its computation complexity is high. In Section 4, we show that the heuristic algorithm reduces the computation overhead by 99% without losing much in optimality in practice.

3.3.1 Brute-force algorithm

The brute-force algorithm lists all the possible combinations of valid groups, performs the permutation for different migration sequences and computes the communication impact. It records the group combination and migration sequence which generates the minimal impact.

Given a set of VMs, the algorithm generates all subsets first, and each subset will be considered as a group. The algorithm eliminates the invalid groups that do not meet the requirement in Equation 3. It then computes all combinations of valid groups that exactly add up to a complete set of all VMs. Figure 4 shows one such combination of two valid groups that add up to a complete set: $\{vm1, vm2\}$ and $\{vm3, vm4\}$. Next the algorithm permutes each of such combination to get sequences of groups, and those sequences stand for different migration orders. The algorithm then computes the communication impact of each sequence based on the traffic matrix and the migration time reported from the intra-group scheduling algorithm. Finally the algorithm will select the group combination and the sequence with the minimal communication impact.

Let n be the number of VMs in the application. The time complexity for the brute-force algorithm is $O(2^n * n!)$, because it takes $O(2^n)$ to compute all the subsets and takes $O(n!)$ to perform permutation for each combination.

3.3.2 Heuristic algorithm

Our heuristic algorithm tries to estimate the minimal impact by prioritizing VMs that need to communicate with each other the most. Given the traffic matrix, we can get a list

L of the communication rates between any two VMs. Each element in L includes $(rate, VM_i, VM_j)$. It represents the communication between node VM_i and node VM_j with $rate$. The heuristic algorithm takes the traffic matrix as input and generates the VM group set S as follows.

- Step 1: Sort the communication rates in L by descending order. S is empty at the beginning.
- Step 2: Repeatedly take the largest rate element $(rate, VM_i, VM_j)$ from L. Check whether VM_i and VM_j are already in S

  - Case 1: Neither VM_i nor VM_j is in S. If the two VMs can be combined into a valid group, insert a new group $\{VM_i, VM_j\}$ into S. Otherwise, insert two groups $\{VM_i\}$ and $\{VM_j\}$ into S.
  - Case 2: Only one VM is in S. For example, VM_i is in S and VM_j is not in S. Find the group which includes VM_i. Check whether VM_j can be merged into the group based on the convergence constraint in Equation 3. If it is still a valid group after merging, then VM_j is merged into the group. Otherwise, a new group $\{VM_j\}$ is inserted into S. For the case that VM_j is in S and VM_i is not, it is similar.
  - Case 3: Both VM_i and VM_j are in S. If the two groups can be merged into one group with convergence constraint, then merge the two groups.
- Step 3: At the end of step 2, we have S which includes the valid group of VMs. The algorithm then compares permutations on the groups to find the one with minimal impact.

The time complexity for the heuristic algorithm is $O(n!)$ because the algorithm is dominated by the last step. Sorting in step 1 takes $O(n^2 log n)$ since there are at most $n(n-1)$ elements in the list L which means every VM communicate with every other VM. Step 2 takes $O(n^2)$. The permutation in step 3 takes $O(n!)$ in the worst case when each VM forms a group.

3.4 Intra-group scheduling

To migrate the VMs in a valid group, one possible solution is to allocate bandwidth equal to the VM's maximal dirty rate to the corresponding VM. Then, we start the migration of all VMs in the group at the same time. The definition of valid group guarantees that we have enough bandwidth to support all VMs in the group migrating concurrently.

However, starting the VMs' migration at the same time is not an efficient use of available migration bandwidth. Figure 5 shows the migration of three VMs during their dirty iteration with different mechanisms to illustrate this inefficiency. Figure 5(a) shows that 3 VMs start dirty iteration of migration at the same time. Different VMs have different migration speeds and dirty rates. Therefore, they finish

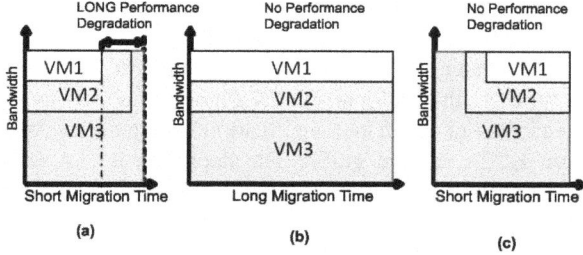

Figure 5. Intra-group scheduling. (a) Start VM migrations at the same time, but finish at different times. Result in long performance degradation time. (b) Start VM migrations at the same time and finish at the same time. Result in long migration time due to the inefficient use of migration bandwidth. (c) Start VM migrations at different times and finish at the same time. No performance degradation and short migration time due to efficient use of migration bandwidth.

migration at different times without coordination. For example, VM_1 takes 5 minutes to migrate most of the dirty blocks or pages. Then it could enter phase 4 to pause the VM and switch over to run in the destination. VM_3 may take 10 minutes to finish. That results in 5 minutes of performance degradation. Recall that the goal of COMMA is to reduce the communication impact during migration. Therefore, the ideal case is that the VMs in the group finish migration at the same time. In order to make them finish at the same time, we could force VM_1 and VM_2 to stay in the dirty iteration and continue migrating new generated dirty blocks until VM_3 is done as Figure 5(b) shows. This mechanism is not efficient because it wastes a lot of migration bandwidth in holding VM_1 and VM_2 in the dirty iteration.

To efficiently use the migration bandwidth, the intra-group scheduling algorithm schedules the migration of VMs inside a group to finish at the same time but it allows them to start the dirty iteration at different times as Figure 5(c) shows.

The design is based on the following observations in practice. (1) Delaying the dirty iteration start time of VMs with light workload can allow for more bandwidth to be allocated to VMs with heavy workload. (2) At the end of the first stage, most of the VM's frequently written blocks are already marked as dirty blocks, and the dirty rate is low at this time. Therefore, delaying the start time of dirty iteration will not significantly increase the number of dirty blocks. (3) Once the dirty iteration starts, it is better to finish migration as soon as possible to save the bandwidth.

While observations (1) and (3) are quite intuitive, observation (2) is less so. To illustrate observation (2), we perform migrations of a file server with 30 clients and analyze its dirty rate. Figure 6(a) shows the migration without any delay for the dirty iteration. From 0 to 280s, migration is in the pre-copy phase and its dirty rate is very stable around 32KBps. Dirty iteration start from 280s to 350s. The dirty

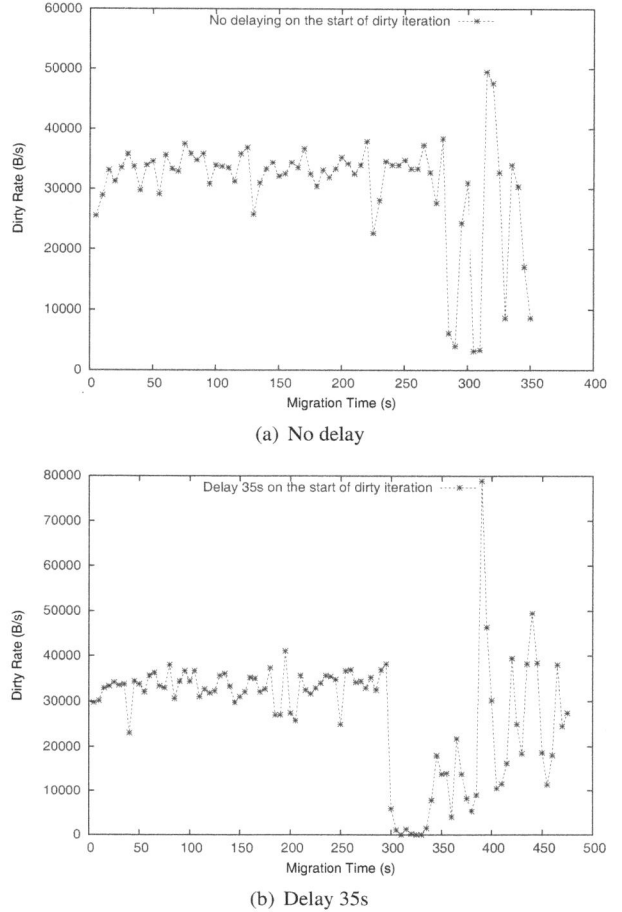

(a) No delay

(b) Delay 35s

Figure 6. An example of delaying the start of dirty iteration for the migration.

rate is very low at the beginning and increases as dirty iteration proceeds. Figure 6(b) show the migration with 35s delay on the start of dirty iteration. During this period, we can see the dirty rate is almost zero. It means there is no more clean blocks getting dirty.

Initially we assume that the minimal required speed for each VM is equal to the VM's maximal dirty rate. We then use the method in Pacer [28] to compute a predicted migration time for each VM. The algorithm would schedule different dirty iteration start times for different VMs according to their predicted migration time so that every VM is expected to finish the migration at the same time.

Available network bandwidth may be larger than the sum of the VMs' minimal required migration speed. If there is extra available bandwidth, the bandwidth will be further allocated to the VMs to minimize the total migration time of the group. This allocation is done iteratively. Suppose the group has N VMs, the extra available bandwidth is first allocated to vm_N, where the subscript indicates the VM's start time order in the schedule. That is, vm_N is the VM that starts the latest in the schedule. The allocation of this extra bandwidth reduces vm_N's migration time, and thus its start time can be moved closer to the finish time target in the schedule. Next, the extra available bandwidth prior to the start of vm_N is given to vm_{N-1}. vm_{N-1}'s migration time is thus reduced also. Then the extra available bandwidth prior to the start of vm_{N-1} is given to vm_{N-2} and so on, until the migration time for the first VM to start is also minimized.

3.5 Adapting to changing dirty rate and bandwidth

When the disk write workload and/or the available migration bandwidth are highly unstable, prediction accuracy will reduce. Fortunately, in the first stage, COMMA periodically updates its predictions based on the latest measurements, such that the pre-copy tasks can still finish at the same time. Furthermore, in the second stage, COMMA will adapt by periodically estimating the maximal dirty rate, measuring the available bandwidth and recomputing the schedule for not-yet-migrated groups. When COMMA detects that available bandwidth is smaller than the sum of any two VM's maximal dirty rate, the migration will be degraded to sequential migration to ensure convergence. In the extremely rare case, if the available bandwidth is smaller than a single VM's maximal dirty rate, throttling is performed to that VM such that the dirty rate is reduced and migration could converge.

4. Evaluation

4.1 Implementation

COMMA is implemented on the kernel-based virtual machine (KVM). KVM consists of a loadable kernel module, a processor specific module, and a user-space program – a modified QEMU emulator. COMMA's local process for each VM is implemented on QEMU version 0.12.50, and COMMA's centralized controller is implemented as a lightweight server with C++.

4.2 Experiment setup

The experiments are set up on six physical machines. Each machine has a 3GHz Quad-core AMD Phenom II X4 945 processor, 8GB RAM, 640GB SATA hard drive, and Ubuntu 9.10 with Linux kernel (with the KVM module) version 2.6.31.

4.3 Application level benefits of COMMA

To directly show the benefits of COMMA during the migration of a multi-tier application, we conduct experiments to migrate RUBiS [20], a well-known benchmark for server performance, using sequential migration, parallel migration, and COMMA. RUBiS is a 3-tier application including web server, application server and database server. We measure the application performance by computing the average response time of the request from clients every second. In the experiment setting, each RUBiS server runs on one VM, and each VM is provisioned on one physical machine. We mi-

grate 3 VMs from 3 source hypervisors to 3 destination hypervisors, with an emulator [3] to emulate a slow link with a round trip latency of 100ms. The architecture of RUBiS is the same as the 3VM setting in Figure 1, which shows real examples of multi-tier application architectures from Amazon EC2's service guide. The deployment and setup of the multi-tier applications in our experiments is based on it. Those 3 VMs have the same image size of 8GB. The memory size of the web server, application server, and database server is 2GB, 2GB, and 512MB. The workload is 100 clients. Figure 7 shows the application performance before, during, and after migration, with the different migration approaches.

In sequential migration, the average response time is 20-25ms before migration. Right after migration starts, response time increases to 30-40ms because of the interference from the migration traffic. At the end of web server's migration, there is a response time spike, because the VM is being suspended for a short downtime to finish the final phase of migration. Immediately after that, the web server starts running on the destination hypervisor, and the communication traffic between the web server and the application server goes through the slow link. As a result, the application performance is degraded to 150-190ms. At the end of application server's migration, there is also a spike, and then the application server starts running on the destination, while the communication between the application server and the database server goes through the slow link. This performance degradation lasts for more than 1000 seconds until the database server finishes migration. In parallel migration, the degradation time is still high at 82 seconds, and there are still three response time spikes because the three VMs finish migration at different times. Finally, we conduct the migration with COMMA. There is only one response time spike, because all the three VM finishes at nearly the same time, and the performance degradation time is only 1s.

4.4 COMMA's ability to minimize the migration impact

In this experiment, we will show that COMMA is able to minimize the communication impact, which is defined in equation 1 of section 2.2. For the experiment setting, we add one more application server to the above RUBiS [20] setup. The purpose is to deploy the 4 VMs on at most 3 physical machines with different placements to mimic the unknown VM placement policy in public clouds. The architecture is the same as the 4VM setting in Figure 1. The number of clients is 300. Each experiment is run 3 times and we show the average results in Table 2.

Table 2 shows that sequential migration has the longest migration time and the highest impact in all cases. More than 2GB of data are affected by sequential migration. Parallel migration reduces the impact to less than 1GB, but this is still much higher than the impact of COMMA. COMMA has

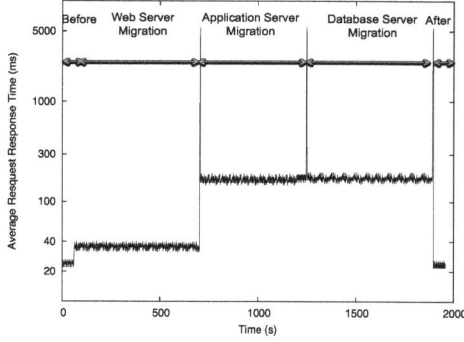

(a) Sequential migration

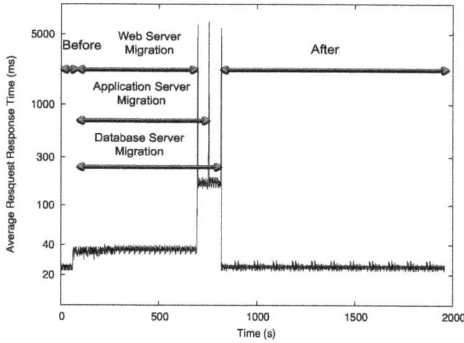

(b) Parallel migration

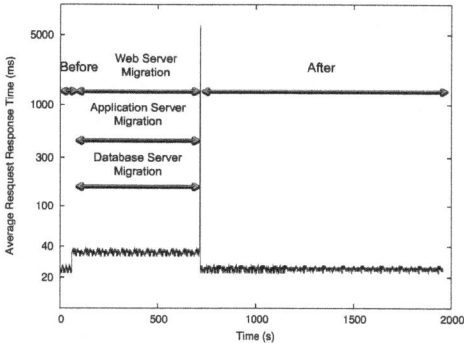

(c) COMMA

Figure 7. Application performance during migration of a 3-tier application. The y axis is in log scale.

up to 475 times of reduction on the amount of data affected by migration.

As the result shows, COMMA has a slightly larger migration time than parallel migration. The reason is that COMMA tries to make all VMs finish migration at the same time, but parallel migration does not. In parallel migration when some VMs finish earlier, the other VMs undergoing migration that share the same resources can take advantages of the released resource and finish migration earlier.

4.5 Importance of the dynamic adaptation mechanism

While the above experiment shows the high communication impact for sequential and parallel migration, one could come

VM Placement	Sequential Migration		Parallel Migration		COMMA Migration	
	Migr. Time (s)	Impact (MB)	Migr. Time (s)	Impact (MB)	Migr. Time (s)	Impact (MB)
{web,app1,app2,db}	2289	2267	2155	13	2188	7
{web,db},{app1,app2}	2479	2620	918	72	1043	2
{web,app1},{db,app2}	2425	2617	1131	304	1336	2
{web}{app1,app2}{db}	2330	2273	914	950	926	2
{web,app1}{app2}{db}	2213	1920	797	717	988	4
{web}{app1}{app2,db}	2310	2151	1012	259	1244	5

Table 2. Comparisons of three approaches for migrating a 3-tier application. {...} represents set of VMs placed on one physical machine.

up with alternative approaches to reduce the communication impact. Some approaches include reordering the migration sequence in sequential migration, or configuring the migration speed based on static migration info such as the VM disk size. However, without the periodic measurement and adaptation mechanism in COMMA, those approaches cannot achieve the goal of minimizing the communication impact, because they cannot handle the dynamicity during migration.

The experiment is based on SPECweb2005 [2]. SPECweb 2005 contains a frontend Apache server with an image size of 8GB and a backend database server with an image size of 16GB. The workload is 50 clients and the experiment is run 3 times. Table 3 shows the results of six migration approaches. The first two approaches are sequential migration with different orders. The sequential migration approach causes a large impact of 265MB and 139MB for the two different migration orders.

The next three approaches are parallel migration with different upper speed limits. In the first experiment, both VMs are configured with the same migration speed limit of 32MBps. They do not finish at the same time, with an impact of 116MB. In the second experiment, the migration speed limit for the frontend VM (8GB) is set to be 16MBps, and for the backend VM (16GB) the speed limit is 32MBps. By setting the migration speed limit proportional to the image size, the user may expect the two VMs to finish migration at the same time. However, this does not happen because the migration cannot achieve the configured speed limits most of the time due to an I/O bottleneck of 15MBps. To avoid this bottleneck, a compromise is to decrease the configured speed limits. In the third parallel migration experiment, the configured speed limits are 5MBps and 10MBps. The degradation time is decreased but is still 36s, and the impact is 9MB. However, the low migration speed brings the side effect of longer migration time. These three experiments show that it is impossible for users to statically pre-determine and configure the migration speed to achieve low communication impact and timely migration at the same time. In a real cloud environment, guessing the proper speed configuration will be even harder with the additional competing traffic or

	Sequential Migr.		Parallel Migr.			COMMA
	frontend first	backend first	32/32 MBps	16/32 MBps	5/10 MBps	
Impact(MB)	265	139	116	122	9	0.2
Migr. Time(s)	1584	1583	1045	1043	1697	1043

Table 3. Manually tuned sequential and parallel migration vs. COMMA's fully automated approach.

Component Type	Image Size	Mem Size	Dirty Set	Max Dirty Rate
Web/App Server Load Balancer	8GB	1GB	100MB	2MBps
Database	8GB	1GB	1GB	15MBps

Table 4. Example VM and workload parameters for numerical analyses.

more complicated dynamics. With COMMA, the controller can coordinate the migration progress of the two VMs automatically. The two VMs finish migration as quickly as possible and have only a communication impact of 0.2MB.

4.6 Benefits of the heuristic algorithm

In this experiment, we evaluate the communication impact and the computation time for both of the brute-force and the heuristic inter-group scheduling algorithms. We perform numerical analyses to evaluate the different migration approaches on the different multi-tier web service architectures shown in Figure 1.

Assume that the VMs have the characteristics in Table 4, and the shared total available bandwidth is 256Mbps. The parameters that we select are image size, memory size, dirty set size and max dirty rate. These are the four key parameters for determining the migration time using the method in [28]. We select a set of representative configurations to enable our numerical analyses. The image size and memory size follow the recommendation from the VMware VMmark benchmark configuration [21]. Dirty set is defined as the written and not-yet-migrated data bytes on the VM's virtual disk at the end of disk image pre-copy. Dirty rate is defined as the speed at which the VM's virtual disk and memory is written. Dirty set and dirty rate settings are from our measurement of the VMware benchmark.

We measure the RUBiS traffic matrix and found that the inter-component communication rates range from 0 to several hundred KBps, depending on the number of clients. Therefore, we generate a random number between 0 and 100KBps to mimic the communication rate in RUBiS. Each experiment is run 3 times with different random number seeds. Table 5 shows the average results. In the first four cases ($VM \leq 5$), all VMs can be coordinated to finish at the same time and the impact is 0. For larger-scale applications ($VM \geq 6$), the coordination algorithm will perform the best effort to schedule VM's migration and achieve the

	Sequential Migration	Parallel Migration	COMMA-Bruteforce Migration	COMMA-Heuristic Migration
2VM	28	3	0	0
3VM	84	3	0	0
4VM	114	3	0	0
5VM	109	3	0	0
6VM	222	INF	1	2
7VM	287	INF	2	2
8VM	288	INF	1	2
9VM	424	INF	9	13

Table 5. Communication impact (MB) with different migration approaches. INF indicates that migration cannot converge.

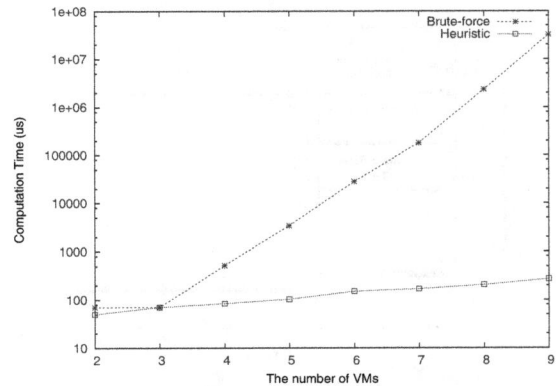

Figure 8. Computation time for brute-force algorithm and heuristic algorithm.

minimal impact. The coordination with the brute force algorithm achieves a slightly lower impact than the coordination with the heuristic algorithm. Take the migration of 9 VMs for example, comparing to the sequential migration, COMMA with the brute-force algorithm could reduce the impact by 97.9% and COMMA with the heuristic algorithm could reduce the impact by 96.9%.

Figure 8 shows the computation time for the brute-force algorithm and the heuristic algorithm. When the number of VM increases to 9, the computation time for the brute-force algorithm rapidly increases to 32 seconds, while the computation time for the heuristic algorithm is a much more reasonable 274us. In other words, the heuristic algorithm reduces the computation overhead up to 99%.

In practice, a multi-tier application could contain tens of components [13]. Fortunately, our heuristic algorithm can handle applications at such size efficiently since the computation time required is still smaller than 10 milliseconds, and the heuristic algorithm only needs to be invoked once every several seconds.

5. EC2 demonstration

To demonstrate COMMA in a real commercial hybrid cloud environment, we conduct an experiment using Amazon EC2 public cloud. The experiment migrates two SPECweb2005 VMs from a university campus network to EC2 instances

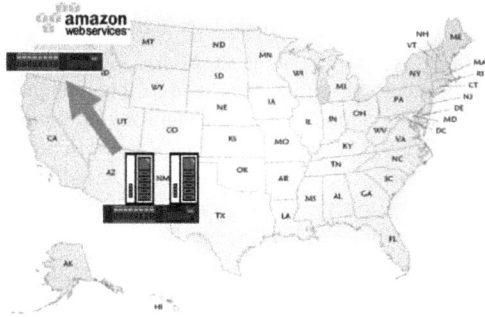

Figure 9. Live migration of multi-tier applications to EC2.

	Sequential Migr.		Parallel Migr.			Coord.
	Migration		Migration			
	frontend first	backend first	32/32 MBps	16/32 MBps	5/10 MBps	
Impact(MB)	28	17	19	6	6	0.1
Migr. Time(s)	871s	919s	821s	885s	1924s	741s

Table 6. Manually tuned sequential and parallel migration vs. COMMA in EC2 demonstration.

with the same settings as the experiment in Section 4.5 except that the workload is reduced to 10 clients. Since KVM cannot run on top of EC2 instances, we run QEMU with the "no-kvm" mode, which reduces the application's performance. Reducing to 10 clients ensures the convergence of the dirty iteration and memory migration phases. We use EC2's High-CPU Medium instances running Ubuntu 12.04.

The result is in Table 6. In the sequential approach, the performance degradation time is equal to the time of migrating the second VM, and thus the migration impact could be as high as 28MB and 17MB for the two different migration orders. For the parallel approach with the same migration upper speed limit for both VMs, the degradation impact is still 19 MB, which is not much better than the impact of sequential approach. We next set the migration speed limit proportional to the size of the VM image. In this case, the impact decreases to 6MB, but this approach does not fully utilize the available bandwidth. Consequently, the migration time increases, especially in the last case with the migration speed limits of 5/10 MBps. For COMMA, migration's impact is orders of magnitude smaller, and the migration time is the shortest because it utilizes bandwidth efficiently. COMMA reduces the communication impact by 190 times compared to that of parallel migration. The above results show that COMMA is able to successfully coordinate the migration of multi-tier applications across the wide area with extremely low impact on application performance.

6. Related work

To the best of our knowledge, no previous work is directly comparable to COMMA, which is the first paper to address the problem of live migration of multi-tier applications. The

goal of COMMA is to reduce the application performance degradation during migration.

There is some related work on performance modeling and measurement of single VM live migration [6, 8, 9, 22, 24, 26]. Wu et al. [24] created the performance model with regression methods for migrating a VM running different resource-intensive applications. Breitgand et al. [8] quantified the trade-off between minimizing the copy phase duration and maintaining an acceptable quality of service during the pre-copy phase for CPU/memory-only migration. Akoush et al. [6] provided two simulation models to predict memory migration time. Voorsluys et al. [22] presented a performance evaluation on the effects of live migration. Zhao et al. [26] provided a model that can characterize the VM migration process and predict its performance, based on a comprehensive experimental analysis. Checconi et al. [9] introduced a stochastic model for the migration process and reserves resource shares to individual VMs to meet the strict timing constraints of real-time virtualized applications. Relative to these previous works, not only does COMMA address a different set of problems which targets multiple VM migrations, COMMA also takes an approach based on real measurements and run-time adaptation, which are found to be crucial to cope with workload and performance interference dynamics, to realize a complete system.

There exists related work on multiple simultaneous migrations [5, 19]. Nicolae et al. [19] proposed a hypervisor-transparent approach for efficient live migration of I/O intensive workloads. It relies on a hybrid active push-prioritized prefetch strategy to speed up migration and reduce migration time, which makes it highly resilient to rapid changes of disk state exhibited by I/O intensive workloads. Al-Kiswany [5] employed data deduplication in live migration to reduce the migration traffic. Their solution VMFlockMS is a migration service optimized for cross-data center transfer and instantiation of groups of virtual machine images. VMFlockMS is designed to be deployed as a set of virtual appliances which make efficient use of the available cloud resources. The purpose of the system is to locally access and deduplicate the images and data in a distributed fashion with minimal requirements imposed on the cloud API to access the VM image repository. Some other work for live migration focuses on reducing migration traffic by compression [12, 15], deduplication [25] and reordering migrated blocks [17, 27]. The purposes of above related work are either to reduce migration traffic or to reduce migration time which are very different from what this paper focuses on.

7. Conclusions

We have introduced COMMA – the first coordinated live VM migration system for multi-tier applications. We have formulated the multi-tier application migration problem, and presented a new communication-impact-driven coordinated approach, as well as a fully implemented system on KVM that realizes the approach. COMMA is based on a two-stage scheduling algorithm to coordinate the migration of VMs with the goal of minimizing the migration's impact on inter-component communications. From a series of experiments, we have shown the significant benefits of COMMA in reducing the communication impact, while the scheduling algorithm of COMMA incurs little overhead. We believe COMMA will have far reaching impact because it is applicable to numerous intra-data center and inter-data center VM migration scenarios. Furthermore, the techniques underlying COMMA can be easily applied to other virtualization platforms such as VMware, Xen and Hyper-V.

Acknowledgments

This research was sponsored by the NSF under CNS-1305379, CNS-1018807 and CNS-1162270, by an Alfred P. Sloan Research Fellowship, an IBM Scholarship, an IBM Faculty Award, and by Microsoft Corp.

References

[1] iperf. http://sourceforge.net/projects/iperf/.

[2] Specweb2005. http://www.spec.org/web2005/.

[3] WANem. http://wanem.sourceforge.net.

[4] iptraf. http://iptraf.seul.org/, 2005.

[5] S. AI-Kiswany, D. Subhraveti, P. Sarkar, and M. Ripeanu. Vmflock: Virtual machine co-migration for the cloud. In *HPDC*, 2011.

[6] S. Akoush, R. Sohan, A. Rice, A. W.Moore, and A. Hopper. Predicting the performance of virtual machine migration. In *IEEE 18th annual international symposium on modeling, analysis and simulation of computer and telecommunication systems*. IEEE, 2010.

[7] Amazon. Aws reference architecture. http://aws.amazon.com/architecture/.

[8] D. Breitgand, G. Kutiel, and D. Raz. Cost-aware live migration of services in the cloud. In *USENIX Workshop on Hot Topics in Management of Internet, Cloud, and Enterprise Networks and Services*. USENIX, 2011.

[9] F. Checconi, T. Cucinotta, and M. Stein. Real-time issues in live migration of virtual machines. In *Euro-Par 2009–Parallel Processing Workshops*, pages 454–466. Springer, 2010.

[10] C. Clark, K. Fraser, S. Hand, J. G. Hansen, E. Jul, C. Limpach, I. Pratt, and A. Warfield. Live migration of virtual machines. In *NSDI'05*, 2005.

[11] Gartner. http://www.gartner.com/newsroom/id/2352816, 2013.

[12] S. Hacking and B. Hudzia. Improving the live migration process of large enterprise applications. In *VTDC'09: Proceedings of the 3rd International Workshop on Virtualization Technologies in Distributed Computing*, 2009.

[13] M. Hajjat, X. Sun, Y. Sung, D. Maltz, S. Rao, K. Sripanidkulchai, and M. Tawarmalani. Cloudward bound: planning for beneficial migration of enterprise applications to the cloud. In *ACM SIGCOMM Computer Communication Review*, 2010.

[14] K. He, A. Fisher, L. Wang, A. Gember, A. Akella, and T. Ristenpart. Next stop, the cloud: Understanding modern web service deployment in ec2 and azure. In *IMC*, 2013.

[15] H. Jin, L. Deng, S. Wu, X. Shi, and X. Pan. Live virtual machine migration with adaptive memory compression. In *IEEE International Conference on Cluster Computing*, 2009.

[16] KVM. Kernel based virtual machine. http://www.linux-kvm.org/page/Main_Page.

[17] A. Mashtizadeh, E. Celebi, T. Garfinkel, and M. Cai. The design and evolution of live storage migration in vmware esx. In *Proceedings of the annual conference on USENIX Annual Technical Conference*. USENIX Association, 2011.

[18] M. Nelson, B.-H. Lim, and G. Hutchins. Fast transparent migration for virtual machines. In *USENIX'05*, USA, 2005.

[19] B. Nicolae and F. Cappello. Towards efficient live migration of I/O intensive workloads: A transparent storage transfer proposal. In *HPDC*, 2012.

[20] RUBiS. http://rubis.ow2.org.

[21] VMWare. VMmark Virtualization Benchmarks. http://www.vmware.com/products/vmmark/, Jan. 2010.

[22] W. Voorsluys, J. Broberg, S. Venugopal, and R. Buyya. Cost of virtual machine live migration in clouds: A performance evaluation, 2009.

[23] T. Wood, P. Shenoy, K.K.Ramakrishnan, and J. V. der Merwe. Cloudnet: Dynamic pooling of cloud resources by live wan migration of virtual machines. In *ACM VEE*, 2011.

[24] Y. Wu and M. Zhao. Performance modeling of virtual machine live migration. In *Proceedings of the 2011 IEEE 4th International Conference on Cloud Computing*. IEEE, 2011.

[25] X. Zhang, Z. Huo, J. Ma, and D. Meng. Exploiting data deduplication to accelerate live virtual machine migration. In *IEEE International Conference on Cluster Computing*, 2010.

[26] M. Zhao and R. J. Figueiredo. Experimental study of virtual machine migration in support of reservation of cluster resources. In *Proceedings of the 2nd international workshop on Virtualization technology in distributed computing*, page 5. ACM, 2007.

[27] J. Zheng, T. S. E. Ng, and K. Sripanidkulchai. Workload-aware live storage migration for clouds. In *ACM VEE*, Apr. 2011.

[28] J. Zheng, T. S. E. Ng, K. Sripanidkulchai, and Z. Liu. Pacer: A progress management system for live virtual machine migration in cloud computing. *IEEE Transactions on Network and Service Management*, 10(4):369–382, Dec 2013.

Friendly Barriers:
Efficient Work-Stealing With Return Barriers *

Vivek Kumar[†], Stephen M. Blackburn[†], David Grove[‡]

[†]Australian National University   [‡]IBM T.J. Watson Research

Abstract

This paper addresses the problem of efficiently supporting parallelism within a managed runtime. A popular approach for exploiting software parallelism on parallel hardware is task parallelism, where the programmer explicitly identifies potential parallelism and the runtime then schedules the work. Work-stealing is a promising scheduling strategy that a runtime may use to keep otherwise idle hardware busy while relieving overloaded hardware of its burden. However, work-stealing comes with substantial overheads. Recent work identified *sequential* overheads of work-stealing, those that occur even when no stealing takes place, as a significant source of overhead. That work was able to reduce sequential overheads to just 15% [21].

In this work, we turn to *dynamic* overheads, those that occur each time a steal takes place. We show that the dynamic overhead is dominated by introspection of the victim's stack when a steal takes place. We exploit the idea of a low overhead return barrier to reduce the dynamic overhead by approximately *half*, resulting in total performance improvements of as much as 20%. Because, unlike prior work, we attack the overheads directly due to stealing and therefore attack the overheads that grow as parallelism grows, we improve the scalability of work-stealing applications. This result is complementary to recent work addressing the sequential overheads of work-stealing. This work therefore substantially relieves work-stealing of the increasing pressure due to increasing intra-node hardware parallelism.

Categories and Subject Descriptors   D1.3 [*Software*]: Concurrent Programming – Parallel programming; D3.4 [*Programming Languages*]: Processors – Code generation; Compilers; Optimization; Run-time environments.

General Terms   Design, Languages, Performance.

Keywords   Scheduling, Task Parallelism, Work-Stealing, X10, Managed Languages.

* This work is supported by IBM and ARC LP0989872. Any opinions, findings and conclusions expressed herein are the authors' and do not necessarily reflect those of the sponsors.

1. Introduction

This paper is concerned with the efficient support for dynamic task parallelism within managed runtimes. Parallelism is a critical concern as improvements in on-chip performance are now delivered through hardware parallelism rather than clock scaling — single nodes can now scale to over one hundred cores.

Dynamic task parallelism is a popular strategy for exposing software parallelism to the underlying hardware. The programmer exposes the parallelism and the problem of scheduling that work is delegated to a supporting library or runtime. Work-stealing has emerged as a popular strategy for scheduling task parallel work [8, 12, 22, 28]. However, there are significant overheads associated with work-stealing, both *sequential* ones, that manifest whether or not stealing takes place, and *dynamic* ones, that manifest when stealing occurs. Our paper addresses dynamic work-stealing overheads, with the goal of improving the efficiency and scalability of intra-node parallelism.

Work-stealing has a long history which includes lazy task creation [26] and the MIT Cilk project [12], which offered both a theoretical and practical framework. It has also been adopted by more recent languages including X10 [8], which we use as the context for the work we present here. X10 is designed to ease programming of scalable concurrent and distributed systems, with explicit constructs for parallelism and data distribution. X10 uses a *finish/async* idiom to capture software parallelism, and its runtimes use work-stealing to efficiently schedule the work. Although the work we present here is evaluated in the context of X10, work-stealing has much broader application, and we hope that our insights will be applicable beyond this specific context.

Kumar et al. demonstrate that work-stealing overheads can be as high as $4\times$. They evaluate work-stealing overheads in X10 and attack the problem of *sequential* overheads; those that manifest independent of the level of actual parallelism. They reduced the sequential overheads due to work-stealing in X10 from around $4\times$ to 15%. They achieved this through three principal means: a) using the victim's execution stack as an *implicit* deque; b) modifying the runtime to extract execution state directly from the victim's stack and registers; and c) using the exception handling mechanism to dynamically switch to different versions of code between the thief and victim.

In this work, we attack the *dynamic* overheads of work-stealing; those that manifest as steal rates grow, and are thus most evident when parallelism is greatest. As core counts increase, dynamic overheads are an increasingly important factor in the performance of work-stealing runtimes. We identify walking the victim's execution stack at every steal as the major dynamic cost. We address this problem by using a *return barrier* [36] to reduce the time spent scanning the stack. This reduces dynamic overheads by around 50%, leading to total performance improvements of up to 20%.

The system we improve upon is already high performance. In Section 6.5 we compare our system directly against the Fork-Join and Habanero-Java frameworks, two other widely used frameworks that use work-stealing, evaluating all three against a straightforward sequential Java baseline. We show that our system is highly competitive. It consistently performs well, and in three out of six workloads it substantially outperforms the other systems (from 50% to 6× better).

The principal contributions of this paper are as follows: a) a detailed study of the *dynamic* costs of work-stealing — costs associated with stealing work from victims; b) an approach for reducing this overhead and c) evaluation of our new design using classical work-stealing benchmarks.

The rest of the paper is structured as follows. Section 2 provides the relevant background. Section 3 discusses our evaluation methodology. Section 4 discusses the motivation for this work. Section 5 explains the design of our new system. Section 6 discusses the performance evaluation of our new design. Section 7 discusses the related work and finally section 8 concludes the paper.

2. Background

This section provides a brief overview of key background material, including return barriers, work-stealing and X10.

2.1 Return Barriers

A return barrier, like a write barrier, allows the runtime to intercept a common event, and (conditionally) interpose special semantics. In the case of a write barrier, a runtime typically interposes itself on pointer field updates, conditionally remembering updates of pointers in certain conditions. On the other hand, a return barrier [36], interposes special semantics upon the return from a method (which corresponds to the popping of a stack frame). One use for a return barrier is to keep track of a 'low water mark' for each stack since some particular event, such as the last garbage collection. In a language where pointers into the stack are not permitted, there is a guarantee that no part of the stack below the low water mark has been changed since the low water mark was set. This information can be used to reduce the overhead of stack scanning. In our work, we use a return barrier to 'protect' the victim from stumbling upon a thief introspecting the victim's stack.

```
1 foo() {
2   val X:Int;
3   val Y:Int;
4   finish {
5     async X = S1();
6     Y = S2();
7   }
8 }
```

Figure 1. X10's `finish-async` style programming model.

2.2 Work-stealing

Work-stealing is a strategy for efficiently distributing work in a parallel system. The runtime maintains a pool of *worker threads*, each of which maintains a set of *tasks*. When local work runs out, the worker becomes a *thief* and seeks out a *victim* thread from which to *steal* work. A steal occurs when a thief takes work from a victim. The runtime provides the thief with the execution context of the stolen work, including the execution entry point and sufficient program state for execution to proceed. The runtime ensures that work is executed exactly once and that the state of the program reflects the contributions of all workers.

2.3 X10

X10 is a strongly-typed, imperative, class-based, object-oriented programming language. X10 includes specific features to support parallel and distributed programming. A computation in X10 consists of one or more asynchronous activities (light-weight tasks). A new activity, S, is created by the statement `async` S. To synchronize activities, X10 provides the statement `finish` S. Control will not return from within a finish until all activities spawned within the scope of the finish have terminated. Figure 1 shows X10's `finish-async` programming model. X10 is implemented via compilation to either C++ (*native X10*) or Java (*managed X10*).

2.4 DefaultWS work-stealing framework

We use as our baseline the low-overhead work-stealing framework, JavaWS (Try-Catch), developed by Kumar et al. [21]. As demonstrated in that previous work, this framework achieves both good scalability and good absolute performance and is therefore a strong foundation for our work. The baseline framework supports managed X10 and uses the Jikes RVM [2] Java runtime. As in [21] the benchmark programs operate directly on Java arrays to avoid the sequential array access overhead of managed X10. In the rest of the paper we simply refer to this system as DefaultWS.

DefaultWS relies on: yieldpoints [3], on-stack replacement [11], dynamic code-patching [32], and exception handling. These fundamental mechanisms are already available in most production JVMs. The key engineering challenge the DefaultWS solves is how to represent the unusual code structure and control flow implied by the `finish-async`

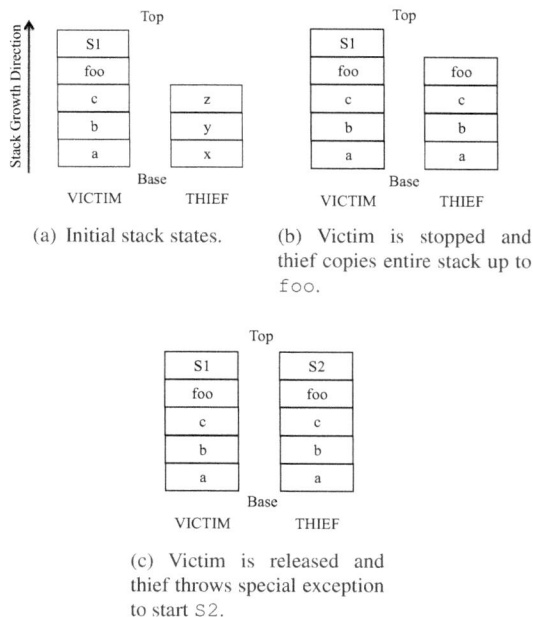

(a) Initial stack states.

(b) Victim is stopped and thief copies entire stack up to `foo`.

(c) Victim is released and thief throws special exception to start S2.

Figure 2. Stack states during a steal procedure.

programming model in a way that facilitates efficient work-stealing. The DefaultWS system does this by re-writing `finish-async` into regular Java and exploiting the semantics Java offers for exception handling, which is very efficiently implemented in most modern JVMs. The result is that the runtime can walk a victim's stack and identify all `async` and `finish` contexts, resulting in a reduction in overhead from $4\times$ to just 15%.

When a thief attempts to steal a task, it first requests the runtime to stop the victim so that it may safely walk the victim's execution stack. If the thief finds a steal-able task, it duplicates the victim's stack before allowing the victim to resume. The thief then runs a modified version of the runtime's exception delivery code to start this stolen task. Figure 2 describes this steal process in DefaultWS. The focus in this paper is on reducing the overheads arising from the thief interrupting the victim, which are incurred every time there is an attempt to steal.

We now conduct a quantitative analysis to characterize the dynamic overheads of workstealing.

3. Methodology

In Section 4 we conduct an analysis to motivate the problem we address. Before presenting that analysis, we briefly outline our experimental methodology, which is also used in the analysis of our solution, presented in Section 6.

3.1 Benchmarks

Because the primary goal of our work is to reduce the cost of steal operations, we have intentionally selected some of our benchmarks with high steal rates (they are available at

http://cs.anu.edu.au/~vivek/ws-vee-2014/). DefaultWS almost completely eliminates the sequential overheads. This avoids the need to control task granularity and enhances programmer's productivity. The programmer only need to expose parallelism without worrying about the sequential per-task overhead. Most of our benchmarks follow this approach.

In each case we ported the benchmark to plain Java (for the sequential case). This sequential version does not have any work-stealing specific calls and also does not have any synchronization constructs. The managed X10 compiler automatically generates the Jikes RVM work-stealing runtime calls from the X10 version of benchmarks. Our six benchmarks are:

Jacobi Iterative mesh relaxation with barriers: 10 steps of nearest neighbor averaging on 1024×1024 matrices of doubles (based on an algorithm taken from Fork-Join).

FFT This is a Cooley-Tukey Fast Fourier Transform algorithm (adopted from Cilk). Input size is 1024×1024.

CilkSort A divide and conquer variant of mergesort (adopted from Cilk) for sorting 10 million integers.

Barnes-Hut A n-body algorithm to calculate gravitational forces acting on a galactic cluster of 100000 bodies. Adopted from Lonestar benchmark suite [20].

UTS The unbalanced tree search benchmark designed in [27]. We have used their tree type T2.

LUD Decomposition of 1024×1024 matrices of doubles (adopted from Cilk).

3.2 Hardware Platform

All experiments were run on a dual-socket machine with two Intel Xeon E5-2450 Sandy Bridge processors. Each processor has eight cores running at 2.10 GHz sharing a 20 MB L3 cache. The machine was configured with 47 GB of memory.

3.3 Software Platform

Jikes RVM Version 3.1.3. We used the production build. This is used as the Java runtime for managed X10. The command line arguments we used are: -Xms1024M -X:gc:variableSizeHeap=false -X:gc:threads=1.

OpenJDK 64-Bit Server VM (build 20.0-b12, mixed mode).

Fork-Join Java Fork-Join work-stealing framework [22]. Version 1.7.0.

Habanero-Java A work-stealing framework from Rice University, which uses X10's `finish-async` style in the Java programming language [7]. Version 1.3.1. We were unable to compile the benchmarks with the adaptive runtime of Habanero-Java. We build with both work-first and help-first policies and report the time from the policy which performs best for a particular benchmark.

We ported JavaWS (Try-Catch) of Kumar et al. from version 3.1.2 of Jikes RVM to version 3.1.3. This also includes one bug fix. In the original system the thief performs a small pause in the case when it fails to find a victim from any worker. After this pause, the thief reiterates searching for a victim. The downside of the pause is minimal in the case of infrequent steals, however even this small pause becomes a measurable overhead in frequent stealing. Hence, we modified JavaWS (Try-Catch) and allow the thief to continuously spin, searching for victims. This same setting is used in default work-stealing implementation of X10.

3.4 Measurements

For each benchmark, we ran twenty invocations, with fifteen iterations per invocation where each iteration performed the kernel of the benchmark. We report the mean of the final five iterations, along with a 95% confidence interval based on a Student t-test. For each invocation of the benchmark, the total number of garbage collector threads is kept as one. We report the mutator time only in all the experiments.

4. Motivating Analysis

Although work-stealing is a very promising mechanism for exploiting software parallelism, it can bring with it formidable overheads to the simple sequential case. Kumar et al. [21] exploited rich features that pre-exist within the JVM implementation to significantly reduce these overheads from around $4\times$ to 15% [21]. We use their system to further attack the problem of *dynamic* overheads — those associated with the cost of each steal — which increase as parallelism increases. Our approach is also to exploit highly optimized features within the runtime.

The principal sequential costs relate to organizing normal computation in such a way as to facilitate movement of a task to another thread if a steal should happen to occur. On the other hand, the principal cost in the dynamic case lies in synchronizing victim and thief threads at the time of a steal to ensure that the thief is able to take the victim's work without tripping upon each other.

Kumar et al. leveraged the runtime's yieldpoint mechanism to yield the victim while each steal took place. The yieldpoint mechanism is designed precisely for preemption of threads and has been highly optimized. When a thief initiates a steal, it sets a yield bit in the victim's runtime state. The next time the victim executes a yieldpoint, it will see the yield bit and yield to the thief. The JVM's JIT compiler injects yieldpoints on method prologues and loop back edges, tightly bounding the time it takes the victim to yield. Notwithstanding the efficiency of the yieldpoint mechanism, this approach nonetheless requires the victim to yield for the duration of the steal, whether or not the steal is successful.

To shed light on the dynamic costs due to stealing and further motivate our design, we now measure 1) the steal

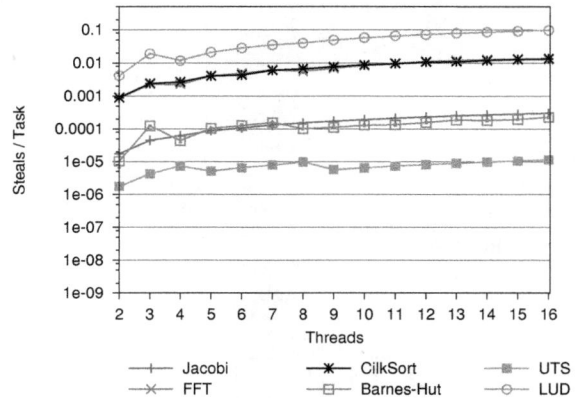

Figure 3. Steal *ratio*, as a function of thread count.

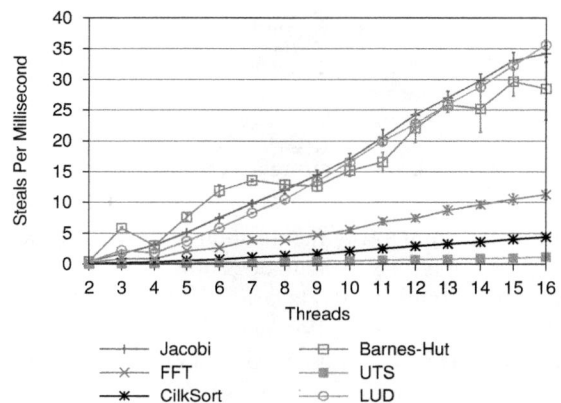

Figure 4. Steal *rate* as a function of thread count.

rate (steals/msec), and 2) the overhead imposed by the steal mechanism upon the victims.

4.1 Steal Rate

The steal *ratio* (Figure 3) is only one dimension of the steal overheads. We also measure the steal *rate* (steals per millisecond), which is shown in Figure 4. Steal rate is calculated by dividing the total number of steals by the benchmark execution time. This indicates how frequently we are forcing the victim to execute the yieldpoint.

From Figure 3, we can notice that the steal *ratio* for Jacobi at 16 threads is as low as 0.0004. However, out of all the benchmarks, Jacobi has the highest *rate* of almost 35 steals per millisecond with same number of threads. This result shows that even a benchmark with very low steal ratio can still have a very high steal rate. In our next study we will explore how the high steal rates can affect the overall performance of the benchmarks.

4.2 Steal Overhead

In this study, we measure the cost of steals as imposed upon the victim by the thief. We measure this by calculating the

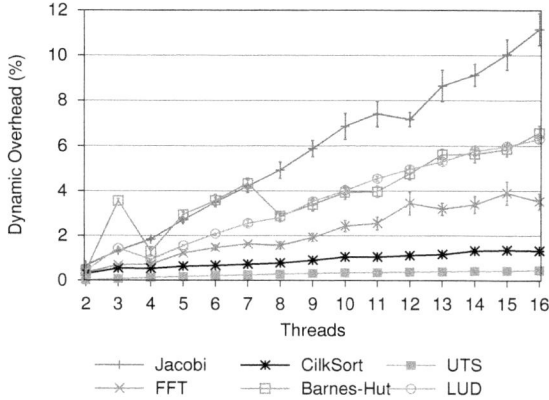

Figure 5. Dynamic overhead as a function of thread count.

percentage of CPU cycles lost by the victim while waiting for the thief to release it from the yieldpoint. For measuring the CPU cycles utilized by the work-stealing threads, we use hardware performance counters. We use the time stamp counter (TSC) [18] for measuring the cycles lost by the victim waiting to be released from yieldpoint. These cycles are summed for all the steals over the benchmark execution. The result in Figure 5 is calculated by dividing these cycles by total program execution cycles obtained from hardware performance counters as mentioned above.

By comparing this overhead in Figure 5 with the steal rate in Figure 4, we can see that higher steal rates correlate with higher overheads. The steal overhead can even be as much as 11.2% (Jacobi with 16 threads). This study clearly shows that forcing the victim to wait inside a yieldpoint at every steal is not an efficient strategy.

5. Design and Implementation

The previous sections identified the problem of dynamic overhead in a work-stealing runtime, highlighting the inefficiency of forcing the victim to wait inside a yieldpoint each time an attempt is made to steal work from it. We approach the problem by using a return barrier [36], to 'protect' the victim from any thief, which may be performing a steal lower down on the victim's stack. The insight is that the cost of the barrier is only incurred each time the victim unwinds past the barrier. So long as the victim remains above the protected frame, it sees no cost at all, and yet is fully protected from any thief stealing work lower down on the stack.

We now discuss the design and implementation of our return barrier, and the modifications made to DefaultWS (section 2.4).

5.1 Return Barrier Implementation

We use a return barrier to 'protect' the victim from stumbling upon an active thief. We do this by installing a return barrier above the stealable frames, allowing the victim to ignore all steal activity that occurs below the frame in which the barrier

is installed. Only when the frame above the return barrier is unwound does the victim need to consider the possibility of an active thief.

A naive implementation of a return barrier would require some (modest) code to be executed upon every return, just as a write barrier is typically executed upon every pointer update. Instead we use an approach similar to that of Yuasa [36]. We hijack the return address for a given frame, redirecting it to point to a special return barrier trampoline method, remembering the original return address is a separate data structure. When the affected frame is unwound, the return takes execution to our trampoline method rather than the caller of the returning frame. The trampoline method executes the return barrier semantics (which may include re-installing the return barrier at a lower frame), before returning to the correct calling frame (whose address was remembered in a side data structure). This barrier has absolutely no overhead in the common case, and only incurs a modest cost when the frame targeted by the return barrier is unwound.

We can use the return barrier trampoline to protect the victim from active thieves — ensuring that the victim never unwinds to a frame a thief is actively stealing. We now discuss the general process of stealing work before detailing how we use the return barrier to perform efficient work-stealing.

5.2 Overview of Conventional Steal Process

Before describing our return barrier-based implementation, we outline the steps used to perform a steal in the prior implementation. In this process the thief steals the *oldest unstolen* continuation from the victim.

1. The *thief* **initiates** a steal.

2. The *victim* **yields** execution at the next yieldpoint.

3. The *thief* performs a **walk** of the victim's stack to find the oldest *unstolen* continuation frame.

4. The *thief* adjusts the return addresses of the callee of the stolen continuation to ensure the unstolen callee is correctly **joined** with the stolen continuation upon return.

5. The *thief* **copies** the frame of the stolen continuation and those of each of its callers onto a secondary stack in the following steps:

   - The *thief* **links** the copied frame on the secondary stack.

   - The *thief* **scans** callee frames to capture any references pertinent to the stolen frames. This is necessary due to the callee-save calling conventions used by many compilers.

6. The *victim* **resumes** execution.

7. The *thief* **throws** a special exception, which has the effect of resuming its execution on the secondary stack (which is now its primary stack).

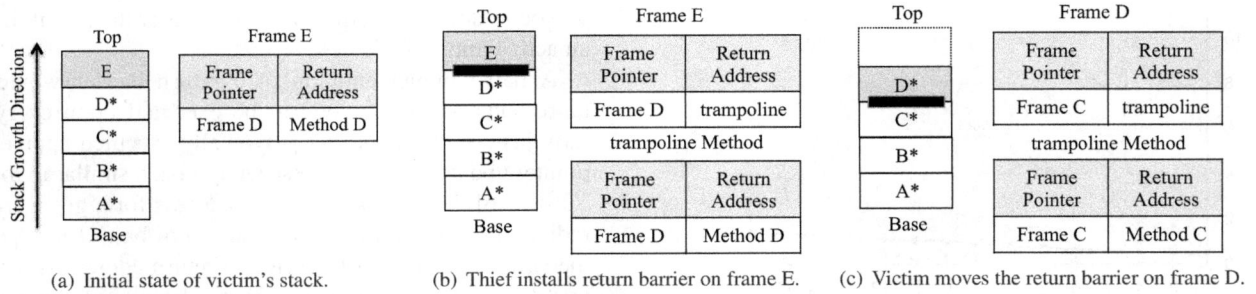

Figure 6. The victim's stack, installation, and movement of the return barrier.

Notice that the victim must yield to the thief throughout steps 2 to 6. We now discuss how the return barrier can be used to avoid such yields when possible.

5.3 Installing the First Return Barrier

Figure 6(a) depicts a typical snapshot of a victim's execution stack. The stack frames with stealable continuations are marked with a * in this figure. The newly executed methods occupy the stack frame slots on the top of the execution stack. Each stack frame is recognized with the help of a frame pointer. The value stored inside this pointer is the frame pointer of the last executed method. The other information of interest to us is the return address, which holds the address where the control should be transferred after unwinding to the caller frame.

Once the thief has decided to rob this victim, it first checks whether a return barrier is already installed on the victim's execution stack. If it discovers that there is no return barrier installed, the thief then stops the victim by forcing it to execute the yieldpoint mechanism (steal step 2). Once the victim has stopped, the thief starts walking the stack frames to identify the oldest unstolen continuation (steal step 3). In our example, it is the frame A. However, before the thief reaches frame A, it notices that the first (newest) available continuation is D. It installs a return barrier to intercept the return from method E to D. The return address and return frame pointer in E is hijacked by the return barrier trampoline. The return address stored in E is changed to that of the return barrier trampoline method. Figure 6(b) depicts the victim's modified execution stack.

The victim holds two boolean fields *stealInProgress* and *safeToUnwindBarrier*, which are now marked as *true* and *false* respectively by the thief. The flag *stealInProgress* is marked as *false* at the end of steal step 5, whereas *safeToUnwindBarrier* is marked *true* at the end of steal step 3. After installing the return barrier, the thief clones the *entire* stack of the victim and then allows the victim to continue. The victim continues the rest of its computation (i.e. frame E), oblivious to the activity of the thief, while the thief proceeds further with the stack walk in steal step 3. However, the thief now switches to the cloned stack of the victim.

5.4 Synchronization Between Thief and Victim During Steal Process

When the victim finishes executing method E, it returns via the trampoline method of the return barrier. It checks whether *safeToUnwindBarrier* is *true*. In this example, we assume it is still *false*.

Apart from the above two boolean flags, the victim also has a fixed size address array (we used size 20) to store frame pointers of its unstolen continuations. During the stack walk up to frame A, the thief updates the victim's frame pointer address array with the frame pointers of C and B (unstolen continuations). However, in reality there could be some unstealable frames in between stealable frames D–A. To make the description simpler, we have chosen this layout. In cases where there are more continuations than the victim's address array size, the thief starts inserting the surplus addresses from the middle index. After completing steal step 3 the thief marks the flag *safeToUnwindBarrier* as *true*. The victim is now ready to unwind to frame D.

There are situations when the frame D is the only unstolen continuation remaining on victim's stack. In this case the flag *safeToUnwindBarrier* will be marked as *true* only at the end of steal step 5. In this case, the victim cannot continue in parallel to the steal procedure so must wait on a condition variable until *stealInProgress* is *false*.

5.5 Victim Moves the Return Barrier

In our running example, the victim is now inside the return barrier trampoline method. The thief has finished steal step 3 and marked *safeToUnwindBarrier* as *true*. Frame C is the first frame pointer inside victim's frame pointer address array. Victim changes the position of the return barrier and reinstalls on frame C. After this the victim safely unwinds to frame D and starts execution of the method D. Figure 6(c) shows this newly modified stack frame of the victim. It keeps on changing the return barrier position until the last available frame pointer in its address array.

Once the steal is complete, the thief sets the victim's field *stealInProgress* to *false* and signals the victim. The victim is now ready to branch to join its part of the computation and become a thief itself. Hence, the return barrier helps the victim continue its computation in parallel to thief's steal steps 3–5.

5.6 Stealing From a Victim with Return Barrier Pre-installed

Once installed, the return barrier removes the need for the yieldpoint mechanism in the steal step 2. Any thief that attempts to steal from a stack with the return barrier installed simply marks the victim's field *stealInProgress* as *true* and continues the rest of the steal steps 3–5 concurrently with the victim's computation. The thief uses the cloned stack of the victim (from the previous thief) to complete rest of its steal phases. We call this type of steal a *free steal*. There is no overhead imposed on the victim (unless the victim waits inside trampoline).

6. Results

We begin our evaluation of return barriers by measuring the reduction in dynamic overhead before evaluating the overall performance gain.

6.1 Dynamic Overhead

We measure the dynamic overhead of work-stealing for both the default system and our system using the return-barrier. Our methodology remains same as that used in Section 4.2; we use the TSC to accurately measure the cycles spent waiting for steals and express that as a percentage of total execution time. Figure 7 shows the dynamic overhead in both the systems as a function of the number of worker threads. With 16 worker threads, the dynamic overhead reduces in Jacobi by 29% (i.e. from 11.2% to 8%), in FFT by 40%, in CilkSort by 46%, in UTS by 60%, in LUD by 24%, and in Barnes-Hut by 30%.

Now we explore how the use of the return barrier affects steal rates. Figure 8 compares the total number of steals in ReturnBarrierWS relative to those in DefaultWS. Values above 1.0 represent higher number of steals in ReturnBarrierWS than DefaultWS and vice versa. We observe from these figures that with the exception of CilkSort (at all thread counts) and Barnes-Hut (low thread counts), all other benchmarks exhibit very similar steal rates in both systems. The higher steal rates at low thread counts in Barnes-Hut show up in Figure 7(d) as nullifying the return barrier advantage. On the other hand, the 15% reduction in steals in Cilk-Sort is consistent with the good result seen in Figure 7(c). Aside from these two outliers, ReturnBarrierWS sees a similar steal rate and consistently reduces the dynamic overhead in all other benchmarks.

6.2 Overhead of Executing Return Barrier

We now examine the cost to each thread of using the return barrier. Recall that this cost is only encountered when the stack unwinds to the point where a trampoline is installed. The trampoline is executed and it will either: a) reinstall itself on the next unstolen continuation frame further down

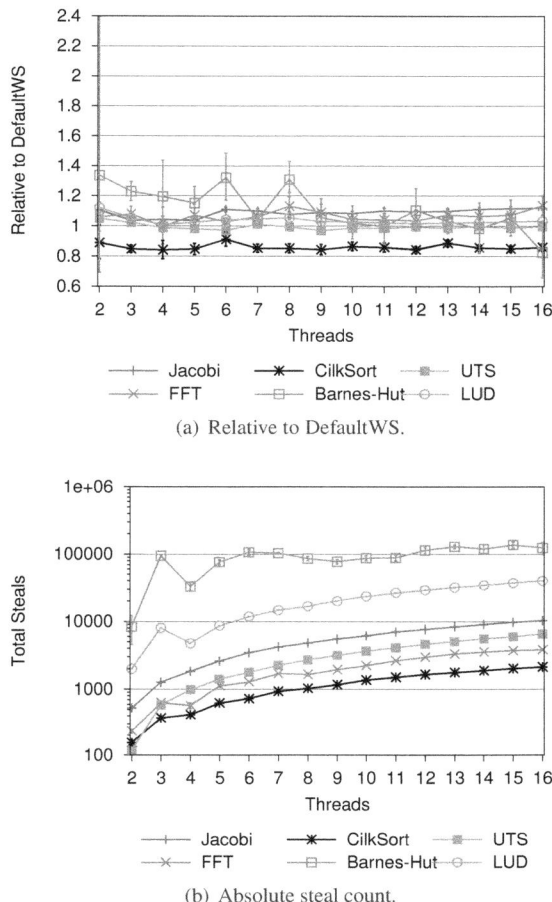

(a) Relative to DefaultWS.

(b) Absolute steal count.

Figure 8. Total steals in ReturnBarrierWS.

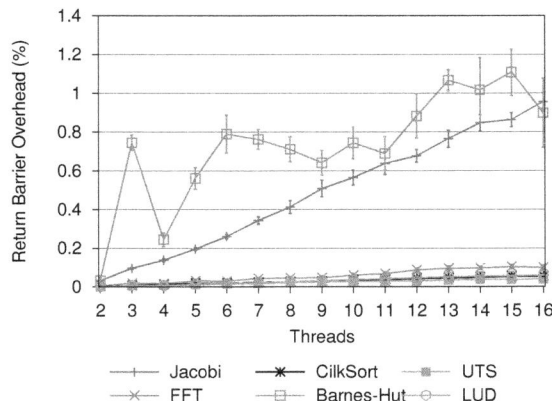

Figure 9. Overhead of executing return barrier in victims.

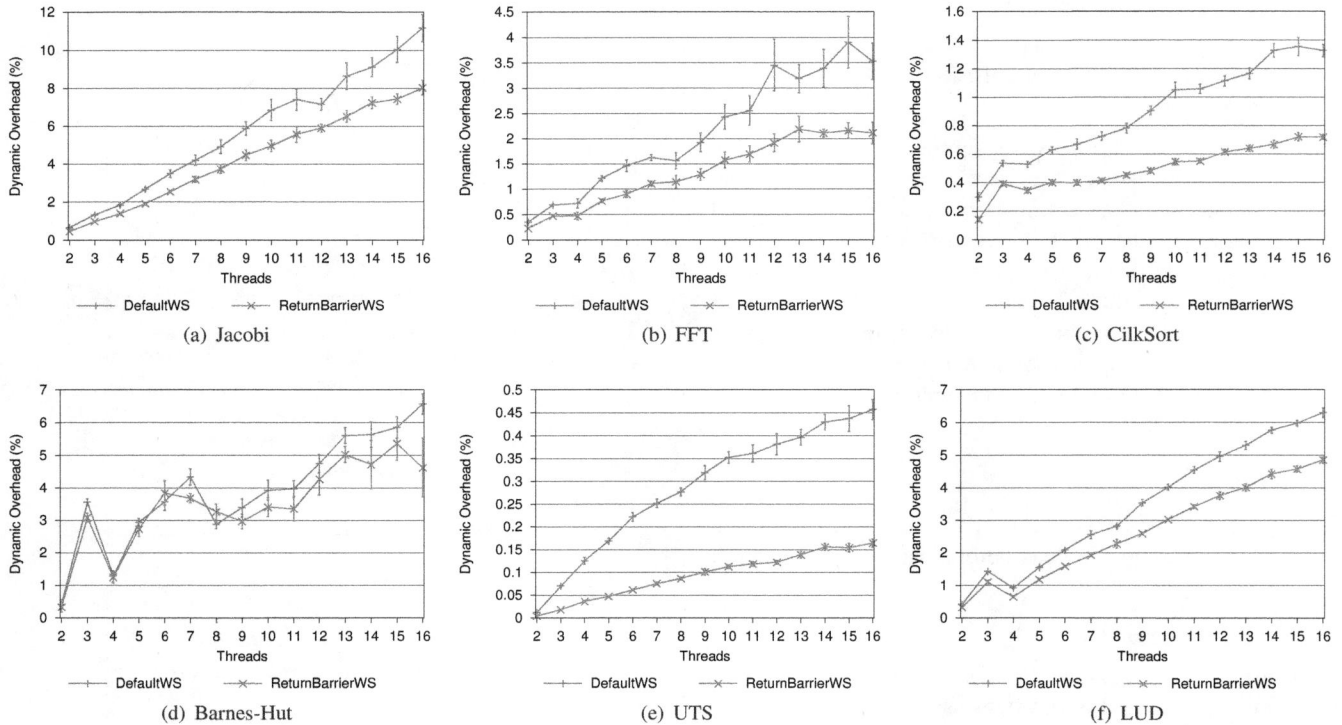

Figure 7. Dynamic overhead in our old and new systems.

before returning to the hijacked frame; or b) wait on a condition lock if there are no more unstolen continuations left and the steal is still in progress. We measure this overhead by using a high-resolution timer and measuring the time spent performing this operation. Figure 9 shows this overhead as a percentage of total program execution. With sixteen worker threads, the maximum overhead is around 0.95% in Jacobi and the minimum is 0.04% in UTS. However, Barnes-Hut shows an overhead of 0.7% even with just 3 threads.

Figure 8(b) shows that Barnes-Hut has the highest number of steals. Even with just three threads, there are around 95000 steals, whereas the closest, LUD, has just 8000 steals. More steals means more frequent trampoline visits by victims. This combined with a shallow stack (Section 6.3) leads to Barnes-Hut showing the highest overhead for the return barrier (max 1.1%).

6.3 Free Steals From Return Barrier

Recall from Section 5.6 that return barriers allow thieves to perform some steals for free. Figure 10 shows the percentage of steals that are free. UTS and CilkSort shows the maximum number of free steals. As the thread count increases, the percentage of free steels for these benchmarks converge close to 30%. FFT has 10% and Jacobi has 7%. Barnes-Hut and LUD have the lowest (3.5% and 1.5% respectively).

A higher free steal count reflects the return barrier staying longer on the victim's stack. This tends to reflect the depth of

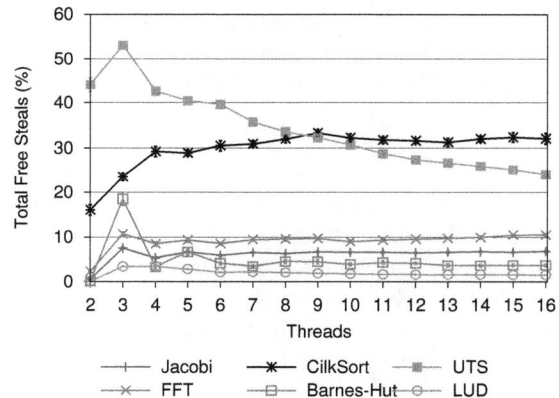

Figure 10. Free steals.

victim's stack. A shallow stack will mean that the victim will tend to more often unwind past the return barrier, meaning that the thief tends to more often require the victim to execute the yieldpoint mechanism. This reduces opportunities for the return barrier to reduce the dynamic overhead. Figure 7 supports this conjecture. LUD and Barnes-Hut benefit the least, whereas UTS and CilkSort benefits the most.

6.4 Overall Work-Stealing Performance

The goal of this work was to reduce dynamic overheads, which are naturally most evident when the level of paral-

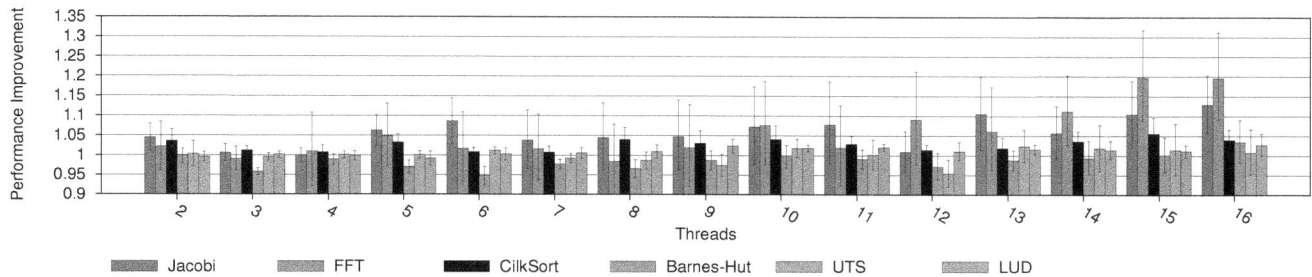

Figure 11. ReturnBarrierWS performance relative to DefaultWS.

lelism is high. Now we explore how the use of the return barrier affects performance when the number of threads grows to 16. In Section 6.5 we add a speedup comparison to the Fork-Join framework and Habanero-Java.

Figure 11 shows speedup relative to DefaultWS for each of the benchmarks on our 16 core machine. The time with n worker threads in ReturnBarrierWS is normalized to the time for n worker threads in DefaultWS. Values above 1.0 reflect a benefit. We can expect benefits at high steal rates, which also happens as parallelism increases. Jacobi reaches the 10% mark with 13 threads. With 16 threads, Jacobi is 13% faster and FFT is 20% faster. CilkSort gets a maximum benefit of 5% (15 threads). UTS, LUD and Barnes-Hut almost remains unchanged.

The absence of a performance improvement in LUD and Barnes-Hut is despite the fact that their maximum dynamic overheads (close to 6%) are even higher than that of FFT (3.5%). The reason for this is little improvement in their dynamic overheads due to the presence of a shallow stack (Section 6.3). On the other hand, UTS already has very low dynamic overhead in DefaultWS (max 0.5%). This results in no benefit in performance even by reducing its dynamic overhead by 60%.

6.5 Comparison to Fork-Join and Habanero-Java

The Fork-Join framework [22], which is now a part of Java 7, is a widely used work-stealing framework. Habanero-Java is another such project, which is inspired from X10 and is actively being used [7, 13, 14, 23, 34, 37]. To determine the performance of our system, we now do a speedup comparison with Fork-Join and Habanero-Java on all our benchmarks. We measure speedup relative to the sequential Java version of each benchmark.

From the speedup graph in Figure 12, we can see that ReturnBarrierWS achieves significantly better speedup on Jacobi, FFT, CilkSort and Barnes-Hut than both the other systems. For UTS, ReturnBarrierWS performs similar to Fork-Join but better than Habanero-Java (threads 2 to 10). LUD performs better in Habanero-Java than both ReturnBarrierWS and Fork-Join. However, the gap in LUD speedup across all the three systems is not very wide.

One interesting point to notice is the poor speedup of Barnes-Hut and Jacobi in Fork-Join and Habanero-Java. Compared to the sequential Java version, single threaded Barnes-Hut is 83% slower in Fork-Join, 95% slower in Habanero-Java and 30% slower in ReturnBarrierWS. Similarly, Jacobi is 70% slower in Fork-Join, 90% slower in Habanero-Java and 10% slower in ReturnBarrierWS. The large slowdown in Fork-Join and Habanero-Java is because of the sequential overheads of work-stealing. Kumar et al.'s work, which we build upon, successfully attacked sequential overheads, leading to the good underlying performance we see here. To verify our findings, we also ran Barnes-Hut and Jacobi on both Fork-Join and Habanero-Java with OpenJDK JVM and observe the same behavior. This verified our belief that its the sequential overhead that is taking the toll on these two benchmarks.

6.6 Summary

These encouraging results demonstrate that our approach is effective at reducing the dynamic overhead and also improves scalability. Our approach therefore promises improved performance with increasing parallelism. However, even for benchmarks with very small dynamic overhead, our approach does not negatively affect performance.

7. Related Work

Stealing overheads In our work-stealing implementation, we steal only one task at a time as in native X10, Cilk, Fork-Join etc. Though stealing one task at a time has been shown to be sufficient to optimize computation along the 'critical path' to within a constant factor [4, 6], several authors have argued that the scheme can be improved by allowing multiple tasks to be stolen at a time [5]. Dinan et al. [10] demonstrate that a 'steal-half' policy gave the best performance in their distributed setting. Stealing multiple tasks in a distributed setting has proven to be better in several other studies [24, 25, 29]. Guo et al. [13] introduce and evaluate the *help first* scheduling policy for the scalability of depth first search algorithms. Cong et al. [9] explore the idea of adaptive task batching for irregular graph algorithms. The thieves steal a batch of tasks at a time, where the batch size is determined adaptively. Several other authors have also ar-

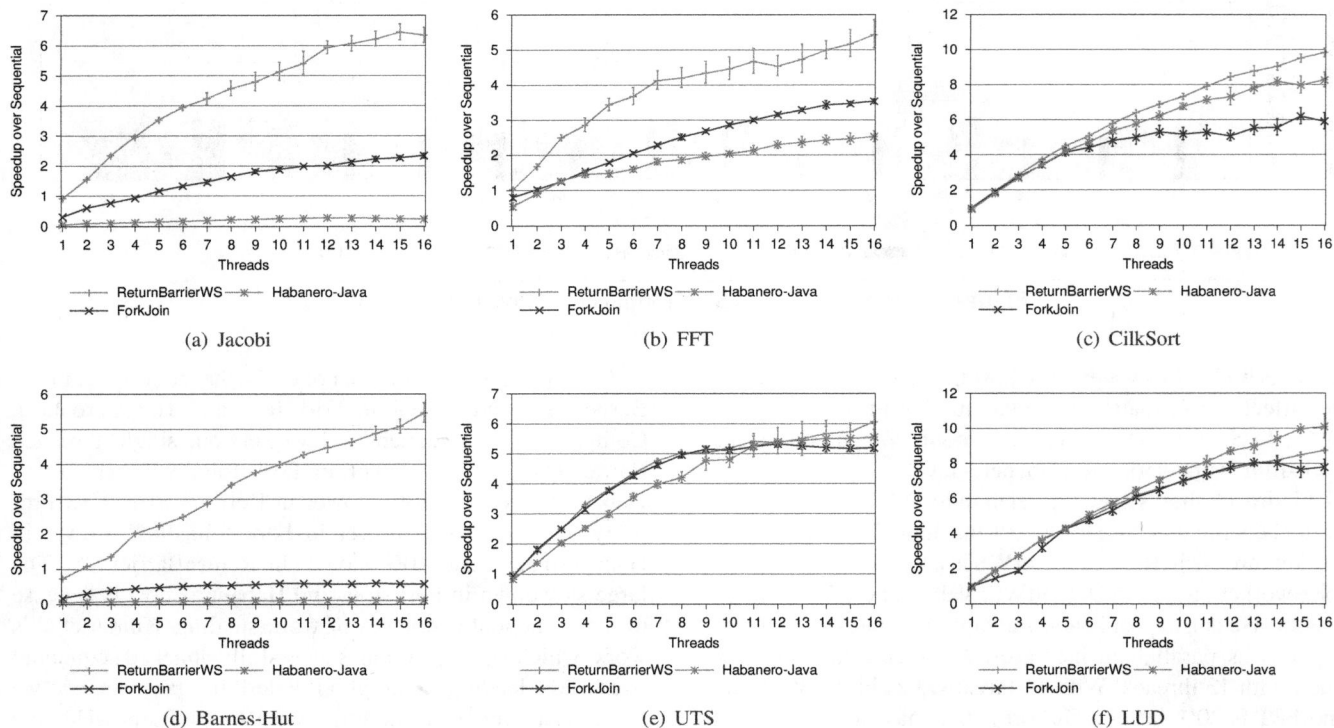

Figure 12. Speedup over sequential Java.

gued that stealing multiple tasks works best in irregular algorithms [1, 15, 16, 31].

These studies show that stealing multiple tasks is better in two cases: a) when performing work-stealing over a distributed setting, where the cost of stealing from remote node is substantial and hence stealing multiple tasks amortizes the communication overhead; and b) in irregular problems, such as depth-first-search algorithm, that do not fit into the divide-and-conquer model. However, not all the workloads are irregular in design nor do all follow the divide-and-conquer style algorithm, where the steal one approach always works better in non-distributed setting. Though we have targeted divide-and-conquer style algorithms, our insight of using a return barrier to reduce the cost of stealing will perform well in irregular algorithms as well.

Our return barrier mechanism for work-stealing and the framework by Kumar et al. on which it is built have some similarity with Umatani et al.'s work [33]. The fundamental insight is the same in both systems: work-stealing overheads can be significantly reduced by deferring operations that most other work-stealing systems perform eagerly. However, the systems are different in a number of ways including: a) In their system a thread starts with stack allocated activation frames. They consider steals to be very infrequent and hence at every steal, the victim heap allocates all of its continuations and stores on its deque. This greatly differs from our system. Frames in our system are always part of exe-

cution stack and simply copied from victim to thief's execution stack (not heap allocated). As reported in Section 4, steals are not always infrequent and hence Umatani et al.'s assumption would lead to large overheads in those cases. b) To start a stolen task, explicitly saved states have to be restored from heap. In DefaultWS, states are already a part of an execution stack and our thief merely throws a special exception to launch the stolen task. c) In their system, when the victim's stack is empty, it tries to get an unstolen heap frame from its deque. This transition between stack to deque can be thought of as a return barrier. For the first steal, victim required synchronization and then again while fetching a heap allocated frame. However, we use explicit return barriers as we treat the victim's execution stack as its implicit deque. d) They used only two microbenchmarks (Fibonacci and Matmul) to evaluate their implementation. We don't have access to their versions of these two tests, but the data presented in their paper suggests that the sequential overhead on their improved system for these two tests is about 57% and 20% respectively. For the same microbenchmarks, Kumar et al. see sequential overheads on JavaWS (Try-Catch) of 35% and 18% respectively. Like Kumar et al., we too use more benchmarks including several real world benchmarks.

Return barriers The return barrier mechanism was first used in [17] in the context of debugging optimized code, to allow lazy dynamic deoptimization of the stack. It has also been used in various garbage collector algorithms [19, 30, 35, 36]. In this work, we exploit the return barrier mechanism to optimize the steal process. To our knowledge, return barriers have not been applied to work-stealing until now.

8. Conclusion

Effectively exposing software parallelism to underlying hardware is a pressing issue, a problem addressed by task-based scheduling offered by systems such as the Fork-Join framework and languages such as X10 and Habanero-Java. These systems use work-stealing to schedule work across the underlying parallel hardware. Unfortunately work-stealing comes with significant overheads. In this work, we identify victim yields as a major source of remaining overhead, and show that a return barrier can be used to greatly reduce this source of overhead. The return barrier allows a thief to steal from a victim's stack without requiring the victim to yield in the common case. Our technique enables improvements of as much as 20% in total execution time. The extremely low dynamic overhead should enable increasing speedups with the increasing parallelism in modern hardware.

References

[1] U. A. Acar, A. Chargueraud, and M. Rainey. Scheduling parallel programs by work stealing with private deques. In *Proceedings of the 18th ACM SIGPLAN Symposium on Principles and Practice of Parallel Programming*, PPoPP '13, pages 219–228, New York, NY, USA, 2013. ACM. ISBN 978-1-4503-1922-5. doi: 10.1145/2442516.2442538.

[2] B. Alpern, C. Attanasio, J. Barton, M. Burke, P. Cheng, J. Choi, A. Cocchi, S. Fink, D. Grove, M. Hind, et al. The Jalapeño virtual machine. *IBM Systems Journal*, 39(1):211–238, 2010. ISSN 0018-8670. doi: 10.1147/sj.391.0211.

[3] M. Arnold, S. Fink, D. Grove, M. Hind, and P. F. Sweeney. Adaptive optimization in the Jalapeño JVM. In *Proceedings of the 15th ACM International Conference on Object Oriented Programming Systems Languages and Applications*, OOPSLA '00, pages 47–65, New York, NY, USA, 2000. ACM. ISBN 1-58113-200-X. doi: 10.1145/353171.353175.

[4] N. S. Arora, R. D. Blumofe, and C. G. Plaxton. Thread scheduling for multiprogrammed multiprocessors. In *Proceedings of the Tenth Annual ACM Symposium on Parallel Algorithms and Architectures*, SPAA '98, pages 119–129, New York, NY, USA, 1998. ACM. ISBN 0-89791-989-0. doi: 10.1145/277651.277678.

[5] P. Berenbrink, T. Friedetzky, and L. A. Goldberg. The natural work-stealing algorithm is stable. *SIAM J. Comput.*, 32(5):1260–1279, May 2003. ISSN 0097-5397. doi: 10.1137/S0097539701399551.

[6] R. D. Blumofe and C. E. Leiserson. Scheduling multithreaded computations by work stealing. *J. ACM*, 46(5):720–748, Sept. 1999. ISSN 0004-5411. doi: 10.1145/324133.324234.

[7] V. Cavé, J. Zhao, J. Shirako, and V. Sarkar. Habanero-Java: the new adventures of old X10. In *Proceedings of the 9th International Conference on Principles and Practice of Programming in Java*, PPPJ '11, pages 51–61, New York, NY, USA,

2011. ACM. ISBN 978-1-4503-0935-6. doi: 10.1145/2093157.2093165.

[8] P. Charles, C. Grothoff, V. Saraswat, C. Donawa, A. Kielstra, K. Ebcioglu, C. von Praun, and V. Sarkar. X10: An object-oriented approach to non-uniform cluster computing. In *Proceedings of the 20th Annual ACM SIGPLAN Conference on Object Oriented Programming Systems Languages and Applications*, OOPSLA '05, pages 519–538, New York, NY, USA, 2005. ACM. ISBN 1-59593-031-0. doi: 10.1145/1094811.1094852.

[9] G. Cong, S. Kodali, S. Krishnamoorthy, D. Lea, V. Saraswat, and T. Wen. Solving large, irregular graph problems using adaptive work-stealing. In *Proceedings of the 2008 37th International Conference on Parallel Processing*, ICPP '08, pages 536–545, Washington, DC, USA, 2008. IEEE Computer Society. ISBN 978-0-7695-3374-2. doi: 10.1109/ICPP.2008.88.

[10] J. Dinan, D. B. Larkins, P. Sadayappan, S. Krishnamoorthy, and J. Nieplocha. Scalable work stealing. In *Proceedings of the Conference on High Performance Computing Networking, Storage and Analysis*, SC '09, pages 53:1–53:11, New York, NY, USA, 2009. ACM. ISBN 978-1-60558-744-8. doi: 10.1145/1654059.1654113.

[11] S. J. Fink and F. Qian. Design, implementation and evaluation of adaptive recompilation with on-stack replacement. In *Proceedings of the International Symposium on Code Generation and Optimization: Feedback-directed and Runtime Optimization*, CGO '03, pages 241–252, Washington, DC, USA, 2003. IEEE Computer Society. ISBN 0-7695-1913-X.

[12] M. Frigo, H. Prokop, M. Frigo, C. Leiserson, H. Prokop, S. Ramachandran, D. Dailey, C. Leiserson, I. Lyubashevskiy, N. Kushman, et al. The Cilk project. *Algorithms*, 1998.

[13] Y. Guo, R. Barik, R. Raman, and V. Sarkar. Work-first and help-first scheduling policies for async-finish task parallelism. In *Proceedings of the 2009 IEEE International Symposium on Parallel & Distributed Processing*, IPDPS '09, pages 1–12, Washington, DC, USA, 2009. IEEE Computer Society. ISBN 978-1-4244-3751-1. doi: 10.1109/IPDPS.2009.5161079.

[14] Y. Guo, J. Zhao, V. Cave, and V. Sarkar. SLAW: A scalable locality-aware adaptive work-stealing scheduler for multicore systems. In *Proceedings of the 15th ACM SIGPLAN Symposium on Principles and Practice of Parallel Programming*, PPoPP '10, pages 341–342, New York, NY, USA, 2010. ACM. ISBN 978-1-60558-877-3. doi: 10.1145/1693453.1693504.

[15] D. Hendler and N. Shavit. Non-blocking steal-half work queues. In *Proceedings of the Twenty-first Annual Symposium on Principles of Distributed Computing*, PODC '02, pages 280–289, New York, NY, USA, 2002. ACM. ISBN 1-58113-485-1. doi: 10.1145/571825.571876.

[16] R. Hoffmann and T. Rauber. Adaptive task pools: efficiently balancing large number of tasks on shared-address spaces. *International Journal of Parallel Programming*, 39(5):553–581, 2011.

[17] U. Hölzle, C. Chambers, and D. Ungar. Debugging optimized code with dynamic deoptimization. In *Proceedings of the ACM SIGPLAN 1992 Conference on Programming Language Design and Implementation*, PLDI '92, pages 32–43, New

York, NY, USA, 1992. ACM. ISBN 0-89791-475-9. doi: `10.1145/143095.143114`.

[18] Intel Corporation. Using the RDTSC instruction for performance monitoring, 1997. URL `http://www.intel.com.au/content/dam/www/public/us/en/documents/white-papers/ia-32-ia-64-benchmark-code-execution-paper.pdf`.

[19] G. Kliot, E. Petrank, and B. Steensgaard. A lock-free, concurrent, and incremental stack scanning for garbage collectors. In *Proceedings of the 2009 ACM SIGPLAN/SIGOPS International Conference on Virtual Execution Environments*, VEE '09, pages 11–20, New York, NY, USA, 2009. ACM. ISBN 978-1-60558-375-4. doi: `10.1145/1508293.1508296`.

[20] M. Kulkarni, M. Burtscher, C. Cascaval, and K. Pingali. Lonestar: A suite of parallel irregular programs. In *Performance Analysis of Systems and Software, 2009. ISPASS 2009. IEEE International Symposium on*, pages 65–76, 2009. doi: `10.1109/ISPASS.2009.4919639`.

[21] V. Kumar, D. Frampton, S. M. Blackburn, D. Grove, and O. Tardieu. Work-stealing without the baggage. In *Proceedings of the ACM International Conference on Object Oriented Programming Systems Languages and Applications*, OOPSLA '12, pages 297–314, New York, NY, USA, 2012. ACM. ISBN 978-1-4503-1561-6. doi: `10.1145/2384616.2384639`.

[22] D. Lea. A Java Fork/Join framework. In *Proceedings of the ACM 2000 Conference on Java Grande*, JAVA '00, pages 36–43, New York, NY, USA, 2000. ACM. ISBN 1-58113-288-3. doi: `10.1145/337449.337465`.

[23] R. Lublinerman, J. Zhao, Z. Budimlić, S. Chaudhuri, and V. Sarkar. Delegated isolation. In *Proceedings of the 2011 ACM International Conference on Object Oriented Programming Systems Languages and Applications*, OOPSLA '11, pages 885–902, New York, NY, USA, 2011. ACM. ISBN 978-1-4503-0940-0. doi: `10.1145/2048066.2048133`.

[24] R. Lüling and B. Monien. A dynamic distributed load balancing algorithm with provable good performance. In *Proceedings of the Fifth Annual ACM Symposium on Parallel Algorithms and Architectures*, SPAA '93, pages 164–172, New York, NY, USA, 1993. ACM. ISBN 0-89791-599-2. doi: `10.1145/165231.165252`.

[25] M. Mitzenmacher. Analyses of load stealing models based on differential equations. In *Proceedings of the Tenth Annual ACM Symposium on Parallel Algorithms and Architectures*, SPAA '98, pages 212–221, New York, NY, USA, 1998. ACM. ISBN 0-89791-989-0. doi: `10.1145/277651.277687`.

[26] E. Mohr, D. A. Kranz, and R. H. Halstead, Jr. Lazy task creation: A technique for increasing the granularity of parallel programs. In *Proceedings of the 1990 ACM Conference on LISP and Functional Programming*, LFP '90, pages 185–197, New York, NY, USA, 1990. ACM. ISBN 0-89791-368-X. doi: `10.1145/91556.91631`.

[27] S. Olivier, J. Huan, J. Liu, J. Prins, J. Dinan, P. Sadayappan, and C.-W. Tseng. UTS: an unbalanced tree search benchmark. In *Proceedings of the 19th International Conference on Languages and Compilers for Parallel Computing*, LCPC'06,

pages 235–250, Berlin, Heidelberg, 2007. Springer-Verlag. ISBN 978-3-540-72520-6. URL `http://dl.acm.org/citation.cfm?id=1757112.1757137`.

[28] J. Reinders. *Intel threading building blocks: outfitting C++ for multi-core processor parallelism*. O'Reilly Media, Inc., 2010.

[29] L. Rudolph, M. Slivkin-Allalouf, and E. Upfal. A simple load balancing scheme for task allocation in parallel machines. In *Proceedings of the Third Annual ACM Symposium on Parallel Algorithms and Architectures*, SPAA '91, pages 237–245, New York, NY, USA, 1991. ACM. ISBN 0-89791-438-4. doi: `10.1145/113379.113401`.

[30] H. Saiki, Y. Konaka, T. Komiya, M. Yasugi, and T. Yuasa. Real-time GC in JeRTy™ VM using the return-barrier method. In *Proceedings of the Eighth IEEE International Symposium on Object-Oriented Real-Time Distributed Computing*, ISORC '05, pages 140–148, Washington, DC, USA, 2005. IEEE Computer Society. ISBN 0-7695-2356-0. doi: `10.1109/ISORC.2005.45`.

[31] D. Sanchez, R. M. Yoo, and C. Kozyrakis. Flexible architectural support for fine-grain scheduling. In *Proceedings of the Fifteenth Edition of ASPLOS on Architectural Support for Programming Languages and Operating Systems*, ASPLOS XV, pages 311–322, New York, NY, USA, 2010. ACM. ISBN 978-1-60558-839-1. doi: `10.1145/1736020.1736055`.

[32] V. Sundaresan, D. Maier, P. Ramarao, and M. Stoodley. Experiences with multi-threading and dynamic class loading in a Java Just-In-Time compiler. In *Proceedings of the International Symposium on Code Generation and Optimization*, CGO '06, pages 87–97, Washington, DC, USA, 2006. IEEE Computer Society. ISBN 0-7695-2499-0. doi: `10.1109/CGO.2006.16`.

[33] S. Umatani, M. Yasugi, T. Komiya, and T. Yuasa. Pursuing laziness for efficient implementation of modern multi-threaded languages. In A. Veidenbaum, K. Joe, H. Amano, and H. Aiso, editors, *High Performance Computing*, volume 2858 of *Lecture Notes in Computer Science*, pages 174–188. Springer Berlin Heidelberg, 2003. ISBN 978-3-540-20359-9. doi: `10.1007/978-3-540-39707-6_13`.

[34] E. Westbrook, J. Zhao, Z. Budimlić, and V. Sarkar. Practical permissions for race-free parallelism. In *Proceedings of the 26th European Conference on Object-Oriented Programming*, ECOOP'12, pages 614–639, Berlin, Heidelberg, 2012. Springer-Verlag. ISBN 978-3-642-31056-0. doi: `10.1007/978-3-642-31057-7_27`.

[35] T. Yuasa. Real-time garbage collection on general-purpose machines. *J. Syst. Softw.*, 11(3):181–198, Mar. 1990. ISSN 0164-1212. doi: `10.1016/0164-1212(90)90084-Y`.

[36] T. Yuasa, Y. Nakagawa, T. Komiyay, and M. Yasugiy. Return barrier. In *Proceedings of the International Lisp Conference*, 2002.

[37] J. Zhao, R. Lublinerman, Z. Budimlić, S. Chaudhuri, and V. Sarkar. Isolation for nested task parallelism. In *Proceedings of the 2013 ACM SIGPLAN International Conference on Object Oriented Programming Systems Languages and Applications*, OOPSLA '13, pages 571–588, New York, NY, USA, 2013. ACM. ISBN 978-1-4503-2374-1. doi: `10.1145/2509136.2509534`.

String Deduplication for
Java-based Middleware in Virtualized Environments

Michihiro Horie   Kazunori Ogata   Kiyokuni Kawachiya   Tamiya Onodera

IBM Research - Tokyo

horie@jp.ibm.com

Abstract

To increase the memory efficiency in physical servers is a significant concern for increasing the number of virtual machines (VM) in them. When similar web application service runs in each guest VM, many string data with the same values are created in every guest VMs. These duplications of string data are redundant from the viewpoint of memory efficiency in the host OS. This paper proposes two approaches to reduce the duplication in Java string in a single Java VM (JVM) and across JVMs. The first approach is to share string objects across JVMs by using a read-only memory-mapped file. The other approach is to selectively unify string objects created at runtime in the web applications. This paper evaluates our approach by using the Apache DayTrader and the DaCapo benchmark suite. Our prototype implementation achieved 7% to 12% reduction in the total size of the objects allocated over the lifetime of the programs. In addition, we observed the performance of DayTrader was maintained even under a situation of high density guest VMs in a KVM host machine.

Categories and Subject Descriptors   D.3.4 [*Programming Languages*]: Processors - Optimization

General Terms   Measurement, Performance

Keywords   Java, Memory reduction, String allocation, Calling context, String sharing

1. Introduction

In a modern datacenter, server machines are virtualized as VMs to improve the utilization of physical servers and to reduce the server management costs. In this environment, increasing the number of VMs on each piece of hardware is a key factor for higher cost effectiveness. For example, a

cloud computing datacenter often uses a separate guest VM for each user to ensure security and isolate those resources from the other users. This kind of configuration runs many small VMs. Even small reductions of the resources used by each VM are important to improve the efficiency of the entire datacenter, especially if more VMs can run on each real machine.

VMs in a cloud datacenter often execute the same middleware on the same OS and even the same applications, since many customers will use standard VM images provided by the cloud service provider. Also, for a Platform as a Service (PaaS) datacenter, the service provider can select the OS and middleware to be used in the VMs, and they usually use the same software stack to reduce management costs. For example, there is a company that provides more than 100 web services by preparing guest VMs for each of their web applications.

In Java-based middleware, a string is one of the most frequently used data type. In IBM WebSphere Application Server Version 8.0 (WAS 8) [3], the cumulative size of string data was 20% of the total bytes for allocating objects by the time the start-up of WAS 8 was completed. In our observations, there are many strings whose values are specified when a guest VM is deployed. One of the reason is that web application servers load many configuration files in XML [11, 13, 21]. Processing the XML files creates many string objects, and they tend to be long-lived since they represent the configurations of the server. Since software stacks and their configurations are similar among the VMs in a single host machine, each of the web application servers holds the same string data, and thus, there is a great deal of duplication in the string data from a host machine's viewpoint. Further, many short-lived string data are created while a web application handles millions of transactions. Many of these string objects are created for SQL statements and JSP pages, which also use a text-oriented architecture. Since a web application server processes many requests for each of functionalities of the web service, string data created during a single transaction is likely to be the same as those created in previous transactions of the same service.

To reduce the duplication of string data, this paper proposes an approach called *String Deduplication*, which enables deduplication inside a single JVM and across JVMs. In our approach, actual deduplication is possible after profiling a target application or middleware to be optimized. For the profiling, we developed a tool named *StringProfiler*, which can detect the identical string values that are created among JVMs and remain in the Java heap. To deduplicate string data across JVMs, we share these string objects across JVMs by using a read-only memory-mapped file. For sharing string data even across guest VMs, we make use of Transparent Page Sharing (TPS) [26], which is a technique in the hypervisor to improve the memory utilization by sharing identical pages after scanning the memory in the background. In contrast, for the deduplication in a single JVM, StringProfiler analyzes which calling contexts create many string objects that have the same values. Based on the results from String-Profiler, we selectively unify the string objects created at application runtime.

We evaluated our approach for a production application server by using a benchmark web application called Apache DayTrader [1] and the DaCapo benchmark suite [9, 10]. DayTrader is one of the J2EE benchmarks that are often used for measuring the performance of WAS. We examined how much the total allocation size was reduced over the lifetime of the programs. With our String Deduplication approach, the size of the total allocation that included all the other objects was reduced by 7% to 12%. We also measured the execution performance of DayTrader running on three guest VMs in a KVM [19] host machine. The execution performance was maintained even under a high density of guest VMs. This result showed that our technique can be used to maintain the quality of web services even when the memory footprint for guest VMs exceeds the limit of the physical memory.

Here are our contributions:

- Analysis of how many string objects hold the same values in real Java applications

- A tool for reducing the duplications of string values based on the results of profiling

- Illustrating the applicability by using WebSphere Application Server with DayTrader and the DaCapo benchmark suite

In the rest of this paper, Section 2 describes how string data are handled in Java and shows that inefficiencies caused by duplications of string values actually exist in real Java enterprise applications. Section 3 explains string profiling and Section 4 proposes String Deduplication. Section 5 evaluates our approach by using real Java applications. Section 6 reviews related work, and Section 7 concludes this paper.

```
1 String getSourcefileName(String clsname) {
2    int index = name.lastIndexOf('.');
3    String srcname;
4    if (index >= 0)
5        srcname = clsname.substring(0, index);
6    else
7        srcname = clsname;
8    return srcname + ".java";
9 }
```

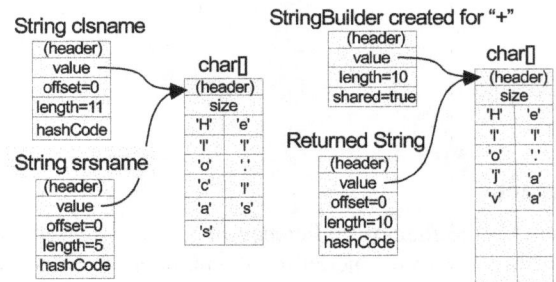

Figure 1. An example that creates `String` and other related objects.

2. String duplication

This section briefly explains how `String` objects are created in Java. Then it shows some of the real cases that create duplicated string values.

2.1 String object creation

In Java, there are three string-related classes: `String`, `StringBuilder`, and `StringBuffer`. Since the `String` object is defined as immutable, its value is never changed after the creation of a `String` object. In contrast, the values of the `StringBuffer` and `StringBuilder` objects can be changed. In typical Java implementations, all these string-related classes use a `char` array (`char[]`) as their instance field to hold the value, although the Java Language Specification [15] does not mention this detail.

`String` objects are created in two ways: one is to explicitly invoke a constructor defined in the `String` class, and the other is to use the `String` literal. A `String` literal is a constant value declared in the Java source code by using double-quotes, such as "literal". The JVM instantiates each literal as a `String` object and a `char[]` object when it is first used in programs with the `ldc` bytecode.

A code snippet in Figure 1 shows an example that creates `String` objects. The `getSourcefileName` method receives a `String` object for the name of a class file and returns a file name with ".java" at the end of its name after eliminating ".class". If the value of the argument `name` includes a dot, the part before the dot is extracted by using the `substring` method in the `String` class. Although the `substring` method creates a new `String` object, its `char[]` object can be shared [6, 25]. Therefore, `clsname` and `srcname` share the same `char[]` object. To concatenate

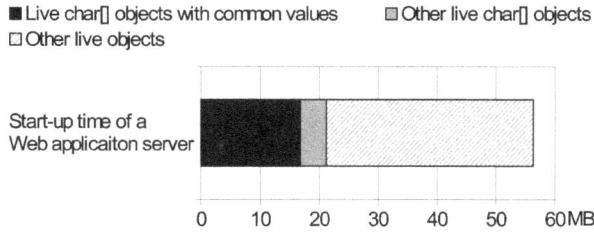

Figure 2. Breakdown of the size of live objects in Machine #2 in Table 1. This result shows that 40% (21.2 MB) of the live objects were char[] objects and 30% (16.8 MB) of live objects were from the char[] objects whose values were commonly found between Machine #1 and Machine #2.

string values, "+" is often used as shown in line 8 in Figure 1. The Java compiler *javac* compiles such program code by using the StringBuilder class. Concretely, the code in line 8 is the same as:

```
StringBuilder builder = new StringBuilder(srcname);
builder.append(".java");
return builder.toString();
```

As shown at the bottom of Figure 1, the constructor of the StringBuilder object creates a new char[] object with a particular array size. This char[] object is reused when a String object is created by the toString method in the StringBuilder class.

2.2 Duplications of string values across JVMs

To assess how many char[] objects with the same values across VMs are created at deployment time of the VM images, we compared the strings created during the executions of two web applications by using physical machines with different versions of WAS on different OS/hardware configurations (Table 1). We measured the live object size of the char[] at the start-up time of each web application server. We used generational a garbage collector (GC) [24] as the GC policy, and also defined long-lived objects as those that survived more than 10 garbage collections.

The result in Figure 2 shows that there are many char[] objects that are commonly created across JVMs. Common

	Machine #1	Machine #2
CPU	Dual-Core AMD Opteron 2.6 GHz	Intel Pentium 4 3.80 GHz
Memory	4 GB	4 GB
OS	RedHat Enterprise Linux 6.1	RedHat Enterprise Linux 6.3
Java	Linux x86-64 IBM J9 Java6 R26SR1FP1	Linux x86-64 IBM J9 Java6 R26GA
WAS	8.5 Liberty Profile	8.0 ND
Application	Tradelite	DayTrader

Table 1. Two physical machines used for confirming the amount of the common strings.

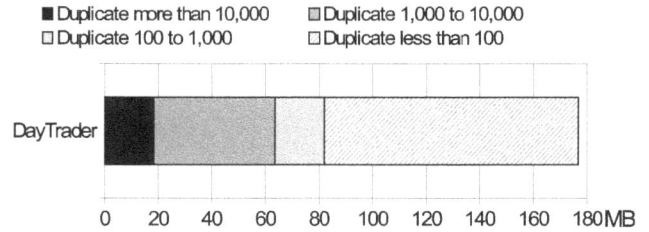

Figure 3. Breakdown by the degree of duplication in the allocated char[] objects that were used by String, StringBuilder, and StringBuffer objects in DayTrader.

char[] objects accounted for around 30% of all of the live objects created during the start-up of the web application server.

Large numbers of common strings were generated by reading configuration files for the web application server. There were many file paths to handle .xml files, .properties files, and the manifest files. Other prominent strings were the tokens generated after parsing the configuration files. When a configuration file or a file path is parsed, the text is split into tokens. Some examples of tokens after parsing a configuration file were "true", "name", and "version=".

2.3 Duplications of string values in a single JVM

To assess how often string values are duplicated, we tracked the allocation events of the char[] objects for the String, StringBuilder, and StringBuffer objects by using a benchmark called Apache DayTrader, which is a J2EE application for simulating stock trading. For simulating user's trading, DayTrader provides more than 20 operations such as buying, holding, and selling stocks. We ran DayTrader on WebSphere Application Server Version 8.0 (WAS 8). The application server runs on IBM's production JVM [8, 16], the J9 Java VM 6.0 for Linux. Figure 3 shows the amount of duplication of string values from the time when DayTrader became ready to the time when it processed 2,000 trade requests.

The size in Figure 3 includes the header for the char[] objects.

The result of the measurement shows that many of the values represented by the char[] objects were heavily duplicated while DayTrader was running. String values that were duplicated more than 10,000 times accounted for 10.4%. The total size of these duplications was 18.3 MB. The ratio became 36% for 1,000 duplications.

Some of the most created strings were parts of SQL statements. By default, WAS 8 uses the OpenJPA library [2] to handle SQL. OpenJPA constructs fragments of SQL statements, and this creates duplicated string values. Many duplications were also created by the JSP during the construction of the HTML text. One such string value was "<FONT color=\"#ff0000\">". Timestamps are also du-

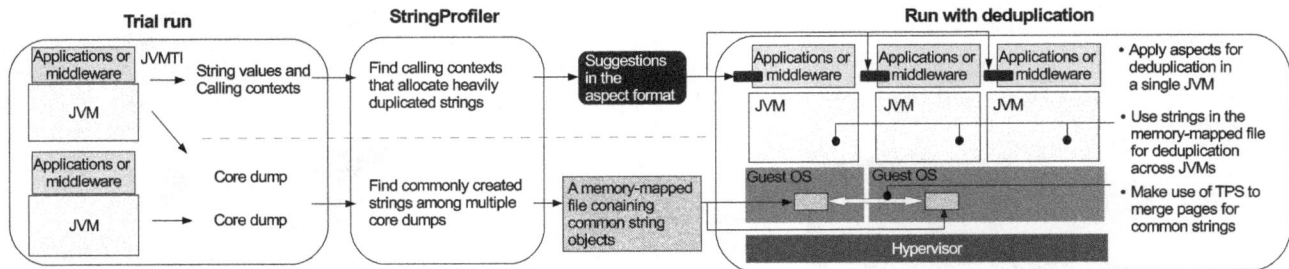

Figure 4. StringProfiler receives two kinds of inputs: calling contexts or core dumps. StringProfiler outputs suggestions in the aspect format, or a memory-mapped file that contains common string objects.

plicated. We found that the year, date, and hours are handled separately, although most of the values of the year and date are duplicated. Web application servers in production systems often provide logging features for monitoring the performance of each running application, and duplicates of those string values are also created frequently.

3. String profiling

To reduce the duplications described in the previous section, we propose two approaches to reduce the duplications of string values both in a single JVM and across multiple JVMs on guest VMs. Both approaches have each profiling step of a target application or middleware.

3.1 Overview

For profiling a target application or middleware, we developed a tool named *StringProfiler*. Figure 4 shows how StringProfiler works in the whole procedure for the deduplications.

Regarding duplication across multiple JVMs on guest VMs, StringProfiler receives several core dumps that JVMs generate, and collects commonly created strings among these core dumps. To share common strings across JVMs in a guest VM, StringProfiler outputs a read-only memory-mapped file, which contains `String` and `char[]` objects with the same object format in the Java heap. To realize this feature, we use the dynamic-link library (DLL). A DLL with common strings is first distributed into each guest VM, and then hypervisors' transparent page sharing, such as KSM [7], merges the read-only section of the DLL. This feature periodically scans pages to detect identical pages and shares them in a copy-on-write manner. Since the common strings in the DLL are stored in the read-only section, KSM merges the pages for common strings into one page.

Regarding the deduplication in a single JVM, StringProfiler receives the information about calling contexts in a trial run of a target application or middleware. Then, StringProfiler automatically generates AspectJ aspects to change the behaviors of applications that selectively unify the `String` objects.

3.2 Multiple JVM string profiling

Since the core dump created by the JVM includes the contents of the Java heap, StringProfiler can collect string values by retrieving the `String` objects in the Java heap stored in the core dump. StringProfiler reads multiple core dumps and finds the strings that are commonly created among them. What developers have to do is to obtain at least two core dumps produced under different configuration of execution environment, such as the one shown in Table 1, to exclude the string values that are specific to a machine or a run.

Since the DLL contains many common strings, it is necessary to have a fast lookup mechanism in the DLL. Therefore, StringProfiler constructs efficient data structures for sharable strings and automatically generates source code of the DLL that uses the data structures. Concretely, StringProfiler separates the sharable strings into small groups to apply the fastest lookup structures for each group. Strings are separated into groups based on criteria such as string length, class files in which the strings are created, and jar files that strings are originally contained. Our prototype implementation uses the string length for the grouping criteria.

As the first step, StringProfiler decides which characters to use for calculating the hash values. Note that this hash value is just for looking up strings in the DLL and differs from the one the `String.hashCode` method returns. StringProfiler chooses only a couple of indices with high information entropy. This is necessary because the length of some sharable strings is more than 30,000 characters, and calculating the hash values using all the characters takes time. For example, in the strings shown below, the fourth and fifth characters are suitable because these characters are completely different, and the hash values will be well distributed.

StringProfiler has a number of predefined hash functions, and chooses the one that produces the fewest collisions of the hash values. For example, `hashFn1` and `hashFn2` below are the functions StringProfiler has.

```
int hashFn1(char ch1, char ch2) {
  int hash = ch1 * ch2;
  return hash * hash;
}

int hashFn2(char ch1, char ch2) {
  int hash = ch1 + ch2;
  return hash * hash;
}
```

StringProfiler also chooses a shifting count that may produce fewer collisions for the index of a hash table. Suppose that we use the L bits as the index for the hash table after shifting a hash value by n bits (n=0,1,..) as shown below. Here, L is a constant that depends on the size of the hash table that stores the sharable strings.

3.3 Single JVM string profiling

The point of our idea is that information about calling contexts plays an important role to decide which strings should be deduplicated because some calling contexts almost always allocate the same string values, while others do not. For the explanation, we use a simple program in Figure 6. The `getString` method is invoked from the `getToken` method, which is invoked from the `parseTable`, `parseView`, and `read` methods. The `read` method is further invoked from the `readCondition`, `readAnd`, and `readTerm` method. The `getString` method creates many duplicated `String` objects whose values are such as "SET", "100", or "WHERE". Although the `getString` method also creates `String` objects with other values, the number of duplications of each of these values is small.

When the `parseTable` method invokes the `getToken` method, only the strings with the value "SET" are created. Thus, we can extract the creation of `String` with "SET" based on the calling context of the `parseTable`, `getToken`, and `getString` methods. The value "WHERE" is created only when the `parseView` method invokes the `getToken` method. Although "WHERE" is created also when the `read` method invokes the `getToken`, many other values are created. Therefore, the calling context starting from the `read` method might not be appropriate for extracting the creation of the value "WHERE". However, when we focus on a caller method `readTerm`, "WHERE" is successfully extracted.

In contrast, there are some values that cannot be extracted based on the calling contexts. `String` objects with the value "100" cannot be extracted even when we focus on

```
"SET":4791 (100%)
 java/lang/String.<init>(II[C)V
*Token.getString()Ljava/lang/String;
 Token.getToken()V
+Parser.parseTable()V
```

Figure 5. An example of suggestion from StringProfiler.

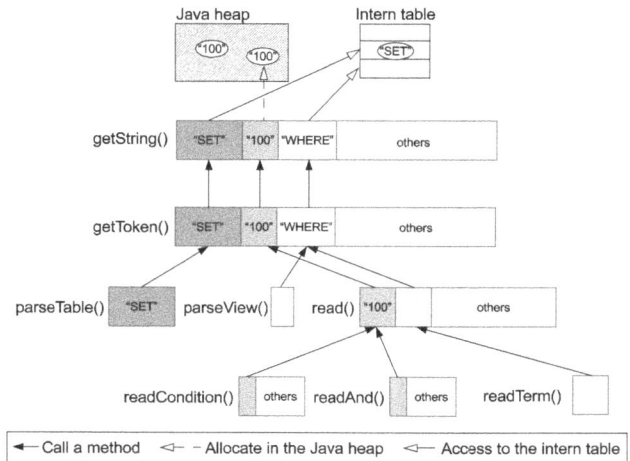

Figure 6. An example of calling contexts that can effectively deduplicate strings "SET" and "WHERE" by checking caller methods, and those cannot find a method to deduplicate string "100" efficiently even if caller methods are checked (the caller methods are shown below).

the calling context starting from the `readCondition`, `read`, `getToken`, and `getString` methods.

In a trial run of a target application, StringProfiler collects the information about the calling context at each allocation of a `String` object. When developers run an application with StringProfiler, it hooks allocation events through JVMTI [4] not only when a `String` object is instantiated, but also when `ldc` loads a `String` object from a constant pool.

After detecting the calling contexts creating duplicated string values, StringProfiler suggests which calling contexts should be optimized. Figure 5 shows an example of the suggestions, which shows what value is created by what kind of calling context. The first line shows the string value and the duplication ratio. From the second line, the method names are listed with two kinds of tags. The tag "+" is attached to the beginning of the calling context for the optimization, and the tag "*" is attached to a method that creates the `String` objects. Note that these tags can be attached to the same method when the optimization on one method is enough without considering the calling context. In addition to these suggestions, StringProfiler automatically generates source code of AspectJ aspects [18].

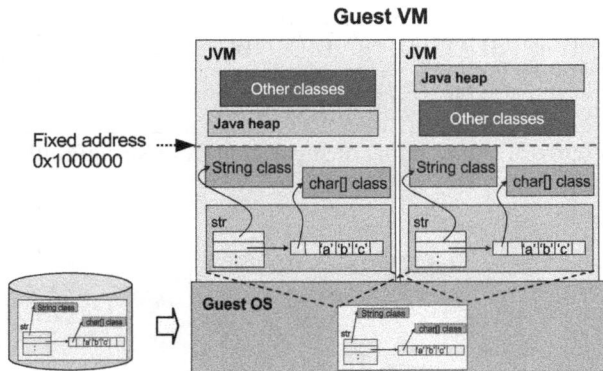

Figure 7. Storing common strings in a DLL enables to share across JVMs. The addresses of the `String` and `char[]` are fixed every time when JVM maps the file so that stored objects can be loaded into a read-only section.

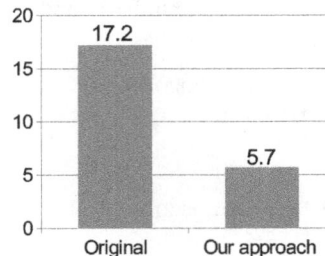

Figure 8. Memory reduction in long-lived `char[]` objects.

4. Deduplication

Actual deduplications become enabled by using two outputs that are generated by StringProfiler.

4.1 Multiple JVM deduplication

Figure 7 represents how the deduplication across multiple JVMs works. To make `String` and `char[]` objects read-only, the addresses of these objects are decided before JVM maps the file into its address space[1]. We modified a J9 JVM to allocate memory areas for the `String` and `char[]` classes at fixed addresses, so that the class pointers of the stored objects can point to the fixed addresses. In Linux, for example, the `prelink` command can decide the exact address of a DLL to be loaded.

The areas for class definitions of `String` and `char[]` are null when a DLL is loaded into a JVM. At the time of class loading, the class definitions of `String` and `char[]` are written into the fixed address.

We revised a couple of String constructors to look up a string from a DLL. As shown below, the `lookupCommonCharArray` method looks up a string from a DLL. Unless the returned value `fromDLL` is `null`, a shared `char[]` object is used. Otherwise, a new `char[]` object is instantiated.

```
public String(char[] data, int start, int length) {
    :
    char[] fromDLL =
        lookupCommonCharArray(data, start, length);
    if (fromDLL != null)
        this.value = fromDLL;
    else {
        this.value = new char[length];
        :
}}
```

---

[1] J9 JVM can remove the lock word from an object by specifying a JVM option. Therefore, we can treat these objects as read-only easily.

One of the benefits of this deduplication approach is that we do not need to modify any application code. In addition, the object identity is guaranteed as long as only `char[]` objects are reused. A `char[]` object that is referred to from a `String` object is encapsulated and the value is never changed.

Both a `String` and its `char[]` objects are reusable from the DLL when the `String.intern` method is invoked, since the `intern` method returns a unified `String` object. We prepared a native method `lookupCommonString`, which returns a reference to a `String` object in the DLL. Also, we revised the `intern` method to invoke the `lookupCommonString` first.

4.2 Single JVM deduplication

For the deduplication of the `String` object, we prepared a `StrUtil` class, which provides `toUnifiedString` methods for various parameter types. For example, based on the suggestion in Figure 5, the invocation of a `String` constructor in the `getString` is converted to an invocation of the `StrUtil.toUnifiedString` only when the `getString` is invoked from the `getToken`, which is invoked from `parseTable`.

AspectJ provides the `cflow` pointcut to specify control flows, but it causes a performance bottleneck. Therefore, our prototype implementation modifies the `parseTable` to record a thread id, and also modifies the `getString` to call the `toUnifiedString` only when the thread id matches. The `toUnifiedString` method returns (or creates) a string in the intern table, so duplicated strings are automatically unified and do not consume memory.

We assume that developers have the responsibility to confirm whether generated aspects are valid. Even if it is hard for developers to decide the applicability of deduplicating `String` objects, our approach still allows developers to deduplicate only `char[]` objects that are referred to from `String` objects.

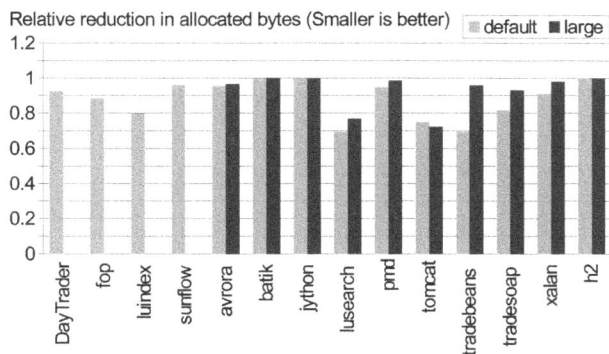

Figure 9. Relative size in allocated objects with the middle and large input data. For profiling DaCapo benchmarks, the small input data was used.

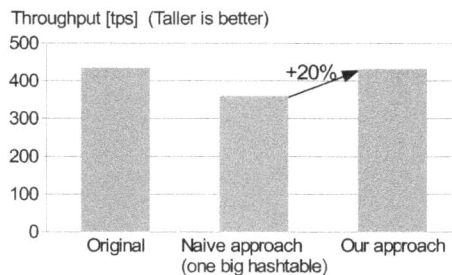

Figure 10. DayTrader throughput to measure search cost on looking up sharable strings.

5. Evaluation

This section discusses the applicability of our approach. We used Apache DayTrader on WAS 8 and the DaCapo benchmark suite released in 2009. DayTrader is one of the benchmarks that are often used for measuring the performance of WAS. As an implementation target, we used IBM's production JVM, the J9 Java VM 6.0 for Linux on x86-64. The measurements were done on a machine with a 2.60 GHz Dual-Core AMD Opteron processor and 4 GB of memory, running the Red Hat Enterprise Linux 6.1 operating system.

5.1 Memory reduction

We measured how much objects in Java heap is reduced by applying our String deduplication.

5.1.1 Memory reduction by sharing

We measured the reduction of long-lived objects due to our string sharing mechanism on DayTrader. We counted the amount of allocated bytes just after the start-up of WAS 8. The result, as shown in Figure 8, was a 12 MB reduction.

A DLL was generated by using two profiling results with two different physical machines as shown in Table 1. The memory use needed for this DLL was 13.3 MB[2]. Since the memory reduction is around 12 MB, we can reduce the memory use when two or more JVMs run.

5.1.2 Memory reduction by selective interning

We also measured how much our approach contributed to heap reduction (Figure 9). In DayTrader, the total allocation size from the time when DayTrader became ready to the time when DayTrader processed 2,000 requests was reduced by 8%. We counted the allocated size before and after reducing the duplicated string values with our approach. Before applying our approach, the cumulative allocation size

of the `String` objects was 11.7 MB and that of the `char[]` objects was 71.8 MB. By using our deduplication approach, the cumulative allocation size for `String` objects was 8.5 MB and that for the `char[]` objects was 65.3 MB.

In DaCapo, to observe the sensitivity of our approach against input data, we changed the size of input data at the time of profiling and measurement. We used small input in profiling phase by enabling *"-s small"* option of DaCapo, but we used the larger sizes of input data (middle and large) at the time of the measurement of the optimized code by enabling *"-s large"* option of DaCapo. In `fop` and `luindex`, there was only the middle-size data. We failed to obtain a measurement result of `sunflow` with the large input data. We also could not measure `eclipse` with both input sizes because StringProfiler failed to analyze the collected data for `eclipse`.

With the middle-size data, we observed a 12% reduction in the total allocated objects on average. When the large data was used for the measurement, the total reduction of allocated objects was 7%. Since our approach for the deduplication is based on the string values that are heavily duplicated, the ratio of reduction depends upon the difference of input data.

The reductions of total allocated objects in `luindex` and `lusearch` were remarkable, even though the numbers of suggestions from StringProfiler were small: 7 for `luindex` and 9 for `lusearch` (Figure 14). The reduction was 20% in `luindex`, and 30% with the middle-size data and 23% with the large data in `lusearch`.

We did not observe any major reduction in `batik`, `h2`, or `jython`. The reason is that the size of the created `String` objects was quite small in `batik` and `jython`. The ratio was 4% and 1% respectively. Although the size of allocation of `String` objects accounted for about 10% in `h2`, StringProfiler could not successfully find the calling contexts that created the heavily duplicated strings, as explained in Section 5.5.

---

[2] The size of the DLL can be smaller than the result of common `char` objects in Figure 2, because Figure 2 includes duplications with the value of the common `char[]` objects.

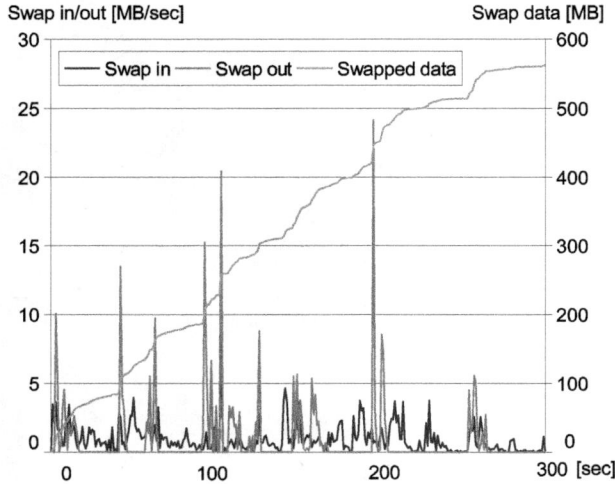

Figure 11. Disk IO rate and total amount of swapped data in original environment.

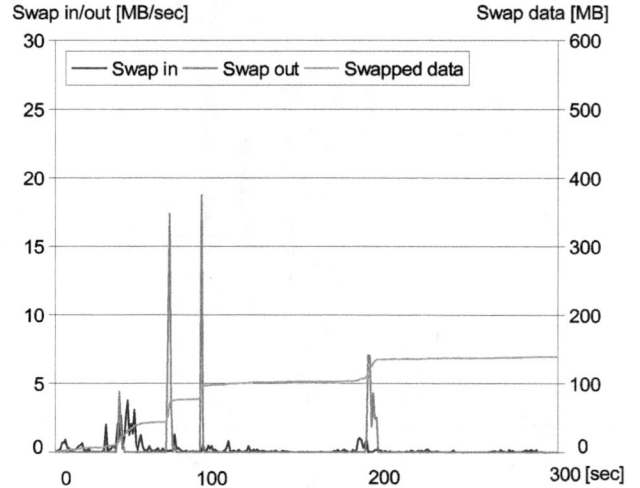

Figure 12. Disk IO rate and total amount of swapped data with our optimization approach.

5.2 Execution performance

Next, we evaluate the execution performance of our approaches.

5.2.1 Verifying negligible performance impact due to sharing

We measured the benefit of our fast look-up mechanism for sharable strings. As shown in Figure 10, the throughput of our approach was the same as the original. Although looking up the DLL each time when a String constructor is invoked has a possibility of performance degradation, we maintained high throughput by separating the strings into small groups and applying the most appropriate data structure for each group.

For comparison, we implemented a string sharing mechanism that uses one big hash table as a naive approach. Figure 10 also shows that our approach was around 20% faster than the naive approach using one big hash table. This result shows that our approach controlled the overhead.

5.2.2 Performance improvement by selective interning with heavy memory usage

Since StringProfiler carefully selects the calling contexts for the string deduplication, our approach can avoid the performance degradation while our approach reduces the memory use as shown in Figure 9. Furthermore, we could see the performance improvement under a memory overcommitted situation.

We measured the memory usage of a machine hosting three KVM guests with 1.5 GB of guest memory. We constructed a special environment with a high density of guest VMs to simulate a situation where the capacity of the physi-

cal resources in a data center is almost full. Each guest VM executed WAS 8 and Apache DayTrader. We used the IBM J9 Java VM included in WAS. Table 2 describes the environment of the real machine and the guest VMs for this measurement. We counted the number of bytes swapped in and out for five minutes of execution on the three WAS processes that DayTrader was running on. DayTrader was continuously accessed from 100 client threads for each VM by using Apache JMeter [5]. Thus, the real machine was accessed by a total of 300 threads. The Java heap size was set to 1.25 GB. Since many short-lived objects are created in DayTrader, 1 GB was used as the nursery space for the generational GC.

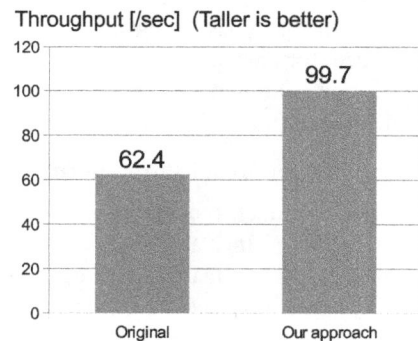

Figure 13. Total throughput of DayTrader in three WAS 8 that ran on three guest VMs. The measurement was done after 300 seconds of warm-up.

184

Physical machine environment	
Machine	IBM BladeCenter LS21
CPU	Dual-core Opteron (2.6 GHz), 2 sockets
RAM size	4.00 GB
Host OS	RedHat Enterprise Linux 6.1 (2.6.32-131.0.15.el6.x86_64.debug)
Hypervisor	KVM (kvm-83-224.el5)
Number of Guest VMs	3 VMs
Guest VM environment	
Virtual CPU	2 virtual CPUs
Guest memory size	1.50 GB
Guest OS	RedHat Enterprise Linux 6.2 (2.6.32-220.el6.x86_64.debug)
WAS version	8.0.0.0
JVM	IBM Java J9 VM for Java 6, 64bit
GC policy	Generational GC
Maximum and minimum sizes of Java heap	1.25 GB
Size for the nursery space	1.00 GB
Size for the tenured space	0.25 GB

Table 2. Execution environment for measuring disk I/O for swap-in and swap-out.

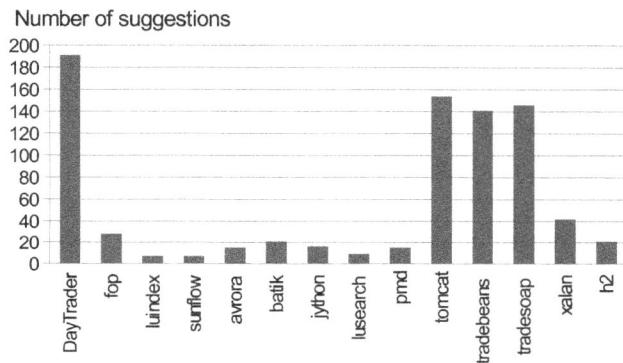

Figure 14. Number of suggestions by StringProfiler.

Figure 11 shows the swapping activity when our deduplication was not used. In this case, large amounts of swapping out occurred periodically during execution, and the total amount of swap space increased by 562 MB in five minutes. Swapping in also occurred continuously during this period. In contrast, Figure 12 shows the results when our deduplication was enabled. In this case, swapping was reduced, and the increase in the total size of the swap space was 139 MB. This indicates that duplicating strings prevents unnecessary swapping.

We also measured the execution performance in these experiments. Figure 13 shows the results, and the throughput with our approach was 1.6 times better than the original run. The throughput in the original run was 62.4. In contrast, the throughput in our approach was 99.7, which was the total of each throughput in three guest VMs. The performance improvement was achieved by reducing the memory used for Java processes and by preventing swapping. Also, the results showed that our technique can be used to sustain the quality of web services when the memory footprint for guest VMs exceeds a limit of a physical memory.

5.3 Suggestions from StringProfiler

We show the numbers of suggestions offered by StringProfiler in Figure 14. For DayTrader, the number of suggestions from StringProfiler was 191. For DaCapo, the average number of suggestions was 48. (Our StringProfiler failed to analyze the collected data on `eclipse`.) Editing the methods suggested by StringProfiler by hand would be time consuming and error prone, so automatic code generation by StringProfiler for deduplication is necessary.

5.4 Duplications of string values across JVMs in DaCapo

We conducted the same experiment as Section 2.2 to look into how many `char[]` objects with the same values across JVMs are created in DaCapo benchmarks. We used two different environment shown in Table 1 to run the same DaCapo benchmarks. We measured the size of `char[]` objects that were live after GC.

Figure 15 shows the size of live objects. On average, live `char[]` objects accounted for 29% in all live objects. The live `char[]` objects that were commonly found accounted for 13% on average. We found that common values were created more than 20% in `luindex`, `lusearch`, and `pmd`, although the size of common values of `char[]` objects were not large.

5.5 Duplication of string values in a single JVM in DaCapo

We also measured how often string values are duplicated in DaCapo benchmarks. We ran each benchmark on J9 Java VM 6.0 for Linux. As shown in Figure 16, string values that were duplicated more than 10,000 times existed only in `avrora`, `eclipse`, `tomcat`, and `h2`. String values that were duplicated more than 1,000 times existed in all benchmarks and the ratio was 7.5% on average. String values that were duplicated more than 100 times existed in all benchmarks and the ratio was 14%.

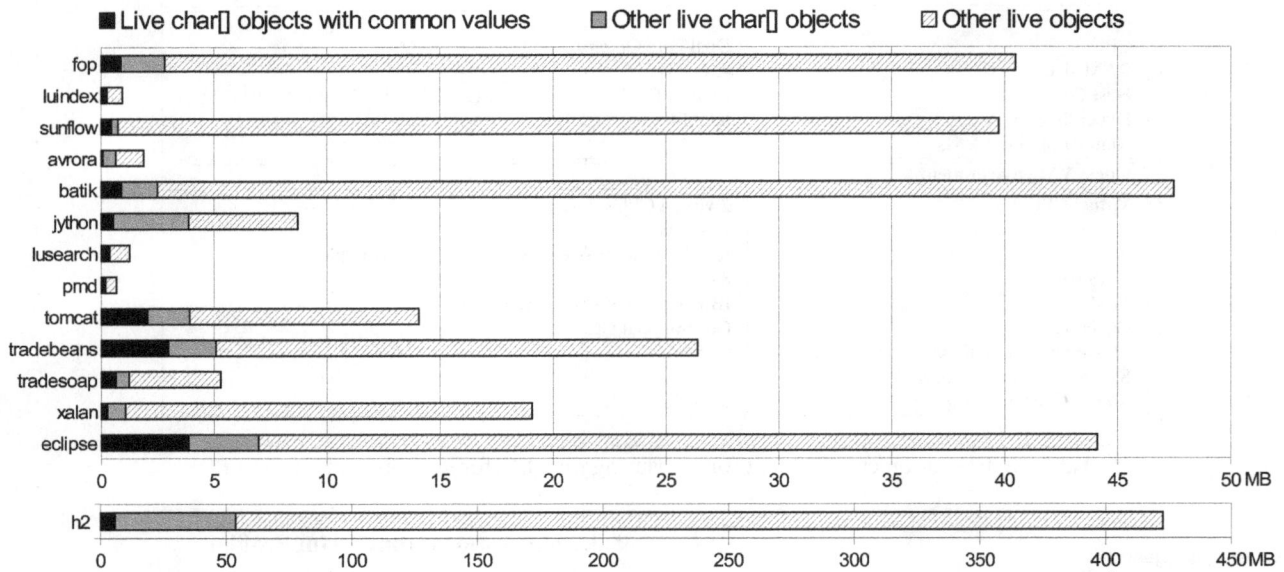

Figure 15. Breakdown of the size of live objects by running DaCapo benchmarks on Machine #2 in Table 1.

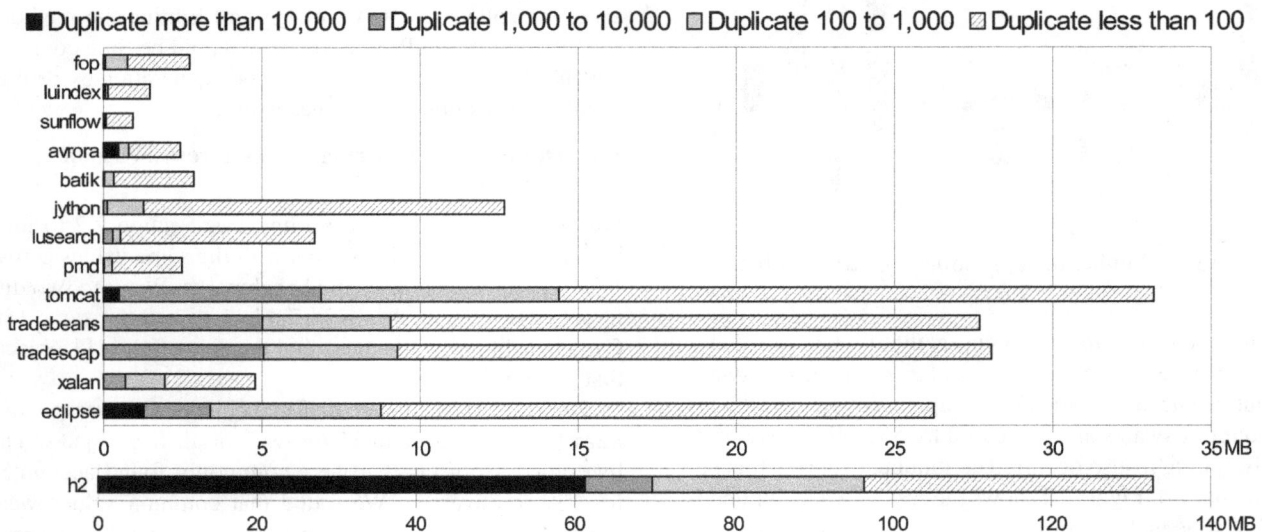

Figure 16. Breakdown by the degree of duplication in the allocated `char[]` objects that were used by `String`, `StringBuilder`, and `StringBuffer` objects in DaCapo benchmarks.

Regarding h2, it is amazing that 46% of strings were duplicated more than 10,000 times. However, StringProfiler did not deduplicate many of the strings created in h2. We found out that all the values that duplicated more than 10,000 times were digits such as "2013" and "-10.00". We also found that there were many calling contexts that create the strings representing digits. There were very few calling contexts in which a single string value is extracted, and thus we obtained only 21 suggestions as shown in Figure 14.

6. Related work

Marinov and O'Callahan presented Object Equality Profiling (OEP), which detects opportunities for replacing a set of equivalent object instances with a single representative object [20]. They studied *mergeability* for arbitrary Java objects. They precisely defined the mergeability problem, and described how to efficiently compute mergeability. In addition, they developed a tool, a combination of an online profiler and postmortem analyzer, which revealed significant amounts of object equivalence in real Java programs. Their motivation to reduce duplicated objects is the same as ours. However, they did not consider efficient ways of unifying the `String` objects. In contrast, our approach avoids the performance degradation by selecting duplicated `String` objects. This is why our StringProfiler gathers the information about the calling contexts to understand how the duplicated strings are created.

StringGC [17] is a technique to reduce the `String` objects in the live heap by restructuring the string-related objects at the time of garbage collections. To reduce the size of the `char[]` objects, StringGC also eliminates unnecessary characters that are not actually used as string values. In contrast, our String Deduplication tries to avoid creating the `String` objects with the same values. Lazy Body Creation partly delays the instantiation of each string literal until the value of the literal is actually used. BundleConverter prevents unused message literals from being instantiated by converting the subclasses of the `ListResourceBundle` class. Both Lazy Body Creation and BundleConverter are techniques to avoid creating unnecessary `String` objects.

There are many other research projects that tackle inefficiencies in memory use. Chis *et al.* listed patterns for wasted memory and one of their patterns is for the primitive array wrappers such as the `String` object [12]. However, they did not focus on the problems with the duplicated string values. Yeti [22] is a tool that summarizes the memory usage to find the cost of the design decisions. Yeti also discovered that the `String` objects have a significant impact in the Java heap although there was no proposal for the deduplication of the `String` objects. Mitchell *et al.* introduced "health signatures" to facilitate assessing the balance between memory consumption and the other requirements such as performance [23]. Our approach can work with their health signatures.

HPROF is a profiling tool provided with Java 2 Platform Standard Edition (J2SE) for analyzing the Java heap and CPU usage in Java programs. It uses JVMTI and bytecode instrumentation to get information on object allocation. StringProfiler uses the same approach to gather calling context information on `String` objects. StringProfiler also records the values and the lifetimes of the `String` objects, while HPROF does not.

For a Software as a Service (SaaS) datacenter, multitenancy is another approach for reducing physical memory usage. It is an approach that runs only a single instance of the middleware and uses separate instances for each of applications that run in the shared middleware. Java has the Application Isolation API (JSR 121) [14] to help implement a multi-tenant server. The advantage of this approach over the VM-based one is smaller memory consumption because the middleware and the OS are shared among all of the applications. The disadvantage is that a misbehaving application may affect other applications running with the same middleware. For example, if one application uses up all of the memory available to the server processes, other applications may crash because of memory shortages. Another example would be if one application crashes upon access to an invalid memory region, so the entire service process can crash.

A problem with multi-tenant servers in a PaaS datacenter is that users of the datacenter may be restricted to certain configurations for their applications. For example, a new user of a datacenter may need to modify the port number of an application if the port number is already used by another user of the datacenter. Also, the user may need to modify the port number later if the application needs more computational resources and needs to be moved to another machine.

7. Concluding Remarks

This paper presented *String Deduplication*, which consists of two approaches of reducing string duplication inside a single JVM and across JVMs. In our approaches, the deduplication is performed after profiling a target application or middleware to be optimized. For the profiling, we developed a tool *StringProfiler*, which can detect which strings are commonly created among the JVMs and remain in the Java heap. To deduplicate string data across JVMs, we share string objects across JVMs by using a read-only memory-mapped file. For sharing string data even across guest VMs, we used TPS, which is a technique in the hypervisor to improve the memory utilization by sharing identical pages in a copy-on-write manner. For the deduplication in a single JVM, StringProfiler analyzes which calling contexts create many string objects that have the same values. Based on the results from StringProfiler, we selectively unify the string objects created while applications are running.

We evaluated our approach for a production application server by using Apache DayTrader and the DaCapo benchmark suite. With our String Deduplication approach, the size of the total allocation was reduced by 7% to 12%. We also measured the execution performance of DayTrader running on three guest VMs in a KVM host machine. The execution performance was maintained even with a high density of guest VMs. This result showed that our technique can be used to keep up the quality of web services, even when the memory footprint for guest VMs exceeds a limit of a physical memory.

Acknowledgement

We thank Samuel Z. Guyer for his valuable comments on this paper. We also thank Graeme Johnson and Michael Dawson of IBM Canada for their various suggestions to our string deduplication work across JVMs. Finally, we are grateful to Adelina Dehelean for her contribution to the analyzing part of the single JVM deduplication during her internship program at IBM Research - Tokyo.

References

[1] Apache geronimo v2.0 daytrader. http://geronimo.apache.org/GMOxDOC22/daytrader-a-more-complex-application.html.

[2] Apache OpenJPA. http://openjpa.apache.org/.

[3] IBM corporation.WebSphere Application Server. http://www-01.ibm.com/software/webservers/appserv/was/.

[4] JVM Tool Interface. http://docs.oracle.com/javase/6/docs/platform/jvmti/jvmti.html.

[5] The Apache Software Foundation. Apache JMeter. http://jakarta.apache.org/jmeter/.

[6] The API documentation of the StringBuilder class. http://docs.oracle.com/javase/6/docs/api/java/lang/StringBuilder.html.

[7] Andrea Arcangeli, Izik Eidus, and Chris Wright. Increasing memory density by using ksm. In *In Proceedings of the Linux Symposium*, pages 19–28, 2009.

[8] C. Bailey. Java Technology, IBM Style: Introduction to the IBM Developer Kit: An overview of the new functions and features in the IBM implementation of java 5.0, 2006. http://www.ibm.com/developerworks/java/library/j-ibmjava1.html.

[9] DaCapo benchmark suite. http://www.dacapobench.org.

[10] Stephen M. Blackburn, Robin Garner, Chris Hoffmann, Asjad M. Khang, Kathryn S. McKinley, Rotem Bentzur, Amer Diwan, Daniel Feinberg, Daniel Frampton, Samuel Z. Guyer, Martin Hirzel, Antony Hosking, Maria Jump, Han Lee, J. Eliot B. Moss, Aashish Phansalkar, Darko Stefanović, Thomas VanDrunen, Daniel von Dincklage, and Ben Wiedermann. The dacapo benchmarks: Java benchmarking development and analysis. In *Proceedings of the 21st Annual ACM SIGPLAN conference on Object-Oriented Programming Systems, Languages, and Applications*, OOPSLA '06, pages 169–190. ACM, 2006.

[11] Shigeru Chiba and Rei Ishikawa. Aspect-Oriented Programming beyond Dependency Injection. In *Proceedings of the 19th European conference on Object-oriented programming*, pages 121–143. Springer, 2005.

[12] AdrianaE. Chis, Nick Mitchell, Edith Schonberg, Gary Sevitsky, Patrick Oḥullivan, Trevor Parsons, and John Murphy. Patterns of memory inefficiency. In *ECOOP '11: Proceedings of the 25th European Conference on Object-Oriented Programming*, Lecture Notes in Computer Science, pages 383–407. Springer Berlin Heidelberg, 2011.

[13] Eric Clayberg and Dan Rubel. Eclipse Infrastructure. In *Eclipse Plug-ins*, pages 107–133. Addison-Wesley Professional, 3 edition, 2008.

[14] Oracle Corporation. Jsr-000121 application isolation api specification.

[15] James Gosling and Billy Joy. *The Java Language Specification, Third Edition*. Addison Wesley, 2005.

[16] Nikola Grcevski, Allan Kielstra, Kevin Stoodley, Mark Stoodley, and Vijay Sundaresan. Java just-in-time compiler and virtual machine improvements for server and middleware applications. In *Proceedings of the 3rd Conference on Virtual Machine Research and Technology Symposium - Volume 3*, pages 151–162, Berkeley, CA, USA, 2004. USENIX Association.

[17] Kiyokuni Kawachiya, Kazunori Ogata, and Tamiya Onodera. Analysis and reduction of memory inefficiencies in Java strings. In *Proceedings of the 23rd ACM SIGPLAN conference on Object-Oriented Programming Systems Languages and Applications*, OOPSLA '08, pages 385–402. ACM, 2008.

[18] Gregor Kiczales, Erik Hilsdale, Jim Hugunin, Mik Kersten, Jeffrey Palm, and William G. Griswold. An Overview of AspectJ. In *ECOOP '01 - Object-Oriented Programming: 15th European Conference, LNCS 2072*, pages 327–353. Springer, 2001.

[19] KVM. http://www.linux-kvm.org/page/main_page.

[20] Darko Marinov and Robert O'Callahan. Object equality profiling. In *Proceedings of the 18th Annual ACM SIGPLAN Conference on Object-Oriented Programing, Systems, Languages, and Applications*, OOPSLA '03, pages 313–325, New York, NY, USA, 2003. ACM.

[21] Hiroshi Maruyama, Kent Tamura, Naohiko Uramoto, Makoto Murata, Andy Clark, Yuichi Nakamura, Ryo Neyama, Kazuya Kosaka, and Satoshi Hada. *XML and Java: Developing Web Applications, 2nd Edition*. Addison Wesley, 2002.

[22] Nick Mitchell, Edith Schonberg, and Gary Sevitsky. Making sense of large heaps. In *ECOOP '09: Proceedings of the 23th European Conference on Object-Oriented Programming*, Lecture Notes in Computer Science, pages 77–97. Springer Berlin Heidelberg, 2009.

[23] Nick Mitchell and Gary Sevitsky. The causes of bloat, the limits of health. In *Proceedings of the 22nd annual ACM SIGPLAN conference on Object-oriented programming systems and applications*, pages 245–260. ACM, 2007.

[24] Jones Richard and Lins Rafael. *Garbage Collection: Algorithms for Automatic Dynamic Memory Management*. Wiley, 1996.

[25] Jack Shirazi. *Java Performance Tuning*. O'Reilly Media Inc., 2003.

[26] Carl A. Waldspurger. Memory resource management in vmware esx server. *SIGOPS Oper. Syst. Rev.*, 36(SI):181–194, 2002.

Shrinking the Hypervisor One Subsystem at a Time

A Userspace Packet Switch for Virtual Machines

Julian Stecklina

Institute of Systems Architecture, Operating Systems Group
Technische Universität Dresden, Germany

Abstract

Efficient and secure networking between virtual machines is crucial in a time where a large share of the services on the Internet and in private datacenters run in virtual machines. To achieve this efficiency, virtualization solutions, such as Qemu/KVM, move towards a monolithic system architecture in which all performance critical functionality is implemented directly in the hypervisor in privileged mode. This is an attack surface in the hypervisor that can be used from compromised VMs to take over the virtual machine host and all VMs running on it.

We show that it is possible to implement an efficient network switch for virtual machines as an unprivileged userspace component running in the host system including the driver for the upstream network adapter. Our network switch relies on functionality already present in the KVM hypervisor and requires no changes to Linux, the host operating system, and the guest.

Our userspace implementation compares favorably to the existing in-kernel implementation with respect to throughput and latency. We reduced per-packet overhead by using a run-to-completion model and are able to outperform the unmodified system for VM-to-VM traffic by a large margin when packet rates are high.

Categories and Subject Descriptors D.4.7 [*Operating Systems*]: Organization and Design; D.4.4 [*Operating Systems*]: Communications Management–Network communication

Keywords Virtualization; Networking; Security

VEE '14, March 1–2, 2014, Salt Lake City, Utah, USA.
Copyright is held by the owner/author(s). Publication rights licensed to ACM.
ACM 978-1-4503-2764-0/14/03. . . $15.00.
http://dx.doi.org/10.1145/2576195.2576202

1. Introduction

A large share of services on the Internet and in private datacenters run in virtual machines [4]. To achieve efficiency, virtualization solutions, such as Qemu/KVM [3], have moved toward a monolithic system architecture in which performance critical functionality is implemented directly in the hypervisor.

Monolithic virtualization layers are a particularly attractive target for attacks, because programming errors can lead to denial of service, disclosure of confidential information, or complete takeover of the virtual machine host by a malicious third party including every unrelated virtual machine on the same host. Security of the virtualization layer is of the utmost importance.

The motivation for having a lean hypervisor with small attack surface can be drawn from the microkernel community, which argues to separate as many components as possible in their own address spaces and thus introduce additional security hurdles for attackers. Despite growing experience in designing microkernel-based systems [8] and applying these design principles to virtualization [28], commodity hypervisors have not adopted the microkernel approach.

In addition to mitigating safety and security concerns, running subsystems in userspace also offers an easy way to update, inspect, and debug them with tools that are familiar to developers of ordinary userspace programs. Yet we still observe the ongoing adherence to monolithic systems even for operating system kernels in general, despite successful efforts to move classic kernel functionality into userspace [13].

Networking is a particularly important and problematic [31] aspect of an efficient virtualization layer. In this paper, we show that an efficient userspace implementation can be achieved for the network path in a commodity hypervisor, and more specifically that network connectivity for virtual machines is possible without any network specific code at all running in the hypervisor or in privileged components.

Our example platform is KVM [14], an efficient and mature virtualization solution for Linux. KVM is interesting in this context, because it relies on the userspace virtual machine monitor Qemu [3]. The per-VM Qemu process provides additional isolation between VMs, but the role of Qemu has shrunk since KVM's inception. As of Linux 3.10 everything regarding interrupt handling and timeouts [18], except their initial setup, is for the sake of performance now done by the KVM module itself. This includes instruction decoding and device emulation of certain timers and interrupt controllers.

With the introduction of `vhost-net`, an accelerator module for paravirtualized networking, network I/O handling is handled in the Linux kernel. Future Linux versions will have in-kernel implementations of paravirtual block I/O as well. Qemu is left to handle the VM bootstrap and any devices that are not deemed worthy of a kernel implementation yet, while the attack surface in the most privileged software component in the system, the hypervisor, is growing.

We introduce *sv3*, a network packet switch implemented as a normal Linux process, which is a replacement for the `vhost-net` acceleration module in the Linux kernel, an in-kernel packet switch, and the `virtio` implementation in Qemu itself. sv3 can also host the driver for the physical network adapter used for outgoing traffic in userspace.

sv3 concentrates networking functionality in a single process, but has all the advantages mentioned earlier. Isolated networking islands can be built by running multiple sv3 instances. Faults in one instance do not spread to subsystems, processes, or VMs that do not depend on it.

Our paper makes the following contributions:

- We design a userspace network switch for virtual machines that relies on existing functionality in Linux (Section 3).

- We evaluate our prototype switch (Section 4) and show that the performance of such a design is comparable to a production in-kernel implementation, while security properties are superior.

- We conclude that implementation of the networking path in the hypervisor itself, including (para-)virtual device emulation, packet switching, and driver for the upstream network adapter is not necessary, because userspace implementations can be equally efficient in a commodity system.

In the following section, we review how Qemu and KVM implement networking. The informed reader may skip to the design of sv3 in Section 3.

2. Networking in Qemu/KVM

Bellard [3] developed Qemu as a standalone emulator for all essential devices of a complete PC[1] and as thus needed no special support by the kernel initially, but suffered high

---
[1] Of course, Qemu also supports different architectures, such as ARM, MIPS, PowerPC and others.

overhead. This situation was resolved by the advent of hardware-assisted virtualization on the x86 platform [29], which made it possible to use virtualization with close to native speeds.

KVM [14], a small abstraction for hardware virtualization features, was introduced to make use of hardware virtualization features and Qemu was modified to support it. The combination of Qemu and KVM is an efficient and stable production virtualization layer.

2.1 `virtio`

Given that the network is usually the only way for a virtual machine to interact with the outside world, access to the network has to be particularly efficient. `virtio` is a network interface specification especially suited for use in virtual machines. It works like other modern NICs by offering the guest a set of DMA queues, at least one receive (RX) queue and one transmit (TX) queue. The guest then chains multiple DMA descriptors together to form a descriptor chain, which represents either a buffer to receive packet data or a buffer that contains a packet ready to be sent. Whenever the guest needs to notify the host, either after queuing packets for transmissions or offering buffers for packet receipt, the guest writes to the `NOTIFY` register of the `virtio-net` device, which may be either an I/O port or a MMIO register depending on the hardware platform. Similarly, if the host needs to notify the guest, it injects IRQs.

The specification offers a way for both parties to see whether the other needs to be notified. Each queue has `NO_NOTIFY` and `NO_INTERRUPT` bits that can be set, when explicit notifications are not necessary.

If both guest and host support offloads, a `virtio-net` device offers a full complement of stateless offloads to the guest, such as checksum and TCP segmentation offload for sending and large receive offload for receiving packets.

A complete description of `virtio` is out of scope for this paper. We refer the reader to Russel [24].

2.2 Accelerating `virtio`

Even with KVM, until the introduction of `vhost-net`, Qemu handled network I/O in userspace and used `tap` devices to pass packets to the kernel. These `tap` devices are usually bridged with a physical NIC to provide access to a network. For a `virtio` network device, sending a packet involves exiting the virtual machine and scheduling the Qemu process. Qemu will pass the packet to the `tap` device with a `write` system call. When sending packets between VMs, this scheme results in up to four system calls and multiple packet copies.

`vhost-net` was introduced to Linux in 2010 in order to reduce virtualization overheads for network-heavy workloads. The main idea is to move the packet handling path of the `virtio` backend into the kernel and remove unnecessary mode switching and packet copying.

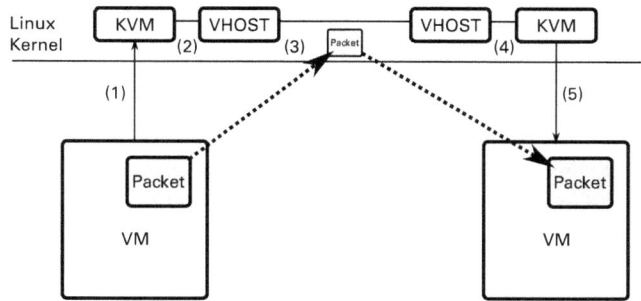

Figure 1. Control flow of packet transmission between two VMs (A and B) with vhost-accelerated network adapters on a single host. Each virtual NIC has a corresponding vhost thread in the host kernel. The sending VM triggers an I/O exit by writing its NOTIFY register (1), which KVM signals to the vhost thread (2). This kernel thread copies the packet data into a kernel buffer and delivers it to the network stack (3). The network subsystem wakes up the receiver's vhost thread, which copies the packet data into a packet buffer of the receiving VM. If an IRQ is necessary, it signals the receiver's vCPU kernel thread to inject an interrupt (4), which delivers the interrupt to the guest (5). No Qemu code executes for packet transmission.

Instead of tying vhost-net to KVM and creating a special purpose solution, the Linux developers used multiple event file descriptors (eventfds) to connect KVM and vhost-net as shown in Figure 1. An eventfd is a file descriptor that can be used to wait for events. In its most basic form, a read on an eventfd will block, until the eventfd is written to.

To process buffers enqueued by the guest in a timely fashion, vhost-net needs to be informed when the guest wrote the NOTIFY register. For this reason vhost creates a thread per virtio device, which blocks on an eventfd. This file descriptor is triggered by KVM, when the NOTIFY register is written.

When packets have been delivered, vhost needs to inject interrupts into the guest. Interrupt injection happens by binding an eventfd to an interrupt source in KVM and giving this eventfd to vhost, which can trigger it.

The actual setup of these event file descriptors is handled by Qemu in userspace. As of Linux 3.10 when running a network benchmark in a properly configured Qemu/KVM, Qemu itself is not involved beyond the initial setup of the VM.

3. sv3: Packet Switch for VMs

During the development of the sv3 switch we strove to solve the following problems.

Per-packet overhead should be minimized, as this will facilitate throughput even when data is arriving in small packets. As seen in Figure 2, in the extreme case of 64 byte packets, only 67 ns are available per packet on average to

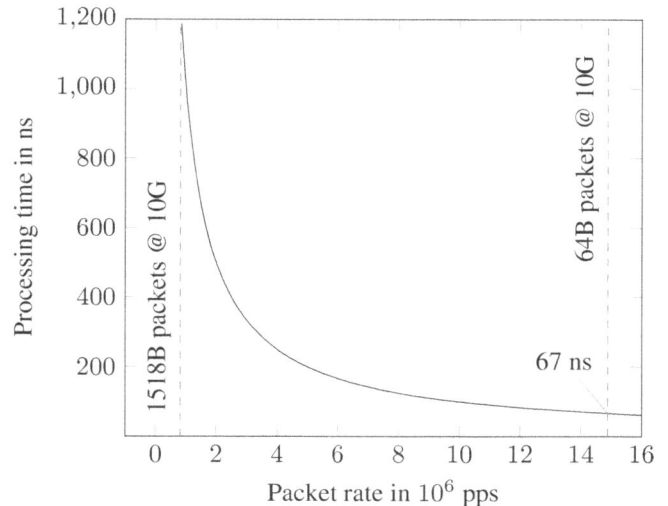

Figure 2. Time available for packet processing for given packet rates on 10 Gbit/s Ethernet. A 64 byte packet must be processed in 67 ns to keep up with line rate. System calls or mutex acquisitions per packet are infeasible.

keep up line rate. While achieving 10 Gbit/s line rate with small packets on commodity hardware certainly remains a challenge, it is clear that heavy-weight operations per packet, such as lock acquisitions or system calls, must be avoided to come close to that goal.

Related to per-packet overhead is the issue of dealing with high notification overhead. We initially believed that our userspace switch will have significant overhead for notifications and IRQ injecting into its client VMs. While this overhead turned out to be less pronounced than we expected (Figure 5), it drove us to abandon the thread-per-VM model of vhost-net.

Memory-bandwidth starts to become a limiting factor as network speeds approach the same order of magnitude. For common operations, our switch should thus not copy data needlessly.

3.1 Qemu Modifications

Just as vhost-net, we concentrate on the virtio network adapter. In vhost-net, the virtio implementation is split between the code handling the setup in Qemu and the packet handling path in the vhost-net module. To avoid this complexity, we strove to implement virtio in a single component only. Because sv3 is meant as a switch for virtual machines, it makes sense to closely tie the implementation of the virtio NIC to the switch itself.

Qemu offers no facility to implement devices out-of-process, so we enhanced Qemu to allow externally implemented PCI devices. Our modified Qemu is able to connect to another process that implements a specific device using a UNIX domain socket.

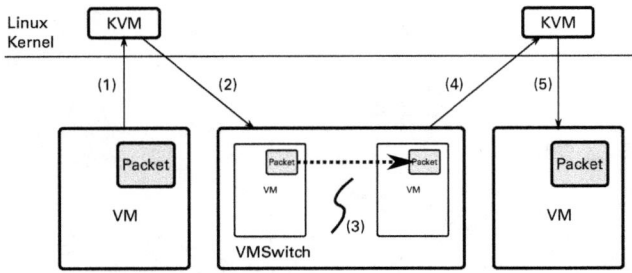

Figure 3. Control flow of packet transmission between two VMs (A and B) with sv3 as packet switch. The sending VM triggers an I/O exit by writing its NOTIFY register (1), which KVM signals to sv3 via an eventfd (2). sv3 is unblocked by the write to the eventfd (3) and copies the packet via its local mappings of VM memory (4). The receiving VM is notified of the packet by signaling an eventfd (5) that is bound to KVM's IRQ injection (6). KVM then injects a virtual interrupt (7).

UNIX domain sockets allow file descriptors to be transmitted between two processes. The modified Qemu creates the guest's memory as a file on a RAM-backed file system and transmits the corresponding file descriptors via the domain socket. The external process can then mmap the guest's memory in its own address space. Further eventfds are exchanged for interrupt injection and I/O notifications.

Our implementation of external PCI devices is complete enough to handle devices with MSI-X interrupts, DMA, and port I/O. This covers virtio, but with minor additions, we can implement other PCI devices in external processes as well.

3.2 Implementing virtio in sv3

Using our Qemu modifications, we are able move the complete implementation of the virtio PCI device into the switch process. This has advantages beyond just simplicity. Because the switch has direct access to virtio DMA queues and can communicate directly with KVM for interrupt injection, there is no involvement of Qemu in packet handling.

Uncritical port I/O by the guest on the I/O addresses of the virtio device are relayed to the switch via the domain socket connection. This is only used during virtio configuration by the guest. Afterwards, the guest only writes to the NOTIFY register of the device. The switch instructs Qemu to attach an eventfd to this particular register. When a write occurs, KVM will trigger this eventfd instead of notifying Qemu of the I/O operation.

3.3 The Switching Loop

The key part in sv3 is its switching loop. Shalev et al. [25] have shown that a single threaded network subsystem is feasible. We build on this result by having a single thread in sv3 to do all packet switching. This thread executes a loop that continuously checks all ports and their queues for work until no port has outgoing packets pending. At this point it will block on an eventfd. Writes by a guest to the NOTIFY register of a virtio device trigger exactly this eventfd, thus unblocking the switch.

In effect, there is no need for mutexes and atomic operations. Operations on switch data structures that rarely change and are modifed outside the switching loop, such as the list of attached ports, are serialized with userspace RCU [7].

While the switching loop is active, sv3 disables notifications for all client VMs. In particular, this means that while the switch is busy copying packets for one VM, another VM need not cause a VM exit to notify the switch of activity in its DMA queues. The busier the switching loop gets the less notifications are needed in the system, until there are no notifications needed at all. sv3 only enables notifications from VMs when it is idle and about to sleep.

Depending on the destination, a packet originating from a virtual machine can take two paths. If the destination is another VM, the packet will be directly copied from the source VM's memory to the receiving VM in a run-to-completion fashion. If the receiving VM does not have sufficient network buffers queued at its virtio device, the packet will be dropped.

While packets that are destined for a VM are either delivered directly or dropped, packets destined for the physical network adapter are sent asynchronously. sv3 translates the packet description given as virtio descriptors into DMA descriptors of the physical NIC. The switching loop then polls regularly to check when the transmission is completed and in turn indicates completion to the sending VM. At this point, the sending VM can reuse its packet buffers. This mode of operation will complete transmit operations potentially out-of-order from the perspective of the guest, a use-case that was already anticipated by Russel [24] in the original virtio design to allow zero-copy transmit. Since only packets delivered to different switch ports may be reordered, the performance of TCP connections is not affected.

As already hinted, with all guest memory directly visible in the sv3 process additional packet copies can be avoided. In contrast to the Linux kernel, where large virtually contiguous in-kernel mappings of user memory are problematic, and where user memory is usually handled pagewise, a userspace solution has the luxury of a simple virtual memory layout: mmaping large files into an application's address space is a common operation.

With packet switching implemented in a single thread, sv3 has to do its own scheduling of how long to service each port. The main tunable parameter in sv3 is the number of packets the switch will deliver from a single queue until it considers packets from another queue. The rationale to set this batch size to values larger than one is to exploit the warmed up cache. Large values obviously affect packet latency.

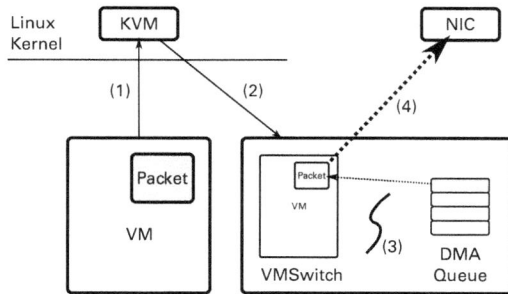

Figure 4. Receiving or sending a packet using the physical network adapter. Step 1 to 3 work as in the VM-to-VM case shown in Figure 3 on the facing page. sv3 translates `virtio`'s packet description to DMA descriptors understood by the NIC. The NIC then reads the packet data directly from the guest's memory.

.

Choosing the optimal batch size is not the scope of this paper. We use a value of 16 by default and note that this can lead to unfair behavior of the switch when different VMs send packets of different average size. In this situation, the switching loop will spend more time servicing the VM sending larger packets.

When latency is of concern, the switching loop can be instructed not to block when the switch is idle, until a certain time has passed. We call this the *idle poll time*. An idle poll time of zero means that the switch will immediately sleep once it has nothing to do. This is the default mode of sv3. A large idle poll time turns the switch into polling mode, where it never sleeps. For the rest of the paper we do not consider poll times other than zero, as it makes the switch behavior hard to compare to `vhost-net`.

The main differences between `vhost-net` and sv3, besides whether they run in the kernel, are their styles of execution. While `vhost` employs one thread per VM, sv3 utilizes a single thread that delivers packets in a run-to-completion fashion.

During overload, i.e. more packets are queued than the network subsystem can handle, sv3 degrades gracefully in that it does not need notifications by VMs anymore, as explained earlier. `vhost` will instead have multiple busy threads that need to synchronize and compete for compute resources with vCPU threads and each other.

3.4 External Connection with Userspace Drivers

Even a packet switch for virtual machines needs an upstream port to transmit packets beyond the boundaries of a single physical host. We decided against using Linux's networking subsystem for this purpose, because it only offers `PF_PACKET` socketsfor high-performance raw packet reception and transmission. We consider `PF_PACKET` sockets limiting, as they require batching of buffer operations and thus introduce unnecessary delays. Additionally, they only sup-

port zero-copy transmission from a fixed kernel-provided memory region, which makes direct transmission from VM memory impossible.

We instead decided to drive the physical NIC in sv3 itself, using the `VFIO` framework [30]. `VFIO` is primarily meant for implementing PCI passthrough in Qemu, but is sufficient for implementing drivers for PCI devices in Linux userspace directly.

`VFIO` allows binding event file descriptors to interrupts. In sv3, we use this feature to unblock the switching loop when the NIC signals incoming packets. This is analogous to how VMs unblock the switching loop by writing to their `virtio`'s `NOTIFY` register.

By including the device driver in the switch, zero-copy packet transmission is possible[2] and the NIC sends packets directly from guest memory. Receiving packets requires an additional packet copy, because the NIC delivers packets before the switch knows where to deliver them.

The switch passes stateless offloads programmed by the guest for a packet to the NIC. Given guests and an upstream NIC that all support TCP segmentation and checksum offloads, the switch never needs to segment packets or compute checksums on its own. The switch also passes Large receives, i.e. TCP packets belonging to the same connection that have been merged into a single packet, on to guests, if they support it.

We implemented a driver for the Intel X520 NIC, a popular 10Gbit Ethernet adapter, from scratch. This particular NIC, as practically all competing 10Gbit NICs, offers a superset of the offloads that are possible with `virtio` and is therefore a good fit for sv3.

4. Evaluation

We evaluated our system on an Intel Core i7 3770S CPU running at 3.1 GHz. Memtest86+ [1] reports 18975 MiB/s memory bandwidth (roughly 159 GBit/s). Memory access is uniform. Our host system uses Fedora 19 with a vanilla Linux kernel version 3.10.18 and has power management and frequency scaling disabled. As already mentioned in Section 3.4, we used an Intel X520 network adapter. Our guests used a stripped down 3.10.10 kernel. We used our modified Qemu based on version 1.5.0 for all tests. Disregarding small changes in how guest memory is allocated, our modifications do not touch Qemu's own `virtio-net` implementation.

4.1 Security

One of the major concerns with code executing in kernel space is its security and safety, since one programming error can crash the system, cause unrelated subsystems to fail,

---

[2] Zero-copy packet transmission is only possible of VM memory is locked. If the system overcommits memory, an additional copy is required, because the NIC cannot DMA into guest memory in this case.

disclose information, or in the worst case allow attackers to gain control of the system.

With respect to sv3, there are two sides to this issue. The first one is *attack surface* and the second the implications of a successful attack. With regards to an attacker that can craft arbitrary packets and fully control one of the connected virtual machines, sv3 shares the same attack surface as KVM used with `vhost-net`, that is the `virtio` interface and those parts of KVM that are necessary for mapping specific VM exits to `eventfds`.

While the latter feature in the KVM module might be superfluous and could be removed from the kernel, if general userspace VM exit handling were fast enough [28], the real value of userspace packet switching lies in the mitigation of attacks.

Because sv3 is an ordinary Linux application, existing hardening techniques, such as sandboxing, can be easily deployed making security relevant flaws harder to exploit for an attacker and attacks themselves easier to detect. Even a successful attack on sv3 will only grant an attacker user privileges on the host, control over the physical network adapter and access to memory of the connected virtual machines.

Access to VM memory can further be restricted by a virtualization layer that emulates an IOMMU [2]. Qemu needs to share only memory that guests mark as DMA-able with a sv3 instance.

Control over the network adapter is also not as valuable as it appears. Due to the use of the host's IOMMU to safely drive the device in userspace in the first place, DMA cannot be used to subvert the rest of the system. The Linux kernel makes sure the application can only establish IOMMU mappings to memory its own memory and an attacker would need to overcome this security feature first.

Finally, sv3 does not need root privileges.[3] It only needs access to its UNIX domain socket and the VFIO device file of the network adapter is supposed to drive. Sandboxing sv3 is trivial.

4.2 Resource Consumption

Low resource consumption is one argument in favor of processes instead of virtual machines as units of disaggregating operating system functionality. Measuring exact memory usage of a Linux process is not straightforward. We measured sv3's memory footprint by observing its *resident set size* (RSS) as displayed by the tool `ps` and subtracted the amount of shared guest memory, as the latter would otherwise be accounted twice, once for the virtual machine and once for sv3. Note that RSS does not include kernel data structures, such as page tables.

Without the upstream network driver sv3 consumes below 2 MiB of resident memory and currently needs 384 bytes

---

[3] Root privileges *are* required for setting interrupt affinity, if that is required, because the VFIO interface is incomplete in that respect. Privileges can be dropped after initialization and before a VM is connected to the switch. We consider adding this capability to VFIO.

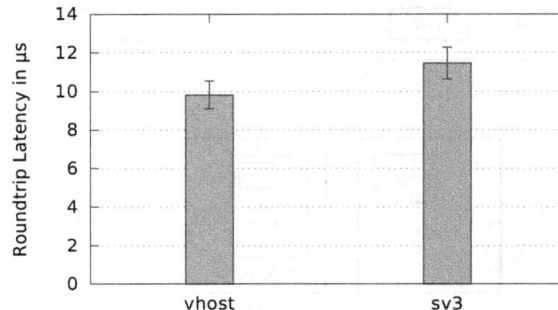

Figure 5. Time between triggering network processing in the guest and receiving an IRQ in the guest for `vhost-net` and sv3 **without** network processing. The overhead for sv3 is caused by traversing the system call layer and switching to userspace. Error bars indicate standard deviation.

metadata per virtual switch port. The Intel X520 NIC driver increases memory usage to 16 MiB, mostly because of a liberal amount of packet buffers.

As a point of comparison, consider recent work by Colp et al. [5], who decompose the privileged Domain 0 in a Xen system by running Domain 0 subsystems in virtual machines. The network backend VM in their systems is allocated 128 MiB of RAM. The smallest VMs in their design use 32 MiB RAM and are confined, unlike sv3, to a very limited programming environment.

4.3 Microbenchmarks

sv3 reimplements a kernel subsystem in userspace. Thus it must use userspace APIs to achieve what `vhost-net` can do with potentially more optimized in-kernel APIs. In this section, we want to measure the direct overhead of using userspace APIs.

In our particular case, sv3 uses `eventfds` to be notified of activity in the guest's DMA queues and to inject IRQs. `vhost-net` uses the same functionality inside the Linux kernel directly and can avoid the kernel to user mode transition.

We modified both implementations to not do any packet processing, but inject an interrupt directly after being notified by the guest. In Figure 5, we measure the time that elapses between triggering network processing from the guest and receiving the IRQ in the same virtual machine. This time includes, for both systems, the same overhead for the actual VM exit and interrupt injection done by KVM. sv3 adds overhead for traversing the system call layer and switching to and from userspace.

The additional overhead is below 2 μs. The design decision to minimize wake ups by using only one switching thread, may thus not be as important as we initially thought.

4.4 Performance

We evaluate the efficiency of sv3 by measuring the CPU utilization of the host system for constant-throughput TCP streams and packet latency. TCP stream measurements were generated using nuttcp [20]. netperf [19] was used to assess latency using its request/response benchmarks. We compare sv3 to vhost-net, which had its zero-copy mode enabled.

We consider two basic scenarios. In the first scenario, an external machine generates the load and a VM on the test system receives it. We use the userspace driver of our Intel X520 NIC, which is built into sv3. vhost-net uses the normal Linux network stack and thus the Linux driver. We tried to use hardware features, such as Large Receive Offload and interrupt rate throttling, in our driver in the same way as the Linux driver to avoid distorting the results.

We throttled the interrupt rate to 10000 interrupts per second for both vhost-net and sv3. This value corresponds to the "bulk latency" setting in Linux' ixgbe driver.

The second scenario moves the load generator into a virtual machine. The traffic stream is thus between two VMs on a single host. No external traffic is involved. Because nuttcp consumes a full core for sending constant-throughput streams, we do not show CPU utilization in this case, because it is always equal to one.

External-to-VM Traffic Figure 6 on the next page shows CPU utilization for TCP streams from the external source with TCP segmentation and large receive offload enabled (left) and disabled (right). With both offloads enabled, nuttcp produced stable results upto 8 Gbit/s. As the receiver does not fully consume its core, the sender must be the bottleneck.

At 8 Gbit/s, sv3 uses 30 % of its core. The CPU utilization for both systems is almost identical. The reason is that both systems use the same architecture to receive packets. The network adapter copies packets into anonymous buffers. After receiving the IRQ, the Linux kernel wakes up the networking subsystem or in the case of sv3 unblocks an eventfd. The thread that is responsible wakes up and copies the packet to the guest VM's memory. Afterwards, the guest is notified of their arrival. The only difference is that sv3 uses eventfds to be notified by the kernel and to notify the guest.

The right part of Figure 6 shows the same setting, but with TCP segmentation and large receive offloads disabled to put more stress on the network path. Instead of large packets the network adapter will now only deliver MTU-sized packets. We used a standard MTU of 1500 bytes. We did not measure vhost-net performance, as we could not disable large receive offload. As with the measurements with offloads enabled, the receive is the bottleneck. At 6 Gbit/s, sv3 uses 55 % of its core.

VM-to-VM Traffic Throughput results for our second scenario, VM-to-VM traffic, are shown in Figure 7 on the following page. With offloads enabled (left), we get stable results with nuttcp up to about 30 Gbit/s. For throughput below 10 Gbit/s, sv3 is slightly more efficient compared to

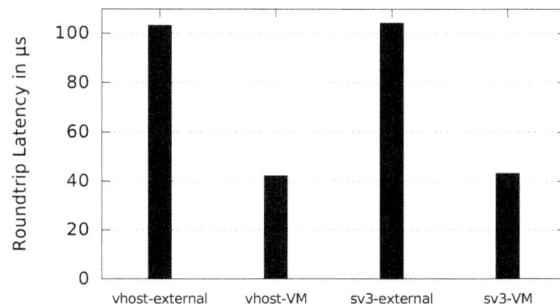

Figure 8. Roundtrip latency for TCP packets between two virtual machines (VM), a virtual machine and an external load generator (external). Standard deviation is below $0.4\mu s$ for all measurements.

vhost-net. With throughput beyond 10 Gbit/s, this effect is more pronounced. Between 12 and 13 Gbit/s the receiving VM starts to fully utilize its core and essentially goes into polling mode, which is reflected in the curve.

The right diagram in Figure 7 shows VM-to-VM traffic with offloads disabled. vhost-net is not able to reach 7 Gbit/s, because it fully utilizes all four cores[4]. For sv3, virtual machines are the bottleneck at 9 Gbit/s as the switching loop consumes only one core at 50%.

Above 7 Gbit/s, when the guest starts to fully utilize its core, sv3's CPU utilization drops. We attribute this to additional batching and less frequent wakeups. The single-threaded model with little per-packet overhead seems especially suited to this scenario.

Latency Judging from our microbenchmarks, we anticipated a modest increase in latency by using sv3 for external traffic and expected a slight decrease in the VM-to-VM case for sv3, because the packets are handled by only one thread instead of two.

Latency results are shown in Figure 8. We observe that with both systems latency is practically identical. We see an increase of roughly one microsecond for sv3 compared to vhost-net.

5. Discussion

5.1 Userspace Switching vs. Driver Domains

Our design shares aspects with the Driver Domain model as it is used in Xen [17]. In particular, it isolates packet processing in a separate component, which is in our case a process in the host system and in Xen's case a dedicated virtual machine.

The overhead of a dedicated virtual machine has lead to architectures, such as Hyper-Switch [21], that optimize network performance by moving the data plane into the hypervisor and leaving only the control plane isolated.

---

[4] As explained earlier, the sending VM's utilization is not shown, because it is always fully utilizing one core.

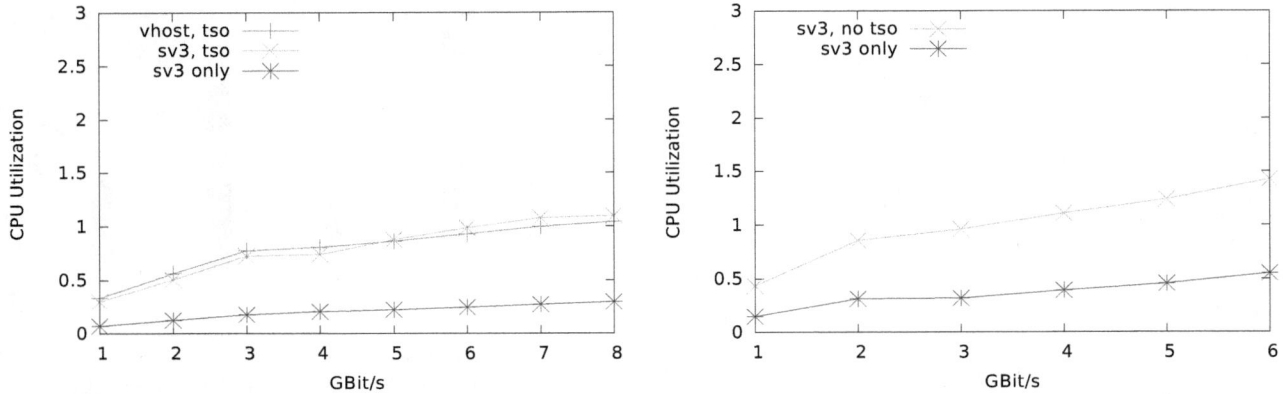

Figure 6. CPU utilization for receiving a TCP stream from an external source. We measured utilization of the whole system, except for the switch-only measurement, which only shows CPU utilization of the software switch itself. The left diagram shows the default configuration with all offloads enabled, the right measurement was done with TSO and LRO disabled. The Linux driver did not support disabling LRO, so it is not shown in the right diagram.

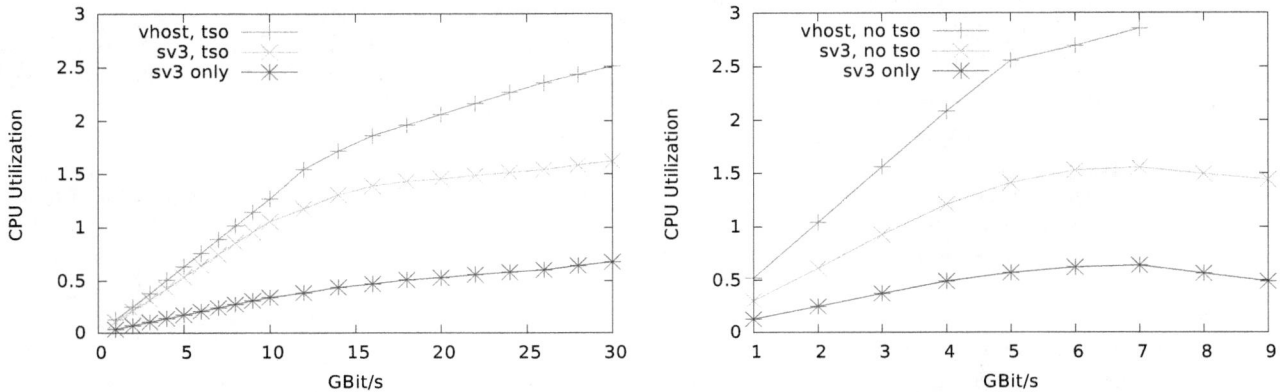

Figure 7. CPU utilization for receiving a TCP stream from another VM. CPU utilization of the load generator VM is excluded. The maximum load of the `vhost-net` configuration is three, when the receiver's vCPU thread and both vhost threads are compute bound. For sv3, the maximum load is two.

We argue that processes offer a lighter-weight abstraction than virtual machines, which still allows the full software switch to run isolated from the hypervisor without special privileges. We detail sv3's memory consumption in Section 4.2.

5.2 Multiserver Operating Systems and SMP

One of the reasons for implementing performance critical functionality in the kernel (or hypervisor) is performance. In a monolithic kernel, components can simply call each other with a function call. Yet the example of `vhost-net` in Figure 1 shows that in realistic scenarios multiple threads interact through asynchronous communication even in a monolithic kernel.

On a modern system with a multicore CPU, each of those threads will execute on a different core, unless the system is overcommitted. Frequent context switches between dif-

ferent address spaces do not happen. In the ideal case, each core executes a single thread in a single address space. The cost of switching an address space becomes meaningless to the overall performance of the system. Isolating subsystems in separate address spaces is practically for free. The performance difference of components running in kernelspace compared to userspace now depends on the efficiency of asynchronous notifications.

By consolidating work onto a single thread, our network switch tries to stay active as long as possible compared to the thread-per-VM model employed by `vhost-net`. sv3 avoids the need for frequent notifications when possible and thus mitigates even this source of potential inefficiency. In return, we get a high-performance subsystem running in userspace.

We believe that this reasoning also applies to other components that are typically implemented in a monolithic kernel. A case in point is the use of asynchronous system calls as in the FlexSC system [27], where system calls are used via shared memory and asynchronous notifications. sv3 can be considered an application of this idea with the twist that our "system call handler" is not running in the kernel.

The design of our userspace network switch is applicable to and inspired by microkernel-based multiserver systems [9, 15, 28].

5.3 A Monolith in Userspace

It seems as if we are just exchanging a monolithic kernelspace component with a monolithic userspace component, but there are important differences compared to the kernel solution.

sv3 can be started multiple times, each time creating an isolated network switch. Errors in sv3 do not propagate to other instances assuming that the underlying kernel is correct. More importantly failures in sv3 do not interfere with kernel subsystems.

The robustness of a single sv3 instance can, of course, be increased. We currently run NIC drivers in the context of the switching loop. A malfunctioning device or bugs in the driver code can potentially wreak havoc on all connected VMs. By making the driver a separate process that speaks the same interfaces as VMs, this scenario can be avoided at the expense of performance.

6. Future Work

6.1 Scalability and NUMA

As demonstrated in Section 4.4, sv3 compares favorably to `vhost-net` for VM-to-VM and external-to-VM communication, because those workloads rarely cause the switching loop itself to be the bottleneck. Especially for high packet rates, such as the measurement in Figure 7 on the facing page with TCP segmentation disabled, the single-threaded run-to-completion approach of sv3 clearly outperforms the model where one virtual NIC is driven by one thread as in `vhost-net`.

For multiple senders, `vhost-net` eventually scales better, because it can distribute packet processing to different cores, whereas sv3 in its current design faces a wall when packet processing chokes a single core, even when virtual network throughput is far from the theoretical maximum dictated by the memory bandwidth of the system. Another issue is that systems with NUMA configurations might exhibit poor performance, if sv3 needs to read and write packet data from distant memory.

One idea to address scalability is to start multiple sv3 instances, one per NUMA domain. VMs are connected to sv3 instances with the same NUMA affinity and, depending on the system, share a last-level cache. Each sv3 instance would still be able to switch packets on the same NUMA node without additional copies. The sv3 instances themselves are connected to each other and use a shared memory region for

each connection to forward packets destined to "remote" virtual machines.

Advantages of such a configuration are that performance scales with the number of NUMA nodes, without introducing complexity in sv3 in the form of multithreading. Additionally, service disruption caused by a crash of one sv3 instance is confined to a handful of VMs.

6.2 Integrating Advanced Interconnects

Cui et al. [6] propose to offer virtual TCP offload engines to VMs and use advanced interconnects, such as InfiniBand, to optimize the networking performance between VMs on different hosts. The implications of this approach are appealing, because what a VM initiates as a TCP connection can be mapped to the most efficient network technology or protocol between two virtual machine hosts, if these hosts cooperate. Instead of speaking TCP between two VMs on the same host, plain `memcpy` with primitive congestion control can be used. For remote connections, data transfer can be implemented using RDMA. The transport mechanism can even be transparently switched, if VMs are migrated. We plan to integrate such functionality in sv3.

7. Related Work

Our paper touches the areas of I/O scalability in the context of virtualization, network stack performance optimizations and operating system design. Additionally, it relates to OS and hypervisor disaggregation efforts.

VALE [23] is a software switch for virtual machines that achieves impressive packet forwarding rates. It reduces per-packet overhead by using a more efficient interface to transmit packets [22], removing VM exits, batching, and the reduction of mutex acquisitions. VALE is implemented in the kernel and shares the same security considerations as the standard `vhost-net` networking path.

Ram et al. [21] present Hyper-Switch, a scalable software switch for virtual machines with a split design to reduce the TCB, which we have already discussed in Section 5.1.

Shalev et al. [25] move the TCP/IP stack of a general purpose operating system onto a dedicated core. The isolated stack (IsoStack) uses queues to communicate with the rest of the system. We adopted design ideas of IsoStack for sv3, specifically the idea to have a main loop that serves all clients, is lockless, and does not need atomic instructions. sv3 shares the major drawbacks with IsoStack. In such a design, it is hard to scale network processing to two or more cores.

With their system ELVIS, Gordon et al. [10] try to remove VM exit and interrupt generation overhead by modifying `vhost-net` to run a single thread polling all guests similar to sv3. ELVIS runs in kernel space and is effective at reducing exits, but fully utilizes a core even for light load. The authors present a heuristic to distinguish latency-sensitive from throughput-oriented workloads that is applicable to sv3 as well. Given the experiences from building sv3, we believe that it is possible to port or reimplement ELVIS in userspace with similar performance to the in-kernel version.

SnabbSwitch [26] is a userspace packet switching and routing framework written in Lua. Its intent is to enable the rapid creation of software-defined networking functionality running on Linux in userspace. Our modifications to Qemu are applicable to SnabbSwitch and may improve its performance significantly.

With their Factored Operating Systems, Wentzlaff and Agarwal [32] rethink the operating system for a many-core system as fleets of servers, where each fleet implements an operating system service. The individual servers in a fleet are bound to particular processing cores and do not directly compete with applications for hardware resources. A future version of sv3 consisting of multiple cooperating instances may be seen as an incarnation of such a service fleet.

Minix 3 [11] uses userspace drivers and components and argues that restartable system components can greatly enhance the reliability of the whole system. Especially, components without or with little state should be easily restartable. sv3 falls into the latter category.

Userspace drivers have been shown to have negligible overhead compared to drivers running in the kernel [16]. Since then, the interfaces for userspace drivers in Linux have been vastly improved [30]. Our switch uses these interfaces.

Hruby et al. [12] agree that dedicating cores to I/O functionality is worthwhile and rearchitect a TCP/IP stack by putting the different layers onto different cores. In contrast to sv3, which follows the run-to-completion philosophy, each networking stack layer is a single threaded program. The authors argue that this is a good design choice for robustness as the layers themselves cannot include concurrency bugs and each layer can be restarted individually.

Colp et al. [5] decompose Xen's monolithic and privileged Domain 0 into several virtual machines according to the principle of least authority. sv3 achieves the same for the networking path in KVM with processes instead of virtual machines with a much lower memory footprint.

8. Conclusion

We have shown that it is possible to reimplement high performance components from an existing monolithic kernel in an unprivileged user process without sacrificing performance. sv3, our userspace network switch for virtual machines, replaces Linux' `vhost-net` subsystem, the in-kernel packet switch, and the device driver for the upstream network adapter. It relies only on basic virtualization functions in the Linux kernel, such as event forwarding and IRQ injection via event file descriptors. No networking code needs to run in privileged mode to achieve high performance networking.

By tightly coupling NIC drivers with the switch, we see identical CPU utilization compared to the in-kernel network-

ing path and negligable latency increase for external-to-VM traffic. VM-to-VM traffic is handled particularly efficient in our implementation, especially at high packet rates, because we reduce per-packet overhead with our design.

The limiting factor of sv3 is that it cannot yet utilize multiple cores for packet processing. For a large number of VMs and sufficient computational resources, it will eventually be outperformed by systems, such as `vhost-net` that use one thread per VM. However, given our microbenchmarks, we are confident that a thread-per-VM design can be adopted for a userspace switch as well.

The source code of sv3 and our Qemu patches are available at `https://os.inf.tu-dresden.de/~jsteckli/sv3.html`.

Acknowledgments

The author would like to thank Björn Döbel for invaluable input on drafts of this paper and Luke Gorrie and the snabb.co team for the occasional dose of motivation and time spent discussing the ideas presented in this paper.

References

[1] Memtest86+ - an advanced memory diagnostic tool. URL `http://www.memtest.org/`.

[2] N. Amit, M. Ben-Yehuda, D. Tsafrir, and A. Schuster. viommu: Efficient iommu emulation. In *Proceedings of the 2011 USENIX Conference on USENIX Annual Technical Conference*, USENIX ATC'11, pages 6–6, Berkeley, CA, USA, 2011. USENIX Association. URL `http://dl.acm.org/citation.cfm?id=2002181.2002187`.

[3] F. Bellard. Qemu, a fast and portable dynamic translator. In *Proceedings of the annual conference on USENIX Annual Technical Conference*, ATEC '05, pages 41–41, Berkeley, CA, USA, 2005. USENIX Association. URL `http://dl.acm.org/citation.cfm?id=1247360.1247401`.

[4] T. Benson, A. Akella, and D. A. Maltz. Network traffic characteristics of data centers in the wild. In *Proceedings of the 10th ACM SIGCOMM conference on Internet measurement*, IMC '10, pages 267–280, New York, NY, USA, 2010. ACM. ISBN 978-1-4503-0483-2. . URL `http://doi.acm.org/10.1145/1879141.1879175`.

[5] P. Colp, M. Nanavati, J. Zhu, W. Aiello, G. Coker, T. Deegan, P. Loscocco, and A. Warfield. Breaking up is hard to do: Security and functionality in a commodity hypervisor. In *Proceedings of the Twenty-Third ACM Symposium on Operating Systems Principles*, SOSP '11, pages 189–202, New York, NY, USA, 2011. ACM. ISBN 978-1-4503-0977-6. . URL `http://doi.acm.org/10.1145/2043556.2043575`.

[6] Z. Cui, P. G. Bridges, J. R. Lange, and P. A. Dinda. Virtual TCP offload: optimizing ethernet overlay performance on advanced interconnects. In *Proceedings of the 22nd international symposium on High-performance parallel and distributed computing*, HPDC '13, pages 49–60, New York, NY, USA, 2013. ACM. ISBN 978-1-4503-1910-2. . URL `http://doi.acm.org/10.1145/2462902.2462912`.

[7] M. Desnoyers, P. McKenney, A. Stern, M. Dagenais, and J. Walpole. User-level implementations of read-copy update. *Parallel and Distributed Systems, IEEE Transactions on*, 23 (2):375–382, 2012. ISSN 1045-9219. .

[8] K. Elphinstone and G. Heiser. From L3 to seL4 – what have we learnt in 20 years of L4 microkernels? In *ACM SIGOPS Symposium on Operating Systems Principles (SOSP)*, pages 133–150, Farmington, PA, USA, November 2013.

[9] genode. Genode operating system framework. URL `http://www.genode.org/`.

[10] A. Gordon, N. Har'El, A. Landau, M. Ben-Yehuda, and A. Traeger. Towards exitless and efficient paravirtual i/o. In *Proceedings of the 5th Annual International Systems and Storage Conference*, SYSTOR '12, pages 10:1–10:6, New York, NY, USA, 2012. ACM. ISBN 978-1-4503-1448-0. . URL `http://doi.acm.org/10.1145/2367589.2367593`.

[11] J. N. Herder, H. Bos, B. Gras, P. Homburg, and A. S. Tanenbaum. Minix 3: A highly reliable, self-repairing operating system. *SIGOPS Oper. Syst. Rev.*, 40(3):80–89, July 2006. ISSN 0163-5980. . URL `http://doi.acm.org/10.1145/1151374.1151391`.

[12] T. Hruby, D. Vogt, H. Bos, and A. S. Tanenbaum. Keep net working - on a dependable and fast networking stack. In *Proceedings of Dependable Systems and Networks (DSN 2012)*, Boston, MA, June 2012.

[13] A. Kantee. Rump file systems: kernel code reborn. In *Proceedings of the 2009 conference on USENIX Annual technical conference*, USENIX'09, pages 15–15, Berkeley, CA, USA, 2009. USENIX Association. URL `http://dl.acm.org/citation.cfm?id=1855807.1855822`.

[14] A. Kivity, Y. Kamay, D. Laor, U. Lublin, and A. Liguori. KVM: the Linux virtual machine monitor. In *Proceedings of the Linux Symposium*, volume 1, pages 225–230, 2007.

[15] A. Lackorzynski and A. Warg. Taming subsystems: capabilities as universal resource access control in L4. In *Proceedings of the Second Workshop on Isolation and Integration in Embedded Systems*, IIES '09, pages 25–30, New York, NY, USA, 2009. ACM. ISBN 978-1-60558-464-5. . URL `http://doi.acm.org/10.1145/1519130.1519135`.

[16] B. Leslie, P. Chubb, N. Fitzroy-Dale, S. Götz, C. Gray, L. Macpherson, D. Potts, Y.-T. Shen, K. Elphinstone, and G. Heiser. User-level device drivers: Achieved performance. *Journal of Computer Science and Technology*, 20(5):654–664, 2005. ISSN 1000-9000. . URL `http://dx.doi.org/10.1007/s11390-005-0654-4`.

[17] A. Menon, A. L. Cox, and W. Zwaenepoel. Optimizing network virtualization in Xen. In *Proceedings of the annual conference on USENIX '06 Annual Technical Conference*, ATEC '06, pages 2–2, Berkeley, CA, USA, 2006. USENIX Association. URL `http://dl.acm.org/citation.cfm?id=1267359.1267361`.

[18] J. Nakajima. Enabling optimized interrupt/APIC virtualization in KVM. In *KVM Forum*, 2012.

[19] netperf. netperf. URL `http://www.netperf.org/`.

[20] nuttcp. nuttcp network performance measurement tool. URL `https://www.nuttcp.net/`.

[21] K. K. Ram, A. L. Cox, M. Chadha, and S. Rixner. HyperSwitch: A scalable software virtual switching architecture. In *Proceedings of the 2013 USENIX conference on Annual Technical Conference*, USENIX ATC'13, Berkeley, CA, USA, 2013. USENIX Association.

[22] L. Rizzo. Netmap: a novel framework for fast packet I/O. In *Proceedings of the 2012 USENIX conference on Annual Technical Conference*, USENIX ATC'12, pages 9–9, Berkeley, CA, USA, 2012. USENIX Association. URL `http://dl.acm.org/citation.cfm?id=2342821.2342830`.

[23] L. Rizzo and G. Lettieri. VALE, a switched ethernet for virtual machines. In *Proceedings of the 8th international conference on Emerging networking experiments and technologies*, CoNEXT '12, pages 61–72, New York, NY, USA, 2012. ACM. ISBN 978-1-4503-1775-7. . URL `http://doi.acm.org/10.1145/2413176.2413185`.

[24] R. Russel. virtio: towards a de-facto standard for virtual I/O devices. *SIGOPS Operating Systems Review*, 42(5):95–103, 2008.

[25] L. Shalev, J. Satran, E. Borovik, and M. Ben-Yehuda. IsoStack: Highly Efficient Network Processing on Dedicated Cores. In *Proceedings of the 2010 USENIX conference on USENIX annual technical conference*, USENIX ATC'10, pages 5–5, Berkeley, CA, USA, 2010. USENIX Association. URL `http://dl.acm.org/citation.cfm?id=1855840.1855845`.

[26] snabb. Snabbswitch. URL `https://github.com/SnabbCo/snabbswitch/wiki`.

[27] L. Soares and M. Stumm. Flexsc: Flexible system call scheduling with exception-less system calls. In *Proceedings of the 9th USENIX Conference on Operating Systems Design and Implementation*, OSDI'10, pages 1–8, Berkeley, CA, USA, 2010. USENIX Association. URL `http://dl.acm.org/citation.cfm?id=1924943.1924946`.

[28] U. Steinberg and B. Kauer. NOVA: a microhypervisor-based secure virtualization architecture. In *Proceedings of the 5th European conference on Computer systems*, EuroSys '10, pages 209–222, New York, NY, USA, 2010. ACM. ISBN 978-1-60558-577-2. . URL `http://doi.acm.org/10.1145/1755913.1755935`.

[29] R. Uhlig, G. Neiger, D. Rodgers, A. L. Santoni, F. C. M. Martins, A. V. Anderson, S. M. Bennett, A. Kagi, F. H. Leung, and L. Smith. Intel virtualization technology. *Computer*, 38(5):48–56, May 2005. ISSN 0018-9162. . URL `http://dx.doi.org/10.1109/MC.2005.163`.

[30] vfio. VFIO driver: Non-privileged user level pci drivers, 2010. URL `http://lwn.net/Articles/391459/`.

[31] G. Wang and T. Ng. The impact of virtualization on network performance of amazon ec2 data center. In *INFOCOM, 2010 Proceedings IEEE*, pages 1–9, 2010. .

[32] D. Wentzlaff and A. Agarwal. Factored operating systems (fos): the case for a scalable operating system for multicores. *SIGOPS Oper. Syst. Rev.*, 43(2):76–85, Apr. 2009. ISSN 0163-5980. . URL `http://doi.acm.org/10.1145/1531793.1531805`.

A Virtualized Separation Kernel for Mixed Criticality Systems

Ye Li   Richard West   Eric Missimer

Computer Science Department
Boston University
Boston, MA 02215, USA
{liye,richwest,missimer}@cs.bu.edu

Abstract

Multi- and many-core processors are becoming increasingly popular in embedded systems. Many of these processors now feature hardware virtualization capabilities, such as the ARM Cortex A15, and x86 processors with Intel VT-x or AMD-V support. Hardware virtualization offers opportunities to partition physical resources, including processor cores, memory and I/O devices amongst guest virtual machines. Mixed criticality systems and services can then co-exist on the same platform in separate virtual machines. However, traditional virtual machine systems are too expensive because of the costs of trapping into hypervisors to multiplex and manage machine physical resources on behalf of separate guests. For example, hypervisors are needed to schedule separate VMs on physical processor cores. In this paper, we discuss the design of the Quest-V separation kernel, which partitions services of different criticalities in separate virtual machines, or *sandboxes*. Each sandbox encapsulates a subset of machine physical resources that it manages without requiring intervention of a hypervisor. Moreover, a hypervisor is not needed for normal operation, except to bootstrap the system and establish communication channels between sandboxes.

Categories and Subject Descriptors   D.4.7 [*Operating Systems*]: Organization and Design

Keywords   Separation kernel, chip-level distributed system

1. Introduction

Embedded systems are increasingly featuring multi- and many-core processors, due in part to their power, performance and price benefits. These processors offer new oppor-

tunities for an increasingly significant class of mixed criticality systems. In mixed criticality systems, there is a combination of application and system components with different safety and timing requirements. For example, in an avionics system, the in-flight entertainment system is considered less critical than that of the flight control system. Similarly, in an automotive system, infotainment services (navigation, audio and so forth) would be considered less timing and safety critical than the vehicle management sub-systems for anti-lock brakes and traction control.

A major challenge to mixed criticality systems is the safe isolation of separate components with different levels of criticality. Isolation has traditionally been achieved by partitioning components across distributed modules, which communicate over a network such as a CAN bus. For example, Integrated Modular Avionics (IMA) [1] is used to describe a distributed real-time computer network capable of supporting applications of differing criticality levels aboard an aircraft. To implement such concepts on a multicore platform, a software architecture that enforces the safe isolation of system components is required.

Hardware-assisted virtualization provides an opportunity to efficiently separate system components with different levels of safety, security and criticality. Back in 2006, Intel and AMD introduced their VT-x and AMD-V processors, respectively, with support for hardware virtualization. More recently, the ARM Cortex A15 was introduced with hardware virtualization capabilities, for use in portable tablet devices. Similarly, some Intel Atom chips now have VT-x capabilities for use in automobile In-Vehicle Infotainment (IVI) systems, and other embedded systems.

While modern hypervisor solutions such as Xen [2] and Linux-KVM [3] leverage hardware virtualization to isolate their guest systems, they are still required for CPU, memory, and I/O resource management. Traps into the hypervisor occur every time a guest system needs to be scheduled, when a remapping of guest-to-machine physical memory is needed, or when an I/O device interrupt is delivered to a guest. This is both unnecessary and potentially too costly for mixed criticality systems with real-time requirements.

In this paper we present an entirely new operating system that uses hardware-assisted virtualization as an extra *ring of protection*, to achieve efficient resource partitioning and performance isolation for subsystem components. Our system, called Quest-V, is a separation kernel [4] design, effectively operating as a distributed system on a chip. The system avoids traps into a hypervisor (a.k.a. virtual machine monitor, or VMM) when making scheduling and I/O management decisions. Instead, all resources are partitioned at boot-time amongst system components that are capable of scheduling themselves on available processor cores. Similarly, system components are granted access to specific subsets of I/O devices and memory so that devices can be managed without involvement of a hypervisor.

Experiments show how Quest-V is able to make efficient use of CPU, memory and I/O partitioning, using hardware virtualization. We show how a Linux front-end (guest) system can be supported with minimal modifications to its source code. An *mplayer* benchmark for video decoding and playback running on a Linux guest in Quest-V achieves almost identical performance compared to running on a non-virtualized Linux system. Similarly, *netperf* running on a Linux guest in Quest-V achieves better network bandwidth performance than when running on Xen, for large packet sizes. Quest-V guest services are able to maintain functionality in the presence of faults in other sandboxed guests, and are also able to communicate with remote guest services using tunable bandwidth guarantees.

The next section briefly describes the rationale for our system. The architecture is then explained in Section 3. Section 4 details a series of experiments to evaluate the costs and performance of using hardware virtualization for resource partitioning in Quest-V. An overview of related work is provided in Section 5. Finally, conclusions and future work are discussed in Section 6.

2. Design Rationale

Quest-V is centered around three main goals: safety, predictability and efficiency. Of particular interest is support for safety-critical applications, where equipment and/or lives are dependant on the operation of the underlying system. With recent advances in fields such as cyber-physical systems, more sophisticated OSes beyond those traditionally found in real-time and embedded computing are now required. Consider, for example, an automotive system with services for engine, body, chassis, transmission, safety and infotainment. These could be consolidated on the same multicore platform, with space-time partitioning to ensure malfunctions do not propagate across services. Virtualization technology can be used to separate different groups of services, depending on their criticality (or importance) to overall system functionality.

Quest-V uses hardware virtualization technology to partition resources amongst separate *sandboxes*, each responsible for a subset of processor cores, memory regions, and I/O devices. This leads to the following benefits:

(1) Improved Efficiency and Predictability – the separation of resources and services eliminates, or reduces, resource contention. This is similar to the *share-nothing* principle of multi-kernels such as Barrelfish [5]. As system resources are effectively distributed across cores, and each core is managed separately, there is no need to have shared structures such as a global scheduler queue. This, in turn, can improve predictability by eliminating undue blocking delays due to synchronization.

(2) Fault Isolation and Mixed Criticality Services – virtualization provides a way to separate services and prevent functional components from being adversely affected by those that are faulty. This, in turn, increases system availability when there are partial system failures. Similarly, services of different criticalities can be isolated from one another, and in some cases may be replicated to guarantee their operation.

(3) Highest Safe Privilege – Rather than adopting a principle of *least* privilege for software services, as is done in micro-kernels, a virtualized system can support the *highest* safe privilege for different services. Virtualization provides an extra logical "ring of protection" that allows *guests* to think they are working directly on the hardware. Thus, virtualized services can be written with traditional kernel privileges, yet still be isolated from other equally privileged services in other guest domains. This avoids the communication costs typically associated with micro-kernels, to request services in different protection domains.

(4) Minimal Trusted Code Base – A micro-kernel attempts to provide a minimal trusted code base for the services it supports. However, it must still be accessed as part of inter-process communication, and basic operations such as coarse-grained memory management. Monitors form a trusted code base in the Quest-V separation kernel. Access to these can be *avoided almost entirely*, except to bootstrap (guest) sandbox kernels, handle faults and manage guest-to-machine physical memory mappings. This enables sandboxes to operate, for the most part, independently of any other code base that requires trust. In turn, the trusted monitors can be limited to a small memory footprint.

3. Quest-V Separation Kernel Architecture

A high-level overview of the Quest-V architecture is shown in Figure 1. The current implementation works on Intel VT-x platforms but plans are underway to port Quest-V to the AMD-V and ARM architectures.

The system is partitioned into separate *sandboxes*, each responsible for a subset of machine physical memory, I/O devices and processor cores. Trusted monitor code is used to launch *guest* services, which may include their own kernels and user space programs. A monitor is responsible for managing special *extended page tables* (EPTs) that translate guest physical addresses (GPAs) to host physical addresses (HPAs), as described later in Figure 2.

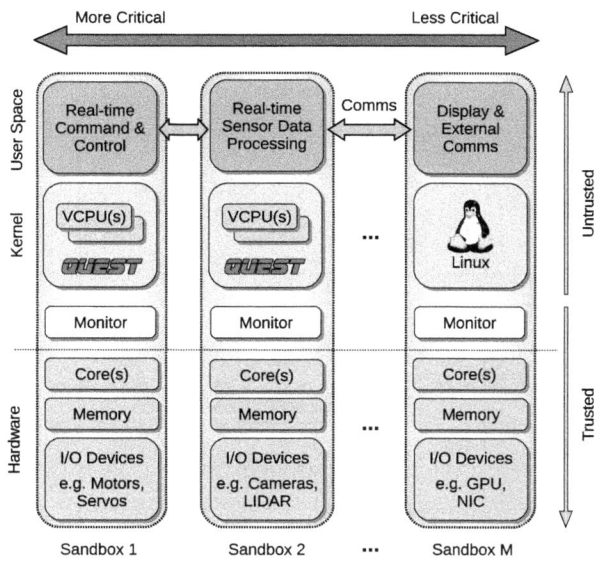

Figure 1. Example Quest-V Architecture Overview

We chose to have a separate monitor for each sandbox, so that it manages only one set of EPT memory mappings for a single guest environment. The amount of added overhead of doing this is small, as each monitor's code fits within $4KB$ [1]. However, the benefits are that monitors are made much simpler, since they know which sandbox they are serving rather than having to determine at runtime the guest that needs their service. Typically, guests do not need intervention of monitors, except to establish shared memory communication channels with other sandboxes, which requires updating EPTs. The monitor code needed after system initialization is about 400 lines.

Mixed-Criticality Example – Figure 1 shows an example of three sandboxes, where two are configured with Quest-native safety-critical services for command, control and sensor data processing. These services might be appropriate for a future automotive system that assists in vehicle control. Other less critical services could be assigned to vehicle infotainment services, which are partitioned in a sandbox that has access to a local display device. A non-real-time Linux system could be used in this case, perhaps also managing a network interface (NIC) to communicate with other vehicles or the surrounding environment, via a vehicle-to-vehicle (V2V) or vehicle-to-infrastructure (V2I) communication link.

3.1 Resource Partitioning

Quest-V supports configurable partitioning of CPU, memory and I/O resources amongst guests. Resource partitioning is mostly static, taking place at boot-time, with the exception of some memory allocation at run-time for dynamically created communication channels between sandboxes.

---

[1] The EPTs take additional data space, but 12KB is enough for a 1GB sandbox address space.

CPU Partitioning – In Quest-V, scheduling is performed within each sandbox. Since processor cores are statically allocated to sandboxes, there is no need for monitors to perform sandbox scheduling as is typically required with traditional hypervisors. This approach eliminates the monitor traps otherwise necessary for sandbox context switches. It also means there is no notion of a global scheduler to manage the allocation of processor cores amongst guests. Each sandbox's local scheduler is free to implement its own policy, simplifying resource management. This approach also distributes contention amongst separate scheduling queues, without requiring synchronization on one global queue.

Memory Partitioning – Quest-V relies on hardware assisted virtualization support to perform memory partitioning. Figure 2 shows how address translation works for Quest-V sandboxes using Intel's extended page tables. Each sandbox kernel uses its own internal paging structures to translate guest virtual addresses to guest physical addresses. EPT structures are then walked by the hardware to complete the translation to host physical addresses.

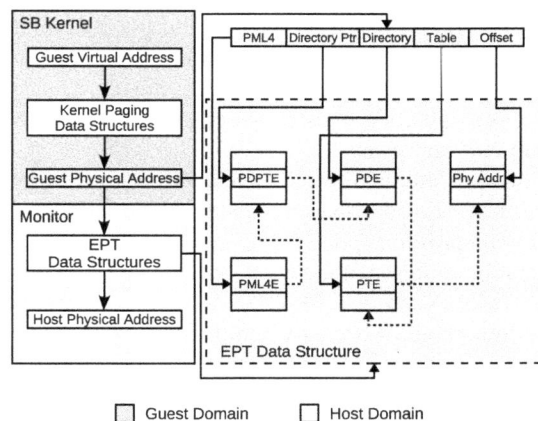

Figure 2. Extended Page Table Mapping

On modern Intel x86 processors with EPT support, address mappings can be manipulated at 4KB page granularity. For each 4KB page we have the ability to set read, write and even execute permissions. Consequently, attempts by one sandbox to access illegitimate memory regions of another sandbox will incur an EPT violation, causing a trap to the local monitor. The EPT data structures are, themselves, restricted to access by the monitors, thereby preventing tampering by sandbox kernels.

EPT mappings are cached by hardware TLBs, expediting the cost of address translation. Only on returning to a guest after trapping into a monitor are these TLBs flushed. Consequently, by avoiding exits into monitor code, each sandbox operates with similar performance to that of systems with conventional page-based virtual address spaces.

Cache Partitioning – Microarchitectural resources such as caches and memory buses provide a source of contention on multicore platforms. Using hardware performance counters we are able to establish cache occupancies for different sandboxes [6]. Also, memory page coloring can be used to partition shared caches [7] between sandboxes. Most of these features are under active development in Quest-V.

I/O Partitioning – In Quest-V, device management is performed within each sandbox directly. Device interrupts are delivered to a sandbox kernel without monitor intervention. This differs from the "split driver" model of systems such as Xen, which have a special domain to handle interrupts before they are directed into a guest. Allowing sandboxes to have direct access to I/O devices avoids the overhead of monitor traps to handle interrupts.

To partition I/O devices, Quest-V first has to restrict access to device specific hardware registers. Device registers are usually either memory mapped or accessed through a special I/O address space (e.g. I/O ports). For the x86, both approaches are used. For memory mapped registers, EPTs are used to prevent their accesses from unauthorized sandboxes. For port-addressed registers, special hardware support is necessary. On Intel processors with VT-x, all variants of `in` and `out` instructions can be configured to cause a monitor trap if access to a certain port address is attempted. As a result, an I/O bitmap can be used to partition the whole I/O address space amongst different sandboxes. Unauthorized access to a certain register can thus be ignored or trigger a fault recovery event.

Any sandbox attempting access to a PCI device must use memory-mapped or port-based registers identified in a special PCI *configuration space* [8]. Quest-V intercepts access to this configuration space, which is accessed via both an address (`0xCF8`) and data (`0xCFC`) I/O port. A trap to the local sandbox monitor occurs when there is a PCI data port access. The monitor then determines which device's configuration space is to be accessed by the trapped instruction. A device *blacklist* for each sandbox containing the *Bus*, *Device* and *Function* numbers of restricted PCI devices is used by the monitor to control actual device access.

A simplified control flow of the handling of PCI configuration space protection in a Quest-V monitor is given in Figure 3. Notice that simply allowing access to a PCI data port is not sufficient because we only want to allow the single I/O instruction that caused the monitor trap, and which passed the monitor check, to be correctly executed. Once this is done, the monitor should immediately restrict access to the PCI data port again. This behavior is achieved by setting the *trap flag* (TF) bit in the sandbox kernel system flags to cause a single step debug exception after it executes the next instruction. By configuring the processor to generate a monitor trap on debug exception, the system can immediately return to the monitor after executing the I/O instruction. After this, the monitor is able to mask the PCI data port again for the sandbox kernel, thereby mediating future device access.

In addition to direct access to device registers, interrupts from I/O devices also need to be partitioned amongst sand-

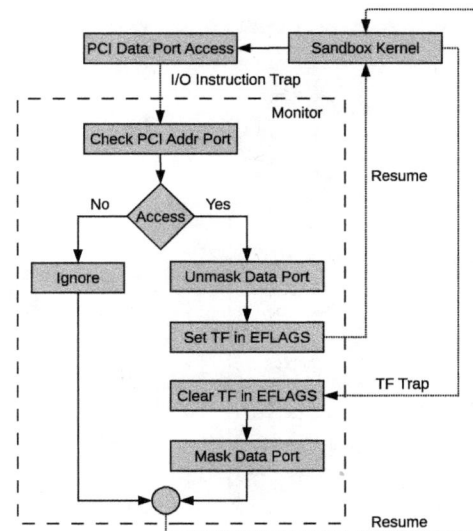

Figure 3. PCI Configuration Space Protection

boxes. In modern multicore platforms, an external interrupt controller is almost always present to allow configuration of interrupt delivery behaviors. On modern Intel x86 processors, this is done through an I/O Advanced Programmable Interrupt Controller (IOAPIC). Each IOAPIC has an I/O *redirection table* that can be programmed to deliver device interrupts to all, or a subset of, sandboxes. Each entry in the I/O redirection table corresponds to a certain interrupt request from an I/O device on the PCI bus.

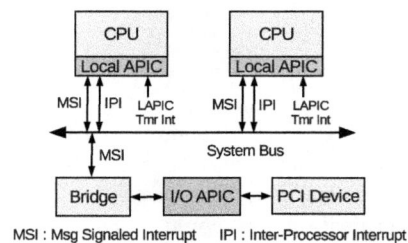

Figure 4. APIC Configuration

Figure 4 shows the hardware APIC configuration. Quest-V uses EPT entries to restrict access to memory regions used to access IOAPIC registers. Though IOAPIC registers are memory mapped, two special registers are programmed to access other registers similar to that of PCI configuration space access. As a result, an approach similar to the one shown in Figure 3 is used in the Quest-V monitor code for access control. Attempts by a sandbox to access the IOAPIC space cause a trap to the local monitor as a result of an EPT violation. The monitor then checks to see if the sandbox has authorization to update the table before allowing any changes to be made. Consequently, device interrupts are safely partitioned amongst sandboxes.

This approach is efficient because device management and interrupt handling are all carried out in the sandbox kernel with direct access to hardware. The monitor traps necessary for the partitioning strategy are only needed for device enumeration during system initialization.

3.2 Native Quest Sandbox Support

We have developed a native Quest kernel for real-time and embedded systems. The kernel code has been implemented from scratch for the IA-32 architecture, and is approximately 10,000 lines of C and assembly, discounting drivers and network stack. Each monitor is given access to a native Quest kernel address space so that direct manipulation of kernel objects during monitor traps are possible.

Real-Time VCPU Scheduling. Native Quest kernels feature a novel virtual CPU (VCPU) scheduling framework, to guarantee that one task, or thread, does not interfere with the timely execution of others [9]. VCPUs form the fundamental abstraction for scheduling and temporal isolation of threads. The concept of a VCPU is similar to that in traditional virtual machines [2, 10], where a hypervisor provides the illusion of multiple *physical CPUs* (PCPUs) [2] represented as VCPUs to each of the guests. VCPUs exist as kernel rather than monitor abstractions, to simplify the management of resource budgets for potentially many software threads. We use a hierarchical approach in which VCPUs are scheduled on PCPUs and threads are scheduled on VCPUs.

A VCPU acts as a resource container [11] for scheduling and accounting decisions on behalf of software threads. It serves no other purpose to virtualize the underlying physical CPUs, since our sandbox kernels and their applications execute directly on the hardware. In particular, a VCPU does not need to act as a container for cached instruction blocks that have been generated to emulate the effects of guest code, as in some trap-and-emulate virtualized systems.

In common with *bandwidth preserving* servers [12][13][14], each VCPU, V, has a maximum compute time budget, C_V, available in a time period, T_V. V is constrained to use no more than the fraction $U_V = \frac{C_V}{T_V}$ of a physical processor (PCPU) in any window of real-time, T_V, while running at its normal (foreground) priority. To avoid situations where PCPUs are idle when there are threads awaiting service, a VCPU that has expired its budget may operate at a lower (background) priority. All background priorities are set below foreground priorities to ensure VCPUs with expired budgets do not adversely affect those with available budgets.

A native Quest kernel defines two classes of VCPUs as shown in Figure 5: (1) *Main VCPUs* are used to schedule and track the PCPU usage of conventional software threads, while (2) *I/O VCPUs* are used to account for, and schedule the execution of, interrupt handlers for I/O devices. This distinction allows for interrupts from I/O devices to be sched-

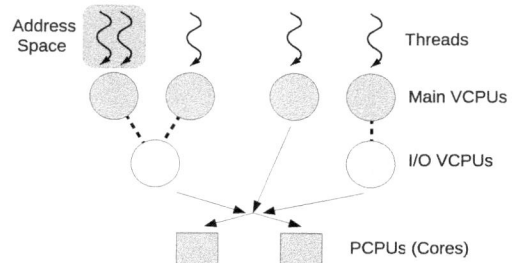

Figure 5. VCPU Scheduling Hierarchy

uled as threads, which may be deferred execution when threads associated with higher priority VCPUs having available budgets are runnable. The whole approach enables I/O VCPUs to be specified for certain devices, or for certain tasks that issue I/O requests, thereby allowing interrupts to be handled at different priorities and with different CPU shares than conventional tasks associated with Main VCPUs.

By default, Main VCPUs act like Sporadic Servers [15, 16], while each I/O VCPU acts as a bandwidth preserving server with a dynamically-calculated period, T_{IO}, and budget, C_{IO} [9]. Each I/O VCPU is specified a certain utilization factor, U_{IO}, to limit its bandwidth. When a device interrupt requires handling by an I/O VCPU, the system determines the thread τ associated with a corresponding I/O request [3]. All events, including those related to I/O processing are associated with threads running on Main VCPUs. In this framework, C_{IO} is calculated as $T_V \cdot U_{IO}$, while T_{IO} is set to T_V for a Main VCPU, V, associated with τ.

Our native Quest kernel is designed for mission-critical tasks in mixed-criticality systems. By sandboxing these tasks in their own virtual machines, they are isolated from the effects of other less critical tasks. By default, all Quest-V sandboxes use native Quest kernels. Even for booting third party systems such as Linux in a Quest-V sandbox, a native Quest sandbox has to be started first.

3.3 Linux Sandbox Support

In addition to native Quest kernels, Quest-V is also designed to support other third party sandbox systems such as Linux and AUTOSAR OS [17]. Currently, we have successfully ported a Puppy Linux [18] distribution with Linux 3.8.0 kernel to serve as our system front-end, providing a window manager and graphical user interface. In Quest-V, a Linux sandbox can only be bootstrapped by a native Quest kernel. This means a native Quest sandbox needs to be initialized first and Linux will be started in the same sandbox via a bootloader kernel thread. To simplify the monitor logic, we paravirtualized the Linux kernel by patching the source code. Quest-V exposes the maximum possible privileges of hardware access to sandbox kernels. From Linux sandbox's perspective, all processor capabilities are exposed except hard-

---

[2] We define a PCPU to be either a conventional CPU, a processing core, or a hardware thread.

[3] E.g., τ may have issued a prior `read()` request that caused it to block on its Main VCPU, but which ultimately led to a device performing an I/O operation.

ware virtualization support. On Intel VT-x processors, this means a Linux sandbox does not see EPT or VMX features when displaying /proc/cpuinfo. Consequently, the actual changes made to the original Linux 3.8.0 kernel are less than 50 lines. These changes are mainly focused on limiting Linux's view of available physical memory and handling I/O device DMA offsets caused by memory virtualization.

An example memory layout of Quest-V with a Linux sandbox on a 4-core processor is shown in Figure 6. Even though the Linux kernel's view of (guest) physical memory is contiguous from address 0x0, the kernel is actually loaded after all native Quest kernels in machine physical memory. Since Quest-V does not require hardware IOMMU support, we patched the Linux kernel DMA layer to make it aware of this offset between guest physical and machine physical memory addresses during I/O device DMA.

In the current implementation, we limit Linux to manage the last logical processor or core. As this is not the bootstrap processing core, the Linux code that initializes a legacy 8253 Programmable Interval Timer (PIT) has to be removed. The 8253 PIT assumes interrupts are delivered to the bootstrap processor but instead we program the IOAPIC to control which interrupts are delivered to the Linux sandbox. In general, our implementation can be extended to support Linux running on a subset of cores (potentially more than one), with access to a controlled and specific subset of devices. Right now, the entire Linux sandbox runs in 512MB RAM, including space for the root filesystem. This makes it useful in situations where we want to prevent Linux having access to persistent disk storage.

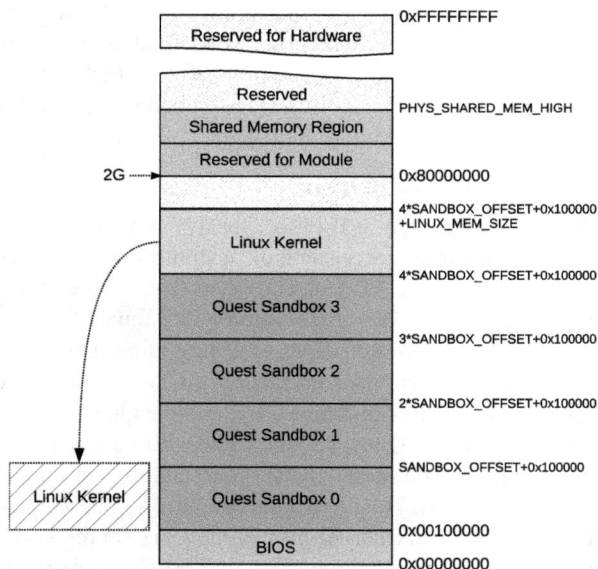

Figure 6. Quest-V Physical Memory Layout with Linux

Whenever a Linux sandbox is present, the VGA frame buffer and GPU hardware are always assigned to it for exclusive access. All the other sandboxes will have their default

terminal I/O tunneled through shared memory channels to virtual terminals in the Linux front-end. We developed libraries, user space applications and a kernel module to support this redirection in Linux.

3.4 Shared Memory Communication Channels

Inter-sandbox communication in Quest-V relies on message passing primitives built on shared memory, and asynchronous event notification mechanisms using Inter-processor Interrupts (IPIs). Monitors update EPT mappings as necessary to establish message passing channels between specific sandboxes. Only those sandboxes with mapped shared pages are able to communicate with one another.

A *mailbox* data structure is set up within shared memory by each end of a communication channel. By default, Quest-V supports asynchronous communication by polling a mailbox status bit, instead of using IPIs, to determine message arrival. Message passing threads are bound to VCPUs with specific parameters to control the rate of exchange of information in native Quest sandboxes. Likewise, sending and receiving threads are assigned to higher priority VCPUs to reduce the latency of transfer of information across a communication channel. This way, shared memory channels can be prioritized and granted higher or lower throughput as needed, while ensuring information is communicated in a predictable manner. Quest-V supports real-time communication between native Quest sandboxes without compromising the CPU shares allocated to non-communicating tasks.

A similar library is under development for communication between processes in Linux and native Quest sandboxes. In the current implementation, a Linux process can only request a memory channel shared with all native Quest sandboxes for non-critical communication.

4. Experimental Evaluation

We conducted a series of experiments to investigate the performance of the Quest-V resource partitioning scheme. For all the experiments, we ran Quest-V on a mini-ITX machine with a Core i5-2500K 4-core processor, featuring 4GB RAM and a Realtek 8111e NIC. In all the network experiments where both a server and a client are required, we also used a Dell PowerEdge T410 with an Intel Xeon E5506 2.13GHz 4-core processor, featuring 4GB RAM and a Broadcom NetXtreme II NIC. For all the experiments involving a Xen hypervisor, Xen 4.2.3 was used with a Fedora 18 64-bit domain 0 and Linux 3.6.0 kernel.

Monitor Intervention. To see the extent to which a monitor was involved in system operation, we recorded the number of monitor traps during Quest-V Linux sandbox initialization and normal operation. During normal operation, we observed only one monitor trap every 3 to 5 minutes caused by cpuid. In the x86 architecture, if a cpuid instruction is executed within a guest it forces a trap (i.e., VM-exit or hypercall) to the monitor. Table 1 shows the monitor traps

	Exception	CPUID	VMCALL	I/O Inst	EPT Violation	XSETBV
No I/O Partitioning	0	502	2	0	0	1
I/O Partitioning	10157	502	2	9769	388	1
I/O Partitioning (Block COM and NIC)	9785	497	2	11412	388	1

Table 1. Monitor Trap Count During Linux Sandbox Initialization

recorded during Linux sandbox initialization under three different configurations: (1) a Linux sandbox with control over *all* I/O devices but with no I/O partitioning logic, (2) a Linux sandbox with control over all I/O devices and support for I/O partitioning logic, and (3) a Linux sandbox with control over all devices except the serial port and network interface card, while also supporting I/O partitioning logic. However, again, during normal operation, no monitor traps were observed other than by the occasional `cpuid` instruction.

Microbenchmarks. We evaluated the performance of Quest-V using a series of microbenchmarks. The first, *findprimes*, finds prime numbers in the set of integers from 1 to 10^6. CPU cycle times for *findprimes* are shown in Figure 7, for the configurations in Table 2. All Linux configurations were limited to 512MB RAM. For `Xen HVM` and `Xen PVM`, we pinned the Linux virtual machine (VM) to a single core that differed from the one used by Xen's Dom0. For all 4VM configurations of Xen, we allowed Dom0 to make scheduling decisions without pinning VMs to specific cores.

Configuration	Description
Linux	Standalone Linux (no virtualization)
Quest-V Linux	One Linux sandbox hosted by Quest-V
Quest-V Linux 4SB	One Linux sandbox co-existing with three native Quest sandboxes
Xen HVM	One Linux guest on Xen with hardware virtualization
Xen HVM 4VM	One Linux guest co-existing with three native Quest guests
Xen PVM	One paravirtualized Linux guest on Xen
Xen PVM 4VM	One paravirtualized Linux guest co-existing with three native Quest guests

Table 2. System Configurations

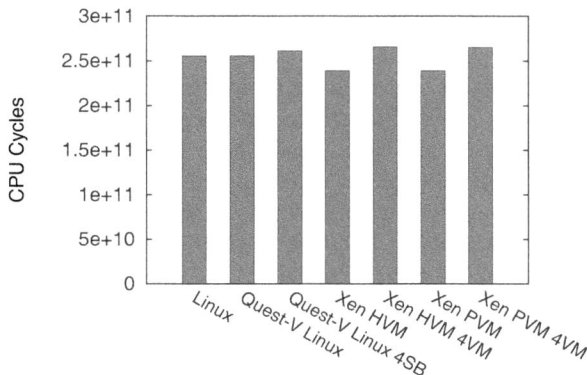

Figure 7. findprimes CPU Benchmark

As can be seen in the figure, `Quest-V Linux` shows no overhead compared to standalone Linux. `Xen HVM` and

`Xen PVM` actually outperform standalone Linux, and this seems to be attributed to the way Xen virtualizes devices and reduces the impact of events such as interrupts on thread execution. The results show approximately 2% overhead when running *findprimes* in a Linux sandbox on Quest-V, in the presence of three native Quest sandboxes. We believe this overhead is mostly due to memory bus and shared cache contention. For the 4VM Xen configurations, the performance degradation is slightly worse. This appears to be because of the overheads of multiplexing 5 VMs (one being Dom0) onto 4 cores.

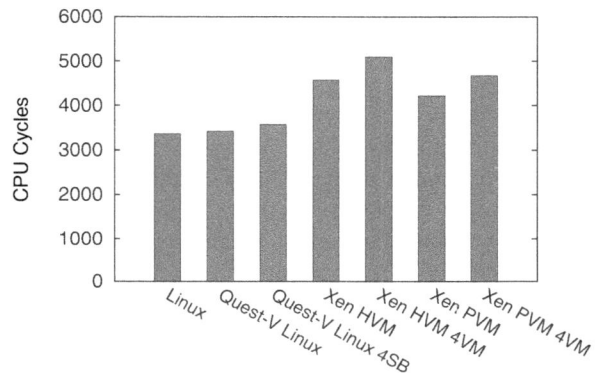

Figure 8. Page Fault Exception Handling Overhead

We evaluated the exception handling overheads for the configurations in Table 2, by measuring the average CPU cycles spent by Linux to handle a single user level page fault. For the measurement, we developed a user program that intentionally triggered a page fault and then skipped the faulting instruction in the `SIGSEGV` signal handler. The average cycle times were derived from 10^8 contiguous page faults. The results in Figure 8 show that exception handling in `Quest-V Linux` is much more efficient than Xen. This is mainly because the monitor is not required for handling almost all exceptions and interrupts in a Quest-V sandbox.

The last microbenchmark measures the CPU cycles spent by Linux to perform a million *fork-exec-wait* system calls. A test program forks and waits for a child while the child calls `execve()` and exits immediately. The results are shown in Figure 9. `Quest-V Linux` is almost as good as native Linux and more than twice as fast as any Xen configuration.

mplayer HD Video Benchmark. We next evaluated the performance of application benchmarks that focused on I/O and memory usage. First, we ran *mplayer* with an x264 MPEG2 HD video clip at 1920x1080 resolution. The video was about 2 minutes long and 102MB in file size. By invok-

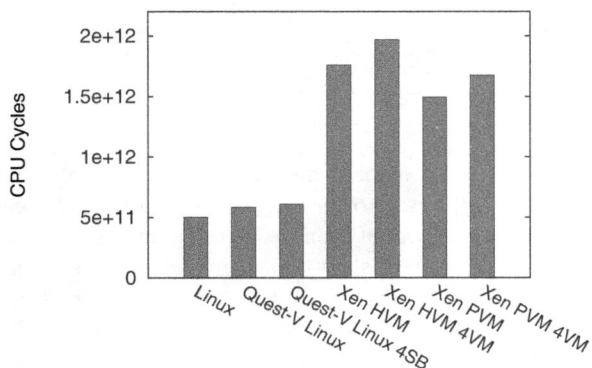

Figure 9. Fork-Exec-Wait Micro Benchmark

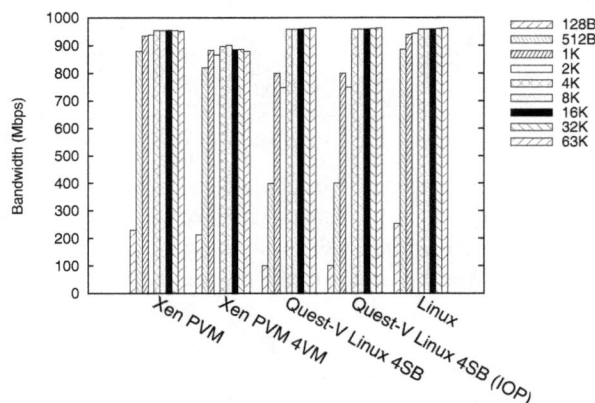

Figure 11. netserver UDP Receive

ing *mplayer* with -benchmark and -nosound, *mplayer* decodes and displays each frame as fast as possible. With the extra -vo=null argument, *mplayer* will further skip the video output and try to decode as fast as possible. The real-times spent in seconds in the video codec (VC) and video output (VO) stages are shown in Table 3 for three different configurations. In Quest-V, the Linux sandbox was given exclusive control over an integrated HD Graphics 3000 GPU. The results show that Quest-V incurs negligible overhead for HD video decoding and playback in Linux. We also observed (not shown) the same playback frame rate for all three configurations.

	VC (VO=NULL)	VC	VO
Linux	16.593s	29.853s	13.373s
Quest-V Linux	16.705s	29.915s	13.457s
Quest-V Linux 4SB	16.815s	29.986s	13.474s

Table 3. mplayer HD Video Benchmark

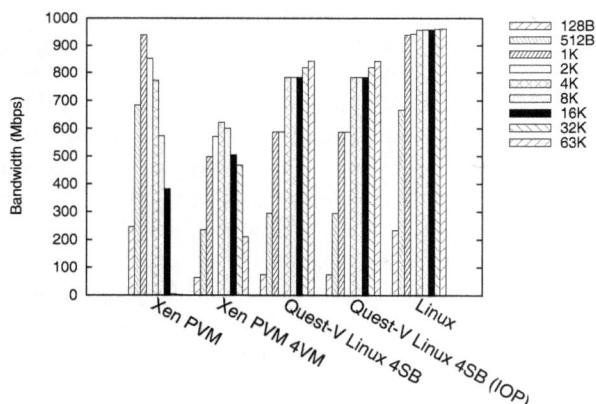

Figure 10. netperf UDP Send with Different Packet Sizes

netperf UDP Bandwidth Benchmark. We next investigated the networking performance of Quest-V, using the *netperf* UDP benchmark. The measured bandwidths of separate UDP send (running *netperf*) and receive (running *net-*

server) experiments, on the mini-ITX machine, are shown in Figures 10 and 11, respectively.

We have omitted the results for Xen HVM, since it did not perform as well as Xen PVM. For Xen PVM and Xen PVM 4VM, virtio [19] is enabled. It can be seen that this helps dramatically improve the UDP bandwidth for small size UDP packets. With 512B packet size, Xen PVM outperforms standalone Linux. In most other cases, Quest-V outperforms Xen with bigger packet sizes and multiple VMs.

I/O Partitioning. We also tested the potential overhead of the I/O partitioning strategy in Quest-V. For the group of bars labelled as Quest-V Linux 4SB (IOP), we enabled I/O partitioning logic in Quest-V and allowed all devices except the serial port to be accessible to the Linux sandbox. Notice that even though no PCI device has been placed in the blacklist for the Linux sandbox, the logic that traps PCI configuration space and IOAPIC access is still in place. The results show that the I/O partitioning does not impose any extra performance overhead on normal sandbox execution. I/O resource partitioning-related monitor traps only happen during system initialization and faults.

However, Quest-V does incur a network performance penalty compared to standalone Linux. This is especially noticeable for small size packets. To determine the cause of this behavior, we ran the same experiments with the server and client running on the same machine for standalone Linux and Quest-V Linux. This eliminated the potential influence from hardware device access and DMA. The results shown in Figure 12 demonstrate that at least part of the overhead is related to memory management rather than just I/O.

We believe that this overhead is caused by multiple factors, including the usage of shared caches and TLBs [20]. For instance, the fact that some of the virtual machine related data structures (e.g. EPT tables) are cacheable could increase the cache contention in a virtualized environment. Further studies are needed to more precisely identify the overheads of virtualization in Quest-V.

TLB Performance. We ran a series of experiments to measure the effects of address translation using EPTs. A

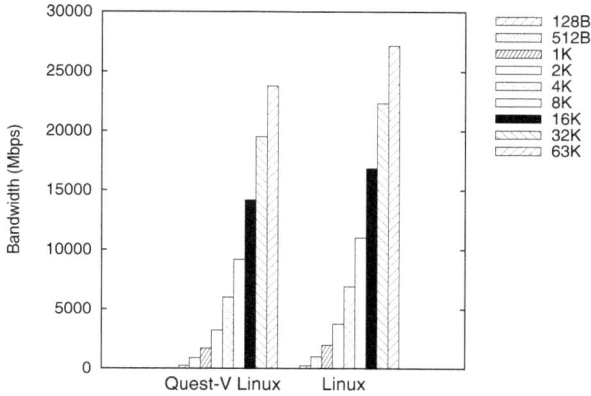

Figure 12. netperf UDP Local Host

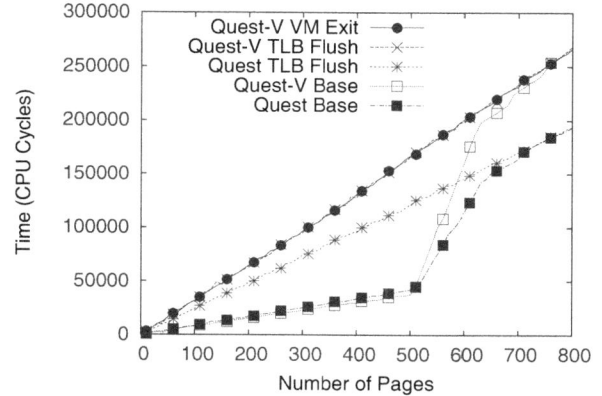

Figure 13. Data TLB Performance

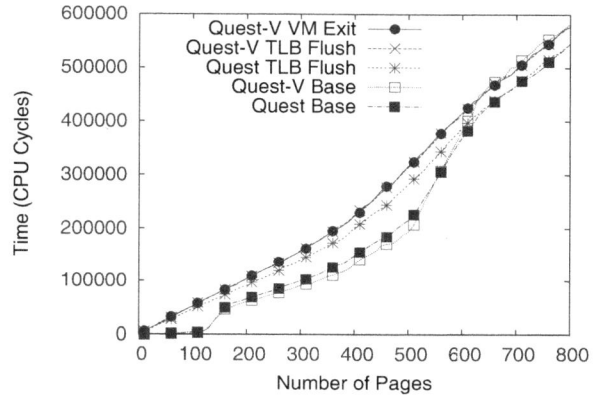

Figure 14. Instruction TLB Performance

TLB-walking thread in a native Quest kernel was bound to a Main VCPU with a 45ms budget and 50ms period. This thread made a series of instruction and data references to consecutive 4KB memory pages, at 4160 bytes offsets to avoid cache aliasing effects. The average time for the thread to complete access to a working set of pages was measured over 10 million iterations.

Figures 13 and 14 compare the performance of a native Quest kernel running in a virtual machine (i.e., sandbox) to when the same kernel code is running without virtualization. Results prefixed with `Quest` do not use virtualization, whereas the rest use EPTs to assist address translation. Experiments involving a `VM Exit` or a `TLB Flush` performed a trap into the monitor, or a TLB flush, respectively, at the end of accessing the number of pages on the x-axis. All other `Base` cases operated without involving a monitor or performing a TLB flush.

As can be seen, the `Quest-V Base` case refers to the situation when the monitor is not involved. This yields address translation costs similar to when the TLB walker runs on a base system without virtualization (`Quest Base`) for working sets with less than 512 pages. We believe this is acceptable for safety-critical services found in embedded systems, as they are likely to have relatively small working sets. The cost of a VM-Exit is equivalent to a full TLB flush, but entries will not be flushed in Quest-V sandboxes if they are within the TLB reach. Note that without the use of TLBs to cache address translations, the EPTs require 5 memory accesses to perform a single guest-physical address (GPA) to host-physical address (HPA) translation. The kernels running the TLB walker use two-level paging for 32-bit virtual addresses, and in the worst-case this leads to 3 memory accesses for a GVA to GPA translation. However, with virtualization, this causes $3 \times 5 = 15$ memory accesses for a GVA to HPA translation.

Fault Isolation and Predictability. To demonstrate fault isolation in Quest-V, we created a scenario that includes both message passing and networking across 4 different native Quest sandboxes. Specifically, sandbox 1 has a kernel

thread that sends messages through private message passing channels to sandbox 0, 2 and 3. Each private channel is shared only between the sender and specific receiver, and is guarded by EPTs. In addition, sandbox 0 also has a network service running that handles ICMP echo requests. After all the services are up and running, we manually break the NIC driver in sandbox 0, overwrite sandbox 0's message passing channel shared with sandbox 1, and try to corrupt the kernel memory of other sandboxes to simulate a driver fault. After the driver fault, sandbox 0 will try to recover the NIC driver along with both network and message passing services running in it. During the recovery, the whole system activity is plotted in terms of message reception rate and ICMP echo reply rate in all available sandboxes, and the results are shown in Figure 15.

In the experiment, sandbox 1 broadcasts messages to others (`SB0,2,3`) at 50 millisecond intervals. Sandbox 0, 2 and 3 receive at 100, 800 and 1000 millisecond intervals. Another machine sends ICMP echo requests at 500 millisecond intervals to sandbox 0 (`ICMP0`). All message passing threads are bound to Main VCPUs with 100ms periods and

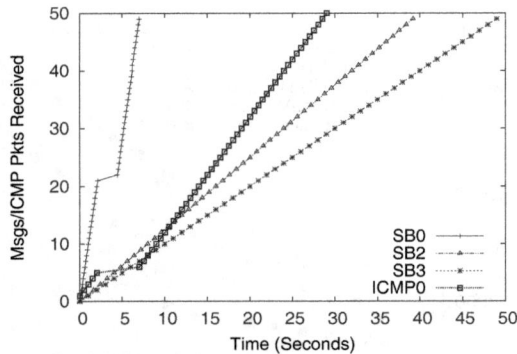

Figure 15. Sandbox Isolation

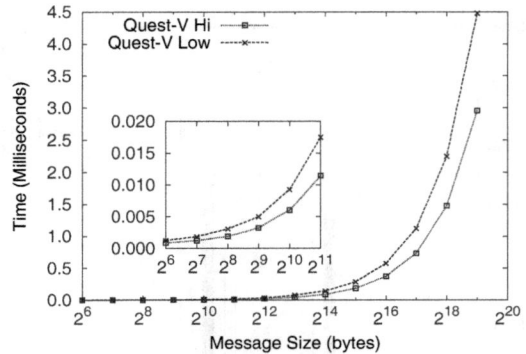

Figure 16. Message Passing Microbenchmark

20% utilization. The network driver thread is bound to an I/O VCPU with 10% utilization and 10ms period.

Results show that an interruption of both message passing and packet processing occurred in sandbox 0, but all the other sandboxes were unaffected. This is because of memory isolation between sandboxes, enforced by EPTs.

Inter-Sandbox Communication. The message passing mechanism in Quest-V is built on shared memory. Instead of focusing on memory and cache optimization, we tried to study the impact of scheduling on inter-sandbox communication in Quest-V.

We setup two kernel threads in two different sandbox kernels and assigned a VCPU to each of them. One kernel thread used a 4KB shared memory message passing channel to communicate with the other thread. In the first case, the two VCPUs were the highest priority with their respective sandbox kernels. In the second case, the two VCPUs were assigned lower utilizations and priorities, to identify the effects of VCPU parameters (and scheduling) on the message sending and receiving rates. In both cases, the time to transfer messages of various sizes across the communication channel was measured. Note that the VCPU scheduling framework ensures that all threads are guaranteed service as long as the total utilization of all VCPUs is bounded according to rate-monotonic theory [21]. Consequently, the impacts of message passing on overall system predictability can be controlled and isolated from the execution of other threads in the system.

Figure 16 shows the time spent exchanging messages of various sizes, plotted on a log scale. `Quest-V Hi` is the plot for message exchanges involving high-priority VC-PUs having 100ms periods and 50% utilizations for both the sender and receiver. `Quest-V Low` is the plot for message exchanges involving low-priority VCPUs having 100ms periods and 40% utilizations for both the sender and receiver. In the latter case, a shell process was bound to a highest priority VCPU. As can be seen, VCPU parameter settings affect message transfer times.

In our experiments, the time spent for each size of message was averaged over a minimum of 5000 trials to normalize the scheduling overhead. The communication costs grow linearly with increasing message size, because they include the time to access memory.

5. Related Work

Xen [2], Linux-KVM [3], XtratuM [22], the Wind River Hypervisor, and Mentor Graphics Embedded Hypervisor all use virtualization technologies to logically isolate and multiplex guest virtual machines on a shared set of physical resources. LynxSecure [23] is another similar approach targeted at safety-critical real-time systems. PikeOS [24] is a separation micro-kernel [25] that supports multiple guest VMs, and targets safety-critical domains such as Integrated Modular Avionics. The micro-kernel supports a virtualization layer that is required to manage the spatial and temporal partitioning of resources amongst guests.

In contrast to the above systems, Quest-V statically partitions machine resources into separate sandboxes. Services of different criticalities can be mapped into separate sandboxes. Each sandbox manages its own resources independently of an underlying hypervisor. Quest-V also avoids the need for a split-driver model involving a special domain (e.g., `Dom0` in Xen) to handle device interrupts. Interrupts are delivered directly to the sandbox associated with the corresponding device, using I/O passthrough. Even though PCI passthrough is supported in recent versions of Xen and KVM, guest virtual machines can only directly access device registers. The hypervisor is still responsible for initial interrupt handling and interrupt acknowledgment. This potentially forces two hypervisor traps for each interrupt. ELI [26] is a software-only approach for handling interrupts within guest virtual machines directly with shadow IDTs. In combination with PCI passthrough, this is similar to the approach Quest-V uses to partition I/O resources. However, Quest-V allows a sandbox to use its own IDT and eliminates monitor intervention on all interrupts instead of only interrupts from a specific device. IOAPIC redirection table access control is used to prevent unauthorized interrupt redirection.

NoHype [27] is a secure system that uses a modified version of Xen to bootstrap and then partition a guest, which is granted dedicated access to a subset of hardware resources.

NoHype requires guests to be paravirtualized to avoid VM-Exits into the hypervisor. VM-Exits are treated as errors and will terminate the guest, whereas in Quest-V they are avoided under normal operation, except to recover from a fault or establish new communication channels. For safety-critical applications it is necessary to handle faults without simply terminating guests. Essentially Quest-V shares the ideas of NoHype, while extending them into a fault tolerant, mixed-criticality system on a chip.

Barrelfish[5] is a multi-kernel that replicates rather than shares system state, to avoid the costs of synchronization and management of shared data structures. As with Quest-V, communication between kernels is via explicit message passing, using shared memory channels to transfer cacheline-sized messages. In contrast to Barrelfish, Quest-V focuses on the use of virtualization techniques to efficiently partition resources for mixed criticality applications.

Dune [28] uses hardware virtualization to create a sandbox for safe user-level program execution. By allowing user-level access to privileged CPU features, certain applications (e.g. garbage collection) can be made more efficient. However, most system services are still redirected to the Linux kernel running in VMX root mode. VirtuOS [29] uses virtualization to partition existing operating system kernels into service domains, each providing a subset of system calls. Exceptionless system calls are used to request services from remote domains. The system is built on top of Xen and relies on both the shared memory facilities and event channels provided by the Xen VMM to facilitate communication between different domains. The PCI passthrough capability provided by the Xen VMM is also used to partition devices amongst service domains. However, interrupt handling and VM scheduling still requires VMM intervention.

Other systems that partition resources on many-core architectures include Factored OS [30], Corey [31], Hive [32] and Disco [33]. Unlike Quest-V, these systems are focused on scalability rather than isolation and predictability.

6. Conclusions and Future Work

This paper introduces Quest-V, which is an open-source separation kernel built from the ground up. It uses hardware virtualization to separate system components of different criticalities. Consequently, less important services can be isolated from those of higher criticality, and essential services can be replicated across different sandboxes to ensure availability in the presence of faults.

Quest-V avoids traditional costs associated with hypervisor systems, by statically partitioning machine resources across guest sandboxes, which perform their own scheduling, memory and I/O management. Sandboxes can communicate via shared memory channels that are mapped to extended page table (EPT) entries. Only trusted monitors are capable of changing entries in these EPTs, preventing guest access to arbitrary memory regions in remote sandboxes.

This paper shows how multiple native Quest-V sandboxes can be mapped to different cores of a multicore processor, while allowing a Linux front-end to co-exist and manage less safety-critical legacy applications. We describe the method by which resources are partitioned amongst sandboxes, including I/O devices. Allowing interrupts to be delivered directly to the sandbox guests rather than monitors reduces the overheads of I/O management. Similarly, allowing sandbox guest kernels to perform local scheduling without expensive hypercalls (VM-exits) to monitor code leads to more efficient CPU usage. Quest-V manages CPU usage using a novel hierarchy of VCPUs implemented as Sporadic Servers, to ensure temporal isolation amongst real-time, safety-critical threads. Since Quest-V attempts to avoid VM-exits as much as possible, except to update EPTs for communication channels, bootstrap the sandboxes and handle faults, the TLBs caching EPT mappings are rarely flushed. This benefit comes about due to the fact that multiple guests are not multiplexed onto the same processor core, and in the embedded systems we envision for this work, sandbox working sets will fit within the TLB reach (at least for critical services in native Quest-V sandboxes).

Quest-V requires system monitors to be trusted. Although these occupy a small memory footprint and are not involved in normal system operation, the system can be compromised if the monitors are corrupted. Future work will investigate real-time fault detection and recovery strategies similar to those in traditional distributed systems. We also plan to investigate additional hardware features to enforce safety and security. These include Intel's trusted execution technology (TXT) to enforce safety of monitor code, IOMMUs to restrict DMA memory ranges, and *Interrupt Remapping* (IR) [34] to prevent delivery of unauthorized interrupts to specific cores [35]. Protection of CPU model-specific registers (MSRs) will be similarly enforced using hardware-managed bitmaps.

Please see www.questos.org for more details.

Acknowledgments

We would like to thank the anonymous reviewers for their valuable comments. This work is supported in part by NSF grants #0615153 and #1117025.

References

[1] C. B. Watkins, "Integrated Modular Avionics: Managing the allocation of shared intersystem resources," in *Proceedings of the 25th Digital Avionics Systems Conference*, pp. 1–12, 2006.

[2] P. Barham, B. Dragovic, K. Fraser, S. Hand, T. Harris, A. Ho, R. Neugebauer, I. Pratt, and A. Warfield, "Xen and the art of virtualization," in *Proceedings of the 19th ACM Symposium on Operating Systems Principles*, pp. 164–177, 2003.

[3] I. Habib, "Virtualization with KVM," *Linux Journal*, vol. 2008, no. 166, p. 8, 2008.

[4] J. M. Rushby, "Design and verification of secure systems," in *Proceedings of the 8th ACM Symposium on Operating Systems Principles*, pp. 12–21, 1981.

[5] A. Baumann, P. Barham, P.-E. Dagand, T. Harris, R. Isaacs, S. Peter, T. Roscoe, A. Schüpbach, and A. Singhania, "The Multikernel: A new OS architecture for scalable multicore systems," in *Proceedings of the 22nd ACM Symposium on Operating Systems Principles*, pp. 29–44, 2009.

[6] R. West, P. Zaroo, C. A. Waldspurger, and X. Zhang, *Multicore Technology: Architecture, Reconfiguration and Modeling*, ch. 8. CRC Press, ISBN-10: 1439880638, 2013.

[7] J. Liedtke, H. Härtig, and M. Hohmuth, "OS-controlled cache predictability for real-time systems," in *the 3rd IEEE Real-time Technology and Applications Symposium*, 1997.

[8] PCI: http://wiki.osdev.org/PCI.

[9] M. Danish, Y. Li, and R. West, "Virtual-CPU scheduling in the Quest operating system," in *Proceedings of the 17th Real-Time and Embedded Technology and Applications Symposium*, pp. 169–179, 2011.

[10] K. Adams and O. Agesen, "A comparison of software and hardware techniques for x86 virtualization," in *Proceedings of the 12th Intl. Conf. on Architectural Support for Programming Languages and Operating Systems*, pp. 2–13, 2006.

[11] G. Banga, P. Druschel, and J. C. Mogul, "Resource Containers: A new facility for resource management in server systems," in *Proceedings of the 3rd USENIX Symposium on Operating Systems Design and Implementation*, 1999.

[12] L. Abeni and G. Buttazzo, "Integrating multimedia applications in hard real-time systems," in *Proceedings of the 19th IEEE Real-time Systems Symposium*, pp. 4–13, 1998.

[13] Z. Deng, J. W. S. Liu, and J. Sun, "A scheme for scheduling hard real-time applications in open system environment," in *Proceedings of the 9th Euromicro Workshop on Real-Time Systems*, 1997.

[14] M. Spuri and G. Buttazzo, "Scheduling aperiodic tasks in dynamic priority systems," *Real-Time Systems*, vol. 10, pp. 179–210, 1996.

[15] B. Sprunt, L. Sha, and J. Lehoczky, "Aperiodic task scheduling for hard real-time systems," *Real-Time Systems Journal*, vol. 1, no. 1, pp. 27–60, 1989.

[16] M. Stanovich, T. P. Baker, A. I. Wang, and M. G. Harbour, "Defects of the POSIX sporadic server and how to correct them," in *Proceedings of the 16th IEEE Real-Time and Embedded Technology and Applications Symposium*, 2010.

[17] AUTOSAR: AUTomotive Open System ARchitecture – http://www.autosar.org.

[18] "Puppy Linux." http://www.puppylinux.org.

[19] R. Russell, "Virtio: Towards a de-facto standard for virtual I/O devices," *SIGOPS Operating Systems Review*, vol. 42, no. 5, pp. 95–103, 2008.

[20] A. Menon, J. R. Santos, Y. Turner, G. J. Janakiraman, and W. Zwaenepoel, "Diagnosing performance overheads in the Xen virtual machine environment," in *Proceedings of the 1st ACM/USENIX international conference on Virtual execution environments*, pp. 13–23, 2005.

[21] C. L. Liu and J. W. Layland, "Scheduling algorithms for multiprogramming in a hard-real-time environment," *Journal of the ACM*, vol. 20, no. 1, pp. 46–61, 1973.

[22] A. Crespo, I. Ripoll, and M. Masmano, "Partitioned embedded architecture based on hypervisor: The XtratuM approach.," in *the European Dependable Computing Conference*, pp. 67–72, 2010.

[23] "LynxSecure Embedded Hypervisor and Separation Kernel." http://www.lynuxworks.com/virtualization/hypervisor.php.

[24] "SYSGO PikeOS." http://www.sysgo.com/products/pikeos-rtos-and-virtualization-concept.

[25] G. Klein, K. Elphinstone, G. Heiser, J. Andronick, D. Cock, P. Derrin, D. Elkaduwe, K. Engelhardt, R. Kolanski, M. Norrish, T. Sewell, H. Tuch, and S. Winwood, "seL4: Formal verification of an OS kernel," in *the 22nd ACM Symposium on Operating Systems Principles*, pp. 207–220, 2009.

[26] A. Gordon, N. Amit, N. Har'El, M. Ben-Yehuda, A. Landau, A. Schuster, and D. Tsafrir, "ELI: Bare-metal performance for I/O virtualization," in *Proceedings of the 17th Intl. Conf. on Architectural Support for Programming Languages and Operating Systems*, pp. 411–422, 2012.

[27] J. Szefer, E. Keller, R. B. Lee, and J. Rexford, "Eliminating the hypervisor attack surface for a more secure cloud," in *Proceedings of the 18th ACM Conference on Computer and Communications Security*, pp. 401–412, 2011.

[28] A. Belay, A. Bittau, A. Mashtizadeh, D. Terei, D. Mazières, and C. Kozyrakis, "Dune: Safe user-level access to privileged CPU features," in *the 10th USENIX conference on Operating Systems Design and Implementation*, pp. 335–348, 2012.

[29] R. Nikolaev and G. Back, "VirtuOS: An operating system with kernel virtualization," in *the 24th ACM Symposium on Operating Systems Principles*, pp. 116–132, 2013.

[30] D. Wentzlaff and A. Agarwal, "Factored operating systems (FOS): The case for a scalable operating system for multicores," *SIGOPS Operating Systems Review*, vol. 43, pp. 76–85, 2009.

[31] S. Boyd-Wickizer, H. Chen, R. Chen, Y. Mao, M. F. Kaashoek, R. Morris, A. Pesterev, L. Stein, M. Wu, Y. hua Dai, Y. Zhang, and Z. Zhang, "Corey: An operating system for many cores," in *the 8th USENIX Symposium on Operating Systems Design and Implementation*, pp. 43–57, 2008.

[32] J. Chapin, M. Rosenblum, S. Devine, T. Lahiri, D. Teodosiu, and A. Gupta, "Hive: Fault containment for shared-memory multiprocessors," in *Proceedings of the 15th ACM Symposium on Operating Systems Principles*, pp. 12–25, 1995.

[33] E. Bugnion, S. Devine, and M. Rosenblum, "Disco: Running commodity operating systems on scalable multiprocessors," in *Proceedings of the 16th ACM Symposium on Operating Systems Principles*, pp. 143–156, 1997.

[34] D. Abramson, J. Jackson, S. Muthrasanallur, G. Neiger, G. Regnier, R. Sankaran, I. Schoinas, R. Uhlig, B. Vembu, and J. Wiegert, "Intel virtualization technology for directed I/O," *Intel Technology Journal*, vol. 10, pp. 179–192, August 2006.

[35] R. Wojtczuk and J. Rutkowska, "Following the white rabbit: Software attacks against Intel VT-d technology," April 2011. Inivisible Things Lab.

Composable Multi-Level Debugging with Stackdb

David Johnson   Mike Hibler   Eric Eide

University of Utah
Salt Lake City, UT USA
{johnsond, mike, eeide}@cs.utah.edu

Abstract

Virtual machine introspection (VMI) allows users to debug software that executes within a virtual machine. To support rich, whole-system analyses, a VMI tool must inspect and control systems at multiple levels of the software stack. Traditional debuggers enable inspection and control, but they limit users to treating a whole system as just one kind of target: e.g., just a kernel, or just a process, but not both.

We created Stackdb, a debugging library with VMI support that allows one to monitor and control a whole system through multiple, coordinated targets. A target corresponds to a particular level of the system's software stack; multiple targets allow a user to observe a VM guest at several levels of abstraction simultaneously. For example, with Stackdb, one can observe a PHP script running in a Linux process in a Xen VM via three coordinated targets at the language, process, and kernel levels. Within Stackdb, higher-level targets are components that utilize lower-level targets; a key contribution of Stackdb is its API that supports multi-level and flexible "stacks" of targets. This paper describes the challenges we faced in creating Stackdb, presents the solutions we devised, and evaluates Stackdb through its application to a security-focused, whole-system case study.

Categories and Subject Descriptors D.2.5 [*Software Engineering*]: Testing and Debugging—debugging aids; D.3.4 [*Programming Languages*]: Processors—debuggers

Keywords   virtualization; virtual machine introspection

1. Introduction

Many virtual machine introspection (VMI) techniques have been developed over the past ten years to analyze, inspect, and reason about the execution of software inside a virtual machine from the outside [3, 5, 6, 11, 17, 22]. VMI-based tools often act like debuggers, using metadata such as debug symbols to interpret data structures and set execution breakpoints. VMI can be a powerful technique to analyze a VM's execution while minimally impacting its internal state. VMI requires no debugging-oriented source-level patches to the software within the VM, and it potentially lowers the odds of detection by the system under inspection.

VMI is often used for whole-system analyses because it can expose the full state of a VM. However, whole-system analyses can be difficult to implement because they involve software components that operate at multiple levels of abstraction over the full software stack: kernel, processes, libraries, and language runtimes. For tasks that involve detailed knowledge of a system's state and structure, such as the analysis of security exploits, a VMI-based tool must overcome the well-known "semantic gap" [2] between the state of a VM and its meaning. For a multi-level analysis, this gap must be crossed at many levels of the software stack.

Crossing the gap is the task of a debugger. Traditional debuggers allow a user to inspect and control one kind of *target* at a time—for instance, GDB [7] supports debugging processes, and KGDB supports debugging kernels [19]. It is uncommon to find a debugger that allows a user to "attach to" a single software system and then debug it at multiple levels of the software stack. For example, if a programmer is using a whole-VM debugger, he or she cannot direct that debugger to also attach to a particular process that is running within the VM under inspection.[1] Moreover, because software stacks are varied, there is a need for a general approach to implementing debuggers that can manage multiple, nested abstractions of a single system. Existing multi-layer debuggers such as Blink [12] and DroidScope [21] do not define general mechanisms for building "stacked" views of a single system.

We developed Stackdb, a debugging library with VMI support that allows users to inspect and analyze software systems at multiple levels of a software stack. In Stackdb, the system being debugged is accessed through one or more

---

[1] A programmer might use debugger facilities, such as GDB command files, to script deep-inspection tasks such as interpreting and walking a kernel's process list, and thereby construct a view of a particular process. However, this approach is limited: the process is still not a target with its own address space, symbols, threads, breakpoints, and other context resources.

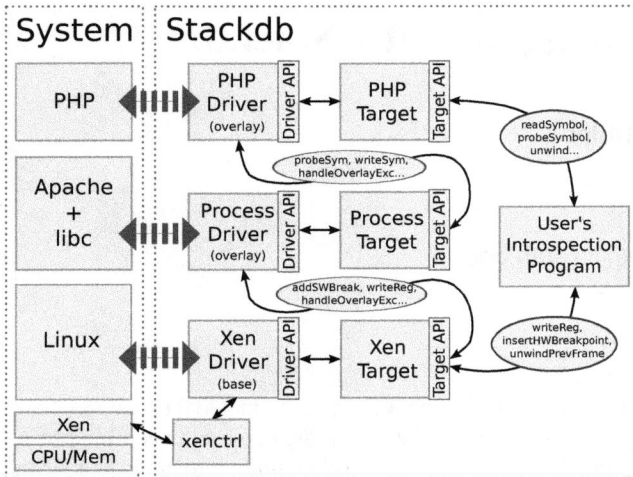

Figure 1. Stackdb applied to a Xen VM running Apache and PHP. In this configuration, three targets provide access to different parts of the system, as shown by wide, dashed arrows. Thin arrows show the actual communication paths.

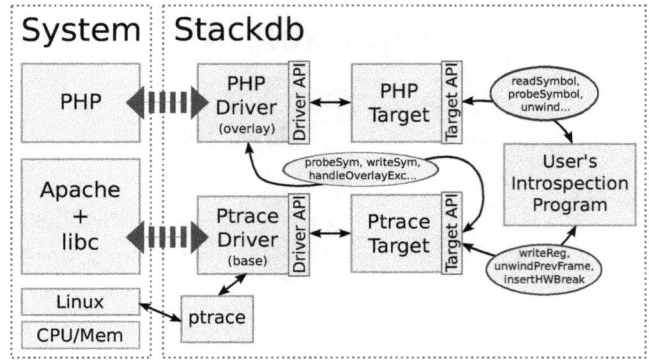

Figure 2. Stackdb applied to a local Apache process and PHP. In this configuration, the PHP driver runs atop a Ptrace target.

target objects, as illustrated in Figure 1. A target corresponds to a particular level of abstraction or a portion of the whole system being debugged. Each provides the features of a complete debugger. By invoking *target API* functions, which are common to all targets, a user can install breakpoints, examine software state and symbols, single-step, and potentially modify execution at the level of a particular target.

Figure 1 also shows that each target is paired with a *driver*, whose purpose is to implement debugger-like inspection and control features for a particular software abstraction: e.g., kernel, process, or language runtime. Although all drivers implement a common *driver API*, we distinguish two primary classes of implementation. A *base driver* interacts directly with the system being debugged, e.g., via a hypervisor-provided interface or ptrace(2). An *overlay driver* interacts with the system through another target, i.e., by "stacking" on top of an appropriate underlying target. The overlay driver communicates with the underlying target through the target API.

Because the target API is implemented by every target, a user can easily instantiate multi-level stacks of targets. In addition, the ability to implement drivers in terms of underlying targets greatly eases the process of developing new drivers, e.g., for new language runtimes. Finally, the target API makes it possible to implement generic analyses and utilities that can be applied to multiple levels of a software stack. We believe the "stackability" offered by Stackdb advances the state of the art for debuggers and that it can enable more powerful and detailed VMI-based analyses.

We have implemented four Stackdb drivers: a *Xen driver* (base) for debugging Linux-based guest OSes; a *process driver* (overlay) for debugging user-space processes within Linux-based guests; a *Ptrace driver* (base) for debugging

local processes; and a *PHP driver* (overlay) for debugging scripts at the PHP level.[2] We chose this set for its practical utility and to exercise Stackdb's APIs. Notably, the PHP driver can sit atop a process target (i.e., a target that uses the process driver) *or* a Ptrace target. The former configuration is for debugging scripts running in a VM; the process driver is an overlay that runs atop a Xen target, so debugging a PHP script within a VM involves two overlays in total (Figure 1). The Ptrace configuration is for debugging PHP scripts in a local web server, as illustrated in Figure 2.

This paper presents Stackdb and describes its application to tracing an example security exploit across software layers within a VM. Our first contribution is Stackdb, a debugger library that supports the development of powerful, programmatic, and whole-system VMI analyses. Our second contribution is Stackdb's design: the architecture that allows overlay drivers to be implemented atop other targets, and Stackdb's solutions to the challenges of implementing stackable targets.

2. Challenges

We encountered several challenges not faced by standard debuggers while building Stackdb because it provides access to a whole system through multiple, coordinated targets.

2.1 Attaching to and Controlling the System

When a Stackdb base driver attaches to a system (e.g., a VM or local process), it does so through an existing API such as ptrace(2). The UNIX ptrace system call allows a debugger to control another process at a fine-grained level, e.g., pausing and resuming threads at will. Kernel-level debuggers such as KGDB [19] rely on internal kernel support or patches that provide a remote debugging protocol.

The existing implementations of these APIs, however, are not available to Stackdb *overlay* drivers. For instance, consider Stackdb's process driver, which provides access

---

[2] We often refer to targets according to the properties of their drivers. For example, a *PHP target* is one that uses the PHP driver. A *base target* uses a base driver, and an *overlay target* uses an overlay driver. Figures 1 and 2 show examples of this convention.

to Linux processes running in Xen VMs (Figure 1). The process driver does *not* use the ptrace facility provided by the VM's guest OS, for several reasons. First, we do not want to prevent the guest OS from using its implementation of ptrace to provide services within the VM; second, we do not want Stackdb to be observed by the guest OS; and third, in newer Linux kernels, using ptrace would require Stackdb to use kmalloc to obtain memory for required data structures, which would alter the state of the guest OS. These arguments apply to the implementation of Stackdb's drivers in general.

To avoid perturbing the system under inspection, an overlay driver cannot depend on debugging APIs that are implemented within that system.[3] Moreover, a developer may want to implement an overlay driver for a part of the software stack that does not implement any internal debugging API. Thus, a key challenge for Stackdb is to support **attachment to and control of parts of a system** without use of that system's internal debugging features. This challenge is addressed by Stackdb's target API and its ability to implement drivers atop the target API (i.e., stacking). A base driver attaches to a system not through that system's internal APIs, but through an API beneath that system: e.g., through a hypervisor-provided interface for VMs. Likewise, an overlay driver does not attach to a system directly via one of that system's internal APIs. Instead, it invokes the target API of an underlying Stackdb target. The underlying target provides a rich debugging interface to the system being controlled.

2.2 Staying in Control

Once attached, a debugger must stay in control. This requires observing and managing the execution of the threads within the system being debugged. In Stackdb, this can be tricky, because an overlay driver may not have control over the scheduling of the threads that it manages. This is a consequence of Stackdb's goal of making it possible to implement overlay drivers without perturbing the system being inspected.

To make this clearer, consider the situations faced by a traditional ptrace-based debugger (e.g., GDB) and Stackdb's process overlay driver when debugging a multithreaded process. When a process thread hits a breakpoint under GDB, the kernel pauses all the other threads in the process. The kernel changes the states of those threads, allowing GDB to handle the breakpoint exception atomically with respect to the process' execution. In contrast, when a thread hits a breakpoint under Stackdb's process driver, Stackdb does not require that the underlying OS suspend the other threads within the process being observed. The process driver must handle the exception without thread-scheduling assistance from the OS within the VM being inspected.

The challenge faced by an overlay driver is **retaining execution control without thread-scheduling assistance.** For

---

[3] One can imagine special overlay drivers that *do* use a system's internal debugging APIs, when circumstances allow. Our goal, however, was to design Stackdb so as not to depend on a system's internal debugging features.

example, consider what happens when a process thread hits a breakpoint: typically, the breakpoint is removed, the thread is single-stepped, and the breakpoint is restored. Without scheduling assistance, it is possible that some other process thread will traverse the breakpoint location while it is temporarily removed—a loss of debugger control. Other problems arise due to thread context switches, thread privilege-level changes, and exceptions that occur while another exception is being handled. These issues are addressed by Stackdb's target implementation and its drivers. In contrast to drivers, which have multiple implementations for different software layers, there is a single implementation of the target API in Stackdb. In OOP terms, all targets are instances of a single class. The target API implementation provides general functions that allow targets' "client" overlay drivers to retain execution control, e.g., by signaling underlying scheduling events "up the stack."

2.3 Minimizing Overhead

All debuggers add overhead, and because Stackdb provides stacked debugger targets, it is important that Stackdb **minimize the performance overhead at each level of the stack.** Every driver must implement Stackdb's driver API for the level of the software stack it addresses. To do this, a driver must find its subject within the system being debugged— e.g., locate a particular process inside a whole VM—and provide debugger-like inspection and control operations for that subject. These parsing and control tasks are potentially expensive. In addition, overlay drivers should be informed of thread and address-space state changes so that they can maintain accurate models of their subjects.

Suppose a developer wants to examine a PHP process spawned by a web server running atop Linux within a Xen VM. To do this, the developer uses Stackdb to create a stack of three targets (Figure 1). If the developer places a breakpoint on a PHP function, the resulting debug exception will cause the entire VM to pause. When the exception occurs, each driver in the stack may need to examine its subject to detect state changes (e.g., new threads, exited threads, and address-space changes) so that it can appropriately handle the exception. A base driver queries the system directly; an overlay driver queries its underlying target.

To minimize overhead, Stackdb provides features to track state changes quickly. These include (1) thread and address-space change notifications and (2) caching of parts of a system's state. These reduce the cost of providing debugging interfaces at every level of the target stack.

2.4 Easing Implementation

To be flexible for whole-system debugging, Stackdb must **simplify the task of adding new overlay drivers.** Beyond the benefits of target stacking, Stackdb eases driver implementation by providing access to an underlying target's debug symbols: variables, functions, types, and data locations. By referring to symbols within an underlying target, an overlay driver can potentially work across many different versions and compilations of the underlying target's software.

Stackdb's process driver, for example, must parse a Linux process control block (PCB) and memory mappings in order to establish control over a process. By accessing the Linux kernel through symbols, rather than hard-coded addresses and offsets, the process driver works atop Linux kernel versions from 2.6.18 to 3.8.0.

To support targets for programs written in different languages, Stackdb's symbol-loading and querying API supports different kinds of symbols: bare ELF symbols; C/C++ symbol, type, and location data encoded in DWARF; and dynamic, variably typed symbols for languages like PHP. Stackdb handles dynamically loaded code, as well as changes to the protections and sizes of memory regions, so that it can manage changes to symbol availability and variable accessibility.

2.5 Handling Heterogeneity

Whole software systems are made from layers that implement different abstractions. The challenge for Stackdb is to **support a variety of different execution models**—from a kernel executing in a VM to an interpreted language running in a user-space process—while retaining a single target API that enables composition through stacking. We addressed this challenge by designing the target API according to a general model of machine-based execution and debugging: a model that includes threads, memory, address spaces, registers, symbols, and breakpoints. The implementation of targets is generic, with layer-specific details modularized within drivers. Not all of Stackdb's target API will apply to all layers, but its uniformity is important for stacking and implementing analyses that can be applied to multiple levels of a system.

3. Stackdb Architecture

Stackdb helps users to write programs that analyze live, whole-system executions. Users write programs that attach to *targets*, where each target provides access to and control over some part of the whole system being debugged. Users' programs then use the *target API* to pause, single-step, and resume targets' execution; query symbol data; modify targets' memory and CPU state; and insert *probes* (breakpoints and watchpoints) that notify user-specified handlers when traversed by a thread of execution. User programs can also load and modify symbol values based on source-language datatype information; unwind thread stacks; disassemble code; and extend the base probe libraries with new kinds of probes.

Figure 1 provides an overview of Stackdb's core abstractions and how they can be combined to debug whole systems. The target API provides a uniform interface to all targets. Internally, each target utilizes a *driver*, which implements control and inspection functions for a particular part of the software stack. A driver attaches to its part of the system being debugged, constructs a model of that part (with address spaces, memory regions, threads, and debug symbols),

Group	Target API	Driver API
	User-invoked	
build	create	*same*
	open	init, attach
	close	detach, kill
model	open	load{Spaces, Regions,Debugfiles}
control	pause, resume	*same; opt. for overlays*
	monitor, poll	monitor, poll, handleExc, handleInterruptedStep; *all opt. for overlays*
	stepStart, stepEnd	*same; opt. for overlays*
overlay	lookupOverlayThread	*same*
	createOverlay	*same*
	User- and Driver-invoked	
sym	lookup{Sym,Addr,Line}, loadVal	readSym; *optional*
value	store, refresh, convert	writeSym; *optional*
cpu	readReg, writeReg	*same; optional*
mem	read, write	*same; optional*
	v2p,{read,write}Phys	*same; optional*
thread	{load,pause,flush}Thread	*same*
probe	probe{SymName,Addr, Line}	{add,del}SWBreak, {add,del}HWBreak
	probeSym	*same; optional*
unwind	unwindStack, prevFrame	*same; optional*
maint	setActiveProbing	*same; optional*
	Driver-invoked	
overlay	notifyOverlay	handleOverlayExc

Table 1. Summary of Stackdb's target and driver APIs

receives and handles debug exceptions, and performs the details of reading and manipulating state and execution. A target communicates with its driver through the *driver API*, which is implemented by all drivers. (However, not all drivers implement every part of the API.) A *base driver* communicates directly with the system being debugged (e.g., via VMI), and an *overlay driver* communicates via an underlying target.

Table 1 summarizes the two APIs and illustrates how target API functions map to driver API functions where applicable. (Many utility and helper target API functions are omitted for brevity; Table 1 lists only the functions that are most important to Stackdb's design.) The table is organized into three parts, corresponding to parts of the target API that are invoked by different clients. The first contains functions that are invoked by user-written analyses and debugging programs. The second lists functions that are called by user analyses and by drivers, and the third lists functions called only by drivers. Although the mapping seems one-to-one for many operations, in fact, the implementations of the target API functions do much driver-independent processing (Section 2.2). Where the mapping is not one-to-one, the table shows the driver API functions called by each target API operation. Optional driver functions are also noted.

3.1 Targets

A target is the primary object with which a user interacts. It corresponds to an executing program: a kernel, a process, or a higher-level execution context such as a script. A target may be created by spawning a new program or by attaching to an existing program, depending on the driver.

Stackdb's target model supports multiple threads that share a single address space. An address space is divided into regions, which are further subdivided into ranges. Typically, a range models a contiguous chunk of memory with uniform protection bits. A region models a related group of ranges (e.g., from a single shared library or executable). For instance, ELF binaries are typically loaded into several ranges: one for program text, another for read-only data, and another for writable data. It is convenient to group these related ranges into a region, since debugfiles usually cover an entire region. (A Stackdb driver will attempt to load a debugfile for each region that contains symbols loaded from a binary program or library.) Helper functions translate between object-file virtual addresses and program-image (linked) virtual addresses.

Stackdb's targets keep state that is sometimes needed for controlling the execution of multithreaded software. Remember that a debugger that supports software breakpoints in multithreaded programs must handle debug exceptions whenever any thread traverses a breakpoint (Section 2.2). When a debugging API (e.g., Ptrace) allows for thread-control operations, the debugger can atomically single-step one thread while all others remain paused. However, Stackdb is designed to allow debugging even when underlying thread-scheduling assistance is not available. For systems that do not support individual thread control, a Stackdb target must keep state associated with the breakpoint being handled. Moreover, since Stackdb supports unlimited single-stepping at a breakpoint, a target must store a stack of states so that it can encounter a new breakpoint while stepping on behalf of a previously hit breakpoint.

CPU state is accessed on a per-thread basis. Memory values are loaded relative to a thread, because some debug-symbol formats encode locations relative to the values of CPU registers.

3.2 Drivers

To attach to a portion of the whole system being debugged, a target uses a driver and invokes its functions through the driver API. A driver corresponds to a particular software layer or abstraction, and some driver API functions might not apply to all drivers: for example, it does not make sense for a PHP script-level driver to provide access to CPU registers. A useful driver, however, should implement as many of the optional API functions as it can.

To attach the driver to its "subject"—i.e., its portion of the whole system being debugged—a Stackdb target invokes functions in the *build* group; it later uses these to detach from and/or terminate the subject. Once attached, a target calls the *model* functions to create a representation of the subject: cataloging its address spaces, regions, ranges, and loading debugfiles for those regions. At this point, a driver can start optimizing its internal maintenance of the model. For example, it can cache symbol values for later use, and it can install probes (Section 3.6) in order to track state changes.

The driver *control* functions allow targets to control the execution of the system being debugged. The system can be interrupted and resumed, and the driver API provides various event-loop mechanisms (blocking, polling, or a combination) that allow one to wait for events. The functions in the *cpu*, *mem*, and *thread* groups allow targets to read and write memory and CPU state. The *readSym* function can be provided by drivers that do not provide raw memory or CPU access, but do provide symbols and values, like Stackdb's PHP driver.

Although Stackdb manages high-level probe creation and state (Section 3.6), drivers provide the low-level implementations of software breakpoints, hardware debug-register-based breakpoints, and watchpoints. Furthermore, for software abstractions that do not expose numeric memory addresses, a driver may implement the *probeSym* function to place a probe on a symbol instead of an address.

Drivers can provide their own exception handlers for breakpoint and single-step events, although the default handlers are very powerful. (The default handlers support probe actions, discussed in Section 3.7.) The *handleInterruptedStep* function allows a driver to handle cases where the driver's subject steps from one thread into another, or into another thread context (i.e., from user to kernel space). This can arise when the driver does not provide individual thread control. In this case, the single-step is effectively paused until the system returns to the thread or context the step was triggered in; then the probe library can continue to handle the stepping thread.

Stackdb also allows drivers to provide their own low-level *unwind* functions to implement the target API's generic unwinder. Stackdb provides a default x86-based unwinder.

The *setActiveProbing* function allows users to control whether or not drivers can actively maintain their internal state. It can be important for a driver to monitor thread events and memory-region changes in its subject; the latter is especially important for handling dynamically loaded code. Rather than rescanning its subject's data structures at each debug exception, or selectively by heuristic, it may be more efficient for a driver to use probes to detect these changes. Stackdb refers to this as "active probing," and a user can enable it when the overhead of active probing is less than the overhead of periodic data-structure scans.

The *overlay* function group is described in Section 4.2.

3.3 Target Personalities

Each target can provide a *personality*, which is implemented by its driver. A personality defines an abstract interface for accessing features common to different types of software that one might want to debug with Stackdb. We envision three common personalities: an *OS personality* that wraps common OS objects, e.g., processes, threads, address spaces, files, sockets, system calls, loadable modules, and users; a *process personality* that abstracts common process-level objects, e.g., command lines, threads, and memory mappings; and an *application personality* that exposes idioms for program runtimes. Stackdb currently defines an OS personality API that provides kernel-version information and a system-call abstraction; the latter is useful to placing probes on the implementations of system calls. Although we are still developing the personality interfaces, we envision that they will simplify driver development and make it easier to stack targets.

3.4 Debugfiles and Symbols

When a driver attaches to its subject, it analyzes the subject and loads as many sources of debug symbols as possible. Drivers can load symbols from the binary files that compose the subject's software, and they can search for more detailed sources of debug symbols (e.g., DWARF debuginfo files) that correspond to those binaries. A target receives the symbol data collected by its driver and makes that data available through the target API. Both user-written programs and overlay drivers use the target API, so both can easily look up symbols, addresses, and source code lines.

Stackdb's *dwdebug* library loads ELF symbols and DWARF debuginfo from binary files and constructs fast search indices. Its core data structures flexibly describe scoped hierarchies of functions, variables, data types, namespaces, and aggregate types like C structs and C++ classes. The dwdebug library also manages location information (telling the target API how to load and locate functions and variables), call-frame information (allowing targets to unwind stacks), source-line information (linking symbols to source code), and address information (linking symbols to the binary compilation). Its core abstractions are general enough to support symbols from radically different languages. We have used it to implement excellent C support, good C++ coverage, and partial PHP support.

3.5 Values

Through the target API, it is possible to read and write the memory of the system being debugged. When possible, however, it is better to load data into *values* rather than employing raw memory access. The functions in the *value* group of Table 1 allow a user to read or write typed values from symbolic locations or raw addresses in the system being debugged. Users can load and display decoded basic types, and they can load members from data structures such as C structs and C++ classes. The target API provides numeric type wrappers, freeing users from size and encoding concerns.

3.6 Probes

Stackdb provides powerful, abstract, per-thread breakpoint and watchpoint support via *probes*. Normally, users register a probe atop a symbol; the details of the probe's manifestation are hidden. Probes support a normal breakpoint interaction pattern. The user supplies a *pre-handler* that is executed before the breaking instruction is executed, and also a *post-handler* that is executed after the breaking instruction has successfully executed. Users may also schedule *actions* (Section 3.7), such as single-steps, that occur between the handlers.

Basic probes may be placed on addresses, source lines, or symbols (that are resolvable to addresses). A *probepoint* represents the implementation of a breakpoint or watchpoint in the system being debugged: e.g., modifications to a CPU's hardware debug registers or the installation of a soft breakpoint instruction inside the program text. Multiple probes can be registered atop probepoints, supporting cases in which different probes care about the same event. When a probepoint's implementation is triggered, the probe's pre-handler is fired. After the instruction at the probepoint is executed, the post-handler is executed. Watchpoints are similar.

Probes are hierarchical: high-level *metaprobes* can register atop basic probes, or other metaprobes, to receive the events that trigger their pre- and post-handlers. This hierarchy can be used to build complex, stateful metaprobes that are composed of many basic probes. This flexible probing infrastructure is key to implementing overlay drivers.

Stackdb's probe library provides several important metaprobes. A *function entry/exit metaprobe* fires its pre-handler when the entry point of a function is reached; it fires its post-handler when any of the exit points of a function are reached. An *inlined-symbol metaprobe* registers atop basic probes placed on all inlined instances of a particular symbol. A *function-instruction metaprobe* allows a user to place basic probes on all instances of chosen x86 instructions within a function; the metaprobe's handlers fire when any of the selected instructions are hit. A *function-invocation metaprobe* allow users to catch invocations of a user-specified function that occur within another function.

A *symbol-value metaprobe* allows a user to register a probe on a function or variable symbol, and additionally place regular-expression filters over named values associated with that probe. When the filters match the values, the metaprobe's pre- or post-handlers are fired. If the probed symbol names a function, the associated values are the function's arguments (and, when the post-handler is fired, its return value). The values are automatically obtained and stringified for easy comparison. If the probed symbol names a variable, the pre-handler is fired if the (string-ified) previous value of the variable matches; the post-handler is fired if the new value of variable matches. Symbol-value metaprobes are particularly powerful because they maintain state. A symbol-value metaprobe on a variable requires the metaprobe to recall the variable's previous value. A symbol-value metaprobe on a function must keep a per-thread stack of invocations of itself, since the post-handler can only be evaluated for firing when the function returns.

3.7 Probe Actions

Probe actions help users script actions to be taken when probes are hit. Actions are executed between the firing of the probe's pre- and post-handlers. Users may schedule one-shot or recurring actions for probes in advance or from within a handler. Actions allow users to single-step a target at a probepoint and/or modify CPU registers and memory.

Stackdb provides a particularly powerful action called "abort." This action does not execute the original instruction at the probepoint, but instead temporarily replaces it with an x86 return instruction, effectively aborting the current function. This is handy for exploring alternate executions or avoiding side effects. For example, it can be used to study malware while suppressing the malware's harmful activity. The abort action attempts to use debug symbol information to determine how much to adjust the stack pointer to clean up the returning stack frame; it can also try to infer this amount via disassembly of the function's prologue.

4. Overlays: Building Stacks of Targets

Stackdb allows a user to debug a whole system at multiple levels of the software stack. It does this by making each level of the stack that the user wishes to debug accessible as an individual target. Stackdb attaches to the lowest-level part of the whole system via a base target. It then allows a user to create overlay targets for each interesting higher level of the system's software stack. A user can interact with an overlay target via the target API, just as he or she would interact with a base target. Each overlay target utilizes an overlay driver, which is "stacked" on top of an underlying target.

Well-designed overlay drivers should be able to sit atop any target that provides the personality they require. For instance, a driver for a higher-level language would sit atop any driver that provides the process personality, for any process that is executing that language's interpreter or runtime. This section discusses the details of implementing overlay drivers for Stackdb.

4.1 Overlay Driver Implementation Strategies

Stackdb supports several strategies for building overlay drivers. A sophisticated overlay driver might receive and process exceptions from its underlying target; act like a base target by subscribing to its own debug-exception stream (Section 5.1); and also forward events to higher-level overlay drivers. A simpler overlay driver might receive and process exceptions only from its underlying target and consume them all, if it is not meaningful to forward them as debug exceptions to a higher-level overlay. The process driver described in Section 5.2 is an example of this simpler strategy. In this case, the higher-level overlay driver stacked atop the lower-level target can insert probes in the lower-level overlay, and fire its own higher-level events when those probes are hit and some set of conditions match.

Overlay drivers can be quite simple: a new one can be built by implementing a small subset of the driver API. For instance, consider developing a new overlay driver supporting a high-level language. This overlay's implementation of the driver API would perform the following steps:

1. Create a single address space containing a single region and range (the *init*, *attach*, *loadSpaces*, and *loadRegions* driver API functions).

2. Create one or more threads corresponding to the threads in the underlying target. Use direct correspondence if the language's threads are 1-to-1 mapped to underlying-target threads, or an $M \times N$ mapping if the language uses virtual threads (the {*load*, *pause*, *flush*}*Thread* driver API functions).

3. Associate a higher-level language debugfile with the region, populate it with symbols, and support loading and interpreting the values of symbols (the *loadDebugfiles* and *readSym* driver API functions).

4. If the language does not provide raw memory or CPU state access, disable those parts of the driver API.

5. Place probes on key functions in the language interpreter, which is accessed through the underlying target. Use these probes to implement the *probeSym* driver API function, and disable support for other kinds of breakpoints and watchpoints.

6. When *probeSym* is invoked (because a client wants to place a probe in the program that the interpreter is executing), implement the requested probe as a metaprobe. The metaprobe sits atop the probes that this driver placed in the language interpreter in step 5.

7. Implement single-stepping and stack unwinding if meaningful. Single-stepping might be implemented by stepping statement executions instead of individual instructions.

8. Reuse the underlying target's functionality for other driver API functions, or do not provide implementations of them because they do not apply.

Section 5.3 describes the implementation of the PHP driver, which generally follows the recipe above.

4.2 API Functions for Overlays

Section 3.2 describes most of core functions that drivers should implement. In this section, we focus on the portions of the APIs that are specific to implementing stacks of targets, shown in the *overlay* group in Table 1.

Recall that the target used by an overlay driver is referred to as that driver's "underlying target." If a target T is to be used as an underlying target, then T's driver must implement the *lookupOverlayThread* function. This function locates threads that can be mapped to threads in an overlay target. For instance, consider a driver that examines an OS kernel. A kernel-only thread in an OS would not support the notion of a thread in an overlay target, but a user thread would, because user threads run programs at higher levels of the system software stack. Thus, the *lookupOverlayThread* function for an OS-level driver would return references to user threads, and not to kernel-only threads.

The driver of an underlying target T must also implement the *createOverlay* function. This is called to help instantiate any overlay driver that will sit on top of T. We involve the underlying target so that it can influence the overlay-creation process. For example, an OS target might help a user create a process overlay target by ensuring the user creates the overlay using the process's thread group leader—a detail that the user might not be aware of, but that matters greatly on Linux.

An overlay driver may need to implement the *handleOverlayExc* function to receive events forwarded from its underlying target. This is necessary when the underlying and overlay targets share an execution model. For example, an x86-based OS and its user processes both execute code on the system CPU, in different privilege levels. In this case, the OS target's driver will be subscribed to the debug exceptions coming from the CPU, and it will receive exceptions that apply to both itself *and* its process overlay targets. The OS target's driver can forward those exceptions that apply to its process overlay targets via the *notifyOverlay* function.

An overlay driver that does not share an execution model with its underlying target does not need to implement *handleOverlayExc*. For instance, the driver for a high-level language can implement its probes by instrumenting key locations within a language interpreter (Section 4.1, steps 5–6). In this case, the triggers for probes at different levels of the software stack are distinct, and do not need to be disambiguated.

4.3 Controlling Threads in Overlay Targets

The semantics of thread control in overlay targets can be confusing. Pausing a single thread in an overlay target generally causes *all* of its threads to pause. Because the overlay cannot use thread-scheduling features that are internal to the system being debugged (Section 2.2), it must instead pause threads through its underlying target. Going down the stack, the base target ultimately pauses the entire system being debugged. Resuming threads in overlay targets is similarly all-or-nothing. For these reasons, we expect that overlay drivers will only rarely implement the *control* driver API functions listed in Table 1. Users can simply monitor, poll, pause, and resume the base target instead. This is not a problem in our experience, since a user can easily pause the base target and then inspect the states of overlay targets.

5. Implementation

Stackdb is written in C and supports the x86 and x86_64 platforms. Its core libraries use the `elfutils` library for reading ELF and DWARF information from binary files, and it uses the `distorm` [4] library for x86 and x86_64 disassembly. Stackdb also provides an SOAP service that

Component	LOC
Target library	21,625
impl. of the target API	
dwdebug library	23,784
handles debuginfo	
Ptrace base driver	5,167
Xen base driver	10,497
Process overlay driver	1,886
PHP overlay driver	2,949

Table 2. Lines of code in Stackdb components

exports both a low-level interface for debugging (e.g., RPCs to install breakpoints) and a high-level interface for running analysis programs written using Stackdb.

Stackdb contains more than 100 KLOC and required approximately two person-years of development effort. Table 2 summarizes the lines of code within several of Stackdb's components. The target and dwdebug libraries provide a significant amount of generic target, thread, probe, and symbol-handling functions to both users and drivers. The Ptrace base driver is a relatively straightforward implementation of Stackdb's driver API on top of the standard ptrace(2) facility. The Xen driver is more sophisticated; much of its complexity stems from the careful exception handling necessary to support both paravirtualized and HVM Xen guests running atop Xen 3.3 to 4.3 hypervisors. Because the Xen base driver handles Linux's inherent complexity, the process overlay driver is relatively simple. Its implementation is focused on interpreting the kernel data structures that define a process; in comparison to the Xen driver, the process driver needs much less code to handle debug exceptions. Similarly, the PHP overlay driver focuses on tasks that are particular to PHP, because process-level details are handled by its underlying target. The data in Table 2 suggests that, in comparison to base drivers, overlay drivers can indeed be simple.

Below, we further describe the implementations of three of Stackdb's drivers. We do not describe the Ptrace driver; its use of the ptrace(2) debugging API to attach to a multithreaded UNIX process is very standard.

5.1 Xen Driver

Stackdb's Xen driver supports Xen hypervisor versions from 3.3 to 4.3, running paravirtualized or HVM Linux guest kernels ranging from 2.6.18 to at least 3.8.0. (We have not tested all kernel versions in that range.)

The Xen driver is a base driver that supports the *overlay* functions shown in Table 1; thus, it supports overlay targets. It uses Xen's standard `xenctrl` library to attach to and control VMs, and to read and write CPU registers and state. It receives debug exception notifications for VMs on Xen's virtual debugger IRQ port. It employs `libvmi` [15] (or its predecessor, XenAccess) to handle virtual-to-physical-to-machine memory translation and mapping.

The Xen driver constructs a model of the VM it attaches to by implementing the *model* driver API functions. In this driver, those functions look up and load key kernel variables and pointers by type. To obtain the list of threads running in the OS, the driver walks the kernel's task list. The driver creates a single address space (since the kernel can address all memory in the VM) and regions corresponding to the kernel program text and to dynamically loaded modules. To obtain loaded-module information, the driver walks the kernel's module list. The driver looks for debugging symbol files corresponding to the kernel and its modules in the dom0 filesystem (where Stackdb runs).

Although the Xen driver is a base driver and ultimately interacts with its VM through `xenctrl`, it also invokes the API functions on its own target in order to reuse the generic features provided by Stackdb's target library. It makes these "self-target invocations" to place probes on key symbols within the VM/kernel being debugged, to look up kernel symbols, and to read kernel data structures in a type-aware manner. Only some driver API functions can use this implementation strategy; in particular, the *build* and *open* function groups should avoid this style of implementation.

The Xen driver uses "self-target invocations" to implement its *setActiveProbing* driver API function. To implement this function, which sets up event notifications for an overlay driver, the Xen driver places probes atop key functions on the kernel's thread-creation and destruction paths, as well as on the module-load and unload paths. This allows a user to configure the Xen driver to actively track new threads and kernel modules instead of repeatedly scanning memory to find new ones (Section 2.4). Without Stackdb's support for debug symbols, the Xen driver could not feasibly support active probing across a wide range of kernels, because the necessary monitoring points change across kernel versions.

A complicating factor for the Xen driver is that it must implement single-stepped execution in two ways: by setting the x86 TF bit in the EFLAGS register for paravirtualized guests, and by setting the Monitor Trap Flag in HVM guests. Xen requires that HVM guests be stepped using the MTF. The MTF is a per-HVM flag that is global to the VM, and unlike like the TF bit in the EFLAGS register, the MTF is not changed at thread context switches. Thus, in an HVM guest, a single-step begun in one thread or context might continue into another thread or context. Single-stepping must therefore be handled carefully to ensure that the Xen driver does not attempt to handle single-steps in user space.

Finally, the Xen driver must support a limited notion of per-thread virtual-to-physical memory translation, since user-space threads have their own virtual address spaces. This is necessary so that the process overlay target can place software breakpoints inside shared libraries. If the breakpoint were placed at a virtual address, and if it were then hit by some process that was not monitored by a process overlay target, the Xen driver would not recognize it as a hit of a valid breakpoint; the Xen driver would assume instead that it was caused by the process itself. The only way for the Xen driver

to recognize these events as valid debug exceptions is to place them on physical Xen target addresses. Depending on the user-space thread in which they occur, the Xen driver will invoke the target API's *notifyOverlay* function to allow the overlay target's driver to handle the exception. If, however, the thread that hits the breakpoint has no associated overlay, the Xen driver must *emulate* the breakpoint in that thread. Otherwise, the thread will suffer a fatal exception.

5.2 Process Driver

The process overlay driver allows a user to debug a Linux user-space process running in a Xen VM. A process has the same execution model as its underlying OS, so the process driver does not need to re-implement much of the driver API, especially the *cpu*, *mem*, *probe*, and *thread* group functions. It can implement those by invoking the target API functions of its underlying target. To model a process's address space, the driver reads the process's memory-mapping data structures from kernel memory, finds the names of files that were mapped or loaded into memory, and searches for matching debuginfo. The process driver implements *handleOverlayExc*, allowing it to receive debug exceptions from its underlying target, and also *lookupOverlayThread* and *createOverlay*, which support overlays atop the process driver.

Two aspects of this driver's implementation are notable. First, its implementation of *handleOverlayExc* must handle cases in which a user-space thread is single-stepped into the kernel. It uses the target library's default implementation of the *handleInterruptedStep* function in this case, to pause handling of the single-step (as well as the breakpoint being handled, if any) until the thread returns to user context. Second, the driver must handle software breakpoints specially by implementing a version of *addSWBreak*. Most modern operating systems allow read-only program text pages to be shared among processes. This means that the process driver must place breakpoints at physical memory addresses in its underlying target, not just at virtual addresses in a process. By setting a breakpoint at a physical address, the underlying (Xen) target can recognize debug exceptions that occur in processes that are not attached to a process overlay.

The process driver's implementation currently has two artifacts that violate the clean stacking semantics that Stackdb seeks to provide. First, it must be placed atop a Xen target. We want the process driver to handle processes in Xen HVM guests, and this requires use of the MTF for single-stepping—but Stackdb does not yet abstract the state of the MTF. Second, the process driver handles only Linux processes. We expect that once Stackdb more fully implements OS personalities—to include abstractions of processes and their metadata—the process driver will be able to sit atop any target that provides the OS personality.

5.3 PHP Driver

The PHP overlay driver allows a user to debug a PHP process *at the PHP-script source level*. Thus, it contrasts with the process driver, which allows the same PHP process to be debugged, but at the C or C++ source level. PHP is an interpreted language with dynamically typed variables, dynamic compilation, and multithread support. Stackdb's PHP driver is a prototype, but still powerful. It supports built-in functions, user-defined functions, and function arguments. It can load values that belong to several PHP datatypes (null, long, double, string), but it does not yet support more complex PHP types (associative arrays and classes). It can install breakpoints on functions, but it does not yet support single-stepped execution. The PHP driver can be stacked atop either the Ptrace driver or the process driver.

Stackdb's other drivers assume a direct and x86-based execution environment, but PHP's engine executes a custom opcode-based intermediate representation. At the source level, it provides no access to raw memory or CPU state. Thus, the PHP driver need not provide the *cpu* and *mem* driver API functions, nor functions to install breakpoints. Instead, it implements the *readSym* and *probeSym* driver API functions so that users can read and install probes on symbols.

The PHP driver uses its underlying target to install probes on important C functions in PHP's execution engine. In particular, these probes monitor functions that handle PHP's opcodes. When the PHP driver is invoked to place a PHP-level probe, that probe is implemented as a metaprobe (Section 3.6) that sits atop the C-level probes. This implementation strategy was previously described in Section 4.1.

When the PHP driver attaches to a process, it unwinds the stack of the underlying target to determine if PHP's execution engine has started executing scripts. If it has, the driver dynamically generates a debugfile containing PHP base types, class types, and both user-defined and internal functions. It does this by applying the target API to its underlying target: loading the C-level data structures that describe PHP types, functions, and values, and converting them into Stackdb datatypes, function types, and values. After this step, a user can then install PHP-level probes onto PHP functions.

The implementation of the PHP driver required about three person-weeks of effort by a skilled developer (the primary author of Stackdb, who has moderate PHP experience). One person-week was spent understanding the PHP engine and developing a driver implementation strategy. These tasks required reading online documentation about how to write PHP extension libraries in C, and also reading the source code for PHP's Zend [16] compilation and execution engine. Implementing the driver to its current level took two person-weeks; a key complication was finding a way to gain access to PHP's thread-local storage to obtain symbol information. Stackdb architecture allowed us to focus our development effort on PHP-specific issues alone. General target issues, and details below PHP's implementation, were handled by other components of Stackdb.

6. Backtracking an Exploit Attempt

We illustrate the usefulness of Stackdb through a case study. Our goal is to showcase the investigatory power of a Stackdb-based analysis that (1) applies to multiple targets, corresponding to different levels of a software stack, and (2) makes use of those targets to analyze cross-layer behavior.

In this case study, we use Stackdb to detect and trace back a privilege-escalation exploit enabled by a buggy PHP script. To set up the scenario, we run a Xen VM containing an Apache web server and a simple PHP script that has a remote command-execution vulnerability. We then use this script to download and execute a published exploit of CVE–2013–1763 [14], an array-index error in the Linux kernel. The steps we follow to detect and backtrack this exploit are illustrated in Figure 3.

Because this is a privilege-escalation vulnerability, a reasonable first step is to watch for threads' attempts to raise their privilege. We therefore start by using the Xen target to place a probe on `commit_creds`, the Linux kernel function responsible for setting thread privileges, and watch for threads that raise their privilege (i.e., become root). In general, we would not know when the exploit will occur and thus would have to insert the probe at system boot time. That would be undesirable, since `commit_creds` is a high-traffic function that would trigger often. Moreover, as becoming root is a common activity, we would be flooded with false positives. Stackdb provides solutions to these problems. It allows a probe to be installed in a disabled state; later, the probe can be enabled as a side-effect of triggering another probe. So we might instead place a probe on the `__sock_diag_rcv_msg` function, mentioned in the CVE as the source of the bad array reference. This function is not frequently used; by placing a probe there, we could dynamically enable the `commit_creds` probe. Stackdb also allows context-sensitive triggering of probes. We can further restrict our `commit_creds` probe to trigger only when it is invoked by the same thread that called `__sock_diag_rcv_msg`.

Once the `commit_creds` probe is triggered (Figure 3, step 1), we are provided with the thread id along with the new credentials as shown. When we detect an escalation to root privileges, the Xen domain is suspended. With the domain suspended, we can run multiple analyses against it.

The second step is to run a Stackdb-based backtracer over the Xen target to obtain a backtrace of all kernel threads and additional information about each thread. The stack trace and information for the offending thread (1081) are shown in the upper-left part of Figure 3, and they reveal crucial information. We see that `commit_creds` was called from a user-mode address with no backtrace information, not from a kernel address. This is a clue that kernel control flow passed through an invalid pointer that wound up in user space. The thread information shows the lineage of the offending thread. Importantly, it is the descendant of an `apache` process.

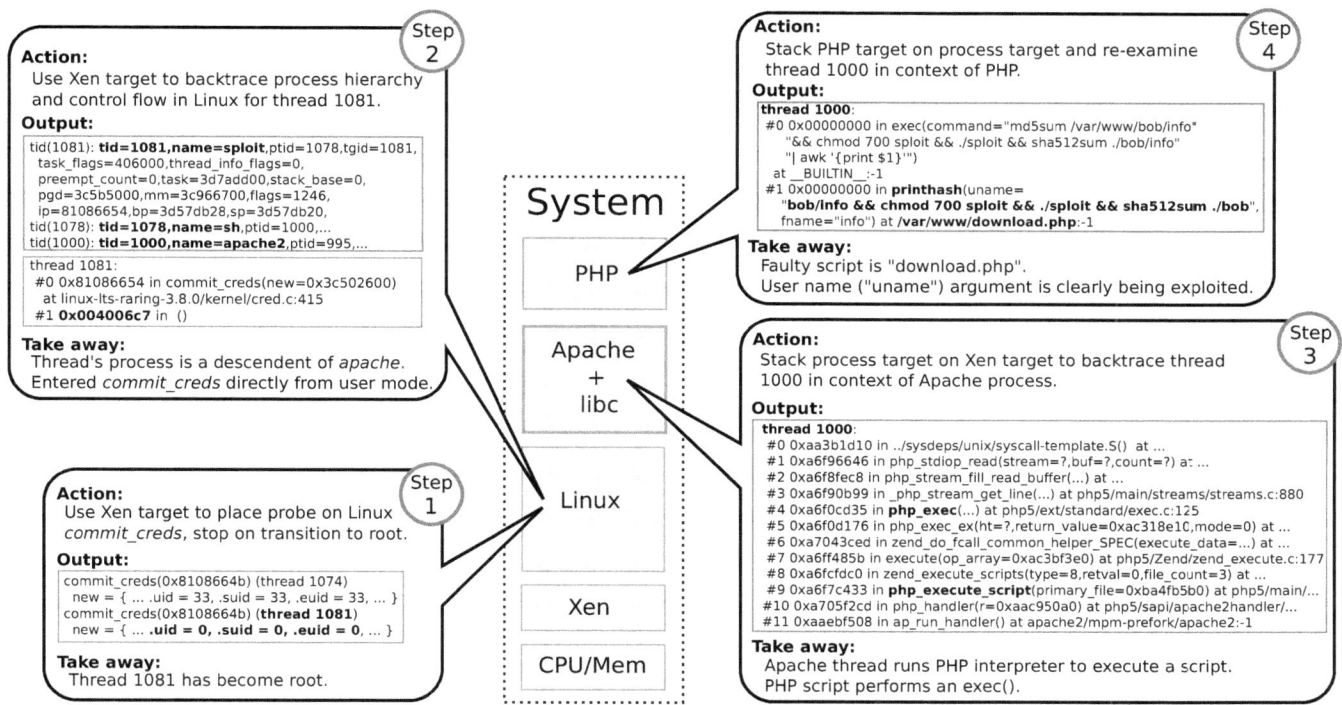

Figure 3. Multi-level analysis of a security exploit using three Stackdb targets

Now we use the multi-target capability of Stackdb. Our Apache server is configured with a fixed set of single-threaded server processes that run PHP. In step 3 (lower right), we run the Stackdb backtracing tool again, this time using a process target to focus on the user process in question (1000). The result is a C-level backtrace, which confirms that the Apache process is running the PHP interpreter and that the PHP script being run made an exec call.

In step 4 (upper right), we stack the PHP target, allowing us to trace back into the PHP code. Again, vital information is revealed. First, we discover the name of the executing script ("download.php"), which we can now examine in light of the stack trace. We also see a PHP exec call that executes multiple commands and clearly does more than just compute the hash of a file. From the arguments to the printhash function, we see that it is the user name (uname) parameter that introduces the multiple commands. By examining the PHP source in a text editor, we find the root cause of the command-injection exploit: the user-name variable is initialized from an unchecked HTML form variable.

7. Performance

We ran a set of experiments to characterize the performance of Stackdb's probes and the overhead introduced by target stacking. We ran our experiments on a Dell R710 with a single quad-core 2.4 GHz 64-bit Xeon E5530 "Nehalem" processor and 12 GB of RAM. The machine ran Xen 4.3 with a paravirtualized Linux 3.8 kernel on an Ubuntu 12.04

LTS base in both dom0 and the domU. The domU ran with a single virtual CPU and 1 GB of RAM.

We wrote two versions of a microbenchmark that calls an open-file function and the corresponding close function in a tight loop for a fixed number of iterations. One version is written in C and uses the Linux open system call; the other is written in PHP and uses PHP's fopen function. We ran our programs in domU and measured the time that each takes to make one loop iteration.

We then ran our programs again, under five configurations of Stackdb. We set up three configurations using the Xen base driver. (In all of these, our programs run in domU, and Stackdb runs in dom0.) The first uses only the Xen target, the second adds the process overlay target, and the third adds the PHP overlay target. We also set up two Stackdb configurations using the Ptrace base driver. (Our program and Stackdb all run in dom0.) The first uses only the Ptrace target, and the second adds the PHP overlay target. For each configuration of Stackdb, we placed a probe on the appropriate open-file function using the target at the top of the target stack. When the Xen target was the topmost (and only) target, we probed the sys_open function in the Linux kernel; when the process or Ptrace target was topmost, we probed the open function in libc; and when the PHP target was topmost, we probed PHP's fopen function. Finally, we ran our microbenchmarks in every Stackdb configuration and measured the time needed to make one loop iteration. The time includes the cost of handling one probe-hit event for the target at the top of the target stack.

Prog. Vers.	Base- line	Xen Base			Ptrace Base	
		Xen	Process	PHP	Ptrace	PHP
C	3.95	1,449	1,308	N/A	391	N/A
PHP	8.15	1,477	1,314	8,897	1,412	3,194

Table 3. Time (μsec.) to execute one open/close iteration of our microbenchmarks with a probe placed at various targets.

Table 3 shows our results. The second column shows the iteration times of the microbenchmark programs when no probes are installed, i.e., without debugger overhead. The next three columns show the timing results under the configurations of Stackdb that use the Xen base driver. The final two columns show the timing results under the Stackdb configurations that use the Ptrace base driver.

The Xen-based configurations rely on VMI-based probes, and our results show that there is significant overhead associated with this mechanism. This is due in part to the cost of virtualization: switching between between domU and dom0 on every probe, and translating addresses and reading memory across the domains. Even with this cost, the absolute performance overhead is not large (1–9 ms), and thus should be acceptable for interactive and scripted debugging.

An apparent anomaly is that probing a Linux-kernel symbol in the Xen target is *slower* than probing a user-process symbol in the process target, which is stacked on the Xen target (column 3 vs. column 4). This is an artifact of the open-file functions that we chose to probe at each level. In column 3, we used Stackdb to probe the Linux kernel's `sys_open` symbol, for which Stackdb found information about the function's arguments. In column 4, we used Stackdb to probe glibc's `open` symbol, and Stackdb did not find type information for this symbol. Every time the `sys_open` probe was triggered, Stackdb read the values of the function arguments, requiring multiple memory accesses. These additional accesses were not performed for `open`.

Columns 5 and 7 show that the PHP driver adds significant overhead. This is not surprising, given the amount of work that it must do to construct a PHP-level view of execution. The cost of reconstructing this view increases with the cost of accessing memory pages in its underlying target.

8. Related Work

Stackdb allows one to examine and control a single software system at multiple levels of abstraction. Overlay drivers and targets allow for multiple views of a system, and effectively, this means that one can combine multiple debuggers in order to better understand a whole system. The Blink debugger by Lee et al. [12] is also based on composition. Blink combines separate single-environment debuggers to create a unified debugger for systems that utilize multiple environments. For example, by sitting atop GDB and JDB, Blink implements a debugger for programs that utilize both C and Java. One can think of this as "horizontal" composition because the composed debuggers operate as peers—independent viewers—

with Blink monitoring and managing the transitions between the two. In contrast, Stackdb can be thought of as "vertical" composition. A Stackdb overlay is not an independent debugger, but is stacked on top an underlying debugger (a Stackdb target). This is different from the composition implemented by Blink and leads to different capabilities. For instance, Blink would not be able to compose a process debugger with a VM debugger in a way that yields a debugger for processes within a VM. This is exactly the style of composition, however, that Stackdb supports.

One of the authors' primary uses for Stackdb is the analysis of VM guests, including both kernel-mode and user-mode processing. The Volatility Framework [18] is a related platform for examining VM guests. Volatility is extended by Python scripts that perform memory forensics, and there are libraries for tasks such as creating objects that represent user-mode processes. In contrast to Volatility, which focuses on the analysis of (static) memory snapshots, Stackdb supports analyses that are driven by the *execution* of the VM guest. Stackdb's target API allows a programmer to write analyses that install probes into a guest, extract data values, and potentially alter the guest's state. The primary challenges in building Stackdb arise from the implementation of debugger services, not just memory-analysis services.

Ho et al. describe PDB, a "pervasive debugger" for debugging Xen-based systems [9, 10]. PDB was integrated with the Xen VMM: a PDB server ran within the hypervisor and received commands from a PDB client, which could run on a separate host. The PDB server could access the VMM, guest kernels, and processes within guests. Like Stackdb, PDB required information about guest operating systems in order to locate process-level data. Unlike Stackdb, PDB lacked an internal abstraction for "stacking" targets in a general way. PDB was removed from the Xen source tree in September 2006 because it was not a core Xen feature [8].

Unlike Stackdb and PDB, which use breakpoints to implement debugger functionality, PinOS uses dynamic binary translation to perform whole-system analyses of Xen guests [1]. PinOS can run unmodified operating systems as Xen guests: it uses Pin [13] to rewrite the code of the guest just before it is executed, and as part of this rewriting, Pin can insert instrumentation as needed for analyses such as whole-system profilers. PinOS and Stackdb are therefore similar in that both are designed to implement analyses of unmodified guests. PinOS is well-suited to fine-grained analyses, such as instruction-level profiling, whereas Stackdb is well-suited to understanding behaviors at the level of source code, e.g., by setting breakpoints and watchpoints on source functions and variables. PinOS and Stackdb differ in the abstractions they provide to analyses. PinOS effectively interposes between the guest and the hardware, where as Stackdb provides whole-system, debugger-like access at multiple levels of abstraction: kernel, process, and application/language.

DroidScope is a platform for analyzing Android malware at multiple levels of abstraction [21]. Using dynamic binary translation, DroidScope tracks the execution of an Android hardware-platform emulator; using its knowledge of the Android software stack, it instruments the emulator's guest in order to find important OS-level and Dalvik VM-level events and data. DroidScope provides three APIs so that analyses can track the guest at the hardware, OS, and Dalvik VM levels. DroidScope is thus like Stackdb in that it provides multi-level debugging APIs, but unlike Stackdb, DroidScope's APIs are different at every level. Stackdb defines a single target API, implemented all targets, used both by analyses and for building target stacks. In contrast, DroidScope does not define an internal abstraction for composing targets.

9. Conclusion

Stackdb is a debugging library that allows a client to observe and control a whole system, such as a VM guest, at multiple levels of the system's software stack. A Stackdb target corresponds to a particular abstraction layer or a portion of the system being debugged. The key insight of Stackdb is that a debugger can be organized as a stack of targets, in which the targets for the higher levels of a system are implemented atop those for the lower levels. Our implementation of Stackdb supports various combinations of targets into stacks, including three-level stacks that provide access to the OS, process, and language-runtime layers of a VM guest. As detailed in our security-focused case study, Stackdb can help to close the semantic gap that is often encountered in VMI-based and whole-system analyses.

Software   Stackdb is open source and available for download at http://www.flux.utah.edu/project/a3.

Acknowledgments

We thank the anonymous VEE '14 reviewers and our shepherd, Galen Hunt, for their comments on drafts of this paper. We performed our experiments on machines provided by the Utah Emulab testbed [20]. This work was supported by the Air Force Research Laboratory and DARPA under Contract No. FA8750–10–C–0242.

References

[1] P. P. Bungale and C.-K. Luk. PinOS: A programmable framework for whole-system dynamic instrumentation. In *Proc. VEE*, pages 137–147, June 2007.

[2] P. M. Chen and B. D. Noble. When virtual is better than real. In *Proc. HotOS*, pages 133–138, May 2001.

[3] J.-H. Chiang, H.-L. Li, and T. Chiueh. Introspection-based memory de-duplication and migration. In *Proc. VEE*, pages 51–61, Mar. 2013.

[4] distorm@gmail.com. distorm - Powerful Disassembler Library For x86/AMD64. http://code.google.com/p/distorm/.

[5] B. Dolan-Gavitt, T. Leek, M. Zhivich, J. Giffin, and W. Lee. Virtuoso: Narrowing the semantic gap in virtual machine introspection. In *Proc. IEEE S&P*, pages 297–312, May 2011.

[6] T. Garfinkel and M. Rosenblum. A virtual machine introspection based architecture for intrusion detection. In *Proc. NDSS*, Feb. 2003.

[7] GDB Developers. GDB: The GNU Project Debugger. http://www.gnu.org/software/gdb/.

[8] A. Ho. Personal communication, Nov. 2013.

[9] A. Ho and S. Hand. On the design of a pervasive debugger. In *Proc. AADEBUG*, pages 117–122, Sept. 2005.

[10] A. Ho, S. Hand, and T. Harris. PDB: Pervasive debugging with Xen. In *Proc. GRID*, pages 260–265, Nov. 2004.

[11] A. Joshi, S. T. King, G. W. Dunlap, and P. M. Chen. Detecting past and present intrusions through vulnerability-specific predicates. In *Proc. SOSP*, pages 91–104, Oct. 2005.

[12] B. Lee, M. Hirzel, R. Grimm, and K. S. McKinley. Debug all your code: Portable mixed-environment debugging. In *Proc. OOPSLA*, pages 207–226, Oct. 2009.

[13] C.-K. Luk, R. Cohn, R. Muth, H. Patil, A. Klauser, G. Lowney, S. Wallace, V. J. Reddi, and K. Hazelwood. Pin: Building customized program analysis tools with dynamic instrumentation. In *Proc. PLDI*, pages 190–200, June 2005.

[14] The MITRE Corporation. CVE–2013–1763, Feb. 19, 2013. http://cve.mitre.org/cgi-bin/cvename.cgi?name=CVE-2013-1763.

[15] B. Payne et al. vmitools - virtual machine introspection tools. http://code.google.com/p/vmitools/.

[16] The PHP Group. PHP at the Core: A Hacker's Guide. http://www.php.net/manual/en/internals2.php.

[17] A. Srivastava and J. Giffin. Automatic discovery of parasitic malware. In *Recent Advances in Intrusion Detection*, volume 6307 of *LNCS*, pages 97–117. Springer, 2010.

[18] Volatile Systems. The Volatility Framework: Volatile memory artifact extraction utility framework. https://www.volatilesystems.com/default/volatility.

[19] J. Wessel. Using kgdb, kdb and the kernel debugger internals. http://www.kernel.org/pub/linux/kernel/people/jwessel/kdb/.

[20] B. White, J. Lepreau, L. Stoller, R. Ricci, S. Guruprasad, M. Newbold, M. Hibler, C. Barb, and A. Joglekar. An integrated experimental environment for distributed systems and networks. In *Proc. OSDI*, pages 255–270, Dec. 2002.

[21] L. K. Yan and H. Yin. DroidScope: Seamlessly reconstructing the OS and Dalvik semantic views for dynamic Android malware analysis. In *Proc. USENIX Security*, pages 569–584, Aug. 2012.

[22] F. Zhang, K. Leach, K. Sun, and A. Stavrou. SPECTRE: A dependable introspection framework via system management mode. In *Proc. DSN*, pages 1–12, June 2013.

Author Index

.